Mind over Matter

Essays on Mentalities in Medieval India

edited by
D.N. JHA
EUGENIA VANINA

Tulika Books

Published by **Tulika Books**
35 A/1 (third floor), Shahpur Jat, New Delhi 110 049, India

First published in India 2009

ISBN: 978-81-89487-47-8

Typeset in Times_CSX+ and Univers at Tulika Print Communication Services, New Delhi; printed at Chaman Enterprises, 1603 Pataudi House, Daryaganj, Delhi 110 002

Contents

Preface

The social, economic and political aspects of the feudal phase of India's history, from the second half of the first millennium to about the eighteenth century, have received much scholarly attention and a substantial corpus of historical literature dealing with them is available. But much work remains to be done on the development of the major thought currents, and people's mental and behavioural patterns during this long period. The present anthology is therefore a modest attempt to focus attention on the working of the medieval mind in relation to state, religion, caste, gender and so on.

The articles included in the volume are based on texts in Sanskrit, Tamil, Persian, medieval 'Hindi' and Marathi. This linguistic diversity of the historical sources naturally gave rise to difficulty in maintaining uniformity in the use of diacritical marks – a uniformity which, despite our best efforts, seemed unachievable beyond a point in a volume like this. We crave the indulgence of our readers if we are found wanting on this score.

We thank Indira Chandrasekhar and Samira Junaid of Tulika Books for seeing the book through the press.

D.N. JHA and EUGENIA VANINA

Introduction

D.N. Jha and Eugenia Vanina

Ever since Indology emerged as a distinct field of research, scholars have been trying to evaluate the tempo of India's historical evolution and its stage of development on the eve of the colonial era. Sharp differences of opinion arose from the very beginning, when Sir William Jones compared the 'golden age of India' with the classical periods of Greece and Rome (Chatterjee 1998: 92), to meet the uncompromising opposition of James Mill, in whose opinion the eighteenth-century Indians were, in terms of historical, cultural and moral development, far inferior even to the primitive tribes of early Britain (Mill 1972: 482). Later, James Todd described medieval Rajput society as analogous to feudal Europe, which also provoked heated criticism from many of his fellow Indologists. This criticism was conditioned by not only the methodological weaknesses in Todd's framework but also by political and ideological reasons. Indeed, if Indian society on the eve of the colonial era was medieval and feudal, then historical evolution was not fully alien to it – therefore the gap between Indians and 'civilized Europeans' was not as deep and wide as hitherto has been supposed, and the 'white man's mission' itself was questionable.

As medieval India studies became established as a separate realm of research, it could, from the initial phase, boast of significant achievements. After long debate the temporal frame of the period in Indian history was delimited from approximately the sixth to the eighteenth centuries. This is a long period, but the term 'medieval' is, according to most scholars, adequate to describe the entire span between the 'ancient' and the 'colonial' epochs. Moreover, this long period has adequate room for the subdivisions 'early medieval' and 'late medieval' and allows for discussions on the possibilities of evolution within the medieval era.[1] Scores of medieval sources were discovered and published, histories of dynasties and states were reconstructed, and various problems of socio-economic relations and administrative structures were discussed. At the same time, celebrated scholars such as V.A. Smith, M. Elphinstone, H.M. Elliott, W.H. Moreland and Sir Jadunath Sarkar studied medieval India not only out of purely academic interest but also to disclose to the reading public the darker side of the 'degraded' society and make

[1] A similar approach to the 'medieval' has been adopted in the present volume.

it aware that, in Sir Jadunath's words, 'happily for India, the death of her old order was immediately followed by the birth on her soil of modern civilization and thoughts' (Sarkar 1949–50, Vol. IV: 347). 'Modern' here meant, no doubt, colonial. The interest in medieval India was likewise a feature of Indian nationalist historiography to which, since the mid-nineteenth century, journalism and belle-lettres were closely linked. Early Indian medievalists, much like novelists, playwrights and journalists, saw their major purpose not just in research but also in making people feel proud of their history and the glory of medieval heroes, be they Shivaji, Raj Singh, Akbar or Guru Gobind.

For the period from the mid-sixth century, however, the focus shifted to socio-economic history. In many cases under the influence of Marxist methodology, there began systematic research into the economic foundations and the social structure of pre-modern Indian society. All aspects of agrarian relations, from peasant landholding to innumerable varieties of land grants, all spheres of administration, taxation and other types of agrarian product appropriation were meticulously studied. There has been considerable research – albeit lacking in detail and comprehension – into craft economy and trade. Different types of social organization were analysed, be it the village community, the trading castes, religious sects or aristocratic clans. There has been a heated discussion on the character of the medieval Indian state described variously by scholars as 'Oriental despotism', feudal or integrative polity and as a 'patrimonial-bureaucratic' system. In the process, medieval Indian studies rose to an internationally recognized level. In spite of all these achievements, the question remained, how to define medieval India and how to situate it within world history. A numerous and highly qualified group of scholars viewing medieval Indian society as feudal is being opposed by a no less numerous and qualified group which denies the applicability of the concept of feudalism to India. Both sides argue their respective postulates on the basis of a wide range of sources and in many cases the same text has been used to argue two contrasting views.

We may briefly note here the essence of the polemic that has continued for around half a century and still shows no sign of nearing its end. Both sides, despite their differences, ground their arguments in a common set of methodological principles. First, their judgement and estimate of medieval Indian society is based exclusively on the data available on economic, social and politico-administrative institutions. These are the core concerns of almost all the participants in the polemic, whatever their attitude towards Marxist methodology.[2] A catalogue of the hitherto published medieval India studies, if one were to make one, would show that,

[2] The question whether this socio-economic plus political exclusivism is really a requirement of Marxist methodology calls for a separate discussion. One may be however reminded of the critical statement of Engels: 'Failing to recognize independent historical development of various ideological spheres playing roles in history, we deny them every possibility of *influencing history*. This attitude is based upon a stereotyped, non-dialectical view of cause and effect as two eternally juxtaposed poles, while their interaction is absolutely ignored' (Engels 1966: 84) .

except for a relatively small number (mainly by scholars who do not define themselves as historians), most of the available works deal with socio-economic and politico-administrative aspects of medieval Indian history.

In contrast, processes and phenomena that belong to the sphere of mentality, religion, culture, scientific knowledge – the very worldview of medieval Indians – have attracted little attention, and mostly as an appendix to the 'fundamental' themes. It is not by chance that the problems of medieval attitudes are usually discussed by those whose field of research is religion, anthropology, culture, philosophy or literature, not history. The typical historical treatise on the medieval period deals with political events, economy (agriculture, crafts and trade), major social groups, their relations and life, the administrative system, taxation and at the end, as a concession, 'a bit of culture' – brief descriptions of religious life, literature and the fine arts. In such a scheme, cultural and mental phenomena are a reflection of socio-economic processes and a secondary source of the latter.

Since feudalism and medieval society as such have been studied more effectively against the backdrop of European history, scholars of medieval India have collectively constructed a model of feudalism, systematizing its main features and its trajectory of development (once again, mainly in the socio-economic and politico-administrative spheres). In this process of model-making the specific features of the various European societies were not taken into consideration; all of them were incorporated into the image of a certain unified and homogeneous 'West' to be accepted as a matrix of not just feudalism, but also its 'real' and 'correct' form. This imagined 'West' emerged as a model because it had been studied more extensively and also because it was supposed to evolve in a known way into capitalism and, depending upon a scholar's ideological position, further on into a post-industrial society or socialism. It was in comparison with this 'correct model' that medieval Indian society was discussed by both sides of the Indian feudalism debate.[3]

As a result, the efforts to estimate the level achieved by Indian society by this or that time in medieval history were reduced to assessing how this or that institution of medieval Indian society matched the European model. And since some of the features (especially socio-economic ones) of this Western feudalism, such as the manor, serfdom, city commune and estate representation, were not found in India, medieval India was either not feudal at all or it was a specific variety of feudalism – an incorrect and underdeveloped version lagging behind the more dynamic and progressive European form. In the latter case then, the researcher's task was to find the reasons for this anomaly – once again, in the economic and social spheres.

No doubt the scholars working within this framework, regardless of what group they belong to, have achieved a lot. But at the same time a sense of disenchantment has been discernible in the last one or two decades. This feeling is

[3] There are, however, exceptions: see the features of Indian feudalism discussed with frequent reference to China, Japan and South-east Asia (Jha 2000: 1–58).

expressed, depending on the scholar's temperament, in the form of either a mild plea for new dimensions to research, or an uncompromising and total rejection of the dominant methodology.[4] When did Indian society become medieval, how did it develop, and at which stage of evolution did it confront colonialism? These questions continue to remain unanswered. The followers of the 'Indian feudalism' concept know almost everything there is to know about medieval agrarian systems and forms of taxation but fail to develop a clear understanding of which of these features were specifically Indian and which belonged to all feudal societies. Their opponents too have a similar understanding of the socio-economic and administrative history of medieval India but expend most of their efforts into proving that medieval India was not feudal than to clarify what it was after all.

This kind of a dead end calls for a different road to be taken, one that differs from the previous approach, which has shown no interest in medieval Indians as human beings with their own worldviews, attitudes and mental and behavioural patterns. There exists another way, one that brings to life a postulate negated by nobody and at the same time forgotten by many: stages of a given society's historical development differ from each other not only in the means of production, economic, social and politico-administrative forms, but also in the way people think and behave, in their values, attitudes and stereotypes – the 'mental programme', as Clifford Geertz (1973: 44–45) put it, that various social groups follow. For medieval studies in general, this postulate is nothing new. Readers are reminded of the contribution of the 'history of mentalities' of the Annales school to the understanding of medieval Europe. A similar history of India, and not only medieval history, is still wanting.

Such an approach may open a new dimension of research and help bridge the gap between the followers and opponents of the Indian feudalism concept. The problem of understanding and estimating medieval Indian society by relying solely on socio-economic and politico-administrative data lies not in methodology as such but in the character of the available sources. In most medieval sources references to the above-mentioned aspects are usually vague and would be unclear to today's reader. It is never easy to discern whether a piece of land mentioned in a document was on freehold, a fief or private property, or whether a named individual was a clan leader, a state official, a feudal lord, a vassal or a tribute payer.

Medieval authors were not interested in the problems that are of interest to us now. They would rather have written dozens of pages glorifying a king's valour and amorous feats than a line to clarify what land property was like in his kingdom. But what medieval texts mention in abundance are social relations, values and the attitudes of people in different walks of life. And it is in these attitudes and relationships, as reflected by the sources, that medieval societies – India was no exception – exhibit both their specific and their common features. Unable to find in medieval texts the data that in our view signifies the progress of property forms, production and social relations, in many cases we deny develop-

[4] See for example, Subrahmanyam (1998); Mukhia (2004: 10–12).

ment to the society in question even though the same sources may refer to crucial changes in values, social attitudes and mental patterns. No doubt, these changes would reflect important developments in socio-economic life as well.

This volume seeks neither to devalue previous approaches to medieval Indian history nor to present the study of medieval values and attitudes as the magic key to all problems. The purpose is to create an interest in the mental and behavioural aspects of medieval society and widen the area of research. The contributors to this volume are from different countries and they adopt dissimilar approaches in their study of medieval India, some accepting feudalism, others rejecting it. It would have been difficult to bring them together if the purpose had been formulated in the old-fashioned way, covering the thematic range of socio-economic and administrative development. But when medieval Indian society is discussed from the viewpoint of ideas, mental patterns and, religious and cultural developments, researchers belonging to various schools and following different methodological approaches, come to certain shared terms and allow their findings to complement each other at a somewhat broader level.

Thus the state may be viewed not only in terms of control, exploitation, extraction and appropriation, but also in terms of practices, ideas and ideologies that were closely linked (among other things) with religion. A specific feature of the medieval state was the legitimation of power through religion. Given all the differences between Hinduism and Islam, Hindu and Muslim states were engaged in legitimizing practices to an almost equal extent, albeit by different means, as the papers of Kesavan Veluthat and Irfan Habib indicate. For legitimacy, early medieval south Indian states needed temples and cults in the orthodox Śāstraic and heterodox *bhakti* garb. For the Delhi sultanate, according to its theorist Baranī, to be legitimate meant to follow the patterns of preceding Islamic states. The rulers of Hindu and Muslim states used religious ideology not only to legitimize themselves but also to de-legitimize their internal enemies: legitimation meant temple/mosque construction; de-legitimation, as is clear in the papers of Eaton and Jha, required their destruction. One may recall that medieval Europeans did much the same, glorifying their kings by building magnificent cathedrals and desecrating the holy places of their enemies, be they mosques in Palestine, non-Catholic churches in Byzantium and Russia, synagogues in Spain, Hindu temples in Goa or even Catholic places of worship in the conquered cities. Even Mughal currency may, as in Najaf Haider's paper, be discussed not only as an instrument of economic transaction and exploitation but also as a symbol of authority, a tool of legitimation and imperial integration.

Medieval society had a specific understanding of the past and of social experience. History, individual or collective, was recorded and reproduced not just to state facts, but also to create patterns for the subsequent generations to follow. This peculiar understanding, common to Hindu bards and Muslim chroniclers as well as their European counterparts,[5] has often been neglected by scholars

[5] For European attitudes see Spiegel (1997).

who bemoan the 'lack of historicity' in Hindu bardic poems and chronicles. Historicity was no doubt present, but in a peculiar medieval sense as discussed in this volume by Stewart Gordon, Eugenia Vanina and Irina Glushkova. They search their respective sources, Sanskrit chronicles, Marathi historical texts and *bhakti* hagiographies, for perceptions and constructions of collective or individual pasts in order to establish the mental and behavioural patterns of royalty and sainthood for generations to follow.

A central feature of medieval society was hierarchy. Hierarchy was embedded in the relations between not only social classes and groups but between individuals and encompassed even intimate feelings and desires. The papers by Vijay Nath, Shalini Shah and Daud Ali address this problematic sphere from various perspectives: gender parity and differentiation, perceptions of the sensual world and sexuality and, in a broader sense, manners and ethical values of attachment and subjection.

Two contributions to this volume bring the reader to the intellectual worlds of medieval India. Sanskrit drama and philosophical and grammatical treatises are analysed by Vishwa Mohan Jha and Sheldon Pollock not as literary or compilatory texts, but as repositories of intellectual, spiritual and emotional experience. Their imagery and stylistics reflect attitudes of the old versus the new, the modes of dissemination and preservation of tradition, as well as of dissent.

Medieval Indian society lacked social and communal conflict only in the musings of Orientalist and romantic nationalist scholars. In the sphere of religion a creed would establish itself through doctrinal, ideological and physical opposition to this or that 'other'. This was true for Christianity, Islam and, as D.N. Jha's paper shows, such Indian-born religions as Hinduism, Buddhism and Jainism. In the realm of social relations Noboru Karashima and Hiroyuki Kotani discuss, on the basis of different sets of sources, how a voluntary or involuntary breach of the established laws of social behaviour was regarded as a sin against both society and religion and describe mechanisms of conflict resolution. The ways in which culprits were imprecated and punished but repenting sinners purified and rehabilitated were peculiar to the Indian milieu in form, but in content similar to those of other medieval societies.

Thus, the papers presented in this volume make a collective effort to denote four components of the medieval Indian 'mental programme'. Many others await research. What is more acutely felt is the need for comparative studies to realize, first, the peculiarities of medieval outlook in various regional cultures of India and second, what in the worldview under research was specifically Indian and what was typically medieval and common to other pre-modern societies. Fully aware of our limitations, we offer this volume as an invitation to our colleagues of whatever school and methodological affiliation to join us in a search for new dimensions in medieval India research.

References

Chatterjee, Amal (1998), *Representations of India 1740–1840: Creation of India in the Colonial Imagination* (London: Macmillan).

Engels, Friedrich (1966), 'Letter to Franz Mering, 14 July 1893', in the *Collected Works by Karl Marx and Friedrich Engels,* Vol. 39 (Moscow: Political Literature Publishers).

Geertz, Clifford (1973), *The Interpretation of Culture: Selected Essays* (New York: Basic Books Inc.).

Jha, D.N. (2000), 'Editor's Introduction', *The Feudal Order: State, Society and Ideology in Early Medieval India* (Delhi: Manohar).

Mill, James (1972), *History of British India*, Vol. I (Delhi: Associated Publishing House).

Mukhia, Harbans (2004), *The Mughals of India* (Oxford: Blackwell Publishing).

Sarkar, Jadunath (1949–50), *Fall of the Mughal Empire*, 4 Vols (Calcutta: Sarkar).

Spiegel, Gabrielle M. (1997), The *Past as Text: The Theory and Practice of Medieval Historiography* (Baltimore: John Hopkins University Press).

Subrahmanyam, Sanjay (1998), 'Reflections on State-Making and History-Making in South India, 1500–1800', *Journal of the Economic and Social History of the Orient*, Vol. 41, No. 3, pp. 382–416.

Instruments of
Legitimation and Delegitimation

Ideology and Legitimation

Early Medieval South Asia

Kesavan Veluthat

I

In this paper I discuss the problem of the use of ideological tools for purposes of political legitimation. More precisely, I concentrate on those aspects of legitimacy achieved or sought through religious symbols. For this purpose I study the present-day states of Kerala and Tamil Nadu in the period between the eighth and the twelfth centuries. Stated briefly, my argument is that the symbols of the Āgamaic/Purāṇic Hindu religion, propagated through the temples and the aggressive *bhakti* movement, were used to legitimize those who were either in power or were aspiring for it. As this religion became firmly established and became a part of the consciousness of certain sections of society, its symbols could be used to achieve ideological domination with great profit.

One of the more important aspects of the religious history of early medieval south India is the emergence of temples dedicated to one of the Āgamaic deities, Śiva or Viṣṇu. The origin of the worship of these deities, traceable to northern India, was itself the result of a great syncretism through which elements of folk cults and practices were incorporated into the classical traditions of Vedic religion. In the earliest historical period in south India, documented elaborately in what is known as the Śaṅgam literature, one does not come across a society in which this religious system had gained acceptance.[1] In that period, which scholars are now inclined to bring down to the fourth or even fifth century AD, what prevailed was a congeries of cults and practices,[2] occasionally sprinkled with Vedic–Śāstraic–Purāṇic ideas (Narayanan 1975), but neither were they standardized in any recognizable form nor reduced to an institutional framework. There is a very strong presence of the Brāhmaṇa, with his Vedic sacrifices, Āgamaic forms of worship

[1] The validity of treating this period as a single entity on the basis of an imagined unity of what has been called the Śaṅgam literature, believed to constitute a single corpus, is now questioned. Poems traditionally included in that corpus are demonstrated to have been composed during a wide span of about a millennium starting from at least the beginning of the third century BC. Nor do those poems represent any one type of society, there being evidence of different levels of social and economic development. As such, to try and seek a uniform 'religion' there is not likely to yield encouraging results.

[2] For a discussion, see Sastri (1972).

and Śāstraic social norms; but sprawling Brāhmana settlements with vast areas of agricultural land under their command and the temple as the pivot around which these functioned had not yet taken shape in that period. They were clearly later arrivals. Perhaps it was the Brāhmanas who introduced the Āgamaic/Purānic religious ideas and institutions into this part of the country in the period that followed immediately.

By the time we reach the seventh–eighth centuries, the picture is significantly altered. A complex socio-economic formation unfolds in this region, its interrelated aspects comprising the opening up of the fertile river valleys for agriculture, the covering of the landscape by a network of big and small Brāhmaṇa settlements, the studding of the territory with a large number of temples commanding vast tracts of land as their property and all the entailing privileges and, of course, the burgeoning of monarchy which anticipated the Coḷa state in the centuries to come (Champakalakshmi 1982). To be sure, these developments were extremely complex and, to a great extent, interrelated – particularly the creation of vast agrarian settlements, the emergence of the Brāhmaṇa settlements and the rise of the temples. In fact, at the risk of over-simplification, one may identify these three – the agrarian settlements, the Brāhmaṇa corporations and the temples – as having been synonymous.

Under the leadership of the corporate body of Brāhmaṇa trustees, the temple served as an agency for efficient extraction of surplus from the peasants on the vast landed estates that it commanded (Narayanan and Veluthat 1981). This resulted in extending agriculture to areas that were hitherto unsettled and transforming the hunter/gatherer people in the twilight zones into peasants, identified as so many new castes. This suited the *varṇa–jāti* paradigm, however inconsistent and contradictory it was, and resulted in restructuring society on *jāti* lines. In fact, the legal fiction of *sankīrṇajāti* was invoked only when convenient, to explain the status of a section of society that had been recently accorded entry into the fold.[3] The general framework of *jāti* and its philosophical justification contained in the *varṇāśramadharma* was, in any case, accepted.

This reorientation of society was to a large extent the concomitant of the extension of agriculture into relatively unsettled regions and the transformation of hunter/gatherers into peasants. The role of the temple-oriented Brāhmana settlements in this transformation was central. The temple commanded the allegiance of the local population in large measure. This allegiance was further strengthened, *inter alia,* by what has come to be known as the Tamil *bhakti* movement. It has been shown that the *bhakti* movement had its institutional base in the Brāhmaṇical temple (Veluthat 1979). The leaders of the *bhakti* movement were leading a temple

[3] For the invocation of the fiction of *sankīrṇa-jāti,* though dating from a slightly later period, see Derrett (1971). In spite of the general acceptance of the principle, it was not extended to the matrilineal communities of Kerala with whom the Brāhmaṇas had alliances. The issues of such alliances belonged to their mother's caste, not their father's nor to any *sankīrṇa-jāti.*

movement; devotion to Viṣṇu or Śiva was reduced to devotion to the deity consecrated in a particular temple. The *bhakti* movement, thus, went a long way in popularizing the temple. The popularity of the temple meant the popularity and acceptance of all that the institution represented, including its norms of social differentiation and the peculiar organization of the forces and relations of production. Thus, what the temple achieved by being a landed magnate and an efficient organizer of production and distribution was further reinforced by the ideology propagated by the *bhakti* movement. To be sure, in the beginning, *bhakti* had an openness about it in matters of caste, but as the movement came to its fruition, it closed ranks and kept the lower sections of society out. In fact, it strengthened the institution of caste. There were various other media too, such as dance, drama, painting and sculpture, as well as scholarly discourses – all made use of in the temples and through which the ideas of the religion were propagated. Thus a particular variety of Āgamaic/Purāṇic religion became part of the consciousness of the people.

II

It is against this background that we can examine how symbols of this religion were used by the ruling classes to achieve ideological domination in general and to seek legitimacy for the ruler in particular. The opening up of the river valleys for agriculture had brought about a major social change in south India. This has been looked upon by historians as one of the significant factors behind state formation in this part of the country (Champakalakshmi 1982). Starting from Toṇḍaimaṇḍalam or the Pallava country in northern Tamil Nadu, this expansion of agriculture led to the crystallization of social stratification and the formation of clear-cut divisions in society. This process extended further south to include the territories of the Pāṇḍyas, and to the south-west, to those of the Ceras, in the centuries that followed. By the ninth century, the Kaveri valley became the core region of a new kind of monarchical state (Stein 1980: 134–40). In other words, the social change resulting from agrarian expansion was reflected in the newly emerging political institutions, beginning in the north of Tamil Nadu in the Pallava country and expanding southward, to find its culmination and fulfilment in the Coḷa country.

An identical trajectory is followed in the spread of the *bhakti* movement (Veluthat 1979). The early Āḷvārs and Nāyanārs were connected with Toṇḍaimaṇḍalam; they sang about the temples of Veṅkaṭam or Kanchi or Tiruvaḷḷikkēṇi. By the time we come to the last of these culture-heroes, they are seen singing about temples in the Pāṇḍyan and Cera country, and in the Coḷa country on either side of the Kaveri. Thus, the *bhakti* movement is directly linked with the expansion of agriculture and the formation of the state based on it.

It is interesting that among the early patrons of the *bhakti* movement we have the names of rulers belonging to the newly established dynasties. The great Appar had Mahendravarman Pallava as his patron; the story goes that he was instrumental in the latter's conversion to Śaivism from Jainism, whereupon a Jain monastery was pulled down to construct a Śiva temple there.[4] Neḍumāṟan, a Pāṇḍya king, is likewise believed to have converted to Śaivism from Jainism under the influence of the minister Kulaiciṟai Nāyanār, and this occasion was promptly celebrated by the impalement of 8000 Jains.[5] The Coḷa Koccenganān, identified by scholars as the grandfather of Vijayalaya (Champakalakshmi 1978), was a Śaiva Nāyanār and so was Ceramān Perumāḷ, identified as the founder of the Cera kingdom of Mahodayapuram.[6] In the early days of these monarchies, the rulers would have found the support of the movement quite useful. The movement, in its turn, derived much benefit from royal patronage, especially in making use of state power in their conflicts with rival creeds even at a physical level. This mutual support is significant.

Even at the deeper levels of society, the *bhakti* movement had a major role to play in reflecting and legitimizing the emerging social order. As the temple gained in popularity, its services and the distinctive language of *bhakti* came to reflect a particular kind of social organization. For instance, the deity in the temple was accorded full royal status, with no detail in the attendant paraphernalia wanting. Thus, *uḍaiyār* or *perumāḷ* meant both the king and the deity, *kōyil* meant both the palace and the temple, and the day-to-day routine of services in the temple followed, to the last detail, the services in the palace (Narayanan and Veluthat 1978: 51–52). However, although the terminology used in all these cases pertains to royalty, it was also applicable to any major landed magnate or local chief: in the political structure of that time every chief or landlord was looked upon as a 'king' in his own right. In fact, the plurality and coexistence of a large number of deities, arranged sometimes in an order of precedence, eminently reflects a political structure with the plurality and coexistence of a large number of lords and magnates arranged in a hierarchical manner with orders of precedence and with strong ties of dependence (ibid.: 51).

If the deity was thus equated with the lord, the devotee was the vassal. The devotee addressed the deity habitually as *uḍaiyār* or *tambirān* (lord) while he described his own position as that of *aḍiyār* (serf). When individuals called themselves 'servant of the servant of the servant' of the deity or 'devotee of the devotee of the devotee' of the deity, we discern the typical feudal pyramid, where, barring the apex and the base, each person at every point was a lord unto his immediate vassal and a vassal unto his immediate suzerain, with ties of allegiance and dependence. By the time we come to Sundaramūrtti, perhaps the last of the Nāyanārs, the Brāhmaṇical character of the movement and its institutional base – the temple – is underlined by the opening verse of his *Tiruttoṇḍattogai* where he describes himself as the 'slave of the slave of the Brāhmaṇas of Tillai' (*Tiruttoṇḍattogai* V.1: 1.1).

[4] See '*Tirunāvukkaraśar Purāṇam*': (*Periyapurāṇam*, 1974: 200–68).

[5] '*Kulaiciṟaiyār Purāṇam*' (ibid.: 268–69): '*Niṉṟaśīr Neḍumāṟar Purāṇam*' (ibid.: 637–38): '*Mangaiyārk-karaśiyār Purāṇam*' (ibid.: 657–58) .

[6] For the identity of Ceramān Perumāl Nāyanār, see Narayanan (1996), chapters on 'Chronology' and 'Religion and Religious Systems'. So also, Kulaśekhara Āḷvār is identified as Ceramān Perumal's immediate successor (ibid.).

This reflection of the existing social order and the re-creation of a parallel world of authority in the realm of religion went a long way in legitimizing the polity that came to be established in this period. Through the creation of an illusion of cutting across caste lines, what was really achieved was to ensure the acceptance of caste and its ideology by all sections of society. The stories of Nantanār who was a Paṟaiya and Tiruppāṇa Āḷvār who was a Pāṇa apparently showed that even people belonging to lowly castes could reach the highest rank in the *bhakti* hierarchy; but in reality it was a statement of what the ordinary Paṟaiya's or Pāṇa's place was. The existing social structure and the power structure, thus, received the necessary sanction and validation from the temple-based religion of Āgamaic/Purāṇic Hinduism, successfully spread by the *bhakti* movement.

III

It was only natural that the symbols embedded in these religious ideas should have been found useful in legitimizing the political order and the ruler as well. Before taking up this aspect of our problem, it is necessary to look at the broad outlines of the polity over which the ruler was presiding. By the time of the firm establishment of the Pallavas in Kanchi, a new form of state had arrived, as it were, in south India, following the model of kingship prescribed in the *śāstra-kāvya-nāṭaka* literature in Sanskrit. This institution found refinement and elaboration in the other monarchies, of the Pāṇḍyās, Ceras and Coḷas. According to their model, the ruler had to be a Kṣatriya, in keeping with the rules of *varṇāśramadharma.* In fact, an elaborate self-image of the monarch was constructed in the expressions of the ideologies in the court, the contours of which were sharpened by elements drawn from various sources (Veluthat 1993).[7] Among the various aspects of this self-image was an attempt to attribute divinity to the king (ibid.; Veluthat 1978). This was, to be sure, not a novel invention in south India; we see it in northern India in the context of the Gupta empire and even earlier. In fact, most of the details were borrowed from this northern Indian source, thereby showing once again that the model of kingship in south India in the period of the Pallavas was derivative. Nevertheless, the conferment of elements of divinity to royalty in the south had a special significance.

In the attempt to elevate royalty to the status of divinity, the divine figures chosen are, significantly, gods of Āgamaic/Purāṇic Hinduism. In the context of the gaining popularity of this religion, with the temple as its institutional base and the *bhakti* movement its ideological organ, its gods, naturally, had greater appeal than the ones worshipped in an earlier period. Similarly, since the entire scheme was within the category of the *varṇāśramadharma,* it was necessary to accommodate even the gods with whom the new 'kṣatriya' rulers were equated into the pattern of the Purāṇic texts. Herein lies the significance of this attempt at divinizing monarchy. At the same time, it needs to be borne in mind that this should not be confused with the 'divine right' theory of kingship (Sharma 1991: 301, 312).

[7] See especially chapter on 'The Self-Image of Royalty'.

The equation of the king with one of the gods was achieved by various means. It is well known that the Pāṇḍya, Cera and Cola dynasties had an autochthonous origin; they figure prominently in what is called the Śaṅgam literature as such. But by the time we come to our period, they were identified as belonging to the *Candravamśa* or the *Sūryavamśa* of Purāṇic fame. The Pāṇḍyas are stated to belong to the *Candravamśa* and the Ceras and Coḷas, to the *Sūryavamśa.* As for the Pallavas, they are stated to belong to a category of *Brahma-Kṣatra,* although there are faint claims to *Candravamśa* origins also. Curious genealogies are invented in all cases, often contradicting the accounts of the *Candravamśa* or *Sūryavamśa* as they figure in the Purāṇas. The origin is invariably traced in all cases to Brahma, not as the Creator but as the very ancestor of all these dynasties. Brahma is depicted as seated in the lotus of Viṣṇu's navel. Again, Purāṇic and divine figures such as Rāma, Kṛṣṇa and Arjuna are introduced at various points in the genealogy so that the king claims descent from these figures as well.

Then there were the numerous traditions that attributed divine status to each of these dynasties. There are a large number of exclusive traditions which the Pāṇḍyas, for example, claimed for themselves, which include participation in the Mahābhārata war, sharing the throne with Indra, acting as messengers of the gods, negotiating peace with Rāvaṇa, etc. These accorded a certain amount of divinity to those who participated in these traditions through the Purāṇic memories which they invoked. Comparable traditions were cherished by the Coḷas – they claimed that the famous Śibi, who is well known for his kindness, and Manu, the ruthless law-giver himself, were among their ancestors (Sastri 1955: 7). The origin myth of the Coḷa dynasty as given in the Kanyakumari inscriptions of Vīrarājendra, by its close resemblance to the Mārīca story, suggests that it might well have been taken from one of the Purāṇas (Spencer 1984). In the case of the Pallavas, the ancestry is traced through sages such as Bhṛgu, Aṅgiras, Bharadvāja, Atri, Śamyu, Droṇa and Aśvatthāman (Subrahmanyan 1966) – another instance of the use of popular religious symbols for claims of special status.

If the above instances show that entire dynasties were accorded a divine status, there are instances in which individual kings were attributed divine qualities. This was achieved with the use of various figures of speech such as the *double entendre,* simile and metaphor. Whole verses in contemporary court poetry employ the *double entendre,* one sense applicable to the king and another to a god. Thus the opening verse of the astronomical treatise called the *Laghu Bhāskarīya Vyākhyā* would yield meanings both in praise of Śiva and of the patron of the poet, Sthāṇu Ravi Kulaśekhara of Kerala (Pillai 1969). The closing verse of what is called the Huzur Office Plates of the Āy king Karunantaṭakkan, who was a local chief in former South Travancore, can be taken to be an invocation of Viṣṇu as well as the ruler (*Travancore Archaeological Services* [*TAS*], Vol. I: 16). Such instances can be multiplied.

A ruler is described in a particular set of terms that remind one of the specific achievements of a particular deity or Purāṇic hero. Narasiṃhavarman's victory over Vātāpi (the Cālukya capital) is almost always a feat comparable to the liquidation of Vātāpi (the demon) by the sage Agastya.[8] The victory of the Cera king Kulaśekhara over Mallaimānagar is described as if he were Mallāri (Viṣṇu).[9] The Coḷa king Rājendra is described as being comparable to Śiva for his capture of Kerala, the land created by none less than Paraśurāma.[10] Such examples are numerous and perhaps unmindful of the uncomfortable questions that could have been thrown up in the process.

More common is the use of simile, the metaphor and a particular adjective for the attributes of a deity or a Purāṇic hero. The Velvikudi Plates speak of the bewilderment of the Pallava ruler at the sight of Pāṇḍya Māravarman, at a loss to explain whether the latter was 'a human, a demon, Śiva, the supreme being (*Para Puruṣa* = Viṣṇu) or Indra'.[11] The same record speaks of Jaṭilavarman as equal to the son of Śiva (*Harasūnukalpa*) (ibid.: l.25). Another Pāṇḍyan record contained in the Srivaramangalam Plates likens the birth of Jaṭilavarman, who was equal to Indra, to the birth of Buddha from the Moon, of Pradyumna from Viṣṇu and of Subrahmaṇya from Śiva.[12] Speaking about Śrīvānavan Mahādēvī, the wife of Parāntaka Vīranārāyaṇa, the Sinnamanur Plates say that she was what Śrī was to Śrīnivāsa and Paulomī to Indra.[13] There are many more such examples.

The titles that the rulers assumed often suggested the qualities of the gods or other Purāṇic figures. Pallava Mahendravarman had among his numerous titles Puruṣottama, Mahendra, Vidhi and Sthāṇu;[14] the earliest known copper plate record of the Ceras describes the Perumāḷ as Rājaśekhara (*TAS*: 81–4); Coḷa Parāntaka called himself Śrīnilaya (*TAS*, Vol. III: I: 142, 1.289); Pāṇḍya Māravarman was Śrīvallabha (Sastri 1929), and so on. This opens the doors to a whole world where the king is presented as the husband of the goddesses of prosperity and of earth (De Casparis 1979). This is a recurring theme in the records of most south Indian dynasties. The titles of Śrīpati and Bhūpati, clear attributes of Viṣṇu, are thus appropriated by the ruler. It is these which are presented in the sharp and brief beginnings of the *meykkīrtti* of Rājarāja: *Tirumagaḷ pōla Perunilaccelviyun tanakkēy urimai pūṇḍamai manakkoḷa* (Sastri 1955: 170). The same idea is repeated, *ad nauseum,* in the *meykkīrttis* of the later Coḷas and of the Pāṇḍyas of what Nilakanta Sastri calls the 'Second Empire'.

At very concrete levels also, there were attempts at 'divinizing' the king. The Coḷas started the practice of consecrating images of the kings in temples as objects of worship. A large number of such 'portrait' images of the Coḷa kings have come down to us (ibid.: 453). Rulers of later dynasties in south India repeated this. Another practice was to name temples after the ruler who endowed them. In

[8] Udayendiram Plates, Subrahmanyan (1966: 126, 1.27).

[9] Cf. Rao (1923: 22). A.S. Ramanatha Aiyar, however, doubts this interpretation (*TAS*, Vol. V: 108).

[10] Tiruvalangadu Plates (*South Indian Inscriptions* [*SII*], Vol. III: 3: 382–439).

[11] Velvikudi Plates (*Pāṇdyar Cappēḍukaḷ Pattu* [*PCP*]: 21, 11.21–23).

[12] Srivaramangalam Plates (*PCP*: 57, 11. 16–19).

[13] Larger Sinnamanur Plates (*PCP*: 149, 11.28–9).

[14] For the titles of Mahendravarman, see Lockwood (1977).

most cases, the deity himself was known by a name or a title of the ruler, the most striking example being that of the Great Temple of Thanjavur. Especially noteworthy is the way in which *Uḍaiyār* Śrī Rājarājadevar boasted of the temple he built for 'Śrī Rājarājeśvaram *Uḍaiyār*' (Nagaswami 1972). The very magnitude of the Coḷa temples inspires awe: they would have fulfilled the legitimating function in a consummate way (Veluthat 2002: 96–110). It may not be entirely out of place to elaborate a little on Great Temple of Thanjavur and the way in which it was pressed into service for political legitimation. It is important that Thanjavur was *not* one of the centres celebrated by the *bhakti* saints of the Śaivites; nor is there any tradition, even in the *Sthalapurāṇas*, linking that place or the temple there with one of the Nāyanārs. It was the nucleus of a cluster of villages on relatively high ground on the Kaveri, where the river begins to fan out into its system of distributaries. What we hear about the place for the first time is that Vijayālaya Coḷa captured it from the Muttaraiyar chiefs and that he built a temple for goddess Niṣumbhasūdinī there.[15] The capture of Thanjavur, in any case, brought a vast resource base, the Kaveri delta, under the control of the Coḷas. By making that place the base of his operations and the ceremonial centre of the state, Rājarāja was not only able to control the resources very strategically but also to make his claims to power loud and clear to all the important magnates of the territory he was controlling. The project was undertaken late in his life, probably after all his military expeditions were complete.[16] He was by then heading a powerful and somewhat centralized state, authoritatively, and the statement he made about that state was bold and unequivocal. The temple was anything but a 'system-maintaining mechanism of a weakly organized polity', which is the way George W. Spencer understands it (Spencer 1969).

The statement that Rājarāja made has two aspects, one directly conveyed and the other symbolic or metaphorical. The number of royal inscriptions present on the walls of the temple, which is the literal aspect of the statement, is well known.[17] The range of activities in the temple, the amount of wealth and other resources that were mobilized for it, and other such details that bring out the importance of the institution require no reiteration. The stupendous nature of the structure, too, has been adequately written about. The megalomania of the king is expressed in architecture nearly in the same impulse which drove the Pharaohs, although one cannot make a comparison between the political structures of the two. The *vimāna* was a metaphor for the structure of the state presided over by Rājarāja – a pyramidal structure with a heavy top. Conceived as *Dakṣiṅameru* (the Southern Meru, Meru being the mythological axis of the earth), it was surrounded by shrines of the guardian deities of the four cardinal directions and the

[15] For example, the Tiruvalangadu Plates of Rajendra I (*SII*, Vol. III: No. 205).

[16] It is important to note that most inscriptions on the walls of the temple are of Rājarāja, that too of his twenty-ninth year (AD 1014), which also happens to be his last known year, (*SII*: II). Was he the proverbial 'old man in a hurry?'

[17] The corpus of inscriptions from the Big Temple of Thanjavur, the bulk of which are of Rājarāja, is remarkable (*SII*: II). See also Nagaswami (1972).

four corners, as a first step in identifying the temple with the cosmos.[18] The chief deity is *Dakṣiṅameru-viṭaṅkar*, also called Śrī Rājarājeśvaram-*uḍaiyār*. As we have seen, by a sleight of words, as it were, Śrī Rājarājēśaram-*uḍaiyār* the deity is equated with *Uḍaiyār* Śrī Rājarāja-*devar*. Thus the temple-cosmos identification goes to the level of the identification of the temple/cosmos with the territory and the god with the king, where what the king presides over is the entire cosmos (Champakalakshmi 1996: *loc.cit*). That the sacred and the secular blend perfectly is also evident in the architectural plan and the sculptural and other artistic details.

The most frequently occurring theme in the sculpture of the temple is that of *Tripurāntaka*. This theme makes its appearance in the sculpture of Coḷa temples for the first time in the age of Rājarāja, and in the environs of Thanjavur. There are about thirty representations of this theme in the temple.[19] Scholars have interpreted this in various ways. There is a fresco in Chamber 11 that recaptures the details of the mythological story in all its magnificence. It depicts Śiva as destroying the *puras* ('towns') of the three demons and reducing them to a state of servitude. Brahma was Śiva's charioteer in this battle and the four Vedas were the wheels of his chariot. Agni was his arrow and Mount Mandāra, his bow. Many gods played a supportive and subordinate role in the battle. Even Viṣṇu is presented in such a role: in the guise of *Māyāmōha*, he is represented as attempting to delude the demons. Śiva destroyed the three *puras* in the battle and took the demons as his servants, two of them as his *dvārapālas* ('doorkeepers') and the third, his drummer. Champakalakshmi has argued that 'By using this myth and the iconographic form in the temple's art in a dominant position and in the narrative paintings, Rājarāja achieved his aim of consolidating Śaivism and subordinating other faiths' (Champakalakshmi 1996: 431). The consolidation of Śaivism and subordination of other faiths may well have been the agenda of Rājarāja; but the political message there should not go unheard. Champakalakshmi does take the massiveness of the *dvārapāla* images to show the power of the king; but not in the context of the *Tripurāntaka* theme.[20] Srinivasan had earlier appreciated the political message by saying that *Tripurāntaka* was Rājarāja's choice as the Śaiva counterpart of the Cakravartin ideal.[21] Sivaramamurti had, as early as 1955, seen this as an emphasis on the warrior aspect of Tripurāntaka and the Coḷa king Rājarāja's choice of this form as indicating his prowess as a warrior (Sivaramamurti 1955: 29). Schwindler argues that Tripurāntaka was Rājarāja's favourite personal deity, *iṣṭadēvatā*, and that he used its unique iconographic symbolism to restore the honour and dignity of his lineage, damaged at Takkolam. For him, it is evidence

[18] For the cosmic symbolism of the temple, see Champakalakshmi (1996: 426–27). Architectural and sculptural details are available in Balasubrahmanyam (1975, Chapter 2) and Srinivasan (1991).

[19] Schwindler (1987: 163–78). For a treatment of the Tripurāntaka episode in the Big Temple of Thanjavur, see Dayalan (1991: 445–48).

[20] Champakalakshmi sees the size and volume of the *dvārapāla* figures as a 'metaphor in stone of power' (1996: 428).

[21] Quoted in Champakalakshmi (1996: 429; n. 24).

of the king's conscious assimilation of the divine and the royal persona (Schwindler [1987] 1989).

Does the political significance of this theme, repeated over and over again, go beyond what has been suggested by these interpretations? Does it allude to the way in which Rājarāja reorganized the Coḷa polity by rolling the juggernaut of the state over the locality chiefs (described as 'feudatories' by historians) and attempting to centralize the administration of the empire? Whereas the locality chiefs had exercised considerable power in their territories in the pre-Rājarāja period, we do not hear of them any more in the age of Rājarāja and immediately thereafter. Rājarāja wiped them off as political chiefs and instead, they functioned under him as the functionaries of the state (the 'bureaucracy' of conventional historiography) – that too in areas far removed from their 'home territories' (Veluthat 1993: 121–24). Here Rājarāja himself is Tripurāntaka, rendering the 'demons' homeless but taking them into his personal service. By depicting the power of those whom he subjugated, as witness the massiveness of the *dvārapālas* in the temple,[22] Rājarāja stressed that his own power was still greater. Thus Tripurāntaka forms an icon of Rājarāja's imperial power and position in every way. It may not be irrelevant that in the same chamber where the Tripurāntaka fresco figures also stands a fresco depicting Śiva as *Rāvaṇānugrahamūrti.*

Caṇḍēśvara, described as the *mūlabhṛtya* of Śiva, is consecrated in a big way in this temple and in a bigger way in the Gaṇgaikkoṇḍacoḷapuram temple. This too is not without significance. The *mūlabhṛtyas* are of great importance in the military–political structure of early medieval south India. 'Companions of Honour' of the kings, they constituted the core of the military establishment (Narayanan 1977). Their role in the Pāṇḍya, Cera and Coḷa states is adequately appreciated (Veluthat 1993: 151–57). In the case of the Coḷa state, where Rājarāja and his immediate successors had taken the military strength of the empire to perfection, it is only appropriate that the *mūlabhṛtya* should have been given importance in the ritual and iconographic schemes of the great royal temples. Taken along with the message and implications of the Tripurāntaka icon, this acquires great significance. Thus, Champakalaksmi is right in her observation that 'the iconographic programme of Thanjavur was indeed the political iconography of Rājarāja' (Champakalakshmi 1996: 432).

Closely related to this was the construction of what are described as sepulchral temples or *paḷḷippaḍai.* These were allied with the cult of Deva-rāja in South-East Asia (Sastri 1955: 452–53; 1978: 149–71; Mabbett 1969: 200–23). Temples were constructed over the mortal remains of kings, princes and princesses. The Ādityeśvara temple at Tondamanad was a *paḷḷippaḍai* erected by Parāntaka over the remains of his father; the Ariñjigai-Īśvara at Melpadi commemorated Ariñjaya who died at Arrur; the Pañcavanmahādevīśvara at Ramanathankoil was in memory of the queen-mother (Sastri 1955: 453) and so on. It is reported that

[22] The *dvārapālas* of Śiva, as worshipped in temples, are Śūlapāṇi (the 'wielder of the lance') and Paraśupāṇi (the 'wielder of the axe').

human bones were discovered under the *sanctum sanctora* of several temples when their renovation was undertaken (ibid., also n. 24). However, this practice appears to have lost its popularity shortly afterwards and was, in fact, looked upon with great disapproval as is shown by the attempt to erase the word *paḷḷippaḍai* in the inscription at Ramanathankoil mentioned above.[23]

Attempts to equate the king with a deity or at least with a Purāṇic hero were not invented in this part of the country and followed only the models obtaining in an earlier period in northern India. This finds standardization in the texts of social conduct and statecraft as well. Incidentally, this north-Indian source of inspiration for this particular aspect of the image of royalty points also to the agency through which that inspiration may have reached the south.

What was the function of this attempt, expressed in various ways, to attribute divinity to the king in the particular context of south India? Clearly, it was one of the means to seek legitimation for the ruler by making use of certain symbols of an ideological apparatus, a religious system, which had already gained acceptance among the people. The historical context in which this attempt was made is significant, worth recapitulating at the risk of repetition. We have seen that the beginning of our period was characterized by, among other things (i) a total re-orientation of society on caste lines accepting the paradigm of *Varnāśrama-dharma* as the organizing principle and with (ii) Āgamaic-Purāṇic-*bhakti* religion as the expression of its religious ideology and all this in tandem with (iii) the formation of a new kind of monarchical state. As the religious ideology had gained acceptance among at least those sections of society with which the ruling classes had to come to terms, the idiom of its symbols suited them to validate their position. In other words, religious idioms provided the necessary legitimacy for the newly emerging power structure and the monarch within it.

References

Balasubrahmanyam, S.R. (1975), *Middle Coḷa Temples* (Faridabad: Thomson Press).

Champakalakshmi, R. (1978), 'Religious Conflict in the Tamil Country: A Reappraisal of Epigraphic Evidence', paper presented at the 4th session of the Epigraphical Society of India (Madras).

——— (1982), 'Introduction', *Studies in History,* Vol. 4, No. 2.

——— (1996), *Trade, Ideology and Urbanization: South India 300* BC *to* AD *1300* (Delhi: Oxford University Press).

Dayalan, D. (1991), 'Hymns of the Nayanmars and the Tripurantaka Episode in Big Temple, Thanjavur', in *Indian Archaeological Heritage* (Shri K.V. Soundararajan Festschrift), Vol. I (Delhi: Agam Kala Prakashan).

de Casparis, J.G. (1979), 'Inscriptions and South Asian Dynastic Traditions', in R.J. Moore (ed.), *Tradition and Politics in South Asia* (Delhi: Vikas Publishing House).

Derrett, J.D.M. (1971), 'Two Inscriptions Concerning the Status of Kammāḷas and the Application of Dharmaśāstra', *Professor K.A. Nilakanta Sastri 80th Birthday Felicitation Volume* (Madras: Prof. K.A. Nilakanta Sastri Felicitation Committee).

Laghubhāskarīya (1969), Vol. I, edited by P.K. Narayana Pillai (Trivandrum: University of Kerala).

Lockwood, Michael (1977), 'The Birudas of Mahendravarman', *Bharatiya Purabhilekha Patrika,*

[23] *Annual Reports of South Indian Epigraphy* (1927: II.13), quoted in Sastri (1955: 453, n. 25).

Proceedings of the Epigraphical Society of India, Third Annual Session held at Udupi (Mysore: Epigraphical Society of India).

Mabbett, I.W. (1969), 'Devaraja', *Journal of South Eastern History*, Vol. 10, No. 2, pp. 202–23.

Narayanan M.G.S. (1975), 'The Vedic-Śāstraic-Purāṇic Elements in the Sangam Literature', *Proceedings of the Indian History Congress*, 36th Session, Aligarh.

——— (1996), *Perumals of Kerala* (Calicut: published by the author).

——— (1977), 'The Companions of Honour', in *Reinterpretations of South Indian History* (Trivandrum: College Book House).

Narayanan, M.G.S. and Kesavan Veluthat (1978), 'The Bhakti Movement in South India; in S.C. Malik (ed.), *Indian Movements: Aspects of Dissent, Protest and Reform* (Simla: Institute of Advanced Studies).

——— (1981), 'The Temple in South India', paper presented at the symposium on 'The Socio-Economic Role of Religious Institutions in India', Indian History Congress, 42nd Session, Bodhgaya.

Periyapurāṇam (1974), edited by K. Subrahmanyam (Srivaikuntham: Kumaraguruparan Sangam).

Rao, T.A. Gopinatha (1923), *History of Srivaishnavas* (Madras: Madras University).

Sastri, K.A. Nilakanta (1929), *The Pandyan Kingdom* (London: Luzac and Co.).

——— (1955), *The Coḷas* (Madras: University of Madras).

——— (1972), *The Sangam Literature: Its Cults and Cultures* (Madras: Swathi Publications).

——— (1978), *South India and Southeast Asia* (Mysore: Geetha Book House).

Schwindler, Gary J. (1987), 'Speculations on the Theme of Śiva as Tripurāntaka as It Appears in the Reign of Rājarāja I in the Tanjavur Area, *c.* AD 1000', *Ars Orientalis*, Vol. 17, pp. 163–78.

Sharma, R.S. (1991), *Aspects of Political Ideas and Institutions in Ancient India* (Delhi: Motilal Banarsidass).

Sivaramamurti, C. (1955), *Royal Conquests and Cultural Migration in South India* (Calcutta: Indian Museum).

Spencer, George W. (1969), 'Religious Networks and Royal Influence in Eleventh Century South India', *Journal of the Economic and Social History of the Orient*, Vol. 12, No. 1, pp. 42–56.

——— (1984), 'Heirs Apparent: Fiction and Function in Coḷa Mythical Genealogies', *Indian Economic and Social History Review*, Vol. 21, No. 4, pp. 415–82.

Srinivasan, K.R. (1991), 'The Peruvudaiyar (Brihadisvara) Temple of Tanjavur: a Study' in *Indian Archaeological Heritage* (Shri K.V. Soundararajan Festschrift), Vol. II (Delhi: Agam Kala Prakashan).

Stein, Burton (1980), *Peasant State and Society in Medieval South India* (Delhi: Oxford University Press).

Subrahmanyan, T.N., ed. (1966), *Thirty Pallava Copper Plates* (Madras: Tamil Varalatru Kazhagam).

Tañjaipperuvuḍaiyār Kōyil Kalveṭṭuagaḷ (1972), edited by R. Nagaswami (Madras: Department of Archaeology, Government of Tamil Nadu).

Veluthat, Kesavan (1978), 'Royalty and Divinity: Legitimization of Monarchical Power in South India', *Proceedings of the Indian History Congress*, 39th Session, Hyderabad.

——— (1979), 'The Temple-base of the Bhakti Movement in South India', *Proceedings of the Indian History Congress*, 40th Session, Waltair.

——— (1993), *The Political Structure of Early Medieval South India* (Delhi: Orient Longman).

——— (2002), 'The Temple and the State: Religion and Politics in Early Medieval South India', in R. Champakalakshmi, Kesavan Veluthat and T.R. Venugopalan (eds), *State and Society in Pre-modern South India* (Thrissur: Cosmo Books).

Two Indian Theorists of the State

Barani and Abū'l Faẓl

Irfan Habib

The pre-modern Indian state has been the subject of discussion in much recent writing, the various theories ranging from the concept of Oriental Despotism to that of Segmentary State. The state's taxation capacities, the extent of centralized control, and the degree of systematic administration tend to be assessed and re-assessed. While these concerns were generally not present in medieval writings on the state (except for the role of despotic authority), there were at least two writers, who, some two and a half centuries apart, provided reflections sufficient in scope and consistency to be given the designation of 'theories'. I propose to deal with them separately, since their premises and conclusions appear in sharp contrast to each other. At the end, I would try to sum up what these contrasts tell us about both the circumstances of the times and the intellectual traditions which produced them.

I

Baranī has been much studied and commented upon as a historian, and since the work of Mohammad Habib and Afsar Khan in the 1950's,[1] his position as a political theorist has also been recognized. The following pages thus partly represent the re-visiting of explored ground; such verification may perhaps perform some service, even where it confirms what was previously known; and, therefore, one may proceed to one's task without a long apology. I begin with a brief reconstruction of Baranī's life, and then go on to analyse his political ideas.

Ẓiyā Baranī,[2] was born in 1285, presumably at Baran (mod. Bulandshahr,

[1] Mohammad Habib and and Afsar Umar Salim Khan (eds), *The Political Theory of the Delhi Sultanate*, Allahabad, n.d.

[2] I write Ẓiyā Baranī because he uniformly styles himself thus. But Ziyā'uddīn Baranī would be equally legitimate; this is how he would have been called by others. Amīr Khwurd accordingly styles him Ziyā'u'l Millat wu'ddin; cf. *Siyaru'l Auliya*', Delhi, AH 1302, pp. 312–13. Apparently, the custom of the time inhibited one from using the full name, which would sound pretentious from one's own lips (Ziyā'u'ddīn meaning 'Light of the Faith'). Baranī's own precursor in the narration of the history of the Delhi Sultanate, the author of the *Tabaqāt-i Nāṣirī*, ed. 'Abdu'l Hai Habibi, Vol. 1, Kabul, 1963, pp. 6, 64, 127, etc. calls himself Minhāj[-i] Sirāj, but Baranī, *Tārikh-i Fīroz-shahi*, ed. Saiyid Ahmad Khan, W. Nassau Lees and Kabir al-Din, Bib. Ind., Calcutta, 1860–62, pp. 20–21, calls him Minhāju'ddīn Sirāj, as did, much earlier (AD 1320), Shaikh

south-east of Delhi), in a family of scholars and officials. Until his father's time he could claim for his father Mu'aiyadu'l Mulk no more than a respectable status (*sharīf*).[3] But Mu'aiyadu'l Mulk married the daughter of an official of some importance, Sipahsālār Husāmu'd-Dīn, who rose to be the *wakīl-i dar* ('chamberlain') of Malik Bektars, the *būrbak* ('court master') of Sultan Balban (1266–86), and was made the police chief (*shaḥnah*) of Lakhnauti during Balban's expedition to Bengal.[4] Mu'aiyadu'l Mulk himself became *nā'ib* (deputy) to Prince Arkalī Khān, son of Sultan Jalālu'd-Dīn Khaljī (1290–96),[5] and, under 'Alā'u'd-Dīn Khaljī (1296–1316), the officer-in-charge (*nā'ib-o-khwājah*) of Baran.[6] Baranī's uncle, 'Alā'ul Mulk occupied a high position in the counsels of Sultan 'Alā'ud-Dīn, having taken part in his plot to assassinate Jalālu'd-Dīn and seize the throne. Upon the success of the plot 'Alā'u'l Mulk was rewarded with the governorship of Kara and Awadh, and then with the office of police chief (*kotwāl*) of Delhi; but he died early in the new Sultan's reign.[7]

Baranī himself, as we can see from his writings, received a very extensive education in Arabic and Persian; he was well trained in Muslim theology and deeply read in history. He had begun writing 'out-of-the-common' (*gharīb*) tracts which he used to show to Khwāja Karīmu'd-Dīn at Ghiyaspur in Delhi, in Shaikh Niẓāmu'd-Dīn's life-time (i.e. before 1325).[8] Baranī in his (later?) work *Ḥasrat-nāma* claimed that he had obtained such proximity to Shaikh Niẓāmu'd-Dīn, the most influential mystic of the time at Delhi, that he was one of the three to be summoned by the Shaikh after his humiliation at a debate (*maḥẓar*) organized by Sultan Ghiyāṣu'd-Dīn Tughluq (1320–24), the other two being Muḥyī'u'd-Dīn Kāshānī and the famous poet Amīr Khusrau.[9] Baranī also asserts in his *Tārīkh* that

---

Nizāmu'ddīn in his conversations recorded by Amīr Hasan Sijzī, *Fawā'idu'l Fu'ād*, ed. Muhammad Latif Malik, Lahore, 1966, p. 396. My insistence on Ẓiyā Baranī being the only correct form (see 'Baranī's Theory of the Delhi Sultanate', *The Indian Historical Review*, Vol. 7 (1–2), 1980–81, p. 99, fn.1) was therefore a piece of misplaced pedantry.

3 Baranī's date of birth is established by his statements in the *Tārīkh*: *573*. On p. 350, Baranī says his 'father was *sharīf*', being a daughter's son of Saiyid Jalālu'ddīn, one of 'the leading and eminent Saiyids of Kaithal'.

4 Ibid., pp. 42, 60–61, 87, 119, for Baranī's 'maternal grandfather', Husāmu'ddīn's position as *wakīl-i dar*, p. 87, also for his appointment at Lakhnauti.

5 Ibid., p. 209; at that time, Baranī, still in his boyhood, used to visit the mystic Saiyid Maulā, later executed on the suspicion of having engaged in a conspiracy against the Sultan (pp. 209–12).

6 Ibid., p. 248, where Baranī also comes round to giving the name (or title?) of his father (Mu'aiyadu'l Mulk).

7 Ibid., pp. 222, 236–37, 248, 250. 'Alā'u'l Mulk is represented by Baranī as an important and honest counsellor of 'Alā'uddīn Khaljī (especially pp. 264–71). He was among those officers of the Sultan who died within the first three or four years of the reign (p. 336).

8 Amīr Khwurd, *Siyaru'l Auliyā'*, p. 315. The author's father knew Baranī and is given the credit of introducing him to Shaikh Niẓāmu'ddīn (pp. 312–13).

9 Baranī's *Ḥasrat-nāma*, which is not extant, is cited for the information here given in the *Siyaru'l Auliyā'*, pp. 313, 531–32. A passage from the *Ḥasrat-nāma*, narrating a conversation with Shaikh Nizāmu'ddīn is quoted *in extenso* in 'Abdu'l Ḥaqq, *Akhbāru'l Akhyār*, ed. 'Abdu'l Ahad, Delhi, AH 1332; pp. 103–5; it is professedly derived from the *Siyaru'l Auliyā*, where, however, at least in the printed edition, it is not to be found.

he had such close relations 'for years' with the two leading poets of 'Alāu'd-Dīn Khaljī's time, Amīr Khusrau and Amīr Ḥasan that the three were inseparable, he himself being the instrument in drawing the two 'masters' together.[10] All this indicates that by the time of Muḥammad Tughluq's accession (1324), Baranī had acquired a certain position in the scholarly and theological circles of Delhi.

But despite such status, and his own family's links with the bureaucracy, a government appointment yet eluded him. This delay in achieving a suitable office could be one of the reasons for Baranī's deep bitterness against lowborn upstarts competing for office with men from established families. At last in 1334–35, when he must have been nearly fifty, he caught the eye of Sultan Muḥammad Tughluq (1324–51), so that he now became 'a servant of the court' (*mulāzim-i dargāh*),serving the Sultan as an aide or companion (*muqarrab*) continuously till the end of the reign.[11] Seventeen years as a courtier gave Baranī an unrivalled proximity to that brilliant and self-willed sovereign, and an opportunity to learn how monarchy in reality functioned, though he was to mourn later that, as one of a set of scholar-courtiers, he remained a pliant yes-man.[12]

Muḥammad Tughluq's death, and the enthronement of his cousin Fīroz brought about an irredeemable fall in Baranī's fortunes. He was dismissed and 'fell among a host of perils', barely escaping execution.[13] He was imprisoned in the fort of Bhatnair for five months.[14] Upon his release he was left penniless, and fell into abject poverty, a condition which engendered in him not spiritual contentment, as alleged in the *Siyaru'l Auliyā,* but a sentiment of deep inner disappointment and resentment.[15] He had failed in the realm of religion, as also the world: nothing but regret (*ḥasrat*) remained.[16]

[10] Baranī, *Tārīkh,* p. 360.

[11] Ibid., pp. 466–67, 497, 504, 516–17. According to Amīr Khwurd, he became the *nadīm* (companion, confidant) of the Sultan (*Siyaru'l Auliyā*, p. 313). It was apparently in this capacity that he was deputed by the Sultan, along with Prince Fīroz, to deliver 100,000 *tankas* to Shaikh Quṭbu'ddīn Munawwar (ibid., pp. 251–55).

[12] Being one of those 'who had learnt to distinguish black and white, had a share of learning from which respectability (*sharaf*) comes, (but) had committed hypocrisy out of worldly greed and ambition, and had become a close companion (*muqarrab*) to the Sultan'. (*Tārīkh-I Firozshahi,* p. 466).

[13] Ibid., p. 557.

[14] Baranī in *Ṣaḥīfa-i Na't-i Muḥammadī,* Riza Library, Rampur, MS, quoted by Mohammad Habib, *Medieval India Quarterly,* Vol. 3 (3–4), 1958: 242. Cf. Baranī, *Tārīkh-i Firozshahi,* 544, where Baranī refers to his presence in the fort of Bhatnair after Fīroz's accession. In the light of these facts, Amīr Khwurd's statement that Baranī voluntarily vacated his position upon the death of Sultan Muḥammad, in lieu of a pension (*māyahtāj*) from Sultan Fīroz (*Siyaru'l Auliyā',* 313) is hardly to be credited. Cf. Mohammad Habib, *Medieval India Quarterly,* Vol. 3 (3–4), 1958, p. 243.

[15] His own statements in his *Tārīkh,* pp. 165, 204–5, 466–67, 548 – how he was old, toothless, he had nothing left, no one would give him even a loan, etc. Amīr Khwurd, who might have witnessed his funeral, says that at the time of his death, 'he did not have a penny (*dām-o-dāng*) on him; he did not even have clothes for his body; on his bier there was just one coverlet above, and one mat [below]'. *Siyaru'l Auliyā',* p. 313.

[16] Baranī, *Tārīkh,* pp. 200–201; also, practically all the statements on the pages of this work cited in fn.14, *supra.*

It was in this phase that Baranī appears to have written his major works They fall into two obvious categories. The first is of a purely religious character The *Ṣaḥīfa-i Na't-i Muḥammadī,* in devotion to the Prophet, was composed when, according to the preface, the author was seventy years of age (1353–54), and had an anxious urge to do something in order to face the reckoning at the Day of Judgement.[17] From what we know from references to it by Amīr Khwurd and 'Abdu'l Ḥaqq, Baranī's *ḥasrat nāma* dealt with sufic matters, including reminiscences of Shaikh Nizamu'd-din;[18] unluckily, it is not extant. To this class also belonged, to judge from their titles, the *Ṣalāt-i Kabīr, 'Ināyat-nāma-i ilāhī,* and *Ma'āṣir-i Sādāt,* mentioned by Amīr Khwurd, as having been written after Baranī's retirement from worldly affairs.[19]

But Baranī wrote prolifically in another sphere too, the worldly one. What was possibly his first work after retirement was frankly designed to win back Sultan Firoz's favour. This was the *Akhbār-i Barmakīyān.* Professedly translated from the Arabic writings of Abū'l Qāsim Tāifi and Abū Muḥammad 'Abdu'llāh, and giving an account of the famous family of 'Abbasid viziers, the work was dedicated to Sultan Fīroz.[20] Apparently with the same intention, Baranī began writing his great history, the *Tārīkh-i Fīroz-shāhī.* Simon Digby was the first to identify an earlier version of this work.[21] The existence of this version may well explain a statement that Baranī makes at the end of his long chapter on Balban: the present Sultan (Fīroz) was well-versed in history, but, though Baranī had named his history after him, he could not even obtain the felicity of presenting it to him.[22] Baranī must doubtless be referring here to the earlier version of his work. By the time that he completed the final version (in 758/1357),[23] the hope of reaching Fīroz and getting his attention had definitely been lost. It is, therefore, likely – though this needs to be confirmed by careful collation of the two versions – that, at least for the period before Fīroz Tughluq's accession, the final version is more free and frank, and less concerned with what Firoz's court-circle would approve than was the earlier one.[24] Since the *Tārīkh-i Fīroz-shāhī.* is a major

[17] S. Nurul Hasan 'Sahifa-i-Nat-i-Muhammadi of Zia-ud-din Baranī', *Medieval India Quarterly,* Vol.1 (3–4), 1950, p. 100. This work is probably identical with the *Ṣanā-i Muḥammadī* mentioned in *Siyaru'l Auliyā*, p. 313.

[18] *Siyaru'l Auliyā*, pp. 313, 531–32; *Akhbāru'l Akhyār,* pp. 103–05.

[19] *Siyaru'l Auliyā*, p. 313.

[20] The work is described by Charles Rieu in his *Catalogue of Persian Manuscripts in the British Museum,* I, p. 333b, and Hermann Ethe, *Catalogue of the Persian, Turkish, Hindustani and Pashtu Manuscripts in the Bodleian Library,* Cols. 161–62. C.A. Storey, *Persian Literature, a Bio-bibliographical Survey,* Vol.1, ii, London, 1953, p. 1082 & n., treats the work as undated, pointing out that Ethe's date for it is based on error. It has been printed, Bombay, 1889; and there are also other and earlier editions.

[21] S. Digby, *War-horse and Elephant in the Delhi Sultanate,* London, 1971, p. 83 ('BTFS', 'BTFSA' and 'BTFSB').

[22] Baranī, *Tārīkh,* p. 125.

[23] Ibid., p. 23.

[24] Baranī, *Tārīkh,* p. 16, has probably this in mind when he says that though the historian 'out of fear and dread' might not be able to speak the truth about contemporary times even in an apologetic form (*ma'zirate*)', he should be free and truthful about the past.

vehicle for the expression of Baranī's political thought, it is important to remember that whatever Baranī says in the *Tārīkh*, except in the last short portion, is probably without any mental reference to the issue of pleasing or displeasing the current regime.

Finally, among the mass of Baranī's worldly writings is the large, repetitive and verbose work, the *Fatāwā-i Jahāndārī*, 'Opinions on Government'.[25] Neither in the short preface nor in the epilogue (defective at the end), does Baranī explicitly indicate the date of its compilation. He calls himself a 'well-wisher of the Sultan's Court' (*du, 'ā-goy-i dargāh-i Sulṭānī*);[26] but does not mention the Sultan's name. If the reference to his having become 'extremely indigent, helpless and perplexed' that is contained in an impassioned prayer to God,[27] is to be treated literally, the work should belong to the last phase of Baranī's life. And if the absence of any reference to Sultan Fīroz by name is to be taken to mean that no hopes of any relief from the throne had now remained, one may suppose it to have been composed after the completion of the *Tārīkh-i Fīroz-shāhī*, a conclusion, which Mohammad Habib drew from his personal impression of the author's declining powers that the work gave him.[28]

For what Baranī says about polity and society, his biography may well set much of the context. He was a theologian and man of culture in the Perso-Islamic mould; he had known a Sultan closely for seventeen years; he had moved in circles where political events and administrative matters formed the fabric of daily discourse; and now, all of a sudden, in his old age he had been removed from his position of dignity and status. He had known the system first-hand; his personal tragedy not only embittered him (despite the solace sought through pious works), but also incited him to locate the defects in the system in which this could occur. He constructed a theory of the history of the Delhi Sultanate in the *Tārīkh-i Fīroz-shāhī* to show how internal contradictions dogged the Sultanate's course, in order to create, in recurring cycles, the fall of successive ruling groups.[29] In the *Fatāwā-i Jahāndārī*, which is constructed in the style of the 'Mirror-for-Princes'

25 This work survives only in single MS (1.0 1149=Ethe, I, 2563) in the India Office Library, London. I have used a rotograph copy of this MS, in the Centre of Advanced Study in History Library, Aligarh Muslim University. An abridged translation of this work by Afsar Begam (Afsar Umar Salim Khan) was published in *Medieval India Quarterly*, Vol. 3 (1–2), 1957, pp. 13–87, and Vol. 3 (3–4), 1958, pp. 151–96, and, then, combined with an introduction and epilogue by Mohammad Habib, 'Life and Thought of Ziauddin Baranī', *Medieval India Quarterly*, Vol. 3 (1–2), 1957, pp. 1–12, and Vol. 3 (3–4), 1958, pp. 197–252, was issued as *The Political Theory of the Delhi Sultanate*, Allahabad, n.d. The translation is a pioneering work and, despite its large omissions and some inaccuracies and unevenness in annotation, has done good service in bringing Baranī's *Fatāwā-i Jahūndārī* to public attention.

26 F. 1b. Not *du'āgoy-i Sultānī*, 'royal chaplain', as in Ethe's *Catalogue*, Vol. I, col. 1377 (No. 2563).

27 F. 246a.

28 *Medieval India Quarterly*, Vol. 3 (1–2), 1957, p. 11 ('probably his last work').

29 I have attempted to reconstruct the theory in my 'Baranī's Theory', pp. 99–115.

books in Arabic literature,[30] Baranī clearly seeks to advise rulers (in the guise of the fictitious 'sons of Maḥmūd') how they should act to prevent, confront or resolve the essential problems of the polity he had lived under.

Here a word of caution may be in order. Baranī makes certain statements explicitly or implicitly as embodying his own opinions; he is here by and large fairly consistent. But, most often, he makes his historical characters discourse on political questions: they speak,[31] then, mostly in terms suitable to their reputations. The particular opinions ascribed to such figures are probably, but need not be in every case, those of Baranī himself. In the *Fatāwā-i Jahāndārī,* Maḥmūd of Ghaznin gives opinions such as a great crusader of the faith might be expected to offer.[32] Sultan Balban, a sovereign of a totally different stamp, becomes in the *Tārīkh-i Fīroz-shāhī,* the vehicle for a series of statements on similar matters that are quite different in thrust or emphasis from those ascribed to Maḥmūd.[33] Baranī does not cite any earlier text on political institutions or law; and he implies no knowledge or reading of either al-Māwardī (974–1058) or Nizāmu'l Mulk Ṭūsī (1018–92) or of the opinions they offer.[34]

As the title of Baranī's tract *Fatāwā-i Jahāndārī* shows, his concern is with the entire matter of *jahāndārī,* 'world-keeping', that is, state or government. The scope of his treatment is not thus confined to royalty alone, though the king

[30] On this genre of literature see Erwin I.J. Rosenthal, *Political Thought in Medieval Islam: An Introductory Outline*, Cambridge, 1962, pp. 67–83.

[31] As especially Maḥmūd in *Fatāwā, passim,* or Balban in *Tārīkh*, pp. 31–58, 82–97.

[32] Baranī, of course, never intended it to be understood that he had obtained the actual texts of Maḥmūd's conversations. The picture he had of Maḥmūd, and which he expected the reader to share, might not be historically justifiable in many particulars. Mohammad Habib, in *Medieval India Quarterly,* Vol. 2 (1–2), 1957: 3, indeed, pronounces Baranī's ignorance of the real Maḥmūd as 'appalling'. Yet the picture that he offers of Maḥmūd is certainly consonant with the one presented also by his contemporary 'Iṣāmī (AD 1350), in his metrical history, the *Futūhu-s Salātīn*, ed. A.S. Usha, Madras, 1948, pp. 34–61.

[33] On Balban's discourses, see Peter Hardy's 'The *Oratio Recta* of Baranī's *Tārīkh -i Firuz-shahi* – Fact or Fiction', *Bulletin of the School of Oriental and African Studies*, Vol. 20, 1957, pp. 315–21.

[34] Baranī's omission of any reference to Niẓāmu'l Mulk Tūsī's *Siyāsat-nāma* (written, AD 1091) is certainly surprising, since it must have been well-known in his time, and much of it consists of anecdotes, using a technique not very dissimilar to the one adopted by Baranī in the *Fatāwā*. Some of the stories used by Niẓāmu'l Mulk are also used by Baranī, but to drive a different point and generally differing in detail. Thus, though like Baranī in the *Fatāwā*, MS.I.O. 1149, ff.3a–6b, Niẓāmu'l Mulk also gives the story of 'Amr Lais and the Samanid *amīr* Ismā'īl (Tūsī, *Siyāsat-nāma*, ed. Ja'far Shu'ūr, Teheran, 1348 Shamsi, pp. 21–27); yet Niẓāmu'l Mulk does not refer to 'Amr Lais in the very hostile terms that Baranī does. The only element in common is that Niẓāmu'l Mulk also says that Ismā'īl declined to accept 'Amr's offer of his treasures, since these were unlawfully acquired. Baranī cites his sources for anecdotes occasionally, but where the authors' names are provided, viz. Ibn Isḥāq, ff.26b, 111b; Aṣma'ī, f.62a; Wāqidī, f.62a; and Ṣa'alibi, f.63b, they are possibly quoted from either memory or simply for effect. Only one author of a Persian source, Mu'īn 'Aṣm (and his son), for the history of the Seljuqid Sanjar, is mentioned (f.203b), but I cannot locate this author, or even be sure of the person's historicity.

is the central element of the polity he treats of.[35] In the preface to the *Fatāwā* Baranī tells the reader: 'the King (*pādshāh*) is one of the wonderful creations of God; and God is the Creator of things, both good and bad'.[36] In other words, in itself, kingship could be good or evil according the character of the King: there was no ordained goodness in the institution. This is a position far more neutral, than the assertions that Baranī puts in the mouths of Maḥmūd and Balban. Maḥmūd is represented as saying in the *Fatāwā* that 'royalty implies the position of a representative of God (*khilāfat-i khudāī*) or vicegerency of God (*niyābat-i khudāī*)'[37] In the *Tārīkh*, Balban is similarly made to claim that 'in the worldly aspect, royalty is (the same as) the vicegerency of God'.[38] Elsewhere, Balban tells his son, Muḥammad: 'The heart of the King is the object of the sight of God (*manẓar-i Rabbānī*): this is a very wonderful object to be viewed, and has no relationship with other objects of sight that the other sons of Adam offer. For until God casts His eye over this object and imparts to this object instructions for the generality of His servants, the affairs of godly people, which depend on the heart and speech of the King, will not be properly managed.'[39] But, though Baranī writes here as if Balban was putting forward a legitimate claim for his own right to the office of King, he knew that, in fact, such pretensions were spurious. This appears from an admission he ascribes to another Sultan. When Jalālu'd-Dīn Khaljī became King (1290) after a long career as an officer and commander, he found no divine light illuminating the throne: 'Royalty (*pādshāhat*)', he is alleged to have declared in his disillusionment, 'is all deception and display. Although externally it has ornamentation and trappings, inside it is weak and contemptible (*zār zār*).'[40] It almost seems as if Baranī sympathises with the resentful response he attributes to 'the vain upstartish young (nobles)' who were then present in the that court. They told each other, 'Royalty (*salṭanat*) is all terror, power and claim to unshared authority; the task does not suit this man.'[41] Here force is recognized in all its nakedness as the real source of royal power; and one can see that Baranī uses the device of introducing Jālalu'd-Dīn Khaljī's disillusionment and the young nobles' realism to remind us of this sordid fact.

It is to be noted that Baranī nowhere even remotely hints at any social contract, which might originally have given rise to monarchy and so to have placed the king and his subjects in a relationship of mutual obligation. Force alone is the source of royalty; and the ruler's self-interest, custom and religion the only constraints upon (or guides to) his action. It is with these compulsions or influences that Baranī largely deals, especially in his *Fatāwā-i Jahāndārī.*

[35] F.160a: 'The substance (*sarmūya*) of *jahāndārī* is that the positive and prohibitive commands of the *Pādshāh* are imposed and enforced on the people'.

[36] Ibid., f.2a.

[37] Ibid., f.167a–b.

[38] Baranī, *Tārīkh*, p. 34.

[39] Ibid., p. 70.

[40] Ibid., p. 179.

[41] Ibid., p. 180.

In a passage in which he introduces one of the imaginary counsels of Maḥmūd, Baranī considers the problems that the sheer reliance on violence poses for royalty. If anyone acquires some power, he seizes a territory by destroying its existing possessor and declaring himself king: thereafter he obtains nobles, supporters and courtiers, 'fifty or sixty thousand men and women, young and old, slaves and children becoming dependent on him and loyal to him'; and, on their support he maintains his rule. But if he dies or is assassinated, another person becomes king; he thereupon destroys 'the establishments and families' of the former ruler's nobility and dependents, to ensure his own firm position by bringing in a 'new' set of supporters; for were he to continue the older one, neither could he trust them, nor they him.[42] Thus there could be no stability in either kingly power or in the ruling groups.

The one way to avoid this could be a firm espousal of the dynastic principle. 'In ancient times, in Iran, Rome, Yemen, Syria and Egypt' this principle prevailed universally and rigorously, so that no one thought of overthrowing the established dynasty. This enabled the kings to continue with an established hereditary nobility, without any danger to their own position.[43] Unfortunately, this salutary system could not survive in Islam. First, the Umayyads ('Mu'āwiya, Yazīd and the Marwānids') destroyed the followers and supporters of the Hashimite house, without which they could not have ruled for eighty (*rect.* ninety) years. And the 'Abbasids similarly destroyed the house of the Umayyads and its adherents to establish their own Caliphate.[44] Baranī had himself seen three dynasties rule (the Balbanids, 1266–90; Khaljīs, 1290–1320; Tughluqs, 1320–1416), and one can appreciate his anxiety on this score, especially since each of the dynastic changes at Delhi had led to the wholesale overthrow of older elements in the nobility – episodes which he chronicles in his *Tārīkh* with great pathos.[45]

Another means of establishing the position of the monarchy was the dazzling display of pomp and splendour, by which the ruler might overawe his subjects. The King needed, therefore, to follow the practices of the Emperors of ancient Iran, which involved such deeds as the construction of 'high palaces', holding grand courts, making people offer prostration (*sijda*), accumulating treasures, seizing properties and grants of (previous) kings, wearing jewels and silk and making others wear them, imposing punishments, and gathering large harems. Such practices, Maḥmūd is represented as saying, were repugnant to Islam, and yet expedient for the ruler.[46] Similar statements are attributed to Balban, who

[42] Baranī, *Fatāwā*, f.223b.

[43] Ibid., f.223a. The necessity of dynastic succession in a strict manner is urged through a different argument attributed to Balban in the *Tārīkh*. Since the King is the vicegerent of God, such 'vicegerency of God cannot consort with the meanness of the mean and the worthless [i.e., the low-born]'; moreover, a King by inheritance ('from grandfather and father') commands prestige, which leads to habitual obedience by subjects without the necessary recourse to force (*Tārīkh*, pp. 34–35).

[44] Baranī, *Fatāwā, f.224a.*

[45] Cf. my 'Baranī's Theory', pp. 107–10.

[46] Baranī, *Fatāwā*, ff.99a–100a.

offers them without the apologetic air with which Maḥmūd is alleged to have made them: 'Unless a king followed the customs of the Iranian Emperors (*Akāsira*, Khusroes) in holding court and in instituting strict ceremonial, he would not excite the necessary awe (*haibat*) among his subjects, so necessary for exacting obedience.'[47]

If monarchy must thus imbibe practices which are un-Islamic, this is surely because the institution as such, after all, does not owe its existence to Islam. Indeed, as we have seen, Baranī spoke appreciatively of pre-Islamic monarchies where happily the institution of dynastic succession was rigorously observed. To him Nausherwān, the Iranian emperor, was an ideal, 'just' (*'ādil*) ruler, so that it could be said of Caliph 'Umar that 'he had followed Nausherwān's practices (*Nausherwānī karda ast*)', though Nausherwān could not anticipate him in his personal modesty and probity.[48] Similarly, Alexander is quoted (through Maḥmūd) in favour of setting limits to royal projects (*'azmu'l-mulūk*): only rulers like the Pharaohs claiming to be divinities could pursue projects irrespective of consequences.[49]

It follows, then, that there could be various functions common between rulers, whether pre-Islamic or Islamic. The initial one, in consonance with general belief, was justice (*'adl*). This involves, says Baranī, through Maḥmūd, two kinds of 'equality-seeking' conduct (*musāwāt tālabī*). In the first (*k͟hāṣ*), the ruler (and any judicial authority) dispenses justice between contending parties, high or low, by treating them with strict impartiality. In the second (*'ām*), the ruler also seeks equality in his own life with his indigent subjects. This latter was, however, achieved only by the early Caliphs of Islam. Clearly, what could be expected from ordinary rulers, both non-Muslim like Nausherwān, or Muslim rulers after the early Caliphs, was justice based on the 'equality-seeking' of the first kind.[50]

It is to be understood – through Baranī is not explicit on the point – that the establishment of equality between two litigating parties for purposes of justice was not to be confounded with seeking equality in general. On the contrary, the essential function of all states was to enforce such laws or regulations as established and strengthened an unequal hierarchical order. Baranī (speaking, again, through Maḥmūd) concedes that 'all sons of Adam are the same in regard to their creation and the same in appearance and body; whatever diversity takes place in the matter of goodness and badness among the sons of Adam is because of the influence of personal qualities and the doing of deeds.' But he goes on to say that 'the higher and the lowly qualities among men were [in fact] marked out at the Beginning and accompanies their souls'. Even 'the callings (*ṣan'at-hā*), noble or ignoble, from that of scribe and horseman to barber and tanner, which people take' is predetermined. The higher moral qualities are only possessed by those belonging to

47 Baranī, *Tārīk͟h*, pp. 31–32.
48 Baranī, *Fatāwā*, ff.136b–137a.
49 Ibid., ff.34a–35b.
50 Ibid., ff.135a–137a. Baranī attributes the distinction between the two kinds of 'equality-seeking' to Ḥanafite theorists.

the nobler professions; and the Kings should ensure that they alone should comprise the ruling class, not 'the lowly and the ignoble'.[51] Baranī is not here speaking of a caste system, with hereditary professions, but of a pre-ordained hierarchy in society to protect which has been a cardinal function of the State, under all good regimes of the past.[52]

Baranī narrates how the famous Bahrām Gor forgot this principle, and appointed a low-born Vizier. This Vizier soon overthrew the older nobility and replaced them by cruel upstarts. Injustice reigned, and, everything collapsing, Bahrām Gor had to take refuge with the Indian King (*Rāi*) of Kanauj. The *Rāi* asked him to draw his nobles only from amongst the high-born; and, when with his assistance, Bahrām reinstated himself, he followed the advice to the letter, duly punishing the low-born Vizier and his associates.[53]

The ancient Iranian monarchy performed its true function once again when it was confronted by Mazdak, who preached a doctrine of communism extending to both property and women, and had ordered that 'the poor should seize the wealth of the rich'. Nausherwān secured the suppression of this dangerous sect.[54]

The Islamic rulers had, according to Baranī, no less a duty to perform than the ancient kings to keep the hierarchical order in place. After describing how the low-born have negative qualities assigned to them by Predestination, Maḥmūd is quoted in the *Fatāwā* as warning that no King should give place in his court to 'the low-born, the market-men (*bāzāriān*), the base, the vile, the worthless (*nākasān*), the mean, the shameless, those of illegitimate birth', since such a course would bring 'ignominy (*fazīḥat*) to royalty.'[55] But the work in which Baranī returns again and again to this matter is his *Tārīkh*.

In the *Tārīkh-i Fīroz-shāhī*, Baranī makes Balban speak forthrightly of

[51] Baranī, *Fatāwā*, ff.216a–219a. Even the Prophet is quoted in support of these propositions (f.218b).

[52] I find it hard to share Professor Mohammad Habib's view that Baranī, while making these statements, was influenced by 'Popular Hinduism', or that he was 'very deeply imbued with the traditions of the Hindu caste system'; cf. *Medieval India Quarterly*, Vol. 3 (3–4), 1958, p. 224. Baranī nowhere argues that one must adopt one's father's profession; he had objection only to upward vertical mobility, not to a horizontal one. Besides, Baranī's argument is throughout steeped in the framework of Islamic thought, which was by no means hostile to hierarchical divisions in society.

[53] Baranī, *Fatāwā*, ff.211a–213a. It is interesting that though the story of Bahrūm Gor's dishonest minister (*wazīr-i khā'in*) occurs in Niẓāmu'l Mulk (Tūsī, *Siyāsat-nāma*, pp. 30–41) as well, the minister is not said to be of low birth, there is no mention of the *Rāi* of Kanauj, and other particulars are also different.

[54] *Fatāwā*, ff.77a–78a. On Mazdak, Baranī's ultimate source was probably Bal'amī [*Tarjuma-i*] *Tārīkh-i Tabarī*, pub. Nawal Kishor, Kanpur, n.d., Vol. 3, pp. 312–17. Baranī, however, does not cite Bal'amī anywhere in his *Fatāwā*. The story is given at length in Tūsī, *Siyāsat-nāma*, pp. 294–318, but none of its special details are present in Baranī's summary account. Moreover, Niẓāmu'l Mulk links Mazdak with heterodox sects which need to be suppressed, while Baranī lays stress more on the hateful values of equality and immorality that Mazdak preached.

[55] Baranī, *Fatāwā*, f.217a.

the duty of the Sultan to keep the low-born away from all offices of government. 'He did not look (merely) to claims of old service and loyalty and did not appoint any one poor, unskilled, miserly, greedy, or low-born, to a position of command (*sarī o sarwarī*).'[56] The definition of a low-born was quite broad, extending from a minister, whose grandfather was descended of a weaver, to the son of a Hindu slave.[57] Such a happy state of affairs where such persons were resolutely excluded from positions of power and pelf, however, did not last, and despotic monarchs, in order to enforce total obedience, recruited pliable nobles from lower, plebeian elements. This was seen under 'Alāu'd-Dīn Khaljī (1296–1316), the most powerful of the Delhi Sultans, when in his last years he put into high positions 'worthless persons(?), clerks, low-born revenue-collectors (*shiqdārān*) and foolish slaves.'[58]

It almost seemed as if the Sultans were driven despite their will to take recourse to such acts. Muhammad Tughluq (1324–51) recounted to Baranī 'stories full of scorn and contempt for the low-born, the base, the mean and the ignoble', and stressed that he 'held the base-born crew to be a greater enemy of his than the false gods.'[59] And yet he went on to fill offices of government with the low-born, giving them to a musician's son, three wine-distillers, a cook, a gardener, a weaver's son, a low-caste *mālī* (gardener), a lowly 'market-man', and a slave ('the shame of all slaves in appearance and conduct'), all named, and including both Muslims and Hindus.[60]

Baranī thus sees that the state in its most powerful moments tends to forget one of its primary functions – the closure of gates of the ruling class to outsiders. His narrative provides a seemingly cogent explanation as to why this happens: the Sultan's need in his drive for despotic power to curb and replace the established nobility by introducing new competing elements. But he himself never explicitly puts forward this explanation.

If the state should maintain stability in the social sphere by confining power to men of high birth, it has a similar duty to ensure stability in the economic sphere by keeping prices under control. The rulers of ancient Iran are said to have collected grain by way of taxes and kept it in reserve to keep down prices and avoid scarcities.[61] Maḥmūd is stated to have held that engrossing (*iḥtikār*) needed to be suppressed and prices fixed to prevent profiteering.[62] In these observations Baranī is surely inspired by his memory of 'Alā'ud-Dīn Khaljī's price-control measures, which he has described in his *Tārīkh*, with exceptional lucidity and

[56] Baranī, *Tārīkh*, p. 29. On p. 38, Sultan Iltutmish is said to have warned that the low-born were not to be appointed just on account of their skill (*hunarmandī*).

[57] Ibid., pp. 36, 39. The definition of the 'low-born' certainly posed a problem. Balban himself was a Turkish slave, and Baranī scornfully regarded him and his group of 'Forty Slaves of Iltutmish' as 'contemptible men and purchased slaves' (ibid., p. 27).

[58] Ibid., p. 337. I cannot make anything of the first word, *yalaflakhān*.

[59] Ibid., pp. 404–05.

[60] Ibid., p. 405.

[61] Baranī, *Fatāwā*, f.103a–b.

[62] Ibid., f.92a ff.

sophistication.[63] This is one clear case where Baranī could well be reading a recent experience into the past and defining a function of the state which could have occurred to few others.

We may finally consider those functions of government, which belonged to states headed by Muslim rulers. Here an obviously simple proposition was that such rulers must enforce the *Sharī'a* or Muslim law. Baranī is aware of this, but is realistic enough to see the distinction between the desirability of the enforcement of the *Sharī'a* in all its rigour and the sheer impracticability of such an enforcement.

Significantly, he does not regard the office of the *Khalīfa* as central to Islamic polity. The destruction of the Caliphate of Baghdad by the Mongols in 1258 delivered the *coup de grace* to an already defunct institution, and Baranī sees the early caliphates as mere episodes in the history of monarchy, and not at all as a parallel institution.[64] The *Sharī'a* is to be enforced now not under the aegis of a Caliph, about whose qualifications for office theologians might argue,[65] but by kings who take office on the strength of military prowess or dynastic succession.

When Baranī makes Maḥmūd speak in consonance with his reputation as an upholder of the faith, he is shown as pressing his sons to have the right faith and fulfil their obligations under it. 'The sign of the firmness of the faith of a King (*Pādshāh*) is that he keeps himself and his subjects on the high road of the *Sharī'a*.'[66]

In order to bring about such a desirable situation, Maḥmūd advised his sons to ensure that *muḥtasibs* or censors are appointed to oversee *Sharī'a* enforcement, that the making of liquor is suppressed, and that prostitutes, minstrels, etc., are banished.[67] One may think that here there was little room left for compromise. But in the *Tārīkh*, Balban is made to suggest that it might be better to stay the righteous hand in such matters. The public display of the prohibited professions was to be strongly suppressed. But if the practitioners of the sinful trades 'retire to mean corners [and] their sins are not visible, such people should not be banned, because otherwise many wicked persons, out of lust, would make inroads into men's harems'.[68]

Baranī is more insistent, on the other hand, on the suppression of the enemies of Islam. The enemies he targets are two: external (Hindus) and internal

[63] Baranī, *Tārīkh*, pp. 303–16. I have analysed this account in 'The Price Regulations of Ala'u'ddin Khalji – a defence of Zia Baranī', *The Indian Economic and Social History Review*, Vol. 21 (4), 1984: 393–414.

[64] Baranī, *Fatāwā*, f.224a. Baranī here speaks of the Umayyads as Sultans (*Salāṭīn-i banī-Umayya*).

[65] Cf. the well-known qualifications laid down by al-Māwardī, for which see Rosenthal, *Political Thought*, p. 29.

[66] Baranī, *Fatāwā*, f.7a.

[67] Ibid., ff.8a–9a.

[68] Baranī, *Tārīkh*, p. 43. At other places, Baranī does not conceal his personal admiration for many practitioners of the sinful arts (pp. 165–66; 199), where he gives the names of the women singers and dancers, with enthusiastic praise of their beauty and art.

(the philosophers). Maḥmūd was naturally a suitable spokesman for an uncompromising stance here. Owing to the obscurity of the position of Hindus in the eyes of Muslim law (in regard to whether they are to be treated as *zimmīs,* and so protected, or as *kāfirs,* infidels, and, therefore, unprotected),[69] Baranī shows Maḥmūd to have been 'an adherent of the Shāfi'ī *mazhab*', and to say that 'Imām Shāfi'ī has said of the Hindus that they are either to be killed, or converted to Islam; it is not permissible to [let them live and] take *jizya* (poll-tax) from them.'[70] Maḥmūd is then shown as regretting the wrong advice of his minister Aḥmad Ḥasan Maimandī, owing to which he had not been able to attempt a 'killing of all Brahmans and converting all Hindus to Islam.'[71] When a scholar advised Iltutmish (1210–36) to slaughter or convert all Hindus, the advice was not accepted on the intervention of his minister Niẓāmu'l-Mulk Junaidī – as Baranī relates in another tract of his.[72] In both cases one is led to infer that expediency was the reason for the rulers' failing to enforce the dictates of the *Sharī'a.*

In the *Tārīkh,* as in the *Fatāwā,* Baranī admits that due to what is judged to be the interests of state itself, Hindus had to be tolerated. Jalālu'd-Dīn Khaljī (1290–96) is made to point out how in his dominions Hindus were wealthy and prosperous and freely enjoyed the right to worship idols and beat drums and celebrate their festivals.[73] In the *Fatāwā* Baranī mourns how in his own days, 'the Kings of Islam' showed respect to 'Hindus, Mongols, polytheists and infidels', by making them sit on the *masnad* (cushion) and in other ways.[74] The Hindus, merely by paying taxes (*jizya ? kharāj*) are allowed to have their temples and celebrations, ride horses, employ Muslim servants, flaunt their titles (*rāī, rānā, ṭhākur, sāh, mahtā, pandit*), etc., right in the capital seats of Muslim rulers.[75] It is, however, singular that in his *Tārīkh,* Baranī himself seems to consider concessions given to the Hindu rural aristocracy or the employment of Hindu officers in high positions in the Sultanate as reasonable; and such measures call forth no protest from him.[76]

Baranī could have claimed greater success in the war against his second target: the 'philosophers' (*falāsifa*) or rationalists within the fold of Islam. He makes Maḥmūd put them at par with the Brāhmaṇs as enemies of Islam and so fit

69 Reuben Levy, *The Social Structure of Islam*, Cambridge, 1957, pp. 254–55, 405–06. There seems no historical justification for Levy's statement on p. 255, as for Baranī's, that Maḥmūd refused to treat Hindus as *zimmīs* in his dominions. Baranī alleges that Maḥmūd did not allow even Jews or Christians to live in his dominions! Cf. *Fatāwā*, f.10b.

70 Baranī, *Fatāwā*, f.12a.

71 Ibid., f.166b.

72 Extract from *Ṣaḥīfa-i Na't-i Muḥammadī*, printed in *Medieval India Quarterly*, Vol. 1 (3–4), pp. 104–5, ed. by S. Nurul Hasan, for whose own comments see pp. 100–103. The result of Iltutmish's decision was, says Baranī, that 'infidelity (*kufr*), polytheism and image-worship took seed amidst Muslims and people of the faith'.

73 Baranī, *Tārīkh*, p. 217.

74 Baranī, *Fatāwā*, f.203a.

75 Ibid., ff.118b–120b. Baranī is obviously painting the picture of contemporary Delhi.

76 This has been dealt with by me in 'Baranī's Theory'; pp. 112–13, where the numerous (relevant) references to the *Tārīkh* are given.

for slaughter.[77] Maḥmūd claimed to have exiled the Mu'tazilites from Khwarizm and regretted that Ibn Sīnā (Avicenna), 'the reviver of the Greek sciences and the chief of the philosophers of Islamic countries', had not fallen into his hands, to be killed and torn to pieces.[78] The animosity to secular sciences and rationalism was by Baranī's time quite widespread; and, especially after Ghazālī (d.1111), it seems to have been fully shared by the sufis.[79]

Rationalism nevertheless survived under the patronage of the Sultans, whose interest in medicine and astronomy (the latter quite possibly promoted out of astrological motives) kept the sciences alive in at least a limited sphere. To Baranī's consternation, his own patron, Muḥammad Tughluq was an unashamed believer in *ma'qūlāt* (application of reason), and allegedly preferred them to the dictates of *manqūlāt* (the received texts). Baranī freely attributed the cruelties suffered by the religious scholars at this Sultan's hand to this fatal weakness in his views.[80]

I have attempted above an analysis of what seems to me to be Baranī's major ideas on the nature, objectives and functions of the state. His earlier interpreters, Professor Mohammad Habib and Dr Afsar Khan have been obviously irritated by his 'fanatical attitude', notably his hostility to Hindus.[81] This element tends to be absent or subdued in writings in countries where, by Baranī's time, the state was not called upon to deal with non-Muslim majorities. The *Siyāsat-nāma,* for example, is more concerned with the suppression of non-orthodox sects within Islam than with any non-Muslim sects. The result is that the contradiction between theory and reality in the relationship between the Sultanate and Hindus (or, for that matter any large body of non-Muslim subjects not identified as 'People of the Book' in the *Sharī'a*) is brought up by Baranī in a manner not to be found in any other leading Muslim writer on the subject.

But Baranī's major contributions could lie in an altogether different field. So far as I know no precursor of his appears to have been concerned with the great anxieties that he harbours over the consequences of violence or force that underlies the state, which makes every possessor of power, individual or dynasty, extremely vulnerable. This would not have concerned Baranī so much, but for the fact that such a situation promotes a lack of trust between the ruler and the established ruling class, and, under any powerful despot, brings about the latter's destruction. There is thus an unending cycle of dynastic change and replacement of ruling groups by new, inevitably lower class, entrants. It is such history that the Delhi Sultanate had witnessed, as presented in his own *Tārīkh,* and Baranī has little to offer by way of a solution other than proposing a strong dynastic principle,

77 Baranī, *Fatāwā,* f.9b.
78 Ibid., f.10b.
79 See the remarks of the Chishti saint, Niẓāmuddīn of Delhi, in Amīr Ḥasan Sijzī, *Fawā'idu'l Fu'ād,* pp. 84–86; 283–84. Baranī was a great admirer of this saint, as may be seen from his *Tārīkh,* pp. 172–77.
80 Baranī, *Tārīkh,* pp. 265–66.
81 *Medieval India Quarterly,* Vol. 3 (1–2), 1957, pp. 5, 21, etc.

the maintenance of monarchical pomp and religious pretensions. The efficacy of such devices in retarding the movement of the fatal cycle may however be doubted, each turn of it inevitably leading to a tragic denouement.

It would be interesting to compare Baranī's narrow perceptions of such cycles, with those of Ibn Khaldūn (1332–1408), his great younger African contemporary. Blessed with a much larger vision and more analytical mind, Ibn Khaldūn too is conscious of the cyclical nature of political regimes, but he attributes the decay of the regimes to social and psychological causes, expressed through the waning of '*aṣabiyya*, the spirit of solidarity in the ruling class.[82] Baranī hardly ever discerns such a sense of solidarity and is not apparently conscious of it. But he still shares one thing in common with Ibn Khaldūn: the great African theorist too had no convincing prescription for avoiding the inevitable downward swing in a state's fortunes.

II

Less than two hundred and fifty years after Baranī had written his *Tārīkh*, there came from the pen of another great master of Persian prose, a theory of the nature and functions of the state, which is entirely different from the one espoused by Baranī. If Abū'l Fazl (1551–1602) shares anything with Baranī in this realm, it is perhaps only this that like Baranī too, his political ideas have not yet been fully explored.[83] In Baranī's case this is, perhaps, due to the fact that he wrote too much although always with a lively and aggressive clarity; in that of Abū'l Fazl, it might, on the other hand, be because of his excessively majestic style, in which the decisive statements often come as concise formulae in the midst of long, suggestive but often ambiguous assertions.

Of Abū'l Fazl's life much is known, from his own pen[84] and from the pen of contemporaries, especially his critic 'Abdu'l Qādir Badāūnī.[85] From later in Mughal times come biographical sketches by Shaikh Farīd Bhakkarī (1650)[86] and Shūh Nawāz Khān (d. 1758).[87] And there are recent studies as well, notably

[82] See Muhsin Mahdi, *Ibn Khaldūn's Philosophy of History*, Chicago, 1964, pp. 193–224; and Rosenthal, *Political Thought*, pp. 84–92.

[83] Saiyid Athar Abbas Rizvi provides a scholarly discussion of Abū'l Fazl's 'political thinking' in his *Religious and Intellectual History of the Muslims in Akbars' Reign (1556–1605)*, New Delhi, 1975, pp. 352–73; but he seems to miss out some of Abū'l Fazl's really bold propositions, such as his rejection of a theocratic regime and his espousal of a species of social contract.

[84] Abū'l Fazl's own autobiography at the end of his *Ā'īn-i Akbarī*, ed. H. Blochmann, Bib. Ind., Calcutta, 1867–77, II, pp. 258–83, is very inadequate for his own career, but there are scattered references to himself in his *Akbarnāma* (the history of Akbar's reign), ed. Agha Ahmad 'Ali and 'Abdu'l Rahim, Bib. Ind., Calcutta, 1873–87, esp. Vol. III.

[85] See his *Muntakhabu't Tawārīkh*, ed. Ahmad 'Ali, Kabiru'ddin Ahmad, and W. Nassau Lees, Bib. Ind., Calcutta, 1864–69, Vols. II and III, passim.

[86] *Zakhīratu'l Khawānīn*, ed. S. Moinul Haq, Karachi, 1961, I, pp. 67–77.

[87] *Ma'āṣiru'l Umarū* ('Abdu'l Ḥai's recension, 1780), ed. 'Abdu'r Rahim and Mirza Ashraf 'Ali Bib. Ind., Calcutta, 1888–91, II, pp. 608–22, which combines Farīd Bhakkarī's account with information drawn from other historical sources.

those by H. Blochmann[88] and S. Athar Abbas Rizvi.[89] In view of this rich material only a short account may be offered of Abū'l Faẓl's antecedents and career, with emphasis on information more relevant to the formation of his thought.

Abū'l Faẓl's father was Shaikh Mubārak (1505–93)[90] of Nagaur (in Rajasthan). Mubarak obtained an orthodox theological education, at Nagaur and Ahmadabad. He then turned to 'sufism and *ishrāq* [the philosophy of Illuminated Wisdom of Shihābu'd-Dīn Suhrawardī Maqtūl, 1155–91]', and 'the truths' of Ibn 'Arabī (1165–1240), the Egyptian Sufi poet, Ibn Fāriẓ (1181–1235) and Ibn 'Arabī's great disciple and interpreter, Ṣadru'd-Dīn (1203–74).[91] These two lines of thought were to exercise much influence on the mind of Abū'l Faẓl.

Mubārak came to Agra in 1543 where he established a reputation for learning and independence.[92] He did not hide his admiration for 'the greatness and mystic status (*wilāyat*) of Saiyid Muḥammad of Jaunpur (1443–1505), the founder of the Indian Mahdawī movement, an anathema to the orthodoxy;[93] and he refused to endorse the theologians' demand before Islām Shāh (1545–54) that the Mahdavī scholar Shaikh 'Alāī be punished.[94] In the early years of Akbar's reign he similarly declined to endorse a judicial opinion (*fatwā*) signed by a number of other scholars permitting people to sell their children into slavery if faced with starvation.[95] Badāūnī alleges that Mubārak successively shifted his allegiance to the Naqshbandī and Hamadānī orders as these sufic orders obtained popularity (or influence at the court?).[96] But if he did so, this did not protect him from the theologians' persecution, which forced him to turn a fugitive, in or sometime after 1569–70, to be saved only by 'the Emperor's compassion.'[97]

By this time Abū'l Faẓl, born in January 1551, had made great progress in his education (mainly obtained from his father, since he mentions no other teacher), until he reached the age of twenty.[98] It was, then, that preceded by his elder brother the poet Faiẓī (1547–95), he obtained access to Emperor Akbar, and began to delight him by contesting the positions of the established theologians in

[88] In the initial portion of his translation of the *Ā'īn-i Akbarī*, I, ed. D.C. Phillott, Bib. Ind., Calcutta, 1972, pp. xxv–lix.

[89] Rizvi, op.cit., esp. pp. 76–140, 339–73, 455–98.

[90] The dates are as given by Abū'l Faẓl in the *Ā'īn*, II, pp. 260–61, 276.

[91] Ibid., p. 261.

[92] Ibid., p. 262.

[93] Badāūnī, *Muntakhabut-Tawārikh* [hereafter cited by author's name only], III, p. 67: Badāūnī recalls here a conversation in which he defended Shaikh Mubārak during the period 1556–60, when he himself was a student of his.

[94] *Ā'īn*, I, pp. 264–5. Badāūnī, III, 74, even alleges a friendship between Mubārak and Shaikh 'Alāī.

[95] Badāūnī, III, pp. 68–69.

[96] Ibid., III, p. 74. He says that Mubārak thereafter turned to favour the 'Irāqīs, by which Badāūnī means the Shi'as; but whether this was before or after he obtained access to the court is not made clear.

[97] *Ā'īn*, II, pp. 266–75.

[98] Ibid., II, pp. 276–78.

discussions in the Emperor's presence at the *'Ibādat-khāna,* in 1578–79.[99] His tendency then to criticize and show the weaknesses of the traditional scholars is noted by Badāūnī, who also quotes him as saying, 'If the Great Imām [Abū Ḥanīfa] had lived in our time, he would have written a different law (*fiqh*).'[100] Ultimately, with Mubārak's influence also rising, the leading theologians were forced into signing a declaration (*maḥẓar*) in 1579 giving Akbar, as a 'just Sultan', the power to grant a final interpretation on the disputed points of law.[101] Mubārak appended to it the statement under his seal that 'this is something I desire with all my heart, and have waited for years.'[102]

However, this was a document which soon became irrelevant, since Akbar, with Abū'l Faẓl as his major confidant in religious and ideological matters, was not content with merely the power to implement a royal version of the *Sharī'a.*[103] The new ideas of religion and the world in general that Akbar began to entertain were expressed by Abū'l Faẓl in different documents drafted on behalf of Akbar and in his own letters;[104] in the official history of Akbar's reign, the *Akbarnāma,* that he began to prepare in 1589 and went on extending till his murder in 1602; and in the *Ā'īn-i Akbarī,* a description of Akbar's empire, with massive statistics of prices, wages and revenue and a detailed account of the culture of India, which he formally completed in 1598.[105] A year-by-year, increasingly critical commentary on the new ideological trend at the court is provided by Badāūnī in his *Muntakhabu't Tawārīkh*. Statements on Akbar's ideas, as well as Abū'l Faẓl's, appear also in the Jesuit accounts (the Jesuits appeared at Akbar's court as early as 1580).[106] By and large, the accounts coincide.

99 Badāūnī, II, pp. 262–63. A letter exists from Mubārak to Faiẓī, expressing some anxiety over the hostility that Abū'l Faẓl was exciting by his debates among 'the black-hearted greybeards' (the theologians) by his use of arguments drawn from the sciences, both rational and scriptural (*'ulum-i 'aqlī o naqlī*), that Mubārak himself had taught him (*Majma' u'l Afkār*, [selection from an 18th-century collection of documents], ed. Iqtidar Husain Siddiqui, Patna, 1993, pp. 22–23.

100 Badāūnī, II, pp. 262–63; III, p. 79.

101 The text of this declaration is given in Niẓāmu'ddīn Ahmad, *Ṭabaqāt-i Akbarī*, ed. B. De, Bib. Ind., Calcutta, 1913–35, II, pp. 344–46; and in Badāūnī, II, pp. 270–72.

102 Badāūnī, II, p. 272.

103 In the *Akbarnāma*, I, p. 269, Abū'l Faẓl comments that the power and function of *ijtihād* or interpretation of Law, assigned by this *maḥẓar* to Akbar, suited 'a status inferior to that of His Majesty's person'.

104 *Mukātabāt-i 'Allāmī* or *Inshā'-i Abū'l Faẓl*, in three parts (*sih daftar*), collected by 'Abdu's Ṣamad (1606–7), many editions: Calcutta, 1810, etc. I have used the Nawal Kishor ed., [Lucknow?] 1864, (cited hereafter as *Inshā'-i Abū'l Faẓl*), edited with glosses by Muḥammad 'Ali.

105 For the relationship between the *Akbarnāma* and the *Ā'īn-i Akbarī* and the dates of their preparation and completion, see Shireen Moosvi, *The Economy of the Mughal Empire, c.1595*, Delhi, 1987, pp. 2–8.

106 The main Jesuit sources (rendered in English) are: *Letters from the Mughal Court: the first Jesuit Mission to Akbar (1580–1583)*, ed. John Correia-Afonso, Bombay, 1980; *Commentary of Father Monserrate*, transl. and ed. S.N. Banerjee and John S. Hoyland, Cuttack, 1922; and Fr. Pierre du Jarric, transl. C.H. Payne, *Akbar and the Jesuits*, London, 1926.

It is to be observed that the dominant influences which led to the formulation of the new views came from within the Islamic tradition.[107] Perhaps, the most significant was the one derived from Ibn 'Arabī. We have seen how Mubārak had read the works of Ibn 'Arabī and the writings of Ṣadrud-Dīn; and Akbar received it from yet another source as well in the late 1570's: Shaikh Tāju'd-Dīn who 'in the knowledge of Unity was a second Ibn 'Arabī', and conveyed in night sessions the matters of 'Unity of Existence' (*waḥdat-i wujūd*) and 'Perfect Man' (*insān-i kāmil*) to the Emperor.[108]

It is true, as modern critics point out, that Ibn 'Arabi's theory does not amount to simple monism, or monotheism.[109] But, however 'transcendental' the unity, once its Reality is recognized,[110] the differences seen in the sensory world are bound to lose their significance and become illusory. From this a world-view followed, which Abū'l Faẓl thus sums up, while introducing his account of Akbar's spiritual views in the *Ā'īn-i Akbarī:*

> When world-ornamenting, wisdom-giving God desires that the essence (*gauhar*) of humankind should come into existence, and when from the diversity in the degree of (spiritual) capacity, the cloud of Duality (*do-rangī*) rises and fashions Religion (*dīn*) and the World (*dunyā*), every creature begins to have a distinct leader (*kār-giyā*), and these become engaged in mutual denunciation. As lack of vision and unwisdom become the touchstone, the knowledge of (true) worth and acquisition of love become scarce. Otherwise, what is Religion, what is World? There is one heart-ensnaring Beauty which casts splendour through many thousands of veils. They have spread an expansive carpet, and it sheds forth many different colours.[111]

This passage may be treated as the starting point of Abū'l Faẓl's political thought. Both religion and the secular sphere ('world') are placed at par, and as equally illusory, being products of a false Duality. This in effect immediately liberates temporal sovereignty from any dictates of theological doctrine.

Abū'l Faẓl can then locate the basis of sovereignty in the needs of the social order. Here his reasoning follows the pure dictates of reason ('*aql*), appealing to the tradition of the philosophers (*filāsafa*) and the scientists (*ḥukamā*). In a sense, Ibn 'Arabī's thought could be used to justify tolerance of reason as of other dissentient or contradictory elements. In the *Ā'īn* Abū'l Faẓl takes special care to stress his knowledge of the classical Graeco-Islamic scientific tradition; and a

[107] It was, indeed, noted by Aziz Ahmad, *Studies in Islamic Culture in the Indian Environment*, Oxford, 1964, p. 179, that Akbar's 'Divine Faith shows a surprising indifference to Hinduism'.

[108] Badāūnī, II, pp. 258–59.

[109] Cf. Henry Carbin, *Creative Imagination in the Sufism of Ibn 'Arabi*, transl. Ralph Manham, London, 1969, p. 203 & ff.

[110] See ibid., pp. 186–88.

[111] *Ā'īn*, I, p. 158. Blochmann's translation of this passage (I, pp. 170–71) is surprisingly inaccurate, and must be entirely discarded.

tradition hostile to him records that he had brusquely brushed aside Ghazālī's criticisms of the scientists with the short remark that Ghazālī 'had spoken non-sense'.[112]

It is, therefore, not surprising that Abū'l Faẓl appeals to a theory of social contract to justify the necessity of political authority.[113] In a chapter entitled 'The Provision of Livelihood (*Rawāī-i Rozī*)', he says:

> Whereas abundant differences are embedded in the nature of humankind, and disturbance, internal and external, is of daily growth, and huge desires spread fast, and anger is quick to break out, in this demon-land of unmanliness, friendship is scarce and justice absolutely non-existent. In all circumstances, in such a place of tumult, relief is not possible except through the punitive power of a single man (*qahrī-i waḥadat*). That life-saving medicine cannot be provided except through the terror (*shikūh*) of just rulers. When a house or inhabited quarter cannot be administered without fear or hope from a perspicuous head (*peshwā*), how is it possible for the disturbance of the world's nest to die down without that recipient of Divine Light (*pazīranda-i farr-i īzidī*) [the righteous ruler] and how would the property, life, honour and religion of the world's people be protected?[114]

He then goes on to argue that the effort of some recluses (*tajarrud-gazīnān*) to appear as 'breakers of old customs' (*khāriq-i 'ādat*), and remedy the troubled state of affairs was unsuccessful because of lack of support from 'exalted Sultans'. This is obviously a dig on prophets trying to be sovereigns on the basis of their creeds, especially, keeping in mind the Islamic experience. Indeed, in such a situation ('burning desert' – *ātishīn dasht*), the tricksters (*ṭilism-kār-o nairanjī-i sha'bada bāz*) have a field day, the innocent being submerged in these 'storms of tumult', and the wise being denounced as 'mad, irreligious and infidels.' A theocracy cannot, therefore, but lead to further disturbance.

It is only 'a just ruler (*kār-giyā*)' who is able 'to convert, like a salt-bed, the impure into pure, the bad into good;' but he can do so only by gathering 'loyal helpers, a large wherewithal for grandeur and a large treasury.' Soldiers were particularly necessary: 'the self-loving base ones (*firo-māyagān-i tabī'at-parast*) cannot listen to the voice of reason, and cannot go beyond their (immediate) senses, and in such saline ground, the water of the sword works, not the wholesome water of argument.'

Accordingly, 'the wages of protection' (*dast-muzd-i pāsbānī*) have to be paid to the sovereign for protecting the four 'essences' (property, life, honour,

[112] I have discussed Abū'l Faẓl's attachment to reason and science in 'Reason and Science in Medieval India', *Society and Ideology in India, Essays in Honour of Professor R.S. Sharma*, ed. D.N. Jha, New Delhi, 1996, pp. 167–69. Abū'l Faẓl's outburst against Ghazālī is related in Muḥammad Raḥīm Kishmī, *Zabdatu'l Maqāmāt*, Lucknow, AH 1302, p. 131.

[113] On this, there will be a comment further on.

[114] *Ā'īn*, I, p. 290.

religion). For such a task no wages or taxes could be too high, but 'just sovereigns do not take more than what suffices for their task and do not soil their hands by desiring more.'[115]

This doctrine justifies temporal sovereignty, but assumes two classes of sovereigns, just and unjust. How a just sovereign should be identified and how he should function are matters that Abū'l Faẓl takes up immediately at the beginning of the *Ā'īn-i Akbarī.*

In this discussion, a third element enters, the influence of the *ishrāq* theory. Developed by Shihābu'd-Dīn Suhrawardī Maqtūl (d. 1191), whose writings were universally read in the Islamic world, its origins went back to Plato's *Republic,* where the Good is presented under the symbol of the Sun. The Sun becomes for the *ishrāqīs* a symbol of God-derived spiritual lights, the *anwār-i qāhira,* each of which 'from degree to degree, illumines the presence of each lower degree' (H. Corbin).[116] Abū'l Faẓl uses the imagery, if not the terminology of the *ishrāq* tradition, when he puts temporal sovereignty at the highest station in the hierarchy of objects receiving spiritual light: 'To the Unique Almighty, there is no higher station than that of the King (*Pādshāh*). . . . Royalty is a light from the Inimitable Almighty and a ray from the world-illuminating Sun, the essence of the books of perfection, the assemblage of excellences. In the language of the day it is called *farr-i īzidī* (divine light); in the ancient [Iranian] language, *kaihān-khwura* (world-illuminating light)'.[117] Thus even if the office of sovereign is not a product of any religion, he yet has authority from God. Abū'l Faẓl refrains from using the conventional Muslim adjective for the ruler, *Zill-i ilāhī,* 'God's shadow'. The sovereign is not a shadow, but rather a recipient of divine light, possessor of illumined wisdom, and the reflector of the light received.[118]

115 *Ā'īn,* I, pp. 290–91, for the original text from which this and the previous paragraphs are drawn. The reader must be warned against depending for these passages on H. Jarrett's translation (*Ā'īn-i Akbarī,* II, revised by Jadunath Sarkar, Calcutta, 1949, pp. 54–56), which is particularly inept here.

116 Quoted in R. Arnaldez, 'ISHRĀK', *Encyclopaedia of Islam,* New ed., IV, Leiden, 1978, pp. 119–20. J.F. Richards has already drawn attention to the connexion between the *Ishrāqī* ('Persian Neoplatonic') theory of Illumination and Abū'l Faẓl's play on Light (J.F. Richards, ed., *Kingship and Authority in South Asia,* Madison, 1978, pp. 260–67; summarized in his *Mughal Empire,* Cambridge, 1993, pp. 45–47).

117 *Ā'īn,* I, p. 2. Abū'l Faẓl surely has in mind here the passage in Shihābu'ddīn Suhrawardī's *Partau-nāma* ('Book of Radiance', ed. and transl. Hossein Ziai, Costa Mesa, Calif., 1998, p. 84): 'Whoever knows wisdom and is assiduous in praising and revering the "Light of Lights" (*Nūru'l Anwār*), as we have stated, they give him the "kingly light" (*khurra-i kayānī*) and bestow upon him the 'luminous ray' (*farr-i nūrānī);* and the 'lightning-flashing (cloud) of God' (*bāriq-i ilāhī*) clothes him in the robe of authority and status' (my own rendering). Can one say that Abū'l Faẓl has in fact inverted Shihābu'ddīn's assertion? Whereas the latter argued that the person with spiritual attainments achieves the supreme status, marked by the possession of 'kingly light', for Abū'l Faẓl it is the just king who possesses not only the 'kingly light', but also the highest spiritual attainments.

118 We have seen above how Abū'l Faẓl calls the just sovereign, *pazīranda-i farr-i Īzidī* (*Ā'īn,* I, p. 290).

But not all worldly sovereigns receive such light. We have seen that Abū'l Faẓl, in speaking of just rulers, implies another category, that of unjust sovereigns. He now blames the simple-minded ones (*salīm-dilān*) for not distinguishing the 'godly ruler' (*farmānfarmā-i ḥaqīqī*) from the self-seeking aspirant for authority (*peshī-jū-i khwūd-kām*), since both have at their command treasure, army, subjects, scholarly servants, numerous craftsmen, and personal attendants. Only the enlightened ones could discriminate between the two: the rule of the 'godly' rulers is long-lasting and marked by peace, justice, etc.; that of the selfish ones is short-lived and marked by terror, cruelty, theft, etc.[119]

It was clearly the just ruler to whom the title of *Pādshāh* was appropriate and who could be the recipient of God's light. As a courtier and, perhaps, sincere admirer, Abū'l Faẓl held Akbar to form a class by himself, and when he speaks of *Pādshāh* and accords him a special station near God, he surely has Akbar as a unique ruler in mind. The concept of 'Perfect Man' in the Ibn 'Arabī tradition could certainly be invoked here, as Badāūnī suspected;[120] but there was another possible source for justifying the exaltation of a particular individual, namely, the doctrines of Maḥmūd Pasikhwānī (d. 1427–28), the originator of the Waḥīdiya or Nuqṭawiya sect.[121] These doctrines certainly had reached Akbar at the critical moment when he was fashioning his new ideas in association with Abū'l Faẓl. In 1577 Sharīf Āmulī, after a chequered career, joined Akbar's court, and he was a follower of Maḥmūd Pasikhwānī.[122] Maḥmūd believed in a kind of metempsychosis through the meeting of the physical elements of a former body or bodies to create a new one, this being in his case, 'a more perfect being' than Muḥammad, whose elements came together in him.[123] One could similarly claim for Akbar an eminent status on the basis of these speculations.[124] It is, however, fair to say that if Maḥmūd's theory of great spiritual souls born at particular periods exercised any influence on Abū'l Faẓl, he does not himself either directly or indirectly give any evidence of it, though he seems to have maintained good relations with the Iranian Nuqṭavīs.[125]

[119] *Ā'īn*, I, p. 2.

[120] Badāūnī, II, pp. 258–9. The central position of *al-insān al-kāmil* in the realm of existence was particularly defined and elaborated by Ṣadru'ddīn Qūnawī, the major disciple of Ibn 'Arabī (W.C. Chittick, 'Ṣadr al-Dīn Qūnawī', *Encyclopedia of Islam*, new ed., VII, Leiden, 1995, p. 754, col. 2.).

[121] A fairly extended account of the founder and his sect is given in Mobad (*c.*1655), *Dabistān* [*-i Maẕāhib*], ed. Qazi Ibrahim, Bombay, AH 1292, pp. 243–47. See also H. Algar, 'Nuktawiyya', *Encyclopaedia of Islam*, new ed. VIII, Leiden, 1995, pp. 114–17.

[122] See Badāūnī, II, pp. 247–8. Badāūnī claims to have read, and been revolted by, Mahmud's tracts, thirteen in number. For *nuqṭavīs* at Akbar's court other than Sharif 'Amili, see ibid., III, pp. 204–07, 378–79.

[123] *Dabistān*, p. 244.

[124] Ṣāni' Khān Hirawī, for example, is said to have invoked Maḥmūd Pasikhwānī's predictions for fixing on AH 990 (AD 1582) as the year when 'the promised person' (*shakhṣ-i ma'hūd*) would appear (Badāūnī, III, pp. 206–7). This would have suited Akbar.

[125] In a *farmān* to the Nuqṭawī scholar Ṣafīu'ddīn Aḥmad Kāshī, Akbar refers to Abū'l Faẓl's favourable opinion of Darwīsh-Khusrau, the principal Nuqt]awī leader in Iran

The true or 'godly' king was rather to be recognized by the functions that he carried out. We may dispense with the display of qualities of strong will, God-worship, quickness in giving relief to seekers, etc., which Abū'l Faẓl enumerates. The two important functions that Abū'l Faẓl assigns to such a sovereign, and which, though suiting Akbar, were in a remarkable manner the very opposite of the functions that, under the *Sharī'a,* Baranī had assigned to the State.

The first such function, says Abū'l Faẓl, is 'the fulfilling [by the sovereign] of the obligations of being father (*pidarī*) to mankind: Different kinds of persons receive comfort from his benevolence and out of the diversity of religion the dust of duality does not rise forth'.[126] This is the tolerance of conflicting faiths, which Abū'l Faẓl subsumed in the term he and his master so often used, *viz., Ṣulḥ-i kul,* 'absolute peace'.[127] Again, this concept invoked Ibn 'Arabī's philosophy. The higher form would be *muḥabbat-i kul* ('absolute love'), when presumably the transcendental unity would be absolutely recognized. For those who could not achieve it, the path of *ṣulḥ-i kul,* the tolerance of all diversity, was prescribed.[128] *Ṣulḥ-i kul* was doubtless something to be pursued and achieved by an individual; in his autobiography Abū'l Faẓl lists his success in 'attaining *ṣulḥ-i kul,* through the favour of His Majesty's attention'. This consists 'sometimes' of turning from speech to silence, sometimes making friendship (*āshtī*) with good men of all communities (*har ṭā'ifa*), and ultimately, 'accepting excuses, make peace (*maṣāliḥa*) with the bad'.[129] For the ruler, this meant a policy of tolerating all religious (and other) differences. Abū'l Faẓl describes how, beginning from 1578–79, Akbar, taking the position of *ṣulḥ-i kul,* opened a discourse with leading men of all religions (including Christians and Brahmans) and appointed men of different faiths to high offices (such a the Sh'iite Iranis, the Sunni Turanis and the Hindus) and quietly faced up to the uproar of denigration and denunciation that arose from the orthodox.[130]

Since *ṣulḥ-i kul* was a philosophical principle difficult for many to follow, Abū'l Faẓl also offered a more popular, Let's-leave-it-to-God argument which he

---

(copy printed in Khaliq Ahmad Nizami, *Akbar and Religion*, Delhi, 1989, pp. 379–80). The *farmān* is dated '4 Azar 94', where 94 must be a mistake for 34 [*ilāhī*], and the date of issue is therefore 26 November 1589. Darwīsh-Khusrau was executed by Shāh 'Abbās I in 1593, and Aḥmad Kāshī not long afterwards.

126 *Ā'īn*, I, pp. 2–3.

127 Cf. M. Athar Ali, 'Sulh-i Kul and the Religious Ideas of Akbar', *Studies in History*, New Delhi, IV(i)(1982), pp. 27–39; and Iqtidar Alam Khan, 'Akbar's Personality Traits and World Outlook – a Critical Reappraisal', *Akbar and his India*, ed. I. Habib, Delhi, 1997, pp. 79–96.

128 *Farman* of 26 November 1590 to A'ẓam Khān, in respect of Jains (Mohanlal Dolichand Desai, *Jain Sahityano Samkshipt Itihas*, place[?], n.d. reprod. of *farmān* [copy], facing p. 545). The *farmūn* bears all the marks of Abu'l Faẓl's penmanship.

129 *Ā'īn*, II, p. 279.

130 *Akbarnāma*, III, pp. 271–73. And not only from the orthodox Muslims. Fr. Monserrate, member of the first Jesuit mission, accompanying Akbar to Kabul in 1581, says distastefully that Akbar 'cared little that in allowing every one to follow his own religion, he was in reality violating all religions' (*Commentary*, p. 142).

put into the regulations (*dastūru'l 'amal*), drafted for the Emperor some time after 1584. Here all officials were enjoined:

> to be vigilant in that royalty and authority mean the giving of protection: they should not object to (the practising of) the faith and religion of the people, for when a wise man does not risk loss in this mortal world, why should one risk loss in the realm of religion which is eternal? If the truth (*ḥaqq*) is on his side, you will be opposing and objecting to the truth; if the truth is with you, and he has, out of ignorance, chosen a position opposite to it, he is a hapless victim of the disease of ignorance; he deserves compassion and assistance, not objection and opposition. Remain friendly (therefore) with the good people of every sect (*har giroh*).[131]

There is no doubt that the urge for the pursuit of *ṣulḥ-i kul,* as state policy, owed much to the position of the Mughal empire, situated in a multi-religious country. It accorded closely with the patriotism for 'Hindustān', which both Akbar and Abū'l Faẓl were so frankly encouraging.[132] The religious tolerance which to Baranī had seemed to be an unworthy compromise, could now be proclaimed as an essential function of the state, required by the highest principles of mystic truth.

The second function of the state is given, in such a brief sentence, that it tends to be missed: The just sovereign 'shall, not seek popular acclaim through opposing reason (*'aql*).'[133] Despite Abū'l Faẓl's extensive use of sufic concepts and beliefs, he remained steadfast in his allegiance to reason and science. One major factor here was the opposition that rationalism offered to orthodox traditionalism. Abū'l Faẓl includes among Akbar's 'happy sayings' the following:

The case for pursuing reason (*'aql pazhohī*) and rejection of traditionalism (*taqlīd*) is so clear that it does not need any argument from me. If tradition is to be held excellent, all prophets would have just followed their ancestral customs.[134]

Abū'l Faẓl himself gives a spirited condemnation of *taqlīd* when he lists reasons why Indian beliefs and culture had not been more closely studied by Muslims:

> Fifthly, the blowing of the heavy wind of *taqlīd* (tradition), and the dimming of the lamp of *khirad* (reason, wisdom). Of old, the door of 'how and why' has been closed; and questioning and enquiry have been deemed fruitless and the act of a pagan (*kufr*). Whatever one received from one's father, teacher,

131 *Inshā'-i Abū'l Faẓl,* p. 61.

132 Cf. M. Athar Ali, 'The Perception of India in Akbar and Abū'l Faẓl', in *Akbar and his India,* op.cit., pp. 215–224. But *ṣulh-i kul* was not seen as a doctrine solely applicable to India. Obviously disturbed by 'Abbūs I's religious persecutions, Akbar wrote in a letter (January 1595), drafted by Abū'l Faẓl, urging him to practise *ṣulḥ-i kul* (*Inshā-'-i Abū'l Faẓl,* p. 31; *Akbarnāma,* III, pp. 659–60).

133 *Ā'īn,* I, p. 3.

134 *Ā'īn,* II, p. 229.

> kinsman, friend and neighbour was considered the wherewithal of Divine favour; and the holder of a contrary opinion was accused of heresy and impiety. Though some of the enlightened have tried a little to pursue a different path, yet they have followed the path of (correct) conduct no more than half-way.[135]

Abū'l Faẓl's stout espousal of the protection of rationalism by the state looks odd when we see him making use of mystic theories and speculations to justify the system of despotism envisioned by him – benevolent, it is true, but despotism all the same. There was little intrusion of reason in the formulation of the basic premises or detailed elements of either the *ishrāq* doctrine or Ibn 'Arabī's speculations; and sufis of all shades had been one with the theologians in denying the autonomy, let alone the supremacy, of the realm of reason. Abū'l Faẓl's obvious theoretical weakness is that he never comes to grips with this contradiction, and makes no attempt to resolve it. This may be one reason why there took place so limited a development of rationalism, even after the Mug͟hal Empire had supposedly extended its protective umbrella over it. It seems that Abū'l Faẓl had hopes that the realm of reason would expand under such protection – he took delight in the fact that his son 'Abdu'r Raḥmān, 'though an Indian by birth, has a Greek temper (*mushrib*)', that is, a philosophical or scientific bent.[136] But the generations after Abū'l Faẓl remained largely barren of creative scientific effort, and even the discoveries of Europe's Scientific Revolution remained undiffused in India. Indeed, in the seventeenth century there existed little rationalism in India that the State needed either to suppress or to protect.

III

Both Baranī and Abū'l Faẓl have elements in their thought that are peculiarly their own and not derived from any known external source. Baranī's dual anxiety that the state should respect and protect the *status-quo,* especially the existing composition of the ruling class, and that the engine of terror should be constrained, especially in relation to members of groups of status, had been generated by his own interpretation of the internal history of the Delhi Sultanate. These coloured his perception of the contemporary state, whose moral justification he could see chiefly in the fulfilment, even if partial, of the dictates of the *Sharī'a,* in respect of the external enemies (Hindus) and internal subverters (philosophers). The actual practice of the Sultanate had been opposite to what he desired of it, whether in constraining its violence or in fulfilling its obligations to the *Sharī'a.* It was, obviously, as far from his ideal state as any polity could possibly be.

With Abū'l Faẓl, the position is the reverse. The Mug͟hal Empire as

[135] *Ā'īn*, II, p. 3. To be fair, Akbar and Abū'l Faẓl did not hold *taqlīd* to be restricted to Muslims. For criticism of Akbar's minister Todar Mal on account of his attachment to his idols, by way of *taqlīd*, see *Akbarnāma*, first version, Br. Mus. Add. 27,247, f.291a; also the final version, Bib. Ind. ed., III, p. 221.137. Cf. *Ā'īn*, II, p. 281.

[136] Cf. *Ā'īn*, II, p. 281.

constructed by Akbar and as governed by him, after he had raised 'the veils' in *c.* 1579–80,[137] was *the* ideal state. There was certainly much in Akbar's regime to justify this beyond the simple claims of a courtier: there were in it a certain element of compassion, a restraint in the operations of its punitive apparatus, a systematisation taken to the extent of creating a quasi-constitution, a degree of religious tolerance found in few other countries at that time.[138] It seemed to meet the two main concerns of Baranī: stable hierarchy and containment of violence. These matters, however, no longer trouble Abū'l Faẓl; he is more concerned with quite different attributes of the State, namely, benevolence and rationality.

We have seen that where Baranī is fairly conscious of the fact that the real basis of the State lies in force, Abū'l Faẓl locates it in a species of social contract and the divine-illumined wisdom of the mystic tradition. In Abū'l Faẓl's view, all its subjects, whatever their faith, have equal claims on the ruler's benevolence; and reason, not theology, is to be the arbiter. One may not be convinced by the logical cogency of Abū'l Faẓl's speculative and mystical premises, while Baranī's insistence on force as the sustaining factor behind the state is far more realistic. But if Abū'l Faẓl's basic assumptions are dubious, the duties he thereby derives for the State are surely unexceptionable, even glorious. Some 'illumined wisdom' must surely have been at work, when he penned his loyalty to *ṣulḥ-i kul,* and *'aql,* not once, but over and over again.

137 Cf. *Akbarnāma*, III, p. 268.

138 M. Athar Ali, Presidential Address ('Mughal Empire in History'), *Proceedings of the Indian History Congress*, 34th session, Muzaffarpur, 1972, pp. 175–88.

Standardization and Empire

A Study of the Exchange Rates of Mughal Currencies

Najaf Haider

In empires encompassing vast territories and diverse customs, the standardization of currencies, exchange rates, weights and measures, was essential for the smooth conduct of economic affairs. Standardization rationalized economic exchange and reduced time and transaction costs. In pre-modern times, standardization often coincided with the establishment of effective sovereign power and the political unification of trading zones. The coincidence between sovereignty and control of standards is especially well illustrated in the realm of exchange and currency circulation in the Mughal Empire.

During the reign of Akbar (AD 1556–1605), a large part of India was unified politically and administratively after territorial conquests and bureaucratic centralization. Akbar exercised the sovereign right to issue coins of standard weight and fineness that differed from those of previous regimes. The Mughal state adopted special measures to standardize the circulation and exchange of currencies. These involved the replacement of non-Mughal currencies by imperial issues and, subsequently, the regulation of internal exchange rates within the ambit of a single coinage. The processes by which the two were realized give us a clue to the conception of money held by the state and the market in the sixteenth and seventeenth centuries.

Revenue Payment, Recoinage and Standardization

In the Mughal Empire, most transactions were conducted in three principal kinds of coin minted by the state, gold (*muhr*), silver (*rūpiya*) and copper (*paisa* or *dāṃ*). Over time and across regions, the demand and supply of the three coins varied and so did their exchange rates. The two constant factors which determined the absolute value of a coin were weight and purity, and Mughal coins were of uniform weight and high fineness (Haider 2005: 137–38). A third factor was the cost of production (brassage) and the imperial tax on minting (seigniorage) which also fixed the mint price of monetary metals (the number of coins delivered by the mint for a given quantity of pure metal). Weight, fineness and minting cost established the exchange rate of the coin against currencies and units of account. The exchange rate of a coin altered if any of these factors changed.

The process of standardization had its origins in exchange-rate alterations in the fiscal sector of the agrarian economy. Even though the economy of the Mughal countryside was not heavily monetized, it contained a huge reservoir of coined money, earned through the sale of agricultural products and paid to the state in the form of land tax. Money was generated in the countryside and spent in the town. Cash was collected by fiscal officers (*'amal-guzār*) with the help of money-changers (*ṣarrāf*) and sent over to the treasury (*Akbarnāma,* OIOC: 323b; *Akbarnāma* 1873–87, Vol. III: 383; Moosvi 1999: 276–83). In an important passage of the *Ā'īn-i Akbarī,* Abū'l Faẓl offers a glimpse into the use of fiscal machinery utilized to force out non-Mughal issues:

> The treasurer (*khazanadār*) should accept whatever *muhr, rūpiya* and *dām* which bears the august name [of the emperor]. He should receive from the cultivator all types of *muhr,* rupee and copper money and their fractions which he may bring, and should not demand any specific coin (*zar-i makhṣūṣ*). He should accept the coin of former reigns (*bāstānī maskūk*) [only] as unminted specie (*nā maskūk*). The treasurer should not levy discount (*ṣarf*) on an imperial coin (*sikka-i muqaddas*) of full weight, but realize the discount [on a lighter issue] on the basis of the weight of the coin (*tafāwat wazn- i maskūk*). (*Ā'īn-i Akbari,* Vol. I: 289)

This statement suggests that land revenue could be paid in all types of coin minted by reigning as well as previous monarchs. However, the imperial issues were valued as coins and the rest as pieces of metal. In other words, non-imperial issues were effectively demonetized, lost the value accrued to them by brassage and seigniorage and commanded a lower exchange rate. As a result, peasants would find it unprofitable to sell their produce in the market for undervalued coins, spurring their demonetization.

In his secretly written history of the Mughal Empire, Akbar's courtier and critic, 'Abdu-l Qādir Badāūnī, refers to an imperial order of AD 1592 effecting general demonetization of non-imperial issues through exchange-rate differences. According to this edict, gold and silver coins of all previous emperors (*pādshāhān-i sābiq*) were required to be melted down and sold as metal, whereas issues of the reigning emperor were to be exchanged at their full value in the market (*Muntakhabu't Tawārīkh,* Vol. II: 380). The official and private versions of the Mughal monetary policy concur on the mechanism adopted by the state to contract the circulation of non-standardized coins and expand the domain of imperial currencies.

The fate of non-imperial issues collected in revenue or sold as bullion is not clear from these statements. As the treasury could neither return them to circulation nor keep them forever, they were in all likelihood sent for recoinage. The list of suppliers of raw materials to Akbar's mint included a merchant who specialized in selling 'billon coins of old mintage' (*kuhn maskūkāt-i misīn nuqra āmēz*) (*Ā'īn-i Akbarī,* Vol. I: 23). The lower exchange rate would have provided the state with the extra cash to meet the cost of recoinage and enabled it to pocket the rest as seigniorage. This was indeed the case with imperial issues that were themselves demonetized, as we shall see. With regular recoinage, obsolete currency was channelled out and replaced by freshly minted coins. Given the amount of revenue collected in cash by the Mughal state in the last quarter of the sixteenth century, the standardization of currency circulation may have been effected on a large scale in this way. Given the success of the measure enforced in the revenue sector, it was extended to cover market transactions in all parts of the empire (*mamālik i mahrūsa*).

Depreciation, Discount and Exchange Rate: The Problem

A more complex issue for the Mughal administration was the standardization of the exchange rates of imperial currencies once they lost weight in circulation. On purely economic grounds, the natural wear and tear resulting in weight-loss, caused by the frequency with which coins were used, was bound to affect their exchange value.[1] Both the market and the state acknowledged that a coin which remained in active circulation lost weight over a period of time as the metal wore out. Added to this continuous loss was the fraudulence of rubbing and clipping coins (*mālish wa jaz*).[2] Thus, at any given time, an unknown quantity of coins that were less than the standard weight was always in circulation, requiring assessment by money-changers (*ṣarrāf*) whenever payments were made in cash. The purpose of this assessment was to levy a discount (Hindi *baṭṭa*; Pers. *ṣarf*) on lighter coins.[3] The travelling French jeweller, Tavernier, whose own mercantile ventures included, among other things, several instances of changing money in the market, was familiar with the reasoning which linked coin weight and exchange rate:

> The Indians are cunning and exacting in reference to coins and payments; for when money has been coined for three or four years it has to lose half per cent, and it continues in the same proportion according to age, not being able, as they say, to pass through many hands without some diminution. (Tavernier 1925, Vol. I: 8)[4]

---

[1] The technical and metallurgical aspects of weight-loss are explored in Aerts (1993: 41–58). Also see Lane and Mueller (1985: 24, n. 1), for methods used by modern historians to calculate weight loss.

[2] Cf. *Ā'īn-i Akbarī* (Vol. I: 27). Clipping is the removal of pieces of metal from the edges of the coin. Rubbing or sweating is a form of abrasion in which metal dust is collected at the bottom of the bag carrying coins.

[3] In Mughal India, *ṣarf-i sikka* or simply *ṣarf* denoted the difference in value in the exchange of specie. The Hindi term *baṭṭa* is derived from *bhaṭṭa* or allowance and is still popular with the petty money-changers of India in the sense of a discount levied on a dated or damaged currency. Elliott (1869: 41) describes *baṭṭa* as a discount on uncurrent or short weight coins. Both *baṭṭa* and *ṣarf* occur as synonyms, and are defined as the difference in the exchange of superior (*sanwāt*) and inferior (*adnā*) specie, in *Yasin's Glossary* (f. 68b, s.v. *ṣarf i sikka*).

[4] And at another place (p. 24): 'the longer a rupee of silver has been coined the less it is worth in comparison with those newly coined, or which have been coined a short time, because the old ones having often passed by hand become worn, and they are in consequence lighter.'

In his description of the currencies of Golconda and the eastern Deccan, Tavernier makes the following observation about the method of qualitative assessment practiced by money-changers:

> If the payment is made in old Pagodas [*huns*], and that the sum amounts to two or three hundred, or three or four thousand, the cheraf [*ṣarrāf*] takes them all, and viewing them one after another, he divides them into five or six parts; and then examining them all, he declares that some are more used than others, and that having passed through many hands, there is a waste of the metal [for] about one per cent. Others, he says, would suffer [a discount] of not above one half per cent; others a quarter. (Tavernier 1679, Vol. II: 596)

The operation of the discount system ideally required that coins be weighed even though the prices of goods were posted in terms of the number of coins rather than weights of gold, silver and copper. But the tedium of the continuous weighing of coins for each transaction led to the prevalence of faster methods of evaluation such as the one noticed by Tavernier in the case of the gold currency of Golconda. In Mughal India, where all silver coins were struck with figures of the current *hijrī* year or the regnal year of the emperor, or both, qualitative assessment was done on the basis of the year of mintage.[5] The money-changers assumed a relationship between age, velocity of circulation and weight-loss in classifying coins into three categories – *sikka*, *chalnī* and *khazāna* – and levied discounts to redeem value and reduce transaction costs. In this system of classification, a newly struck silver coin was designated *sikka* (from *sikka-i tāza* or fresh coin) and exchanged at a premium against coins minted in previous years. After one or two years, *sikka* rupees were considered old enough to be given a new name, *chalnī* (or *pēth* in Bengal), in order to be discounted against freshly minted coins (*sikka*). Both the *sikka* and the *chalnī* rupees carried a premium over the coins belonging to the preceding regimes circulating concurrently. These coins, which acquired the name *khazāna* (lit. treasure) after Akbar's regime, occupied the lowest position in the hierarchy of exchange and suffered maximum discount (Habib 1961: 4–5 and notes; Mukherjee and Habib 1988: 293; 1989: 247). Foster (1928: 48) describes the 'Cajana ropee' as the 'smallest' (in value). The three categories were not entirely rigid and operated with flexibility, particularly when a transition took place from one regime to another. The system was arbitrary and open to abuse, but was popular with both money-changers and state officials for reasons of convenience and profit.[6] Some major problems with these categories were that full-weight coins were discounted after a year, under-weight coins of previous mintages suffered a double discount, and coins of identical weight and fineness fetched

[5] An exception was the deliberate minting by Akbar of coins bearing the date *alf* before AH 1000 (Haider 2006: 76–83).

[6] Tavernier (1925, Vol. I: 25) indeed mentions that 'the poor people who do not know how to read the year when these rupees or paisa were coined are liable to be cheated, because something is always deducted from them, one paisa or half paisa on a rupee, and on the paisa three or four cowries'.

different values.[7] In addition, qualitative assessments of this kind encouraged clipping and sweating which thrived on the custom of counting rather than weighing coins.

With coins of similar denominations circulating at different exchange values, any transaction involving money was bound to be contentious.[8] There was no remedy for this except that each payment had to be clearly specified for a particular coin type and account books needed to be meticulously adjusted to maintain uniformity in balances, especially when the business involved partnerships, dealings in bills of exchange or investments through correspondents.[9] For some partners in a business venture, the practice of receiving money in one type of coin and keeping the account in another constituted a violation of trust and mercantile ethics and provided an opportunity for earning unaccounted profit through exchange-rate differences.[10] Such an opportunity seems to have existed at all times in unsupervised undertakings and we have the details of a case in the records of the English East India Company. In an enquiry launched to investigate the misappropriation of Company funds, it was noticed that their Agra factor always made payments in inferior rupees (*kachchā ānth*) while he received 'good money' (*pakkā ānth*) from Surat in bills of exchange. The difference (*baṭṭa*) between the two sets of rupees, 1 to 2 per cent depending on demand and supply, remained unaccounted for in the Agra ledgers of the Company (*Original Correspondence*: 217a–b; Foster 1906–27, Vol. 1651–54; 80–81, 105–06). While these matters could largely be resolved within the business community through greater trust, supervision and proper book-keeping, the problem faced by the state administration was of a different nature.

Depreciation, Discount and Exchange Rate: The Policy

For the Mughal state, the decision to standardize the exchange rates of under-weight legal tenders was motivated by interests of political sovereignty and fiscal management on the one hand, and concerns of liquidity and uniformity in the exchange economy on the other. It was important for the reigning monarch to ensure the wider circulation of currencies carrying his name, regal protocol and regnal year. It was also ideal for the state and imperial household to conduct

[7] '[T]he shroffs value the chalani rupee at from 1 to 2 per cent above the Khazana though the coins are identical in weight' (Pelsaert 1925: 29).

[8] For Tavernier's dispute with the treasurer of the Mughal noble, Shaista Khan, over payments received in lighter silver coins see Tavernier (1925, Vol. I: 28).

[9] Keeping this in mind, Tavernier advises his fellow merchants that 'when you make a sale it is necessary to say that you require to be paid in Shahjahani rupees, that is, in new silver, otherwise your payment will be made in rupees coined fifteen or twenty years or more, upon which there may be up to 4 per cent of loss' (Tavernier 1925, Vol. I: 25).

[10] In a letter of protest, a scribe, Balkrishna Brahman, mentions to his partner, a *mahājan* of Hissar called Lakhmidas, that the accounts were not kept in rupees of higher exchange value (*jins-i Shāhjahānī awwal awwal*) sent to him. Instead, Brahman was credited with a type of rupee (*chalnī wa barārī khazāna*) which exchanged at a discount (*ṣarf*) of 3.25 per cent (*Maktūbāt-i Balkrishna Brahman*: ff.27a–b).

expenditure in the same specie that the treasury received in taxes. But the circulation of imperial coins at their full exchange value, no matter how deficient they were, would have encouraged the culling of superior specie through the application of Gresham's law, which states that bad money drives good money out of circulation. There was already a strong tendency among money users to receive payments in the new coins and to get rid of the old ones (Tavernier 1925, Vol. I: 24–28; Roques 1676–86: 226–27; Crawfurd 1971: 267). By not granting full exchange value to coins of standard weight, the state would have promoted the circulation of lighter coins and a decline in the aggregate stock of precious metal coinage. Gresham's law could be rendered inoperative if all lighter coins were removed from circulation and reminted. But such standardization was inconceivable for any medieval economy with an optimum demand for currency. Also, to effect such uniformity in currency circulation a control system far beyond what was feasible for the Mughal monetary authorities had to be established.

The Mughal state approached the problem of currency depreciation by accepting the principle of discount.[11] But the acceptance of the principle did not mean the acceptance of the method of applying these discounts. The method of assessing coins by age was unfair to users because it snapped the link between weight and exchange value. The intention of the administration was to strengthen the link, at least in the case of imperial issues, as is quite clear in the instructions given to the treasurer. In order to expand the circulation of coins minted by the reigning sovereign and retain the system of discount, the Mughal state adopted three general principles. First, no discount should be permitted on imperial issues of full fineness and weight (*naqd-i durust 'aiyār tamām wazn*), no matter how old they were.[12] On coins minted by emperors of the reigning dynasty, a standard discount based on age could still be allowed (Sarkar 1906: 252–23; Moosvi 1992: 204). Second, discount rates should give credence to real loss and remain in line with the market. Any discrepancy between the official and the market rate of discount could trigger arbitrage transactions by treasury officials for profit.[13] Third,

[11] Tavernier (1925, Vol. I: 25–26) tells us that the money that goes into the treasury 'is carefully examined by the Changers of the Emperor, and the great nobles also employ their own'. The rupees were 'placed by the thousand in sacks with the seal of the grand treasurer, to which is added the number of years since they have been coined'.

[12] *Akbarnāma* (OIOC, Vol. II: 275b); Habib (1961: 5, n. 3). Cf. *Muntakhabu't Tawārīkh* (1864–69, Vol. II: 380) ['All types of *ashrafī* and *rupiya* which have the royal stamp, whether old or new, should be given equal currency and no deduction should be made on the basis of the year of mintage (*tafāwat-i sanwāt aṣlan manzūr na bāshad*)'].

[13] In an incident reported during the reign of Aurangzeb, the official discount (*dastūr quṣūr*) on the rupees of Shah Jahan was higher than the market rate (the latter was 2.25 per cent or 102.25 *shāhjahānī* rupees for 100 '*ālamgīrī* rupees). As a result, when revenue officials received *shāhjahānī* rupees in payment (say 103 for each tax claim of 100 '*ālamgīrī* rupees) they exchanged the amount in the market for '*ālamgīrī* rupees (102.25 for 100), paid taxes in the new coins and pocketed the difference (0.75 rupees). The state prohibited such exchanges and decreed that revenue records should specify each payment in coin type as well as list the money collected in discount separately ('Malikzāda' 1882: 78).

to control the circulation of underweight issues as well as the endless deterioration of currency, a line should be drawn between legal tender and coins deemed unfit for circulation. This too was based on weight loss, but with the understanding that the treasury should function as the main instrument of recoinage by accepting the most deficient coins in revenue payment and then withdrawing them from circulation. Here the role of the treasury as the extended apparatus of the mint was the same as in the case of non-Mug͟hal currencies. The legal limit set by the monetary authority for demonetization and recoinage required a feasible balance between the total supply of currency in demand and the volume of mint output. The recoinage of underweight coins tended to reduce the physical volume of money and impinge on the minting of fresh supplies unless there was a proportional increase in the size of the mint work force or production hours. But once the limit of demonetization was set, the market and treasury were authorized to give currency only to legal tender.

Such a policy had a dual advantage for the state. It facilitated the payment of revenue in cash by freeing the peasants from the obligation of tendering currency of a particular type or weight (*zar-i makhṣūṣ*) insisted upon by the officials, or yielding to a high discount rate in case they failed to comply. At the same time, it allowed the treasury to get hold of all coins to be withdrawn from circulation that could not be brought voluntarily to the mint by the users.

These principles were first reflected in a policy formulated by Todarmal, Akbar's minister in charge of state finances in AD 1582. By then, revenue collection had been centralized for five years, and the imperial administration had come face-to-face with the realities of fiscal management and monetary circulation. Two types of gold and silver coins were then current as imperial issues. The first was the *ashrafī* and rupee current from the beginning of Akbar's reign until AD 1578. In this year, these were replaced by a second type of coin, square in shape and with new names (Table 1). It is important to note that in the same year (AH 990 or AD 1582), Akbar had decreed the freezing of the year of mintage on gold and silver coins, apparently under the influence of Nuqtawi ideas of the

TABLE 1 **Gold and Silver Coins of Akbar: 1556–91**

Years of Mintage	*Designation*	*Metal*	*Shape*	*Legend*	*Weight (rice grains)*	*Weight (troy grains)*
1556–78	*Akbarshāhī ashrafī*	Gold	Round	*Kalima* & caliph mint & *Hijrī* year	528.0	169
1556–78	*Akbarshāhī rupiya*	Silver	Round	*Kalima* & caliph mint & *Hijrī* year	552.0	178
1578–91	*Lāl-i Jalālī muhr*	Gold	Square	*Kalima* & caliph mint & *Hijrī* year	586.5	188
1578–91	*Jalālī rupiya*	Silver	Square	*Kalima* & caliph mint & *Hijrī* year	552.0	178

Source: *Āʼīn-i Akbari*, Vol. I: 25, 27–28 and Museum Catalogues of Mug͟hal Coins

Islamic millennium (*alf*) but with serious implications for the popular method of assessment based on age. From AD 1582 to 1589, gold and silver coins carried a single numismatic date (*alf*), year after year.

Todarmal drew up a schedule of exchange rates for gold and silver coins in money of account which reflected discount rates based on fixed bands of depreciation. The minister also set the limits for coins to remain legal tender (Table 2). The rates were designed to raise money from discounts as well as regulate the circulation of each coin type through demonetization and recoinage. In the case of gold coins (*akbarshāhī ashrafī*), discounts were charged on weight losses ranging from a maximum of 9 rice grains (1.5 *rattī*) to a minimum of 3 rice grains (0.5 *rattī*). Marginally deficient coins (up to 3 rice grains) were exchanged at their full value, on account of tolerance or permissible deviation from the mint standard, while those which passed the maximum limit were exchanged as gold bullion (*tila).* In order to reduce the quantity of lighter issues, the state separated the most deficient legal tenders (7–9 grains) collected in taxes for reminting.

This measure applied only to the round *muhr* of old mintage, and the square *lāl-i jalālī muhr* introduced four years before it escaped the net of discount. This was done probably because the state was aiming to limit the circulation of this coin by listing all issues for demonetization except those which were of full weight (*Ā'īn-i Akbarī*, Vol. I: 27–28; *Akbarnāma* 1873–87, Vol. III: 383). Two years later, the *kalima*-bearing *lāl-i jalālī muhr* was replaced by a new gold coin of identical weight and fineness which had the *ilāhī* year as well a new legend (*Allāhu Akbar Jall-i Jalāla*) inscribed on it. In order to reduce the quantity of lighter issues, the state separated the most deficient coins (7–9 grains) collected in taxes for reminting.

In comparison with gold, a higher rate of weight-loss was acknowledged for silver coins and a higher limit for demonetization was set. This was probably based on the understanding that even though gold is the softer metal, the rupee was used more intensively than the *muhr* and was hence more susceptible to wear and tear. The old *akbarshāhī* rupee was allowed to circulate with a deficiency of up to 6 rice grains (1 *rattī*) at a discount of 1 *dām* (2.5 per cent). Any weight-loss beyond this level and up to 12 rice grains (2 *rattī*) subjected the rupee to a discount

TABLE 2 **Weight Loss and Discount on Gold and Silver Coins: AD 1582–84, 1585–89**

Name of coin	*Weight loss (rice grains)*	*Weight loss (%)*	*Exchange rate (dām)*	*Discount (dām)*	*Discount (%)*
Akbarshāhī ashrafī	0–3	0.57	360	0	0.00
Akbarshāhī ashrafī	4–6	1.14	355	5	1.39
Akbarshāhī ashrafī	7–9	1.70	350	10	2.78
Jalālā rupiya	0–12	2.17	40	0	0.00
Akbarshāhī rupiya	0–6	1.09	39	1	2.50
Akbarshāhī rupiya	7–12	2.17	38	2	5.00

of 2 *dām* (5 per cent) and the custody of the treasury. All rupees which passed the maximum limit were demonetized and reckoned as silver bullion (*nuqra*). The effective discount on the demonetized issue was 5.28 per cent, the cost of silver minting.

The exchange rates of rupees were set out in a way that overvalued the new rupee (*jalāla*), introduced four years before, against the old rupee (*akbarshāhī*) of the same weight and fineness. While the under-weight new rupee exchanged at its full value up to 12 rice grains, the full-weight old rupee was discounted from the start (Table 2). The stock of the most deficient legal tenders accepted by the treasury but reserved for reminting also had a much higher proportion of the old rupee, since the limit for withdrawal was kept lower, at 6 rice grains (*Ā'īn-i Akbarī*, Vol. I: 27–28; *Akbarnāma* 1873–87, Vol. III: 383).

From the coins collected at the various levels, only those permitted to remain in active circulation were deposited in the treasury, while the rest were separated and placed with the custodian (*taḥvildār*) with their full details recorded by the accountant (*mushrif*) in the daily register of receipts (*roznāmcha jama*'). These registers were sent regularly to the headquarters. Todarmal's regulations dealing with discount rates incorporated instructions for mint officials to send newly struck coins to the imperial treasury in exchange for older currencies (*sikka-i-sanwāt-i guẕashta*).

Todarmal's regulations were only partially successful in meeting the precise equivalence between weight-loss and discount. The major discrepancy between the official and market practices was that an under-weight coin was discounted at a rate higher than the mint price of bullion. For instance, the price of 6 rice grains of gold was fixed at a level (5 *dāms*) that artificially inflated the exchange rate of a full *muhr* by 80 *dāms* (440 instead of 360 *dāms*). Similarly, the price of 6 rice grains of silver (1 *dām*) was set at a much higher level than the exchange value of a full-weight rupee (92 instead of 40 *dāms*) (*Ā'īn-i Akbarī*, Vol. I: 28). Also, the absence of discount on the under-weight new rupee would have set into motion, through arbitrage sales, the flow of full-weight coins out of the treasury and a reverse flow of lighter coins.[14]

The inconsistencies in Todarmal's regulations were addressed two years later by his successor, an Iranian intellectual and administrator, Fatḥullāh Shīrāzī. Operating with the simple idea that discounts should serve to restore the deficient coin to its full exchange value, the new minister brought down the rates to agree with the mint price of coined bullion (Table 3). Shīrāzī also eliminated the difference between the two types of rupee by bringing the exchange rates of the old on a par with the new (*Ā'īn-i Akbarī*, Vol. I: 28). The new rupee was in circulation for about six years and there was no reason for it to be privileged with a premium. Both rupees now enjoyed a tolerance of up to 6 rice grains (*birinj*).

Shirazi's measures were implemented, set aside by Todarmal, and then

[14] See note 13 for arbitrage sales which brought new rupees into the treasury.

TABLE 3 **Weight Loss and Discount on Gold and Silver Coins: AD 1584–85**

Name of coin	*Weight loss (birinj)*	*Weight loss (%)*	*Exchange value (dām)*	*Discount (dām)*	*Discount (%)*
Akbarshāhī ashrafī	3	0.57	360.00	0.00	0.00
Akbarshāhī ashrafī	6	1.14	355.91	4.09	1. 14
Akbarshāhī ashrafī	9	1.70	353.87	6.13	1. 70
Jalālā rupiya	6	1.09	40.00	0.00	0.00
Akbarshāhī rupiya	6	1.09	40.00	0.00	0.00
Akbarshāhī rupiya	12	2.17	39.00	1.00	2.50

finally restored by Akbar.[15] Till then, Akbar had taken little personal interest in the details of the discount business. In 1591, after receiving more complaints, he looked into the matter and endorsed Shirazi's regulations. Akbar, however, decreed that the tolerance of 3 and 6 rice grains extended to gold and silver coins should be repealed, since it was open to abuse. The reasons given for the repeal were that the mint officials could be encouraged by the leeway to strike lighter coins, and the treasurers would find it profitable to remit such issues to the treasury even when the actual payments were made in full-weight coins.

The final implementation of Shīrāzī's regulations was accompanied by the standardization of the lowest unit of weight used for weighing precious metals and coins. This too was linked to the working of the discount system, but had not been addressed so far. As in the case of other administrative measures, the idea of standardization stemmed from practical problems. It was reported that lighter rice grains (*birinj hā-i sabuk*) were used by 'thievish people' (presumably money-changers) to enhance discounts fraudulently. This was particularly serious in the case of gold coins, since the 'deficiency of a *muhr* was raised from 3 rice grains to 6 and from 6 rice grains to 9' and a 'large amount of money was pocketed' in this way. Akbar introduced quartz grains (*bābā ghurī birinj*), which were smaller than rice grains and therefore more useful for weighing precious metals and coins. The absolute weight of the higher units (*rattī*, *māsha* and *tola*) remained unchanged (ibid., Vol. I: 28; Vol. II: 60).

It was one thing to decree uniform standards of currencies, weights and exchange rates for the empire, but quite another to enforce them. The imperial ordinances were generally accompanied by a warning to all 'greedy persons' (*tama' dārān*), the usual beneficiaries of currency manipulation in the eyes of the state, to refrain from 'temptations' in the future. Among specific measures were

[15] When Todarmal resumed the office of the *dīwānī* a few years later, he restored his own regulations. Abū'l Fazl notes with disapproval that this was done out of vanity (*ta'sub-i manishī wa sukhan parastī*). After Todarmal's eventual departure in 1589, the new minister, Qalij Khan, raised the discount on the old *ashrafī* by twice as much as the prevailing rates, and reduced the level of weight loss permissible for the old rupee by half, from 12 to 6 rice grains. It seems that the intention was once again to replace old with new issues by setting a lower threshold for the demonetization of the former (*Ā'īn-i Akbarī*, Vol. I: 28).

sworn statements taken from the *ṣarrāfs* to comply with the prescribed regulations. There were special officers to deal with offences and the penalties were unremitting (ibid., Vol. I: 29; *Akbarnāma* 1873–87, Vol. III: 651; *Muntakhabu't Tawārīkh*, Vol. II: 380; Monserrate 1922: 207). The paucity of sources does not allow us to evaluate the degree of success achieved by Akbar's administration, but it seems that the two pillars of standardization, a fair equivalence of weight loss and discount, and displacement of demonetized currencies held up well in the seventeenth century. The following text of an imperial order, summarized in the local history of Ahmedabad, brings out the three principles of standardization adopted by Aurangzeb's administration, viz. acceptance of all types of imperial issues by the treasury in revenue payment; discount based on weight; and demonetization of heavily underweight issues:

> In this year [AD 1684], it was brought to the emperor's attention that the revenue officials of *parganas* do not accept the money which peasants bring to the treasury on the pretext that an imperial order binds them to accept coins of only superior quality. The peasants therefore have to change money in the market to pay good quality coins (*zar hai jins-i ā'la*) into the treasury, and the course of [money] changing causes delay in revenue collection. An imperial order was issued that from the beginning of the autumn harvest, whatever type of rupee of less weight and inferior variety (*kam wazn wa jins- i zubun*) that the peasants may bring, the treasury should accept it and never refuse (lit. return). . . . The rupee which is [deficient in weight by] one *surkha* (*rattī*), two *surkha* and three *surkha* should be reckoned as [current] rupee. If the rupee is less than the standard weight, which is 11 and $^1/_2$ *māsha*, the difference should be made up by [adding] silver on the scale till it reaches 11 and $^1/_2$ *māsha*. One rupee of full weight is then to be taken as its equivalent. Previously, a rupee of one *surkha* [deficiency] was considered a full weight coin and no discount (*wajh-i quṣūr*) was levied. Since the discount is now fixed by weighing [the coins] on the scale (*ba wazn-i tarāzū*), deductions should also be made on the basis of weight on the scale. Further, if the rupee is underweight beyond 3 *surkha*, it should be reckoned as [bullion] silver and, at the price of silver fixed at one rupee per *tola*, should be sent to the treasury. (*Mīrat-i Ahmadī*, Vol. I: 308)[16]

In the later years of Aurangzeb's reign, complaints were received by the administration from the people of Ahmedabad that the money-changers had manipulated the circulation of older coins (*chalnī*) to impose heavy discounts. There was a shortage of newly minted coins in the city and an opportunity for *ṣarrāfs* to recycle older issues. When people suffered recurring losses (*nuqsān*) and market transactions came to a standstill, an order was passed once again to fix

[16] For the standard weight of the rupee, read *yāzdah* (eleven) instead of *pānzdah* (fifteen) of the printed text. The correct figure (pointed out first by Habib in 1961) is given in OIOC, MS Isl. 222: 199b.

the rate of discount and the limit of demonetization. Treasury officials and money-changers were instructed to send all demonetized coins to the mint (*dār uz zarb*) for recoinage (ibid.: 327–28, 337).

The widespread prevalence of the system of discount on different varieties of coins, and the administrative problems it caused, intensified with the eighteenth-century fragmentation of political authority (Sinha 1965, Vol. I: 133–39; Datta 1978: 171–202). The problem had been present ever since precious metal coinage came into common usage and was so deeply entrenched in the mercantile milieu that it was difficult for any political authority to set it right definitively. The growing influence of money-changers and state officials entitled to exchange money was itself a reflection of the process of depreciation arising out of increasing transactions in metallic money. Tensions were manifest in policy formulations when different officials approached the problem with different convictions while imposing the authority of the state over the manipulative money market.

The system of discount had implications for hoarding and the velocity of circulation, the two concepts which generally elude comprehension in concrete historical situations. It appears from commercial correspondence that whenever the system of reckoning value by age prevailed, merchants and money users preferred spending a good coin before the premium was lost (OIOC *Factory Records, Hugli*, Vol. 10: 208; van Dam 1927–54, Vol. I, part II: 91). Obviously, the propensity to spend not only discouraged hoarding but also increased the velocity of circulation. There is evidence also to suggest that depreciation encouraged deposit banking by allowing money-changers and bankers (*ṣarrāfs*) to acquire control over liquid resources while certifying payments (Tavernier 1679, Vol. II: 597). How important this factor was in the general determination of either the degree of hoarding or the velocity of circulation is of course very difficult to determine, as both were influenced by other factors as well. It does, however, seem that depreciation was not always chaotic and hoarding not always endemic in Mughal society that used precious metal coinage on an extensive scale.

The problem of depreciation and discount also reflected the perceptions about money held by the state and understood in the market. There were two broad streams of thought within which the status of money was articulated in the medieval world, cartalism and bullionism. Cartalism is the idea that money derives its value from convention or law, whereas bullionism locates the value of money in its intrinsic worth.

The Mughal state visualized money as a symbol of political authority and its emission as the sole prerogative of the emperor. This conception was cartalist to the extent that the state controlled the weight, fabric and fineness of currencies and standardized monetary circulation. Regulations concerning discount were also directed towards ensuring fixed value relations in monometallic exchange and fair transaction. The cartalist conception of money had implications for the market, the biggest supplier of monetary metals and the recipient of coined money. The market held to the core idea of bullionism and thrived on exchange-rate differences. At the same time, it was obliged to function within a legal–political framework.

Currency circulation was therefore an area in which the possibilities of conflict and cooperation arose in tandem, between state and market.

References

Aerts, Erik (1993), 'Metal Loss in the Monetary Circulation of the Southern Low Countries (Fifteenth–Eighteenth Centuries). Sources and Methods' in E. Aerts *et al* (eds), *Studia Historica Oeconomica. Liber Alum norum Herman van Der Wee* (Leuven: Universitaire Pers Leuven).

Akbarnāma by Abul Fazl, Oriental and India Office Collection (OIOC), British Library, London, MS Add. 26207.

Akbarnāma by Abul Fazl (1873–87), edited by Ali Agha Ahmad and Abdur Rahim (Calcutta: Bibliotheca Indica).

Ā'īn-i Akbarī by Abul Fazl (1872–77), edited by H. Blochmann (Calcutta: Bibliotheca Indica).

Crawfurd, John (1971), 'A Sketch of the Commercial Resources and Monetary and Mercantile System of British India, with suggestions for their improvement, by means of Banking Establishments (1837)' in K.N. Chaudhuri (ed.), *The Economic Development of India under the East India Company 1814–58. A Selection of Contemporary Writings* (Cambridge: Cambridge University Press).

Datta, Kalikinkar (1978), *Survey of India's Social Life and Economic Conditions in the Eighteenth Century 1707–1813* (New Delhi: Munshiram Manoharlal).

Elliot, Henry Miers (1869), *Memoirs on the History, Folklore and Distribution of the Races of the North Western Provinces of India*, 2 Vols, revised by John Beames (London: Trṃbner).

Factory Records, Hugli, OIOC, Series G/20.

Foster, William, ed., (1906–27), *English Factories in India* (13 Vols, each sub-titled by the year[s] it covers) (Oxford: Clarendon Press).

——— (1928), *A Supplementary Calendar of Documents in the India Office relating to India or to the Home Affairs of the East India Company, 1600–1640* (London: India Office).

Habib, Irfan (1999), *The Agrarian System of Mughal India* (New Delhi: Oxford University Press).

——— (1961), 'The Currency System of the Mughal Empire', *Medieval India Quarterly*, Vol. 4, Nos. 1 and 2, pp. 1–22.

Haider, Najaf (2005), 'The Monetary Integration of India under the Mughal Empire', in Irfan Habib (ed.), *India: Studies in the History of an Idea* (Delhi: Tulika).

——— (2006), 'The Monarch and the Millennium: A New Interpretation of the *Alf* Coins of Akbar', in Himanshu Prabha Ray (ed.), *Coins in India: Power and Communication* (Mumbai: Marg Publications).

Lane, Frederic C. and Reinhold C. Mueller (1985), *Money and Banking in Medieval and Renaissance Venice* (Baltimore: John Hopkins University Press).

Maktubāt i Bālkrishna Brahman, OIOC, MS Add. 16859.

Nigārnāma i Munshi by 'Malikzāda' (1882) (Lucknow: Nawal Kishore).

Mirāt i Ahmadī by Ali Muhammad Khan (1927–30), edited by Nawab Syed Ali (Baroda: Oriental Institute).

Monserrate, S.J. (1922), *The Commentary of Father S.J. Monserrate, on his Journey to the Court of Akbar (1590–91)*, translated by J.S. Hoyland and S.N. Banerjee (London, Bombay: Oxford University Press).

Moosvi, Shireen (1988), 'Todarmal's Original Memorandum on the Revenue Administration, March 1582', *Proceedings of the Indian History Congress*, 49th Session, Dharwad. Reprinted in, Shireen Moosvi (2008), *People, Taxation, and Trade in Mughal India* (New Delhi: Oxford University Press).

——— (1992), 'Aurangzeb's Farman to Rasikdas on Problems of Revenue Administration', in Irfan Habib (ed.), *Medieval India* (Delhi: Oxford University Press). Reprinted in, Shireen Moosvi (2008), *People, Taxation, and Trade in Mughal India* (New Delhi: Oxford University Press).

Mukherjee, Tarapada and Irfan Habib (1989), 'Land Rights in the Reign of Akbar. The Evidence of the Sale-deeds of Vrindaban and Aritha', *Proceedings of the Indian History Congress*, 50th Session, Gorakhpur.

——— (1988), 'The Mughal Administration and the Temples of Vrindavan During the Reigns of Jahangir and Shahjahan', *Proceedings of the Indian History Congress*, 49th Session, Dharwad.

Muntakhabu't Tawārīkh by Abdul Qadir Badauni (1864–69), edited by William Lees and Ali Ahmad (Calcutta: Bibliotheca Indica).

Original Correspondence 2071, OIOC, Series E/3.

Pelsaert, Francisco (1925), *Remonstrantie*, translated by W.H. Moreland and P. Geyl as *Jahangir's India* (Cambridge: W. Heffer & Sons).

Roques, Georges (n.d.), *La maniere de negotier dans Les Indes Orientalles dedice a mes Chers amis Et Confreres Les Engages de la Royalle Compagnye de France, MS Fonds Francais* 14614, *Bibliotheque Nationale.*

Sarkar, Jadunath (1906), 'The Revenue Regulations of Aurangzib (with the Persian texts of two unique farmans from a Berlin Manuscript)', *Journal of the Asiatic Society of Bengal*, New Series, Vol. 2. No. 6, June, pp. 234–35.

Sinha, Narendra Krishna (1965), *The Economic History of Bengal From Plassey to the Permanent Settlement*, Vol. 1 (Calcutta: Firma K. L. Mukhopadhyay).

Tavernier, Jean-Baptiste (1925), *Travels in India*, translated by V. Ball, edited by William Crooke (London: Oxford University Press).

——— (1679), *Les Six Voyages de Jean Baptiste Tavernier, en Turquie, en Perse, et Aux Indes* (Paris: Chez Gervais Clouzier et Claude Barbin).

van Dam, Pieter (1927–54), *Beschryvinge van de Oostindische Compagnie*, edited by F.W. Stapel and C.W. Th. van Boetzelar (Gravenhage: M. Nishoff).

Yāsīn's *Glossary*, OIOC, MS Add. 6603.

(Re)construction of Experiences

Epistemologies Concerning the Past in Maharashtra

Stewart Gordon

Introduction

This article began some years ago when I read Ranajit Guha's *Dominance Without Hegemony.*[1] In his opening chapter he appears to have found only one sort of liberal history in the nineteenth and twentieth centuries in India. He argued that there could be no 'real' critique of the colonial situation because both the colonizer and the colonized accepted this sort of history. Equally straightforward was the author's characterization of history before colonialism. There was only one kind of 'feudal' history. Guha selected the well-known mid-eleventh century Sanskrit Kashmiri chronicle, the *Rājataraṅgiṇī,* to stand for all pre-colonial historical writing in India (Guha 1997: 1–11).

As I thought about this position, I realized that it was neither new nor was it unique to Guha. In fact, all widely recognized schools of historical writing on India work with the same assumptions and periodization. British colonial histories written in the nineteenth century, nationalist histories of the twentieth century, Marxist writing, the Cambridge school and the Subaltern collective, all – from various political perspectives – agree that there was a 'pre-colonial' period with its characteristic forms and mentality followed by a 'sharp rupture' that was in turn followed by the 'colonial' period with its characteristic forms and mentality. Such a characterization and periodization is now widely accepted and reflected in course syllabi, theses and research topics.

My paper does not attempt an answer to the broad question of whether there was a single 'mentality' in the 'pre-colonial period'. Rather, it aims to answer a specific portion of that question: was there a single unified way to establish the truth about the past, or, conversely, were there different and diverse

[1] I had the pleasure of presenting some of these ideas at the Association for Asian Studies, 2001, in a panel organized by Kumkum Chatterjee. Ranajit Guha was in the audience and was gracious in his response to my questioning a core Subaltern hypothesis. He commented at some length that the study of people's actual experience of history, what he termed 'historicality', was a crucial and understudied area of South Asian history. I wish to thank four colleagues for helpful criticism: Richard Eaton (history), Lee Schlessinger (anthropology), Madhav Deshpande (language and literature) and Robert Frost (information technology).

ways? The finding of multiple epistemologies would cast doubt on a single pre-colonial mentality. As data relevant to this question, let us consider six types of Marathi literary genres concerned with the past, written in the seventeenth and eighteenth centuries. We will consider the search for 'truth' as a contingent social construction, appropriate to its venue. Let us begin, however, with that epistemology concerned with the past that for Guha is representative of the whole of the 'pre-colonial' period.

The *Rājataraṅgiṇī* [The River of Kings]

The following quotation gives the flavour of the early portion of this Sanskrit epic written by Kalhaṇa (from the same translation to which Guha refers). Finding himself unable to judge a Brāhmaṇa accused of murder, the king resorted to a sacred fast.

> After three nights of fast there, the best among the sleepless gods, he whose vehicle is Garuḍa, spoke in a dream to the king who was true to his word. . . .
>
> 'Yielding to your spiritual power this will be carried out of once; in this place when he [the Brāhmaṇa] is doing the circumambulation three times, if behind the imprint of his footsteps is seen the trail of the foot-steps of Brahmahatya then he being the murderer will deserve a suitable sentence; this procedure should be carried out at night, by day the sun is the remover of evil.' (*Rājataraṅgiṇī*: 125)

Overall, in the first half of the *Rājataraṅgiṇī*, we have all the characteristics of what we might term an 'epic' epistemology. First is its fabulist causality: omens, foretelling, and signs successfully predicting future events. Second, time is cyclical. The needs of each 'age' are similar; a great leader arises in each age to meet the crisis. Third, supernatural causality dominates the story. Humans have little agency without divine and semi-divine supporters. Human and divine worlds thoroughly interpenetrate. Fourth, events cluster around morally correct actions. Good succeeds, transgressions are punished, and *dharma* destroys its evil opposite, *adharma*. Lives are edited down to a handful of 'significant' events in which *dharma* triumphs over *adharma*. Fifth, numerical usage is notational and suggestive. Armies are composed of *lākhs* or multitudes. Finally, the *Rājataraṅgiṇī* is only about kings, the title means a 'River of Kings' flowing down through history. Lowly folk appear, but only in their moral interactions with kings.

Within this 'epic' epistemology, how does one know that an event is true or important? Broadly, the event is closely homologous to an unchanging pattern of previous significant events. Human nature and the gods remaining the same, problems too remain unaltered, and moral behaviour remains consistent. This is why omens can foretell events. Notational numbers downplay 'facts' (such as the number of men on a battlefield) that might weaken the homologies. Within this epistemology, it is the duty of educated writers (Brāhmaṇas) to notice and record patterns of significant events. To our modern eye, these 'epics' would not seem to be history at all, but a playing out of unchanging, repeating patterns of moral interaction between gods and men, suspended in a timeless present. They would be primarily about the reinforcement of collective memory and the legitimation of kingly power.

The reality however, is rather complex. As recounted events emerged from the distant past to a time closer to the writer's, in this genre, he had to make choices about what was the 'problem of the age' and who, exactly, has been pre-ordained to solve it. Events close to the writer's own time were even more problematic. There might well be courtiers with memory of how many were actually on the battlefield and whether anyone foretold the outcome. The writer's patron and his status were intertwined with whom he portrayed as the moral saviour of the age. As Ronald Inden (2000: 73–91) has recently shown, subtle shifts in emphasis in various versions of these epics and the homologous relation to recent political events were actually reflective of power plays by competing religious orders. The second half of the *Rājataraṅgiṇī* being closer to the author's own time, has a less epic quality. Here is a sample passage describing what happened in AD 949, a century-and-a-half before Kalhaṇa wrote the epic.

> Then placing the infants' guardian, the grandmother, on the royal throne, Parvagupta [the minister] wielded power with five ministers, Bhūbhaṭa and others. In the course of time having killed the grandmother and the others, he became powerful by aggrandizement and the sole master in the royal domain. Unable to uproot the king owing to fear of conflict with the Ekāṅgas, for the destruction of the infant he made use of sorcery. [The sorcerer speaks] 'On the first of caitra the crown will justly belong to you and your line, but if you act otherwise your family and life will soon be destroyed.' Having thus harkened during the night to the spirit's voice and pondering over the futility of witchcraft he was more perturbed. [The minister took advantage of a heavy snowstorm that immobilized local resistance, seized the palace, killed the king, and took the throne.] He who was born in Parevíśoka, the son of Saṃgrāmagupta, who was the son of a clerk named Abhinava, then became king. The few who formerly vowed to make a stand against him – all of them being afraid of him, the very next morning made their submission. (*Rājataraṅgiṇī*: 238–40)

Here, we have fewer elements of the epic epistemology. Omens still foretell future events, the focus still remains firmly on the king, and the point of the story is the result of good and bad action. There is, however, no direct divine intervention. Rather, there is human agency. The minister chose to assassinate the inconvenient king. Time is linear, not cyclical. He performs the assassination on a particular snowy day. With such epistemology in mind, let us now turn to ways of 'knowing' the past in seventeenth and eighteenth century Maharashtra.

The Courtly Epic

There was a genre in Maharashtra that sounds much like the *Rājataraṅgiṇī* and broadly matches its epistemology. Kavīndra Parmānanda wrote the *Śiva*

Bhārata, an epic poem likely commissioned by Shivaji around the time of his coronation (1675). It consciously adopts forms and conventions from classical epic poems, especially the *Mahābhārata*. Consider this quote from the opening of the *Śiva Bhārata*.

> Tell us, o knower of all!
> O Brāhmaṇa, praised for piety,
> The entire tale of that king:
> The famed tale of Raigad's king:
> The ascetic Shivaji who rules
> By the grace of Tulja Bhavānī,
> An avatār of lord Viṣṇu
> And of the World Guardians'
> A man content, restrained in mind,
> Yet more terrible than Bhīma. . . .
> Protecting gods, brāhmaṇa, and cows
> He rescues those seeking refuge
> And is loving of his subjects (Laine and Bahulkar 2001: 44–45)

Here we find many of the characteristics of what I call 'epic' epistemology. There is fabulist causality. Omens, foretelling, and signs successfully predict future events. Time is cyclical. Numerical usage is notational and suggestive. The needs of each 'age' are similar and a great leader arises in each age to meet the crisis. Supernatural causality dominates the story. Human and divine worlds thoroughly interpenetrate. Events cluster around morally correct actions. The *Śiva Bhārata* edits the incidents of Shivaji's life down to a handful of 'significant' ones in which *dharma* triumphs over *adharma*. Frequent references by simile and metaphor connect the work to classical stories. Note the comparison of Shivaji to Bhīma in the extract given above.

This connection between the classical epics and the *Śiva Bhārata* was predictable and intentional. Kavīndra Parmānanda wrote in Sanskrit for an audience fluent in Sanskrit and predominantly Brāhmaṇa. In the poem, Shivaji shows his moral superiority by support of cows, Brāhmaṇas and gods, coupled with his defeat of those who oppressed them. Overall, the *Śiva Bhārata* acted as a political resource for legitimating Shivaji.

Like the later portions of the *Rājataraṅgiṇī*, the homologous 'fit' is less than perfect between epic events of the past and even carefully selected stories of Shivaji. These dissonances arise because the story of Shivaji was unavoidably anchored in historical events within the memory of its earliest audiences. For example, though Muslims generally play the evil 'other' in the text, the author could not avoid the fact that Shivaji's father faithfully served Muslim kings during his entire career and was well rewarded for his service. The author also had to concede that several Muslim rulers were just and tolerant toward Hindus and had to be appreciated for this. Also, the author wanted to connect Shivaji with a Rajput lineage, but had to conclude his genealogy at his grandfather, Maloji. Earlier generations clearly had not been Rajputs, though a powerful family (Deshmukhs) from northern Maharashtra. Still, making the local story 'like' the epic gave grandeur and coherence to the story of a local king. Casting an important local ruler in epic terms also strengthened awareness and power of the older, more general epics.

If the *Śiva Bhārata* were the only sort of epistemology concerned with the past written in Maharashtra in the seventeenth and eighteenth centuries, there would be a strong case for a single type of pre-colonial 'history' and, by extension, mentality. But there were several other types of genre common in Maharashtra in the same period we must now consider, namely *powada, bakhar* literature, court depositions, revenue appeal documents, and tax projections.

Powāḍās

The *powāḍā* is a bardic ballad genre that first made an appearance in the mid-seventeenth century. The first known *powāḍā* was composed in 1659 to celebrate the victory of Shivaji over Afẕāl Kh̲an. The *powāḍā* is different from the courtly epic in four important aspects. First, all *powāḍās* were written in Marathi (not Sanskrit) and were intended for a popular, mainly Maratha, audience. Second, *powāḍās* were performed by travelling bards, Maratha devotees of Bhavānī known as Gondhalis, and not by Brāhmaṇas. Third, the performances were for gatherings in homes or outdoors (not for courts) and were often associated with a life cycle ceremony, such as a birth or a marriage. Fourth, while the performance included stories of the gods and sometimes spirit possession of the performer by Bhavānī, many *powāḍās* centered on historic events – heroic deeds, dangerous rescues, hairbreadth escapes, and victories against great odds. These stories celebrat-ed bravery, sacrifice, martial prowess, and honour, rather more than the virtues of a Sanskritic king who protected Brāhmaṇas, cows and gods (Arbuthnot 1894: xxxii–xxxv; also Divekar 1981: 13–14).

The following section is from the Ballad of Tanājī Mālsure, composed some time in the eighteenth century. After a brief intervention by Bhavānī at the beginning of the *powāḍā*, the piece is mainly about the guts-and-glory of Mālsure's attack of the Sinhgarh fort. Tanājī alone scaled the wall and confronted the fort commander while his troops attacked the gate below. In this section, the commander demanded to know who had invaded his fort by night.

> I greet thee brother, who art thou?
> Thy name, thy monarch, tell us now.
> Answered the chief, Behold in me
> Tanaji subhadar my name
> Son of a clown unknown to fame,
> The Moslem cried, 'a turban place
> About thy neck, and kneel for grace.'
> 'Nay, thou,' so Tanājī replied
> 'Beneath thy shoes thy visage hide;

'And twixt the teeth a straw is fit
'For curs who arm but to submit.
'But if thou will'st to fight with words,
'Here let us sheathe our useless swords;
'If not, then let thy words be few,
'And show what Sidi arms can do.' (Acworth 1894: 43–44)

The important point here is that *powāḍās* have fewer characteristics of the epic epistemology than either the *Rājataraṅgiṇī* or the *Śiva Bhārata.* Note that time is strictly linear, not cyclical. Omens and divine intervention appear briefly at the beginning of the narrative, but it is human courage that carries the day. Numbers are not notational but painfully precise. The Marathas know that they are badly outnumbered by the fort troops. The point of the battle is not to restore a world of gods, cows and Brāhmaṇas, but to right a particular affront to the deity Bhavani and to further the fortunes of Shivaji. The story is not of a king, but an ordinary man – a Maratha who gained glory by his courage.

Bakhar Literature

The earliest Maharashtrian *bakhar* dates from the sixteenth century. The written genre developed slowly in the seventeenth century, proliferated in the eighteenth, and continued its popularity in the nineteenth century. More than a hundred *bakhars* are still extant. In general, the genre relates the story of a family, a king, a minister, or an important battle. They are often concerned with position, honour and inheritance. Unlike *powāḍās, bakhars* are never meant for large-scale performance. They are a written form, possibly read out to 'tell the story' of a family's deeds, honour and holdings. We can get a flavour of *bakhar* literature from the *Sabhāsad Bakhar,* a well-known recounting of Shivaji's family, written in 1697 (about a decade after the *Śiva Bhārata*). The quotation below comes from the same story of Shivaji and Afẓāl Khan excerpted above from the *Śiva Bhārata.* As any Indian school child would know, the Sultan of Bijapur dispatched Afẓāl Khan, a high-ranking general, to put down the rebellion of upstart Shivaji. As the *Sabhasad Bakhar* tells the story, Afẓāl Khan in his misplaced arrogance violated the shrine of Tuljapur and its goddess, Bhavānī, the patron gossess of Shivaji's family.

> Then the whole force came together and formed a vast camp. It came to Tuljapur, and made a halt there. The Goddess Bhavani, patron goddess of the Maharaja's [Shivaji's] family was broken, pounded, to dust. No sooner was Bhavani broken than a heavenly voice was heard –
>
> 'Afzal Khan! thou! wretch! On the twenty-first day from this I will behead thee; the whole army of thine I will destroy and satiate the nine crores of Chamundas with their blood'. (Sen 1920: 9–10)

Though this passage sounds like the *Śiva Bhārata,* there are crucial differences. Here, for example, in a typical passage are Shivaji's functional instructions once he arrived at the fortress of Pratapgarh.

> Netaji Palkar Sarnobat was instructed to come up the ghat [coastal mountains] with his forces. 'I shall invite Afzalkhan to Javle', so he was told. 'Meet him offering to make peace, and draw him near me by inspiring confidence. You should come to the Ghat Matha, and block the road.' Ragunath Ballal Sabnis was sent with him. And it was arranged that Moropant Peshwa would also come from the Konkan, bringing with him Shamrao Nilkanth and Trimbak Bhaskar. (Sen 1920: 12–13)

The *Sabhāsad Bakhar* undoubtedly has fabulist causality, divine intervention, and a selection of events that demonstrate the triumph of *dharma* over *adharma*. Other elements of the epic form, however, are missing. The worlds of the divine and humans do not tightly interpenetrate. Shivaji marshals the troops for an upcoming attack. The connecting of the story by metaphor and simile with classical epics is also absent.

In general, in the *bakhar* literature, divine intervention occurs early in a family's history, often as an explanation of how they became 'notables' rather than being peasants. A god or a semi-god gives them a gold hoard or a sword or a horse. Otherwise, the divine rarely intervenes in these family histories. These *bakhars* all move from one event to the next, from one generation to another. Throughout, there is a very clear sense of what the family acquires, how, and when, and through whose individual efforts. Some *bakhars* contain great detail about the family holdings, down to individual villages, including the quite worldly reasons for holding them. Crucially, the *bakhars* were composed in Marathi and probably were intended for a Maratha audience. They spend little time on a changeless morality based on the protection of cows or Brāhmaṇas. They are, for the most part, much more concerned with the family's place in the world, both its property and elite status, than in proving the supremacy of *dharma* over *adharma*.

A Different Epistemology

Powāḍās and *bakhars* seem to represent a rather different way of understanding the 'truth' of the past than the Sanskrit epic as represented by the *Rājataraṅgiṇī* and the *Śiva Bhārata*. The events described in *powāḍās* and *bakhars* are both true and important, not because they are homologous to events in the epics, rather, because (1) they actually happened in a way that can be confirmed (in broad outline if not in detail) and because (2) they confirm the traits and characteristics of a group who are the sponsors and patrons.

It was the performer's or writer's obligation to provide dense detail to buttress the truth of what actually happened. Detail was equally important to establish the bravery, loyalty and honour of the hero, the position of the family, or the blame for a failure in battle. As an epistemological position, we might label *powāḍās* and *bakhars* 'practical empiricism'. I mean only that, as with any empiricism, 'truth' was established in these genres by 'mapping' events on an external reality, thereby showing whether the events were true or false. This attention to evidence includes shared concepts of time, space, causality and the nature of objects. The *powāḍā* and *bakhar* literature stretched these agreements to include shared group characteristics, such as bravery and honour.

Court Depositions

A less well-known truth-constructing genre concerned with the past is the court deposition. The Maratha government adjudicated disputes over portions of Maharashtra in the seventeenth century and much larger areas (including portions of Madhya Pradesh, Gujarat, Orissa, and the Delhi and Nagpur areas) in the eighteenth century. In a dispute over land, rights or privileges, both sides gave their version of a past in which they either enjoyed the disputed right or were denied it. To get a flavour of these court depositions, consider the following case that involved Shivaji's family. When this deposition was taken in 1716, the dispute had been ongoing for fifty years.

> Deposition of Piraji Yadav of Pargana Karad. In the time of the Adilshah [apparently about 1640], Rangoji Nimbalkar was disrupting the area. Our ancestor fought him, but the Badshah sided with Nimbalkar and cancelled our rights. Later they passed to the vazir at the court and after that to Randullah Khan [*c*. 1660], the whole of the rights passed to Shivaji [*c*. 1680], then to Sambhaji [Shivaji's son], then to Raja Ram [*c*. 1700]. We have served Raja Ram and once again received the rights and are currently enjoying it. So that our children will not raise a dispute over it, we are here of our own volition to divide the rights and request that you prepare a document of division.
>
> The judge replied, 'For a long time you have not had these rights, how did you first get them?' [There follows more than ten pages of detail on who in the family first acquired the rights, how they acquired them, and in exactly which villages the family held rights. The next poignant section outlines the con-sequences to the nuclear family of Jastoji Yadav when Rangoji Nimbalkar, at the direction of the Bijapur sultan, expelled them from their holdings.]
>
> Jastoji Yadav started at night and arrived at dawn the next day at the town held by his brother. 'We have not eaten all day and all night.' He said, 'Stay here and eat.' Jastoji said, 'We cannot get into the gate.' So, four brothers took food out to them. After dinner, Jastoji raised the issue of deshmukhi rights. . . .
>
> [The four brothers who still enjoyed government-sanctioned land rights were unwilling to share them, so the Jastoji Yadav was reduced to ordinary trooper/soldier status.] (Pawar 1969: Document No. 332)

Note that there were no claims to godly intervention in the acquisition of the rights in the first instance. No one claimed that omens foretold the loss of the rights. When expelled from the rights, the family did not stop to pray at the family shrine. The events in the deposition were not edited down to the few that established morality on one side. Rather, the judge requested detail; the deposition above, for example, went on for more than sixty pages. Time was not represented as cyclical. The consequences of one-time events continued for generations.

Throughout the deposition, numbers were not notational, but quite exact – the revenue of the villages, the percentage of taxes the family retained, and the number of troops they furnished. Argument was by evidence and chronological succession, not by simile and metaphor as in the classical epics. Moral claims took a back seat to the rules of evidence, especially documentary proof. We may note that, as a genre, the court deposition was probably more common than the *powāḍā* and certainly more common than the *bakhar.* The Pune Daftar, the archive of Maratha government and family records (located in Pune) houses thousands of similar court depositions from every district of Maharashtra and many from later Maratha conquests in the North.

Revenue Appeals

Another genre concerned with the past consists of letters to the central government about the proper degree of taxation, both for a single year and over the long term. The initiative for these appeals emerged at the local level when a taxation situation was deemed unacceptable. Local leaders (Deshmukhs) had a letter drafted to explain the problem. Typically, many local landholders and local officials signed the appeal (making their mark if they were illiterate). Here is a government summary of one such interchange during the Maratha conquest of the Tapti valley in the 1750s. The translation is mine and the prose is a good bit drier than the heroic warfare of the *Śiva Bhārata.* In essence, this was the situation. The Maratha general Malhar Rao Holkar tried to double a category of taxes termed *ghāssdāna.* Local officials and landholding families appealed to the central government of the Maratha state to return the tax to the level it had been under the former Mughal government.

> Malharji Holkar having represented the item of 'forage money' (*ghassdana*) of the Pargana Adavad, held by government from former years and fixed at Rupees 750, has at present been increased to Rupees 1500, which the peasants find difficult to pay and therefore requested that it be returned to Rupees 750 for the current year forward. The amount of 'forage money' from the said Pargana to the government has, therefore, been fixed at Rupees 750. . . . Rupees 750 have been fixed for the collection every year in order to save the said Pargana from further molestation. (Gordon 1994: 50–60)

Like the court depositions, there was nothing epic here. Past usage had a legal weight that rested on a shared linear time. Gods, moral homilies, and metaphors that connected the problem to the classical epics were conspicuous by their absence. These documents were about contractual obligations. There are tens of thousands of such documents in the Pune Daftar. All come from the countryside and involve local landholders.

An Epistemology of Practical Empiricism

Court depositions and local revenue appeals had a clear and coherent logic and a means to establish true knowledge about the past. More than the *powāḍā* and the *bakhar*, the revenue appeal and the court deposition seem firmly placed in 'practical empiricism'. The court had rules of evidence and precedence. Written evidence carried more weight than oral testimony. Judges made careful examination of signatures and marks on a document. They looked for forgery. They looked for inconsistencies in the oral testimony. Government officials vetted tax appeals in the same way, reviewing documents and sifting through oral testimony. Throughout, there was an attempt to arrive at a 'true' rendering of the past and a rejection of a 'false' view.

Tax Projections

There was a genre concerned with the past and produced in great numbers in Maharashtra in the pre-colonial period that is even less epic in its epistemology than court depositions and tax appeals. To get a sense of these documents, we must know a bit more about Maratha taxation at the time. Taxes came mainly from sedentary agriculture and were paid – as under the earlier Mughal government – by groups of villages termed a *parganā*. In the most settled and productive *parganās*, tax demands were not made on a yearly basis, but in the form of multi-year contracts that would hold for five, seven, or even ten years. These areas generally had decades of detailed revenue statistics before a collector would take out a long-term collection contract. He typically had records that showed the number of productive, recently colonized and vacant villages, plus the names of the owners and field sizes of the cultivated land in all the cultivated villages, the quality of land, and the crops grown. He had the costs of the garrisons in the area and the overall costs of administration, plus long-term records of taxes paid and outstanding balances for each village and the names of those responsible for local collection (Gordon 1994: 50–57).

The central government analysed this complex of local data and revenue history and arrived at increased levels of local taxation possible for a particular *parganā* in the forthcoming years. Combines of Pune Brāhmaṇa bankers analysed the same data and arrived at the level of risk involved for advancing loans to the government against a *parganā's* current and future taxes. The result was an interest rate for loans to government against future local taxes. Across the Maratha dominions, this interest rate topped out at 60 per cent for virtually unconquered lands and dropped to less than 6 per cent per year for stable, peaceful areas. Successful negotiations between the banking community and government depended on a quantifiable perception of the past of a pargana, as well as the relation of that past to a predictable future. Then, as now, bankers used hard evidence to assess risk, which is essentially a projection of the past into the future. This approach to the 'truth' of the past was sufficiently routine and credible, and bankers regularly formed combines of investors based on it (Kulkarni 1973: 180–205).

An Epistemology of Practical Pragmatism

What distinguished loan assessments from court cases or revenue appeals was the sophisticated use of history to make a prediction regarding the future and the confidence to lend money based on that analysis. It is certainly no surprise that there was, in these revenue projections, no cyclical time, no divine intervention and no moral homilies. Numbers were exact, down to the last fraction of a rupee. Agency was human, not divine. Numbers could hardly be notational; wealthy people staked their financial future on the accuracy of the projections. Prediction was based not on omens, but on numerical calculation. In this epistemology, which we term 'practical pragmatism', Brāhmaṇa financial combines and the government constructed a model of the environment (a connected past, present and future) with the aim of solving a problem (the rate of interest to charge against future tax receipts). The model was then refined, based on actual results, and probably also on hunches and rules-of-thumb based generations of experience. Overall, we might term this a domain of epistemological 'practical pragmatism' that was completely different from the epic epistemology with which we began.

The Subsequent History of these Epistemologies

Let me remind the reader of the all-important fact that these genres – epic, *powāḍā*, *bakhar* and several other magisterial genres – and epistemologies existed simultaneously in seventeenth and eighteenth century Maharashtra. They were not sequential or in phases. Now, let us turn to how these various genres, concerned with history in Maharashtra, fared in the colonial period. The Sanskrit epic was never produced in great numbers, but there was some new production through the nineteenth century and two have been written just in the last decade. At a more popular level, comic books on Indian epic heroes abound, as do television spectacles based on the epics.

Powāḍās fared quite well in the colonial period. They were oral, public, and in Marathi, making them a continuing form of popular entertainment. These were the myths on which a regional nationalism was built in the nineteenth century. *Powāḍās* were critical public performances in the mass mobilization strategies of Tilak in the first decades of the twentieth century. The epic stories of Shivaji and other heroes of Maharashtra are at least as popular now as they have been over the last three centuries. There have been scholarly papers written recently that compare Shivaji's qualities to Kṛṣṇa. Heroic, epic statues decorate many cities. Comic books that portray Shivaji much as the *powāḍās* did can be found in every bookshop. *Powāḍās* are still regularly performed as a part of concerts.

Grounded in their own hard-empiricist cultural epistemology, British colonial historians of the nineteenth century generally dismissed *bakhars* as being fanciful, self-serving, and inaccurate. Such judgment hardly stopped the flow of new *bakhars* (or *khafīyats* as they were also known). *Bakhars* showed the age, nobility, and importance of a family. They probably became more important in the nineteenth century than earlier, as actual chances to prove military prowess waned. Hundreds of *bakhars* were commissioned in the nineteenth and twentieth centuries, many complete with photos of family members and home places. Nationalist historians generally accepted the British colonial historian's low opinion of *bakhar* literature but lauded the collection and publication of any original family documents embedded in such histories.

Depositions, appeals and numeric projections suffered a far different fate. After British troops captured the Peshwa's archive at Pune (1818), the Bombay government was divided as to what to do with it. One faction wanted to simply sell it as waste paper (a sentiment that recurred regularly through the nineteenth century). The successful rival faction knew that the documents would be needed for inevitable court cases over land rights throughout Maharashtra. The papers subsequently became part of the legal system and could only be consulted in connection with a pending court case. They were firmly and absolutely closed for historical research. (Incidentally, the long cases over land rights in the seventeenth and eighteenth centuries make similarly extended cases in the colonial period seem normal rather than an irritating feature of Indian character as many colonial officials thought.)

From internal discussions within the Bombay government in the later decades of the nineteenth century, we know that many officials were aware of the potential these documents had for a nationalist agitation. The papers showed that India (or at least the part ruled by the Marathas) was not in a state of 'anarchy' and in no need of British intervention. At the very least, government had been predictable enough for money to be loaned against future receipts. The documents showed that the British were hardly bringing 'civilization' to Maharashtra, but were, in a sense, replacing a more financially sophisticated system by a less sophisticated one.

Through the colonial period in the twentieth century, the Bombay government never made the documents available for research and carefully vetted those published to ensure that they were politically non-controversial. For example, the government published no 'runs' of documents on a single person or office or area, so that no comparison to the colonial situation could be documented. What was published was a confusing batch of documents from various areas and periods on rather innocuous subjects.

The closure of the richest archive of Maratha history meant that these court and revenue records were not available for research until well after Independence and are still not well known.

The great Maratha historians of the first half of the twentieth century, however, recognized that the closure of the Peshwa archive was a colonial affront to their history and treated the collection of family and regional records as important nationalist work. As a result of these efforts, there are now several major private research collections in the state, as well as a steady stream of books of private and family documents from the period.

The suppression of depositions, appeals and tax projections from the Maratha period had important results. There is now some awareness that 'modern' forms of epistemology ('practical empiricism', for example) concerned with the past were not introduced by the British colonial government in the nineteenth century, but were, in fact, the most common quotidian epistemology in pre-colonial

Maharashtra. India was not, as British colonial historians asserted and nationalist historians largely accepted, lost in an ahistorical epic epistemology. Instead, there was great continuity between ways of establishing historical truth in the pre-colonial and colonial periods. These continuities are especially clear in the tax appeals and court cases from the colonial period.[2]

Conclusions

We sell Maharashtrians short if we presume that they could not handle the various approaches to the past that we have found in the seventeenth and eighteenth centuries. Epic, *powāḍā*, *bakhar*, deposition, appeal and numeric projection were all operating in Maharashtrian society at the same time. There is every reason to believe that people could go to a performance of a *powāḍā* at night and go to court in the morning. It is important to note that the genres that showed an 'empiricist' epistemology (*powāḍā*, the *bakhar* and more so, depositions and appeals) were probably more popular and common in the countryside than the epic genre. For example, every year each cultivator had to consider the past to settle his tax contribution for the coming year. The installments were due on the stated date and no god intervened if the payment was late. We see no evidence that these various genres were found only in some sort of transition period from status to contract, or 'feudal' to bureaucratic. Note also that each genre had aspects of orality, and it is not as if the more textual forms somehow crowded out the less textual forms (Thomas 1992: 128–153). Though, for obvious reasons, with the rise of the 'modern' nation state the more empirical epistemologies enjoy ascendancy, the genres we have considered continue right to the present. How else are we to explain godly intervention in many Bollywood movies, the popularity of televised epics, or epic-based comic books? These epic forms coexist alongside the epistemology found in today's court depositions, narrative histories and economic projections.

If it is conceded that there were several distinguishable epistemologies of the past operating simultaneously in Maharashtra in the seventeenth and eighteenth centuries and that these must necessarily form a part of anything we might call a 'mentality', then any assertion of a simple, unified pre-colonial mentality seems highly questionable. Equally simplistic and questionable is the assertion that the colonial period produced a 'sharp break' with the past. We have found no evidence of an abrupt end to any of the earlier epistemologies of the past in the nineteenth century. Rather, all of these forms continued (and several flourished) in spite of the gradual development of document-based history writing in the nineteenth century.

I am indeed not suggesting a 'changeless' India with unchanging epistemologies as an alternative to the 'sharp break' periodization. All of the genres discussed

[2] This survey does not exhaust the genres that dealt with the past in pre-colonial Maharashtra. Lee Schlessinger suggested two more, the family genealogies kept at pilgrimage sites such as Pandarpur and lineage genealogies such as the one kept by the Bhonsle house. To these, I might add a third, the court chronicles of the Muslim court of Ahmadnagar. The genres analysed are perhaps enough to make the point of several coexisting epistemologies.

arose in a specific period associated with the emergence of a relatively independent Maratha political power. They catered to real social and economic needs – to celebrate great deeds, win court cases in order to retain family holdings, or judge the risk of loans to government. Nor am I suggesting that important changes did not take place under the early colonial regime. Of course they did. In the Maharashtra region, the new structure of the Bombay army halted centuries of military entrepreneurship that had catapulted families into land holding. The Maratha government had routinely repaired dams and weirs damaged in war. The cash-strapped Bombay government could not. The Bombay army relentlessly attacked forest dwellers such as the Bhils, settling those it could, and marginalizing the rest.

All I am suggesting is that for the indigenous production of genres associated with an analysis of the past, the conquest of Maharashtra by the British did not represent a 'sharp rupture'. It did not stop either the need or the patronage for these various genres. We have yet different concurrent epistemologies in Maharashtra because they 'worked' in different venues. The same Brāhmaṇa might listen to an epic then go back to work on the year's tax projections. In the colonial period, change was slow as new patronage and institutions developed. In general, old forms rattled on next to new forms (Deshpande 2001: 119–28). Old forms sometimes took on new political functions, such as the use of *powāḍās* in nationalist organizing. The process was complex, subtle, nuanced and continues to this day. We need to respect this lived experience in any larger theoretical periodization.

References

Acworth, Harry Arbuthnot (1894), *Ballads of the Marathas* (London: Longmans, Green, and Co.).

Bhausahebanci Bakhara (1984), translated by Ian Raeside as *The Decade of Panipat (1751–1761)* (Bombay: Popular Prakashan).

Deshpande, Madhav M. (2001), 'Pandit and Professor: Transformations in the 19th Century Maharashtra' in Axel Michaels (ed.), *The Pandit: Traditional Scholarship in India* (Delhi: Manohar).

Divekar, V.D. (1981), *Survey of Material in Marathi on the Economic and Social History of India* (Pune: Bharata Itihasa Samshodhaka Mandal).

Gordon, Stewart (1994), *Marathas, Marauders and State Formation in Eighteenth-Century India* (Delhi: Oxford University Press).

Guha, Ranajit (1997), *Dominance without Hegemony: History and Power in Colonial India* (Cambridge: Harvard University Press).

Inden, Ronald, Jonathan Walters and Daud Ali (2000), *Querying the Medieval: Texts and the History of Practices in South Asia* (Oxford: Oxford University Press).

Kelkar, Y.N. (1928), *Itihasik Powade* (Pune: Y.N. Kelkar).

Kulkarni, G.T. (1973), 'Banking in the 18th Century: A Case Study of a Poona Banker', *Artha Vijnana*, Vol. 15, No. 2, pp. 180–200.

Laine, James W. and S.S. Bahulkar (2001), *Kavindra Parmananda's Sivabharata: Translation and Study* (Hyderabad: Orient Longman).

Pawar, D.A., ed. (1969), *Tarabaikalin Kagadpatra* (Kolhapur: Sivaji Vidyapitha).

Rajataraṅgiṇī by Kalhaṇa (1968), translated by Ranajit Sitaram Pandit and entitled *Rajatarangini: The Saga of the Kings of Kashmir* (New Delhi: Sahitya Akademi).

Sen, Surendranath (1920), *Śiva Chhatrapati, being a translation of Sabhsad Bakhar with extracts from Chiṭnīs and Śivdigvijaya, with notes* (Calcutta: University of Calcutta).

Thomas, Rosalind (1992), *Literacy and Orality in Ancient Greece* (Cambridge: Cambridge University Press).

Wad, G.C. and D.B. Parasnis (1907), *Selections from the Satara Rajas and the Peiswas' Diaries* (Poona: Deccan Vernacular Translation Society).

Describing the Common, Discovering the Individual

A Study in Some Medieval Indian Biographies

Eugenia Vanina

For nearly two centuries it was accepted that ancient Indians had neither a historical consciousness nor an interest in the past and its recording for the future generations, and that the tradition of history writing was introduced by the Muslim invaders. This concept became a key constituent of the image of India created by the European Orientalists, irrespective of their 'Indomania' or their 'Indophobia' (Trautmann 1997: 62–130). Only a few Orientalists were brave enough to challenge this belief and to state, like the Russian Sanskritist K.A. Kossovich (1815–83), 'They say that India has no history. If history is a depiction of the destinies of a nation that has developed independently under the influence of the ideas worked out by the course of its own life, if "the history-minded nations" are those who have succeeded in organizing their statehood against the spacious background of all possible manifestations of free thought and creativity, if there are impregnable monuments and literary testimonies of their life, then the Indians are nothing inferior to the most historical-minded peoples of the world'.[1]

The notion of the 'a-historicity' of the Indians seems itself to have become a part of history along with the other Orientalistic constructions; vestiges of it, however, are still traceable in some later works (Larus 1979: 9–10; Chandra 1976: 2–3). Nevertheless, thanks to the efforts of a number of scholars, we now have a clear notion of the development of historical consciousness in India from ancient times onwards and its reflection in various genres of literature (Pargiter 1922; Pathak 1966; Warder 1972; Thapar 1986).

My paper attempts to discuss a peculiar dimension of history writing in medieval India, which is personal history – biography and autobiography. The subject will be treated neither from the persepective of a literary form or genre, nor in relation to language and modes of expression. My interest is in the changing perceptions of man as reflected in a few works of this class. The purpose of this limited effort is to trace societal and cultural changes as reflected in the changing perception of man in this corpus of literature, as well as to try and suggest a new topic for the discussion on medieval Indian society and dimensions of change.

[1] Quoted in Serebryakov (1985: 13).

It has become an established tradition in studies in medieval Indian history to discuss the society in question, irrespective of the scholars' view of it as stagnant or dynamic, almost exclusively within the framework of socio-economic relations (primarily in the agrarian sphere), administration and political developments. What emerges as a result is a world of land grants, rents, feudal hierarchies, royal policies and commercial networks that is devoid of any understanding of the social ideals, values, behaviour and attitudes. The very concept of man as worked out by the society in question and as developed through its history finds no place in scholarly description. Literary works belonging to the genre of biography and autobiography have hitherto evoked little interest among historians of medieval India unless they contain some valuable data on socio-economic or political life. Moreover, quite a significant number of scholars are prejudiced against medieval literature, especially when it does not comply with the canons of chronicle writing (established by the celebrated historians of the Delhi sultanate and the Mughal empire). Historical poems (*mahākāvyas),* dynastic histories (*vaṃśāvalīs*), panegyrics (*praśastis*), biographies (*caritas*, *vārtās*, etc.) and such sources are regarded as unreliable because of their 'mixing past with legends' (Chandra 1976: 2–3) or their inability to 'symbolize research and factual truth' (Sinha 2000: 118).

The problem of 'factual truth' is of special interest in the medieval context. Doubts have been cast upon even celebrated chronicles and epigraphic records, on which generations of scholars have relied. Yet 'factual truth' was for medieval historians neither an aim nor a value to abide by.[2] But for the purposes of the present study, what is of importance is the way historical reality had been correlated with personal life and with the specific purposes of biography-writing. These purposes themselves are worthy of a historians' attention. Questions such as why the society needs an individual life-story to be recorded for present and future generations, why someone writes a biography of a certain person and why an individual thinks it necessary to record and make public the events of his/her life are important indicators of the characteristic features of a society and of the developments within it.

Valour and Glory

As has been observed by David Arnold and Stuart Blackburn in the Introduction to their recently published volume, 'life histories have been a historically persistent and socially pervasive form of cultural expression' in South Asia (Arnold and Blackburn 2004: 6). Biography writing was known in ancient India: one can refer to the *Buddhacarita*, and the *Rāmāyaṇa* too, as a biography, or at least as having been composed along biographical lines. Yet, as V.S. Pathak has shown, it was the early medieval period that truly gave birth to this specific genre, depicting the life and exploits of not only the divine sages and heroes of yore like Rāma or the Buddha, but also of existing individuals, in many cases personally known to

[2] This theme has been extensively and convincingly elaborated on the basis of medieval West European historiography by Spiegel (1997: 85).

the writer (Pathak 1966: 21). Oral tradition apart, the life and exploits of the kings were depicted in numerous epigraphic records, but the trailblazer for the biographical genre was of course the celebrated *Harṣacarita* of Bāṇa (seventh century). Bāṇa's masterpiece was followed by a number of other works in Sanskrit and regional languages, such as the *Vikramāṅkadevacarita* of Bilhaṇa (eleventh century), *Pṛthvīrājrāsau* by Cand Bardāī and so on. Apart from biographies, there were chronicles, *mahākāvyas*, *vaṃśāvalis*, *praśastis* and bardic poems[3] in which life histories (both of the hero and of the author himself) found an important place.

For a long time these works have been discredited as sources. In Pathak's colourful description, these narratives remained 'an outcaste on the margins', 'craving' the scholar's permission 'to join the company of historical writers' (ibid.: 81). Indeed, it is a difficult task to sieve 'factual truth' out of the huge layers of poetic imagery, romantic exaggeration and simple adulation of the rulers by the court poets. Nevertheless, these works are helpful if we are interested not just in 'facts' but in the way medieval biographical writing reflects the prevalent perceptions of man, time and society.

Perhaps I should pause here for a while to anticipate the readers' query: how can one be sure that the perceptions described in medieval biographies and other literary works were really prevalent at the time of their composition? In the opinion of Chattopadhyaya, 'the choice of the premises to be projected in the written text, whether the text is that of a land-grant inscription or of a *mahākāvya*, was of a literate elite who, in the process of creating the text, was drawing upon a well-established pool of conventions, motifs and symbols'; therefore this choice 'cannot be material for construction of public consciousness, but only of dominant premises' (Chattopadhyaya 1998: 22).

Medieval Indian literature, especially in Sanskrit, has for quite a long time been reproached for its elitist character and complete separation from the everyday life of common people. Many Sanskrit literary works, however, were distinguished by their realistic descriptions of social milieus and an acute awareness of the social problems of their time. Moreover, it was the educated elite that was able to express itself in this or that written form, while the illiterate majority had no such opportunities; for the major part of ancient and medieval history, with the exception of some stray cases in various texts like Buddhist poetry or the Tamil Śaṅgam lyrics, the voice of the masses was not heard until the period of *bhakti* poetry. This situation was by no means peculiarly Indian: a well-known Russian scholar of medieval European history and culture has named his book on popular mentality, *Medieval World: The Culture of the Mute Majority* (Gurevich 1990). Therefore, rightful as it would have been to study literature of both the

[3] Stuart Blackburn is right to denote such genres of Tamil literature as 'ballads' and to view them as somewhat analogous to Scottish and Border ballads (Blackburn 2004: 208). I suggest that similar comparison would be correct for the Rajput and Maratha poems as well.

elite and the masses of medieval India, in reality such a research agenda would hardly be practicable, and we have no other way but to content ourselves with what has been and is available now. Moreover, we know that neither of the two layers constituted a homogeneous whole and that a certain interaction did exist between them: folklore had an undoubted influence on Sanskrit literature, while vernacular adaptation of some parts of the latter, did become a part of mass culture. Thus it may be suggested that the medieval *kāvya* and *carita* did reflect, albeit in a peculiar way, the prevalent socio-cultural perceptions, including ideas about man, and the social and temporal aspects of his life.

According to Thapar, the *carita* emerged as a complement to the *vaṃśāvalī* or dynastic history and contributed to the legitimation of rulers of the post-Gupta feudal states (Thapar 1986: 378). The purpose was, no doubt, an unabashed eulogy of the royal patron; at the same time, the court poet strove for reward and glory too, and a well-written *carita* might have been a means to realize personal ambitions. Raṇchoḍ Bhaṭṭa, the author of the *Rājpraśastiḥ Mahākāvyam*, a eulogy of Rāj Singh, the ruler of Mewar,[4] described the relationship between the court poet and his patron in the uncompromising terms typical of the feudal exchange of services, in which each side provides for the other's fame:

> *Vyāsavālmīkivadvanyo bāṇaśrīharṣavannṛpaiḥ*
> *Sa saṁskṛtkavi rājñām yaśoṅgasthāpakaściram*

> [Men like] Vyasa and Valmiki should be glorified by the rulers [in the way] Sri Harsha glorified Bana:

> It is due to the Sanskrit poets that the limbs of the royal glory are kept firm forever. (Raṇchoḍ Bhaṭṭa 1973: 17)

Medieval biography writing was distinguished by well-established personal relations between the author and his hero. The poet was obliged to the royal patron for favours, this made him neglect other possible topics for his work. The *Pṛthvīrājrāsau* features a curious episode of discussion between the author, Cand Bardāī, and his wife. The latter reminds her husband about the illusory character of the mundane world and requests him to sing the praise of Hari. The poet does not object, but says that he must first fulfil his duty to his patron Prithvīrāj and the royal family of the Cauhāns (*rin aphphau cahuvān ko*). The wife insists and requests Cand not to eulogize a mortal man (*nar kittī nana gāī*) (*Pṛthvīrāj-rāsau* 1955, Vol. I: 30–34). In order to escape from this pressure the poet begins *Das Avatār Kathā* (The Story of Ten *Avatāras*) and even incorporates it into the text of his main work, but breaks it, saying that it takes too much time to sing about Rāma and Kṛṣṇa, a poet could hardly live so long.

[4] This eulogy (composition began in 1661) was inscribed on 25 huge stone slabs that decorate the dam of the artificial Rajsamundar lake, 40 miles to the north from Udaipur.

Vālmīk rikhirāj, kisan dīpāyan dhārī /
koṭi janme sambhavai toi hari nām apārī //
manucchi mand mati gand tan, puvv bhār cahuān sir /
jī kahyau alap mati sulapkari, suhari citt cyantau suthir //

Through millions of births Valmiki and Krishna Dvaipāyana (Vyāsa)
Were not able to fully [eulogize] the countless names of Hari.
A [common] man with slow mind and impure body, previously loaded with [obligations] to the Chauhans,
With firm concentration upon Hari, [I sing] as it suits my weak mind. (Ibid.: 80)

This lively episode is truly interesting as it throws light on significant aspects of royal biography writing. First, it appears that this kind of literature, mundane and secular in its character, was in that epoch viewed by society as somewhat inferior to religious poetry. The poet himself is of the same opinion, and with a habitual self-humiliation admits that it is only his own inferiority as a person and author that makes him compose the *carita* of a mortal man. Second, the poet's obligations as a hereditary bard of the Cauhān family are a heavy load on his head. The work was, however, profitable, as Cand and other royal biographers never failed to mention thc lavish gifts and land grants they received from their patrons (ibid.: 138). The rulers, in their turn, felt it necessary to secure the favour of the poets by all possible means; they never forgot to please those on whom their glory and legitimacy depended to a considerable extent. Thus the Rajput bard Khiḍiyā Jagā in his *Vacanikā*, a poem that eulogized the heroic death of the Rajput Rājā Ratan Singh Raṭhor in the Dharmat battle (April 1658) against the army of the rebellious princes Murad and Aurangzeb, made a graphic description of his hero's preparations on the eve of the decisive battle. Having arranged his armies, Ratan Singh worships all the gods, distributes gifts among the Brāhmaṇas and then organizes a lavish feast for the poets who, in chorus, sing the glories (*kavi japai jaikār*) of the valiant and generous hero (Khidiya Jagā 1960: 28–29). This feasting of the poets on the eve of the decisive battle is depicted as a ritual on a par with religious ceremonies.

Curiously enough, at the very beginning of his poem Cand noted that he had been asked by a certain 'sexy beauty' (*kāminī kal keli*) to narrate the heroic deeds of Prithvīrāj (*Pṛthvīrāj-rāsau* 1955, Vol. I: 13).[5] Moreover, he acknowledged that, singing the glory of the Cauhāns he might become a laughing stock – someone who made public the things already known to everybody:

[5] In the modern Hindi rendering of the text the editor chastely presents her as the poet's 'wife' but, as readers can see from the previously discussed episode, it was not the one who criticized Cand for eulogizing a mortal man. That latter lady was styled by Chand as merely *vāmā* – woman, wife. The mention of the 'sexy beauty' seems to stress once again that this type of literature was looked upon as somewhat light, more suitable for entertaining a mistress. Bāṇa also narrated his *Harṣacarita* to please his friends.

Phūli kittī cauhān kī, juggani jugg nivās /
app matti sarasai sabal, matī karau kabi hās //

The glory of the Chauhans lives through the epochs,
It is mighty and delightful by itself; oh poets, mock me not! (Ibid.: 2)

Apart from the poet's humility and aspiration to praise his patron these lines also emphasize the peculiarity of the biography: the author describes contemporary events, known, at least to some extent, to his audience.

What kind of a personality did the *carita* writers portray? When a modern reader looks through this kind of literature, (s)he has two kinds of impressions. First, irrespective of the epoch, region or language, most royal biographies seem to depict one and the same person. Harṣa, Prithvīrāj, Rāj Singh or any other ruler, all possess the same character and perform nearly the same feats of valour, generosity and love. Even the events described by various authors are nearly similar: endless wars, feuds and skirmishes, hunting expeditions, love affairs with matchless beauties, marriages, lavish feasts and the distribution of immeasurable wealth to the temples, Brāhmaṇas, poets, warriors and the needy. And the heroes' behaviour under these standard circumstances is standard as well – not because the poets copied each other's works or just followed some well-established literary canons, but because they depicted what Duby called a 'collection of mental images which form the real core of the notion of *nobilitas*'. This observation, made on the basis of medieval French sources, is fully applicable to medieval India as well (Duby 1990: 217). Secondly, one can hardly detect any difference between the real historical personages as depicted in biography and heroes of the epic or of folklore or medieval literature. Little distinction can be traced between the real Prithvīrāj Chauhan as portrayed by Cand Bardāī and the literary or folklore personages, like Udayana, Mṛigāṅkadatta, Bhoja, Bisāldev, Ālha or Ūdal. Like these imaginary heroes, Prithvīrāj is a paragon of bravery and generosity; he is handsome 'like a statue of Kāma' and intelligent: his education has made him an unrivalled expert in not only martial arts, but in six languages, music, painting and other arts – seventy-four in all (*Pṛthvīrāj-rāsau* 1955, Vol. I: 27–30). Actually the royal hero of the *caritas*, Harṣa, Prithvīrāj, Vikrama or Hammīra, or any other, is a model ruler and model Kshatriya warrior – more an ideal than a real human being.

If that be so, then should we not agree with those who dismiss the *caritas* and allied literature as fiction, devoid of historical value? Or should we agree with Hart that Indian classical literature, including medieval biography 'deals not with reality but with archetypes – models and examples that can be used for experience and conduct' (Hart 1995: 169)?

It seems to be a core feature of any medieval society, India being no exception, to perceive people not as individuals distinguished by certain traits of character and peculiarities of physique, but as members of a certain social group, estate, caste, corporation, religious community or clan. Pertaining to each and every such group was a definite set of values, or, to quote Duby once more, 'models of behaviour, exemplary types of human achievement' (Duby 1990:

219) that a member of this community was supposed to follow or at least strive to follow, as a respected and righteous person. Since ancient times each *varṇa* was supposed to be distinguished by a clearly defined set of values, and the Kṣatriyas, to whom the majority of the epic heroes and *carita* personages belonged, were perceived as people endowed with manhood (*vīrya*), might (*ojas*), bravery (*sāhasa*) and so on. Other key words for them were power or rule (*rāj*), realm or domain (*rāṣṭra*) and, of course, glory (*kīrti*) (Smith 1994: 30–31). The latter was especially significant as the main social indicator of a person's success in imbibing his *varṇa* ideals. In the medieval period the above-mentioned set of values, with some additions like lavishness and the generous expenditure of all wealth acquired by the sword, was established as the ethos of the feudal military castes, especially those reckoning themselves among the Rajputs (Kolff 1990: 73; Gordon 1994: 183–87). Thus the heroes of medieval romances, bardic poems and *carita*s had, according to their authors, no other way but to embody these values. By depicting Harṣa or Prithvīrāj as the ideal Kṣatriya, the *carita* writer, no doubt, flattered his patron and claimed a handsome reward, but at the same time he contributed to the preservation of social ideals and the behaviour patterns of his patron's caste and estate, also legitimizing his rule. In other words, he worked not just for the present but also for the future – the future of the caste and the state.

Therefore, medieval Indian literature, biography included, did deal with archetypes, and Hart was right to emphasize this. Yet his juxtaposition of archetypes and reality is questionable. Medieval biographers dealt with the reality not of concrete events, but of actual social ideals and caste values. Hence, in the words of Chattopadhyaya, medieval *carita*s and *kāvya*s were both 'biographies' and 'not biographies', as 'the portrayed life was the reflection of an ideal reality which, of course, had to match the specific station of the hero' (Chattopadhyaya 1998: 26).

The character depicted by medieval biographers was thus determined by his birth in a valiant family of Kṣatriya warriors and therefore all the traits and features were inherent in him from the very beginning of his life. Nothing in this character was acquired under these or that circumstances, nothing was changed or developed: from the moment of birth in the glorious house of the Cauhāns, Prithvīrāj possessed the whole set of virtues pertaining to his caste and clan. And this is relevant to all heroes of medieval biographies and romances. Moreover, strange as it may seem to a modern reader, since the hero's adversaries also belong to the same noble warrior families, they are depicted by the poet as nothing inferior to the hero: they fight bravely and strive for glory, and the author and his hero are the first to acknowledge this. Even the Turkish invaders are depicted in the *Rāsau* as *vīr gorī* (hero Ghorians) (*Pṛthvīrāj-rāsau* 1955, Vol. II: 450). Glory is the only thing that is eternal in this perishable world (ibid., Vol. I: 166–67). Even amorous adventures are depicted more as military pursuits than a part of an individual's emotional or sexual experience. Marriage with celebrated beauties, mostly the daughters of mighty rulers, also contribute to Prithvīrāj's glory and increase his military might by adding new forces to his army. If a maiden is carried off against the will of her family, as it happened with the Yādava princess Padmāvatī or the most famous of his wives, Sanyogitā, it only enhances the fame of the valiant Cauhān. Moreover, it is only with the fame of Prithvīrāj that the fair princesses fall in love, as none of them is able to see him before marriage. Consequently, while love adventures abound in the royal *caritas*, passion in the modern sense is rarely depicted; the emotional component of the narratives is on the whole, often poor or vague.

If Aries is right in stating that up to the twelfth century, medieval Europe had neither a perception of childhood as a distinct period in physical and mental development of a person, nor the tradition of portraying it, nor a place for childhood in its social and cultural life (Aries 1973: 31), I suggest that in this sphere medieval India was different. Colourful and moving descriptions of little children as charming creatures dear to the hearts of their parents and enjoyable to the eyes of all people are not unusual for Sanskrit and Prakrit literature. In *Pṛthvīrāj-rāsau* there is a description of the baby Prithvīrāj crawling, tottering and playing. But at the same time the author never forgets that he is not an ordinary child but a great hero who is unusual from his very birth, hence *barakh baḍhai biy bāl, pithth baḍhḍhai ik māsah* (Prithvīrāj developed in a month like other children develop in a year) (*Pṛthvīrāj-rāsau* 1955, Vol. I: 26). Such descriptions seem to have become a tradition in medieval biography writing. Centuries after Cand Bardāī, Lāl Kavi, a Bundela poet who eulogized the celebrated Rājā Chatrasāl of Panna and his victories over the neighbouring princes and the Mughals in *Chatraprakāś*, described the childhood of his hero in the same way. According to him, from Chatrasāl's very birth, *cakkavatni ke cinh sab aṅgan aṅgan rākhi* (every part of his body bore the signs of the great emperor) (*Chatraprakāś* 1916: 23). While still a child, Chatrasāl too attained perfection, both physical and mental:

> *khelan bolan calan mẽ, sab kaũ det anand /*
> *bālāpan te baḍhi calī, din din buddhi buland //*
> *baḍhī buland buddhi kachu aisī / ya jug māh nāhinai jaisī//*

> [His] playing, speaking and walking made everyone happy.
> As the child grew his wisdom increased day by day.
> His wisdom grew as no one's in that epoch. (Ibid.: 25)

Moreover, since the character of a person was viewed as fully determined by his caste or estate, inherent in him, temporal changes were only qualitative and not quantitative ones. The difference between a child and an adult was viewed within the framework of the oppositions like 'small – big', 'weak – strong', 'foolish – wise' and so on; a child was perceived as a man in miniature. The charming baby whom Cand Bardāī described as crawling and tottering was, nevertheless, even at that tiny age, a Prithvīrāj Cauhān, imbued with all the virtues of a Rajput warrior. According to the *Rāsau*, Prithvīrāj was born in VS 1206/AD 1149 (*Pṛthvīrāj-rāsau* 1955, Vol. I: 23); thus on the fateful day of the Tarain battle (1192) he was forty-three. However, his physique and behaviour at that time show no difference from that of the teenager and the youth Prithvīrāj. From his boyhood up to the end of his life he remains unchanged. His personal traits are estimated by other people from the viewpoint of his complying with the standards of behaviour prescribed by his Rajput origin. These standards seem to be comparable with those prescribed for a European knight, and the words of Grierson, who viewed the Rajput folk heroes Ālha and Ūdal as 'worthy of a seat with the noblest heroes of the Arthurian table' (Grierson 1990: 20) are fully applicable to Harṣa, Vikrama, Prithvīrāj, Chatrasāl and Rāj Singh – perhaps not the real ones, but as depicted by their court biographers.

Devotion and Humility

There has been another trend in biography writing, also known from ancient times: describing the life stories and achievements of the great sages and spiritual leaders. A significant number of such works was contributed by Buddhists and Jainas, and later by the Hindus too. But the real blooming of this kind of literature was connected with the mystical sects and movements of medieval India, primarily with those pertaining to the rainbow of *bhakti* traditions.[6]

It would be unreasonable here to give a detailed description of the *bhakti* sects, their vast literature including the ocean of hagiography, and peculiar features of religious outlook. Suffice is to remind the reader that the *bhakti* type of religiosity implied direct mystical contact between a devotee and his *iṣṭadevatā* (chosen, desired god). This made unnecessary any intermediary between god and believer, especially in the form of an officiating priest; at the same time it provided for the pivotal role of the guru or spiritual guide who opened the pathway to God for the seeking soul. Therefore a critical attitude to professional priesthood, which was an important part of the *bhakti* doctrines, went hand-in-hand with extreme reverence to the most distinguished saints who disseminated the doctrines, and in many cases their deification. Thus the life stories of the *bhakti* luminaries emerged as the most significant part of the literary legacy of medieval Hindu mysticism.

The spiritual leaders of the *bhakti* traditions belonged to various castes, from Brāhmaṇas to untouchables. Their life descriptions, authored by disciples and followers, were composed with a clearly spelt purpose: to disseminate the ideas of *bhakti* and to set a pattern of moral behaviour for all adherents and others as well, including the foolish and the vicious. As Jan Gopāl wrote in his *Janma līlā* (*c.* 1620), the biography of the celebrated Gujarati saint Dādū Dayāl (XVI, 18–19), the life story of that great *bhakta* would not only bring joy and happiness to all those who possess the true knowledge of *bhakti*, but even make fools intelligent (*mūriṣ sunai ta bidyā pāvai*). Meanwhile, a wicked man would become sorrowful and turn his heart and mind to God (*sunai asant hoī dukh bhārī / hirdai sudh hoī banvārī*) (Callewaert 1988: 87, 125).

The task of the *bhakti* hagiographers was thus much more complicated than that of the royal *carita* writers. Unlike Bāṇa or Cand Bardāī, they had no uniform pattern of caste virtues to establish or proclaim through the deeds of their

[6] The scope of this article does not permit a discussion of sufi Sikh hagiography.

heroes. They had to emphasize a new set of values and ethical norms that had to unite, to a certain extent, Dñyāneśvar the Brāhmaṇa and Cokhāmelā the 'untouchable'. And the way of *bhakti* devotion was viewed was as open to everybody, including the poor, the depressed, the ignorant and the weak.

If we try to bring together at least a part of the *bhakti* hagiography it may be of interest to work out patterns in the descriptions of the life and mission of the *bhakti* saints, patterns not artificially created by someone, but developed by the very interrelation of a number of factors: events in the saint's life, the biographer's own background, and the ideology and ethics that were to be disseminated. The main aspects of the saints' lives are described below.

Family Origin, Pre-Birth and Birth

The *bhakti* saints came from various ethnic groups, castes and social strata, but most biographers found it necessary to emphasize that the parents of the future saints were pious, highly religious and virtuous people. In many cases, the future saint is born as a long-expected offspring of the childless parents who thus receive this heavenly gift as a special reward for their piety and devotion. This does not differ much from the royal hero *carita* pattern: the latter too was usually born to the parents who themselves embodied all the values and virtues of the Kṣatriyas and, after years of religious austerities and sacrifices, received the boon of the long-desired son from a god.[7] This story of a long-expected child born as a special gift to a childless family owes much to folklore as well. To make the folklore association even stronger, there are innumerable cases of the saints being born not from a woman's womb, but in this or that fabulous, mysterious way. Thus the aged couple, Dāmājī and Goṇāī, prayed for a son and obtained a divine baby Nāmdev floating in a shell down the Bhima river; when Goṇāī lifted the child her breasts miraculously filled with milk (*Bhaktavijaya* 1988, Vol. I: 58–60).[8] A child born or acquired in such a wondrous manner was especially loved by his parents.

Thus the people in whose families the future saint is born are usually depicted as pious, spiritual, generous and staunch devotees of God; they are loving and caring parents. Some exceptions, however are also available, the most vivid being that of the parents of the great Vaiṣṇava saint poet Sūrdās. Born blind, according to his biographer Harirāy, he knew no parental love: 'neither mother, nor father, nor other family members loved him. What kind of a son is he who has no eyes! No one even spoke to him' *(so mātā pitā ghar ke sab koī insõ prīti kare nāhī̃. Jāne jo nenn binā kau putr kahā! Tāsõ insõ koī boltau nāhī̃)* (Harirai vs 2008/1951: 3). Unlike other saints, Sūrdās had parents who were worldly, egoistic, cruel and merciless. They considered Sūrdās an evil omen for the family and realized the real value and spiritual gift of their son only when the six-year old found, in spite of his blindness, the golden coins stolen by rats. Only then, 'love appeared

[7] See for example Blackburn (2004: 210).

[8] A similar story is told about the birth of Kabīr (*Bhaktavijaya* 1988, Vol. I: 78–80).

[in the hearts] of mother and father' (*so mātā pitā kõ moh utpann bhayau*) (ibid.: 4). This seems, let me repeat, an exception; in most cases, a future saint is born into a pious and loving family.

However, what makes the *bhakti* biographies special as compared to the royal *carita*s is the concept of *avatāra* origin. The majority of the *bhakti* saints are depicted in their biographies as *avatāras*: Dñyāneśvar, of Viṣṇu, Sūrdās and other *aṣṭachāp* poets of Kṛṣṇa's *sakhā*s (playfellows); Tulsīdās of Hanumān, Nāmdev of Kṛṣṇa's friend Uddhav, etc. (Hailey 1984:15; *Bhaktavijaya* 1988, Vol. I: 138; Vol. II: 191).

This concept was central to the deification of the saints and was in its turn immediately related to the *bhakti* type of religiosity in which the guru who 'passed the torch' to the path-seeking adapts was venerated, worshipped on almost equal terms with the god. But a second aspect is noteworthy too.

It has been noted here already that the medieval perception of a person was fully based on caste, estate and community origins. Social attitude to individuals was determined by the way they conformed to the behavioural patterns prescribed for a particular caste. Unlike the modern epoch, which judges a person by what we call his/her individuality, original and innovative thinking, or, in simple words, *being unlike other people*, in the Middle Ages a person was respected and approved of only when he or she *was like other people* of his/her estate, caste or community.

Originality, innovation or just deviation from the prescribed pattern of thinking and behaviour were viewed as a serious social transgression and sin. Medieval authors found it necessary to emphasize that their writings were not at all original and just followed the thinkers and poets of yore or a popular tradition. In the case of the saints, however, the hagiographers were confronted with two sets of problems: how to justify unusual behaviour and how to explain spiritual feats. According to the dominant view, a son of a tailor like Nāmdev or of a Muslim weaver like Kabīr, not to mention the untouchables Cokhāmelā or Rāidās, could not become a great saint, a sage or a spiritual leader. Thus a tool, well-tested by folklore and medieval literature (a low-born but virtuous and beautiful heroine as an *apsarā*, *vidyādharī* or goddess damned or incarnated to live among the mortals) (Bali 1977: 206–40; Vaisya 1972: 210) had been found. The saint born into a low-caste family was in reality an *avatāra* of the god himself or of his close associate. This helped to preserve the main principle of man-evaluation intact. Moreover, when we read the hagiography by Mahīpati we come across a curious hierarchy: the god or his closest and revered associate (like Hanumān, Vālmīki, Vyāsa, etc.) is usually re-incarnated as a saint of Brāhmaṇa origin, such as Dñyāneśvar, Rāmdās, Eknāth or Narsī Mehtā (and in that case he is born in a natural way) (*Bhaktavijaya* 1988, Vol. I: 5–10). But low-caste saints like Namdev or Kabīr are usually depicted as the incarnations of God's associates of a less important degree and are born in a wondrous way (from a shell, a lotus, etc.). Hence, the saint was not 'polluted' by birth in a low-caste family and for a tailor or a Muslim weaver the divine associates were only step-fathers. This helped to avoid a clash between *bhakti* ideas and the predominant view of society.

Pathway to God

For a majority of the saints their spiritual elevation began, in hagiography, at a very early age. Sūrdās first exhibited his superhuman vision when he was six (Harirai 2008: 3). The child Eknāth was never interested in the games of other children: in his play, he imitated the worship of gods or pilgrimage to Pandharpur (*Eknāth* 1927: 3–4). Such an approach tallied well with the perception of the child as a small adult; if a person was born as a great *bhakta*, all the saintly traits of his character had been already inherent in him from his very birth.

It has to be noted that although in a majority of cases *bhakti* hagiography describes the saints as spiritually-elevated devotees from early childhood, if not from birth, there are vivid exceptions too. Nāmdev and Tukārām had to take long and laborious routes to their *iṣṭadevatā*. For a certain period, their aspiration for the mystical communion with the god bore no fruit: sometimes the desperate *bhakta*s even abused the god in a harsh and even obscene way – this served as a bright and contrasting background for the bliss consequently achieved.[9]

In the path to God, the guru, of course, plays a pivotal role and the meeting with him, occasional or deliberate, becomes a turning point. Some saints underwent great labour and trouble to become the disciples of their chosen guru – like Kabīr whom the great *bhakti* sage Rāmānanda first turned down and then tested in a cruel way, or Eknāth who served his preceptor Janārdan like a slave, cleaned his toilet room and even drank the contents of his spittoon (*Bhaktavijaya* 1988, Vol. I: 112–17; *Eknāth* 1927: 9–17; Lorenzen 1987: 108–09). Such episodes, eloquently narrated, stressed the nearly-divine status of the gurus and, at the same time, the dedication, devotion and humility of the saints who succeeded in fully suppressing their self. In a number of cases, however, the role of the guru in the spiritual development of a saint remained but nominal and was mentioned by hagiographers just as a tribute to the tradition.

World Renunciation

The majority of the *bhakti* saints did not approve of asceticism in the sense it was viewed by orthodox high-caste Hindus who retired to the woods or mountains to practise austerities. Many *bhakta*s were married, had children and followed their professions. Their ideal was to renounce the world while formally being a part of it, to remain a householder fully absorbed in the god and at the same time indifferent to worldly affairs. That meant working without any concern about result or remuneration, and getting married and having children without being preoccupied by sensual pleasures, family life and parental feelings. To illustrate this, the hagiographers created tearful and shocking stories of the people who easily sacrificed their near and dear ones to the god and to *bhakti*. Family members were martyrs to the *bhakta*s' exclusive concentration on the god, so that their wives, children and aged parents starved and begged.

The holy men who disseminated the ideas of divine love and compassion

[9] Discussed in more detail by Glushkova (2000: 262–63, 270).

to every creature were depicted as extremely cruel and indifferent towards their own kith and kin. Great renunciation was exhibited by Cokhāmelā who, when his wife was going to deliver a child, rushed away from 'this bloody mess' and left her to suffer alone (Zelliot 1999: 93–99). Biographers spared no colours in describing how a grocer, whom Kabīr's wife asked for some foodstuffs to cook for the visiting saints, agreed to do so on condition that she would spend the coming night with him and how Kabīr not only consented but himself carried the woman on his shoulders to the grocer's house. All are perhaps surpassed by Gorā Kumbhār who, being totally absorbed in God, trod his own child into the clay he was wedging – when his wife's wailing disturbed his concentration he felt, not sorrow for the child but anger with the wife and wanted to strike her with the wheel handle (*Bhaktavijaya* 1988, Vol. I: 179–84, 286–87). Such stories may be disgusting for a modern scholar but not so for the medieval audience,[10] nor indeed for present-day devotees, who see there nothing but evidence of renunciation, devotion and self-sacrifice. Moreover, to prevent the readers' possible doubts the evergreen principle 'all's well that ends well' is faultlessly employed: God assists Cokhāmelā's wife in her labour, restores Gorā's child back to life and makes the vicious grocer repent. This allowed the hagiographers to once again proclaim the omnipotence of God, who, in reward for his *bhakta*'s sacrifices and renunciation, always comes to their help.

There is however another important aspect of the renunciation as depicted by the *bhakti* hagiography. In more than one case, wives and parents of the saints were opposed to their spiritual pursuits and viewed them as madness, insolence or cruelty, and the main cause of the family's suffering. Women were especially active: the angry voices of Nāmdev's mother Goṇāī and Tukārām's wife Jijābāī (the latter was especially known as *karkaśā* (a peevish wife), are clearly heard in the hagiography and *bhakti* poetry. They tried desperately to bring their men back to normal family life, but then some of them reconciled themselves to their fate and followed the saints in their renunciation; others, like Jijābāī, never surrendered and continued to shower lamentations and abuses upon their husbands and on the god himself (*Bhaktavijaya* 1988, Vol. I: 72–73; Glushkova 2000: 262–63). The opposition of family members was especially strong and violent in the case of the women saints, Lāl Ded, Mīrā Bāī, and Bahinā Bāī, since the deviant behaviour of a woman was, of course, more intolerable than that of a man, and all possible measures, including corporal punishment and even murder, were employed by the outraged men. In many cases, like that of Bahinā Bāī's husband, the men simply envied the spiritual successes and popularity of their women (Abbott 1985: 13, 23–24).

Thus, the spiritual pursuits of quite a number of the *bhakti* saints are

[10] Some medieval thinkers too would, however, protest against such extremities. See how the thirteenth-century Liṅgāyat writer Pālkuriki Somanātha interpreted the story of a *bhakta* who killed his son and cooked his flesh to feed Śiva, disguised as a wandering saint (Shulman 1993: 63–65).

shown against the background of a deep and sometimes traumatic family conflict. The other side of this conflict, that is, parents, wives or husbands, is depicted as an active and self-sufficient force whose arguments cannot be easily dismissed. In this aspect the *bhakti* hagiography differs significantly from the royal *carita*s in which the protagonist never experienced conflict with his family (with the only exception of rival brothers who strove for the crown) which is usually depicted either as a colourless background or a collective of persons reflecting the main traits of the hero's character. Even with the enemies, there was no real conflict as they belonged to the same social order and represented the same values; their collision with the hero was a competition between two equal characters, two similar outlooks. On the contrary, the *bhakti* hagiography depicted not just a conflict between a saint and his wife or mother, but the collision of different values and views. True, in a majority of cases these conflicts ended in a compromise, so habitual for Indian thought and way of life: even Bahinā Bāī's husband repented his hostility to Tukārām and embraced *bhakti* and she realized her duties as an obedient Hindu wife (ibid.: 25–29).

Tests, Persecutions and God's Assistance

An important element of medieval Hindu hagiography (and its counterparts in other religions too) was the motive of establishing the moral and spiritual superiority of the saint over the opponents of his doctrine, rivals of various kinds and those who just tried, consciously or unconsciously, to test the abilities and generosity of the *bhakta.* Among the latter there were thieves who tried to rob this or that saint and whom the holy man's kindness and indifference to worldly wealth made repent (*Eknāth* 1927: 166–69; Callewaert 1988: 39–40, 93–94). However, of much more importance were the sceptics who doubted the saint's superiority and closeness to the god, and also the open enemies of the *bhakti* doctrine. Especially hostile were, of course, the Brāhmaṇas, and nearly all hagiographical stories abound in episodes depicting their attempts to revile the saint, to punish or even kill him. Even if some of these episodes were a later addition to comply with the already established literary canon of hagiographical writing, it can be safely presumed that they testify to the real persecution of the *bhakti* saints by Brāhmaṇas who, as is vividly demonstrated in Dādū's biography, never hesitated to join hands in this matter with the Muslim authorities (Callewaert 1988: 37, 92). But of primary importance for the hagiographers and their audience was the role of God himself, who always came to the aid of his *bhakta*s and saved them in this or that miraculous way. The written text of the panchayat resolution threatening anyone visiting Dādū with a fine of Rs 500 changed wondrously, prescribing the fine to those who *would not* visit the saint; Eknāth's manuscript drowned by the Brāhmaṇas in the river came out unspoilt; Kabīr, subjected to all kinds of tortures, survived and felt no pain (Callewaert 1988: 37, 92; Lorenzen 1987: 109–10).

God does not just save his saints when they are in danger but in many cases helps them in other ways too. Rāma and Lakṣmaṇa with their bows guard Tulsīdās' house to repel the robbers, Rāma weaves for Kabīr and serves his guests;

Kṛṣṇa rebuilds the damaged hut of Nāmdev and grinds corn for his maid, herself a devout *bhakta* (*Bhaktavijaya* 1988, Vol. I: 42–45, 81–82, 340–46). More than once the God disguises himself as the saint, especially in the cases when the latter faces some danger. Such episodes[11] were to symbolize, on the one hand, the equal validity of the object and subject of mystical love, and on the other, the reciprocity and personal intimacy of relations between the God and his devotee.

Of no less interest were the hagiographical stories of encounters with the kings, including such historical figures as Sikandar Lodī, Shivaji and Akbar: the latter was especially favoured by hagiography writers who made him meet quite a number of saints, including those who historically speaking could by no means have done so. All these encounters are centred on two main themes: the saint poet is offered lavish gifts and requested to eulogize the king; both the offer and the request are turned down as the saint is in no way tempted by worldly wealth and feels it possible to praise only God. All the rulers depicted by the hagiographers treat the saints with extreme reverence; the only exclusion perhaps was Sikandar Lodī who persecuted Kabīr: this later made the tenth Sikh Guru, Gobind Singh, remark that a trace of that ruler remained in history only because the great saint Kabīr lived during his reign (Macauliffe 1909, Vol. VI: 113; Kharak Singh and Gurtej Singh 1995: 77). As for Akbar, according to the hagiographers, he exhibited wonders of patience when the saints spoke to him without even minimal respect, and expressed, like Kumbhan Dās, their irritation ('What has a *bhakta* to do in [Fatehpur] Sikri? To come, to go back, to break shoes and forget the name of Hari!')[12] and when requested by the Emperor to ask for a boon answered like Sūrdās: 'Never call me again, never meet me any more' (*hamkõ kabhī̃ phir mat bulīiyo, aur mosõ kabhī̃ miliyo mat*) (Harirāy 2008: 31). Akbar fully acknowledged the superiority of the saints and embraced some of their views: Jan Gopāl alleged that it was after the meeting with Dādū that Akbar 'stopped hurting living beings' (*jīv na satāyau*) (Callewaert 1988: 54, 103).[13]

In many hagiographies it is Akbar who is a respectful companion and admirer of the saints, even those who were not his contemporaries, because of his celebrated religious policies. But there is another point of interest here. Analysing the Indian ṣūfi hagiographies, Muzaffar Alam lays special emphasis on 'competitive spirituality' as described in the stories of the sufi saints competing with the Brāhmaṇas and establishing the superiority of their faith (Alam 1989: 41–44). Although the *bhakti* saints never made it a clearly-spelt purpose to convert people, 'competitive spirituality' was not totally foreign to them. They met Emperor Akbar (not Aurangzeb, of course) and triumphed over him, even made him their follower.

[11] Compare these with the Vallabhite *bhakti* poetry motif of Kṛṣṇa and Rādhā exchanging clothes during love play (Hailey 1984: 83).

[12] '*Bhaktā̃ kā̃ kahā̃ sīkrī kām / āvat jāt panhayī ṭūṭī, bisar gayau Harinām*' (Mital 1949: 102).

[13] For more details of Akbar's encounter with the saints see Sangari (2000).

Wonders of Life and Death

A saint could hardly be revered if he did not produce wonders. The majority of the wonders as depicted in the *bhakti* hagiography were performed by God, but saints too had to their credit a number of miracles. They brought dead men back to life (Tulsīdās and many others), made a buffalo recite the Vedas or made their own back a pan for baking bread (Dñyāneśvar) or made a stone bull eat and jump (Eknāth). These episodes were also important to silence sceptics. The death of saints, too, was in most cases depicted as unusual: Dñyāneśvar took *samādhi* in a cave and nearly three centuries after that was still alive, coming in a dream to Eknāth and asking him to remove the roots of the tree that had choked him (the present day *Vārkarīs* believe he is still alive there). Eknāth drowned himself in the river and after the cremation of his body the holy plant *tulsī* sprouted out of his ashes along with the tree that later fulfilled the desires of the devotees. Tukārām mysteriously disappeared from his native village, Dehu (*Eknāth* 1927: 135, 238–39; *Bhaktavijaya* 1988, Vol. II: 294); after the death of Kabīr, his body – which his Hindu and Muslim followers fought over – was miraculously transformed into a heap of flowers. Thus the worldly life of the saint ended; in most cases, we may note, was depicted as the *bhakta*'s voluntary act of final communion with God, to quote Jan Gopāl, 'like salt dissolves in water' (Callewaert 1988: 84, 123).

It would be of interest to find out what new features the *bhakti* hagiography brought to medieval Indian biography. Hart opines that, unlike other kinds of pre-modern Indian literature, 'bhakti literature does not set any archetypes, it violates them, often systematically and quite consciously' (Hart 1995: 171). This seems an exaggeration. True, for orthodox Hinduism the behaviour and outlook of the *bhakti* saints was deviant if not heretic. This was fully reflected by literature. Nevertheless, at the same time, the approach to man as expressed by the hagiographers remained to a considerable extent similar to the one displayed by the writers of the royal *caritas*. The character of the saint remains unchanged throughout his lifetime; all the traits and spiritual qualities are inherent in him at birth and determined by the very status of the saint; therefore the hagiographies too, composed by different writers and depicting different saints, seem to portray one and the same person. Differing from other people, the saint is similar in deeds and thoughts to other members of his community, both in the sense of his *panth* (pathway) of *bhakti* and in that of the whole conglomerate of saints.

Moreover, it has to be borne in mind that not all the great *bhakta*s rebelled against established ways of social behaviour: more than one of them, at least as their hagiography describes, criticized the caste system and the idea of Brāhmaṇa superiority, but lived by them in real life (Lorenzen 1987: 105). Time was not moving for the hagiographers and their personages: the child saint exhibited the same wisdom, piety and devotion as he exhibited when an old man. There was no problem for the hagiographers to 'arrange' a meeting of saints who had really lived in different epochs, for instance to make Dñyāneśvar and Nāmdev together visit Kabīr (Mahīpati 1988, Vol. I: 185). While in many ways violating traditional norms of behaviour, the *bhakta*s as described by their biographers (and themselves too) set new norms, imitated by their spiritual successors and prescribed for their followers as a social and spiritual ideal. The writings of Harirāy, Jan Gopāl and Mahīpati were the means of bringing these patterns to the grassroots. Thus, violating one kind of archetype, *bhakti* hagiography spared no effort to establish another. This is evident not only in the life stories of the immediate successors of this or that saint, but more so in the biographies of nineteenth- and twentieth-century saints, religious preceptors and 'godmen'.

Discovering the Individual

At the same time *bhakti* literature, including hagiography, did contribute considerably to the development of a new approach to man, one that realized and valued individuality. This was relevant to the very foundations of the *bhakti* doctrines, which described the pathway to God as a matter of individual choice. The saints chose not only their *iṣṭadevatā* (sometimes different from *kuladevatā* or family patron deity) but also the guru and way of life, in more than one case different from that of their caste and family. They had to pursue their spiritual goal against the background that was anything but friendly and withstand pressure from their wives and parents, fellow castemen, rival Brāhmaṇas and tyrannical rulers. No hero of the royal *caritas* had to confront such adversities. This peaceful struggle that the *bhaktas* waged through their lives against hostile forces required courage and, more important, individual effort.

The emotional component of *bhakti* religiosity was incomparably richer than what we find in the royal *caritas* and other genres of medieval heroic literature. Ecstatic love in all its aspects from parental to sexual, admiration, tenderness, hope and despair, submission, sorrow, vexation, wrath, even friendly punching and mockery – this is only a small part of emotional colours of the saint's inner life. These emotions are addressed almost exclusively to their God, while people with the exception of the *bhaktas*, are usually treated with calm indifference. Nevertheless, medieval *bhakti* literature played a pioneering role in depicting the inner life of an individual. It is noteworthy that the *bhakti* poets, more than other medieval writers, used the first-person singular in their compositions.

The late medieval period saw considerable changes in many spheres of socio-cultural life, where, along with the old some new approaches came into being. This is to a considerable extent reflected in biographical literature. For example, the *Janma līlā* by Jan Gopāl has all the features of medieval *bhakti* hagiography and at the same time exhibits a number of new elements. Like other life stories of the *bhakti* saints, it describes (Callewaert 1988, I, 7–18) the beginning of Dādū's career, starting with an encounter with a certain old man (*bābā būḍhai*). Some variants of the text state that this was God himself. To test Dādū, then a child of eleven playing with other boys, the old man begged for money and only Dādū willingly gave him some. The old man blessed the generous child, put a betel roll in his mouth, and with that gave him the 'everlasting [cognition] of Rāma' (*rā̃m deī meṭai ko nā̃hī̃*), thus initiating him as a *bhakta*. What is important is that at that moment the 'child's mind understood nothing' (*bālak budhi jā̃ni nahĩ līnaũ*). Only after seven years passed in doing other things (*bariṣ sāt auraũ kṛt kīnaũ*) did Dādū have a vision of Hari with which began his journey as the *bhakti* preceptor (ibid., 35, 91–92).

This small episode displays certain novel approaches. Unlike other saints who were devotees at birth, had no interest in playing and exhibited unusual spirituality as toddlers, Dādū at eleven behaves like an ordinary boy and there is nothing unusual in his kindness to the old beggar. Blessed and initiated by God himself, he understands nothing; the author, contrary to other *bhakti* hagiographers, realizes that the abilities of a child of eleven, even if this child is a Dādū, are limited. Only seven years later does Dādū became conscious of his spiritual mission.

Unlike many other hagiographical works, the *Janma līlā* abounds in dates (in Vikram Saṃvat era) marking the most important events; in the end, the chronology of Dādū's life is repeated in a condensed way (ibid.: 88, 125). The text mentions a number of historical personages and presents perhaps the most lengthy and detailed account of the saint's encounter with Akbar than any other work of *bhakti* hagiography; this meeting, which took place in 1585, is described by Jan Gopāl in a rather realistic way and may be credited as a historical event. All in all, it can be suggested that the *Janma līlā* represents a transitional form from hagiography to true historical biography; linked in more than one way with the centuries-old tradition, it exhibits a number of novel approaches to man and time, both personal and historical.

A similar coexistence of old and new approaches is traceable in a number of other biographical works of the late medieval period. For example, in Abū'l Faẓl's celebrated *Akbarnāma* and *Ā'īn-i Akbarī*[14] there are two different and rather contrasting approaches to personality as applied by the author to Emperor Akbar and to himself. In both the texts, Akbar is described in a way that fully coincides with the canons of both hagiography and royal biography, in their Hindu and Muslim garb.[15] He is depicted as an ideal ruler, a Perfect Man (fully complying with the ṣūfi doctrine of *insān al-kāmil*) and even a saint and spiritual guide. He is endowed at birth with divine wisdom and human perfection; he neither errs nor hesitates and publicly admits some of his mistakes and makes people aware of his

[14] I may be reproached here for turning to the 'Muslim' biographical tradition while all my previous examples were from the 'Hindu' one. David Arnold and Stuart Blackburn discuss 'Muslim' biography as 'another stream' of South Asian tradition of life history (Arnold and Blackburn 2004: 7). But as they themselves show, this 'other stream' consisted of the same literary genres (ṣūfi hagiography and royal/heroic biography, the latter including memoirs and chronicles) and, let me add, followed almost the same perceptions of man and life history. Therefore I do not know why we should not view both 'Hindu' and 'Muslim' as one medieval Indian tradition of biography writing which, of course, may be as complex and heterogeneous as India itself.

[15] Again, I am not discussing here the differences between the two. Suffice is to note that despite confessional and cultural dissimilarities, they did have much in common. Abū'l Faẓl, perhaps more than any Muslim writer of the epoch, absorbed Muslim and Hindu cultural trends and was one of the best representatives of their synthesis. His representation in the written sources owed much to the popular traditions (Sangari 2000: 80–83).

modesty and humility. At the same time, Akbar's character as depicted by Abū'l Fazl has more individual features than that of any other hero of royal biographies, thanks to the writer's attention to the minute details of the Emperor's life: so we learn about Akbar's tastes in food and dress and his hobbies. Therefore, his character is static, an embodiment of the socio-political and religious ideas that were in the foundation of his reforms. When the author talks about himself, however, we see a personality that changes through time and under the influence of various circumstances, an inner life that reflects aspirations and doubts, ups and downs; last but not least, we see an attempt to trace the influence of the narrator's family background and early life circumstances on his character (*Ā'īn-i Akbarī* 1978, Vol. III: 478–524).

It deserves a special note that the late medieval period was distinguished by the significant development of autobiography as a genre.[16] To a considerable extent India owes this to the *bhakti* literature and the saints who made public their individual experiences in finding God. Autobiography as such was initially different from biography, since unlike those who narrated the life stories of others (rulers and saints), a person could not eulogize him/herself – this would have been regarded as immodesty. The didactic aspect of literature is indeed traceable in autobiography, but this did not prevent the writers from giving a more objective and detailed narration of their inner and outer life, from making public their doubts and mistakes too, and thus warning their audience about their foibles.

Among late medieval autobiographies, we may consider the work of the celebrated Marathi saint poet Bahinā Bāī (seventeenth century). This autobiography provides a unique insight into the life and spiritual pursuits of a woman who, after a long and painful struggle, succeeded in reconciling her *dharma* as a dutiful Brāhmaṇa wife to her *bhakti* devotion to god Viṭṭhal and saint Tukārām – a rare example among Indian women *bhaktas*.[17] In her narration the main emphasis is her path to *bhakti* against the extremely hostile background of her parental home, her husband, and a prejudiced society. Her life and inner world are to a certain extent typical for a Hindu woman of that period; in the words of Anne Feldhaus, 'Bahinā is important, not for any particularity of her life story but because its outcome is universal. Bahinā's name, which means simply "Sister", might best be translated as "Everywoman"' (see Abbott 1985: vii). However, Bahinā, as it appears from her autobiography, is not 'Everywoman' in the sense that in her behaviour and spiritual activity, she has violated, calmly and without open rebellion, many a rule of conduct prescribed for a Brāhmaṇa wife. Her reconciliation to the duty of a *pativratā* woman comes out as the result of a painful inner struggle in which she doubts even the significance of 'Viṭṭhal who is a mere stone and Tukā of whom I have simply dreamed', in contrast to the happiness of being a loyal wife (ibid.: 26). Thus both conflict and compromise are described as her conscious

16 According to Georg Misch, in Europe too, autobiography re-appeared only during the Renaissance as 'one of the innovations brought by cultural advance' (Misch 1951 I: 5).

17 Discussed in detail by Anne Feldhaus in her Foreword to Abbott (1985: vi–vii).

choice; the whole narrative bears the imprint of individuality, of an inquiring mind and the sorrowful heart of a spiritually gifted and lonely woman surrounded by a hostile society.

We have, last but not least, a nearly contemporary work fully centred on an individual life. It is the *Ardhakathānaka*, a biography-cum-family history of a Jain merchant family, completed by Banārasī Dās in 1641. This gem of medieval Indian biographical literature may – with good reason – represent a third type of biography writing which came into being, unlike the previously-discussed two, in the late medieval period and reflected a number of important socio-cultural developments of the epoch. It narrates, in elegant verse, the previous history of a middle-class family and then the life of Banārasī Dās, merchant, poet and thinker. The author described political events from afar, as they were perceived by the unsophisticated townsfolk who had neither knowledge of nor an interest in court affairs (the only exception was the death of Akbar viewed by Banārasī and his neighbours as a great personal loss) (*Ardhakathānaka* 1981: 38–40, 242–43). A unique historical consciousness is evident: the text abounds in dates, sometimes very precise (month and day), which presuppose the author's usage of family records or diaries; the dates refer to both family history and political events.

In the *Ardhakathānaka* one sees a considerable departure from the canons of medieval biography-writing and, what is more important, the general perception of man. Against the background of a rather typical merchant family history (births, marriages, diseases, deaths, business travels, commercial losses and gains, family conflicts, natural calamities, etc.) the life of an individual unfolds with the narrator's attention centred on his inner world, feelings and emotions and the various stages of his spiritual life. Within a span of fifty-five years, Banārasī does not just grow from childhood to maturity, he changes psychologically, searches for the true path to God, sometimes strictly follows the tenets of Jainism, sometimes becomes a sceptical free-thinker, abjures his religion for Hinduism and then returns to his paternal faith (in both cases for purely practical reasons). Sometimes he turns to ascetic practices, sometimes he indulges in sensual pleasures. These ups and downs are described by the author with sincerity, a good sense of humour and irony, mostly directed at himself. Especially funny is the episode of Banārasī being cheated by a wandering *yogī* who had advised him to bury a golden coin in the lavatory and daily chant a certain *mantra* there in order to obtain a treasure. There is also satirical exposition of some superstitious practices of his family members.

The *Ardhakathānaka* is remarkable also because it depicts an extremely significant conflict of values in the family. Banārasī's parents and kinsmen wanted him to be a businessman like themselves, to fully reproduce the way of life as prescribed by their caste and community. But by nature Banārasī was a poet and a thinker, and in many cases rebelled against caste prescriptions. He was interested more in learning and in poetry-writing than in profit-making, to the disgust of his elders who were sure that *bahut paḍhai bāmbhan aru bhāṭ / banikputr tau baiṭhe hāṭ* (too much learning behoves a Brāhmaṇa or a *bhāṭ* / a merchant's son should sit in the bazaar) (ibid.: 33, 239). The author lays special stress on the fact that business operations were against his inclination and interests; hence his numerous commercial losses, described with sincerity and humour. As a result Banārasī was in a never-ending conflict with his beloved father. He had to compromise for the sake of family peace and to make his own two ends meet. Only at the end of his life did Banārasī allow himself to concentrate on poetry, learning and the activities of a religious reformer.[18]

The text abounds in complex, multi-dimensional characters: Banārasī's relatives, friends, business partners and others whom he had met. The way they are depicted bears the imprint of the narrator's subjective attitude and at the same time is objective enough to create a vivid and realistic image. Even Banārasī's father, Khaḍagsen, adored by the author as the ideal merchant and Jain householder, combines in himself some controversial traits of character: he generously refuses, in favour of his orphaned cousin, a huge legacy from his deceased uncle but grows hysterical when his son Banārasī fails to make a profit on his trading expedition to Agra. The writer seems to be interested in the individuality of each person he encountered as well as of himself. The characters he depicts are not stereotypes of their caste or religious community: we see merchants, parsimonious and wasteful, generous and mean; we see Mughal officials, benevolent and cruel, reasonable and foolish; and we see the narrator, sinning and repenting, rebelling and compromising, suffering and laughing at himself. In the end he produced an analysis of his own character with a detailed list of its good and bad features.

Changing approaches to man, as reflected in some late medieval biographies and autobiographies, are relevant to some extremely important changes that medieval society and culture experienced, especially at the end of the period. Such changes took place in various spheres of life – economic, social, ethnic, cultural, political and ideological. Some impregnable postulates of social behaviour and world outlook were questioned by heterodox religious leaders and by the rationalist free-thinkers like the associates of Emperor Akbar, known as the 'enlightened philosophers' and their successors. Some even dared to question the very core aspect of social life, that is, the necessity to live according to the patterns set by forefathers. Akbar himself was recorded as saying

> Commending obedience to the dictates of reason and reproving a slavish following of others need the aid of no arguments. If imitation were commendable, the prophets would have followed their predecessors. . . . Many simpletons, worshippers of imitating custom, mistake the traditions of the ancients for the dictates of reason and garner for themselves eternal perdition. (*Ā'īn-i Akbarī* 1978, Vol. III: 427–28)

Abū'l Faẓl lamented 'the blowing of the chill blast of inflexible custom and the low flicker of the lamp of wisdom. . . . Whatever has been received from father, kindred, friend or neighbour, is considered a deposit under Divine sanction and a malcontent is reproached with impiety' (ibid.: 4–5). Late medieval society

[18] Discussed in more detail in Vanina (1995: 217–24).

became more interested in human individuality and more sensible to temporal change. Unlike earlier periods, most late medieval literary works were dated and some writers, in sharp contrast to their predecessors, were aware of the movement of time, both personal and historical, as well as the changeability of social and political institutions. It is not by chance that in the miniature painting of the late sixteenth and early seventeenth centuries, portraiture emerged as a popular genre. Initially nothing but a symbolic and canonized depiction of a man as an embodiment of the idea of royalty, saintliness, statesmanship, etc., it gradually became more sensitive to the personality age and physique of the subject.[19] The seventeenth and eighteenth centuries saw biography and autobiography emerge as popular literary genres. Some of them, like the biography and diaries of the Tamil merchant Ānanda Raṅga Pillai, autobiographies of the Maratha statesman Nānā Phaḍnīs and the celebrated Urdu poet Mīr Taqī Mīr,[20] may be viewed, in David Shulman's words, as 'proto-modern biography' (Shulman 2004: 196), 'modernity' in this case being a result of not the Western influence, but of indigenous development. Biographical compendia and dictionaries came into vogue. Compiled mainly by Muslim authors, these dictionaries narrated the life stories of Muslim and Hindu celebrities without any communal bias. Highlighting major political and cultural events as reflected in the lives of the elite, the writers paid adequate attention to the individual traits of character and peculiarities of behaviour of each person, pointing to negative features of even those denoted as 'perfect men'.[21]

Such developments in no way overwhelmed or displaced preceding forms, they appeared and coexisted with the centuries-old traditions, proving, however, that medieval Indian society possessed a certain dynamism that allowed for a revision of old values, thus preparing (the educated elite, of course) for the novel approaches of the forthcoming modernity.

References

Abbott, Justin E. (1985), *Bahinā Bāī. A Translation of Her Autobiography and Verses* (Delhi: Motilal Banarsidass).

Ā'īn-i Akbarī by Abū'l Faẓl Allami (1878), Vol. III, translated by H.S. Jarret (Delhi: Munshiram Manoharlal).

Alam, Muzaffar (1989), 'Indo-Islamic Interaction in Medieval North India', *Itinerario*, Vol. 13, No. 1, pp. 37–60.

Ardhakathānaka (1981), translated by Mukund Lath as *Ardhakathānaka: Half a Tale* (Jaipur: Rajasthan Prakrit Bharati Samsthan).

Aries, Philip (1973), *Centuries of Childhood* (Harmondsworth: Penguin Books).

[19] Cf. Grek, a Russian art historian, who had made a comparative analysis of miniature portraits of Mughal emperors and nobles created during their lifetime by various painters: Grek (1972: 237–54).

[20] For the biography of Mīr Taqī Mīr see Naim (1999). The English translation of Nānā Phaḍnīs' biography is available in Raeside (1984). For life and works of Ānanda Raṅga Pillai see Shulman (2004).

[21] See, for instance, Desai (1993: 53–54, 101).

Arnold, David and Stuart Blackburn (2004), 'Introduction. Life Histories in India' in Arnold David and Stuart Blackburn (eds), *Telling Lives in India. Biography, Autobiography and Life History* (Delhi: Permanent Black).

Bali, Indu (1977), *Madhyakālīn Hindī premākhyānõ ke kathānak kā adhyayan* (Delhi: Risarch).

Bhaktavijaya by Mahīpati (1988), translated by Justin E. Abbott and Pandit Narhar R. Godbole as *Stories of the Indian Saints* (Delhi: Motilal Banarasidass).

Blackburn, Stuart (2004), 'Life Histories as Narrative Strategy: Prophecy, Song, and Truth-Telling in Tamil Tales and Legends', in Arnold David and Stuart Blackburn (eds), *Telling Lives in India. Biography, Autobiography and Life History* (Delhi: Permanent Black).

Callewaert, Winand M. (1988), *The Hindi Biography of Dādū Dayāl* (Delhi: Motilal Banarasidass).

Chandra, Prabha (1976), *Historical Mahākāvyas in Sanskrit (Eleventh to Fifteenth Century)* (Delhi: Sri Bharat Bharati).

Chattopadhyaya, Brajadulal (1998), *Representing the Other? Sanskrit Sources and the Muslims* (Delhi: Manohar).

Dhakkira ul-Khavanin by Shaikh Ahmad Bhakkari *(A Biographical Dictionary of Mughal Noblemen)* (1993), translated by Zia ud-Din Desai, Pt. I (Delhi: Idarat-i Adabiyat-i Dehli).

Duby, Georges (1990), 'The Diffusion of Cultural Patterns in Feudal Society', in Maurice Aymard, Harbans Mukhia (eds), *French Studies in History*, Vol. II: *The Departures* (Delhi: Orient Longman).

Eknāth by Mahīpati (1927), translated from the *Bhaktalilamrita* by Justin E. Abbott (Poona: Scottish Mission Industries).

Glushkova, Irina (2000), 'Viṭṭhal: Sometimes Adored, Sometimes Rejected. Changes in Theological Pattern', in Mariola Offredi (ed.), *The Banyan Tree. Essays on Early Literature in New Indo-Aryan Languages* (Delhi: Manohar).

Gordon, Stewart (1994), *Marathas, Marauders and State Formation in Eighteenth Century India* (Delhi: Oxford University Press).

Grek, T.V. (1972), 'Mogolskiye miniatury XVII v s izobrazheniyami dvortsovikh priyemov-darbarov (sravnitelnaya kharakteristika gruppovikh portretov) (Mughal miniatures of the seventeenth century depicting Palace receptions – durbars (A comparative characteristic of group portraits)', in *Strani i Narodi Vostoka (Countries and Peoples of the Orient)*, Vol. 14 (Moscow: Nauka Publishers).

Grierson, G.A. (1990), 'Introduction', in W. Waterfield and G. Grierson (tr.), *The Lay of Alha* (Gurgaon: Vintage Books).

Gurevich, Aaron (1990), *Srednevekovy mir; kultura bezmolvstvuyuschego bolshinstva* (*Medieval World: The Culture of Mute Majority*) (Moscow: Nauka Publishers).

Harirāy (VS 2008/AD 1951), *Go.Śrī Harirāy jī kṛt Sūrdās kī vārtā*, edited by Prabhudayal Mital (Mathura: Agraval Press).

Hart, George L. (1995), 'Archetypes in Classical Indian Literature and Beyond', in David Shulman (ed.), *Syllables of Sky. Studies in South Indian Civilization in Honour of Velcheru Narayana Rao* (Delhi: Oxford University Press).

Hawley, John Stratton (1984), *Sūr Dās. Poet, Singer, Saint* (Seattle and London: University of Washington Press).

Kharak Singh and Gurtej Singh (1995), *Episodes from the Lives of the Gurus. Parchian Sewadas. English Translation and Commentary* (Chandigarh: Institute of Sikh Studies).

Khiḍiyā Jagā (1960), *Vacanikā Rāṭhauḍ Ratansiṅghjī rī Mahesdāsaut rī Khiḍiyā Jagā rī kahī*, edited by Kasiram Sarma and Raghubir Singh (Delhi: Rajkamal Prakasan).

Kolff, D.H.A. (1990), *Naukar, Rajput and Sepoy. The Ethnohistory of the Military Labour Market in Hindustan, 1450–1850* (Cambridge: Cambridge University Press).

Lāl Kavi (1916), *Lālkavi racit Chatraprakāś*, edited by B.A. Syamsundardas and Krishnabaldev Varma (Kashi: Nagari Pracarini Sabha).

Larus, Joel (1979), *Culture and Political Military Behaviour. The Hindus in Pre-Modern India* (Calcutta: Minerva).

Lorenzen, David N. (1987), 'The Social Ideologies of Hagiography: Śaṅkara, Tukārām and Kabīr', in Milton Israel and N.K. Wagle (eds), *Religion and Society in Maharashtra* (Toronto: Centre for Asian Studies).

Macauliffe, M.A. (1909), *The Sikh Religion. Its Gurus, Sacred Writing and Authors*, Vols. V and VI (Oxford: Clarendon Press).

Misch, Georg (1951), *History of Autobiography in Antiquity*, Vol. I, translated by E.W. Dickes (Cambridge, Mass.: Harvard University Press).

Mital Prabhu Dayal (1949), *Aṣtachāp Paricay: Vallabha sampradāy ke vivaraṇ sahit Aṣtachāp kā ālocnātmak jīvan-vṛttant aur kāvya-saṅgrah* (Mathura: Agrawal Press).

Naim C.M. (1999), *Zikr-i Mir, The Autobiography of the Eighteenth Century Mughal Poet: Mir Muhammad Taqī 'Mīr'*, translated and edited by C.M. Naim (Delhi: Oxford University Press).

Pargiter, F.E. (1922), *Ancient Indian Historical Traditions* (London: Oxford University Press).

Pathak, V.S. (1966), *Ancient Historians of India* (Bombay, etc.: Asia Publishing House).

Pṛthvīrāj-rāsau by Cand Bardāī (1955), edited by Kavirao Mohan Siṅgh (Udaipur: Sahitya Samsthan, Rajasthan Vidyapith).

Raeside, Ian (1984), *The Decade of Panipat (1761–71)* (Bombay: Popular Prakashan).

Raṇchoḍ Bhaṭṭa (1973), *Mahākavi Rañchoḍ Bhaṭṭa praṇītam Rājprasastiḥ mahākāvyam*, edited by Motilal Menariya (Udaipur: Sahitya Samsthan, Rajasthan Vidyapith).

Sangari, Kumkum (2000), 'Tracing Akbar. Hagiographies, Popular Narratives, Traditions and the Subject of Conversion', in Neera Chandhoke (ed.), *Mapping Histories. Essays Presented to Ravinder Kumar* (Delhi: Tulika).

Serebryakov, I.D. (1985), *Literatury narodov Indii (The Literatures of the Peoples of India)* (Moscow: Vysshaya Shkola [High School Publishers]).

Shulman, David (1993), *The Hungry God. Hindu Tales of Filicide and Devotion* (Chicago: University of Chicago Press).

——— (2004), 'Cowherd or King? The Sanskrit Biography of Ānanda Raṅga Pillai', in David Arnold and Stuart Blackburn (eds), *Telling Lives in India. Biography, Autobiography and Life History* (Delhi: Permanent Black).

Sinha, A.K. (2000), *Readings in Early Indian Socio-Cultural History* (Delhi: Anamika Publishers).

Smith, Brian K. (1994), *Classifying the Universe. The Ancient Indian Varṇa System and the Origins of Caste* (Delhi: Oxford University Press).

Spiegel, Gabrielle M. (1997), *The Past as Text. The Theory and Practice of Medieval Historiography* (Baltimore: The John Hopkins University Press).

Thapar, Romila (1986), 'Society and Historical Consciousness: The Itihāsa-Purāṇa Tradition', in S. Bhattacharya and Romila Thapar (eds), *Situating Indian History: For Sarvepalli Gopal* (Delhi: Oxford University Press).

Trautmann, Thomas R. (1997), *Aryans and British India* (Berkeley: University of California Press).

Vaisya, Rukmini (1972), *Kuśala Lāāha ke sāhitya kā loktattvik adhyayan* (Jaipur: Panchsheel).

Vanina, Eugenia (1995), 'The Ardhakathānaka by Banārasī Dās: A Socio-Cultural Study', *Journal of the Royal Asiatic Society*, Third Series, Vol. 5, No. 2.

Warder, A.K. (1973), *An Introduction to Indian Historiography* (Bombay: Popular Prakashan).

Zelliot, Eleanor (1999), 'Women in the Homes of the Saints', in Irina Glushkova and Rajendra Vora (eds), *Home, Family and Kinship in Maharashtra* (Delhi: Oxford University Press).

Marathi Saint-Poets

Statics versus Dynamics, or Contradictions Ignored

Irina Glushkova

Marathi saint-poets (*sant*) of the thirteenth to seventeenth centuries are probably more popular today than they have ever been. They constitute an intrinsic part of the concept of Maharashtrian *asmitā,* understood as the indigenous identity of the region. Scrutinized in hundreds of PhD theses and praised in everyday columns in Marathi dailies, their hymns are sung in temples and by amateur chorus groups. The saint-poets' life stories, preserved in mainstream legends and local interpretations, are taken as practical and ethical teachings. These nourish Maharashtrians of the twenty-first century who, inspired by them, take off to search for spiritual bliss in various places connected with the names of Dñyāneśvar, Nāmdev, Eknāth, Tukārām and Rāmdās.[1]

A. Bharati (Leopold Fischer) was perhaps the first scholar to treat Indian pilgrimage as a separate academic subject. He wrote:

> Desire for emulation of the preceptors' total way of life provides a psychological clue for a paradox which is really but apparent: all the saints who have minimized the importance of pilgrimage have constantly been on pilgrimage themselves, most of them having spent their lives as mendicants and minstrels who sang their songs at places of pilgrimage for the benefit of the pilgrim. Thus, it has become customary for the pious Hindu to go on pilgrimages, to believe in their merit, and yet to state that pilgrimage is not important – just as their preceptors kept doing. (Bharati 1963: 144)

This statement provides for the reconciliation of contradictory ideas, but also raises a lot of questions. What is the range of the phenomenon of 'pilgrimage', or, to be more precise, *tīrtha-yātrā*?[2] Could one neglect a difference between pilgrimage (*tīrtha-yātrā, tīrthāṭan*) – many-goaled movement (transit) among *tīrtha*s (Hindu sacred places) – on the one hand, and wanderings (*deśāṭan*) – a life mode that implies non-attachment to a starting point and living or roaming elsewhere, instead of the inevitable return? Who are the saints who behaved in accordance

[1] The dates are as follows. Dñyāneśvar: thirteenth century; Nāmdev: thirteenth–fourteenth; Eknāth: sixteenth century; Tukārām and Rāmdās: seventeenth century.

[2] Glushkova (2000, 2004, 2006a, 2006b, 2008).

with Bharati's statement? Is the information about their pilgrimages reliable? Finally, what were their own thoughts regarding pilgrimage practice in general?

In the Marathi-speaking region of India five saint-poets (*pañc santkavi*), who composed the main body of Marathi devotional poems, are glorified and occasionally contraposed to one another, but normally brought together as creators of 'people's literature' in Maharashtra. It is also habitually reiterated that 'Any home where [the songs] of these five sants has [sic] not entered . . . is not a Maharashtrian one' (cited from Novetzke 2003: 113). Dñyāneśvar, Nāmdev, Eknāth and Tukārām were proponents of the Vārkarī *panth.* This religious way is characterized by devotion to Viṭṭhal (Viṭhoba) at the sacred town of Pandharpur. Viṭṭhal is recognized as a local manifestation of Kṛṣṇa, and is looked upon as a 'beloved mother' by Vārkarī devotees, who perceive themselves as his/her children. Rāmdās, the fifth poet, was the founder of the Rāmdāsī *panth,* which gives priority to Rām and his devoted servant, the monkey god, Maruti (Hanumān). Rāmdās is acknowledged as an ideological preceptor, and Rāmdāsīs serve their gods as servants.

Both the Vārkarī and the Rāmdāsī traditions have preserved a good deal of evidence suggesting an ambiguous attitude towards the practice of pilgrimage. This ambiguity is expressed even formally, as the contradictory aspects – rejection and recognition of *tīrtha-yātrā* – are divided between different genres of medieval literature. The religious poems of these poets are either silent on this matter or reject going to sacred places altogether. The following observation by a scholar of Rāmdāsī literature demonstrates a general comprehension of this gap: 'We do not know sufficient details about the tour of Rāmdās, the difficulties he had to face and the several people whom he met. Some miraculous incidents in the Satpuda ranges [sic], Kashi, Ayodhya, the holy places in the Himalayas, Kashmir, and such other places are related by traditional writers, some names of convents and Rāmdāsī disciples are mentioned, but not in Ramdas's writings' (Bokil 1979: 277). In the case of compositions that take a positive approach to pilgrimage, well-founded doubts arise regarding the authorship and date of those works. For example, this is the case with the *Tīrthāvaḷī*[3] ascribed to Nāmdev. Another 'pilgrimage' poem, the *Ānandavanbhuvan* by Rāmdās, contrary to the Rāmdāsī tradition and to the poem's interpretation by some scholars restrained by the same tradition or by the rules of political correctness, does not have a pilgrimage theme at all.

At the same time, the Marathi hagiographic literature that emerged in the seventeenth century abounds in details of saint-poets' journeys to sacred places. Vārkarī hagiographies even succeeded in a particular framing of the medieval period of the Vārkarī tradition (from Dñyāneśvar to Tukārām). The frame begins with the narration of a *tīrtha-yātrā* of Viṭṭhalpant which eventually brings him to Alandi and to his marriage to Rakhumābāī – thus forming the marital union of Dñyāneśvar's future parents. After Viṭṭhalpant leaves to go on pilgrimage again,

[3] The term *tīrthāvaḷī (tīrtha+avaḷī,* a row) can be translated as both 'pilgrimage' and a 'list of sacred places.'

he is brought back by a certain Rāmānand, who has met Rakhumābāī on his way to the sacred place Rameshvaram, and helps this woman get him back and bear their children. The framed period ends with Tukārām's departure from his native village of Dehu.[4] As one version suggests, he goes on a *tīrtha-yātrā.* As for the Rāmdāsī tradition, its ideological basis is said to be rooted in the experience acquired by Rāmdās during his twelve years of travel, which are interpreted as a pilgrimage.

Saint-Poets Say 'No' to Pilgrimage

It is said that the Vārkarī poets knew only one-way motion – towards Pandharpur to embrace the feet of Viṭṭhal, ever eager to meet his children. They did not need the ritual mediation of Brāhmaṇa-priests and they were not curious about the world devoid of their god. As normatively described by *māhātmyas* (Dhere 1970; Raeside 1965; Sand 1990, 1992), Pandharpur had been recognized as both a *tīrtha* and a *kṣetra* and as such was regularly visited by pilgrims. But at some unspecified time the collective movement of the Vārkarīs to this town began to be called a *vārī,* and thus the language itself makes the annual movement of the Vārkarīs distinct from a *tīrtha-yātrā* as perceived in the 'Great Tradition' (for details see Bhardwaj 1983). As P. Engblom puts it, 'for a *Wārkarī* there is a clear difference between making his *wārī* to Pandharpur and doing a *yātrā.* The one he does regularly and punctually every year; while the other he *may* also occasionally do as an additional, supererogatory merit-earning action' (Engblom 1987: 24).

As for the *bhakti* of Rāmdās, much diffused in the traditional ritual activity, it had a bias in favour of acquiring theological knowledge; travel with the objective of begging for alms was looked upon as a means for taming one's ambitions and arrogance.

Dñyāneśvar

Though there is no consensus whether Dnyaneśvar had ever visited Pandharpur at all, public opinion in Maharashtra names him as the founder of the Vārkarī tradition. R.C. Dhere builds a sequence of selected verses from the *Dñyāneśvarī,* an Old Marathi commentary on the *Bhagavad-gītā,* to present Dñyāneśvar's position on the common Hindu *tīrthas* (Dhere 1998). Dñyāneśvar believed that 'true persons' (*satpuruṣ*) and their mere glance could purify a man and transform his inner world much more effectively than would have been achieved by a visit to a *tīrtha.* A 'true person' endowed with this quality was similar to a *tīrtha* (*tīrtharūp*), and it was he who gave *tīrthas* their *tīrtha*-ness, i.e. made them sacred.[5] Dñyāneśvar gave the highest title 'king of *tīrthas,*' not to the

[4] Both Alandi and Dehu are located on the Indrayani river close to the city of Pune, and nowadays are viewed as sacred places of the Vārkarī tradition.

[5] 'The *Skandapurāṇa* says that a spot of the earth resorted to by ancient good men for the collection of merit is called *tīrtha* and that the main thing is to go to (i.e. associate with) holy men and pilgrimage is only a secondary object' (Kane 1953: 555). A detailed treatment of the term *tīrtha* is found in Eck (1981).

sacred town of Prayag as was traditionally done, but to those personalities whose mere sight (*darśan*) helped people to recognize their life objectives. Hence, one would not need to undertake a long journey to famous sacred places to get purified and acquire merit; the sacred water of *tīrthas* would not remove the filth of the soul unless it was accompanied by a person's own efforts. M.S. Kanade and R.S. Nagarkar state that 'the opinion of Dñyāneśvar, [the author] of the *Dñyāneśvarī*, is not favourable towards pilgrimage' (Kanade and Nagarkar 1996: 194). Marathi *sants* are known to keep repeating that it is the nature of the water, especially that used for washing the feet of a *guru*, to purify, therefore one should not undertake an 'erroneous whirling' (*sakaḷ tīrthe nivṛttīcyā pāyī / tethe buḍī deī mājhyā manā // ātā mī na karī bhrāntīce*[6] *bhramaṇ*) [291];[7] one's parents and the company of *sants* are considered the best *tīrthas* – 'these are both tirtha and kshetra and in this world they are sacred' (*to tīrtha to kṣetra / jāgī toci pavitra*) (Dhere 1998: 183–85).

Besides the *Dñyāneśvarī* there are approximately 1000 *abhaṅgs* that are accepted by the Vārkarīs and by many scholars as having been composed by Dñyāneśvar. Some of those *abhaṅgs*, flavoured with a touch of *advaita* philosophy, reject the journey to the *tīrtha* because the source of all *tīrthas* is God, who can be found in one's heart (*aṣṭottarśe tīrthe jayācyā caraṇī / to tujhā hṛdaybhuvanī ātmarāmu // dev javaḷī*[8] *astā jāsī ānā tīrthā* [497]). Moreover, even the grandeur of sacred places such as Kashi, Ayodhya, Avanti (Ujjain), Kanti and Mathura (of the seven cities granting salvation) does not help them to get to Pāṇḍuraṅga (Viṭṭhal) (*kāśī ayodhyā āvanti kānti / mathurā māyā gomtī / aiśī tīrthe ityādike āhetī / pari sarī na pavtī pāṇḍuraṅgī* [64]). However, this theme appears more often in reverse: it is the *tīrthas* that arrive at Pandharpur. Some *abhaṅgs* (like those from the *Haripāṭh* group) stress the uselessness of visits to *saṅgams*, *triveṇīs* and other *tīrthas* if a pilgrim does not concentrate on [God's] name (*triveṇī saṅgamī nānā tīrthe bhramī/ citta nāhī nāmī tari vyartha* [746]). Failure is also the destiny of those who lack fervent faith (*tīrthas vrat nem bhāveviṇ siddhi / vāyāci upādhī karisī janā* [748]), while merit gained at the time of pilgrimage may also be achieved by many-faceted attachment to Hari's name (*harivaṃś purāṇ harināmsaṅkirtan / harivīṇ saujanya neṇe kāhī // tayā narā lādhle vaikuṇṭh joḍle / sakaḷhi ghaḍle tīrthāṭan* [754]). Thus, *tīrthāṭan* is not recognized for itself but is taken as a criterion for the evaluation of the results of spiritual practice.

Nāmdev

The symbols of the Vārkarīs include Viṭṭhal; the *bhakta* Puṇḍalika who is said to have been the cause of Viṭṭhal's permanent stay on the bank of the Bhima (Chandrabhaga) river; the town of Pandharpur; and the village of Alandi.

[6] *Citta* is the word used in some editions.

[7] Numbers referring the *abhaṅgs* of Dñyāneśvar and Nāmdev correspond to Joshi (1967, Vol. I); those of Eknāth and Tukārām – to Joshi (1967, Vol. II); the additional numbers in the case of quotations from Tukārām correspond to Tukārām (1950).

[8] Another reading is *deh devaḷī*, which produces a different meaning.

In the *abhaṅgs* of Nāmdev they are normally treated as *tīrthas* (*tīrtha viṭṭhal kṣetra viṭṭhal* [362]; *sarva tīrthāñce heci mūḷ* [1022]; *aise tīrtha sarvottam* [1023]). The superiority of Pandharpur and Alandi is also substantiated through a reference to the 'other', 'all', or '108' *tīrthas* which reach Pandharpur at midday to worship local sacred objects (*aisī paṇḍharī manī dhyātī / tyāsī tihī lokī gati / te āṇikā tīrthā jātī / tī vanditī tayāsī // . . . sakal tīrthe mādhyānhakāḷī / yetī puṇḍalikājavaḷī/ karitī aṅghoḷī / vanditī caraṇ* [402], *sakaḷ tīrthe viṭhobāce caraṇī* [412], *pāhtā deūḷāci pāṭh / tīrthe ghaḍlī tīnśe sāṭh* [413], *aṣṭottarśe tīrthe sarī / aghe ālī alaṅkapurī* [1037]). Moreover, the *tīrthas* are said to be genetically related to Pandharpur, which is called their 'parents' home' (*aise sakaḷ tīrthāñce māher / tīrtha nāhī yāparte thor* [412]).

These sequences of comparisons and equations, by affirming the superiority of the Vārkarī symbols, either disclaim the necessity of travel to other pan-Indian *tīrthas* or belittle its importance. As a concept and a dense substance (*tīrthapaṇ*), holiness 'accumulates' in the hearts of Hari's servants and is then relegated to sacred places, which are also created by devotees of Hari (*jayāceni tīrthā āle tīrthapaṇ / kelī sāṭhavaṇ hṛdayī tī // naval mahimā haridāsā jīvī / tīrthe upajavī tyāce kusī* [859]). Instead of the necessity of going to *tīrthas* located beyond the Vārkarī domain Pandharpur is seen as Kashi, Prayag, Narasimhapuri and other renowned sacred places (*kāśī he paṇḍhari / prayāg, nīrā nṛsiṃhapurī* [412]). At the same time the original city of Kashi, embracing numerous *tīrthas* within itself, comes to worship Pandharpur and Viṭṭhal's feet, and Kashi's presence in Pandharpur constitutes an additional pretext for a visit to the abode of the Vārkarīs (*sakaḷ tīrthe vārāṇasī mādhyānhakāḷī yetī paṇḍharīsī / ovāḷtī viṭhobāsī / viśvanāth mhaṇoniyā // mhaṇaūni vegī calā paṇḍharpurā* [412]). This figure of speech serves also as an indirect recognition of the importance of sacred places other than those of Vārkarīs. This 'algebraic equalization' can be traced here and there in the Sanskrit *māhātmyas* (Feldhaus 2003: 157–84[9]), which were aimed at drawing devotees to a particular sacred place. Stylistically and theologically, too, this device brings together orthodox Hindu compositions and *bhakti* poetry. It is worth mentioning that a detailed knowledge of Kashi's topography is traced in an *abhaṅg* signed with the name 'Viṣṇudās Nāma'. Many scholars judge this *mudrikā*, along with differences in style, to be an alien element, and exclude the poems signed in this way from the body of 'genuine' Nāmdev's poetry (Deshpande 1977: 476–94).

Other religious technologies, such as austerities, offerings of gifts, etc. are disclaimed along with pilgrimage. The substitution suggested is a visit to Pandharpur and/or devotion to the name of God (*tū jāū nako jethe tethe / jarī tuj muktīce ārte* [419], *vrat tap na lage karṇe sarvathā / na lage tumhā tīrthā jāṇe tayā* [2042], *pṛthvīvarī tīrthe ahet apār / parī paṇḍhrīcī sar ekā nāhī* [410]).

The *Tīrthāvaḷī* [913–73], or List of *Tīrthas*, invariably included in all

[9] In an unpublished work on place-rhetoric in the poems of Vārkarī saint-poets, Feldhaus (n.d.) includes snatches from this poetry which she interprets differently.

editions of Nāmdev's poetry and recognized unconditionally by contemporary Vārkarīs, is not a 'list' at all. Instead of an account of pilgrimage there is a philosophic discussion between Dñyāneśvar and Nāmdev, while their 'journey towards sacred places is nothing else but a confluence (*saṅgam*) of knowledge and bhakti' (Khanolkar 1977: 159), with considerable bias in favour of *bhakti*, or '*bhakti*-whirling' (*bhakti-bhramaṇ*) (Kanade 1970). In *abhaṅg* 931, just nineteen *abhaṅgs* after the beginning of the trip, the two pilgrims turn back, and Dñyāneśvar, who initiated the pilgrimage, confesses to Nāmdev, '[One] should not go on pilgrimage or undertake anything [else], [when] listening to your singing is happiness' (*tīrthayātre jāṇe nalage kāhī kāraṇe / aikonī tujhe gāṇe sukhrūp*). The next *abhaṅg* tells about the end of the pilgrimage; Nāmdev expresses his regret about the journey in almost every line of this *abhaṅg*: 'My mind was full of ignorance [which] made me wander from a place to a place . . . [I] visited many great *tīrthas* still the Chandrabhaga was in my mind' (*adñyānācā bhāg hotā mājhe manā / hiṇḍavile mhaṇonī deśodeśī // ... udaṇḍ tirthāñcī aiko jāy prauḍhī / pari citta mājhe voḍhī candrabhāgā*). Then there follows a long narration of a brāhmaṇa-feeding ritual, concluding with the direct statement 'Pilgrimage is not needed' (*Nalage tīrthāṭan* [968]).[10]

Eknāth

The greatest number of references to *tīrthas* is found in Eknāth's *Paṇḍharī māhātmya* (318–479). Although the main idea of *abhaṅgs* praising the sacred town is expressed by the adjective 'incomparable' (*anupamya*), implying the futility of comparison with other *tīrthas*, comparison – implicit and explicit – is found here and there in such expressions as 'such a superior place, the best among the best (*aise śreṣṭha kṣetra uttamā uttam*)' [342], 'there is no need to search for a comparison . . . [as] a place [like this] does not exist anywhere' (*nāhī dyāvayā upamā . . . aisā nāhī koṭhe ṭhāv*) [348], '[one will] not see a place similar to Pandharpur anywhere on earth [or] in three worlds' (*paṇḍharīsārkhe tīrtha mahīvarī / na dekho carācarī trailokyāt*) [354], and 'the space of the seven cities is holy and easily [achievable]; Pandharpur is the best of all' (*saptapuryā kṣetra pavitra sopār / tayāmājī śreṣtha paṇḍharpūr*) [448]. The 'seven cities' that grant salvation from the circle of rebirth are the set most frequently said to be inferior in all respects to Pandharpur. Some other famous places of pilgrimage are also mentioned: 'there exist Prayag and ten million other sacred places' (*prayāgādi kṣetre āhet kalpakoḍī*) [350], Kashi, the Ganga, Sagara, Prabhas and 'other sacred places yield to Pandharpur' (for example, *prabhāsādi kṣetre saptapuryā astī / parī sarī na pavtī paṇḍharīcī* [355, 360, 1653]).

As a rule, the toponyms mentioned are not specified and singled out. This is evident from the constant usage of the extension *ādi* – 'and so on', and recurring collective pronouns like *sakaḷ*, *sagaḷe* and *avaghe* etc: '[Viṭṭhal] is the

[10] The *Tīrthāvaḷī* is analysed in detail in the following sub-chapters.

most eminent among all gods, all *tīrthas* salute to his feet' (*sakaḷ devā siromaṇī / sakaḷ tīrthe vaiditī caraṇī*) [605], 'all *tīrthas* come together [and] reiterate the [God's] name, even gods – each one is better than the other – are running ahead; look, all *tīrthas* come as menials to the houses of Vaiṣṇavas' (*sakaḷ tīrthe / ghaḍtī karitā nāmsmaraṇ // devādhi dev uttam / tohī dhāve sāmorā // pahāho vaiṣṇavāñce gharī / sakaḷ tīrthe kāmārī* [1658]). The last examples reinforce the motif of the Vārkarī tradition regarding the preferability of movement towards Pandharpur. Moving away from Pandharpur is treated as much less attractive for various reasons, including the dominance of Brāhmaṇa priests at *tīrthas* (*sāṅgatī saṅkalpa brāhmaṇ / teṇe nirphal tīrtha jāṇ* [2611], *brāhmaṇāce tīrtha ghetā trās moṭhā* [2718]). This one-directional movement is substantiated by the 'incomparability' of Pandharpur due to its being, simultaneously, *tīrtha*, *kṣetra* and god, thus providing for the realization of all human dreams at this one specific spot (*parī purtī manorath paṇḍharīye* [361]). Consequently, any other *tīrtha-yātrā* becomes irrelevant. Pandharpur is more 'accessible' (*sugam*) [342] and 'reachable' (*sopār*) [448] than other places; it is better because it is simpler. For Pandharpur one need not carry out laborious rituals, such as shaving the head, torturing the body, fasting, spending money and emotions (*muṇḍan tī kāyā nirāhār rāhṇe / yethe na muṇḍane kāyā kāhī // mhaṇonī sarva tīrthamājī uttam ṭhāv* [350], *sarva tīrtha mārga vividhiyukta āhe / yethe ubhā pāhe pāṇḍuraṅg* [406], *kāśī kṣetra śreṣtha sarvāt pavitra / parī tethe veñce jīvitva śreṣtha// taise nohe jāṇā paṇḍharī he / . . . nalage veñcṇe dhan vitta jīv / mukhya ek bhāv pure yethe* [447]).

Verbs of vision that occur here and there in Eknāth's *abhaṅgs* provide additional verification of the poet's statements: '[I] have seen the layout of many kshetras but learn! – Pandharpur [is nothing else but] Vaikuṇṭh . . . , [I] have seen Sāgara and other *tīrthas*, but my mind is attracted to Pandharpur' (*udaṇḍ kṣetrāñcī pāhilī racanā / paṇḍharī te jāṇā bhūvaikuṇṭh // tīrtha āṇi dev santsamāgam / aise sarvottam koṭhe nāhī // sagarādi tīrtha pāhtā pāhile / parī man he vedhle paṇḍhrīye* [356], *sakaḷīk tīrtha pāhtā ḍoḷā / nivānt nohe hṛdaykamaḷā // pāhtā tīrtha candrabhāgā / sakaḷ doṣ gele bhaṅgā* [365]). Such 'visual' rhetoric aimed at the other *tīrthas* is strengthened by an impressive command ('learn!') and succeeds in imparting to the idea of Vaikuṇṭh – Viṣṇu's heavenly abode – a sense of reality.

Besides Pandharpur and its constituents, *sants*, too, are understood as *tīrthas*. Contact with them is said to bring purification and a substitute for pilgrimage: water used for washing their feet washes the Vārkarīs' flags (*santāñce caraṇtīrtha ghetā anudinī / pātakāñcī dhuṇī sahaj hoy* [1544]); no *tīrthas* can match the power of the *sants*' company (*kāśī prayāgādi tīrthe barī / bahut astī mahīvarī // parī santsamāgamācī thorī / tīrthe na pāvtī sarvadā* [1653]). God, too, prefers devotees who give up pilgrimage and austerities and replace them with service to *sants* (*tīrthāṭan guhāvās / śarīrā nāś na karṇe // samāgam santsevā / heci devā āvaḍte* [1657]); such people, whose intentions are pure and who recognize a divine core in every being, are destined to dwell in *tīrthas* as the latter approach them on their own (*je ṣucirbhūt śuddhmatī / iśvar mānitī sarvābhūtī/ te sarvadā vastī tīrthī / tīrthe vastī tyāñcyāsāṅge // . . . to sakaḷ śiṣṭāñcā dhātrā /*

tīrthe karitī tyācī yātrā / pādodakālāgī pavitra / tīrthe māthā vodhavitī // . . . sakaḷ tīrthe nāmsmaraṇī / ghaḍtī santsaṅghaṭani / yethe saṃśay nāhī [1618]).

Besides a visit to Pandharpur and contacts with *sants*, recitation of the *Bhagavad-Gītā* is one more device that Eknāth places on the same footing as the most precious pilgrimages to the three worlds and Kashi or Varanasi. According to him, constant recitation of the *Gītā* absorbs the might of all *tīrthas* and movement among them (*gītā dhyāī nar sarvadā to sucī / sarva tīrthāñcī mahimā tethe // tīrtha kṣetra yātrā devāce pūjan / yadñyayāg dān udyāpan* [3546]; *trilokīce tīrthāṭan ghaḍle tyāsī // vārāṇaśī yātrā teṇe kelyā apārā* [3548]).

So, along with other rituals, Eknāth rejects going to sacred places (*nako tīrthāṭan nako mantrāvaḷī / vedśāstra jāḷī guntū nako* [2803]). This rejection accompanied by multiple clarifications and specifications pertinent to the *bhakti* ideology, is reiterated again and again. He also condemns people who set off to *tīrthas* erroneously thinking they will find God there, instead of searching for him within their own hearts, and those who while lacking firm faith (*bhāv*) are busy pursuing mercenary objectives related not to the improvement of the human spirit but to gaining fame or merely food (*karū jāy tīrthayātrā / govile man vicārā* [2606], *tīrthayātrāyoge kīrtihī pāvlī / buddhi suddhi jhālī nāhī teṇe // śānti kṣamā dayā nāhī pai antarī / vāyā yerjhārī kaṣta kele* [2644], *āhārālāgī karī tīrthāñce bhramaṇ / āhāre jiṅkile man sarvaparī // āhārālāgī karī tīrthapradakṣaṇā / āhā re vyāpile janā ekmay* [2674]).

Tukārām

Tukārām expressed his views quite clearly by speaking about the tradition of performing the *vārī*, or annual pilgrimage to Pandharpur, in his family. Consequently, he denounced travelling to other sacred places and making vows as contradicting the Vārkarī ideology (*paṇḍharīcī vārī āhe mājhe gharī / āṇīk na karī tīrthavrat* [2241, 2351]). Tukārām equates a visit to Pandharpur with five pilgrimages to Kashi and three to Dvarka, arguing that the latter drain a body or just 'burn' it (*kāśīyātrā pāc dvārkecyā tīn / paṇḍharīcī jāṇ ek yātrā // kāśī deh viṭambṇe dvārke jāḷṇe* [4427] (Tukārām 1950). According to his convictions, *tīrthas* are nothing but 'stones' and 'water', and approaching them is a waste of time, because the true God is found in virtuous people (*tīrthī dhoṇḍa pāṇī / dev rokaḍā sajjanī* [89, 114], *dev āhe antaryāmī vyartha hiṇḍe tīrthagrāmī* [4482], (Tukārām 1950). Tukārām finds God everywhere, and consequently any water turns into a *tīrtha* or Ganga water (*jālyā tīrtharūp bāvī nadī kūp / avaghe gaṅgājaḷ jāle* [1848, 1830]). Whoever thinks that God dwells only in *tīrthas* but is absent elsewhere, displays a fault (*dev tīrthī yer dise jayā os / toci tyā doṣ jāṇtiyā* [2565, 3232]). Tukārām denounces those who have 'visited over ten million *tīrthas* but failed to have a [single] look at Pandharpur', as the touch of Viṭṭhal's feet brings as much merit as visiting 'uncountable' *tīrthas* (*tīrthe kelī koṭīvarī / nāhī dekhilī paṇḍharī // jaḷo tyāce jyalepaṇ / . . . tukā mhaṇe viṭṭhal pāyi / anant tīrthe ghaḍli pāhī* [324, 685]). On the whole, anyone who aspires to go to *tīrthas* is miserable, as he is searching for a place at a distance, ignorant of the fact that it is situated next to him (*tīrthāciye panthe cāle to nidaiv / pāvije ṭhāv antray* (3189 [Tukārām 1950]). Tukārām also speaks ironically of those who, having gone on a pilgrimage or having performed austerities a single time, start 'mooing', publicly proclaiming this feat and thus showing false pride (*tīrthāṭaṇe ek tape humbartī / nāthile dharitī abhimān* [1024, 1520]). Austerities and pilgrimages increase one's arrogance (*tap karūni tīrthāṭaṇ vāḍhavilā abhimān* [65, 90]). Some of Tukārām's statements do acknowledge some significance in the *tīrtha*s, but at the same time he clearly indicates their imperfection. Thus, there exist many *tīrtha*s but in comparison to the favours acquired swiftly in Pandharpur these *tīrtha*s are slow in granting rewards (*paṇḍharīcā mahimā / detī āṇīk upamā //. . . āheti sakaḷ / tīrthe kāḷe detī phal* [88,113]) . They might purify faults committed elsewhere while the faults committed at *tīrtha*s proper remain forever (*anyatrīñce tīrthī nāse / tīrthī base vajralep* [887, 1385]).

At the same time, Tukārām does not tire of praising the sacred abode of Viṭṭhal, the Chandrabhaga river, the god himself and his trustful devotees. Tukārām calls the Lord of Pandharpur the 'root of *tīrthas*, a fruit of vows' (*tīrthāñce je muḷ vratāñce je phaḷ / brahma te kevaḷ paṇḍharīye* [971, 1473]). The main Hindu gods – Viṣṇu, Śiva, and Brahmā – are astonished at the festivities in the sacred town of Pandharpur. They come with 330 million gods, and transform the place into a divine realm (*hari hara brahma tīrthāsahit bhīmā / dev koṭī tehtīs re / vismit hoūni ṭhakle sakaḷ jan / amrāvatī kelī os re* (195 [Tukārām 1950]) . The Ganga comes too, and other *tīrtha*s arrive as well, hoping to be purified by the dust from the *sants*' feet (*yetī tīrthāvaḷī / parvakāḷ sakaḷ* [1544, 2754], *tīrthe parvakāḷ / avaghi pāyāpe sakaḷ* [26, 51], *tīrthe tyācī icchā karitī nityakāḷ / vhāvayā nirmaḷ āpnāsī* [685, 1242]).

According to Tukārām, Pandharpur draws not only the gods but also people. Here they are at ease, free from the various bans and limitations characteristic of stays at other holy places, and need do nothing but sing hymns for their salvation (*kelā na sahāve tīrtha upvās / kathevin doṣ sādhan te* [2121, 2181]). If at other *tīrtha*s, a devotee is required to show off his faith, here, in the proximity of *sant*s, even ignorant ones turn out worthy (*tīrthī bhāv phaḷe / yethe anāḍ te vaḷe* [89, 114], *tīrthīñcī apekṣā sthaḷī vāḍe dharma / jāṇāve te varma bahu puṇya* [2312, 2416]). By annihilating their bad qualities anyone can be transformed into a *tīrtha*, and just glancing at such a person will bring salvation; hence there is no need to proceed to Varanasi (*mokṣāce tīrtha na lage vārāṇasī / yetī tyāpāsī avaghī jan // tīrthāsi tīrtha jālā toci ek / mokṣa teṇe darśane* [28, 53]). Finally, Tukārām, known for his occasional arrogant utterances, remarks that his songs, imbued with passionate love for Viṭṭhal, are sweeter and better than a stay in paradise and therefore are able to stop anyone from going on pilgrimage (*tīrthabhrāmakāsī aṇīn āḷas / kaḍu svargavās karīn bhog* [3609, 1589]).

Rāmdās

As a part of his instructions related to various aspects of human and divine life in the didactic text *Dāsbodh* (Belsare 1981), Rāmdās repeatedly mentions *tīrthas* and movements to or among them. He does not differentiate between sacred places at all, and keeps stressing their multiplicity and diversity (*nānā*). Nowhere does he treat pilgrimage as a self-efficient or a worthwhile religious technique. *Tīrthas* are mainly included in standard sequences enumerating various kinds of ritual orthodoxy, such as ablutions, meditation, recitation, vows, gifts, austerities, inhaling smoke whilst hanging head down over a fire (*dhūmrapān*), or performing penance amidst the five fires (*pañcāgnī*) prescribed for Brāhmaṇas (*snān sandhyā jap dhyān / tīrthayātrā bhagvadjan / nityanem pavitrapaṇ* [2-9-20], *tīrthe vrate tape dāne / ja na joḍe dhūmrapane / pañcāgnī* [5-6-29], *nānā tīrthe. . . / śamadamādi... / nānā granthantare* [5-8-38], *dev dharma tīrtha vrat* [6-6-8], *nānā vrate nānā dāne / nānā tape nānā sādhane / nānā yog tīrthāṭaṇe* [7-8-25], *nānā sādhane puruścaraṇe nānā tape tīrthāṭaṇe* [13-3-47] etc.). These sequences may vary slightly, and sometimes their inner logic is broken by incorporating notions of *bhakti*, such as the performance of *kīrtans* describing qualities of the favourite god and of intense faith (*bhāv*) (*tīrtha yātrā dān puṇya / bhaktikathā nirūpaṇ / mantra pujā jap dhyān* [5-7-47], *nāvaḍe bhakti nāvaḍe bhāv / nāvaḍe tīrtha nāvaḍe dev / vedśāstra* [2-6-24] etc.).

Rāmdās looks at pilgrimage as an auxiliary means that should or should not be resorted to depending on the context. Thus, to get rid of viciousness (*pāpkṣayākāraṇe*) it is recommended that a person be either absorbed in acquiring knowledge or visit *tīrthas* or concentrate on the right articulation of a *mantra* (*puraścaraṇ*) [2-4-8]; spiritual realization of God can be achieved both by looking at an ascetic or a pilgrim, at a person who is busy repeating *mantras* or someone who has managed to restrain his mind (*man*), at a great yogi or a person known for his versatile knowledge [1-8-11].

Rāmdās does not object to spatial movement in principle: in the *Dāsbodh* he even recommends it. However, in speaking about it he does not use terms related to visiting *tīrthas*, rather he uses words that are void of religious meaning, such as 'transit along the country' (*deśāṭan*), 'roaming here and there' (*paribhramaṇ*), and the oblique expression 'meet anybody [anywhere]' (*jyālā tyālā bheṭī dyavī*). Besides, these instructions also mention several reasons for motion that are unrelated to pilgrimage. One can start on a journey to collect alms[11] (*nitya nūtan hinḍāve / udaṇḍ deśāṭaṇ karāve / tarīc bhikṣā māgtā barve* [14-2-8]) or to expand one's mental outlook by getting acquainted with new people and with different views (*sṛṣṭimadhe bahu lok / paribhramaṇe kaḷe kautūk / nānā prakārīce vivek / āḍaḷo lagtī* [19-8-1], *yeke ṭhaī baison rāhilā / tarī mag vyāpaci buḍālā / sāvadhpaṇe jyālā tyālā / bheṭī dyāvī* [15-1-34] etc.).

In the teachings of Rāmdās, the *tīrtha-yātrā* is supplanted by an affirmation that different values belong to various value systems. The highest knowledge, *ātmadñyān,* can be received only from a guru and not by the performance of

[11] A special word is constructed to refer to this activity – *bhikṣāṭan.* Feldhaus treats *bhikṣāṭan* as 'merely the normal begging rounds of a wandering renouncer' (personal communication).

rituals or going on pilgrimage (*tīrthe . . . je prapt navhe* [5-6-9]). The knowledge received brings ten million more virtues than a journey to *tīrthas* (*sakaḷ tīrthāñcī saṅgatī . . . tyāhūni dñyānācī sthitī / viśeṣ koṭiguṇe* [5-4-35]). These values are drawn from *bhakti* ideology in general, and the Vārkarī tradition in particular; the latter is found in strained relations with later generations of Rāmdāsīs. For instance, *tīrthas* are said to get purified by the *darśan* of *sants*, and lose their importance if the latter do not come to them (*sādhudarśane pāvan tīrtha / pūrti tyāñce manorath / sādhu na yetā jiṇe verth / tayā puṇya kṣetrāñce* [1-10-11]), and *kīrtan*, which is a general mode of worship in *bhakti*, is said to be great because it brings satisfaction to the Supreme God and embraces all *tīrthas* and even the world soul within itself (*mhaṇoni kīrtanācā agādh mahimā / kīrtane santoṣe paramātma / sakaḷ tīrthe āṇi jagadātma / harikīrtanī base* [4-2-31]).

Saint-Poets Say 'Yes' to Pilgrimage

It would be tendentious to overlook those statements of saint-poets that do not diminish the importance of going to *tīrthas*. Mutually contradictory proclamations are found in abundance in the writings of all of them. We could take an exclusivist approach, resorting to grammatical and semantic criteria, to attribute ambiguous or obscure texts to 'a few' or 'other' Dñyāneśvars, Nāmdevs, Eknāths, Tukārāms and Rāmdāses distributed through time and space.[12] Alternatively, by an inclusivist approach, a scholar may detect the 'highest truth', which unites the antinomia of thought (Mitchell 1982: [Tukārām] 58); calling it a 'mobile perspective', he/she might invent a special vision that functions as a cultural integrator and changes the evaluation of an event or phenomenon according to the point of view (Lamshukov 1989), explain disparities in a text by the many-layeredness of a context (Kiehnle 1992, 1997a, 1997b), or differentiate between genres bound to the various epistemological systems (Gordon, this volume). Undoubtedly, the methods of bringing together diverse and contradictory data are not limited to these two approaches.

Dñyāneśvar

The style and trend of the hymns ascribed to Dñyāneśvar differ drastically from the *Dñyāneśvarī*, if only in the fact that none of the *ovīs* of the commentary mention the god Viṭṭhal, while the majority of the hymns praise no one but him. These *abhaṅgs* discuss *tīrthas* and the advisability of movement towards them more often than the *Dñyāneśvarī* does. Although they express total delight with regard to Pandharpur (a true *bhakta* visiting this town himself becomes similar to a *tīrtha* — *toci tīrtharūp sadā* [62]), the possibility of a journey to other sacred places is not excluded. Thus, in one of the *abhaṅgs* of the *Paṇḍharīmāhātmya* Dñyāneśvar reproaches those who do not go on pilgrimage themselves and yet

[12] The problem of authenticity is often realized by scholars but normally is of no importance to devotees or adepts of the Vārkarī and Rāmdāsī traditions. There are numerous studies of this aspect (too many to be included in the Bibliography).

stop others from doing so, and foretells their descent into hell (*Āpaṇ na karī yātrā dujiyāsi jāvo nedi / . . . na karitī tīrthayātrā tayā narakī biḍhāre* [72]). In another *abhaṅg* he displays his knowledge of various *tīrthas*, both within Maharashtra and outside, every new toponym preceded by the affirmation, 'I will go to [this place] / I will see [that place]' (*vārāṇaśī yātre jāīn / prayāg tīrtha pāhīn . . .*) and concludes with the refrain, 'I will not be exhausted [by it]' (*pari mī vīṭ navhen* [78][13]). Judging from the fact that the position of the author of the *Dñyāneśvarī* is not favourable to pilgrimage, Kanade and Nagarkar (1996) eliminate all such *abhaṅgs* from the corpus of Dñyāneśvar's works.

Nāmdev

The motif of Varanasi emerges unexpectedly in the description of the sainthood of *sants* which otherwise is not attached to a particular place because it is places that are dependent on a holy person. Nāmdev states, 'one who dies in Varanasi might be liberated by repetition of the name of Cakrapāṇi (Viṣṇu)' (*vārāṇasī prāṇī mare antī koṇī / tayā cakrapāṇi nāme tarī* [859]). Pilgrimage as such is recognized in at least two groups of poems ascribed to Nāmdev, – the *Ādi* [884–909] and the *Tīrthāvaḷī* [913–73]. The first enumerates various toponyms and talks about two pilgrimages (*tīrthāṭaṇ*) of Viṭṭhalpant, the father of Dñyāneśvar. These adhere to the norms of the *tīrtha-yātrā* that is a successive movement to a considerable number of places glorified in mythological sources (Glushkova 2004). These places (Prayag, Dvarka etc.) are mentioned and talked about in clichés (*mag puṣkārādi tīrthe pāhāvā samasta / anutāp citte dharielā // . . . nighālāse bhakti tīrthāṭaṇa // viṭṭal vandūnī mātāpitā donhī / saṅg tīrthāṭaṇī muhūrta kelā* [887], *mārgīñcī tīrthe karūnī samaste* [888], *dvārkādi tīrthe karūnī ālo* [889], *parī viṭṭhalāce man tīrthāṭaṇī //. . . gaman kele teṅe tevhā tīrthāṭaṇā / mukhya sthānā anukrame* [890]).

The oldest copy of the *Tīrthāvaḷī* mentioned above dates to 1631 and is ascribed by various scholars either to Nāmdev or to Dñyāneśvar.[14] C. Novetzke describes it as 'veritably an anti-travel, anti-pilgrimage narrative' (Novetzke 2003: 51). There are also several other *Tīrthāvaḷīs* ascribed to Nāmdev. The manuscript of one of them, found by P.S. Subandh in the library of the Bhandarkar Oriental Research Institute, is dated 1581 (*Śake* 1503). The same Institute houses another

[13] The line '*pari mī vīṭ navhen*' is difficult to interpret. Sadanand More, a philosopher and a descendant of Tukārām, looks upon the word *vīṭ* as the brick from under the god Viṭṭhal's feet in his temple in Pandharpur, and treats the whole *abhaṅg* as anti-pilgrimage ('It recommends not to go on pilgrimage and asserts the unobtainability of brick – the state [sic] which is superior to the merits by such actions as [going to] Varanasi' (personal communication, 8 March 2006). Feldhaus interprets the whole poem as pointing out the 'defects of other holy places'. She explains that Dñyāneśvar 'laments the inability of various specific holy places . . . and a number of kinds of ascetic practices to make him the brick on which Vithoba stands' (Feldhaus n.d.).

[14] 'The oldest version of the text, dated 1631 CE, credits authorship to Jñāndev, *not* to Nāmdev. However, the Vārkarī tradition and other Nāmdev followers attribute the story, as well as this very text, only to Nāmdev' (Novetzke 2004: 5).

manuscript of the text, dated 1787 (*Śake* 1709). The *Tīrthāvaḷīs*[15] consist of fourteen *abhaṅgs*, textually closely related, and mention neither Dñyāneśvar nor his taking the lead in the pilgrimage. They narrate, in the first person, visits to an enormous number of *tīrthas*. The 'anti-pilgrimage' *Tīrthāvaḷī* on the other hand is narrated in the third person; therefore Novetzke calls the latter 'biographical' to distinguish it from the 'autobiographical' *Tīrthāvaḷīs* of 1581 and 1787: 'The two versions of the *Tīrthāvaḷī* – the biographical and the autobiographical – are starkly different. There is hardly a mention of place in the biographical version and hardly a mention of anything other than place in the autobiographical version' (Novetzke 2003: 283). Besides, 'Nāmdev is praised in the [biographical] text as the most exalted of all Kṛṣṇa devotees, a characterization not found in his supposedly autobiographical songs' (Novetzke 2005: 5).

According to the 'autobiographical' versions, Nāmdev travelled alone, starting from the confluence of the Bhima and the Nira at Narsimhapur. He then went to Nasik, leaving the Marathi-language area to proceed to the Tapi river and Dvarka in Gujarat, and stayed there for a while before visiting Prabhas and Ambadi. The Rukmavati river in western Gujarat, D(h)apulpur to the north of Gwalior at the border of Rajasthan and Madhya Pradesh, the mountain of Saraneshvar next to Sirohi in Rajasthan, and the Pushkar lake are also mentioned. Then came Pehoa at the Saraswati river in Haryana, Hastinapur near Dehradun, and Rishikesh. The next verses deal with the sacred places of the Himalayas, Nepal and Tibet, from where Nāmdev turned to the south. He visited the Ganga plain, Ayodhya, Vrindavan, Mathura, Varanasi, and Gaya; Jagannath-Puri in Orissa, Ujjain in Madhya Pradesh, D(r)aksharaman in Andhra Pradesh and Arunachal in Tamilnadu. From Kanyakumari he went up along the Kerala coast, on reaching the Deccan visited Mahabaleshvar and Kolhapur, and then returned to Pandharpur. Both manuscripts refer to other places too, speaking of them along with the names of mythological characters and epic episodes.

Eknāth

The *abhaṅgs* of Eknāth display a sense of displeasure and discontent with regard to general moral degradation, especially the loss of religious commitment in the *Kaliyug*, including visits to *tīrthas* (*na cale karmāce ācaraṇ / vidhinisedhāce mahimān / loplī tīrthe jāṇ / devpratimā pāṣāṇ* [2576], *dev bhajan santpūjan tīrtha mahimān na kaḷe mūḍha / aise kaliyugī jāle jāṇat dagaḍā* [2580], *janmay prāṇ na ghaḍe sādhan / nohe tīrthāṭan vrat tap* [2581]). The section 'Non-believers, scoundrels and bad people' comprises *abhaṅgs* that enumerate negative qualities and denounce people who are indifferent to Viṭṭhal, as well as those who, while

[15] I am profoundly grateful to Christian Novetzke, who drew my attention to different versions of the *Tīrthāvaḷī* and generously shared with me his translation of the 1581 Subandh version and a Marathi copy of the 1787 version. His translation of the 1581 version is followed by detailed comments on the geography and mythology in the original. Novetzke also supplied me with his own studies, still in manuscript form, including his doctoral dissertation (Novetzke 2003, 2004), which turned out to be very insightful.

searching for 'better feet',[16] do not go on pilgrimage. The latter are said to be possessed of 'wooden' instead of real feet (*uttam pad te sobhtī / pari tīrthayātre na jatī* [2741], *pāyi tīrthayātrā na ghaḍe / pay nohet te keval̤ lākaḍe* [2742]). Those who start on a pilgrimage but in their mind keep clinging to home are also blameworthy (*tīrtha jātī udaṇḍ / tyāce pāthimāge toṇḍ* [2643], *tīrthayātre jāye saṃsār cintā vāhe* [2965]). In one of the *abhaṅgs* (*Kāśī-mahimā*), Eknāth reveals a sound knowledge of the sacred objects that normally attract devotees to Kashi: the presiding god Viśvanāth, the Ganga–Bhagirathi river, the deity Kālabhairav, the ritual circumambulation of Kashi (*pañckrośīcī pradakṣiṇā*), and the merit obtainable there. He concludes with a line that can be interpreted as 'Overjoyed is Eknāth by staying daily in Kashi' or 'Overjoyed is Eknāth by his stay in Kashi' (*eka janardanī nitya kāśīvās / param sukhās pātra jhālo* [3481]). Whatever the interpretation, this line suggests the possibility that Eknāth did visit Kashi.

Tukārām

Like Dñyāneśvar, Tukārām too is unlikely ever to have visited Pandharpur. Be that as it may, all editions of his lyrics bring together sixty *abhaṅgs* narrating his suffering at being separated from Viṭṭhal. This suffering is the content of the letter Tukārām is believed to have sent to Viṭṭhal along with the Vārkarīs travelling to Pandharpur [3540–3605, 1909–1974]. Some editors have brought together another three *abhaṅgs* and entitled the whole group 'A letter to the Bhagirathi [river] passed by Tukārām to pilgrims' [1675–1677, 1656–1658]. These *abhaṅgs* contain three easily recognizable symbols: the Bhagirathi river (the Ganga), the god Viśvanāth, and the ritual of *gayāvarjan*, or ancestor-worship practised in Gaya, the town traditionally visited along with Prayag at the time of *kāśī-yātrā,* also known as *tristhalī*/*tirsthaḷī* [movement to three places]. These *abhaṅgs* perhaps testify to Tukārām's curiosity about traditional *tīrthas*; he also calls the Ganga a remover of great faults, and the sovereign of all sacred places (*bhāgīrathī mahādoṣ-nivāraṇī / sakaḷā svāmiṇī tīrthāciye* [1675, 1656]). True, in another *abhaṅg* Tukārām denounces this statement by saying that he 'has seen Varanasi, Gaya, [and] Dvarka', and that they cannot be even compared to Pandharpur (*vārāṇasī gayā pāhilī dvārkā* [2405, 2409]).[17] In several *abhaṅgs* Tukārām seems to quite unequivocally salute those who start for *tīrthas* and those who encourage them to do so (*namo tīrthpanthe cāltī tayāsī / yetī boḷvit tyāsī namo* [3958, 452]). He urges his listeners with conviction to keep going on pilgrimage, as it is beneficial (*tava tū āpule svahit pāhe / tīrthyātre jāy cuko nako* [4056, 655]). He also accepts various kinds of ritualism, including going to *tīrthas*, if it is accompanied by non-stop praise of Hari (*tap*

[16] This might be an allusion to other gods' feet or imply *viṣṇu-pad*, the 'foot-prints' of Viṣṇu.

[17] On asking More if there are some family beliefs regarding Tukārām's movement to sacred places outside Maharashtra, I got this answer: 'That he did not go to any other place is a false impression created by those who wanted to show some drawback or the other in Tukārām' (personal communication, 8 March 2006).

tīrtha dān vrat ācaraṇ / gātā hariguṇ vāru naye [996, 1490]). Consequently Tukārām condemns those who 'perceive a *tīrtha* as water, an image as a stone, sants as worthless' (*tīrtha jal dekhe pāśaṇ pratimā / sant te adharmā māṇsāise* [1425, 2636]) and those who ignore *tīrthas* altogether (*kāhī santāñce pūjan / na ghaḍe tīrthāñce bhramaṇ // yamācā āndaṇ siṇ thor pāvel* [97,122]). In one of the *abhaṅgs*, which eludes a straight translation, Tukārām exclaims that 'nothing is done to no purpose' with pilgrimage (*na vaje vāyā kāhī keliyā tīrtha* [1028][18]) as an example.

Of special interest is *Niryāṇ abhaṅg*, a group of poems in which Tukārām bids farewell to everybody and gets ready to ascend to Vaikuṇṭh in a chariot that has arrived for this purpose. In most editions this group consists of twenty-three *abhaṅgs* (Tukārām 1928; Joshi 1967b; Jog 1990; Neurgavkar 1978), while the authoritative 'state-sponsored' edition published in 1950 to commemorate the tercentenary of Tukārām's 'departure', along with the 'Dehu edition' published fifty years later for the 350th anniversary (Tukārām 1950; Tukārām 2001) gives this group another title (*Svāmīnī kāyā brahma kelī, te abhaṇg*) and adds a twenty-fourth *abhaṅg* that talks about Tukārām's safe arrival in Kashi (*vārāṇasīparyant aso sukharūp / sāṇgāvā nirop santāsī hā // yethūniā āmhā jāṇe nidhāmā* [1609, 1604]).[19]

Rāmdās

The more Rāmdās devalues the idea of pilgrimage the more he speaks of it as an important part of human life. According to him, a person disengaged from worldly affairs should wander from *tīrtha* to *tīrtha* (*virakte phirāvī tīrthāṭaṇe / virakte karāvī nānāsthāne / param ramṇīy* [2-9-25]). Rāmdās also states the necessity of such travel for those who are imbued with the best quality of *satva*, i.e. those who embody truth and light, and he finds it possible to substitute a pilgrimage for the feeding of and granting gifts to Brāhmaṇas or for ablutions in the months of *kārtik* and *māgh* (*kātiksnāne māghsnāne / trate udyāpaṇe dāne / ni:kām tīrtha upoṣaṇe / to satvaguṇ* [2-7-17]).[20] His admission of this alternative signals his acknowledgement of the principle of pilgrimage. In his instructions Rāmdās describes those who neither know *tīrtha* or *kṣetra* nor are aware of other varieties of orthopraxy as 'unclean', 'stupid' and 'collectors of ant shit'(*na manī tīrtha na manī kṣetra / na manī ved na manī śāstra / pavitra kuḷī jo apavitra / to yek paḍhatmūrkha* [2-10-24], *neṇe tīrthī neṇe vrat / neṇe atit abhyāgat / muṅgīmukhīñce je*

[18] This *abhaṅg* is absent in Joshi (1967, Vol. II); the number corresponds to Tukārām (1950).

[19] As per More's suggestion, 'You can interpret that he had reached Varanasi' (personal communication 8 March 2006), 'however, even if this *abhaṅg* is accepted as authentic it will not help you. As it was the parting abhang there are no chances of returning and describing the experience of Varanasi' (e-mail communication, 1 April 2006).

[20] The Purāṇas attach importance to bathing in rivers during these months, placing three ablutions in the Ganga in the coldest month of *māgh* on the same footing as a gift of one hundred thousand cows; the explanation is that ten thousand *tīrthas* and ten million other rivers are present in the Ganga during this period (Feldhaus 1995: 89).

sit / tehi veñcūn sañcī [3-3-5]). He also dismisses as 'meaningless' the efforts of those who follow ritual practices and visit *tīrthas* but still remain full of doubts (*vyartha saṃśayāce vrat / vyartha saṃśayāce tīrtha / vyartha saṃśayāca paramārtha / niscayeviṇ* [5-10-17]) . A section of the *Dāsbodh* contains a wide-ranging discussion on pilgrimage between two participants. While one speaks positively of it, the other calls it a hardship resulting in meeting 'rock' and 'water' and in suffering at the time of bathing because of water getting in one's eyes and mouth. The exchange of opinions ends with a remark that *darśan* of *tīrthas* leads to the extinguishing of great sins (*yek mhaṇtī sāṇḍī vācāḷī / agadh mahimā bhūmaṇḍaḷī / darśanmatre hoye hoḷī / mahāpatakācī* [8-10-17, 18, 19]).

Besides the *Dāsbodh*, references to places of pilgrimage are found in the 'spontaneous' (*utsphurta*) poems of Rāmdās. Many of these have not yet been published; they are preserved in bundles (*bāḍ*) in a depository (Shrisamarthavag-devatamandir) established in the town of Dhule in 1935 by S.S. Dev, a collector, publisher and interpreter of Rāmdāsī literature. Dev cites a statement of Rāmdās that 'a Brāhmaṇa should roam' (*brāhmaṇu hiṇḍtā barā*) and talks about two poems, of 60 and 75 *ovīs* respectively, enumerating various toponyms: Kashi, Kanti, Kolhapur, Kashmir, Kushavarta and so on (Dev 1944: 230). Dev cannot explain the idea behind these enumerations and is also unable to find a referent for each and every toponym, but he still makes a general list of over one thousand places which he believes Rāmdās might have visited at the time of his pilgrimages (Dev 1944: 231–35).

Textual Ambiguity as a Condition of Efficacy

The (biographical) *Tīrthāvaḷī* [913–973], normally ascribed to Nāmdev, informs of Dñyāneśvar's arrival at Pandharpur to negotiate with Nāmdev about the idea of a joint pilgrimage. Nāmdev is not interested, and Dñyāneśvar tries to convince him. He explains to Nāmdev that even holy persons exonerated from future births, even those who have achieved the highest knowledge and have become purified, should not abandon gods, *tīrthas*, or *bhajans*. He urges that earthly sacred places, and the *sādhus* and *mahants* dwelling in them, should be seen with one's own eyes and that one's own life should be imbued with [this high] goal [914]. Nāmdev yields to persuasion and asks for Viṭṭhal's permission. Eventually, both saints make their ablutions in the Bhima–Chandrabhaga river, put their foreheads on Viṭṭhal's feet, and cross the river [917]. On the way – the description of which is totally absent – Nāmdev pines for Viṭhobā, but still both travellers experience bliss daily (*ānand*) [923]; Dñyāneśvar distracts his companion's attention with discussions of *advaita*, *karma*, *dharma*, and other philosophical concepts. It is said that they visit Prabhas, 'other places', Dvarka, and 'all cities [that grant] *moksha*', they miss nothing on the way and also wash away the 'sins of their passions' [928]. It is noteworthy that they leave Pandharpur in *abhaṅg* 918 and turn back already in *abhaṅg* 928; they carry on their conversation for three more *abhaṅg* and then step in to Pandharpur in *abhaṅg* 932. The following thirty-eight *abhaṅgs* depict the joy of their reunion with Viṭṭhal and describe vividly the ceremony of *udyāpan*, the feeding of Brāhmaṇas, which preludes and concludes any important religious event. The final line of *abhaṅg* 970 states, 'Nāmdev has finished the book', but then there appear three more *abhaṅg*s, rather different in style, that narrate a story of Dñyāneśvar's visit to Kashi and his cordial welcome by the god Viśvanāth.

As a matter of fact, the authorship of the *Ādi* and the *Tīrthāvaḷī* is not yet ascertained though there is little doubt that besides 'that very Nāmdev (a contemporary of Dñyāneśvar), the author of the *Dñyāneśvarī*, and / or the person who signed his work with the *mudrikā*s 'Dñyāneśvar' or 'Dñyāndev' there were several other 'Nāmdevs' who lived in different centuries and used for a *mudrikā* the renowned name and some other similar sounding forms (like Viṣṇudās Nāma). R.C. Dhere, for example, rejects Nāmdev as the original author of Dñyāneśvar's biographical trilogy, which, along with the *Ādi* and the *Tīrthāvaḷī*, comprises the *Samādhī*, and he names the composer of all parts as *ādikar*, or the 'creator of the Adi' (Dhere 1970, 1990).

There is a diversity of opinion regarding the authenticity of the 'bibliographical' *Tīrthāvaḷī*. Some scholars and fans of Marathi literature denounce any link between Nāmdev of the thirteenth and fourteenth centuries and this text, which linguistically should be placed in the seventeenth or eighteenth century (Pendse 1972; Dhere 1990; Novetzke 2003).[21] Others wholeheartedly recognize as authentic not only the 'biographical' *Tīrthāvaḷī*, traditionally included in every edition of Nāmdev's *abhaṅg*s, but also the 'autobiographical' ones of 1581 and 1787 mentioned earlier. Composed in the first person, both accounts enumerate any number of geographical and mythological places. According to Novetzke, they are 'quite positive about pilgrimage, travel, and the glories of other religious traditions and legends' and slip 'into obscurity from the end of the eighteenth century to the present' (Novetzke 2005: 47, 49). After a thorough comparison of the available versions of the *Tīrthāvaḷī*, Novetzke remarks: 'In the autobiographical version, Nāmdev ends each stanza by comparing whatever place he finds himself to Pandharpur, and each time Pandharpur wins the contest. In the biographical version, there is no contest: Pandharpur triumphs in a knock-out within the very first round' (Novetzke 2005: 283).

Vārkarīs do not reject the 'autobiographical' versions in public but prefer to sing the 'biographical' one at the time of their *kīrtan* and *bhajan* programmes: the discourse of their leading *sant*s is much more relevant for them than the geographical absurdity of the text. Hence, they invent a company of *sant*s consisting, besides Dñyāneśvar and Nāmdev, of Dñyāneśvar's brothers (Nivṛttināth and Sopān) and sister (Muktabai) and other famous Vārkarī poets – Gorā Kumbhār, Savtā Mālī etc. Vārkarīs today accept the pilgrimage narrative as fact but define its

[21] Novetzke states, referring to (though not naming) another work of his, that 'the biographical *Tīrthāvaḷī* seems to be a compilation of songs by various sants, perhaps organized by Nāmdev (or a Nāmdev), and various [sic] attributed to Nāmdev or Jnāndev' (Novetzke 2003: 30, n. 6).

main objective in the spirit of their saints' teachings, as a purification of sacred places polluted by human sins. Those scholars who support the image of Nāmdev as a pilgrim treat the *Tīrthāvaḷīs* of 1581 and 1787 as incontestable evidence of pilgrimages being performed (Kavitkar 1970, 1970–71; Bartakke 1970–71). G.V. Kavitkar, for example, dates the joint journey of the two to the period 1291 to 1296, paying little attention to the impossibility of such a long journey in the short life-span of Dñyāneśvar (1271/75–1296). Kavitkar speaks of five pilgrimages of Nāmdev, each lasting for several years ('He started from Maharashtra and made up to Mysore in Karnataka and Rameshvaram in Tamilnadu in the south; in the north direction he travelled up to Saurashtra in Gujarat, Sindh, Rajasthan, Madhya Pradesh, Uttar Pradesh, Punjab, Himachal Pradesh. . .'). He even retells a legend about a meeting between Nāmdev and a Muslim ruler which supposedly took place on Nāmdev's way to Kashi – the strength of this testimony is said to be its source, a chapter from the *Mahikāvatīcī bakhar*, which does not belong to the Vārkarī tradition. The weakness of this argument is that Kavitkar dates the *bakhar* (chronicle) to the fourteenth century, while it is known that some chapters were written between the fifteenth and seventeenth centuries (Rajvade 1923). But even Kavitkar, who has succeeded in detecting the maximum number of pilgrimages of Nāmdev, does not believe that the poet was driven by a desire to see *tīrthas*: 'Having realized that "God is everywhere" Nāmdev did not perform the *tīrtha-yātrās* for the sake of *tīrtha-yātrās*. . . he considered expansion of bhakti (*bhagavat-bhaktīcā prasār*) to be his life goal' (Kavitkar 1970–1971: 90–91; 1970: 702–11). S.D. Pendse holds the view that the itinerary described in the 'autobiographical' *Tīrthāvaḷīs* could not be fulfilled between 1290 and 1296 (Pendse 1972: 382).

Between the two poles of rejection and acknowledgment, there is a view that explains the *tīrtha-yātrā* in the 'biographical' *Tīrthāvaḷī* as a philosophical explication, including a thesis on the superiority of *bhakti-mārga* in comparison to *dñyān-mārga*. S.M. Deshmukh, for example, explicating the interpretation of the hagiographer Mahīpati Tahrabadkar, treats the reference to *tīrtha-yātrā* as a 'pretext invented by Dñyāneśvar in order to engage in free discussion with Nāmdev'; Dñyāneśvar also allegedly planned to draw Nāmdev's attention to the consequences of the Muslim invasion in the north of India, and thus to stimulate Nāmdev to popularize *bhakti* – 'which Nāmdev eventually did' (Deshmukh 1970: 130–34). Kanade (1970: 155) even resorts to a different lexeme – *bhaktibhramaṇ*, 'roaming [for the sake of] *bhakti*' – to describe the movement of Dñyāneśvar and Nāmdev. M.G. Deshmukh, on the one hand, expresses the opinion that 'human narrow-mindedness is removed by visiting various places, and that was the case of Nāmdev'; and, on the other hand, he treats the journey as Nāmdev's victory over Dñyāneśvar, and consequently as *bhakti's* victory over *yoga*, illustrating it with a story of getting water from a deep well[22] (Deshmukh 1970–71: 11–12). S.T.

[22] Dñyāneśvar used his powers of *yoga* to diminish his size and get down to the bottom of the well, while Nāmdev appealed to Viṭṭhal who made the water flow over the wall of the well.

Akkole believes that the near absence of toponyms in the 'biographical' *Tīrthāvaḷī* proves that the 'description of tirtha-yatra could by no means at all be the theme', which was rather a convincing show of the might of Nāmdev's *bhakti* over Dñyāneśvar's knowledge, resulting in the spiritual growth of the latter [Akkole 1970: 276–77]. Discounting the details, S. More defines the 'biographical' *Tīrthāvaḷī* as an ideologically condensed product of Vārkarī thought: '... even if Nāmdev is not the author, it does not imply that the event as such is not historical. And more importantly, it does not in any way harm the traditional Vārkarī philosophy it contains' (More 1994: 171).

The position of compromise is characteristic of the 'state-sponsored' edition of Nāmdev's *abhaṅgs* too, which, as in the case with 'state-sponsored' editions of other saint poet's writings, is considered the most competent. It was published on the occasion of the septacentenary of the poet and, like critical editions, is based on multiple manuscripts. Novetzke observes:

> Among the manuscripts collected by the government was a version of the autobiographical *Tīrthāvaḷī* (a version of which was published for the first time by Subandh in 1949) found in Pandharpur with the date saka 1503 (1581), making it the oldest manuscript the Government committee consulted. . . . The editors gave this long narrative its own appendix since it otherwise bore no resemblance to the biographical *Tīrthāvaḷī* included in the main body of the anthology, and thus could not be collated into that more popular version. The editors do not mention the discrepancy between the two versions of the *Tīrthāvaḷī*, nor do they note the obvious anti-pilgrimage sentiment of the biographical *Tīrthāvaḷī*, and thus the apparent psychological incongruity of Nāmdev's choice to take yet another pilgrimage to the North. (Novetzke 2003: 115–16)

At the same time, while calculating the dates of Nāmdev's birth and death on the basis of a song attributed to him and evidence in the north Indian hagiographies and the hymns of Eknāth and Narsī Mehtā of Gujarat, the editors suggested that 'Nāmdev's life coincided with Jnandev's for several years, allowing enough time to complete a short journey to one or two places in the north. Thus the essential story of the biographical *Tīrthāvaḷī* is more likely to be historically accurate, in their view' (Novetzke 2003: 118).

True, evidence from reliable sources should be taken into consideration to reject or accept the joint pilgrimage, but the medieval *bhakti* literature often supply emotions, not facts. Some Vārkarī poets are referred to for substantiation of the pilgrimage. Most often it is Janābāī and four *abhaṅgs*, 331 to 334 (Joshi 1967, Vol. I), under the rubric *Tīrthāvaḷī* and concluding with the *mudrikā* 'Says Jani'. Their earliest version is dated 1631 (Novetzke 2004: 15). Janābāī, a servant in the household of Nāmdev, tells a story of Dñyāneśvar requesting Viṭṭhal to let Nāmdev accompany him on a pilgrimage. Viṭṭhal consents, and instructs Dñyāneśvar, his brothers Nivṛtti and Sopāndev, and the *yogī* Cāṅgdev to take full care of Nāmdev: to remove thorns from his path, not to go too fast as Nāmdev is not in the habit of walking, not to let him starve, etc. All this implies the participation of the persons mentioned in a *tīrtha-yātrā* (*yājbarobar cālāvī ho vāṭe / moḍtīl kāṇṭe sāmbhāḷāve // haḷ haḷ jāve karū nakā ghāī / cālāyācī nāhī savay tyāsī // lātāci bhūk na dharī ha nirdhār / ghyāvā samācār kṣaṇkṣaṇā* [333]). Janābāī's *Tīrthāvaḷī* ends with a description of Viṭṭhal's suffering on the departure of his favourite devotee. There is no mention of the *tīrthas* visited nor any information regarding where and when of the pilgrimage.

Eknāth, too, hints at Nāmdev's pilgrimage in two lines of his *Nāmdev-caritra* [3551–632] (Joshi 1967, Vol. II). At the end of the last *abhaṅg,* he speaks of Prahlād, Aṅgad and Uddhav, the earlier earthly incarnations of Nāmdev, born a saint-poet during the *Kaliyug,* he then names the *tīrtha-yātrā* as a means of spiritual advancement (*tīrthayātrā sarva kelāse uddhār/sarva tyācā bhār cālavilā* [3632]). At the same time it is hard to think of a reasonable explanation for the fact that none of Dñyāneśvar's siblings (Nivṛttinath, Sopāndev and Muktābāī) – all poets themselves! – ever mentioned the pilgrimage of their renowned brother. It is also inexplicable that no one in Nāmdev's extended family who comments in detail on Nāmdev's failure to provide for his relatives, has made a single reference to his prolonged absence!

Similar to discussions of different versions of the *Tīrthāvaḷī,* alternative interpretations of the *Ānandavanbhuvan* of Rāmdās have not resulted in a consensus regarding the referential meaning of the title of this poem (Pangarkar 1989: 422–26). Almost every verse of this poem ends with the locative form of *Ānanda-vanbhuvan* taken as a toponym; the content narrates the hardships of the country under the yoke of invaders who placed the people of the country in an ongoing state of moral degradation. Still, under the guise of a dream which is believed to form the body of the poem, it prophesies forthcoming victories and the restoration of the [Hindu] faith. Depending on the argument that one learns about the condition of one's country by travelling through it, many scholars assume that Rāmdās composed the *Ānandavanbhuvan* in Kashi, where he made a stop after his journey along the Indian peninsula and his visits to various sacred places, including those in the Himalayas. The fact that *Ānandavanbhuvan* is also a traditional epithet for the sacred town situated on the Ganga might have contributed to this understanding (Pendse 1980: 51, 343–72). The identification of *Ānandavanbhuvan* with Kashi, in turn, is accepted as testimony to Rāmdās's travels outside Maharashtra. An opposite view, i.e. that *Ānandavanbhuvan* refers to Maharashtra, is held by those who are convinced that the meaning of each *ślokā* can be applied only to the reality of Maharashtra. Many scholars quote from Hanumant,[23] who in 1793 wrote an authoritative prose biography of Rāmdās. The hagiographer refers to Rāmdās's own use of the name *Ānandavanbhuvan* for the area between Nasik and Karvīr

[23] Hanumant-swāmī was a great-grand-grandson of Rāmdās's brother. In 1793 he wrote a biography of his great ancestor, basing it mostly on the work of Giridhar, and later added some more details. Some of the events mentioned by him are supported by an account of four pages from a diary of one Gopāl Ambājī which he wrote four days after the death of Rāmdās in 1681 (Deming 1990: 21–23).

(Kolhapur), the region of Maharashtra known as the Desh (Pangarkar 1989: 422). A third group of scholars find Kashi in some lines of the *Ānandavanbhuvan,* and Maharashtra in others (Mate 1957: 237–53).

Evidence of Rāmdās's alleged travels is further extracted from an even earlier biography, entitled *Samarthapratāp* (The Might of the Powerful One, i.e. Rāmdās), written fifty years after his death in 1681 by Giridhar (d. 1728) (Dev 1912). There are multiple mentions in the *Samarthapratāp* of the fact that Giridhar met the great teacher when still a young pupil of one of his followers; there are also references to pieces of information Giridhar learned from the immediate circle of Rāmdās. At the same time, the god Rāma is named the primary source of the information, as he narrated a story to Veṇābāī, a pupil of Rāmdās, who handed it over to her own pupil Bāyābāī, who eventually passed it on to Giridhar. The third chapter informs us that 'Samartha moved within India, Samartha blessed the *tīrthas*' (*Samarthe bhāratkhaṇḍī aṭaṇe kelī / Samarthe tīrthe pāvan kelī* (Dev 1912: 18); the sixth chapter names a few *tīrtha*s of pan-Indian significance, includ-ing Kashi – which is called Muktipuri, i.e. 'salvation [granting] city' (Dev 1912: 34), and not *Ānandavanbhuvan.* Eventually, on several pages of the tenth and eleventh chapters, there are inscribed the names and native places of more than two hundred of Rāmdās's pupils; this made some scholars link those places to an itinerary of Rāmdās's journeys. Interestingly, no other alternative scenarios are taken into consideration, though they occur here and there in the *Samarthapratāp:* for example, the departure of pupils initiated by Rāmdās and his followers for other places (*Veṇābāīpāsūni kitek mahant jāle / uttarbhūmīsī bahudhā gele)* (Dev 1912: 72), or a metaphorical approach to the universe identified with a community (*maṭh*) founded by Rāmdās and/or his pupils (*Samarthāñca koṇ ho maṭh / avaghā brahmāṇḍ yāñcā maṭh*) (Dev 1912: 82).

A poem by Giridhar called the *Kāśīyātrākathan*, or Story of a pilgrimage to Kashi, which praises Kashi, Gaya, Prayag and Ayodhya, contains no information about any real journey to these sacred places (Dev 1912: 28–30). As Dhere (1969: 35) observes, at that time 'Giridharswami Bidkar, who was a great-grand-pupil of Samarth, went on pilgrimage to Kashi and memorialized it in a short poem (106 *kaḍve*) that contains neither the experience of the pilgrimage nor the description of sacred places. Giridhar only managed to express his bhakti in regards to those places'.

Pilgrimages of the Saint-Poets as Presented in their Hagiographies

The earliest mention of the pilgrimage theme in relation to the *pañc santkavi*, appears in manuscripts dated to the end of the sixteenth century. A revival of interest in Dñyāneśvar and Nāmdev probably resulted from the conscious efforts of Eknāth, who, by his own account, tried hard to revitalize the Vārkarī tradition.[24] Be that as it may, the first references to Nāmdev's travels have been

[24] It is known from Eknāth's poems that he traced Dñyāneśvar's lost *samādhī* and found the saint-poet still alive inside, with a copy of the *Dñyāneśvarī* by his side; Eknāth reintroduced this text to Maharashtrian society.

traced not in the Marathi-speaking region but in the Indian north, in hagiographies or biographies by Vyās (1580), Anantadās (1588), Nābhādās (1600), and several others (Khanolkar 1977: 237; Novetzke 2004: 15). Novetzke affirms that 'the idea of Nāmdev as a traveller is one that flourishes in northern India, but is unsettled in Marathi sources and in the Vārkarī lore' (Novetzke 2003: 192–93). In Maharashtra proper the assertion of the pilgrimage practice of the saint-poets in the collective consciousness of the region goes back to the eighteenth century when a certain Mahīpati Tāhrābādkar began to compile anthologies of the life stories of all Maharashtrian (and non-Maharashtrian) *sants*.[25]

Mahīpati, according to his own declaration, was guided not by his imagination but by literary sources, and drew heavily on the *Ādi*, the 'biographical' *Tīrthāvaḷī,* and north-Indian hagiographies. In the section of the *Bhaktavijaya* (1762)[26] entitled, by its interpreters J.E. Abbot and N.R. Godbole, 'Vithoba's wanderings', Mahīpati tells the reader about the pilgrimages of Dñyāneśvar's father Viṭṭhalpant, who dreamed of visiting the famous *tīrtha* of Pushkar. With the consent of his parents, he 'gave himself up to the worship of Hari', went to Dwārāvatī, bathed in the Gomati river, prostrated to the image of Kṛṣṇa, and proceeded to Piṇḍārakā, Maṅgalahudā, Dwarka, Sudampurī (Porebunder), Mulmādhav, Bhaluka, Prabhāsliṇga, Soraṭhi–Somnāth (Kathiawar), etc. He visited places described in the Purāṇas – such as a spot 'where God became an *avatār* in the form of a fish' and 'the place where Kalayavan was burnt to ashes by Muchakund'. Mahīpati states that Viṭṭhalpant omitted none of these places. Nevertheless, the more realistic places in the list lie within Maharashtra, as they might have been better known to Mahīpati: Viṭṭhalpant paid respects to Ādimāyā in Saptaśriṅgī, bathed in the Arūṇāwarūṇā, from where he travelled eastward to the Godavari river, visited Kapileshwar, bathed in Kuśāvart, circumambulated the Brahmagiri, etc., and reached Alandi (Abbot and Godbole 1988: 124–26).

It is in Alandi, after he married Rakhumāī (a daughter of a local village accountant) that Viṭṭhalpant conceived the idea of visiting Pandharpur. He presumed that 'If Pandhari is compared to other sacred places, any such comparison seems deficient. . . . The moment it is seen it burns up mountains of sin' (Abbot and Godbole 1988: 128). His wish fulfilled, Viṭṭhalpant started on another pilgrimage, this time northwards. This journey too is described as a mixture of geographical and Purāṇic localities interwoven with gods and mythological characters: the Mount Śaila, Mallikārjuna and Nivritte Saṅgam, Ahobāl, Narasiṃha, Vasudev and Lord Vyāṅkat in Mount Giri, and Mount Arum, Chidambaram, Gokarṇa and Hatakeśwar. Mahīpati testifies that he 'saw with his eyes the mountain from which Hanumant

[25] Mahīpati authored four volumes of hagiographies – the *Bhaktavijaya*, the *Santīlīlāmṛta*, the *Bhaktalīlāmṛta*, and the [incomplete] *Santvijaya*, created between 1762 and 1789, and some other works (Khanolkar 1977: 237–38).

[26] The volume that I have used consists of two parts with different pagination. Page numbers from the first part imply references to Dñyāneśvar and Nāmdev, and those of the second, references to Eknāth.

flew in search of Sita'. He made it as far as Rameshwar and came back via Kolhapur after bathing in the Panchganga and at the confluence of the Kṛṣṇa and the Vena in Mahuli.[27] After some time, he left Alandi anew, almost secretly, and reached Benares, only to proceed to Prayag, return to Benares, and make for Pushkar again (Abbot and Godbole 1988: 129–32).

Mahīpati begins the story of Dñyāneśvar's wanderings with the following words addressed to Nāmdev, 'Although a *Jivanmukta* (free while living) has become free from sin, he should not leave off the worship of his *guru*, of God or of sacred places. I desire to see all the sacred places on the surface of this earth in your company' (Abbot and Godbole 1988: 159). As in the 'biographical' *Tīrthā-vaḷī*, Nāmdev does not appear stimulated by this project. Viṭṭhal is surprised too: 'Just so, Dñyāndev, why do you want to wander to sacred bathing-places with useless thoughts in your mind? Why wander about uselessly?' To this Dñyāneśvar replies, 'True, true. What you say is perfectly right, but I want association with such a God-loving *bhakta* as Nāma is. I want the joy of association with him, and so make my life worth living' (ibid.: 161). Satisfied with this explanation, Viṭhobā lets Nāmdev go. On the way, Dñyāneśvar and Nāmdev are busy discussing various aspects of *bhakti*. Their discussion is suspended only when Mahīpati tells us of their arrival at Delhi, which had never been a *tīrtha*.[28] Then Mahīpati resumes the pilgrimage narrative: 'If I should mention in detail these sacred bathing places in the various countries, this book will be extended too much. Nāmdev visited all of them and finally came to Anandavan (modern Benares) . . . Nāmdev remained there for four months, (ibid.: 178). Traditionally, the duration of a stay in this sacred town was dictated not only by the four-month period of the rains (*cāturmāsya*), which kept a pilgrim in one place, but by a dense ritual programme and local *tīrtha-yātrās* performed inside and around the town. Mahīpati does not bother to mention these, but uses the reference to Benares as a pretext to introduce legends related to Kabīr, a resident of this town, and to talk about his encounters with Dñyāneśvar and Nāmdev, who lived at least two centuries earlier. Moreover, Dñyāneśvar plays the role of a mentor, explaining to Nāmdev and Kabīr their lofty aims: 'The *bhakti mārga* (the way of devotion) has become soiled. All mankind was sunk in worldly concerns, and you came to this world of action to save them', and invites Kabīr to visit Pandharpur (ibid.: 185–86).

Further, Mahīpati simply enumerates Gaya, Prayag, Ayodhya, Gokul, and Dwārāwatī and goes into the details of a competition between the yogic powers of Dñyāneśvar and the *bhakti* feeling of Nāmdev that took place, according to him, in a desert in Rajasthan (ibid.: 187–91). This episode is followed by a new list of names of places and gods: Badrikāśram in the Himalayas, Jagannāth of

[27] This is the sequence as rendered by Abbot and Godbole. Feldhaus comments, 'It seems unlikely that he would have gone to Kolhapur *after* the Krishna-Vena sangam in Mahuli'.

[28] There follows an account of Nāmdev's re-animation of a cow killed by a Muslim ruler. Other sources locate this miracle in the vicinity of Ahmadnagar in Maharashtra.

Odhyā, Oṅkār, Amaleśwar, Kedār, Mahākāleśwar at Ujjain, Paraḷīvaijanā [Paraḷī Vaidyanāth], Soraṭhisomnāth, Śrī Śaila, Ghriśneśvar and so forth.[29] 'Thus taking one after another the most important sacred bathing places on the surface of this earth, among which the most distinguished of them are mentioned as well-known and with high reputation in the *Puranas*. Ayodhya, Mathura, Kanti, Benares, Dwarawati, Avanti. . . .To these may be added the celebrated twelve Jyotirliṅgas. I have mentioned only these; still there are many on the earth which remain to be mentioned, but to what length should I go in speaking of them in this book?' (ibid.: 191–92).

Mahīpati deviates from the accounts in his own previous works, but keeps drawing from even earlier accounts. The *Bhaktavijaya*, the first hagiography written by him, contains two chapters on Eknāth (ibid.: 154–71, 172–88), which do not mention Eknāth's departure from the Marathi-speaking region at all. As G.V. Tagare states in his introduction to the *Bhaktalīlāmṛta* (1774), the *Pratiṣṭhāna-caritra*, the earliest available biography of Eknāth, written by Kṛṣṇadās Jagadānanda in 1698, just a century after Eknāth's death, does not contain an account of Eknāth's pilgrimage either (Abbot 1983: xvi). This gap is more than compensated for in (Mahīpati's) *Life of Eknāth* from the *Bhaktalīlāmṛta*, which significantly enriches Eknāth's life-story with the version created by Keśav-swāmī in 1720 (ibid.: viii).[30]

Like Nāmdev, Eknāth did not undertake his first pilgrimage on his own initiative, he was led by his guru Janārdan, who felt a desire to bathe in the Godavari river and to see 'with his own eyes' Nasik, Pañcavaṭī and Trimbakrāj (Tryambakeśvar) – the holy trio of northwestern Maharashtra.[31] Better versed in *tīrthas* within Maharashtra, Mahīpati digresses to give some realistic details: while preparing to start on the pilgrimage, Janārdan 'assigned to Eknāth a mare to ride on. A horse for their things, and one for himself. He appointed a Brāhmaṇa cook, and all promptly started. Whenever they found a beautiful spot there they rested for the night' (ibid.: 35).

The next time also it was Janārdan who took the lead. He thought to himself, 'I must send Ekoba on a pilgrimage to the sacred watering places. This earth will be made holy thereby'. He then elaborated his idea to Eknāth:

> Go and visit at least once all the sacred watering places that this earth possesses. Make a three nights' rest in some places, a five nights' rest in others. Whenever you meet with what is related to God you should make *namaskara*. Though you go for the purpose of a pilgrimage, you will at the same time meet with Saints. Sri Krishna Himself will provide for all your daily needs. Go as far as

[29] Feldhaus has drawn my attention to the fact that this is a combination of the four *dhāms* and the twelve *jyotirliṅgas*, the clichés that stand for an idea of pilgrimage in general.

[30] I have been unable to check the content of the second volume of hagiographies – the *Santīlāmṛta* written by Mahipati in 1767.

[31] These holy places are called the Maharashtrian *tristhaḷī*.

> Badrinath, and view that northern lake, Manas, with your eyes. To the south, visit Ramesvara, and then return to me here. (Ibid.: 41–42)

Like Nāmdev, Eknāth submitted to the command, but his mind was filled with Janārdan:

> He saw only him in all the animate and the inanimate of the three worlds. He visited many sacred watering places and shrines to set an example to the people. Wherever he found a restful place he tarried a three-night. In some places finding a company of saints he would remain a five-night. He would worship and bathe at such places, and leave whenever it so pleased him. He visited the great river watering places, the Purna, Payoshni, Tapati, Narmada. The sight of Mahakalesvara at Avanti brought peace to his mind. He visited also Mathura, Gokul and Vrindavan. . . . (Ibid.: 51)

Staying five days in Benares (Varanasi), Eknāth bathed in the Maṇikarṇikā and 'worshipped before Viśveśvara'. He visited Prayag, where he bathed at the confluence of the three rivers; reached Gaya, where he 'bowed with love before the feet of Sri Vishnu'. Mahīpati does not see traditional pilgrimage routes through the lens of orthodox ritualism but fills them with the essence of *bhakti*:

> Those who with an undivided devotional spirit place body, speech and mind at the feet of Vishnu, by that very fact perform the ceremonies at Gaya. Those who are wholly devoted to the feet of Sri Hari, are by that very fact performers of all good deeds. And as their feet touch the *tīrthas* these watering places become purified. The rivers Yamuna, Godavari, Bhagirathi, Krishna, Venya, Sarasvati, Narmada, Tapi, Bhimarathi, all long for the coming of the saints. Janaradan had known of their desire and had compassion on them. He therefore had commanded Eknath to visit all the sacred watering places. (Ibid.: 52)

Then Mahīpati mentions Ayodhya and explains Eknāth's attachment to places connected with Viṣṇu; he also names Badrināth, as well as Pushkar, at the sight of which 'all filth of the Kali yuga is immediately destroyed'. Still 'this place also was purified by the coming there of Eknath'. After that, Mahīpati once again brings his hero to the Himalayas, and then moves him to Dvarka for a one-month stay to observe the 'morning, noon and evening offerings and worship, and listening to the praise services [of Krishna]. . . . Thus having visited the northern *tīrthas* thoroughly, and having seen the twelve chief Śiva shrines, and the seven chief cities, he danced in the fullness of joy'. The pilgrimage made him a different person. 'He had conquered his appetite in restraining his senses. He was no longer conscious of what was sweet to the taste. Whether he was honoured or dishonoured was alike to him. . . . It was with this thought that Eknāth had visited the *tīrthas* and now had arrived here at Pratishthana' (ibid.: 54).

Mahīpati mentions another visit of Eknāth to Kashi, when he was summoned by Kashi pandits who were annoyed that his commentary on the *Bhāgavata-*

purāṇa was in Marathi instead of Sanskrit. Mahīpati calls the journey to Kashi the 'Great Pilgrimage', but stresses that this time Eknāth did not have time to prepare well, and left his native Paithan in the company of the Kashi pandits' pupils and without his own servants, who joined him later (ibid.: 178, 180).

Though from among the 'five saint-poets' Rāmdās was almost the immediate predecessor of Mahīpati – the latter was born in 1715, only 34 years after Rāmdās's death in 1681 – the hagiographer refers to the pilgrimage experience of Rāmdās neither in the *Bhaktavijaya* (Abbot and Godbole 1988: 189–200) nor in the many-paged *Rāmdās* that is a part of the *Santavijaya*, Mahīpati's last work (Abbot 1932), 1674 to 1690,[32] but left unfinished. Yet the Rāmdāsī tradition routinely speaks of the twelve-year pilgrimage of its founder. It could be that Mahīpati was not aware of the biography of Rāmdās, the *Samarthapratāp* by Giridhar-swāmī, which later became the most authoritative source on Rāmdās. Be that as it may, there is no mention of Giridhar in the detailed biography of Rāmdās that forms a part of the *Santavijaya*, though there is an explanation of why Mahīpati conceived of writing a new account of Rāmdās's life: 'I related his story as far as I was able, in the book called the Shri Bhaktavijaya, but it was a very brief account.[33] I . . . now begin [the story of Ramdas] in very commonplace language, through the authority given me by the saints. The Husband-of-Rukmini has given me the command, and I am therefore unable to hold back the expression of my thoughts' (ibid.: 2). It cannot be ruled out either that Mahīpati failed to trace the pilgrimage in Giridhar's account, the very pilgrimage that has become a core of the teachings of Rāmdās's followers.

Despite the variety of versions, the Marathi-speaking region holds in high esteem the stories presented by Mahīpati. In his introduction written in 1926 Abbot explained why he had translated the later version of Eknāth's biography by Mahīpati instead of the earlier version by Keśav-swāmī: he had learned about the latter only after the translation work had been completed. He also added that Mahīpati's account was the 'popular version for all modern references to Eknāth. The two modern Eknāth's *caritas* by Sahasrabuddhe and Pangarkar and Ajgaonkar in Marathi are but resumes of this *Bhaktalīlāmṛta* account' (Abbot 1983: viii; Pangarkar n.d.). To this the author of the authoritative 'Dictionary of Marathi Literature' adds: 'He did not aim at realistic life-accounts of sants based on consequent narration of facts. Mahīpati was an expert in picking out those events that would make readers happy and would serve to strengthen the Bhagavata dharma' (Khanolkar 1977: 238).

Mahīpati's persistence in sending Dñyāneśvar, Nāmdev and Eknāth (but not Tukārām or Rāmdās, chronologically closer to him) on prolonged journeys to

[32] The date of the *Santvijaya* varies from 1674 in Abbot and Godbole (1988) to 1690 in Jog (1973: 376), depending on the dating of Mahīpati's demise and some other events.

[33] This section is absent in the English translation of the *Bhaktavijaya*. A small section from the second part: tells about another Rāmdās, Kṛṣṇa's devotee from Dakur (Abbot and Godbole 1988, Vol. II: 1–6).

sacred places could be compared to the persistence of hagiographers of multiple saints in going into details about the personal (friendly) contacts of great *bhaktas* with each other or with other famous historical characters from different epochs and regions. Thus the absolute importance of the genre for the reconstruction of core values characteristic of pre-colonial Indian society (Vanina, this volume) and for an idea of the dynamics of their formation. The further a hagiographer strayed chronologically from the hero of his account, the more sacred places he included in the itinerary of the main character. Later this device was used by modern promoters of both traditions, who said the statements that Tukārām stayed at home were myths invented by his ill-wishers and introduced more and more details about Rāmdās's twelve-year wanderings.

Tīrthā-Yātrā as the Highest Value

As it happens, *sant* poetry (in Maharashtra and outside) is saturated with disparities of the kind mentioned above, and the hagiographies are full of illogical treatment of the subject of pilgrimage. It is this situation that might have caused Bharati to make the statement quoted at the beginning of this essay. If the medieval poets' minds seem to have been divided between a traditional prescription of movement to sacred places and an understanding of the futility of various ritualistic contrivances, in the beginning of the twenty-first century their alleged movements along the Hindustan peninsula are not questioned any more but taken for granted. The creation of this 'reality' allows Novetzke to speak of the efforts of nationalist politicians and historians who, for instance, allot to Nāmdev the function of pan-Indian integration because his 'perambulations [are] imagined as a boundary; the areas through which he is said to have travelled thus circumscribe the boundaries of the modern Indian nation – to his followers, a map of India to come' (Novetzke 2003: 290–91, 304).

Modern propagandists of the five saint-poets in India and/or scholars who might also belong to the same devotionalist trend as a poet they write about, are usually not content to advocate the verity of prolonged *tīrtha-yātrās* of the Marathi *sants*, but by elaborating concrete details do their bit to (re)construct the pilgrimage theme in general. Popular books of biography printed in large fonts and decorated with drawings usually include a separate chapter entitled *Tīrtha-yātrā.* Normally it talks about a collective pilgrimage made by ideologically related *sants*, 'Visoba Khechara, Goroba Kumbhar, Sawata Mali, Chokhamela and Bamka were among the saints who accompanied them [i.e. Dnyaneshwar and Nama Deva]' (Khanolkar 1990: 43). This kind of writing also attempts to explain what caused the main character to go on *tīrtha-yātrā.* R.R. Gosavi and V.R. Gosavi (1997: 91–92) hold the opinion that pilgrimage was an important stage in the life of Dñyāndev 'because the best Maharashtrian saints from the "eighteen-turbans castes" [decided to] join him. He himself dreamed of spreading an ideal of spiritual equality all over India. Undoubtedly, there was a need to beat the drums of *bhakti* everywhere, but he clearly intended to show all strata of the society how to achieve the ideal. Otherwise why would Dñyāneśvar, who said, "One should not stick to vows / [and] get one's body exhausted / One should not go long distances visiting *tīrthas*', himself go on pilgrimage?. Further, taking advantage of some data from the bibliographical *Tīrthāvaḷī*, these scholars recreate the atmosphere of the collective pilgrimage of Dñyāndev, Nāmdev, Narharī Sonār, Cokhāmelā, Gorā Kumbhār, Viṣobā Khechar, Savtā Mālī, Senā Nhavī and other great *sants* – 'filling the air with the non-stop recital of the [God's] name', 'embracing each other', etc., they tell us about the bliss of the *sants*' meetings and specify their itinerary: Prayag, Kashi, Gaya, Ayodhya, Gokul, Vrindavan, Dvarka, Girnar' (ibid.: 92). 'During his youth, he [Namdev] went on two pilgrimages to the Indian north. The first pilgrimage lasted from 1293 to 1295 (or took place sometime between the two dates), and Namdev was accompanied by Dñyāneśvar and other Maharashtrian *sants*. The second journey took place around 1336. Both times, while moving across northern India, Namdev visited Gujarat, Rajasthan, and Panjab . . .' (Javarkar 1994: 21).

The propagation of this idea has long since crossed the limits of Marathi-language works, and has become an intrinsic part of English and regional-language treatments, spreading the message all over India: 'Jnanadeva took Namadeva with him and travelled up to Banaras visiting all the holy places in the Northern India and all the country resounded with their sweet kirtans' (Bahirat 1984: 14). 'Dnyanadeo went on a pilgrimage to Banaras as a part of his apostolic mission. He was accompanied by a number of his admirers prominent among whom was the Saint Namdeo. On his way he held meetings which were attended by thousands of men and women. The pilgrimage over, Dnyanadeo considered his life's mission fulfilled and made preparations for its voluntary renunciation' (Dandekar 1969: 9).

In the Marathi biography of Eknāth by Gosavi and Gosavi quoted above, the two authors, seeking an acceptable explanation of the contradictions ask: 'What need was there to go on pilgrimage after God's revelation (*sākṣātkār, darśan*)? Naturally, everybody will ask himself this question as [it is known that] movement towards sacred places and other obligatory actions are performed for accumulation of merit. At least, this is a traditional idea, but it is wrong. Life stories of sants who got revelation give testimony in this respect. They all set off for pilgrimage after they had the revelation. . . . The real reason for this was the realization that God, who manifested himself in the image of the whole world (*viśvarūp nārāyaṇ*), dwells everywhere, in each and every creature, and this realization formed the base of the revelation'. To find substantiation in concrete experience, 'they wandered for a while under the pretext of tirtha-yatra, and that goal made Janardan guide Eknāth to go on pilgrimage' (Gosavi and Gosavi 1998: 58–59). 'A sprout cannot shoot up if it grows under a tree' or one's personality stops developing when one stays in the same place. 'That is why Janaradan sent Eknāth to have a look at various tirthas, and . . . to spread the Bhagavata dharma.' Contemporary authors make Eknāth, too, pursue an 'integrating itinerary' – from Badrīnāth–Uttarmānas in the north to Rameshvaram in the south. They break their own logic of philosophical reasoning and reinvent Janārdan's instructions: 'Come back famous!' (Gosavi and Gosavi 1998: 68–69).

Each and every popular writing or research scholarship related to Rāmdās generally refers to the data collected by Dev and the interpretation in the Introduction to Giridhar-swāmī's three-volume biography of Rāmdās (Dev 1912; 1944; 1998). Dev elaborated on the pilgrimage theme in two chapters of his own version of Rāmdās's biography. The seventh and ninth chapters, called 'Tirtha-yatra: Northwards (1632–1639)' and 'Tirtha-yatra: Southwards (1640–1644)' contain several extracts from the *Dāsbodh*, a few 'spontaneous' poems of Rāmdās, and some extracts from Giridhar's and later Rāmdās's hagiographies, which generously expand the earlier versions. Generous quotation alternates with Dev's comments that the twelve-year period from age twenty-four to thirty-six was the most important in terms of forming Rāmdās's world view. At the same time he regrets that there is no trustworthy information on this period. 'Nobody has ever written a word, and if anybody has written down where, when, and with whom he was, what did he do, whether there was anyone at his side or not, and what his daily practice was – it has not yet been found' (Dev 1998: 83).

This accurate observation did not prevent Dev from freely interpreting various statements by Rāmdās as indications of journeys around sacred places outside Maharashtra. That is how, for example, a poem entitled *Tīrthāvaḷī daṇḍīgāṇe* (Songs [accompanied by a stringed musical instrument] *dandi* [to be sung] during pilgrimage) found its way into the chapter on visiting northern *tīrtha*s. This poem praises the main features of various sacred places of pan-Indian significance both in the north and in the south, but does not arrange them in a logical or geographical sequence. This is also the case with two other poems mentioned above – to distinguish among the three, Dev calls them a song, an *abhaṅg*, and a *pad* respectively – that enumerate *tīrtha*s almost everywhere in India and the gods of these *tīrtha*s. Dev prefaces his edition by confessing: 'I think they enumerate the tirthas visited by him [Ramdas]'. He indicates that the song uses the word '*pohā*', referring to 'a group of pilgrims' of which Rāmdās could be a member. Another word, *pāhile*, the past tense of the verb 'to see', might be taken as testimony that Rāmdās based the description on his own visual experience. It is not clear though why Dev resorts to '*pohā*' in particular, leaving aside '*yātrā*' or '*samudāv*', both of which have the same meaning. He also ignores the general usage of third-person plural verb forms, like 'people go' or 'take darshan'. Dev uses equally, with other kinds of evidence, legends from various sources, including stories of the god Rāma presenting Rāmdās with warm clothes in the Himalayas and stopping him from jumping into a well. The latter story is found in the *Samarthapratāp* by Giridhar, and includes an *ovī* that quotes Rāma as saying: 'During two [periods of] of twelve years I was taking care of your body because of [your duty] to restore dharma' (*donī tape tumcī rakṣilī kāyā he / dharmasthāpṇekārṇe*) (Dev 1912: 92). This statement specifies two periods of twelve years that are invoked not for calculation but as a unit of folklore time used to distinguish different stages in Rāmdās's life – a static stage of study and austerities at a particular place (Takli) and a dynamic stage of movement among various unnamed places (compare with the twelve-year absence of Eknāth).[34] In the chapter on the south as well, Dev interprets a number of extracts from *abhaṅgs*, connecting their meanings to various sacred places but also commenting, 'It is impossible to specify which mountains are spoken about here – the Himalayas or the Vindhyas, the Satpudas or the Sahyadris. But are there other personalities who overcome so many hardships for the sake of their country and *dharma*, for the sake of the divine grace and world salvation?' (Dev 1998: 114).

Thus, it is not surprising that henceforth nobody feels obliged to search for evidence but just reiterates what has become generally accepted. For example, in the *Śrīsamarthacaritrāmṛt*, V.D. Palnitkar not only mentions *tīrtha-yātrās* – both northern and southern – but also rediscovers additional details and beautifies these pilgrimages with stories of wonders extracted from various sources. For example, he reminds his readers that a priest of the Viśveśvar temple in Kashi did not allow Rāmdās to enter, and then found that the *śivaliṅgam* had disappeared. Simultaneously he heard Śiva's order; 'Bring back the person you have just driven away and submit to him'. Rāmdās was allowed to pay his respects to Viśveśwar and, eventually, he established the image of Māruti at Hanumān-*ghāṭ* on the bank of the Ganga; he also listened to the *Ayodhyā-māhātmya* in Ayodhya, visited Gokul, Vrindavan and Dvarka, and then Badrīnārāyaṇ and Badrīkedārī in the Himalayas, and took *darśan* of 'White Māruti', who presented him with warm clothes. Rāmdās also initiated many pupils, founded monasteries (*maṭhs*) in various locations, and nominated his disciples as their heads (Palnitkar 1957: 28). He made it to Rameshvaram in the south, and from there was brought by Māruti to Lanka, to the realm of the king Vibhīṣaṇa of the *Rāmāyaṇa*. The latter reminded him that Dñyāneśvar and Nāmdev had already visited this island and made everybody happy by performing *kīrtans*. When Vibhīṣaṇa asked Rāmdās to do the same, the poet felt obliged to meet the king's request and stayed on in Lanka for two months (Palnitkar 1957: 28–29).

V.P. Bokil affirms (1979: 76–97) that the alleged pilgrimage of Rāmdās corresponds to established norms, as manifested earlier by the wanderings of Rāma after he had completed his studies at the abode of the sage Vasiṣṭha, or by the journey throughout the whole country by the early medieval philosopher Śaṅkarācārya; Bokil also mentions the examples set by Dñyāneśvar and Eknāth. Drawing from biographies composed within the Rāmdāsī fold, Bokil states that Rāmdās visited 1028 sacred places: 'The places visited by Ramdas during the pilgrimage have been taken from three poems composed by him, in one of which the word "seen" is used. Some non-believers, however, say that he might not have

[34] 'Twelve years' as 'a next period in turn' are usually invoked at a breach of plot linearity, i.e. when one episode ends and the next, not caused by the previous one, starts. 'Twelve years' might be used to mark the transition from one age group into another. In such cases the function of this number gets more complicated as it also signifies the end of a fairy-tale static phase and the beginning of a dynamic development (Glushkova 1979: 67). In relation to Rāmdās, 'dynamics' can be linked to the beginning of his propagatory activity in Maharashtra.

visited all [of them]'. But the version used here is that of the traditional biographers (Bokil 1979: 79). Contrary to Bokil and the like, other scholars are more reserved about the *tīrtha-yātrā* of Rāmdās, and do not go into details. For example, V.S. Deming deals with this theme in one page (Deming 1990: 33–34), and S. Khanolkar has taken recourse to a condensed cliché accepted by general opinion: 'From 1632, Ramdasa spent another 12 years visiting *tirthas*. He prayed before the 12 Jyotirlingas, resided in the seven eternal cities and reached the four Maths at the confines of Bharata'. He adds, 'The precarious state of the religious *tirthas* constantly under threat of pillage and desecration and the floods of forcible conversions appalled him, and he began to see Hinduism as being in danger of extinction' (Khanolkar 1990: 162–63).

It is in this way that details with potential reference to pilgrimage began to be manipulated and *tīrtha-yātrā* came to be perceived as the highest value. Thus the belief that saint-poets went on pilgrimage became predominant, and movement between *tīrthas*, though not supported by solid evidence, came to be a predictable element in religious biography and a part and parcel of sainthood! It became, to use S. Gordon's expression, 'a single unified way to establish the truth about the past' (this volume).

Western scholars prefer to build their deductions on the basis of anti-pilgrimage utterances of saint-poets. In the introduction to *The Sants* volume K. Schomer writes that the *sants* rejected the outer forms of Vaiṣṇava practice but shared the 'Vaishnava belief in the saving power of the divine Name and the spiritual benefit of keeping company with true devotees' (Schomer 1987: 9). Vaudeville, who reflects the Western understanding of *bhakti* being in contrast with orthodox Hinduism, makes a similar point: 'Association with true Sants is often compared to pilgrimage to the Hindu *tīrthas* accompanied with a purificatory bath: the Sants themselves stand as the true *tīrthas*. This belief is common to the Sants and to Hindus in general though the northern Sants do not countenance the common Hindu practice of *tīrtha-yātrā*' (Vaudeville 1987: 35).

However, E. Zelliot takes the saints' pilgrimage for granted and draws our attention to a different aspect – Maharashtra's bent for north-Indian stereotypes: 'The connection between the Marathi-speaking area and the north seems to have been strong at this time. Eknāth had made the pilgrimage to the north evidently expected of the devout, and in the words of the eighteenth-century biographer of all the Sants, Mahipati, "Thus having visited the northern *tīrthas* thoroughly, and having seen the twelve chief Shiva shrines, and the seven chief cities, he danced in the fulness of his joy"' (Zelliot 1987: 94–95). This bent, as expressed by the equation, comparison and affirmation of the superiority of Maharashtrian sacred places over northern (rarely, southern) ones, is almost algebraically proved by A. Feldhaus (2003: 157–84). And Novetzke, without taking sides stresses the integrating functions of Nāmdev's pilgrimage as described in both 'autobiographical' *Tīrthāvaḷīs* and carried out within the borders of today's India. It has 'organizational, physical, and architectural presentation in the many societies that exist in cities, large and small, as well as in the form of temples, shrines, and other memorials to Nāmdev that dot the landscapes of Maharashtra, Gujarat, Rajasthan, Himachal Pradesh, Uttar Pradesh, Bihar, and Punjab' (Novetzke 2003: 24).

The Art of Interpretation

To sum up, the poems of medieval *bhaktas* do not give us a straightforward answer regarding the institution of pilgrimage. Followers of either saint-poet do not feel confused by this fact, and, to appear sensible, suggest distinguishing between the various stages of maturity of these renowned personalities by arranging their utterances into seemingly coherent sequences. The explanation for the purificatory impact of a *sant* upon *tīrthas* is neither new nor original: the idea of spiritual authorities exercising this power is pertinent to traditional Hindu texts, along with the idea of the possibility of *tīrthas*' going towards the embodiment of higher merit. Thus, in Śrīdhar's popular Marathi version of the *Padma-purāṇa*, Puṇḍarīka (Puṇḍalīka)[35] stopped at the abode of the sage Kukutta on the way to Kashi. At night Puṇḍalīka saw three rivers, the Ganga, the Yamuna, and the Vāgīśa (Saraswati) arriving at the sage's place to be purified from the world's pollution that they had absorbed (Sand 1990: 52). In the *bhakti* version, Puṇḍalīka stops at the place of Rohīdās, a north-Indian cobbler, and observes the Ganga and the Yamuna sweeping his courtyard (Feldhaus 1995: 62).

As mentioned above, detached observers did not fail to notice the contradictions. Efforts were made and hypotheses were framed to seek a solution. Speaking of the antinomy of Tukārām's thoughts, M. Mitchell saw the reconciliation of mutually opposed statements in their unification in the form of 'ultimate truth' (Mitchell 1982: 58). However, given the present-day realization of the impact of Orientalist pressure in the epistemology of the Orient, one should not overlook the resistance of European thought, which is guided by the principle of non-contradiction: no thing or event can be ascribed a quality and its opposite at the same time. Nevertheless, Vārkarīs do not feel misguided by the jet-black colour of Viṭṭhal, who is still called 'Pāṇḍuraṅga', or of pale colour; or by the fact that a Viṣṇuite god is decorated with headgear resembling a *śivaliṅgam*. No Vārkarī is perplexed that both Dñyāneśvar and Nāmdev acknowledged as their guru a representative of the Śaivite Nāth tradition while the guru of Eknāth was a ṣūfī or a Datta Sampradāy follower. Nobody finds it strange that Dñyāneśvar and Nāmdev set off in the direction of Dvarka, the very place that their favourite god Viṭṭhal, who resides permanently in Pandharpur, hails from. And why should one think of 'seven cities' granting salvation if the ideal of *mokṣa* prevents a *bhakta* from a new meeting with his beloved god?

Nowadays, Vārkarīs display a wide range of theological tolerance: en route to Pandhapur for a reunion with Viṭṭhal, they do not fail to make a detour to visit Shri Shikharshingapur for the *darśan* of Śambhū-Mahādev; they also combine devotion to a *saguṇ*, i.e. in possession of qualities, form of god, with the ideal of

[35] The Vārkārī tradition holds that it was Puṇḍalīka who was responsible for Viṭṭhal-Krishna's appearance in Pandharpur.

a *nirguṇ* form, and so on. V. Lamshukov discovered in such antimonies the relativistic principle of the 'mobile perspective', a kind of motley ethnic and social 'cultural integrator' meaning that Hindu consciousness, being less dogmatic than is usually believed, can change the angle of vision in accordance with the urge of the moment (Lamshukov 1989). Kiehnle, while not dismissing the fact that poetic texts composed by different authors in different times are brought together under the name of Dñyāneśvar, reveals through evidence of textual disparity the multilayered structure and heterogeneity of the context, which had lost its clarity for later generations (Kiehnle 1997a; 1997b). In terms of various genres, S. Gordon speaks in this volume of several distinguishable 'epistemologies' of the past operating simultaneously in Maharashtra in the seventeenth and eighteenth centuries. If applied to the subject of this paper, these various epistemologies do operate in various genres, even within the frame of one genre with the 'angle of vision' changing according to the requirements of either orthopraxy or orthodoxy.

In their turn, the hagiographies drawing from various sources created norms to be followed and made every effort to send saint-poets (even resisting their lack of interest, as in the case of Nāmdev and Eknāth) on prolonged wanderings between *tīrthas*. Later, the majority of Indian scholars of these saint-poets took this construction for granted. In the absence of authentic information, it is easier to assert the pilgrimage element and to ignore the anti-pilgrimage mindset of some of the saint-poets. Contrary to Viṭṭhalpant of Nāmdev's 'biographical' *Tīrthāvaḷī*, the father of Dñyāneśvar, who, following the classical epic model, began his pilgrimage from Pushkar lake, the saint-poets moved absolutely chaotically: the narratives bring into proximity Ayodhya, Badrinath and Pushkar, or Kashi, Kanti, Kolhapur, and Kashmir, or Ayodhya, Kashi, Kolhapur and Mathura, and so on. The imagined details of the wanderings became widely known only in the twentieth century, when the advent of low-cost book-printing facilities resulted in mass produced editions.

However, brought together, these details reveal a mysterious similarity: it looks as if *sants* were sent on pilgrimage only *post factum*, i.e. by the invention of later generations. The fact that all versions of any of Nāmdev's *Tīrthāvaḷī* are unmistakably late testifies to this assumption, as does the complete lack of information on saint-poets' *tīrtha-yātrās* in the earlier hagiographies (of Eknāth, for instance) or even the first works of Mahīpati, who, as a matter of fact, sent neither Tukārām nor Rāmdās on pilgrimage. The pilgrimage motif, containing as a rule a reference to Kashi, emerges precisely at the very end of some series of poems, and the presence of such *abhaṅgs* in some editions alternates with their absence in others. This is the case of the three final *abhaṅgs* attached to the 'biographical' *Tīrthāvaḷī*, which do not correspond in style or meaning to the main text; this is also the case of the last, twenty-fourth *abhaṅg* from the *Niryan* series of Tukārām. Even the *Nāmdev mahimā* by Eknāth contains a mention of Kashi, if only in the concluding part of the last *abhaṅg*! Interestingly, rare external evidence that *sants* did leave Maharashtra is available in the *Mahakāvatīcī bakhar*, which mentions Nāmdev's visit to the same Kashi, and the *Ānandavanbhuvan* of Rāmdās is identified with Kashi because it would have been strange to overlook this opportunity. Finally, there emerges 'material' evidence of dislocations: for example, D. Chauhan discovered at a Kashi monastery a column that bears the name of Dñyāneśvar and the date of his visit to this sacred city.[36]

If the remark of A. Blasi that 'Medieval pilgrimages began with an individual state of *anomia*' (Blasi 2002: 160) – i.e. a breach of harmony resulting from deviation from traditional behavioural norms – is applied to medieval Indian *bhaktas*, the anomia would have been noticed first by the norm-makers and preservers, the Brāhmaṇas. That the saint-poets (with the exception of Rāmdās, who also broke some norms) were in one or another way harassed by Brāhmaṇas is a fact recorded both in the lyrics and in their hagiographies, compiled, normally, by the Brāhmaṇas. The latter not only responded to new parameters of behaviour established by charismatic personalities, but were guided by values accepted within their fold, including ritual visits to pan-Indian *tīrthas*. Hence anyone who was becoming, due to his own popularity, an ideal to be followed should adopt a prescribed itinerary. Anyone who tried to compile a life-account had as an objective 'to disseminate the ideas of *bhakti* and to set a moral pattern of behaviour for all who adhered to this doctrine and even those who did not, including the foolish and the vicious' (Vanina, this volume). He was also obliged to encourage his audience to go on pilgrimage.

As G.D. Khanolkar states, 'Mahipati was an expert in picking out those events which would make readers happy and would serve for strengthening of the Bhagavata dharma' (Khanolkar 1977: 238). The events mentioned might be nothing but stories of pilgrimages. Albeit some sections of society could think differently – as is seen for example in a usage peculiar to Marathi: 'Visit Benares thrice, say our Maratha people, "and you become a thorough scoundrel"' (Mitchell 1882: [Pandharpur] 152). Marathi speakers also use the term *tristhalī*/*tirsthaḷī* (pilgrimage to the three holy places, viz. Kashi, Prayag, and Gaya) in the sense of 'vexatious or vain journeying from place to place; running hither and thither on fruitless errands etc.' (Molesworth 1975: 381).[37]

Many questions that engaged scholars in their study of saint-literature and were considered to be of primary importance once, have gradually fallen into oblivion. This happened not because the questions have been satisfactorily resolved

[36] Cited in Pendse (1972: 384); see also Khanolkar (1977: 160). It is worth mentioning that S.D. Pendse treats this information critically, and picks up contradictions in D.V. Chauhan's arguments presented in his article *Dñyānobā śake 1216 Kāśī yātrā Kelī* (Dnyanoba Went on Pilgrimage to Kashi in Shake 1216 [1294]). For example, the house of the *maṭh*'s owner was built on land purchased in the reign of Aurangzeb (the middle of the seventeenth century). At the same time Chauhan does not inform us whether the name and date are painted or engraved. Notwithstanding this disparity Khanolkar takes this information for granted and uses the word 'engraved' (*korlelī*) while introducing it into the *Dictionary of Marathi Literature*.

[37] There are other proverbs and sayings on pilgrimage available in Date and Karve (1942: 289–90).

but because by the beginning of the twenty-first century they no longer seem to be urgent given the new realities. For example, inclusion of both 'biographical' (with no indication of actual movement) and 'autobiographical' (filled with enumeration of numerous toponyms) *Tīrthāvaḷīs* in the state-sponsored edition of Nāmdev's works, published on the occasion of his birth-septecentenary, signifies a politico-administrative intervention exercised with the help of printing facilities. The same may be said about the ambitious volume titled *Śrīnāmdevdarśan,* published on the same occasion by Relekar, Inamdar and Mirajkar: the fly-leaf of this volume has a map showing Nāmdev's movements around India. This is also the case with the state-sponsored and 'family' (i.e. published in Dehu) editions of Tukārām, with the twenty-fourth *abhaṅg,* which talks about Tukārām's safe arrival at Kashi, included in both volumes.

Monumental corroboration of the thesis that some important issues related to saint-poets have been lost is found in a grandiose work of sculpture erected on the outskirts of Pune in 2000. The sculpture depicts a meeting between Tukārām and Shivaji, 'a union of *bhakti* and *shakti*' – its very construction seems to annihilate any discussion about whether this meeting ever took place at all. The saint-poets have become cultural symbols of the Marathi-speaking region and as such are insured against any doubt regarding their life and creative activity; simultaneously, academic verification has been confronted by political correctness and the hyper-sensitivity of various social groups.[38] Nowadays, distrust regarding the claim that the author of the *Dñyāneśvarī* (which does not mention the god of Pandharpur), also wrote the *abhaṅgs* praising Viṭṭhal that are ascribed to Dñyāneśvar, is not verbalized much; works treating the problem of authorship might draw public rather than scholarly attention and cause undesirable agitation. The fact that there are two *samadhīs* of Nāmdev – one in Maharashtra and the other in Punjab – is taken for granted, and the different versions of the *Tīrthāvaḷī* are used to substantiate both Nāmdev's importance in the Vārkarī tradition and his role as a propagator of *bhakti* at the pan-Indian level. Instead of the kind of discussion of the authorship of the *Dāsbodh* that used to take place in the beginning of the twentieth century (Deming 1990: 142–44), the twenty-first century faces the recital of verses of the *Dāsbodh* at sessions of hobby groups. At the same time, the *Ānandavanbhuvan* has become accepted as a prophetic dream seen by Rāmdās during his stay in Kashi at the time of his twelve years of wanderings among the sacred places; these years, along with multiple miracles that he is said to have performed, form the core of the Rāmdāsī tradition. Thus the pilgrimage theme has found a stable place in both traditions and keeps influencing the adepts and scholars of both.

[38] With this background it would not have been very surprising to come across another sculpture, for example, depicting a meeting between Rāmdās and Vibhīṣaṇa in Lanka. This is not very likely, however, given present trends in Marathi-speaking society.

Acknowledgement

I owe many thanks to Anne Feldhaus who generously commented upon and edited this paper on my request. Some of her comments are presented in the footnotes.

References

Abbot, J.E. (1932), *Ramdās, Translation of Mahīpati's Santavijaya* (Poona: N.R. Godbole).

——— (1983), *The Life of Eknāth. Śrī Eknāth Charita. Translated from the Bhaktalīlāmṛta* (Delhi: Motilal Banrsidass).

Abbot, J.E. and N.R. Godbole (1988), *Stories of Indian Saints. Translations of Mahipati's Marathi Bhaktavijaya* (Delhi: Motilal Banarsidass) (reprint).

Akkole, S.T. (1970), 'Nāmdevkṛt santcaritre', in N.N. Relekar, H.V. Inamdar and N.D. Mirajkar, (eds), *Śrīnāmdevdarśan* (Kolhapur: Namdev Samajonnati Parishad Prakashan).

Bahirat, B.P. (1984), *The Philosophy of Jñānadeva* (Delhi: Motilal Banarsidass).

Bartakke, M.G. (1970), 'Śikhāñcyā ādigranthātīl nāmdev', in N.N. Relekar, H.V. Inamdar, and N.D. Mirajkar, *Śrīnāmdevdarśan* (Kolhapur: Namdev Samajonnati Parishad Prakashan).

Bharati, A. (1963), 'Pilgrimage in the Indian Tradition', *History of Religions*, Vol. 3, No. 1, pp. 135–67.

Bhardwaj, S.M. (1983), *Hindu Places of Pilgrimage in India. A Study in Cultural Geography* (Berkeley: University of California Press).

Belsare, K.V., ed. (1981), *Sārth śrīdāsbodh* (Pune: Pracharya Dandekar Dharmik, Samskrutik va Shaikshnik Vanmay Prakashan Mandal).

Blasi, A.J. (2002), 'Visitation to Disaster Sites', in W.H. Swatos and L. Tomasi (eds), *From Medieval Pilgrimage to Religious Tourism: The Social and Cultural Economics of Piety* (Westport: Praeger).

Bokil, V.P. (1979), *Rajguru Ramdas* (Poona: Master Kamalesh P. Bokil).

Dandekar, S.V. (1969), *Dnyanadeo* (New Delhi: Maharashtra Information Centre).

Date, Y.R. and C.G. Karve (1942), *Mahārāṣṭra Vāksampradāy Koś*, Vol. I. (Pune: Prasad Prakashan).

Deming, W.S. (1990), *Ramdas and the Ramdasis* (Gurgaon: Vintage Books).

Deshmukh, M.G. (1970–71), 'Sant nāmdevāñce vyaktimattva', in *Sant Nāmdev: Sāt Vyākhyāne* (Kolhapur: Shivaji Vidyapith).

Deshmukh, Sh. M. (1970), 'Nāmdevāñce tīrthāṭan', in N.N. Relekar, H.V. Inamdar, and N.D. Mirajkar (eds), *Śrīnāmdevdarśan* (Kolhapur: Namdev Samajonnati Parishad Prakashan).

Deshpande, A.N. (1969), *Prācīn Marāṭhī Vāṅmayācā Itihās, Bhāg Dusrā* (Pune: Vhinas Prakashan).

——— (1977), *Prācīn Marāṭhī Vāṅmayācā Itihās, Bhāg Cauthā* (Pune: Vhinas Prakashan).

Dev, Sh. Sh., ed. (1912), *Śrī Rāmdās āṇi Rāmdāsī*, Bhāg 8: *Giridharsvāmī, Samarthapratāp* (Dhule: Satkaryottejak Sabha).

——— (1944), *Śrīsamartha-caritra, śrīsamartha-sampradāy. Tisrā Khaṇḍ* (Mumbai: Keshav Bhikaji Dhavle).

——— (1998), *Śrī Rāmdās āṇi Rāmdāsī*, Bhāg 121: *Śrīsamartha-caritra, Pratham Khaṇḍ* (Mumbai: Keshav Bhikaji Dhavle).

Dhere, R. Ch. (1969), *Santāñcyā Ātmakathā. Prācīn Marāṭhītīl Ātmakathānātmak Vāṅmayāce Darśan* (Pune: Puspak Prakasan).

——— and A.P. Kamat (1970), *Śrīnāmdev: Ek Vijayyātrā* (Pune: Vishvakarma Sahityalay).

——— (1977), 'Dñyāndevāñcī kulsvāminī' in *Śodhśilpa* (Pune: Vishvakarma Sahityalay).

——— (1990), *Śrīviṭṭhal: Ek Mahāsamanvay* (Pune: Shrividya Prakashan).

——— (1998), 'Santāñcī tīrthasaṅkalpnā', in *Sant, Lok āṇi Abhijan* (Pune: Padmagandha Prakashan).

Eck, D.L. (1981), 'India's *Tīrthas*: "Crossings" in Sacred Geography', *History of Religions*, Vol. 20, No. 4, pp. 323–44.

Feldhaus, A. (1995), *Water and Womanhood. Religious Meanings of Rivers in Maharashtra* (New York: Oxford University Press).

——— (2003), *Connected Places. Region, Pilgrimage, and Geographical Imagination in India* (New York: Palgrave Macmillan).

——— (n.d.), Place Rhetoric in the Poems of Vārkarī Poet-Saints (forthcoming).

Glushkova, I.P. (1979), 'Simvolika chisel sem' i dvenadtsat' v volshebnoy skazke hindi i marathi (Symbolics of numbers 'seven' and 'twelve' in Hindi and Marathi fairy-tales)', in V.I.

Semanov (ed.), *Literatura dvuh Kontinentov* (Moskva: Izdatel'stvo Moskovskogo universiteta).

——— (2000), *Indiyskoye palomnichestvo: metafora dvizheniya i dvizheniy metafori* [Indian Pilgrimage: the Metaphor of Motion and the Motion of Metaphor], (Moskva: Nauchniy Mir).

——— (2004), 'Moving God(s)ward: The Idea of *Tīrtha-yātrā*' in *Bulletin of the Deccan College Post-Graduate and Research Institute* (Deemed University), Professor Ashok R. Kelkar Felicitation Volume, Vols 62–63 (2002 and 2003).

——— (2006a), 'Moving God(s) ward, Calculating Money: Wonders and Wealth as Essentials of a *tīrtha-yātrā*' in *South Asia*, Vol. 29, No. 2, August, pp. 215–34.

——— (2006b), '*Tīrtha-yātrā* in Maharashtra: Recorded and Imagined', *Annals of the Bhandarkar Oriental Research Institute*, 2005, Vol. 86, pp. 179–201.

——— (2008), '*Mārg(a)kramaṇ* of Maharashtrian Princely Families: a Search for Self within the Boundaries Made for Others', in M. Naito, I. Shima and H. Kotani (eds), *Mārga: Ways to Liberation, Empowerment, and Social Change in Maharashtra* (New Delhi: Manohar).

Gosavi, R.R. and Gosavi, V.R. (1997), *Śrī dñyāneśvar caritra* (Pune: Sarthi Prakashan).

——— (1998), *Śrī eknāthmahārāj caritra* (Pune: Sarthi Prakashan).

Javarkar, P.V. (1994), 'Śrīmant Nāmdev caritra', in *Nāmyācī sārth abhaṅgvāṇī* (Amravati: Vaishnav Prakashan).

Jog, R.Sh., ed. (1973), *Marāṭhī vāṅmayācā itihās. Khaṇḍ tistrā* (Pune: Maharashtra Sahitya Parishad).

Jog, V.N. (1990), *Sārth Tukārāmācī Gāthā*, Parts 1 and 2 (Pune: Varda).

Joshi, K.A., ed. (1967), *Śrīsakalsantgāthā*, Vols. I and II (Pune: Shreesantvangmay Prakashan Mandir).

Kanade, M.Sh. (1970), 'Nāmdevāñcā jīvan-paṭ', in N.N. Relekar, H.V. Inamdar, and N.D. Mirajkar, (eds), *Śrīnāmdevdarśan* (Kolhapur: Namdev samajonnati parishad prakashan).

——— and R.Sh. Nagarkar (1996), *Śrīdñyāndevāñcā Sārth Cikitsak Gāthā* (Pune: Suvidya Prakashan).

Kane, P.V. (1953), *History of Dharmaśāstra (Ancient and Medieval Religious and Civil Law in India)*, Vol. IV (Poona: Bhandarkar Oriental Research Institute).

Kavitkar, G.V. (1970), 'Dñyāndīp lāvū jāgī', in N.N. Relekar, H.V. Inamdar and N.D. Mirajkar (ed.), *Śrīnāmdevdarśan* (Kolhapur: Namdev Samajonnati Parishad Prakashan).

——— (1970–71), 'Sant nāmdevāñce āntarbhāratīce ek darśan', in *Sant Nāmdev: Sāt Vyākhyāne* (Kolhapur: Shivaji Vidyapith).

Khanolkar, G.D., ed. (1977), *Marāṭhī Vāṅmaykoś. Khaṇḍ pahilā. Marāṭhī granthkār i.sa. 1050–1877* (Mumbai: Maharashtra Rajya Sahitya Samskruti Mandal).

Khanolkar, S. (1990), Saints of Maharashtra (Bombay: Bharatiya Vidya Bhavan).

Kiehnle, C. (1992), 'Authorship and Redactorship of the Jñāndev Gāthā', in R.S. McGregor (ed.), *Devotional Literature in South Asia, Current Research, 1985–1988* (Cambridge: Cambridge University Press).

——— (1997a), *Jñyāndev Studies I and II. Songs on Yoga. Texts and Teachings of the Maharashtrian Nāths.* Institut für Kultur und Geschichte Indiens und Tibets, an der Universität Hamburg, 48.1 (Stutgart: Franz Steiner).

——— (1997b), *Jñyāndev Studies III. The Conservative Vaiṣṇava. Anonymous Songs of the Jñyāndev Gāthā.* Institut für Kultur und Geschichte Indiens und Tibets an der Universität Hamburg, 48.2 (Stutgart: Franz Steiner).

Lamshukov, V.K. (1989), 'Printsip podvizhnoy perspektivi (A principle of mobile perspective)', in N.I. Prigarina and A.S. Sukhochev (eds), *Literaturi Indii* (Moskva: Nauka, GRVL).

Mate, S.M. (1957), 'Ānandvanbhuvan mhaṇje Vārāṇasī kī Mahārāṣṭra?', in *Sant, Pant, Tant* (Pune: Thokal Prakashan).

Molesworth, J.T. (1975), Preface: Dr. N.G. Kalelkar, *Molesworth's Marathi-English Dictionary* (Pune: Shubhada-Saraswat).

More, S. (1978), '"Namadeva's" *Tīrthāvaḷī* and the Vārkārī Tradition', in A.W. Entwistle and F. Mallison (eds), *Studies in South Asian Devotional Literature* (New Delhi: Manohar).

Murray, Mitchell, J. (1982), 'Tukārām', *The Indian Antiquary, A Journal of Oriental Research*, Vol. 2, pp. 57–66.

Neurgavkar, S.K. (1978), *Śrītukārām Mahārājāñcī Sārth Gāthā* (Pune: Pracharya Dandekar va Samskrutik Vanmay Prakasan Mandal).

Novetzke, C.L. (2003), *The Tongue Makes a Good Book: History, Religion, and Performance in the Namdev Tradition in Maharashtra*, PhD Thesis, Columbia University.

——— (2004), 'A Family Affair', in G. Beck (ed.), *Alternative Krishnas* (Albany: State University of New York Press).

Pangarkar, L.R. (n.d.), *Śrīdñyāneśvar mahārāj. Caritra āṇi granth vivecan* (Mumbai: Sumangal).

——— (1989), *Śrīsamartha Granth Bhāṇḍār* (Pune: Keshav Bhikaji Dhavle).

Palnitkar, V.D. (1957), *Śrīasamarthacaritrāmṛt, Sajjangad* (Satara: Shrisamartha Seva Mandal).

Pendse, S.D. (1972), *Mahārāṣṭrācā bhāgavatdharma, Dñyāndev āṇi nāmdev* (Pune: Continental Prakashan).

——— (1980), *Mahārāṣṭrācā bhāgavatdharma. Rājguru Samartha Rāmdās* (Pune: Continental Prakashan).

Raeside, I.M.P. (1965), 'The Pāṇḍūraṅga-Māhātmya of Śrīdhar', *Bulletin of the School of Oriental and African Studies*, University of London, Vol. 28, No. 1, pp. 81–100.

Rajvade, V.K. (1923), *Kesavācāryādikṛt Mahikāvatīcī ūrf Māhīmcī Bakhar* (Pune: Chitrashala Press).

——— L. Joshi, ed. (1967), *Rājvāḍe Lekh-Saṅgrah* (Mumbai: Sahitya Academy/Popular Prakashan).

Relekar, N.N., H.V. Inamdar and N.D. Mirajkar (1970), *Śrīnāmdevdarśan* (Kolhapur: Namdev Samajonnati Parishad Prakashan).

Sand, E.R. (1990), 'The Legend of Puṇḍarīka: The Founder of Pandharpur', in H. Bakker (ed.), *The History of Sacred Places as Reflected in Traditional Literature: Papers on Pilgrimage in South Asia* (Leiden: E.J. Brill).

——— (1992), 'The Bhīmāmāhātmya: A hitherto Unpublished Source for the Study of Pandharpur' *Acta Orientalia*, Vol. 53, pp. 86–105.

Schomer, K. (1987), 'Introduction. The Sant Tradition in Perspective', in K. Schomer, and W.H. McLeod (eds), *The Sants. Studies in a Devotional Tradition of India* (Delhi: Motilal Banarsidass).

Tukārām (1928), *Śrī Tukārāmmahārājāñcī Sāmpradāyik Gāthā* (Pune: Aryabhushan Press).

——— (1950), *Śrī tukārāmbāvāñcyā Abhaṅgācī Gāthā, Bhāg pahilā, bhāg dusrā* (Mumbai: Government Central Press).

——— (2001), *Jagadguru Santṣreṣṭha Srī Tukārām Mahārāj Yāñcyā Abhaṅgāñcā Gatha* (Dehu: Shri Vithoba-Rakhumai devsthan samsthan).

Vaudeville, Ch. (1987), 'Sant Mat: Santism as the universal path to sanctity', in K. Schomer and W.H. McLeod (eds), *The Sants. Studies in a Devotional Tradition of India* (Delhi: Motilal Banarsidass).

Zelliot, E. (1987), 'Eknath's *Bhāruḍs*: The Sant as link between cultures', in K. Schomer and W.H. McLeod (eds), *The Sants. Studies in a Devotional Tradition of India* (Delhi: Motilal Banarsidass).

Hierarchization of Attachments

Gender Differentiation or Gender Parity

The Puranic Evidence
(A Study based mainly on Matsya and Mārkaṇḍeya Purana)

Vijay Nath

Gender differentiation is structurally inbuilt into a patriarchal social order and there can only be variations in the degree and extent to which women are subjected to male dominance. This would depend largely on the level of material culture reached by that society. The more it outgrows its subsistence character and acquires a surplus base that gives less scope to women (especially those belonging to the upper stratum) to participate in economic activities, combined with the growing importance of issues such as the inheritance of landed property, gender differentiation will grow; women will become increasingly marginalized and excluded from important areas and sources of power, including rights to education and property. This is borne out in the case of the early Brāhmaṇical society of Dharmasūtra and early Smṛti texts, which are generally assigned to the period spanning the later part of the first millennium BC and the opening centuries of the Christian era.

However, the society revealed by the Purāṇas (composed over a period of almost a thousand years beginning around the second quarter of the first millennium) is found to be heterogeneous in more than one way. Besides cultural and ethnic diversity, it was also marked by sectarian plurality. It was a society in which Brāhmaṇas continued to represent the dominant category of religious ideologues, but had to make major compromises due to significant changes taking place in material culture that directly affected social structure and polity during this period. The authors of the Purāṇas are found to adopt a more liberal stance towards the marginalized sections of society, especially women and Śūdras, who had by then been clubbed together to an extraordinary degree. As a genre of literature the Purāṇas are stated to be composed chiefly for the edification of these two segments of society. According to a verse of the *Devī Bhāgavat Purāṇa* (I.3.21), since women and Śūdras are denied access to the Vedas, the Purāṇas have been composed especially for their benefit.

This study is based on two major Purāṇas, the *Matsya* and the *Mārkaṇḍeya Purāṇa*. The date of composition of the *Matsya Purāṇa* is between AD 200 and 400 according to P.V. Kane (1958: 852) and between the fourth and eleventh century according to R.C. Hazra ([1940] 1975: 50). The *Mārkaṇḍeya Purāṇa* is ascribed to a date not later than AD 600 by Kane (1958: 903) and to 500 AD by Hazra

([1940] 1975: 12). Both Purāṇas are believed to have been composed in the western Deccan (ibid. [1940] 1975: 52; *Mārkaṇḍeya Purāṇa*: viii–ix) and reflect conditions prevailing in that region during early medieval times.

A significant development that would seem to have had considerable bearing on gender equations as reflected in the Purāṇas was the unprecedented growth and popularity gained by the Śakti cult. Whereas in the preceding period the female principle in her manifestation as Sarasvatī, Lakṣmī and Pārvatī, the divine consorts of Brahmā, Viṣṇu and Śiva respectively, had remained essentially subservient to the dominant male triad, through the Purāṇas the cult centering on the Devī not only emerged as an independent and potential rival of most existent sects, but also came to permeate them via Tāntric beliefs. The *Mārkaṇḍeya Purāṇa*, in fact, contains an entire section styled the *Devī-mahātmya* (chapters 78–90), which is regarded by Barth (1963: 197) as the 'principal sacred text of the worshippers of Durgā in northern India'. Besides focusing on the origin and exploits of Devī, it also lists the innumerable names and epithets with which she came to be designated and the variety of attributes and functions with which she was associated. Accounting for the origin of Devī in her aspect of Durgā Mahiṣāsuramardinī, it relates how the gods, feeling threatened by the great demon Mahiṣāsura, approached the three great Gods, but that the latter were unable to rescue them on their own and decided to merge their respective powers to create the great Goddess Durgā. The latter, fully armed with every possible divine weapon and mounted on a lion, succeeded in rescuing the gods by completely vanquishing the great demon. The latter perhaps represented some Buffalo-totem cult that outgrew its tribal roots and gained wider popularity and posed a threat to some of the established religious cults of the time (Rao 1968: 354). It is significant to note that in the Mahiṣāsuramardinī myth, whatever the contribution of the male principle in her initial empowerment, once invested with power Durgā emerged as a mighty deity in the Purāṇic pantheon, not only challenging male dominance but also appropriating the powers and functions of the male triad. According to the *Devī-mahātmya* (*Mārkaṇḍeya Purāṇa* 78.43, 53, 56–57) she is the cause of the creation, preservation and dissolution of the universe. She is also said to bestow knowledge, prosperity, enjoyment, heaven and liberation (ibid., 89.34; 88.6–7, *bhuktimukti pradāyinī*). According to a legend contained in the *Devī Bhāgavata* (III: 4, 6–10) Brahmā, Viṣṇu and Śiva were transformed into women before they were allowed to see Devī in her highest form. Some more powerful and fierce manifestations of Durgā included Mahā-Caṇḍī, Bhadra-Kālī, Cāmuṇḍā, Mahā-Māyā, Rakta-Dantikā and Kātyāyanī. But we also come across the benign aspect of Devi in her manifestation as Kumarī, Ambā, Umā, Gaurī and Pārvatī.

Besides bringing out Śakti's ambivalent character through her legion manifestations, another important theological concept that gained prominence through the Purāṇas was that of *Ardha-Narīśvara* (*Matsya Purāṇa* 60.25, 192.28, 260.1–10). The earliest iconic representation of *Ardha-Narīśvara* has been found at Mathura and is dated around the late Kuṣāṇa or early Gupta period (Yadav 2002). The concept emphasized not only the fusion of the male and female principles, but also parity in the sharing of power and functions between the two. According to the myth contained in the *Brahmāṇḍa Purāṇa* (II.27.98, IV.5.30, IV.44.48) Śiva became *Ardha-Narīśvara* by worshipping Śakti.

It needs to be determined whether the two developments, the emergence and growing prominence gained by the Śakti cult during the later half of the first millennium on the one hand and the changing gender equation as revealed by the Purāṇas on the other had any symbiotic connection and also whether the very conception of Śakti, especially in her aspect of Durgā Mahiṣāsuramardinī, was essentially a mythic representation of an empowered womanhood or else merely represented a prominent tribal cult that found its way into the Purāṇic pantheon and came to dominate it.

Here it needs to be pointed out that the growing popularity of the Śakti cult is very closely linked with the rise of Tāntricism. The latter became a major ideological force in the early medieval period, dominating the religious ideology of not merely the later Purāṇas but all existent religious sects of the time, including non-conformist ones like Buddhism. Noteworthy in the present context is the fact that it also deeply affected the gender-related social restructuring process. As a religious system Tāntricism is regarded as being rooted in the ritual practices and beliefs of preliterate societies. There is also evident a strong symbiotic linkage between Tāntricism and fertility cults with a prominent rural agrarian base. It was, therefore, largely due to two concurrent developments during the later part of the first millennium, namely agricultural expansion into tribal zones in the wake of a prolific issue of land-grants and the momentum gained by the forces of acculturation, that the rise of Tāntricism became almost a natural corollary. However, what is significant about Tāntric ideology is the prominence that was given to women as the most powerful symbol of reproduction and fertility. The centrality of women in Tāntricism, both in its belief-system and ritual practices, is so overbearingly manifest that its matriarchal leanings can scarcely be doubted. Significantly, a large number of preliterate groups even today are known to have matriarchal moorings. The resurgence of ideas related to fertility, magical and orgiastic rites and other ritual practices involving indulgence in drinking and meat-eating were clearly developments having a strong tribal bearing. That Tāntric ideas infiltrated into the Purāṇic fold via tribal traditions is now generally conceded. We have to recognize, therefore, the role of Tāntricism in bringing about a visible change in the Purāṇic attitude to women, especially as compared to that of the Dharmaśāstras. Perhaps the phenomenal popularity gained by Tāntricism explains why it became necessary for Brāhmaṇical ideologues not only to reinterpret and redefine gender relations, but also to do a lot of rethinking as far as their general attitude towards that substratum of society was concerned. In their role as Purāṇa composers they were able to achieve this mainly by modifying existing forms of ritual and inventing a wide range of new ones and also by making extensive use of legends and myths, both pantheon-centric and of a general nature. The portrayal of women in a more traditional light was done mainly with the help of didactic aphorisms and narratives very often lifted directly from the Dharmasūtra and Smṛti texts.

My analysis of the Purāṇic content reveals a certain dichotomy in the way women have been depicted in the Purāṇas. Their composers at times appear to adopt an ambivalent if not occasionally a self-contradictory stance towards gender differentiation. On the one hand we find women are increasingly represented as chattel and bracketed with Śūdras and property (*Mārkaṇḍeya Purāṇa* 137.5; *Agni Purāṇa* 173.44) and the practice of *satī* is upheld as the ultimate ideal and the acid test for the truly devoted wives (*Mārkaṇḍeya Purāṇa* 20.32, 21.13, 115.20, 131.37). On the other hand women are often said to observe a very lax code of sexual morality as is apparent in the case of Śarmiṣṭhā who uninhibitedly seeks sexual gratification from her friend's husband. Furthermore, whereas women in the Dharmaśāstras had been steadily excluded from all forms of Vedic ritual, in the Purāṇas they are increasingly projected as being integral to all domestic (ibid.: 67.23) and collective rituals such as bathing in sacred rivers and tanks and visiting *tīrthas*. Thus, according to the *Vāmana Purāṇa* (36.79), 'persons belonging to the four varṇas and women, when they bathe in *tīrthas* with devotion, see the highest goal'. In this regard some of the Purāṇa composers were not merely disregarding but actually overruling the stern Smṛti dictum that '*japa*, *tapas*, pilgrimage to holy places, becoming an ascetic, efforts to gain mastery over *mantras* and worshipping deities (as a priest), lead to sinfulness in the case of women and śūdras' (Kane 1953: 568–69). Even though the Smṛti stipulation does find an echo in some Purāṇic texts like the *Skanda Purāṇa* (V.3.103.22), yet in other Purāṇas women visiting *tīrthas* and performing *pūjā*, far from being denounced are actually lauded. It is even made mandatory for the husbands to have their wives by their side while performing these ritual acts, if they want to procure the desired results. By allowing women, albeit with the consent of their men-folk, to visit *tīrthas* and temples and even publicly bathe in holy tanks and rivers or actively participate in religious festivals of a folk nature (*utsav*/*parv*) like the *ratha-yātrā*, *Durgā pūjā* or even *Kumbha* and *Ardha-Kumbha*, the Purāṇas were certainly ceding greater freedom of movement to them, and more opportunities to step out of the household and, inevitably, into proximity with strangers. That pilgrimage and participation in festivals tend to erode all forms of segregation including those based on caste and gender is well recognized by anthropologists (Tribhuwan 2003: 130). Consequently greater latitude in the freedom of movement allowed to women, especially in the case of those belonging to the lower stratum, can be presumed on the basis of the Purāṇic evidence, particularly when the latter is juxtaposed to that of the Dharmaśāstras.

Women's rights to be priestesses and teachers (*guru*) is also occasionally conceded in the Purāṇas, though it has been done strictly in the Tāntric context. Similarly though an ascetic mode of life is deemed unconventional and even sinful for women in the Dharmaśāstras, we come across numerous Purāṇic tales and legends about women becoming *yoginīs*. The fact that the practice of asceticism by women found approval in the Purāṇas is, therefore, a significant development, more so since such a way of life was not recommended only for widows. Both married and unmarried women are frequently described as becoming *yoginīs*. In fact, adoption of an ascetic mode of life by women in no matter how small a number clearly bespeaks an attempt to challenge male control over their sexuality. It is also symptomatic of an assertion of the will to opt for an alternate way of life or even forsake it. Acchodā lost all her powers, earned over thousand years of penance, just because she decided to marry. Interestingly she is much derided by the Purāṇa composer for succumbing to such weakness. Besides women like Arundhatī, Pivari, Kṛtvī, Ekaparṇā who are described as great *yoginīs* (*Mārkaṇḍeya Purāṇa* 16.90; 21.66–67; 49.33; *Matsya Purāṇa* 13–14), references are also forth-coming in the Purāṇas to some great scholarly ladies called *brahmavādinī.* Menā and Dhāriṇī, the two daughters of Svadhā, are said to be such erudite ladies (*Mārkaṇḍeya Purāṇa* 49.33). Similarly Madālsā, an extremely devoted wife and mother, was also intellectually competent to expound on such varied subjects as polity, ethics and religious dogma (*Mārkaṇḍeya Purāṇa* 27–35).

How far the Purāṇa composers were compelled to give consent to the pursuit of asceticism by women mainly to wean them away from the fold of heterodox faiths like Buddhism and Jainism, which had all along claimed a large female following, needs to be ascertained. That the authors did labour under considerable pressure from rival sects is acknowledged by most scholars. This could to some extent account for the enunciation of a less stringent code of conduct for women in the Purāṇas. But it must be reiterated that the number of such intellectually proficient women could not have been so large as to make a pronounced impact on society. Moreover, no matter how much respect they were able to gain by their accumulated ascetic powers and intellectual capabilities, this could not have necessarily translated into financial independence or a total de-linking from all forms of social control. On the contrary, they must have continued to function very much within the family framework, conforming to social traditions. Nevertheless, as compared to the Dharmaśāstras, more frequent references contained in the Purāṇas to scholarly women taking to asceticism or displaying their skills in a field that had traditionally been man's preserve undoubtedly indicates a certain dilution of Brāhmaṇical chauvinistic bias. What makes it all the more glaring is the fact that the Purāṇa writers have openly admitted to the presence of such cerebral women in contemporary society.

Even more surprising is the projection of the female child in a very conflicting light in the Purāṇas. The author of the *Skanda Purāṇa* at one place regards a daughter as a constant source of grief (*kanyāsadādukhakārī,* I.1.20.64), but elsewhere in the same Purāṇa, young girls below the age of puberty are said to be objects of worship (VI.36.53). According to the *Devī Purāṇa* (Kane 1958: 170), Durgā is not so much gratified by *homa, japa* and *dāna* as she is by honouring maidens (*kanyā-pūjana*). On ritual occasions such as *Navarātra,* young girls were worshipped under such names as Kumārikā, Kalyāṇi, Kālī, Caṇḍikā, Sambhavī, Durga, etc., thus clearly indicating that they supposedly substituted for these goddesses. Hemādri quotes a long passage from the *Skanda Purāṇa* that enjoins the performer of *navarātra vrata* to feed the girls from the first to the ninth *tithi* on a rising scale (Kane 1958: 170) That much of this development is to be ascribed to the overpowering Tāntric influence so much in evidence during this period, cannot be denied. But whatever the influences or constraints, some degree of attitudinal change on the part of Purāṇa writers has to be conceded. This can be inferred from the fact that despite a very large number of *vratas* being enumerated in the Purāṇas for begetting sons, their composers are occasionally also known to prescribe methods of ensuring the birth of a daughter as is especially apparent from the evidence furnished by the *Viṣṇu Dharmottara Purāṇa* (2.55.9). Besides referring to the vow called *putriyāṣṭami*, meant for begetting both sons and daughters, it enjoins a person desirous of a daughter to offer *jāti* flowers dipped in clarified butter (ibid.: 2.125.1). The particular time and day of the year is recommended for such a person to approach his wife for the purpose of procreation (ibid.: 2.85.2–3). According to the *Padma Purāṇa* (*Sṛṣṭi khaṇḍa*, 40.154, 156) a virtuous daughter is equivalent to ten sons, while according to the author of the *Liṅga Purāṇa* (I.5.31) the word *putrī* means a daughter who saves her parents from the hell called *put*. The changing attitude towards female progeny may be discerned also from the story of king Aśvapati, who by offering the Lakṣahoma sacrifice to goddess Sāvitrī (*Viṣṇu Dharmottara Purāṇa*, 2.36.3–4) is said to have been blessed with a daughter. We also come across instances of people willingly adopting daughters as would appear to be the case of Pṛthā being adopted by Kuntibhoja (*Mātsya Purāṇa* 46.7). In the *Viṣṇu Dharmottara Purāṇa* (2.125.23) the recitation of a particular Vedic mantra is considered to be especially efficacious for the female child.

Another important issue that engaged the attention of the Purāṇa writers and suggests a more humane and considerate attitude towards women is that of adultery and of the abduction and rape of a woman, married or unmarried. Thus even though the lack of chastity is considered to be one of the greatest faults of a woman, according to a Purāṇic injunction a woman sexually enjoyed by another person must never be given up (*Skanda Purāṇa* IV.40.47) and may be purified by continuous austerity. She is, however, subject to certain restrictions, such as not being able to cook food for the ancestors or for the gods, or to participate in worship (*Brahmavaivartta Purāṇa* II.47.40). It is further stipulated that in the case of sex with a woman against her will, she could become pure through expiation (ibid.: II.47.39), but if she was sexually outraged by a strong man then even the need for expiation was not there and purity of mind was enough in her case (ibid.: I.58.106). It is even stated, and more than once, that women can never be sexually polluted by anyone for they are always pure (*Skanda Purāṇa* IV.40.37, VI.144.130,133; *Agni Purāṇa* 165.6; *Garuḍa Purāṇa* I.214.23). That this was not mere theorizing but was actually practised, is more than apparent from the story of Mamatā, who despite being sexually assaulted by her brother-in-law Bṛhaspati was not abandoned by her husband Ūsij (*Matsya Purāṇa* 48.32). One may also recall the story about Tārā's abduction by Soma and the war waged by her husband to recover her (ibid.: 23.29).

Contradictions prevailing in the standards of morality upheld by the Purāṇas, however, come to the fore when we consider one of the mythical explanations offered in the *Padma Purāṇa* (*Sṛṣṭi khaṇḍa* 23.86) for the genesis of the institution of prostitution. According to the Purāṇa the wives of gods and Asuras, on being ravished by members of the other side, were told to follow the life of prostitutes. They were asked to go and stay as prostitutes at temples, or at the house of king or Brāhmaṇas. Nevertheless a certain change in the Purāṇic world-view is perceptible, especially in the attitude towards a segment of women, who were traditionally known to be held in very poor social esteem. Unlike the Dharma-śāstric treatment of prostitution as a professional calling, the Purāṇa writers not only give due recognition to it (*Brahma Purāṇa* XVII.68–70, 81–89 contains references to prostitutes who were accomplished in music and dance), but also offer helpful tips to make the profession lucrative. Prostitutes are advised not to love any one particular person especially if he is poor and that their main purpose should always be money, irrespective of the client being handsome or deformed (ibid.: 23.106–09). Moreover, instead of being looked down upon, the sight of a prostitute came to be regarded as a highly auspicious omen (*Brahmavaivartta, Śrī Kṛṣṇa khaṇḍa*, 70.25). The author of the *Matsya Purāṇa* has listed prostitutes among objects that portend good luck. This would appear a far cry from the Dharmaśāstric dictum that forbids eating food cooked by a *gaṇikā* (*Manusmṛti* IV.209; *Yājñavalkyasmṛti* I.160–67). In the Purāṇas their ritual participation in major festivals became almost mandatory. In the festival of lights, after the banishment of Alakṣmī, a prostitute accompanied by other women was supposed to go from house to house uttering auspicious words and heralding the advent of the goddess of good fortune, Lakṣmī. Significantly, in north-eastern India a handful of earth from the threshold of a prostitute's house is still required for the making of the image of Durgā. A change in the social esteem enjoyed by prostitutes is apparent also from the myths woven around their heavenly counterparts like Menakā, insulting whom (by refusal) was now a grievous sin (*Brahmavaivartta* 32.11).

Such references to women in the Purāṇas certainly do not suggest an excessive marginalization. Rather, it bespeaks an ethos that was very different from that reflected by the Dharmaśāstras and a society which was definitely more indulgent to women. It reveals not only a higher level of female self-confidence and considerable degree of aggression and self-assertion, but also a more open avowal of sexuality. For instance, in the *Matsya Purāṇa*, Śarmiṣṭha, seeking sexual gratification from her friend's husband, tries to convince him by arguing that 'one's own husband and the husband of her companion are equal – and as you are the lord of my companion you must take me as being wedded to you'. But even in the case of women projected in a more conservative light we find that they are shown to be extremely strong women capable not only like Sāvitrī (*Matsya Purāṇa*) of bringing back their deceased husbands from the world of the dead, but also like the devoted wife of the Brāhmaṇa Māṇḍavya who stopped the Sun from rising, extracting boons from the gods. But in their case the moral and spiritual strength they exuded had its source mainly in fidelity and devotion to their husbands, so that instead of challenging male dominance in any way they were only augmenting it further. In fact, there is hardly any evidence forthcoming in the Purāṇas to show that women had been allowed even nominal participation in the political field, which continued to exclusively remain a man's domain.

Before further enlarging upon the changed condition of women we now need to probe the precise nature of the compulsions that led the ideologues to compose an entirely new genre of literature and also to change their attitude to women and Śūdras. The third and fourth centuries mark a watershed in the history of India when the market economy almost broke down and there was a resurgence of agrarian development. Whereas the former can largely be attributed to a decline in the demand for Indian goods in foreign markets following the collapse of the Roman Empire along with a corresponding decline in commodity production and the money economy, the resurgence of an agrarian system was accompanied by pressure on land as the principal means of production. Since the core civilizational zone, especially the Indo-Gangetic plain, had already been subjected to near optimal agricultural growth and exploitation, further expansion was possible only in the outlying areas, which naturally became subject to colonizing activities, expectedly spearheaded by religious agencies such as Buddhist and Jaina monks who were followed in their wake by the Brāhmaṇas.

The situation was further aggravated by the absorption of a large number of foreign groups such as Yavanas, Śakas, Kuṣāṇas, Parthians and Huṇas into the Indian population, thereby adding new ethnic strands and cultural dimensions to the latter. Right from the outset the more ambitious amongst these peoples had begun to stake their claim to political power. They were thus anxious to gain recognition and validation for their power from whichever existent Indian religious system was willing to provide it, in return for munificent benefactions. This inevitably intensified religious rivalry and accelerated proselytization by such heterodox sects as Buddhism and Jainism. The latter, in order to win over new categories of donors and patrons, were willing not only to revamp their religious ideologies and monastic systems (as can be seen particularly in the case of Buddhism), but also to venture into uncharted territories sparsely populated by preliterate groups. Through their colonizing activities in such peripheral zones as Gujarat and trans-Vindhyan Deccan, indigenous groups there were exposed to mainstream cultural influences. The latter thus emerged as yet another potential religious clientele who needed to be wooed by all sects engaged in an intense fight over surplus-sharing.

The Brāhmaṇical leaders could not ignore or remain unaffected by these developments for very long. For sheer existential reasons it became absolutely necessary for them to become equal contenders in this race for new donors, especially in the more outlying areas. But this entailed giving up their uncompromisingly elitist stance and affecting certain fundamental changes in the existent belief-system, so that the latter could hold greater appeal for the preliterate masses, who had till then been treated with contempt and condescension. It was necessary to give Brāhmaṇism a more popular base and character, without, of course, eroding in any way the dominance and interests of the Brāhmaṇas as a priestly class. This had to be done in a manner to maximize both the size of the Brāhmaṇical clientele and their own share in surplus sharing.

A factor that further lent urgency to the problem and which rendered the need to acculturate preliterate groups even more imminent, was the fast growing practice of making land grants in favour of religious beneficiaries. Since the royal donors through these grants besides seeking to earn social prestige and spiritual merit also aimed at bringing virgin tracts under the plough, most of the land donated by them (particularly during the initial phase) lay in peripheral areas like Gujarat, Bengal, Assam and Orissa. In order to make *brahmadeya* land that was received in gift but lay in distant tribal zones an economically gainful proposition it was essential for the Brāhmaṇa beneficiaries to make them cultivable. But this could be possible only by mobilizing tribal labour. That was not an easy proposition, rooted as the latter were in totally antithetical socio-economic and cultural traditions. They could not be expected to not only just give up their traditional mode of subsistence but also take to a completely alien mode of production. It was thus a matter of sheer economic survival for the Brāhmaṇa beneficiaries not only to conciliate and win over the tribal people on whose lands they were clearly encroaching, but also to influence and absorb them, so that they could become more amenable to the adoption of new agricultural techniques based on the use of the ploughshare and extensive utilization of cattle wealth. All this, however, could be achieved only by readapting and refurbishing Brāhmaṇical ideology. That the Brāhmaṇical ideologues were largely successful in achieving this end, namely that of absorbing a large preliterate segment into its fold, would be apparent from the phenomenally inflated size of the Śūdra stratum during the post-Gupta centuries and also the transformation of Śūdras into a predominantly agricultural class, as is indicated by the statements of Hiuen-Tsang and Alberuni. The proliferation of caste and sub-caste groupings with strong occupational, residential and regional affiliations was another major fallout of the same process of agricultural expansion in outlying areas.

Thus conditions were ripe for significant changes to be brought about in the Brāhmaṇical attitude towards not only the lowest *varṇa* stratum but also towards tribal segments in general including both foreign and autochthonous groups, who had up till now been denigrated as Mlechha, Asura, Rākṣasa etc. and whose very touch and sight were considered to be polluting. The Brāhmaṇa ideologues, moreover, were forced to do a certain amount of rethinking also with regard to their attitude towards women. The role and status of women in a tribal social order is vastly different from the one they are assigned in a male-dominated class-divided society, the kind reflected in the Dharmasūtra and Smṛti texts. In the latter kind of social order, the availability of a large social surplus rules out the scope and possibility of women of the upper strata being actively engaged in economic pursuits and contributing to family earnings, but the presence of the firmly-entrenched institution of private property and the attendant issues of inheritance are bound to curtail the freedom of women. This is largely due to the fear of their going astray and thus subjecting the issue of paternity of their male offspring and heirs to the family property to doubts. Anxiety to preserve and protect the purity and continuity of family lineage would also lead to social evils like child marriage and polygamy. Other restrictions in the form of women being deprived of education and property and the right to independently participate in religious ceremonies would be other forms of disability. The birth of a girl, therefore, would always be regarded as a misfortune or even a curse.

Women in a preliterate social order on the other hand are generally known to participate more freely in most economic, social and religious activities, which gives them a fair amount of freedom of movement (Thompson 1952: 15–16). Although the degree of parity enjoyed by them would depend on the traditions to which a tribal group subscribes, nevertheless, as active contributors to family earnings women generally remain fairly esteemed members of the family. In fact in a tribal society a daughter instead of being regarded as a serious liability is considered an asset to the family and anyone depriving the latter of her services is made to pay a bride-price. Women moreover are allowed considerable freedom to choose their own spouse.

In order to draw the tribal segments living in areas far removed from civilization within the vortex of mainstream cultural fold it became necessary not only to devise an effective instrument of acculturation and absorb tribal cults and practices into Brāhmaṇism, but also to show respect for at least some tribal social traditions such as that of according a certain amount of parity to their womenfolk. It is in this context that society as revealed by the Purāṇas has to be viewed and assessed.

In fact, as compared to that of the Dharmaśāstras, the Purāṇic world-view in some ways reveals a closer affinity to a tribal more than a fragmented and caste-based society. Unlike the earlier Brāhmaṇical texts of a purely didactic nature, the Purāṇas constitute a literary genre which was suited not so much to self-perusal and study but to folk-recital, which constitutes an integral feature of preliterate social life and is a major source of reaffirming tribal values and tradition and reinforcing the unity and identity of the group. The format of the Purāṇas is so conceived as to simplify even complex theological constructs by repeated questioning and elaboration with the help of popular anecdotes and parables. It shows a clear distancing of the authors of the Purāṇas from those of the earlier Brāhmaṇical texts, a fact that immediately puts a question mark on the true identity of the former. As I have tried to point out elsewhere (Nath 2001), in view of the fact that many of the Purāṇas are known to have been composed in such peripheral zones as western Deccan, Bengal and Orissa, it is reasonable to assume that their authors must have been people of those areas, so familiar with local culture that these seeped into their work, giving it a certain tribal and local veneer.

Once we recognize the nature of the compulsions working behind the composition of the Purāṇas and the purpose for which they were written, as well as the socio-cultural antecedents of their authors, it becomes easy for us to account for the changed tenor and ethos reflected by those texts. As already mentioned, this is especially evident in the projection of women. In fact, it furnishes perhaps the only rationale for the dichotomy in such a portrayal. Thus on the one hand we hear of such archetypal role models as Satī, Madālsā and Sāvitrī who are projected as the epitome of wifely virtues and whose funeral rites, in case they happened to predecease their husbands, had to be accompanied by the performance of an Agnihotra (*Viṣṇu Dharmottara Purāṇa*). On the other hand we come across such tales as that of Bṛhaspati lustfully approaching his brother's pregnant wife Mamatā, who instead of being scandalized puts up a mild protest, requesting him to wait until she has delivered the baby (*Matsya* 48.32–36). The *Matsya Purāṇa* also contains references to girls proposing marriage to men, at times being rejected, as happened in the case of Devayānī proposing marriage to Kāca. We also hear of women indulging in bouts of drinking and merry-making in the forest (*Matsya Purāṇa* 30).

References to customs such as levirate (*niyoga*) may be treated more in the nature of Purāṇic authors looking back at the past and drawing upon it freely, for some of these practices do seem to have become obsolete by their time. Thus we come across Bali beseeching Dīrghatamas to beget progeny from his (Bali's) wife Sudeṣṇā (*Matsya* 48.60). Other famous instances of this practice are likewise drawn mainly from the *Mahābhārata*: Kuntī begetting her three sons from three different gods, or Madri conceiving her two sons Nakula and Sahadeva from the two Aśvinī Kumārs. This practice, moreover, drew its rationale chiefly from royal concerns about preventing a break in the line of inheritance or succession rather than a sanction for a lax code of sexual morality more characteristic of a tribal order. But what is really significant is the nonchalance displayed by them while narrating such tales. This is in sharp contrast to the tenor of even the *Mahābhārata* (I.113.4.7), which, though brimming with such tales, contains a scathing indictment of the wanton behaviour and extraordinary sexual freedom enjoyed by the women of Uttara Kuru and Mahiṣmati. Even in other contemporary literary works such as Rājaśekhara's *Karpūramañjarī* (I.22) and Kṣemendra's *Dasāvatāracarita* (Bhattacharya 1987: 124) promiscuity in general and Tāntric rituals in particular (especially those involving drinking and orgiastic rites) have been strongly depreciated. The Purāṇa composers on the other hand seem to take a more tolerant and perhaps even a pragmatic view of the composite cultural makeup of contemporary society. In the *Matsya Purāṇa* there is more than one reference to kings willing to be rid of their numerous daughters by marrying them off (44.49–50; 45.22); yet there is awareness of unbridled sexuality common amongst some sections of society. Labelled *go-dharma*, it is expounded by the son of the divine cow, Surabhi: 'We bother not about the propriety of a thing to be done or not; equally to us there is no distinction in the matter of mating' (48.49–50).

Such conflicting Purāṇic tales about women can be interpreted either as reflecting the ethos of two completely disparate social groups that had been thrown into close cultural proximity due to agricultural expansion in tribal zones or else, as stated above, may be regarded as attesting the culturally heterogeneous character of the emergent Purāṇic society. In both cases they indicate a striking departure from the Dharmaśāstric code laid down for women. But more than anything else they serve as an index to the changing social attitude towards women in general as also to a certain amount of complacency that the Purāṇa writers had begun to exhibit in this regard, very much in contrast to their Dharmaśāstric counterparts. Significantly, even in the later period when some of the late Smṛti works were being composed, their authors continued to maintain an unrelenting attitude towards women. How does one account for such contradictory attitudes displayed by the authors of two different sets of Brāhmaṇical texts being composed almost at the same time? Perhaps one simple explanation could be that whereas the Smṛti writers were concentrating entirely on women of the mainstream as also of the upper stratum, the focus had drastically shifted in the case of the Purāṇas to those belonging to the marginalized tribal groups, who constituted a fairly large segment of the clientele they were actively seeking to win over.

It needs, however, to be noted that the authors of the Purāṇas, by juxtaposing such narratives about less conventional women with other stories of a more edificatory nature (wives cast in a completely traditional mould and willing even to immolate themselves at the death of their husbands), certainly sought to uphold the latter as the true ideal and the standard point of reference for the targeted (though not so discerning) Purāṇic audience, necessarily composed of a sizeable tribal segment. For instance the author of the *Mārkaṇḍeya Purāṇa* (121.29) goes out of his way to emphasize that 'self-reliance is the quality of men; women (*abalā*) are always dependent on others'. Moreover, extraordinary emphasis came to be laid on chastity as the prime virtue and chief adornment of any woman. According to one assessment (Bharadwaj 1999), chastity was the dominant theme underlying the *vratas* as propounded in the Purāṇas, through which the *pati-vratā dharma* and social control of women was sought to be ensured.

Another significant dichotomy in the Purāṇic depiction of women is the manner in which they have been regarded as chattel and clubbed with property at a time when their right, however limited in nature, to own and inherit family property had come to be actually conceded by the Dharmaśāstra writers (Nath; Bhattacharya 1987). Thus, in the *Matsya Purāṇa* (31.22), a woman has been compared to a servant or a son, who is always poor because the wealth acquired by them belongs to their masters. But as pointed out elsewhere (Nath 1993–94), women have been bracketed with property essentially in two contexts in the Purāṇas: where the need to protect property is emphasized, and where property is described as yielding prestige and status. With landed property and the attendant issue of inheritance gaining in importance due to unprecedented developments in the field of agricultural expansion, the very stability of the family was now considered to be dependent upon the protection of its women and property, which had also come to constitute the chief source of its prestige and status. Consequently, wherever emphasis had to be laid on family prestige or the need to protect property, women, particularly wives came to be mentioned.

Considerations related to the inheritance of property would seem to have weighed quite heavily with the Purāṇa composers for them to severely denounce remarriage in the case of women. According to the *Mārkaṇḍeya Purāṇa* a man who has married a widow is a sinner (14.82) and one who gives his daughter twice is doomed to be reborn a worm (ibid.: 15.13). On the rare occasions when the remarriage of a widow was condoned, it was with the brother of her deceased husband, a practice not quite uncommon amongst some tribal groups. Such marriages are called *pat* in Maharashtra, *natra* in Gujarat and *udki* in the Canarese districts (Kane 1941: 615). But even in a tribal order, where women primarily figure as producers of food, they tend to be regarded as equivalent to food and hence virtually akin to property. In fact they are also known to figure as important items of exchange between two groups or clans. So even in the context of ongoing acculturation the clubbing of women with property can be said to have been a factual statement, essentially in consonance with the cultural spirit and ethos of the time.

The origins and growing popularity of the Śakti cult in tandem with the changing gender equation during this period also needs some probing. We may begin with the cult of Durgā, who has received so much importance in the *Mārkaṇḍeya Purāṇa* and who, according to Majumdar (1906–07: 355–62), does not find mention in any literature or epigraphic record prior to the fifth century (except in the *Mahābhārata*). Majumdar regards Durgā as a non-Aryan tribal goddess in origin and has tried to establish the genesis and linkages of this goddess with Kumārī-Osā worship. The latter is still prevalent amongst the Śūdra castes-dwelling in the Oriya-speaking hill tracts of Sambhalpur district, which lies on the south-western border of Bengal. 'In this out of the way place all the different tribes retain to this day their old manners and customs, unaffected by Brāhmaṇic influence' (ibid.). According to Majumdar considerable ritual similarities between the tribal cult and the way *Durgā pūjā* came to be celebrated in Bengal, such as the singing of obscene songs on the Navamī, the throwing of the idol into water after the completion of worship and the worship of Vana-Durgā (represented by a plantain tree covered by a piece of cloth and placed on the right side of the main idol), speak of a close linkage between the latter and its tribal counterpart. This is further affirmed by four Mahiṣāsuramardinī Durgā idols that were discovered in the predominantly tribal areas of Bolangir and Kalahandi districts and are presently lodged in the Sambhalpur University Museum (Mishra 1988: 176). It is interesting to note that according to the *Bhāgawat Purāṇa* (Bhagawati 1988: 93), the girls of Vraja worshipped the goddess Kātyāyanī Durgā by constructing an image of her with sand. Moreover, the fact that in the *Devī-Mahātmya* (*Mārkaṇḍeya Purāṇa* 80.34) the Devī is referred to as drinking some intoxicant (*pāna*) during her fight with Mahiṣāsura would definitely indicate her tribal affinities. A similar impression is augmented by her other manifestations as Śākambharī, Bhramarī and Vindhyavāsinī. Hazra too has attributed a non-Aryan origin to the female deity in the Purāṇas (Hazra 1963: 16). Whereas the tribal origins of Durgā are indisputable, then, her entry into the Purāṇic fold and the dominance she gained in the pantheon underscore the impact of ongoing cultural interaction between the so-called Great and Little traditions on Purāṇic society and religion, as well as the fact that it was never a one-sided cultural movement.

In fact, that the Purāṇas serve as an effective instrument of cult assimilation and play a significant role in the making of a regional tradition is well recognized by scholars (Chakrabarti 2001). From the sixth century onwards a large number of epigraphic records are forthcoming which bear references to female deities with tribal affiliations: Ghatavāsinī, Araṇyavāsinī, Khīmalatā, Śaṅkaramātā and Vatyākṣiṇidevī (*Epigraphia Indica* [*EI*], Vol. IX: 187; Vol. XI: 229, 301–02; Vol. XIV: 176; Vol. XX: 97, 122). We also come across remains of temples dedicated to such goddesses as Harṣatamātā, Ānandīmātā and Khokrimātā, which too bear out how widespread the cult was during this period especially at a more local and regional level. As we find in the case of the assimilation of Durgā Mahiṣāsuramardinī, the phenomenon of the emergence of Śaktism as a dominant sectarian force both in the Purāṇas and otherwise can be explained only in the context of changes in the social order and a cultural syncretism taking place in the wake of agricultural expansion in peripheral zones.

The two developments, the changing gender equation and the dominance gained by the mother goddess cult in the Purāṇas, can therefore be attributed to the same source. In fact, scholars regard the 'female-oriented world view manifested in Śaktism and the Tāntric forms of religious systems' to be directly linked with the 'social customs and institutions like matrilineal descent and inheritance, matrilocal marriage and residence, and other allied features which quite commonly characterize tribal life in India' (Bhattacharya 1987: 120). According to Briffault, the development of agriculture without an intervening pastoral phase enhanced the position of women not only as owners and heiresses of the land but also, because of their traditional association with agricultural magic and religion, for a long period, the women retained the role of priestesses (Briffault 1954: 251). In fact, the significance of *Kumāri-pūjā*, which is widely recommended in the *Śākta Purāṇas*, can be understood chiefly in the context of the worship of the Great Mother in the person of a virgin to which the Tantras attach special importance. *Kumāri-pūjā* is still current in Nepal and its rationale lies in the belief that the country belongs to the Kumārī, a young girl elected from time to time and worshipped as the living form of Kālī or Durgā, so that each year the king has to take a fresh mandate from her in order to legitimately rule the land (Bhattacharya 1987: 121).

The growing recognition of mother-right in the Purāṇas is therefore undeniable. There is a need, however, to determine the degree of gender parity that the authors sought to concede through such instruments as rituals, myths and legends. It needs also to be remembered that the Purāṇas were primarily Brāhmaṇical texts that claimed to derive their authority and sanctity from the Vedas and also that their authors themselves were so steeped in patriarchal traditions that they could scarcely be expected to negate the latter and promote an alternate value-system with absolute gender-parity, something which may be hard to find amongst totally preliterate or even the most emancipated groups. And yet the pressures and demands of a changing material milieu were so great that they could not be easily overlooked. Moreover, for existential reasons arising out of the challenges thrown by heterodox sects, it became necessary for them to strike some sort of balance: so even though we come across a continual reiteration of the Dharmaśāstric norms for women, at the same time there is also to be found an open avowal of ethnic and cultural diversity.

The Purāṇa authors appear to have been fully cognizant of the implications of the widening of geographical horizons, the establishment of new relations of production based on the feudal pattern, and the need to adjust to a new mode of patronage connected not so much with commercial enterprise but with tribal chiefdoms and agricultural production. If, in the case of the latter, fertility rites seemingly played an important role, as would be apparent from the growing popularity of Tantric rites and practices, the aspirant chiefs, tried to exploit local beliefs to augment their power. In fact, there had taken place a major change in the nature of the clientele of the Brāhmaṇa priests.

This explains the shift from *homa*-centric ritualism to more innovative and wide ranging forms of *dāna*, as also to newer types of folk-based rituals: observing *parv*, visiting *tīrthas*, listening to *kathā* recitals, worshipping in shrines and observing *vratas*, all supposed to secure great rewards. Thus, in response to a query 'how can a poor man reach God?' it is stated in the *Varāha Purāṇa* (39.17–18; 23–24) that he could do so by observing fasts and *vratas*.

In fact, in keeping with their rather favourable predisposition towards women, the Purāṇa composers are known to have devised a range of special vows (*vratas*) to be exclusively observed by married and unmarried women, such as the *saubhāgya śāyaṇa vrata* prescribed in the *Matsya Purāṇa* (60.41; 62.38; 63.27–28); 64.25). There were also introduced numerous vows to be observed by widows (54.5) and still others by prostitutes (69.58–60; 70.44–45). Even though the aim of such *vratas* was social control by instilling in women patriarchal values such as fidelity and undying devotion (*pati-bhakti*) and chastity (duties of a chaste woman receive detailed exposition in the *Varāha Purāṇa* 207), indirectly they also reveal a concern for women's individual needs and aspirations which could find expression and symbolic fulfilment through the observance of these vows. Other religious practices, the *Kumārī-pūjā* for instance, and special ritual offerings made to *suhāgans* (that is, women whose husbands were alive) on the occasion of particular *vratas* like the *Saubhāgyasundarī vrata* (Kane 1958: 367) must have also resulted in a certain increase in the level of women's involvement and participation in ritual performances. This was a decidedly conspicuous shift from the earlier Dharmaśāstric position, when women had been debarred from active participation in sacrificial and *homa*-centric rites.

The compulsions to appease and win over a clientele drawn chiefly from preliterate and marginalized sections of society must have placed the Purāṇa composers in an ideological quandary. The only way they could overcome their predicament and justify the contradictions besetting their society was by taking recourse to the myth of the Kali age. The latter proved to be a master stroke that not only enabled them to resolve the anomalies and ambiguities arising out of the fusion of disparate cultures, but also to effectively meet the challenges thrown up by the changing material milieu. By declaring those changes in the Brāhmaṇical tradition that were at sharp variance with that of the Dharmaśāstras as symptomatic of the Kali age, the Purāṇa writers were able to both justify and condone them. A salient feature of the Kali age according to these authors was the promiscuity of women, which led to *varṇa-saṅkara* and became ultimately responsible for the rise and proliferation of mixed castes, a development that was so marked during the early medieval period. The Kali age myth, along with its addenda, *kalivarjya* and *kalidharma*, thus served as useful and facile instruments in the hands of the Purāṇa composers to vindicate and validate the contradictions that had become so prominent in the delineation of women's rights in the Purāṇas. Thus, as compared to the Dharmaśāstras, the Purāṇas, focusing on a much wider cross-section of society, reveal a slight upward trend in favour of women as far as the gender equation is concerned. But this was more notional than actual, for relatively greater gender parity is perceptible in the case of women of the lower social strata than in the case of women of the elite.

References

Barth, A.B. (1963), *Religions of India*, translated by J. Wood (Varanasi: Chowkhamba).

Bhagawati, G.K. (1988), *The Bhāgawat Purāṇa – A Socio-Cultural Study* (Allahabad: Vohra).

Bharadwaj, R.M. (1999), 'Brahmanical Patriarchy & Religious Vratas during Early Medieval India', *Indian History Congress Proceedings*, 59th Session, Bangalore (Delhi: Indian Council of Historical Research).

Bhattacharya, N.N. (1987), *History of Tāntric Religion* (Delhi: Manohar).

Briffault, R. (1954), *The Mothers, A Study of the Origins of Sentiments and Institutions*, Vol. II (London: Allen and Unwin: New York: The Macmillan Company),

Chakrabarti, Kunal (2001), *Religious Process: The Purāṇas and the Making of a Regional Tradition* (Delhi: Oxford University Press).

Epigraphia Indica (EI), relevant volumes (New Delhi: Archaeological Survey of India).

Hazra, R.C. ([1940] 1975), *Studies in the Purāṇic Records on Hindu Rites and Customs* (Delhi: Motilal Banarsidass).

——— (1958), *Studies in the Upapurāṇas*, Vol. I (Calcutta: Sanskrit College).

——— (1963), *Studies in the Upapurāṇas*, Vol. II (Calcutta: Sanskrit College).

Kane, P.V. (1930), *History of Dharmaśāstra: Ancient and Medieval Religious and Civil Law*, Vol. I (Poona: Bhandarkar Oriental Research Institute).

——— (1941), *History of Dharmaśāstra: Ancient and Medieval Religious and Civil Law*, Vol. III (Poona: Bhandarkar Oriental Research Institute).

——— (1946), *History of Dharmaśāstra: Ancient and Medieval Religious and Civil Law*, Vol. IV (Poona: Bhandarkar Oriental Research Institute).

——— (1958), *History of Dharmaśāstra: Ancient and Medieval Religious and Civil Law*, Vol. V (Poona: Bhandarkar Oriental Research Institute).

Majumdar, B.C. (1906–07), 'Durgā: Her Origin and History', *Journal of the Royal Asiatic Society of Great Britain*, Vol. 38, pp. 335–62.

Mārkaṇḍeya Puraṇa ([1904] 1969), translated by F.E. Pargiter (Varanasi: Indological Book House).

Mishra, P.K. (1988), 'Some Rare Durgā Icons', in K.K. Dasgupta, P.K. Bhattacharya and R.D. Choudhury (eds), *Shraddhānjali: Studies in Ancient Indian History: D.C. Sircar Commemoration Volume* (Delhi: Sundeep Prakashan).

Nath, Vijay (1993–94), 'Women as Property and their Right to Inherit Property up to Gupta Period', *The Indian Historical Review*, Vol. 20, Nos. 1–2, pp. 1–15.

——— (2001), *Purāṇas and Acculturation: A Historico-Anthropological Perspective* (Delhi: Munshiram Manoharlal).

Rao, T.A. Gopinath (1976), *Elements of Hindu Iconography*, Vol. I (Delhi: Motilal Banarasidass).

Gender and Sexuality in Early Medieval Sanskrit Literature

Shalini Shah

My paper sets out to discuss what has been described in the Indian tradition as *kāma puruṣārtha.* This was one of the four goals of human life, *dharma, artha* and *mokṣa* being the other three. While the patriarchal tradition completely subordinated women's goals in the spiritual and material spheres to the dictates of men (by following the *pativratā dharma* or the duty of an ideal chaste wife, a woman was said to achieve both *artha* and *mokṣa*); in the *kāma* tradition, on the other hand, a woman seemed to have a far more visible (though not always subjective) role to play. Perhaps this was because within the Indian tradition, unlike the Greek for instance, *kāma* was conceived predominantly in heterosexual terms.

In analysing the issues of gender and sexuality in early medieval India (the seventh to the thirteenth centuries) I utilize the classical Sanskrit literature. Not all of it belongs to one genre, and obviously the issues of gender and sexuality in the different genres will be framed differently. Thus, for instance, while the *āyurvedic* discourse is concerned with procreation, the *kāmaśāstrīya* discourse concerns itself essentially with the regimen of pleasure. The *dharmaśāstrīya* discourse, on the other hand, gives expression to the normative Brāhmaṇical view of gender relations. We also need to be sensitive to the variety of ways in which *kāma* has been conceptualized within the major philosophical discourses of this period, in the ascetic, materialist and Tāntric streams of thought. Secular courtly literature is yet another source material wherein a gendered view of female sexuality is richly reflected. Within this genre we will analyse *kāma* under the two broad rubrics of *prema* (love) and *śṛṅgāra* (the erotic). Since this paper grapples with the issues of female sexuality, it becomes imperative to clarify that 'women' cannot be perceived as an unproblematic generalized category. Thus an attempt will be made to unravel the differences in the conception of the female sexuality of girl, wife, widow and prostitute, as also the free woman outside patriarchal society.

It is a truism that sources need to be analysed not only in a given chronological context, but also within a spatial setting. However, the latter is difficult. An interesting historical fact of this period is that, while there was an increasing immobility of the peasantry, and trading-class mobility too suffered on account of an increasingly closed economy, the elite Brāhmaṇa class was on the move. Bilhaṇa, a Kashmiri Brāhmaṇa, travelled far from his native place to the court of the

Cālukyas of Kalyāṇa, as poet and scholar. Rājaśekhara was a Brāhmaṇa from Maharashtra who served the Pratīhāra court in Kanauj. Daṇḍin hailed from Saurashtra but was patronized by the Pallavas of Kanchipuram. So it is difficult to situate certain texts in a particular regional context.

A striking feature of all types of sources is their pronounced gender bias. It would not be an exaggeration to state that classical Sanskrit literature was authored by men for male listeners and a male readership. The *nāgaraka* is the focus of *kāmaśāstrīya* discourse, and *rasika/sahṛdaya* of the courtly literary productions. The *āyurvedic* discourse addresses itself to either the learned person (*paṇḍita/vidvāna*), or to the physician (*vaidya* or *bhiṣaja*); none of these Sanskrit terms have a feminine equivalent.

For a historian of societal norms human sexuality is a valid area of research. Few human emotions are more fundamental or more pervasive than sexual needs and feelings. Just as the influence of sex on culture is a universal phenomenon, human sexuality is never culture-free (Smith-Rosenberg 1975: 195). An analysis of sexuality offers the historian an opportunity to explore possible relationships between sexual practices, social structures, and the normative values of a place and age. Sexuality cannot be perceived as just a biological necessity and we cannot assume that there is the same interest in it among men and women. After all, sexual interaction is essentially between men and women who have differential access to social, economic and political power. The asymmetry of the power equation is translated into asymmetric sexual relationships. In this study of the patriarchal sexual-social world I write of 'emphasized femininity' and 'hegemonic masculinity'. The latter concept implies the dominance of men over women, a denial of status to women so that they cannot assert themselves or maintain autonomy of behaviour and desire. This masculinity is offset by female compliance, and is oriented towards accommodating the interests and desires of men. Within this discourse of hegemonic masculinity, a woman exists only as a fetishized object under the male gaze. Associated with emphasized femininity are the qualities of sociability, sexual passivity and the acceptance of domesticity and motherhood. Wherever this model of emphasized femininity was transgressed, women were labelled either whores or pushed outside patriarchy as *rākṣasī* or *dākinī*. The latter were perceived as particularly dangerous.

The seventh to thirteenth centuries saw the making of early medieval India. These were the centuries that saw the crystallization of feudal relationships in much of India. There is now a growing realization that these centuries need not be seen as an unchanging monolith in economic terms, and that the closed feudal economy witnessed, around the mid-tenth century, a revival of trade and urbanization. R.S. Sharma (1980) in fact talks of 'cracks' in the system. Nonetheless, the validity of arguing in favour of a feudal socio-economic and political setup for the early-medieval period still remains. From the slow stirrings of economic revival one cannot deduce any change in the feudal ethos. Politically too, much of India witnessed the formation of a number of principalities – all regional powers and none a pan-Indian one. Even the tripartite conflict for the control of Kanauj (which had been an imperial capital under Harṣavardhana) did not succeed in giving either the Pratīhāras, the Pālas or the Rāṣṭrakūṭas an all-India presence. In the early medieval period, the feudal polity triumphed over the idea of a united realm. Furthermore, the constant rivalry between warring principalities resulted in a pervasive atmosphere of vainglorious machoism, in which *bhoga* or enjoyment of the earth was linked to the *bhoga* or enjoyment of the women. Both inscriptional and textual evidence attest to this fact. It is this complete identity of women and property which characterizes the strongly patriarchal feudal phase (Sharma 1983).

I

The philosophical ideas of a given culture are a significant medium through which sexual behaviour is represented. In fact, when we use the term sexuality, we refer not just to the sexual act, but to all behaviour, attitudes, values and beliefs that may be seen to have some sexual significance in a society. Of all the philosophical discourses the normative *dharmaśāstrīya* discourse has always been the dominant one, because it was the framers of this discourse, the Brāhmaṇas, who enjoyed unparalleled hegemony in ancient India. Since the *dharmaśāstrīya* texts were concerned not with pleasure but with norms for social regulation, in the man–woman relationship it was the procreative and not the erotic angle that was important. Cohabitation was a duty, and it was enjoined on men that a woman's *ṛtukāla* not be wasted (*Manubhāṣya* 3.45; 9.4). Since sex was to be for the reproduction of the species, heterosexual coitus was the norm and deviance in the form of male homosexuality – tellingly referred to by Manu (*Manusmṛti* 11.68) as *klībya* or impotence, and lesbianism earned the ire of the Brāhmaṇas (ibid.: 11.174; 8.369–70). The *dharmaśāstrīya* writers were also obsessively concerned with the upper-caste widow's position. A widow was enjoined to be patient of hardship, self-controlled and chaste (*Manubhāṣya* 5.156–60). Later *Dharmaśāstra* authorities were even more explicit about the widow's existence. *Vṛddhahārita* (Kane 1974: 584) states that she should 'give up chewing betel nut, wearing perfume, flowers, ornaments and dyed clothes, taking food from a vessel of bronze, taking two meals a day, applying collyrium to the eyes, she should wear only a white garment, curb her senses and anger, and sleep on the ground'. This meant that a widow should become an ascetic within the home. Her sexuality, which in marriage had served familial and social goals, was now of no use to the patriarchal household. Even more than the unmarried menstruating girl or nubile wife whose husband was away, the widow was the object of moral panic. Girls could be controlled, but the sexuality of the widow could not be similarly treated. She had to be completely 'unsexed' (Chakravarty 1995: 2250–51). Although a widow was permitted procreation for the continuation of the patrilineage in an earlier period, the trend in the early medieval period was to prohibit *niyoga*, particularly for the *dvija* caste. Medhātithi (*Manubhāṣya* 9.59), for instance, permits *niyoga* only if the widow undertook it under the instruction of the elders of the husband's family.

The control mechanism operated at two levels. At an ideological level, female sexual prowess was greatly exaggerated. Women were *pramadā*, possessed of an insatiable and threatening innate sexual lust. Medhātithi (*Manubhāṣya* 11.137–38) uses the term 'inconstant' (*anavastithā*) for those women who are sexually promiscuous like prostitutes. Yet, at another level, women were depicted as *abalā*, who had to be forever under male tutelage (*Manubhāṣya* 9.3). We thus see that women could not exist in the *dharmaśāstrīya* discourse as autonomous individuals, but only as members of a 'type' – either *sādhvī/pativratā* or else *svairiṇī*.

Within this overall patriarchal structure we can detect spaces where patriarchy was not functional at all or was greatly diluted. Thus we find a variety of sons listed in the *Dharmaśāstra: kānīna* (son of a maiden), *sahoḍha* (son of a pregnant bride), and *paunarbhava* (son of a twice-married woman) were accepted as part of the family (*Manubhāṣya* 9.158–160). The very manner of the birth of these sons allows a more lenient view of female sexual behaviour. This leads us to believe, that, in spite of constraining norms, women could negotiate the consequences of their desires.

A rabidly masculine offshoot of the *dharmaśāstrīya* concept of *saṅyāsa* was the ascetic ideology which tended to demean the notion of *kāma*. In the ninth century Śaṅkarācārya was one of the greatest representatives of the ascetic tradition. In his commentary on the *Brahmasūtras* (Chattopadhyaya 1959: 2) he equated the crude mob (*prākṛitjana*) with the followers of the lokāyata view. Women as inciters of desire in men were even more vilified. For Śaṅkara, women symbolized ignorance; therefore, in his *advaita* philosophy, *māyā* was the feminine principal of ignorance, and in the pursuit of an ascetic life (Śaṅkara never married and his monastic order was exclusively for men) women were a snare.

In none of the mainstream discourses was *kāma* renounced as a *puruṣārtha* or goal of human life. Although it had a lower priority than did *dharma* and *artha*, it was an essential aspect of life. But the ascetic tradition was unique in that it developed as an antithesis to *kāma,* most specially its erotic aspect. And since sexual desire was conceived essentially in heterosexual terms, the renunciatory ideology acquired a gendered aspect as well. Dumont (1960: 63) sees renunciation as a sort of universal language of India, and the renouncer being for him a creator of values. Thapar (1979: 70–71) presents the ascetic renouncer as a representative of a counter-culture who exercised a great deal of moral authority in society. But from a gender perspective the ascetic and his philosophy of renunciation were not a counter-culture. He was very much within the mainstream of a patriarchal society whose norms had misogyny as its leitmotif. The ascetic tradition indulged in wholesale woman bashing – woman as *kāminī* (lustful mistress) was the temptress. In Jalhaṇa's *Sūktimuktāvalī* (449.24–25) the verses under the *vairāgya paddhati* underline that because of women there is desire. If one abandons women, one abandons desire for this world, and leaving this world entitles one to happiness (*yasyastrī tasya bhogecchā, strīyam tyaktvā jagatyaktam, jagatyaktvā sukhī bhaved*).

Much of the misogyny of the ascetic tradition stems from the fact that women were viewed as objects of sexual desire and were seen as representing through their reproductive functions, a hold on the family. They were therefore disruptive and threatening to the male ascetic's quest for liberation. Perhaps it will be easier to understand the misogyny of the ascetic tradition if we link it to somatophobia. The body was seen as a source of all undesirable traits a human being could have, and women's lives were seen as manifesting those traits. As Bhartṛhari says in his *Vairāgyaśataka* 'unborn man suffers a painful confinement in a woman's foul womb' (*Śatakatrayam*, vs. 199). He further notes, 'with all her emotions, woman enchains us' (ibid., vs. 79). The ascetic perspective thus made woman a symbol of rebirth, and the ascetic in order to achieve *mokṣa* had to transcend this rebirth cycle. This was the reiteration of the patriarchal dichotomy between men/masculinity and transcendence on the one hand, and the woman/femininity and immanence on the other.

One only has to contrast this somatophobia of the ascetic tradition which was inextricably linked with misogyny, with the Tāntric tradition and its liberating potential for women in their corporeal existence (see Vijay Nath, this volume). Many female *siddhas* played a significant role in preaching and popularizing Tāntric Buddhism of *sahajayāna* in the early medieval period. Shaw (1998), in her study of Tāntric Buddhism, points out that within this philosophical system enlightenment was possible through heterosexual intercourse undertaken within specific ritual and spiritual contexts. This was a major break from the earlier Buddhist tradition within which the renunciation of sexual relations was a prerequisite for attaining liberation. Bhagwatī Lakṣmīṅkara in the eighth century boldly projected the new theory of *sahajayāna,* wherein she declared that truth can only be realized by reverence of the body which is the abode of all gods, with concentration of the mind or *sahajayoga* (cited in Bhattacharyya 1999: 239). Here we do not notice any dichotomy of body and mind. One is not valorized at the expense of the other. Furthermore, as against the misogyny of the ascetic tradition, Lakṣmīṅkara forcefully underlined the need to venerate women. She said that no hatred should be expressed towards those who were the embodiment of the Goddess *Prajñā* (see Bhattacharyya 1999: 239).

Tāntricism was unique in that it did not have the inbuilt androcentricism of other ancient Indian religious systems. The *Śaktīsaṅgama tantra,* thus, states that 'there is no *tapas* better than a woman, no *tīrtha* better than a woman, no *yoga* better than a woman, and no *japa* better than a woman' (cited in Bhattacharyya 1982: 346). This grand valorization of women had to do with a cosmogony in which the woman's generative organ (*bhaga*) had a life-giving symbolism (ibid.: 128). Among the *pañcamakāras* of Tāntricism, one was *maithuna* (intercourse), viewed as the human counterpart of the cosmic creative process. According to the *Kaulāvalīnirṇaya, maithuna* was the only means by which an aspirant could become a *siddha.* It was thus looked upon with reverence and was not associated with guilt or sin (Shaw 1998: 154–55). In Tāntric discourse sex is salvation.

In Tāntric philosophy, the *puṅsa* or male is passive and *prakṛti* or the female is dynamic. This was a reversal of the traditional hierarchy of Vedic literature. Not only was the hierarchy reversed, but also perhaps the heterosexual love itself was challenged within this discourse. Within the Tāntric system, for instance, among the *sahajīyas* the male devotee had to worship the female principle as a woman. As Bhandarkar (see Chattopadhyaya 1959: 284) observed, 'the ambition of every pious follower of the system is to become identical with the Tripurasundarī, and one of his religious exercises is to habituate himself to think that he is a woman. Thus, the followers of the *Śākta* school justify their appellation by the belief that god is a woman and it ought to be the aim of all to become a woman'. Similarly, speaking of *Sahajīyas*, Bose (ibid.) remarked that 'the *Sahajīyas* believed that at a certain stage of spiritual culture the man should transform into a woman, and remember he cannot have the experience of true love so long as he cannot realize the nature of the woman in him'. The divine principle here is the feminine, and the worshipper, even a male, in order to be considered a true devotee had to invoke in himself his latent femininity. From the gender perspective this was truly liberating. For this meant, as far as men were concerned, a reversal of status. From the point of view of sexual love the Tāntric system can be interpreted as encouraging love between women.

The Lokāyatas, also known as Cārvākas, had a radically different notion of *kāma*. Their philosophy identified the self with the senses and spoke of the satisfaction of the senses (Radhakrishnan 1953: 133–38). The materialists were of the view that worldly pleasure is the only thing that is true and good. The only reasonable end for men is the gratification of their senses – *kāmevaika puruṣārtha*. Therefore, bodily pleasures were not deprecated (*Naiṣadhcaritam* 17.48: 50–51). Since the Cārvākas did not suffer from somatophobia, they had no misogynistic views either. As the *Naiṣadhcaritam* (17.42), quoting materialists, says 'Fie on those who boast of family dignity! They hold women in check out of jealousy; but do not likewise restrain men, though the blindness of passion is common to both'. The Cārvākas also exposed the hypocrisy of the patriarchal ascetic tradition: 'those other-worldly fellows, ready to perform sacrifices, did they renounce their passion? For even after death they long for heaven, the quintessence of which is its gazelle-eyed nymphs' (*Naiṣadhcaritam* 17.68).

II

Let us now focus on the female body as conceived in the *āyurvedic* and *kāmaśāstrīya* discourse. This emphasis on the body to understand the social reality follows from the anthropological theory that the body represents or encodes social meanings. The body is thus seen as a metaphor for society (Douglas 1966). If gender is indeed constructed, then it is not psychology or biology but really, as Butler remarks, 'culture that becomes destiny' (Butler 1990: 8). A body is perceived as the instrument or medium of culture. A culture's grip on the body is the fact, and woman in relation to her body is dominated by culture.

The *āyurvedic* discourse tended to marginalize if not exclude women. The only expression of the female body framed within this discourse is what is of significance to men. Thus, when the *āyurvedic* texts deal exclusively with female pathology it is with reference to diseases of the uterus or *garbhavyāpta* as they are referred to in the *Aṣṭāṅgasaṅgraha*. The *āyurvedic* texts also talk at length about the diseases of the women's reproductive system *yonivyāpta* (*Caraksaṃhitā, Cikitsā* 30; *Suśrutasaṃhitā, Uttaratantra* 38; *Aṣṭāṅgasaṅgraha, Uttarasthāna* 38.34). In the *Mādhavanidāna* (*Nidānaparisiṣṭam* 27), Madhavkar deals with the latter and with abortion, the post-natal period, lactation, and infertility. Of the *aṣṭāṅga* or eight branches of medicine enumerated by Vāgbhaṭṭa, there is one devoted to *bālacikitsā* (paediatrics), one branch to *vṛṣacikitsā* which deals with restoring the virility of men, but women do not figure anywhere as a subject in this specialized list of eight. Men are advised to balance their diet in order to maintain good health, while women's health is discussed only (in the contexts of pregnancy and childbirth). Furthermore, if at all *āyurvedic* texts were concerned with diseases of the uterus, it was because a healthy uterus was crucial to the birth and health of progeny. Says Vāgbhaṭṭa (*Aṣṭāṅgasaṅgraha, Uttarasthāna* 2.40), *strī hi mūlapatyānām, strī hi rakṣati rakṣitā* (Woman is the chief cause for progeny, if she is protected progeny is protected). The stance of the *āyurvedic* writers was pro-antenatalistic. Their intent was to protect women's fertility and the fruit of that fertility. Vāgbhaṭṭa and Caraka[1] thus confine their attention to problems of women's reproductive organs.

As woman mattered only as a potential mother, her impregnation by man was also something that engaged the attention of these writers. Caraka, Ḍalhaṇa and Vāgbhaṭṭa state that what is today called the missionary coital position is the best means of impregnating a woman. Ḍalhaṇa (*Suśrutasaṃhitā, Cikitsāsthāna* 24.120), listing the don'ts for a man during intercourse, mentions coitus enjoyed by lying back and holding the woman on one's bosom. In another place, he (*Suśrutasaṃhitā, Śarīrasthāna* 2.42–44) describes impotence and says that it develops when a man behaves like the female partner while performing intercourse; a boy so conceived will behave like a woman and will be incapable of discharging. If a girl is so conceived, then she will behave like a man. Vāgbhaṭṭa says the same thing. It follows, then, that 'masculinity' according to *āyurvedic* writers was an achieved state and not an anatomical fact, and in order to achieve the required degree of masculinity it was necessary to follow a virile model of the sexual act.

Lesbian love and autoeroticism were denounced. Ḍalhaṇa (*Suśrutasaṃhitā, Śarīrasthāna* 2.47) tells us that a 'boneless monstrosity' (*alpakomalāsthi*) is the outcome of a sexual act in which both the partners are female and their sexual secretions unite somehow or the other in the womb of one of them. Ḍalhaṇa (ibid.: 48–49) also says that a lady who has had a bath after her menstrual period then in a dream experiences the pleasure of intercourse, the *vāyu* pushes the menstrual blood into the uterus and converts it into a foetus. Such a foetus (*kalalam*) is devoid of paternal qualities. Ḍalhaṇa (ibid.: 52), therefore declares that all such foetuses should be considered the outcome of deadly sin and the atheism of the parents in Vāgbhaṭṭa (*Aṣṭāṅgasaṅgraha, Śarīrasthāna* 1.44) notes that at the time

[1] Although the *Carakasaṃhitā* was originally a work of the third century, the extant text is a redaction of Dṛḍhabala dated to the ninth century. At that time Dṛḍhabala also added a chapter entitled *Siddhisthāna* to it.

of intercourse women secrete *śukra,* but since it is of no significance for conception, he does not elaborate on it. It is clear that for *āyurvedic* experts woman was nothing more than a uterus. She only had a reproductive life and nothing beyond.

Yet a description of a woman's role in intercourse appears in the chapter entitled *Śarīrasthāna* which deals with the formation of the embryo. For Caraka (*Carakasaṃhitā, Śarīrasthāna* 2.20), one reason for the birth of deformed progeny is the lack of a mother's arousal. Desire of both partners is underlined as an important element in the making of a foetus in the first place. The (*Carakasaṃhitā, Śarīrasthāna* 8.7) states, 'when they are stimulated well and are favourably disposed for coitus (*sañjātaharṣamaithune*), they should go to bed well-perfumed'. Vāgbhaṭṭa (*Aṣṭāṅgasaṅgraha, Śarīrasthāna* 1.12) also opines that in the process of begetting children a man and woman should be healthy, in love with each other, and desirous of intercourse. Describing the kinds of women whom men should not have sexual intercourse with, Ḍalhaṇa (*Suśrutasaṃhitā, Cikitsāsthāna* 24.114–16) lists one who is not amorously disposed, who is inimical to men, or one who is leading the life of a nun. Having intercourse with such women leads to a waste of semen. Thus, medically speaking, women's desire and sexual pleasure were seen only as aids to the conception of the child.

Interestingly, where female desire transcended the virile model, it usually got classified under the diseases of the genital tract. Vāgbhaṭṭa (*Aṣṭāṅgasaṅgraha, Uttarasthāna* 38.34), enumerating twenty diseases of the genital tract, says that one of the diseases is caused by the use of an unnatural thing for coition. Ḍalhaṇa (*Suśrutasaṃhitā, Uttaratantra* 38.15), describes nymphomania as a kind of uterus that does not know satiation. Mādhavkar (*Mādhavanidāna* 62.9) and Caraka (*Carakasaṃhitā, Cikitsāsthāna* 30.18) refer to the *aticaraṇā/acaraṇāyoni* as one which is unable to retain semen and suffering pain due to over-indulgence in sex. Caraka (*Carakasaṃhitā, Cikitsāsthāna* 30.17) describes satyriasis in women when he refers to intense itching. Women afflicted by this ailment, he says, constantly desire sexual intercourse. Ḍalhaṇa's (*Suśrutasaṃhitā, Uttaratantra* 38.16) description of the *acaraṇāyoni* is an illustration of a woman experiencing orgasm before male ejaculation is complete. He says, that in an *acaraṇāyoni* a greater quantity of ovum is secreted before male ejaculation. Referring to *acaraṇā* as *pārkcaraṇā*, the *Madhukoṣa* commentary on *Mādhavnidāna* (Vol. 2: 828–29) says that it cannot get impregnated. Thus we see that what can be construed as sexual pleasure for women, was associated in the *āyurvedic* treatises with difficulty in procreation. Perhaps the control of women's sexuality was also sought by instilling a fear of genital diseases.

The medical discourse also valorizes semen, the male organ, and ejaculation. There are therapies for enhancing virility. While the *āyurvedic* writers were aware of the biological fact of menopause, it did not evoke any special concern. The very definition of *vājikaraṇa* underlines the *āyurvedic* writer's bias towards privileging the male desire. Suśruta says, and Ḍalhaṇa (*Suśrutasaṃhitā, Cikitsāsthāna* 26.4–5) agrees, that a youth in sound health, regularly taking some sort of aphrodisiac remedy may enjoy pleasures every night in all the seasons of the year.

Old men and persons weakened by excessive sexual activity should subject themselves to a course of *vājikaraṇa* therapy. Virility was not only sexual prowess but also the fertility which it made possible. Caraka (*Carakasaṃhitā, Cikitsāsthāna* 2.1: 16–23) says, 'one desirous of progeny as well as sexual pleasure should use an aphrodisiac regularly'.

Women, on the other hand, were not the focus of these aphrodisiac prescriptions. According to Vāgbhaṭṭa (*Aṣṭāṅgasaṅgraha, Uttarasthāna* 50.118–23), woman is the best aphrodisiac. Caraka (*Carakasaṃhitā, Cikitsāsthāna* 2.1: 4–7) tells us that the foremost of the aphrodisiacs is the exhilarating young woman who is beautiful, submissive and skilled. Such a woman is the best aphrodisiac (*sa strīvṛṣyatamāmata*). A woman's sexuality thus lies in her capacity to arouse desire in that male. Can then one legitimately ask, as MacKinnon (1982: 533) does, 'Is women's sexuality its absence? If being for another is the whole of woman's sexual construction.'

Feminists (MacKinnon 1994: 260–61) have tended to argue that sexuality is not a discrete sphere of interaction, feeling or behaviour in which social divisions may or may not be played out. Rather, it is a dimension along which gender occurs and through which gender is socially constituted. Thus 'woman' is defined by what men desire or require for arousal and satisfaction, and is socially tautological with 'female sexuality' and the 'female sex'. The restrictions and constraints, the servility and the display, the enforced passivity, are all included in the content of sex in the case of women (ibid.). This theoretical position is best illustrated in the *kāmaśāstrīya* texts of our period.

All the *kāmaśāstrīya* texts were written by men, for men. The purpose was to educate men on the mechanism of sexual principles that govern men and women's sexual relations and, thus, control women. As Kokkokā says in his *Ratirahasya*, 'the aim of the *kāmasāstra* is the easy attainment of a woman who can be attained with difficulty, to erotically arouse the one who is already attained and to enjoy complete sexual pleasure with her' (*Ratirahasya* 1.6). He says 'a man who is puzzled about the nature, type, disposition and gestures according to the place of a origin of a woman and who is ignorant of the doctrines of sexual pleasures (*ratitantra mūḍa*) will not know what to do even when he is in the presence of a young woman, just like an ape does not know what to do after having acquired a coconut' (*Ratirahasya* 1.8).

Kāmaśāstra theoretically granted access to sexual knowledge to both men and women, for the latter too were involved in its practice. But, women's access to this knowledge was circumscribed. Yaśodhara (*Jayamaṅgalā* 1.3.2) tells us that a girl should learn the *kāmaśāstra* before marriage in her father's house because after marriage she will not be independent. He also warns that if a married woman tries to gain this knowledge without her husband's permission he is likely to doubt her virtue and may think her promiscuous. Besides, girls/wives could imbibe this knowledge only in a select circle of women, mostly kinswomen. Thus, an entire 'network of control' (Roy 1996: 162) existed to regulate women's access to such knowledge. No wonder then, that in these texts women are rarely allowed their own preferences and the texts hardly ever focus on women's pleasure or satisfaction.

It could be argued that inequity was central to such texts as they articulate a set of statements about social hierarchy. The society was feudal and patriarchal with polygynous households; the *nāyaka* was the focus of socio-sexual relations and in control of them. Women came to be classified as the object of sexual relations in a very comprehensive way. The ideal woman was defined in terms of physical and psychological attributes, and also according to the region from which she came. There was a striking dichotomy between the construct of the *nāyaka* where the ideal seemed to be a universal kind of man but where women were diverse (Roy 1996: 158). The *nāyikās* were differentiated almost *ad infinitum* from men and from each other and what was important in this classification was the sexual ties to the man. They are either accessible to a single man on to two men on to all men, or they are inaccessible on account of incest taboos, class/caste considerations and so on (*Jayamaṅgalā* 1.5.29). One suspects that the sheer diversity of the women came not only from flights of erotic fancy, but also have to be seen in a social context in which women for sale (*vikretvyatulya*).

Given the feudal patriarchal setting of these texts, sexual access to women was presented as an index of male status. Yaśodhara's (*Jayamaṅgalā* 5.5.5–6) description of women's sexual exploitation is distressing in its nakedness. He tell us that women of the lower classes (*carṣaṇī*) performing forced labour for high-status men may be made the target of sexual advances. Yaśodhara (*Jayamaṅgalā* 5.5.7–10) goes on to list a number of state officials who may use their position to gain sexual access to women. In fact, men who were at the receiving end in this feudal polity were encouraged to buy protection through the sexual gift of their wives/women. Theoretically, lower-class men could gain access to royal apartments, which would signify the overturning of social/sexual hierarchies, that is, women inviting outside men, defying the powerful high status of their father or husband. But this was not perceived as desirable. The solution consisted in guarding women (*Jayamaṅgalā* 5.6.39). To prevent a man being cuckolded, Yaśodhara (*Jayamaṅgalā* 1.5.29) while enumerating women who should not be visited sexually, lists royal women among them. The *Ratirahasya* (13.6) advises that *paradārā* should be from the non-*dvija* (*advija*) caste only so that the class/caste hierarchy was not adversely affected.

Since men were initiators of sexual relationships and at the same time controlled them, it was only natural that primacy was given to the male desire. Woman was the passive recipient of male desire and had no subject position. In this set-up her desire was to 'be desired'. And to make herself desirable, woman was required to present herself as a beautiful thing. We see in the *kāmaśāstra* literature tips on cosmetics and *Ratirahasya* (15.80) gives tips on how a newly delivered woman can regain a youthful body. It is stated explicitly that by following such tips and achieving the desired results women will entrap the hearts of men (*rasikahṛdaya*). Yaśodhara (*Jayamaṅgalā* 4.1.13) says women should approach their husbands properly dressed and made up, or else face indifference. Women's bodies were thus 'subjected' in the sense that they were made to conform to the ideal of the male gaze. An entire aesthetic of femininity was thus built up which women were supposed to uphold, yet not for their own sakes. In Kumāradāsa's *Jānakīharaṇa* (8.42) is a verse wherein Rāma decorates Sītā, but she does not show any desire to see herself in the mirror, because for women the entire purpose of dressing is to please the husband. Not only did women have to have the right physical proportions but they also had to be the right age in order to be sexually desirable for men. An old menopausal woman beyond the age of fifty, states the *Nāgarasarvasvam* (16.2–3), was prohibited for sexual intercourse (*suratotsava-varjitā*).

In the *kāmaśāstra* texts the heterosexual coitus prioritized male pleasure so much that even when the texts (*Nāgarsarvasvam* 37.6–10) focus on the details of a woman making love, the verses do not convey her pleasure. Rather, the emphasis is on what the woman should do to enhance male pleasure. It was expressly stated that she should give herself totally to the pleasure of man. A *nāyikā* who was indifferent to sexual intercourse was to be forcibly seduced (*Ratirahasya* 10.4). In fact, love was described as a sexual war[2] in *Ratirahasya* (10.53), and as *kalaharūpa* by Yaśodhara (*Jayamaṅgalā* 2.7.1). But in this combat while men had the right to strike, women could only respond with shrieks and moans and this behaviour is justified on the grounds that men are by nature rough and impetuous, but women are passive and weak (*Jayamaṅgalā* 2.7.22). It follows from this that masochism is associated with women and the sadism with men.

In the *kāmaśāstrīya* discourse, not only is the idea of sexual love largely narcissistic and chauvinistic from the male viewpoint, it is also conceived as the pursuit and capture of the *nāyikā*. In the realm of body language the various ways of carrying oneself are culturally encoded and can even define social status. Thus, in patriarchy men are the predators while women in order to be sexually attractive must be passive, shy and given to flight so that their pursuit becomes that much more desirable for men. The theme of the chase as a metaphor indicates dominance and submission as inherent in sexual activity. It is significant that in the classification of *nāyikās* according to nature, *padminī* is described as the best while *chitriṇī, śaṅkhinī* and *hastinī* are successively lower in appeal (*Ratirahasya,* 1.10). This text goes on to describe *padminī,* the most desirable of the *nāyikā,* as deeply shy, while *hastinī* is totally devoid of shame (*Viṭalajjā*). *Saṅkhinī* too is sexually forthcoming (*Ratirahasya* 1.17) and quick to make nail and tooth marks on her lover's body. We thus see that female sexuality is supposed to lie in physical receptiveness and a passive and submissive personality. Thus *padminī* women were more desirable than the *śaṅkhinī* and *hastinī.*

Heterosexual sex in the *kāmaśāstra* literature was essentially conceived in terms of a virile penetrative model that was the outcome of a patriarchal phallic

2 Van Gulik (1961: 76) makes a similar observation about ancient China. He points out that in Chinese literature sexual congress was often referred to as a battle. In fact, some manuals in ancient China worked out the details of the coitus as military moves on the battlefield and were therefore mistaken to be manuals of war.

culture (here the term phallic signifies the dominance of men over women). Female pleasure was conceived in terms of successful and more frequent penile penetration. In other words, intercourse was seen as an invitation to mount and the penis was seen as the primary organ of sexual pleasure for both sexes. This being the case, men with soft and small penises, says *Nāgarasarvasvam* (12.1) cannot satisfy women. So men are advised to follow a regimen that would make their penises hard like iron and such men (*Nāgarasarvasvam* 12.4) become conquerors of women. This emphasis on the male genitals and on man's inexhaustible, voracious sexual appetite as the only formula in the success of erotic relationships tends to devalue the notion of desire per se (with its emotional and mental connotations) and on erotic reciprocity in the sexual relations between the two partners.

The valorization of male virility resulted in the marginalization of such postures in which women were active. In the *puruṣāyita* erotic posture, there was a reversal of the penetrator-penetrated hierarchy and, therefore, it was described as *viparītarata.* The very use of the term *viparīta* (opposite) is significant for it conveys departure from the norm. Here the man was receptive. Yaśodhara states (*Jayamaṅgalā* 2.8.39) that in this posture women make their desires more apparent. It seems that in this position women could finally 'own' desire. *Ratirahasya* (10.49–50) describes a woman atop a man who says that 'now you rogue, you have been laid down by me, I shall kill you, hide yourself, you have been rendered humble'. Kokkokā points out (*Ratirahasya* 10.65) that becoming too used to this position and adopting it frequently is neither desirable nor cultured. While Yaśodhara (*Jayamaṅgalā* 2.8.1) warns women that they should adopt this posture only if the *nāyaka* is tired and she has his permission or else be considered shameless. He further says (*Jayamaṅgalā* 2.8.2–3) that a woman can initiate this posture on her own only if she is very sure of her man and knows that he enjoys this form of copulation.

III

In the classical Sanskrit literature, the *veśyā* is one of the *nāyikā* types. She is variously described as *sāmānyā, sādhāraṇa strī, prakāśanarī, bāhyā* etc. In nearly all these appellations for the *veśyā* what is stressed is her sexuality, which was the opposite of the sexuality of the domestic women of patriarchy. In Dāmodaragupta's *Kuṭṭanīmatam* (vs. 637), a *veśyā* is described as one who uses her sexual skills for a livelihood. But in this process of commodifying desire (*kāma*) she, unlike the *kulavadhū*, managed to acquire control over her own *dharma* and *artha.*

There is a tendency to view the prostitute as a sexy person, but there was more to her than just a body on sale. The courtesans (*gaṇikā*) among the prostitutes were more famous for their cultural accomplishments than for their erotic appeal. It was intellectual and artistic accomplishments, that made a *gaṇikā* worthy of respect from even the king. The connoisseur showered praise on her, and she was sought out as a teacher (*prārthanīya kalopadeśārthina*) (*Jayamaṅgalā* 1.3.17–18). Unlike the *kulastrī* who had to have a low voice (*Kuṭṭanīmatam*, vs. 848) or be altogether silent, the prostitute was articulate. This is evident from the fact that in literature the 'clever speech' of the courtesan had a proverbial status even if non-prostitutes resorted to it. This was how the speech of princess Vegavatī was described in Buddhaswāmī's *Bṛhatkathāślokasaṅgraha* (canto XV.46). Not only were prostitutes articulate as a rule, they were in many cases among the only women in classical Sanskrit literature who were entitled to speak Sanskrit as is the case with the *gaṇikā* Vasantasenā in *Mṛcchakaṭikam*.

Yet sexuality was the most important characteristic of the *veśyā*, for they were sex workers. In the patriarchal discourse, non-marital, non-reproductive and libidinous female sexuality was 'deviant'. Even for many feminists, the prostitute's sexuality is essentially a dominated one and, therefore, bad. Pateman (cited in Overall 1992: 722) argues that the prostitute's sexuality is the recognition of men as sexual masters. It puts submission on sale as a commodity in the market. Irigaray (cited in Bell 1994: 74, 88) also sees prostitution as sex that is not one's own and is constructed according to the desire of the other. A prostitute is, in Irigaray's words, merely an obliging prop for the enactment of men's fantasies. Thus she explicitly links the prostitute body to (male-defined) female sexuality. For Mackinnon (1982: 515–44), since heterosexuality institutionalized male dominance and female submission, there can be no scope for prostitute 'agency' in commercial sexual encounters. But Mackinnon (Bell 1994: 80) tends to ignore the existence of the multiplicity of desires, some of which do not conform to the requirements of the masculinist system. Liberal feminists like Vance (1984) and Rubin (1984) argue against treating any kind of sexual practice as either 'bad' or 'abnormal'. Heterosexual coitus itself cannot be taken as a mark of women's sexual subordination for even their own sexual choices are often exercised.

A careful analysis of the literary sources of our period would confirm the liberal feminist view of prostitute sexuality. If one juxtaposes the socialization of the *kulavadhū* against the *vāravadhū* (prostitute) the latter appears far removed from 'domination'. The notion of shame is important in patriarchy, where the female body is controlled and regulated both at the level of the individual and the group. In fact, patriarchy rests on the foundation of controlled female body. Along with purity and pollution, honour and shame are two of the most prominent cultural ideologies of Brāhmaṇical patriarchy; and they have played an important role in controlling women's behaviour and the spaces that they can occupy, as also the limits of their socio-sexual relations. In the *bāhyā* and the *abhyāntarā* (women of the household) classification of the *nāyikās* we see the operation of the *purdah* system. Sociologically speaking (Papanek and Minault 1982), purdah delimits the spheres that women can legitimately occupy. The *Kuṭṭanīmatam* (verse 895) tells us that the veil was what distinguished respectable (*ārya*) ladies from ordinary (*anārya*) ones. These ordinary women were usually prostitutes. In *Samayamātṛkā* (2.54) Kṣemendra refers to a mischievous courtesan who passed herself off as the daughter of a high-ranking royal officer by half-covering her face. In *Dhūrta-viṭasamvāda* (*Śṛṅgārahāṭa* 74) a *kulavadhū's* veil is called *lajjā-paṭa* (i.e. what covers the shame). Women of good family not only had to have a veil on their faces, they were also required, says the *Kuṭṭanīmatam* (vs. 848), to have humility, a low voice and slow movements. The *bāhyā*, on the other hand, was without veil. In the *Mṛcchakaṭikam,* Vasantasenā was without a veil till the king's announcement declared her the bride of Cārudatta, and immediately Śarvilaka veiled her. The wearing of the veil also affected the way the sexuality of women was perceived. In the *Nāṭyaśāstra* (24.225–228) it is said about the courtesan that when she goes out to meet her lover she decorates her body with various ornaments and goes forth to meet him . . . with (a display of) passion and joy. The *abhyāntarā nāyikā* (*Nāṭyaśāstra* 24.227), on the other hand, walked the street covering her face with a veil, timidly her limbs contracted, and often turned her face away or looked down. According to the *Nāṭyaśāstra* (24.163–165) a *bāhyā nāyikā* could be depicted displaying her love – 'she expresses her passion by casting side-long glances (*kaṭākṣa*), touching her ornaments, itching ears, scratching the ground with her toes, revealing the breasts and the navel, cleaning the nails and gathering her hair'. But a high-born lady shows the signs of love differently (*Nāṭyaśāstra* 24.166–167) – 'she looks continuously with blooming eyes, conceals her smile, speaks slowly and with a downcast face, replies with a smile, conceals her sweat and appearance, has throbbing lips and is trembling'. Not only was a prostitute allowed greater freedom of expression, but she was also entitled to greater freedom as far as her bodily gestures were concerned. Bharata notes in the *Nāṭyaśāstra* (24.240–42) that higher-class women could not be shown using cosmetics (unguents and collyrium), painting the body, coyly handling their breasts on combing their hair. They could not be shown dressed poorly (*nāpavṛtā*) or wearing only one garment (*ekavastra*).

The notion of 'shame' acquired a totally different meaning for the prostitute. In the *Kuṭṭanīmatam* (vs. 306) we are told that 'for a *veśyā* covering her lower body is not out of "shame" but to arouse desire in others'. Prostitutes were open about discussing their sexual experiences with all types of clients. In a comic verse (*Kuṭṭanīmatam*, vs. 399) a *veśyā* tells others how, when she closed her eyes in the ecstasy of sexual pleasure, her inexperienced paramour ran away thinking her dead. So we see that, compared to the circumscribed sexuality of the patriarchal women, the prostitute enjoyed greater freedom of sexual expression. We get an interesting example of Madanamañcukā in the *Bṛhatkathāślokasaṅg*raha (canto XIV.113), who was the daughter of a *veśyā*. She took the vow of constancy, and thus was transformed as an ideal *pativratā*.

Much is said about a prostitute's sexuality being commanded by the man, who as a client, pays for it. But if one contrasts the location of the man's wife in the inner apartment and that of the *veśyā*'s life outside, we find the former completely closed and its occupants, the wife/wives, owe complete fidelity to their husband. The husband–wife tie was one that did not necessarily depend on the existence of an erotic relationship in order to constitute itself. The sexual relations between the two were carried on the basis of a statutory relationship that empowered the husband to 'demand' from his wife all services including sexual ones. The *pativrata* ideology ensured compliance. Within the confines of the *antaḥpura*, the marital partners were hierarchically placed. While *kulavadhūs* were thus relegated to a private sphere and their status was in being *asūryaspṛśyā*, the *gaṇikās* (significantly enough called *prakāśanarī*) (*Mṛcchakaṭikam* Act III.7) were the women par excellence of the public sphere. Vasantasenā is appreciatively described as *nagarasyabhūṣaṇam* and *Nagarsṛī* in the *Mṛcchakaṭikam* (Act VIII.23; VIII.39). In *Daśakumāracarita* (p. 130), *veśyā* Kāmamañjarī was similarly described as an ornament of the city of Campa. These *gaṇikās* and their paramours met in public places such as brothels, gardens, or the temples of *Kāma*. All these were open areas in which everyone moved around freely. Freedom of space also dictated the freedom of choice. One could not in such a case exercise statutory authority. A *gaṇikā* was thus free to accept or reject any proposition – Vasantasenā used this choice quite tellingly, rejecting the king's brother-in-law for impoverished Cārudatta. In order to secure her consent, no *pativrata* ideology could come to the rescue. Her favours (which many were in a position to refuse) had to be secured by persuasion and very often this took the form of gifts that outshone those offered by the rivals.

It is my submission that it was the prostitute's autonomy that introduced an element of male anxiety in the *veśyā*–client relationship. It was this precariousness of relation, which was most often used by the *veśyā* to milk her clients. Irigaray (see Bell 1994: 89–91) sees the prostitute as a 'speaking subject' who actively intervenes in the male exchange economy (which had the exchange of women at its foundation).[3] A prostitute took herself to the market and named her price, and in so doing she intervened in the male exchange economy. Should then the prostitute be seen as an empowered person who set the terms for the encounters?

In the sources of our period the sexual life of the prostitute – the unlimited freedom and the unbounded pleasure of intercourse with any partner – is often portrayed in a positive light. Kṣemendra in *Kalāvilāsa* (see Sternbach 1953: 65) says that because of this independence they are envied by some women who thought 'fortunate are courtesans who enjoy life without restrictions, with many young men'.

We find aphorisms which state that a good wife is one who behaves in bed like a *veśyā*. This notion does attribute a degree of agency to her. In fact, the free sexual behaviour or sexual experience of the prostitute is seen as giving greater pleasure than does consorting with wives. This is pithily expressed in Īśvardata's *Dhūrtaviṭasaṃvāda* (*Śṛṅgārahāṭa* 1960: 74) where a young man announces that he is about to be married. The *viṭa* or narrator expresses surprise that the young man wants to leave a *veśyā mahāpatha* for *kulavadhū kumārageṇa*. He also wonders how pleasure can be had from consorting with *kulavadhūs* who are blind to sexual pleasure, who talk inaudibly, are so shy that they have never seen their bodies and are no better than a yoked animal. The prostitute, then, is not so much a 'deviant' as a 'teacher'.

[3] French anthropologist Levi Strauss had argued that the circulation of women among men is what establishes the operation of society. The use, consumption and circulation of women are the foundation for society.

Far from being a mere 'obliging prop' for the enactment of male fantasies we find from our sources that prostitutes found pleasure in their lives. In the *Bṛhatkathāślokasaṅgraha* (canto XVIII. 63–66) we are told about the *veśyā* Gaṅgādattā who openly desires the hero, Sannudāsa. In fact the sexual encounter between Gaṅgādattā and Sannudāsa (*Bṛhatkathāślokasaṁgraha*, XVIII.73–75) is described as a mutual exchange of bodies on equal terms. In *Kuṭṭanīmatam* (verses 389, 575), we see a *veśyā* performing the *puruṣāyita* or *viparītarata* form of coitus. Yaśodhara in his *Jayamaṅgalā* (6.6.44; 2.6.48) refers to many patrons uniting with one *veśyā,* and this is referred to as *goṣṭhiparigṛha.* It is important to note, that one woman uniting with many men is not acceptable to Vātsyāyana and his commentator Yaśodhara.[4] In Book II of the *Kāmasūtra* (2.6.45) where Vātsyāyana described various sexual practices including orgies, he attributes such a practice as one woman sexually uniting with many men as taking place in a woman's kingdom.[5] Yaśodhara (*Jayamaṅgalā* 2.6.45) refers to the men who partner women in these orgies as those who live like kept women. Such descriptions put a question mark on the notion of a prostitute's sexuality as being completely male dominated. One could argue that a feature of sexual activity with a prostitute is the opportunity for men to escape conventional heterosexual roles that placed a heavy emphasis on masculine prowess and domination. In fact, the *veśavāsa* or prostitute quarters were those liminal places where socially acceptable practices could be transgressed.

Apart from prostitutes, we also find references to other free women who were outside the constricting patriarchal social and sexual norms. Prominent among them were the *rākṣasī* and the *māyāvinī.* In the literary sources of our period these two communities of women were specifically associated with erotic autonomy. In the *Mahāvīracaritam* of Bhavabhūti the *rākṣasī* women of Dakṣiṇāpatha live a life of freedom (social, political and sexual) as compared to the circumscribed life of the patriarchal Aryan women (Dikshit 1964: 198). Given their free lifestyles and assured social standing, it is not surprising that Sūrpanakhā of *Mahāvīracaritam* (Act IV: 177) had no shame in desiring a younger Rāma either, for she was enamoured of his good looks. In the *Nalacampū* (see Miller 1975: 662) of the tenth century, while referring to the adulterous passion of Rādhā for Kṛṣṇa, Trivikrambhaṭṭa describes Rādhā as a *māyāvinī* who, he says, committed the fault of giving up modesty, ignoring the virtuous elders and set her passion on the highest other man (*parāpuruṣa*).

On the other hand, the daughters and the wives of the patriarchy lived their entire lives circumscribed by rules. Within the patriarchal family the girls were guarded against sexual transgression as breaking the rules would bring disgrace to their entire families. In Bāṇa's *Kādambarī* (*pūrva bhāga*: 213) Mahāśvetā's tragedy arises from the fact that she could not decide whether she should follow

[4] In none of the narrative or *kāvya* texts is this practice mentioned.

[5] These have traditionally been seen as the marginal areas outside the Brāhmaṇical patriarchy, where 'normal' practices are suspended. Although sometimes (*Jayamaṅgalā* 2.6.38, 48) the royal women of prācya land indulge in the practice, it is done in secret.

her heart and go to her lover or stay back within the parental four walls. She tells her friend Taralikā of her predicament thus: 'my senses are perplexed. . . . If in the first place, like an ordinary maiden leaving off shame, relinquishing firmness of mind, casting off modesty, not regarding the evil talk of the people not minding his birth, accepting infamy . . . not permitted by my father and not allowed by my mother, if I approach him of my own accord and make him accept my hand, then it will be a grave breach of duty'. . . . While it was important for the girls to remain chaste and restrained, it was equally important not to be averse to marriage as Subandhu's Vāsavadattā (1967: 110) was. Princess Vāsavadattā's father was eager to avoid the sin that would accrue from her passing youth. In the marriage-oriented world of patriarchy, it was crucially important for girls to make a commitment. Thus, in Vidyākara's *Subhāṣitaratnakoṣa* there are fifty verses[6] on adolescence age (*vayasandhi*), and except for a solitary verse (no. 353) on a young boy, all the other forty-nine are about girls slowly awakening to the other sex. In this view, female sexuality was just waiting to open up to male contact. The male eye and male touch were the *summum bonum* of that growing up for adolescent girls.

In the patriarchal social world, wifehood was the most significant milestone of a woman's life. Throughout her girlhood she was groomed for this role. In *Bṛhatkathāślokasaṅg*raha (canto IV.79–80) a woman bereft of a husband was likened to a house with walls but no roof. If the husband was the roof or provided a roof over her head, he also extracted privileges for it. In order to ensure that the wife was bearing only her husband's child, she had to be completely loyal (*satī*) to him. A verse in Jalhaṇa's anthology *Sūktimuktāvalī* (122.6) hails the wife who is loyal (*satī*) to her husband, sweet-speaking, works for the husband in the day and smells nice and is ornamented by night. Given the illegitimacy of the sexual transgression by a wife, in the erotic *kāvya* poetry female adultery is always depicted as love on the sly. Since her adultery is a secret tryst, the husband's awareness of it is never alluded to in the literature. There is, thus, no cheated *nāyaka* in classical Sanskrit literature. In a patriarchal polygynous setting, free sexuality of the wife that could make the husband jealous was not possibile. As for the husband, society did not demand strict fidelity from him. On the other hand, if a woman was to be unfaithful, she would cease to be noble, and Sanskrit poetics does not permit emotional concern of the *nāyaka* over the loss of what had already lost its value (Ingalls 1965: 15). In a rare example where the husband has full knowledge of his wife's adultery, the woman happens to be from a lower class while her paramour belongs to the elite. A verse from *Āryāsaptaśatī* (312) refers to a weaver taking pride in the beauty of his wife which has made her an object of desire among the elite. This gives him a certain status among his kin and makes it difficult for him to keep his feet on the ground.

[6] In Śridharadāsa's *Saduktikarṇāmṛta* all verses under *vayasaṅdhi* refer to the adolescent female.

IV

Bhoja, in his seminal treatise *Śṛṅgāra Prakāśa* (p. 39), talks of two kinds of *kāma*: *sāmānyarūpa* and *viśeṣarūpa*. While the former is the pleasurable experience of the five senses and the mind, the latter is pleasure born of love for a sweetheart. This *viśeṣarūpa kāma* is further sub-divided into *pradhāna* (foremost in the sense of touch in the sweetheart) and *apradhāna* (joy in thinking of her beauty. We thus see that Bhoja tends to make a distinction between love that is mental and love that is corporeal. In my analysis of the classical Sanskrit literature, I have found that it is possible to establish a binary divide between love (*prema*) and the erotic (*śṛṅgārī*) traditions. While love is essentially a feminine tradition, the erotic is inherently masculine. While love is about reciprocity and emotions that may or may not be physical, the hegemonic masculinity of the erotic tradition objectifies women and is, therefore, particularly lacking in emotions or sensitivity. Within this tradition a woman is a fetishized object. For instance, *Nakhaśikha-varṇana*, where the physical charms of women are listed in a determinedly systematic manner, is ubiquitous in both the prose and poetry forms of classical Sanskrit literature. Every single body part of the woman from *keśa* to *jaghana* and *uru* are painstakingly described in these texts. In fact, it would not be an exaggeration to state that the writer's imagination luxuriates in the rich complexity of the woman's body. Not only was the *śṛṅgārī* poetry erotic, it was erotic for men alone. This lends strength to Irigary's view (see Robinson 1987: 256) that the gaze is inherently masculine. She claims that the kind of look that separates the subject from the object of the gaze and projects desire on to that object is essentially masculine.

In the classical Sanskrit literature men are 'bearers of looks', and women 'merely images'. Mulvey (1989: 19) would argue that in a world ordered by sexual imbalance, pleasure in looking has been split between active male and passive female. The determining male gaze projects its fantasy on to the female figure, which is styled accordingly. Women are simultaneously looked at and displayed, with their appearance coded for strong visual and erotic impact so that they can be said to connote a kind of 'to-be-looked-at-ness'. Women depicted as objects of the male gaze is the leitmotif of erotic *śṛṅgārī* poetry.

An analysis of the verses in just one anthology, *Subhāṣitaratnakoṣa*, tends to reinforce the truth of Mulvey's argument. In one verse (vs. 347) we find the term *netrekapeyamvapuḥ*, i.e. figure that forms the sole drink for one's eyes. Here it is an adolescent female who is an object of the male gaze. In yet another verse (410), is the phrase *netraviśrāmapātram tvā mukham,* your face is the sole place where I rest my eyes. Here a young woman or *yuvatī* is the object of the male gaze. In a very interesting verse (476) the poet writes about the pleasure that is derived from gazing at a passive object. 'My eyes with difficulty pass her thighs, to wander long in the land about her hips; then at her waist. . . . But now at last, like the travellers parched by thirst, they have climbed the mountains of her breasts. . . .' Similarly in Rājaśekhara's play *Bālarāmāyaṇa* (Act III: 24–25) Rāvaṇa is gazing at Sītā who has appeared in the *swayaṃvara sabhā*. Ravana dwells on each feature of Sītā and fantasizes about her.

These references strengthen the argument about the power of the male gaze to objectify and eroticise the woman's body. We can also confirm the truth of Mulvey's argument (1989: 20) that men alone can gaze and women are mere images. In the classical Sanskrit *kāvyas* woman's beauty is overwhelmingly described in physical terms – all anthologies and *mahākāvyas* contain a section which describes women's physical anatomy in minute detail. In contrast, masculine beauty is a matter of character; it is inherent and lies in man's heroism, nobility, tenacity and gravity etc. (cited in Kulashrestha 1997: 62–64). These qualities are inherent and also autonomous, without women as points of reference. In the *Naiṣadhacaritam* (1.1–10), for example, verses on king Nala's beauty refer to the radiance of his fame, his virtue, learning and might. Similarly Kumāradāsa's *Jānakīharaṇa* an extensive *nakhaśikha varṇana* of Kauśalyā and Sītā, but devotes just three verses on Rāma's beauty (*Jānakīharaṇa* VI. 56–58). And in one of these verses that talks of Rāma's eyes, there is nothing physical in the description; rather it is metaphorical where emphasis is on Rāma's great knowledge and his vision. Numerous virtues of this kind can be found in classical sanskrit texts (for example, *Daśakumāracaritam* of Daṇḍin, *Vāsavadattā* of Subandhu, *Saduktikarṇāmṛta* of Śrīdharadāsa and *Daśarūpaka* of Dhanañjaya, etc.). John Berger (1972: 45) was not too far off the mark when he pointed out that according to usage and conventions, the social presence of a woman is different in kind from that of a man. He states that 'a man's presence is dependent upon the promise of the power which he embodies. If the promise is large and credible, his presence is striking. If it is small or incredible, he is found to have little presence. Man's presence suggests what he is capable of doing to you or for you'. In contrast, a woman's, presence says Berger (ibid: 46), is 'intrinsic to her physical person. So, to be born a woman has been to be born within an allotted and confined space into the keeping of men'.

If women were simply eroticized and objectified, that by itself may not have been a bad thing, since objectification may be an inherent component of both male and female eroticism. Sexual excitement, as Stoller (cited in Simon 1996: 149) suggests, inevitably involves objectification or fetishization of the other, because she or he is the carrier and bearer of what elicits sexual response. But what is crucial for our argument is that (Snitow *et al.* 1983: 311) men do not simply look. Their gaze carries with it a suggestion of action and possession, something that is lacking in the female gaze. Women receive and return the gaze, but cannot act on it. Much is said about the specifically[7] female gaze (*kaṭākṣa*) in the literary sources of our period. The female sidelong glance,[8] is essentially erotic. A verse of the *Subhāṣitaratnakoṣa* (395) states: 'I sing the praise of lovely-eyed women, who are victorious over three-eyed Śiva; who by their glances (*kaṭākṣa*) resurrect that love which he consumed by his'.

[7] In *Naiṣadhacaritam* (canto VI.22) there is reference to king Nala's side-long glances but the use of the term *kaṭākṣa* here is very different from that of female side-long glances. Nala being in women's inner apartment without permission did not want to look fully and distinctly so he resorted to side-long looks only to negotiate the space.

[8] While men have the privilege of looking fully, women can only look sideways.

However the erotic sidelong glances of a woman do not objectify the male, rather, she invites that male to objectify her. Thus, in *Kathāsaritsāgara* (Vol. 8: 15) a *nāyikā* says, 'I looked with sidelong glances at him whose eyes were fixed on me'. In a verse of the *Subhāṣitaratnakoṣa* (466) the male protagonist says, 'The glances of your eyes, which stretch to your ear, darker than a water-lily, were enough to steal a heart; what need is there pretty lass, with such ado pretending to bind your loosened braid, to show your armpit, camphor-dusted and marked with the lover's nail?' When women do look they are shy and hesitant about it. In *Kathāsaritasāgara* (Vol. I: 23), when princess Pātalī beholds Putraka in her apartment, there was 'a contest between shame and love in her eyes, which were alternately fixed on his face and averted'. In the same text (ibid.: 135) when Udayana and Vāsavadattā behold each other for the first time his eyes are fixed on her but Vāsavadattā's eyes are modestly averted. We never get any reference to a man dropping his glances when a female looks at him.

In Jalhaṇa's *Sūktimuktāvalī* we get verses under two heads, viz. *nāyikāvalokanam* and *nāyakāvalokanam.* While in the former *paddhati* there are twenty-four verses, and in all these verses the *nāyikā's* body is depicted as a fetishized object of the male gaze, in the latter *paddhati* there are only three verses. All the three verses are culled from a single Sanskrit *kāvya* called the *Bhikṣāṭankāvya* of Utprekṣāvallabha. In these verses there are references to women looking at a man who is actually Śiva in disguise. The poet says: 'A certain girl who was forbidden by her mother to go out, reached the grilled window of the house to gaze at Śiva; her eyes when seen from the road resembled for a moment a fish that was caught in the net spread by a fisherman' (*Sūktimuktāvalī* 177.26). What is interesting in this verse is the statement that a girl looked, in spite of having been forbidden by elders. Also, while the verse opens with a woman's gaze it actually ends up with her being gazed at in return. Many such examples support Mulvey's view (1989: 20) that within a patriarchal culture women can only exist as images, never as the bearers of looks. A woman alone will be displayed for the gaze and enjoyment of men. Within this masculine system the male figure cannot bear the burden of sexual objectification in the woman's gaze.

The love tradition of the classical Sanskrit *kāvya* is best represented in the writings of Bhavabhūti. For him love does not start from the citadel of the body. At no place in his plays *Uttararāmacarita* or *Mālatī-Mādhava* does Bhavabhūti expend his energy describing the physical charms of the *nāyikās.* Mādhava, admitting his powerful desire for Mālatī, avoids reference to her physical charms. He says, 'Some internal affection (*vikāra kāmajo kopayanti*), which is past exact determination, which baffles all power of expression, which again was never before experienced by me, and which is impenetrable owing to the great infatuation (*mahāmohagahano*) growing in strength on account of the total destruction of discrimination, stupifies and affects me simultaneously' (*Mālatī-Mādhava* Act I.30). It is thus obvious that Mādhava's emotions were deeply affected. He does not talk in terms of his seduction by Mālatī's physical form. The emphasis, is instead on feelings. Mādhava says, 'I was thus subdued by this disclosure of the feelings which could be inferred as proceeding from love of her *(sneharasa)* who was bewitching to the heart in every way' (ibid., Act I.29). Thus for Bhavabhūti love is not bodily sensation but philosophical and spiritual.

If for Bhavabhūti love is worthy of being treated as an expression of highly spiritual truth, that is because he is among those rare litterateurs in the field of classical Sanskrit literature who gave pre-eminence to *karuṇarasa* over the *śṛṅgārarasa.* Rejecting as he did the primacy of *śṛṅgārarasa,* Bhavabhūti could not but view love as a communion of souls. He notes about love in *Uttararāmacarita* (Act I.39), that fulfilment is 'deeply desired by all men. It remains constant in happiness and sorrow in all states. It is the perfect repose of the heart. It is the love (*rasa*) that cannot be removed by old age. In time, it turns into the mature essence of affection as the couple becomes more aware of one another's inner lives'. Reminiscing about the time spent with Sītā in the forest, Rāma says in the *Uttararāmacarita* (Act I.27), 'Lying close to each other as we talked together softly, secretly, cheeks closely pressed to cheek, while our arms were buried in their tight embrace and the night was gone without our knowing the hours as they passed.' The mutual affection in such a love relationship was powerful enough for the *nāyaka* and *nāyikā* to claim to know each other perfectly. Sītā says about Rāma, 'I know his heart and he also knows mine' (*Uttararāmacarita* Act III: 215). The ideal love relation which Bhavabhūti envisaged was monogamous, even connubial. Kāmāndakī notes in *Mālatī-Mādhava* (Act VI.18), 'The husband to woman and the lawful wife to man are the dearest objects, friends, all relatives put together, all things that the heart covets, a treasure and life itself, let this be mutually known'. The usual love intrigues (Śrī Harṣa's plays), and subterfuges in an *antaḥpura* setting do not thus find a place in Bhavabhūti's plays. In fact Bhavabhūti's *nāyaka* sets much in store by the singularity of his devotion to the *nāyikā.* Rāma says, offering his arm as a pillow to Sītā in *Uttararāmacarita* (Act I.37), 'Ever since the time of my marriage, whether in the house or in the forest, in childhood and after that in youth, this arm of Rāma has been thy pillow lulling thee to sleep and not resorted to by any other woman'. Bhavabhūti further makes his *nāyaka* Rāma describe his wife (*Uttararāmacarita,* Act I.38) as the 'prosperity of my house, collyrium pencil of ambrosia to the eyes, and her touch like a balm of sandalwood on the body'. Thus, for Bhavabhūti's Rāma the very act of desertion of such a wife was like ending his own life. He says in *Uttararāmacarita* (Act I.46), 'The purpose of Rāma's life is at an end today. The earth is now a sterile withered wilderness, worldly life is without interest, full of worry is the body; I have no refuge left'. The sorrow of Rāma on separation from his wife was not just mental but physically debilitating. In the *Uttararāmacarita* (Act III.1) he is depicted as exceedingly wasted (*parīkṣīṇo*). Bhavabhūti's view of women and more importantly man's love for woman was a totally new presentation, almost entirely non-physical and deeply emotional, it was a major departure from the vast corpus of classical Sanskrit literature. Bhavabhūti's *nāyaka* reserved his roman-tic love for a single woman, his *svīyā.* Although the later litterateur Rājaśekhara was fond of seeing himself as an incarnation[9] of Bhavabhūti, I see no similarity with Bhavabhūti in the treatment of the notion of love. Although Rājaśekhara's play *Viddhaśālabhañjikā* had a romantic setting, Rājaśekhara was pre-occupied with the idea of physical love and its satiation. Unlike Bhavabhūti there is no celebration of monogamous love. In fact in the *Viddhaśālabhañjikā* Vidhyādharamalla marries two women at one stroke. The play has nothing to say about the two women's feelings. In the very first act of the play, Vidhyādharmalla 'falls in love' (if at all this phrase can be used here) with Kuvalayamālā who he happens to eye just after her having bathed in the Narmada. The King's Vidūṣaka calls him '*mahilā lampaṭa jāta'*.

Lee Siegel has argued that the notion of love in Jayadeva's *Gītagovinda* was qualitatively different from the courtly erotic love of the predominant Sanskrit *kāvya* literature – 'That which is an art, cultivated and mannered emotion rather than something more spontaneous, natural and fundamental?'. I would argue, that the content of the *Gītagovinda* and the treatment of the Rādhā–Kṛṣṇa relationship there transcend the usual *nāyaka–nāyikā* relationship in Sanskrit *sṛṅgārī* poetry. Jayadeva's text is unique in the sense that it overturns many of patriarchy's cherished norms. First, it valorizes the woman's adultery. Benoy Kumar Sarkar (1986: 42) calls Rādhā a revolutionary, for she had transgressed the conventional morality of her surroundings. In the *Gītagovinda* Rādhā and Kṛṣṇa's adulterous union is actually apotheosized.[10] In one verse (5.7) the place of their love-making is referred to as *nikunjamanmathamahātīrtha.* The epithet *gopavadhū* (wife of *gopa*, as against just *gopī* which means milkmaid) (in 2.18) for Rādhā is an important indication of her married status.[11] In fact, the *Gītagovinda* also describes Vrindavana itself as a place where adulterous love relations exist. In social terms the illicit love affair of a man does not threaten patriarchal societal structures. But for a woman adultery is an infringement of the order of patriarchy. Woman's adultery would constitute a break from worldly relations and a substantial bid for autonomy. It is the social regimentation of the patriarchal family which gives female illicit love its special daring. Rādhā not only harboured an illicit love for Kṛṣṇa but was also an older woman who dared to love the adolescent Kṛṣṇa. In the very opening verse of *Gītagovinda* we are told that an older Rādhā is asked by Nanda (Kṛṣṇa's foster father) to be Kṛṣṇa's escort, and she used this opportunity to establish an erotic relationship with him. Here she transgresses the established norms.

The *Gītagovinda* also discards the *śṛṅgārī* ideal of heroic lover (for whom no woman is exceptional and who wants all of them), whose passion and intensity of love for Rādhā matches hers for him. The deep emotional sentiment and recipro-

[9] Rājaśekhara in his *Bālabhārata* makes this claim, cited in Poddar (1974: 1).

[10] In the *sṛṅgārī* poetry on the other hand the adulterous desires of women are placed under the heading of *asatī / kulaṭā* and they are usually illicit.

[11] Significantly, Kṛṣṇa in contemporary literature is also presented as an adulterer par excellence. In *Puṣpabāṇavilāsa* (vs. 1) Kṛṣṇa is foremost among the paramours.

city of their love is evident from a verse (5.7) where it is said, 'Mādhava still waits for you in love's most sacred thicket, where you *perfected love together*' (emphasis added). If Rādhā seeks Kṛṣṇa, he too seeks her. He says (10.4), 'You are my ornament, my life, my jewel in the sea of existence. Be yielding to me forever, my heart fervently pleads!' He also begs her forgiveness (3.9): 'Forgive me now! I won't do this to you again. Give me a vision, beautiful Rādhā!' He understands Rādhā's anger and curses himself because she saw him surrounded in the crowd of women and went away. 'I was *too ashamed, too afraid* to stop her. Damn me! My wanton ways made her leave in anger' (emphasis added). And as Kṛṣṇa's attachment grows, he discovers that he would rather serve (*Gītagovinda*, 11.2, 22; 12.3,6) and adore Rādhā than vanquish and demand. Jayadeva tells us (3.1–2). 'Feeling for Rādhā bound his heart with a chain of memories buried in other-worldly lives . . . as he searched for Rādhā in vain, arrows of love pierced his weary mind and Mādhava repented as he suffered in a thicket on the Yamuna river bank'. According to Kakkar and Ross (1986: 79), 'As a tale of love this transformative moment, from desires' sensations to love's adoration, gives the story of Rādhā and Kṛṣṇa its singular impact'. Siegel (1978: 93) notes that while Rādhā's longing is typical of the the *gopīs* of Vraja, it is Kṛṣṇa's attitude to Rādhā in the *Gītagovinda* that is a completely new development – 'Krishna becomes a more humanized person, subject to the pain of love which in prior literature he had inflicted but not himself felt'. As a supplicant and adorer of Rādhā, Kṛṣṇa overturns the dominant gender/spiritual status given to him.

This conception jettisons the status of Kṛṣṇa as the supreme godhead in the *Bhāgavata Purāṇa.* Miller (1975: 670) points out that in the *Bhāgavata Purāṇa* there is an allusion to the arrogant girl (*dṛptā*). If this is a reference to Rādhā (who is never mentioned by name), then it seems to be rejecting her relationship with Kṛṣṇa as an inappropriate model for the devotee. The possessive attitude manifested in her secret encounters with Kṛṣṇa is antithetical to the values presented in the *Bhāgavata.* Rādhā is criticized for being perverse (*daurātmya*). It is not un-likely that the authors of the *Bhāgavata* knew a rival cult centering on Kṛṣṇa and his *gopī* consort, and were critical of it. Ranajit Sarkar (Sarkar 1974: 5) says much the same thing. He feels that perhaps Rādhā was already the centre of the *rasa* in the popular *pre-Bhāgavata* legends, which the Bhāgavatas tried to suppress, foreseeing the danger of such individualization. Thus, the Rādhā of *Gītagovinda* stands as a consort in relation to Kṛṣṇa, says Miller (1975: 668). She is neither a wife, nor a devoted rustic playmate; rather she is an intense, solitary and proud figure who is Kṛṣṇa's partner in mature, exclusive love. Rādhā contrasts (*Gīta-govinda* 2.1) her love for Kṛṣṇa with his affair with other *gopīs*, which is described as common. Rādhā and Mādhava have an 'exclusive love relation' which was a rejection of the *Bhāgavata* principle of devotion to Kṛṣṇa. It is Kṛṣṇa who turns into a devotee of Rādhā in the *Gītagovinda.* He declares himself her slave (12.6) and even attends to her toilet like a personal maid (12.12–20). Rādhā in the climax of her union with Kṛṣṇa is *svādhīnapatikā,* (12.11), or one whose lover is in her power. Unlike the usual *nāyikā* of the *sṛṅgārakāvya*, in the *Gītagovinda* the *nāyikā* Rādhā has a remarkable agency vis-à-vis her desires. She is active in pursuance of that desire. She says at one place (*Gītagovinda* 7.4), '*yad-anugamanaya niśi gahanam api śīlitam*', i.e. in search of whom, at night I have frequented the woods even though they are deep. Rādhā's subjectivity in her love relations with Kṛṣṇa flows from the fact that in Jayadeva's conception she is Kṛṣṇa's equal (6.5). We see her loosing the consciousness of the duality of existence and in that moment she thinks of herself as Kṛṣṇa, a fact noted and expressed by Jayadeva (2.12–17).

Sukumari Bhattacharji (1993: 161) notes that 'real poetry of love is conspicuously lacking in Sanskrit literature. What passes for love poetry is only poetry of lust, where physical desires substitute emotional depths'. This assessment is correct if by love poetry she was referring to the *śṛṅgārī* poetry. However, this analysis will not hold for the love verses by women poets. The primary focus of the love verses of women is on bonding with their male beloved. And when the desire for emotional/erotic reciprocity on the part of the *nāyikā* is thwarted by an indifferent/straying *nāyaka*, there is great pathos, as in Śīlābhaṭṭarikā's famous verse, '*Yaḥ Kaumāraharaḥ*' (Chaudhuri 1941: vs. 82) and Vijjikā's '*Gatepremābandhe*' (ibid.: 113). Śīlā bemoans the indifference of the husband who had once been the stealer of her virginity, and had sported with her on the river-bank at night. Vijjikā is equally evocative in registering her sorrow. 'When the ties of love have come to be rent asunder, when the heart's high esteem has disappeared, when a friendly relation has ceased, when he passes before me like an (ordinary) individual; I do not know the reason why, my dear friend! my heart is not being rent to a hundred pieces thinking about those very same past days, spent in that way, i.e. happily before estrangement (see Shah 2008).

I have argued in the course of this paper that it would be both simplistic and ahistorical to conceive of *kāma* or sexual desire as a natural given. I have tried to establish that, far from being a biological, it was a socially mediated practice and, therefore, had specific class/caste and gender connotations. Furthermore, far from being a uniform monolithic construction it was conceived differently in different discourses even within the wider stream of the classical Sanskrit literature.

References

Āryāsaptaśati by Govardhanācārya (1965), edited and translated by Ramakanta Tripathi (Varanasi: Chowkhamba).

Aṣṭādhyāyi by Pāṇini (1962) edited and translated by Sirishchandra Vasu (Delhi: Motilal Banarsidass).

Aṣṭāṅgasaṅgraha by Vāgbhaṭṭa (1995–97), edited and translated by K.R. Srikantha Murthy (Varanasi: Chowkhamba).

Bālarāmāyaṇa by Rājaśekhara (1984), edited and translated by Gangasagar Rai (Varanasi: Chowkhamba).

Bell, Shannon (1994), *Reading, Writing and Rewriting the Prostitute Body* (Bloomington and Indianapolis: Indiana University Press).

Berger, John (1972), *Ways of Seeing* (London: Penguin Books).

Bhattacharji, Sukumari (1993), *History of Sanskrit Literature: Classical Age* (Hyderabad: Orient Longman).

Bhattacharyya, N.N. (1982), *History of the Tāntric Religion* (Delhi: Manohar).

Bhattacharyya, N.N., ed. (1999), *Tāntric Buddhism* (Delhi: Manohar).

Bṛhatkathāślokasaṅgraha by Buddhasvāmin (1986), edited and translated by R.P. Poddar (Varanasi: Tara Printing Works).

Butler, Judith (1990), *Gender Trouble, Feminism and the Subversion of Identity* (London: Routledge).

Carakasaṃhitā (1981–85), 2 vols, edited and translated by P.V. Sharma (Varanasi: Chowkhamba).

Chakravarty, Uma (1995), 'Gender, Caste and Labour: Ideological and Material Structures of Widowhood', *Economic and Political Weekly*, September 9, pp. 2248–55.

Chattopadhyya, D.P. (1959), *Lokāyata: A Study in Ancient Indian Materialism* (Delhi: People's Publishing House).

Chaudhuri, J.B. (1941), *Sanskrit Poetesses: Contributions of Women to Sanskrit Literature*, Vol. 2, Part A. (Calcutta: author).

Daśakumāracarita by Daṇḍin (1965), edited and translated by Kedarnath Sharma (Varanasi: Chowkhamba).

Daśarūpakam by Dhanañjaya (1969), edited and translated by Shrinivasa Shastri (Meerut: Sahitya Bhandar).

Dikshit, R.D. (1964), *Women in Sanskrit Drama* (Delhi: Meharchand Lachhman Dass).

Douglas, Mary (1966), *Purity and Danger* (London: Routledge and Kegan Paul).

Dumont, Louis (1960), 'World Renunciation in Indian Religions', *Contributions to Indian Sociology*, Vol. 4, pp. 33–62.

Gītagovinda by Jayadeva (1977), edited and translated by B.S. Miller (Delhi: Oxford University Press).

Gulik Van (1961), *Sexual Life in Ancient China* (Leiden: E.J. Brill).

Ingalls, D.H.H. (1962), 'Words for Beauty in Classical Sanskrit Poetry', in *Indological Studies in Honor of W. Norman Brown* (New Haven: American Oriental Society).

——— (1965), 'Introduction in *Subhāṣitaratnakośa* (Harvard: Harvard University Press).

Jānakīharaṇa by Kumāradāsa (1967), edited and translated by Brijmohan Vyasa (Allahabad: Mitraprakashan).

Jayamaṅgalā, Commentary on Kāmasūtra by Yaśodhara (1995), 2 vols, edited and translated by Madhavacharya (Bombay: Khemraja Shrikrishna Prakashan).

Kādambarī by Bāṇabhaṭṭa (1968), *Pūrvabhāga*, edited and translated by M.R. Kale (Delhi: Motilal Banarsidass).

——— *Pūrva* and *Uttarabhāga* (1965), edited and translated by Ramteja Shastri (Kashi: Pandit Pustakalaya).

Kakkar, Sudhir and J.M.Ross (1986), *Tales of Love, Sex and Danger* (Delhi: Oxford University Press).

Kāmasūtra by Vātsyāyana (1995), 2 vols, edited and translated by Madhavacharya (Bombay: Khemraja Shrikrishna Prakashan).

Kane, P.V. (1974), *History of Dharmaśāstra*, Vol. II, Parts I & 2 (Poona: Bhandarkar Oriental Research Institute).

Karpūramañjarī by Rājaśekhara (1974), edited and translated by R.P. Poddar (Vaishali: Research Institute of Prakrit).

Kathāsaritsāgara by Somadeva (1968), edited by N. Penzer, translated, by C.H. Tawney (Delhi: Motilal Banarsidass), reprint.

Kulshrestha, Sushma, ed. (1997), *Erotics in Sanskrit and English Literature: Kālīdāsa and Shakespeare* (Delhi: Eastern Book Linkers).

Kuṭṭanīmatam, by Dāmodaragupta (1961), edited and translated by Atrideva Vidyalankara (Varanasi: Indological Book House).

Mackinnon, Catharine (1982), 'Feminism, Marxism, Method and State: An Agenda for Theory', *SIGNS: Journal of Women and Culture in Society*, Vol. 7, No. 3, pp. 515–44.

Mādhavnidān by Mādhavkara (1950), edited and translated by Dinanatha Shastri (Delhi: Meharchand Lakshmandass).

Mahāvīracaritam by Bhavabhūti (1968), edited and translated by Ramachandra Mishra (Varanasi: Chowkhamba).

Mālatī-Mādhava by Bhavabhūti (1928), edited and translated by M.R. Kale (Second edn) (Bombay: Gopal Narayan and Co).

Manubhāṣya by Medhātithi (1920–26), Vols. I and II, translated by Ganganatha Jha (Calcutta: Calcutta University).

Manusmṛti (1992), translated by Wendy Doniger and Brian K. Smith (London: Penguin).

Miller, Barbara S. (1975), 'Rādhā: Consort of Kṛṣṇa's Vernal Passion', *Journal of the American Oriental Society,* Vol. 95, No. 4, October–December, pp. 655–671.

Mṛcchakaṭikam by Śūdraka (1962), edited and translated by M.R. Kale (Bombay: Book Seller's Publishing Co.).

Mulvey, Laura (1989), *Visual and Other Pleasures* (Bloomington: Indiana University Press).

Nāgarsarvasvam by Padmaśrī (1994), translated by Babulal Shukla Shastri (Delhi: Eastern Book Linkers).

Naiṣadhacaritam by Śrī Harṣa (1965), translated by K.K. Handiqui (Poona: Deccan College Postgraduate Research Institute).

Nāṭyaśāstra by Bharatmuni (1967), translated by Manomohan Ghosh (Second revised edn) (Calcutta: Manisha).

O' Flaherty (1981), *Sexual Metaphors and Animal Symbolism* (Delhi: Motilal Banarsidass).

Overall, Christine (1992), 'What's Wrong with Prostitution? Evaluating Sex Work', *SIGNS: Journal of Women and Culture in Society.* Vol. 17, No. 4, pp. 705–24.

Papanek, Hanna and Gail Minault, eds, (1982), *Separate Worlds: Studies Purdah in South Asia* (Delhi: Chanakya).

Poddar, R.P. (1974), *An Introduction to Karpūramañjarī* (Vaishali: Research Institute of Prakrit).

Porter and M. Teich, eds, (1994), *Sexual Knowledge, Sexual Science: The History of Attitudes to Sexuality* (Cambridge: Cambridge University Press).

Puṣpabāṇavilāsam by Kālidāsa (1969), translated by Somnath Shastri, edited by Satkari Mukhopadhyaya (Varanasi: Chowkhamba).

Radhakrishnan, S., ed. (1953), *History of Philosophy: Western and Eastern* (London: George Allen and Unwin).

Ratirahāsya by Kokkokā (1994), edited and translated by Ramananda Sharma (Varanasi: Chowkhamba).

Robinson, Hilary, ed. (1987), *Visibly Female: Feminism and Art An Anthology* (London: Camden Press).

Roy, Kumkum (1996), 'Unravelling the Kāmasūtra', *Indian Journal of Gender Studies,* Vol. 3, No. 2, pp. 155–70.

Rubin, Gayle (1984), 'Thinking Sex: Notes for a Radical Theory of the Politics of Sexuality', in Carol S. Vance (ed.), *Pleasure and Danger: Exploring Female Sexuality* (London, Routledge and Kegan Paul).

Saduktikarṇāmṛta by Śrīdhardāsa (1965), edited by S.C Banerji (Calcutta: Firma KLM).

Samayamātṛkā by Kṣemendra (1967), edited and translated by Ramashankar Tripathi (Varanasi: Chowkhamba).

Sarkar, B.K. (1986), *Love in Hindu Literature.* Delhi: Award Publishing House.

Sarkar, Ranajit (1974), *Gita Govinda: Towards a Total Understanding.* (Groningen: Publikaties van Het Instituut voor Indische inculturin).

Śatakatrayam by Bhartṛhari (1967), translated by B.S. Miller (New York: Columbia University Press).

Sharma, R.S. (1980), *Indian Feudalism c. AD 300–1200* (Delhi: Macmillan).

——— (1983), *Perspectives in Social and Economic History* (Delhi: Munshiram Manoharlal).

Shah, S. (2008), 'Poetesses in Classical Sanskrit Literature: 7th–13th Centuries C.E.', *Indian Journal of Gender Studies,* Vol. 15, No. 1, January–April, pp. 1–27.

Shaw, Miranda (1998), *Passionate Enlightenment: Women in Tantric Buddhism,* (Delhi: Munshiram Manoharlal).

Siegel, Lee (1978), *Sacred and Profane Dimensions of Love in Indian Traditions As Exemplified in the Gītagovinda of Jayadeva* (Delhi: Oxford University Press).

Simon, William (1966), *Post Modern Sexualities* (London: Routledge).

Smith-Rosenberg, Carroll (1975), 'The New Woman and the New History', *Feminist Studies,* Vol. 3, No. 1–2, pp. 185–98.

Snitow, Ann, *et. al.,* eds, (1983), *Power of Desire: The Politics of Sexuality* (New York: Monthly Review Press).

Sṛṅgārahāṭa: *Caturbhāṇi* (1960), edited and translated by Motichandra and V.S Agrawala (Bombay: Hindi Grantha Ratnakar).

Sṛṅgāramañjarīkathā by Bhoja (1959), edited and translated by Kalpana Munshi (Bombay: Singhi Jaina Series, 30).

Sṛṅgāraprakāśa by Bhoja (1963), translated by V.R. Raghavan (Madras: Vasanta Press).

Sternbach, Ludwik (1953), *Gaṇikā Vṛtta Saṅgraha: Texts on Courtesans in Classical Sanskrit* (Hoshiarpur: Vishveshvarananda Institute Publication).

Subhāṣitaratnakoṣa by Vidyākara, (1957), edited by V.V. Gokhale and D.D. Kosambi (Harvard Oriental Series, 42).

——— (1965), translated by D. Ingalls (Harvard: Harvard University Press).

Śukāsaptati (1966) edited and translated by Ramakanta Tripathi (Varanasi: Chowkhamba).

Sūktimuktāvalī by Jalhaṇa (1938), edited by E. Krishnamacharya (Baroda: Oriental Institute).

Suśrutasaṃhitā with commentary of Ḍalhaṇācārya, (2003), edited by Vaidya Trikamji Acharya (Varanasi: Chowkhamba).

Thapar, Romila (1979), 'Renunciation: The Making of a Counter Culture?', in *Ancient Indian Social History: Some Interpretations* (Hyderabad: Orient Longman).

Uttararāmacarita by Bhavabhūti (1962), edited and translated by P. V. Kane and C.N. Joshi (Delhi: Motilal Banarasidass).

Vance, Carol, ed. (1984), *Pleasure and Danger: Exploring Female Sexuality* (London: Routledge and Kegan Paul).

Vāsavadattā by Subandhu (1967), edited and translated by Shankardeva Shastri (Varanasi: Chowkhamba).

——— (1962), translated by Louis H. Gray (Delhi: Motilal Banarsidass).

Viddhaśālabhañjikā by Rājaśekhara (1965), edited and translated by Ramakanta Tripathi (Varanasi: Chowkhamba).

Romantic Love, Self-Regard and the Courtly Environment in Early Medieval India*

Daud Ali

This essay will consider the rise and prominence of certain notions of erotic love that grew up in and around the Sanskritized courts of early medieval India. Previous studies have interpreted these notions as expressions of civilizational uniqueness, particularly in the light of Indian theological notions of family structure.[1] This essay will offer an alternative explanation of the evidence, one which follows more closely the contours of love as set out in medieval texts and which situates its conventions in a more specific social context. Particularly, it will highlight the explicit connection between discourses of self-mastery on the one hand and erotic love on the other, and analyse this nexus in terms of social relationships in the courtly world.

It must be noted at the outset that romantic or sexual love, as revealed by the evidence we have available to us from early medieval India, was class-defined. Normative treatises on the subject addressed themselves to those possessed of good birth, wealth, urbanity and beauty (*Kāmasūtra* 1.4.1–2; cf *Pañcasāyaka* 1.4). The most immediate context for this literature was typically the royal court or the associations of refined city-living men who were drawn to the court for their livelihoods. Given its close correlation to the rise of classical Sanskrit literary culture, it may also be said that conceptions of romantic love developed in tandem with the evolution of a particular type of class society. Its terminology was covalent with theories of affiliation more widely current in the court circles of early medieval India, and, as we shall see, some of its key dynamics embodied the preoccupations

* This essay is a revised and reworked version of 'Anxieties of Attachment: The Dynamics of Courtship in Medieval India', *Modern Asian Studies* Vol. 36, No. 1 (2002), pp. 103–39.

[1] For the former, see O'Flaherty (1973) and Siegel (1983). These scholars have argued, using the paradigm of J. C. Heesterman, that Hindu thought is best characterized by the tension between the violent exigencies of the immanent world and the drive for the spiritual transcendence – abandon *for* the senses and abandonment *of* the senses. Shulman (1985) has applied the following model to Indian kingship, arguing that the king's personality reveals this larger civilisational conflict. More recently, this argument has been used within a putative historical frame to discuss the sexuality of Nāyaka kings in late-medieval south India (Narayana Rao, Shulman, Subrahmanyam 1992). For the latter interpretation, see Kakar and Ross (1986).

of that society. Its rise and prominence may be effectively traced through the proliferation and development of Sanskrit *kāvya*, at royal courts from the second century AD, but particularly from around AD 400.

The evolution of *kāvya* exhibits an increasing complexity in manners and conventions among the elite from Gupta times. This was as much the case with love as it was with elements of personal comportment, social disposition and ethical refinement. If we compare the story cycle of the courtship of Nala and Damayantī as it appears in the *Mahābhārata,* dated perhaps to the first centuries of the Christian era, with the *Naiṣadhacarita* of Śrīharṣa, composed nearly a millennium later, during the reign of the Gāhaḍvāla king Jayacandra of Kanauj (1170–93) in the twelfth century, it is immediately apparent that romantic love had become a far more discursively elaborated process, one imbricated with the concerns of personal refinement and 'ornamented' with various embellishments which characterized the wider preoccupations of courtly life. Developments in form and genre that separate these two cycles are themselves indicative of the evolution of a tradition of courtly love among the ruling classes. Indeed, erotic love emerged as perhaps the chief preoccupation of the literary imagination of these classes, so much so that by the time of Bhoja (eleventh century) it was deemed to be the pre-eminent aesthetic sentiment.

Courtly poetry, however, must be put into the context of other types of sources. This paper will also draw on the Śāstraic literature regarding *dharma*, *artha* and *kāma*. Particularly relevant are the treatises on *kāma* or pleasure – most notably Vātsyāyana's *Kāmasūtra* (third to fifth century) which often contain, *inter alia*, sections devoted entirely to the characteristics and relations of lovers. Perhaps even more important for the interpretations below are the treatises on *artha* (acquisition) and *nīti* (policy) which together roughly correspond to the domain of polity. Taken together, these prescriptive knowledges had as their audience the ruling elite. Also important are inscriptions, usually royal orders (*śāsana*) which mention in their poetic preambles particular conceptions of the relations between agents at court. Finally, the aphoristic and didactic verses often referred to as *subhāṣita* (meaning literally 'well-spoken'), sayings or counsel that circulated orally in courtly circles and echo through the expanse of Sanskrit literary culture, providing an invaluable index to the themes of concern, delectation and even collective ethical problematization among these classes. Read together, these various sources illuminate the courtly preoccupation with erotic love in a different way.

Understanding the discursive provenance of the terms which come to refer to romantic love in medieval India is particularly difficult because their interrelation shifts over time between aesthetic and religious traditions. Nevertheless, reading the early texts, one can distinguish between two different types of words: those that refer to the physical desire for and pleasure arising from sexual union, which generally include terms like *kāma* and *rati*, and those terms which refer to adoration, attachment, affection, and the participation that lovers were to share to varying degrees with one another, typically designated by terms like *rāga*, *anurāga*, *śṛṅgāra* and *bhakti.* In drawing this distinction, I am not suggesting that these terms functioned to distinguish between physical sex and a higher form of love. Both of these sorts of terms must be distinguished from sexual union itself (*sambhoga, surata*) and were uniformly deemed to arise within the mind and heart of the lover. Some schools of theology certainly did counterpose various of these terms against one another, for example, Kṛṣṇa in the *Gītā* recommends *bhakti* over *kāma.* But in the case of the relations between lovers as described in the *Kāmasūtra, Nāṭyaśāstra,* and other courtly texts, these two types of terms are seen to be related and complementary rather than opposed. Moreover, the admonitions to avoid too much *kāma,* (which incidentally formed as much part of the *Kāmasūtra* tradition as it did that of putative 'religious' sphere) apply equally to the terms like *anurāga.* More widely affective terms like *anurāga* and *śṛṅgāra* were sometimes thought to encompass *kāma* within themselves. The wider provenance of terms like *anurāga* and *bhakti* meant that they were often used more generally to characterize relations between various men in medieval Indian society. Finally, the rise of these terms in political discourse chronologically parallels the rise of *kāvya* as a discursive form and love as a courtly theme. And it is through some attention to the wider usages of these terms that we may learn something of the preponderance of erotic themes among the ruling discourses of medieval India.

It shall not be assumed here that modes of self-discipline in early India were repressive forces restraining passions and desires. Recent scholarship has too often understood self-discipline and enjoyment as inimically opposed domains. Their interaction has been interpreted as the more or less successful impingement of repressive forces, usually in the form of transcendentalizing Brāhmaṇical orthodoxy, on the instincts and impulses of the popular. Much work remains to be done in the Indian context even from this vantage point. In European sociology, Elias has been instrumental in suggesting that development of mechanisms of 'restraint' – or civilizing processes – such as manners and courtesy reflect social compulsions. In the Indian context, the history of erotic love thus could be connected to the growth of courtly manners within a framework akin to the now apparently unpopular paradigm of 'Sanskritization'.

In European sociology, the alternative to this tradition of scholarship has been most clearly articulated by Foucault. This 'repressive hypothesis' is a distorted self-perception of modern bourgeois societies. Disciplinary mechanisms have provoked far more desire than either their architects or opponents have assumed. Foucault has read disciplinary practices in pre-bourgeois societies as parts of regimes of self-discipline connected with the formation of ethical subjecthood and agency. This paper will read the 'repressive traces' in courtly texts not as vestiges of a network of codes negating pleasure, but instead as disciplines integral to the *production* of desire. While there is certainly an antagonistic relation between self-mastery and sensual pleasure, the effects of this relation were not always negative in relation to the pursuit of pleasure. While for the ascetic life the conquest of the senses involved a subdual, or sublimation of pleasure, in elite circles this same conquest entailed a *cultivation* of desire. The enjoyment of pleasures was thus not understood as a straightforward release of libidinal impulse, as is clear from Vātsyāyana's eloquent argument in the *Kāmasūtra* (1.2.18–24) that *kāma* required the application of 'means' (*upāya*). These means, the 'rules of engagement' that the erotic texts lay out in great detail, both through specific conventions and general principles, were explicitly understood as a form of self-mastery. The desires of the court-centred texts, thus, are encouraged and formed *positively* and *internally* by the call to self-mastery. In fact, according to the texts, the proper exercise of pleasure is a form of self-mastery. Self mastery did not bear down upon desire, but cultivated it and operationalized its practices and discourses.

A short example from the Nala story will illustrate my point. In the *Mahābhārata's* (3.50.17–18) account of the initial love-sickness of Nala and Damayantī, we find the following description of Nala: 'unable to bear his desire in his heart, Nala at once left secretly and sat in a grove besides the women's quarters.' In Śrīharṣa's rendition, this event is preceded by a rather long conceit about Kāmadeva's attempt to subdue Nala through the form of Damayantī – a conceit which is significant in itself as we shall see – in which Damayantī's excellence is said to be 'made by the king the guest of his ears'. After Damayantī enters Nala's heart, Śrīharṣa says that:

> The powerful Nala, though consumed by desire, did not ask the king of Vidarbha for the hand of his daughter, as the proud would rather renounce both life and happiness than forsake the single vow never to beg. Feigning to be depressed on account of something, he concealed the succession of his sighs caused by his separation from her, and denied his paleness by attributing it to an excess of camphor in the sandal paste applied to his body. Luckily, even while in company, he was able to conceal during the *vīṇā* players music both his words to his beloved uttered under delusion, as well as the fact that he fainted. The king who had a reputation of being the foremost among those whose senses were conquered, was ashamed when the irresistible power of Kāmadeva became by degrees manifest in him. Neither the power of discrimination nor other virtues could restrain Nala's disquiet; for where there is desire, Kāmadeva produces an unrest that is never restrained – such are the ways of the world. When, in spite of his efforts, he became unable to sit in the royal assembly even for a moment, without betraying signs of being in love he desired to retreat to a secluded place under the pretext of recreation in his pleasure garden. (*Naiṣadhacaritam* 1.49–55)

While both accounts precede Nala's entry into the garden, in the *Naiṣadhacaritam* his problems worsen as a host of flowers afflict his mind and make him pine even more, but Śrīharṣa's elaboration is significant. He dwells on the afflictive condition of Nala's growing affection for Damayantī, whether as the designs of Cupid or simply as an indication of his 'weakness' at court. How should we understand the elaboration of distress and 'shame' (*sāpatrapatā*) at the manifestation of his condition, and his efforts to conceal his feelings before members of the court? Should we see this elaboration as the result of increased imposition on the part of Brāhmaṇical orthodoxy on the desires of the hero? The approach here will instead see the elaboration of romantic love not merely as part of the 'restraining' compulsions of the social, but also as part of the productive agency of self-formation that such compulsions encouraged.

Self-Discipline

We may begin with the conception of the self in early medieval India. While courtly theories of the self are related to and draw from those formulated by monastic and liturgical orders of post-Vedic India, it would seem that worldly life of the court presented its own set of exigencies and problems which demanded particular strategies and solutions. This was so much the case that the care and discipline of the self was foundational for all of the 'scientific' knowledges which were to organize human life, and particularly (for our purposes) that of *nīti*, or 'politics'. The problems taken up in these texts were 'ethical' to the extent that they were driven by the need to formulate the postures and dispositions that a man was to take with those around him. This training, according to the texts on polity, was to begin with an active relationship toward the self. The basic idea of the self we find mentioned in the texts and manuals on political conduct was a concentrically arranged structure which may be represented visually, following Kāmandakī's *Nītisāra* (1.33–36) in Figure 1.

The central constituent of the self, which could stand in for the self as a whole, was the *ātman*. In Kāmandakī the next element was the mind, or *manas*, but in other formulations evolutes or layers like *buddhi*, *cit* and *ahaṃkāra*, collect-

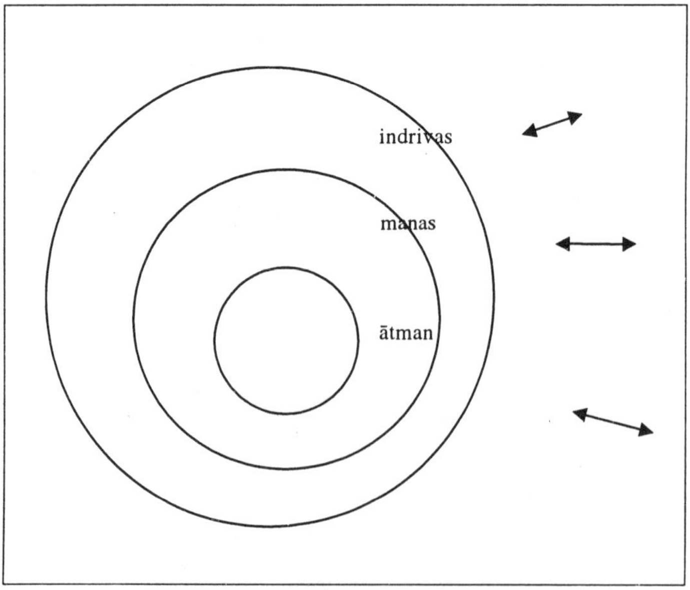

ively known as the 'internal organs' (*antaḥkaraṇas*).[2] The outermost constituents of the self were the five sensory organs or *indriyas* (ears, skin, eyes, tongue and nose) along with five other organs (the sexual organ, the anus, hands, feet, and mouth), which together formed the ten faculties of action and cognition. Taken together, these formed a particular order which may be grasped in a number of ways. The spatial arrangement was concentric, and operated with a logic very similar to that of the court or the kingdom. The self's most important and defining element, the soul (*ātman*), stood at the centre, comparatively inactive, preferring instead to act through the agency of less permanent sheaths that surrounded it in successive layers. Consequently, the outer layers of the self surrounding the *ātman* were considered to be *karaṇas*, 'instruments' or 'means' of knowledge and action, ultimately in the service of their master. The *karaṇas* were further divided into 'internal' and 'external' instruments or organs (*antaḥkaraṇa, bahiṣkaraṇa*). Each of these organs had an activity (*kriyā*) appropriate to it, according to Kāmandakī. The most important of these were the sensory organs (*indriyas*) which had as their activities sound, touch, vision, taste and smell, while the other external organs performed speech, movement, the giving and accepting of objects, and excretion. The major activity of the sensory organs was of course to engage with their appropriate fields (*viṣaya*). The more complex processes of the internal elements of the self presupposed the activities of the sensory organs. In a process called *saṃkalpa*, the mind (*manas*) organized indeterminate sensory data into determinate perceptual forms. From this process a series of both affective and volitional states arose: doubt, imagination, and, relevant to the topic at hand, pleasure and desire. The mind was crucially situated: it formed the link between the outer sense organs and the more internal parts of the self. It was the first element of sentience in perception.

Relations between elements of the self were not simply based on function, but also implied hierarchy and mastery. One of the earliest images of the self was that of a chariot. Each of the components of the self was compared to a part of the chariot as driven by its ruler, the *ātman*. In an eighth-century inscription of the Rāṣṭrakūṭa king Amoghavarṣa, the soul is compared to the king, the mind his minister, the group of senses his circle of feudatories, and speech and the other organs to servants conforming to the prescribed rules of *dharma* (*EI* XVIII: 26). This is repeated by spiritual discourses as well. A thirteenth-century Śaiva Siddhāntin text, the *Civajñāṉapōtam* contains a similar description of the soul ruling over the inner senses (*antaḥkaraṇas*) of *manas, cit, buddhi* and *ahaṃkāra* just as a king ruled his kingdom through his ministers. Such metaphors not only underscore the

[2] Kamandakī is aware of this elision. He states elsewhere that 'perfect knowledge (*vijñāna*), the heart (*hṛdaya*), consciousness (*citta*), the mind (*manas*) and the intellect (*buddhi*) are synonymous and are caused by the *ātman* to discriminate between what should be done and what should not be done' (*Nītisāra* 1.30). Elsewhere he includes the *ātman* along with the *manas* among the *antaḥkaraṇas* (*Nītisāra* 1.35). This would seem atypical. He implies in verse 1.30 that the *ātman* has a more determinative role. For different formulations of the *antaḥkaraṇas*, see Grimes (1996).

evolution of political structures and the importance of the social relations of the court, but just as importantly, reveal something about the actual relation that the twice-born man was to have with himself. The normal and proper 'functioning' of the self was one that implied relations of internal hierarchy, mastery and even coercion. The mind's activity of resolving indeterminate sensory matter received from the *indriyas* into coherence (*saṃkalpa*) was not simply a generic psychic process, but a marshalling and disciplining of the senses as instruments in the same manner as a minister bearing the burden of rule effected the will of his master in regard to his feudatories. The mind was ruler of all the external organs through which a person communicated and commanded the objects of the senses, which were regarded as its 'domains', or fields (*viṣaya*) of mastery.

So it is that we find that the first dictum of *nīti* or policy in the theoretical texts is that the king should master the various elements of his own self, particularly his senses. This (*indriyajaya*) was of utmost importance for the king. The texts on polity are emphatic on this point. According to Kāmandakī, the conquest of the senses made a candidate fit for the knowledge of the Śāstras, as only one who had mastered his senses was fit to receive its meaning. This mastery of the senses was effected through, and synonymous with, self-discipline or *vinaya* (*Nītisāra* 1.22). The term *vinaya*, one of the most general virtues of courtly life, was conceptually (and etymologically) related to concepts of proper 'policy' (*nīti*) and proper 'directed conduct' (*naya*) integral to life at court. While *naya* and *nīti* generally referred to conduct in relation to the external world, *vinaya* most often denoted conduct towards oneself. The position of the texts is that an individual's conduct and policy at court presupposed and sprung from 'self-policy' or self-discipline. As Kāmandakī puts it, 'self-discipline (*vinaya*) is the root (*mūla*) of policy (*naya*)' (*Nītisāra* 1.21). This is because, according to Kāmandakī, perfect knowledge of the Śāstra could only be obtained through discipline. For Kauṭilya, self-discipline in the various knowledges is the cause of mastery over the senses, which is in turn considered the essence of the Śāstras on policy (*Arthaśāstra* 1.6.1–3). In either formulation, we begin with the practice of self-discipline as the means to mastery over the senses. So the first coercion that the king was to exercise, the first agonistic relation in which he was engaged, which was to form the basis of all his subsequent policy, was with respect to his own mind and body. Megasthenes' observation about Brāhmaṇas would seem to apply, judging from the texts on *nīti*, to the king as well: 'they regard the body as being the fruitful source of wars, and, as we have already shown, fight against it like soldiers in battle contending against the enemy' (*Indika*, Fragm. 54).

So far we have explored the mastery of the self in relation to the pursuit of *artha*, but perhaps not surprisingly, the mastery of the senses was also deemed a prerequisite for the proper pursuit of *kāma*. Judging from the texts, self-discipline was as general a characteristic of the people at court in love as it was in other matters. The *Nāṭyaśāstra* (34.18–19), for example, includes *dhīra*, being self-controlled, as an integral characteristic in all of its categorizations of *nāyakas*. The penultimate verse of the *Kāmasūtra* (7.2.58) recommends that 'he who knows the principles of this Śāstra is one who has conquered his senses (*jitendriya*) and will be able to conduct himself in the world and firmly guard *dharma*, *artha* and *kāma*'. It is perhaps peculiar to conceive of the enjoyment of pleasures as entailing a conquest of one's senses. While the true dynamics of this conquest will become apparent in the following sections, Vātsyāyana's general definition of *kāma* is telling enough for the moment: 'the activity of the sense-organs, the ear, the skin, eyes, the tongue and the nose, when favourably disposed in their fields of operation, as overseen by the mind (*manas*) along with the soul (*ātmasaṃyukta*)' (*Kāmasūtra* 1.2.11). The senses must be engaged, 'in contact' as the succeeding verse specifies, with their particular fields (*viṣaya*), but simultaneously they were to be 'overseen' or 'directed' by the mind. The word here is *adhiṣṭhita*, literally to 'stand over' or 'superintend'. This was to be the particular posture of the mind with regard to the senses in general and particularly with regard to pleasure. We may see now that 'victory' over the senses did not entail their eradication, but rather their subordination and control by an appropriate superintending agent, the mind. The mind ruled the senses in the enjoyment of pleasure and it was in the mind that the experience of *kāma* was thought to arise, through resolution (*saṃkalpa*), giving rise to the epithets 'mind-born' (*manasija*, *manoja*) and 'will-born' (*saṃkalpaja*). We shall return presently to the importance of the mind in the actions of the self, but here it will suffice to note that enjoyment of pleasure is not conceived in opposition to self-discipline and mastery of the senses, but as a function of it.

The Dangers of the Senses

Why was such self-discipline necessary? Each of the five senses, according to the *Nītisāra* (1.52ff.), was sufficient to bring about the ruin (*vināśa*) of a person. Kāmandakī gives an example, for each sense, of an animal killed by its hunter – a deer lured by the melodious sound of the hunter's flute, an elephant ensnared by his desire for the touch of a cow-elephant, and so on. For man, the vices that could arise from the improper influence of the senses were many, and a list of six enemies (*ṣadarivarga*) is routinely cited by courtly texts as consisting of desire (*kāma*), anger (*krodha*), greed (*lobha*), conceit (*māna*), rashness (*mada*) and delight (*harṣa*) (*Arthaśāstra* 1.6.1, 1.7.1; *Nītisāra* 1.57; *Kāmasūtra* 5.5.38). Avoiding these effected the conquest of the senses according to Kauṭilya. These 'enemies', however, like the senses themselves, were not inherently harmful. All of them in adequate measure could bring benefit, but in excess were capable of transforming themselves into vices destructive of a man's interest and fortune. Kāmandakī's commentator, for example, explains *harṣa*, a term usually positive in connotation, as 'joy taken in the killing of beings without sufficient reason' (*Nītisāra* 1.57 comm). A number of vices arose from anger and desire, the relative ranking of which was a matter of debate among these Śāstra authors. Despite their status as 'enemies' anger and desire had their utility (the former being necessary for the suppression of evil and the latter for the enjoyment of fruits) in the words of one author cited in the *Arthaśāstra* (8.3.8–12). Though Kauṭilya seems to differ on this point, he elsewhere asserts that the king should not deprive himself of pleasures but serve *kāma* without contravening *artha* and *dharma* (*Arthaśāstra* 8.3.13–22).[3]

Control over the senses, then, was 'avoidance of error' (*avipratipatti*) in relation to each of the senses (*Arthaśāstra* 6.1.2). These errors most often took the form of indulgence, excessive pursuance of a particular sensory domain. The mind (*manas*), as the superintendent of the senses, was ultimately responsible for the control of the senses, and in the case of their straying, was complicit in such excess. Kāmandakī says that the mind excites (*prerayati*) the senses with greed for sense-objects as if they were meat preparations (*Nītisāra* 1.29). Goaded on by an undisciplined mind 'running wildly like an elephant in the forest of the sense-objects' (*Nītisāra* 1.27), the senses become fixated on their objects to the detriment of the self. In the hierarchic logic of self-structure, the command of the mind included mastery over all that he should command. The conquest of the senses, in other words, began with the mind. Kāmandakī asks 'how can one who cannot subdue the mind (*manasaḥ saṃnibarhaṇe*), conquer the earth bounded by the oceans?' (*Nītisāra* 1.39).

The consequences of the mind and senses going astray were manifold. They could involve a violation of the hierarchical principles of 'law', or *dharma*. The Śāstric literature cites such examples in abundance. The Bhoja king Dāṇḍakya, for example, out on a hunt, saw a Brāhmaṇa girl and abducted her, to perish along with his family and kingdom as the result of her father's curse (*Arthaśāstra* 1.6.5; also *Kāmasūtra* 1.2.44). Such admonitions would seem to imply a 'repressive' code. The pursuit of sensual pleasure was not to contravene the proper exercise of *dharma*. In fact, a varied set of dangerous eventualities awaited the man who indulged his senses. The excessive pursuit of one's senses left one exposed to one's enemies. So a king overcome by desire for the objects of the senses was vulnerable to attack like an elephant (*Nītisāra* 1.40).

But the most general danger in the pursuit of the senses was what various sources, both courtly and monastic, called 'attachment'. In its broadest sense, attachment referred to life in the world, as opposed to liberation from the world. More precisely, attachment referred to a specific relation of *involvement* on the part of the self, through the mind and the senses, with the outside world. Renunciative philosophies attributed it to different cognitive and mental errors.[4] Release and liberation from the fetters of worldly life thus began with a detachment from the objects of the senses. 'Attachment', however, was an equally important concern at court. One of its implications features prominently in medical texts concerning the health of the king, particularly around a disease known as *rājayakṣman*, 'the

[3] Kauṭilya differs with the cited author, Bhāradvāja, over the issue of the relative seriousness of *kāma* and *krodha* (the topic of much of this chapter) and not on their status as vices as such. His remarks are, thus, somewhat curious, given that Bhāradvāja, not considering these qualities as vices, is not concerned at all with their relative seriousness. For Kauṭilya's positive remarks on *kāma*, see *Arthaśāstra* (1.7.3).

[4] See the discussion of the term *rāga* in relation to orthodox schools of philosophy in Dasgupta (1922).

royal disease' or 'king of diseases'.[5] The medical treatise *Carakasaṃhitā* gives a detailed account of its origin, etiology and treatment. According to this text (6.8.4ff.), Dakṣa, or Prajāpati, gave his twenty-eight daughters to the Moon (Soma) in marriage. But the Moon became overly attached (*atisakta*) to one of them Rohiṇī, and neglected his own body, which suffered a diminishment of unctuous substance (*snehakṣaya*) or loss of vital fluids. Because the Moon had married all the daughters of Prajāpati but did not deal with them equally, the god became angry and exhaled his anger from his mouth. And 'despised by the great, treating his wives unequally, filled with *rajas* and weakness, the Moon was attacked by *yakṣmā*' (*Carakasaṃhitā* 6.8.7). After seeking the refuge of the gods, Prajāpati was pleased and allowed the Moon to be treated by the divine physicians, the Aśvins, who cured him. *Yakśmā* was then despatched to the human world by the Aśvins, where it enters into human beings through various etiologies.

The invective here is not against pleasure as such. The cause of the moon's affliction is his over-attachment to one of his wives and the consequent neglect of his others, literally the 'non-enjoyment' (*asaṃbhoga*) of his other wives (*Carakasaṃhitā* 6.8.5). Among the etiologies of the disease in the human world was 'excessive thinning' (*atikarśana*) which again could be caused by a variety of factors, notable among which, for our purposes, are pining for a lover (*utkaṇṭhā*) and overindulgence in sexual intercourse (*ativyavāya*) (*Carakasaṃhitā* 6.8.24). The emphasis here is on 'excessive' sensual indulgence which initiated a physical wasting.

The final book of the *Raghuvaṃśa* ends with the story of king Agnivarṇa. Installed on the throne by his father, the king conducts his affairs for some years in person, and then consigns them to his ministers, and devotes himself wholly to the pursuit of pleasure. Kālidāsa describes at length his dalliances with the various women of the palace – his wives, courtesans, dancers and attendants. But he hints that all is not right. Unable to bear even the interval of a single moment without the enjoyment of the objects of the senses (*indriyārtha*), spending day and night in the interior (of the palace), he had no regard for his subjects. If upon the coun-sel of his ministers he deigned to give appearance (*darśana*) to his expectant subjects, he did so by dangling a foot from the opening of a window (*Raghuvaṃśa*, 19.6–7). The dependants (*anujīvin*) of his court bow and honour his extended foot.

The king's neglect of his subjects and supplicants forebode the worst. Though he is powerful and safe from his enemies, he begins to thin (*akṣiṇot*) from a disease 'born of attachment to pleasure' (*ratirāgasaṃbhava*) (*Raghuvaṃśa*, 19.48). Agnivarṇa ignores the counsel of his physicians as the *rājayakṣman* disease becomes apparent. His face pales, his voice weakens, he is unable to adorn himself, and can walk only when supported by his servants. Raghu's family, according to Kālidāsa, was now like the sky with the moon on its last digit. The comparison is significant. The Moon, or Soma, who was progenitor of the rains, and the waters,

[5] The double-meaning of *rājayakṣman* is noted and discussed by Zimmerman (1987: 177).

was the first victim of *rājayakṣman*. His 'thinning', according to the *Carakasaṃhitā*, was due to a loss of unctuousness (*snehakṣaya*), specified by its commentator as the loss of semen and vital life fluid (Zimmerman 1987: 177). The king's loss of fluid, like that of the moon, led to the inevitable drying up of the domains which they 'watered'. Interestingly, in the case of *rājayakṣman* we see that the indulgence in intercourse, which ordinarily causes a tumescence and plumpness of the body, may also lead, if excessive, to the reverse process of desiccation, and in some cases death. Agnivarṇa is not as fortunate as Soma; he eventually dies in his palace garden, attended by his ministers and the royal physician.

Overattachment and its attendant wasting were not just dissipation, but instead a disarticulation of selfhood. The wasting of *rājayakṣman* could in some cases, the *Carakasaṃhitā* (6.8.24) tells us, be caused by loss of weight from prolonged pining for a lover. In his discussion of liaisons with other men's wives, Vātsyāyana enumerates ten 'stages of desire' (*kāmasthāna*). He begins with pleasure of the eyes (*cakṣuṣprīti*), followed by a fixation of the mind (*manahsaṅga*), and then the arising of resolve (*saṁkalpa utpatti*).[6] After a progression from the senses to the mind, which becomes slowly attached to the object of desire with 'resolve' (*saṁkalpa*) there is a steady progression of attachment, and loss of sleep, physical emaciation, turning away from (other) objects of the senses, loss of shame, madness, fainting and finally, as in *rājayakṣman*, death (*Kāmasūtra*, 5.1.4.4–5). The advice given (5.1.3) to avoid physical degeneration, is 'When he sees desire progressing from one stage to the next, then, with the goal of preserving his own body from harm, he may approach another's wife'. So self-preservation in the face of wasting away from over-attachment becomes a pretext for Vātsyāyana to prescribe the violation of patriarchal privilege by sleeping with another man's wife. In some cases, then, the dangers of attachment could be avoided by entering into liaisons rather than curtailing them. Dāmodaragupta says that while sexual intercourse with one's wife was necessary for progeny, sexual intercourse with servants may be necessary for the abatement of sickness (from excessive desire) (*Kuṭṭanīmata* 812). The problem of attachment, then, was not about morality and did not take the form of a body of consistent interdictions against particular acts, behaviours or liaisons. It instead concerned the disposition that the self was to have with the external world as a whole. The senses posed the danger of a loss of self-mastery.

Attachment and Autonomy: The Dynamic of Relations at Court

To grasp the full significance of attachment in *kāvya*, it is necessary to view attachment and mastery from another angle. We have seen that there were, according to the policy manuals, good reasons for the noble man to avoid attachment to sensual pleasure. Further, his self-restraint was seen to be a token of his fitness to stand above his social inferiors. In this sense, the condition of self-mastery

[6] The term *saṃkalpa*, as noted, refers to the mind's organization of the diffused sensations coming from the senses into desire, will or volition.

stood in contradistinction to various states of dependence and servitude. In this world self-restraint is a mark of freedom.

The life of men at court may be viewed in relation to two poles, *svatantra*, or dependence on oneself, and *paratantra* or dependence on another. Much of the gnomic and didactic literature of the court denigrates dependence and elevates independence. A ninth-century inscription which records the victory of the Pratīhāra king Nāgabhaṭṭa over Cakrāyudha of Kanauj, who was in the service of the Pāla king Dharmapāla, says that Cakrāyudha had a 'lowly demeanour clearly obvious from his dependence on another' (*EI* XVIII: 13). As the hero of one story in the fifteenth-century *Puruṣaparīkṣā* (1.3.2) puts it, 'cowards, children and women live by taking refuge in others'. Such attitudes, however, must be placed in the context of multiple and complex political dependencies. Most men of rank at court enjoyed varying degrees of autonomy by virtue of their service to higher lords as princes, generals, retainers, or ministers. It is these men who formed the larger audience for the prescriptive and aesthetic literatures of the court, and whose world-perspectives are encoded in these literatures.

Autonomy and dependence were often viewed in relation to the acquisition and disposition of wealth. What constituted independence in terms of wealth was a perennial theme for the moralists of the court. Again and again they are clear on this point. According to the *viṭa* in Īśvaradatta's *Dhūrtaviṭasaṃvāda* (59)

> There are three ends of money: making gifts, enjoyment and hoarding. Of these gifts and enjoyments are superior, and hoarding has been censored. Why? In hoarding money there is no benefit, and being without benefit, it creates no satisfaction. Hence hoarding is improper.

Bhartṛhari adds another point of view:

> Giving, enjoying and losing are the three ways through which the amount of one's wealth can be lessened. The wealth of a man who neither gives nor enjoys his wealth can only be lessened by the third way. (*Subhāṣitatriśatī*, 1.34)

Giving and enjoying, then, are the most honourable ways of disposing of one's wealth. Preserving money, on the other hand, were signs of the vice of 'miserliness'. Significantly, the *Puruṣaparīkṣā* (1.7.1) calls miserliness a form of cowardice (*kātarya*): if a man is fearful about his life he was called a coward; if he was fearful about his wealth he was known as a miser.

Generosity, by contrast, was among the most praiseworthy of virtues, the best complement to wealth. All the prescriptive texts are in agreement as to the good benefits of giving wealth, and verses abound in the aphoristic literature praising giving (*dāna*). Generosity was a sign of independence as it presupposed not only self-subsistence, but the ability to make others dependent upon oneself. Through generosity one became a refuge for others. Put more cynically, in the shrewd words of Īśvaradatta's *viṭa*, 'making gifts was a means of bringing others under one's control' (*Dhūrtaviṭasaṃvāda* 29ff.). Generosity was the necessary complement of wealth according to texts on the court. Courtly aphorisms tirelessly reiterate that being generous attracted others to oneself regardless of one's birth and other virtues (*Nītisāra* 5.60). Considering that the concept of largesse formed the dominant 'rationality' in the distribution of wealth among the ruling classes, its importance can hardly be underestimated.

Such an ethic could, however, also contribute in adverse circumstances to sudden penury and force a regional ruler to attend the court of a greater king. Similarly, for others of rank, the loss of fortune portended the abandonment of one's own retinue and entry into the service of others. This is precisely the background of that peculiar character of courtly life who forms the comic and wry narrator of the *bhāṇa* monologue plays cited above, the *viṭa*. The *viṭa* was a well-regarded man, learned in the arts of pleasure, who according to Yaśodhara, the commentator on the *Kāmasūtra* (1.4.45 and comm.), once led the lifestyle of the *nāgaraka*, but having subsequently consumed his wealth, was now a dependent for his livelihood on courtesans and *nāgarakas*. The *viṭa* possessed all of the qualifications of the *nāyaka* except for financial independence, and therefore was deemed a lesser member of 'good society'. According to Kṣemendra, he was broken by debts (*Deśopadeśa* 5.24). His knowledge of the affairs of pleasure, however, was legion, and in Sanskrit drama he acted as an advisor to *nāyikā* and *nāyaka* (*Kāmasūtra* 1.4.47). In the *bhāṇa* monologue plays, the *viṭa* walks through the courtesans' quarters in conversation with those he meets on the street. The *Nāṭyaśāstra* (34.14–16) places the *viṭa* among the mixed characters of the drama, who, despite his birth, knowledge and refinement, was unsuitable for the role of *nāyaka* because his poverty made him a low character. The leading character, the *nāyaka*, was one who succeeded in fortune, who was literally 'elevated' or 'lifted up' from adverse conditions (*Nāṭyaśāstra* 34.23). Such was the fate of the virtuous Brāhmaṇa Cārudatta in Śūdraka's *Mṛcchakaṭika*. This play begins with Cārudatta's pathetic lament on his new-found poverty, poignant verses which take their place among the best of the maxims on the subject in Sanskrit literature. The 'burning' thing about poverty, according to Cārudatta, is that guests avoid a house of diminished wealth and people slacken their friendship with one whose wealth is destroyed (1.12, 13). By the play's end, however, Cārudatta has gained a position of favour at the king's court, which enables him to bestow largesse once again.

Poverty in the eyes of Cārudatta, as for the hundreds of courtly maxims on the subject, was painful because it prevented the display of generosity and favours that structured relations at court – between members of equal rank in the form of hospitality and friendship, and between men of rank and their inferiors in the form of the provision of livelihood. Ultimately, poverty destroyed one's autonomy and subjected one to greater and greater dependence on others. The anxiety over wealth apparent in court-centred aphorisms reflected a perception of the precariousness of autonomy: there was a chain of greater and lesser dependencies which characterized the feudal élite in medieval India. For every maxim that wealth and power drew retainers and made one a refuge of the world, another followed, that losing one's wealth and failing to provide honours, brought calamity.

Good men would abandon an impoverished lord like a calf abandoning its mother's udder when its milk was dry (*Nītisāra* 5.59, 62, 63; *Arthaśāstra* 5.5.12; *Cāṇakya-rājanīti* 181). To round off the discussion, the ethical problem that faced men at court was this: how was it possible to maintain autonomy within a world of dependence? How was a man to negotiate his relations with others, precariously but ineluctably situated between the poles of autonomy and dependence? That this situation constituted a concern is clearly indicated by the persistent exaltation and derision of wealth and poverty, and the states of mastery and service they implied, within the discourses of the court.

The relation between superiors and inferiors, between relatively autonomous and relatively dependent agencies, was expressed in a specific and limited set of expressions and practices, several of which will be relevant for the discussion at hand. From the very inception of political discourse, but particularly from Gupta times, inscriptions and court texts frequently describe the relations of lords and their subordinates through the language of attachment.[7] 'Attachment' in these contexts referred not merely to a person's disposition towards the external world in a general sense, but more specifically to the particular relationship he or she had with other individuals. That is to say, the most common form of attachment we find in the discourses of the court is one person's 'attachment' to another. The term most often used to describe this relationship is *anurāga*. The root *rañj* (lit. 'reddening') meant to be affected or attracted by someone or something. Preceded by the purposive suffix *anu,* 'to follow', *anurāga/anurakta* had an even stronger sense of being 'attracted to' or 'attached to' someone. The allied term *bhakti* denoted a disposition of 'devoted participation' toward a superior agent which involved subordinate participation in one's master's lordship. A few examples will give a sense of this vocabulary. In the famous Junagadh rock inscription, datable to the Gupta era in the fifth century AD, one Parṇadatta, a 'servant' (*bhṛta*) of Skandagupta appointed to rule Saurāṣṭra, is described as 'devoted' (*bhakti*) and 'attached' (*anurakta*) to his lord (*CII* III: 14). An early sixth-century inscription from Eran records that the wife of one Goparāja, who died on the battlefield in the service of his lord Bhānugupta, being devoted (*bhakti*) and 'attached' (*anurakta*) to her husband, followed him to heaven on the funeral pyre (*CII* III: 21). The famous court poet of Harṣa (606–47), Bāṇabhaṭṭa, writing at the beginning of the seventh century, describes kings from various countries who attend the court of Harṣa as 'attached' to his splendour (*pratāpānurāgagata*) (*Harṣacarita* 60). And finally, an eighth-century inscription from western India refers on the one hand to the hereditary servants of a dynasty as 'attached to the king through affection' (*anurāgānurakta*), and later refers to *sāmantas* paying obeisance to the king through the 'attachment produced by his splendour' (*pratāpānurāgapraṇatasamastasāmanta*) (*CII* III: 39).

[7] For two pre-Gupta examples, see Khāravela's Hathigumpha inscription which refers to the king Khāravela as 'pleasing the people' (*rañjayati pakatiyo*) (*EI* XX: 7); and the Junagadh rock inscription of Rudradāman which claims that his subjects were attached to him (*prakṛti anuraktena*) (*EI* VIII: 6).

Viewed as a process, *anurakta* denoted the attraction or drawing of one person to another and courtly representations usually mention the virtues and powers that attract others to oneself. Virtues generally had the effect of making one 'attractive' – literally 'pulling' others toward oneself. Numerous inscriptions mention the bonds of service and affiliation being based on the attraction or attachment to the qualities of one's lord. A typical attribute that attracted others to a king for example, was 'splendour' (*pratāpa*). A later inscription refers to Kalinga king Anantavarman as having an entire circle of vassals (*sāmantas*) attracted to him by virtue of the excellence of his threefold power (*śaktitrayaprakarṣānurañjita*) (*EI* XXIV: 17).[8] But inscriptions often make more general reference to the virtues of kings and lords. A southern Śilāhāra grant of the eleventh century describes a Rāṣṭrakūṭā king as 'attractive by his royal qualities' (*nṛpaguṇaramanīya*) (*CII* VI: 40). In the famous Mandasor inscription which recounts the emigration of a guild of silk weavers to Daśapura and their request for favours from the reigning king of the region, the silk weavers proclaim that they are 'attracted to the virtues' (*guṇāpahṛta*) of the king (*CII* III: 18). Together, these inscriptions make explicit one of the chief goals of self-cultivation and moral perfection – to gain the attachment of others in the world. The texts on polity like the *Nītisāra* (4.6.8) and *Arthaśāstra* (6.1.3) exhort the king to develop virtues within himself which are called *ābhigāmika guṇas*, literally, 'qualities which invite'. Having inviting qualities would attract dependants and allies. A seventh-century inscription of the Kāmarūpa king Bhāskaravarman is explicit about it: the king is described as having people 'attached to his inviting qualities' (*ābhigāmikaguṇānurāga*) (*EI* XIX: 19).[9] In an eighth-century inscription, even the goddess of fortune is attracted to the inviting qualities of the Gurjara king Ahirola (*CII* IV: 24).

Attachment as Subjection

What constituted this attachment? In the inscription of Ahirola, the poet tells us that it is the mind of Lakṣmī that was fervently attached to the king (*CII* IV: 24; cf. *CII* IV: 12). In the preceding discussion we learned that it was the mind that oversaw the relation of the self with the external world. If we see the problem of attachment as one not simply between the self and the world but *between* selves, then we may see the role of the mind in courtly discourse somewhat differently. The mind was the 'zone of engagement' for the dynamics of attachment and detachment which articulated the relations of members of the court. As the locale of social dispositions and sentiments, the mind was the place where affiliation resided, and where the battle of affections took place. The texts most often speak of the attachment of people's minds as a sort of 'capturing'. We may see early examples of this in some of the hymns of the *Atharvaveda*, the methods of which

[8] The threefold-power, according to the *Arthaśāstra* (6.3.33), refers to the power of counsel, might and effort. Counsel consisted of the power of knowledge; might, the power of the treasury and army; and effort, the power of valour.

[9] See also the eighth-century inscription of the Gurjara king Ahirola which claims that even the goddess of fortune is attracted to the inviting qualities of the king (*CII* IV: 24).

were later appended to the knowledges of the *Arthaśāstra* and *Kāmasūtra* as 'secret' (*aupaniṣadika*). In one rite to attain 'victory' in the assembly (*sabhā*), the performer was to eat milk-porridge, take hold of the pillars of the assembly hall and pay respect to the assembly hall while reciting the following hymn: 'If your mind has wandered to a distance or been tied here or there, then we draw it here. May your mind take delight in me' (*Atharvaveda* 7.12).[10] In another *Atharva* hymn (6.94) which sought to procure harmony within the assembly, the performer was to chant:

> We cause your minds, vows, plans, to bend (*namāmasi*).
> Those devoted to other purposes (*vivratā*) we cause to bend.
> I seize your minds with my mind (*gṛhṇāmi manasā manāṃs*).
> Your thoughts will follow my thoughts (*citamanu cittebhireta*).
> I place your hearts in my control.
> Direct yourself toward me after my course.[11]

These hymns, connected with secret rites, were only to be employed in special circumstances, when policy and strategy as detailed in the bulk of the *Arthaśāstra* and *Kāmasūtra* failed. In a peculiar way they thus reveal quite well the unveiled ambition of court practice. Although they do not use the term *anurakta*, they anticipate its logic by referring to the untying of the opponent's mind from its current mooring and drawing it close to where it may 'take delight'. The goal of policy and strategy at court was to bend and capture the mind of others and thereby to cause them to submit in some way to oneself. The imagery of 'seizing' another's mind or 'causing it to bend' is highly significant. The comportment of the body was ultimately linked to the disposition of the mind, and becoming attached to someone entailed bodily gestures which reflected the condition of the mind. One bowed because one's mind was drawn in a deferential manner toward another person. Attachment was envisioned as a 'leaning toward' or an 'inclination' of the mind, which led to the inclining of the body in the direction of another. So it is perhaps not surprising that in the eighth-century inscription cited above, feudatories are said to bow down to their lord from excessive attachment to his splendour (*CII* III: 39). From the vantage point of the self, it's internal order was disrupted as it literally gravitated, through attraction, to another. Attachment meant the partial surrender of one's own self-mastery, through a re-direction of the disposition of the mind and the external 'instruments' (*karaṇas*) which it ruled (the senses as well as the motor organs) to the service of another being.

This submission entailed 'control' of others, a concept indicated in Sanskrit by the term *vaśa*, often translated as 'influence' or 'subjugation'. The *Atharva* hymn cited above speaks of placing the heart of one's opponent 'in the control' of

[10] For practices associated with this hymn, based on Keśava's commentary on *Kauśikasūtra*, see Bloomfield (1897: 543).

[11] This hymn appears with six others which together are designated as 'designed to bring harmony' (*sā.manasyāni*) and is associated with rituals which include eating the pickled flesh of young calves. For details see Bloomfield (1897: 360–61).

the reciter. Subjugation could be exercised over a number of domains, first and foremost of which was one's own self. We hear of rulers as being 'self-controlled,' a condition which presupposed the conquest of the senses and the restraint of the mind (*CII* III: 14). Conversely, attachment to pleasures, is often said to entail a disorder or the control of the mind by the senses. In Harṣa's *Ratnāvalī* a woman is observed to be moving unsteadily during the spring festival because she is 'controlled by passion' (*madanavaśa*). The term *vaśa* also referred to the effecting or extension of one's wishes over another person, akin to the modern notion of 'influence'. A thirteenth-century inscription of the later Rāṣṭrakūṭas refers to a counsellor who exercised 'fascinating control (*vaśikāram*) over his friends' (*EI* XIII: 3a). The goal of royal policy, according to the *Arthaśāstra* (1.4.2), was for the king to use the benefits of livelihood, along with his wealth and the army, to 'bring under his control' both his own and other parties. In reviewing the importance of *daṇḍa*, Kauṭilya cites a school of thought which held that coercion was the most effective means of political control (*Arthaśāstra* 1.4.6). While Kauṭilya disagrees with the proposition that coercion should be the sole instrument of rule, he hardly differs on the goal. Bringing other parties under one's control was most effectively achieved through peaceful means, as when a *viṭa* remarks at a salon of refined men (*Dhūrtviṭasaṃvāda* 29) that giving gifts was a means of bringing the people of the world in general – and courtesans in particular – under one's control.

The language of capture and seizure, however, indicates that relations of attachment were also in part agonistic. Attachment was essentially a submission of one mind to another. It compromised the relative autonomy of the servant and secured the relative autonomy of the master. Expectedly, then, 'attachment' could also be achieved through the direct or indirect threat of force. When an eighth-century inscription from western India describes *sāmantas* who bow down to king Kharagraha because they had been 'violently subdued by excessive attachment (*atiprakṛṣṭānurāga*) more than a hint of coercion is implied (*CII* III: 39). In the *nīti* texts the submission of a defeated king to a victor was expressed as the attachment of the defeated king's self/mind as ruler of its own organs/instruments with their external domains, to a new lord.

We may sum up the discussion as follows. Relations between men at court were characterized by strategies that entailed drawing others to themselves by attracting or 'capturing' their minds. In such relations the self remained relatively unattached, with the proviso that its own autonomous agency was enjoyed only by virtue of its attachment to even higher agencies. The loss of independence was an anxiety behind all courtly action. The *Mudrārākṣasa* (3.4) says that acting in the interests of others causes one's own interests to suffer and one becomes servile; and being dependent on another, it was impossible to experience the taste of pleasure. The goal of royal policy, in a sense, was to limit the internal mastery of all servants, companions and rivals within and beyond the king's sphere of mastery and thus gain their submission or attachment, while remaining relatively 'unattached' within these relations himself.

The same antagonism could potentially underlie the servant's relation with his lord. As the *Gathāsaptaśatī* (3.65) puts it, 'though being self-dependent (*ātmavaśa*), a good man of noble birth may submit to another, even if hated, with the complexion (or attachment – *rāga*) of his face unchanged, and follow his wishes'. The *nīti* texts recommend that the king placate his dependants, or else be abandoned or even killed by them (see *Nītisāra* 5.68). The courtier's advancement through circles of the court and his gaining of superior favour could often entail antagonistic policies toward his lord, as when in the *Puruṣaparīkṣā* (1.3.1ff.) the prince Malladeva, who attends the court of Jayacandra, leaves the court of his lord in order to challenge him to battle in the hope of gaining the king's favour by a display of valour. The jackal-minister Damanaka in the first book of the *Pañcatantra* (1.18ff.), when he sees his own sovereign Piṅgalaka's weakness, confides to his friend that 'this very day I will catch him while he is overcome with fear and by the power of my intelligence bring him under my control'. In these cases an internal constituent of the kingdom, one of the king's own 'instruments', attempts to exercise his will over his master, and is ultimately successful.

The mutual antagonism which could underlie relationships at court is best revealed, I submit, by a persistent ambivalence to attachment and dependence in the aphoristic literature. Servitude, devotion, and attachment were on the one hand elevated to the most perfect of virtues and on the other denigrated as the basest of conditions. It was better to go to the forest than to be dependent on another. Moralists of the court decried servitude and denigrated lords for their pride and cruelty, while at the same time blaming servants for their greed. Thus the apparently simple posture of devotion that a servant was to have toward his lord, and the reciprocal disposition of favour the lord was to display toward his dependant (relations which formed the very sinews of affiliation at court), were undergirded by complex antagonisms which the language of attachment was fully capable of sustaining.

Courtship and the Language of Paramours

Before turning to the 'ideological' dimension of courtship as it is represented in court poetry, it will be useful to make a brief reconstruction of the contexts in which 'courtship' may actually have occurred. In the higher forms of marriage laid out in the Śāstras, to be practised by the upper *varṇa*s and deeply enmeshed in the acquisition and perpetuation of property and/or authority, prospective wives were to be secured by arrangement, through the 'selection' (*varaṇa*) and/or 'gift of a maiden' (*kanyādāna*). Marriage was an institution explicitly used to build political alliances and open avenues of exchange between 'houses'. For the ruling elite of medieval Indian courts, of putative Kṣatriya lineage, selection and marriage constituted the most important method of sealing political alliances between kings. Wars between rival kings were often concluded with the defeated house offering women in marriage to the victors. The practice of *kanyādāna*, as Trautmann (1981: 26) has demonstrated, tended to establish the superiority of the groom's family over the bride's. Even for others of standing, selection seems to have been the dominant form of marriage. Vātsyāyana begins his book on 'acquiring a wife' with a discussion not of the relations between the *nāyaka* and *nāyikā*, but between the *nāgaraka* and the family of the prospective bride, implying the context of *varaṇa* or *kanyādāna*. Among Kṣatriyas, marriage was in some cases arranged through a *svayaṃvara*, or 'self-choice', where the daughter of a superior king chose from a group of suitors drawn from allies or powerful underlords of her father. The *svayaṃvara* also ended with a bestowal of the daughter, but may not have indicated the subordination of the giving king (see *Naiṣadhacaritam* 16.10–12). An important event in the *Mahābhārata*, the *svayaṃvara* became an increasingly popular theme in later *kāvya*, particularly the story of Nala and Damayantī.[12] The *svayaṃvara* would seem to offer a context for the display of male virtue vaguely akin to conceptions of chivalric romance in medieval Europe. It was certainly not, however, the dominant mode of brokering marriages among the courtly elite, and seems to have been more of a literary theme than anything else. The romance which unfolds in the Nala–Damayantī story is peculiar in that the protagonists fall in love and begin to pine without ever having seen one another, a fact which highlights the role of 'fame' (female beauty as much as male prowess) in drawing families together in marriage, rather than the rudiments of courtship.

In both the *kanyādāna* and *svayaṃvara*, as in the more embracing rites of 'selection' of which they were variants, the scope for *premarital* courtship was limited. Only one form of marriage sanctioned by the Śāstras, the *gandharva*, was understood as the culmination of the mutual affection and obviously entailed premarital courtship.[13] Whatever the prevalence of this form of marriage, the context of courtship presumed in the bulk of the *Kāmasūtra*'s discussion of the acquisition of a wife revolves around 'creating confidence' in the bride during the first few days *after* the marriage ceremony. This was no doubt the typical marital context for courtship, and one that was undoubtedly complicated by the existence of co-wives and other women in the house sexually available to the patriarch. Both the *Kāmasūtra* (3.2.1) and later manuals like Kokkoka's *Ratirahasya* (11.8) recommend three nights of restraint after the marriage ceremony, to which Vātsyāyana adds another seven, before the groom was to begin wooing the bride. Both texts are

[12] Noted by Meyer (1995: 78) and Yadava (1973: 70). In addition to Śrīharṣa's *Naiṣadhacarita*, versions of this story include the *Nalodaya* of Kālidāsa; the *Nalacampū* of Trivikramabhaṭṭa (ninth century); the *Naiṣadhānandanāṭaka* of Kṣemīśvara (ninth-tenth century); the *Sahṛdayānanda* of Kṛṣṇānanda (thirteenth century); and the *Nalābhyudaya* of Vāmanabhaṭṭabāṇa (fifteenth century).

[13] Vātsyāyana begins the third chapter of his book on acquiring a wife by advising the man who lacks the proper qualifications for the marriage negotiation, not to enter into the selection ceremony because he would not be able to obtain a maiden (*Kāmasūtra* 3.3.1ff.). In this case he was to win her over himself by courting that began in her childhood. Vātsyāyana then cites Ghoṭamukha's opinion that this type of wooing, in a girl's childhood, pure and according to *dharma*, is praiseworthy (*Kāmasūtra* 3.3.4). Following chapters provide various strategies for the cultivation of a mutual attraction between the prospective partners before marriage. The *gandharva* marriage, according to Vātsyāyana, was the superior form because it was attained without much difficulty, without a ceremony of 'selection', and was based on mutual affection or attachment which was said to be the 'fruit' of all marriage in any event (*Kāmasūtra* 3.5.29–30).

emphatic that the husband avoid rash or untimely sexual advances without first gaining the confidence of the bride (*Kāmasūtra* 3.2.4–6; *Ratirahasya* 11.8). This is because, we are told, when a man approaches a woman suddenly, he engenders fear, disgust on dejection, and when she feels no affection, she is ruined by anxiety and may come to hate men in general or later go to another man (*Kāmasūtra* 3.2.43–44; *Ratirahasya* 11.21–22). It is concluded that a man who knows how to win the confidence of women, increase their attachment, and arouse their affection for him, comes to be loved (*Kāmasūtra* 3.2.41; cf. *Ratirahasya* 11.20). Post-marital courtship suggests a clear recognition that marriage and affection, though related, were distinct. Courtship formed a way of 'regulating' the initial period of marriage, one potentially fraught with tension given the context, typical among the elite, of polygamy and concubinage. The result of courtship, 'affection' (*anurāga*) was considered to be a 'fruit' of marriage rather than marriage being the culmination of courtship and affection (*Kāmasūtra* 3.5.30).

Indeed, if we follow the texts on *kāma*, it is clear that the conjugal relations formed only one of the potential contexts for courtship. After recommending the norm of same-caste liaisons with unmarried virgins for the purpose of procreation, the *Kāmasūtra* (1.5.3) says that relations may be enjoyed with lower *varṇas* not fully rejected from the social order, including courtesans, and widows or women once married. On this basis, Vātsyāyana concludes that *nāyikās* were of three basic varieties: unmarried girls (*kanyā*), married women seeking the company of a man out of wedlock, and courtesans (*veśyā*).[14] Excepting virgins of the same caste married for children, other women of these categories were to be enjoyed for pleasure alone.

Judging from *subhāṣita* literature, for many men of rank the courtesan was the preferred liaison. Relations with courtesans (*gaṇikā*), the highest rank for a prostitute, entailed elaborate courtship, explicitly detailed in the *Kāmasūtra* and the theme of numerous literary works, including an entire genre, the *bhāṇa* monologue play. Many aphorisms compare the courtesan favourably with the wife: in contrast to courtesans, according to one saying, wives had the uninterrupted course of their youths destroyed by continually having children, had no respect for the games, diversions, and sentiments of the salon of refined men (*goṣṭhī*), avoided the manners of the courtesan, and were devoid of passion (*Gaṇikāvṛttasaṃgraha* 28).[15] Numerous sayings recommend that the perfect wife strive to be like a prostitute in bed (ibid.: 18–21).

[14] Vātsyāyana goes on to engage various contemporary authorities (no longer extant) over the question of other categories of *nāyikās*, implicitly conceding two more varieties, the married woman enjoyed for some other purpose (*pākṣikī*), and those of the 'third nature,' classified as neither man nor woman (*Kāmasūtra* 1.5.5, 27). Varieties of *tritīya-prakṛti* are discussed in more detail in *Kāmasūtra* (2.9.1–8), in connection with the practice of *auparisṭaka*.

[15] Judging from the sources, the institution of marriage was no bar to relations with them. One need only think of Śūdraka's famous play, the *Mṛcchakaṭika*, in which the hero, the Brāhmaṇa Cārudatta, falls in love with the courtesan Vasantasenā.

Another context of courtship for men of rank, but particularly princes, must have been the affections they received from palace women as they reached maturity. Such episodes are mentioned in the accounts of princely lives contained in the *Buddhacarita*, *Raghuvaṃśa* and *Kādambarī*. Though these descriptions at one level underscore the attractiveness of the young prince, they nevertheless point to an important context for sexual liaisons which were not structured by the interests of marriage. Such episodes in the young prince's life, Śākyamuni's case only being an extreme example, were meant to demonstrate an ability to master the senses and remain aloof from such attachments. King Agnivarṇa of the *Raghuvaṃśa*, whose sad fate was mentioned above, begins his life of pleasure in his youth at the palace, and never emerges from it. These episodes point to an important dimension of courtship in the life of the court which we shall be exploring in the remainder of this paper. Courtship introduced young men to some of the most important 'lessons' and 'rules' of court life as a whole. It formed the perfect 'training ground' for the virtuous. After learning the sciences, young princes were 'tested' in the company of women before they assumed the throne. In courtship they were to perfect the controlled display and interpretation of dispositions, exhibit courtesy, generosity and other virtues, and most important, exercise self-mastery at all times.

Whatever the context of courtship, there is a tendency in its representation, in both the texts on poetics and the poetry itself, to dissociate lovers from their contexts. We tend to find a world of hermetically sealed lovers who solicit, create confidence and win each other over by various stratagems. The context of the courtly world, however, may be dimly discerned by attention to the dynamics of the lovers themselves. I suggest that the ubiquitous inclusion of this theme in court poetry may be understood as a tableau onto which the ruling class projected its larger concerns and anxieties, particularly those around the problems of autonomy and dependence outlined above. The prominence of erotica in the literature of the courts of medieval India has much to do with the fact that 'courtship' became the arena where the ethical problems of courtly life were reflected upon and learned. And so the rise of the dominance of this theme in court poetry is quite clearly related to and explained by the spread of 'feudal' relationships in medieval India.

The link between erotica and the wider problems of court life as sketched in the previous sections of this paper is, in the first place, underscored by the fact that a number of the key terms used in the discussion above – *anurāga*, *vaśa*, *mano grah* – are usually encountered first by modern scholars of Sanskrit literature not to describe political, but instead erotic relationships. This congruence of language deserves serious consideration, for the agonism of affection is even more apparent in the discourse on courtly love. Perhaps the most obvious parallel is the use of martial terms in descriptions of courtship. This takes numerous forms. The most common images connect the bodies and gestures of lovers to weaponry in general, as when Bhartṛhari says that a woman's sidelong looks, darting glances with raised eyebrows, soft speech, shy laughter, and playfully indolent movement all constitute at once ornaments (*bhūṣaṇa*) and weapons (*āyudha*) (*Subhāṣitatriśatī* 2.3). More particular is the iconography of Kāmadeva, the bowman of love, who pierces the hearts of lovers with his flower arrows. This set of comparisons form among the most popular images of courtly *kāvya*. The most developed imagery is resolved around the eye, with the eyebrow compared to the bow, the eyelash to the bowstring and the glance to the arrow. In a typical example from Vidyākara's anthology, the female's glance is likened to a poison arrow, bringing paralysis, dizziness of mind, fever and, in the last event, loss of consciousness (*Subhāṣitaratnakoṣa* 496). In Sanskrit erotica desire was afflictive, not simply as a generalization of the self's relation to the world (as it has been read by scholars of religion), but much more specifically as violence of one person against another. Once again, a hymn from the *Atharvaveda* (3.25.2) makes this explicit. To gain success in love, one could perform a ritual incantation: 'With that arrow, winged with longing, whose shaft is love, whose neck is resolve – with that Kāma, well aimed, I shall pierce your heart'. Vātsyāyana remarks that erotic pleasure takes the form of combat because it is essentially a contest and because of its contrariety, his commentator Yaśodhara explains the latter as arising 'because man and woman each tries to accomplish their own goal by overcoming the other' (*Kāmasūtra* 2.7.1 and comm.).[16]

The *Kāmasūtra* makes it clear that the goal of this combat was gaining the attachment of one's 'opponent'. Creating confidence and trust and soliciting were all included in the larger strategy of 'winning over' a lover – what Vātsyāyana calls 'causing one to be attached (*anurañjayati*)' (*Kāmasūtra* 3.3.2). The idea was to gain the attachment of one's paramour without oneself becoming attached. For men, according to the *Mṛcchakaṭika* (4.14), 'no attachment (*rāga*) should be had to women; women insult the attached man; only the woman who is herself attached should be enjoyed'. In preparing for courtship, the idea was to make oneself 'attractive'; the suitable *nāyaka*, just like the king, was to have inviting virtues. The courtesan Vasantasenā repeatedly remarks in the *Mṛcchakaṭika* (1.6 *passim*) that she is attached to the virtues (*guneṣvanurakta*) of Cārudatta.'

The drawing of a lover to oneself, just as drawing a dependant and gaining his or her attachment, was fraught with potential antagonism. Each lover tried to 'catch' the mind of the other, and having done so, to exercise 'control' or 'influence' (*vaśa*) over it. Typical are two ninth-century graffiti from Sigiriya in Sri Lanka addressed to paintings of heavenly maidens: 'having looked at you my mind is as if subdued (*visī*); by the mere sight of you I am enslaved'; 'you have bent and subdued my mind.'[17] Wives were recommended to seek control over their husbands, particularly in the polygamous context. Vātsyāyana says that a king or minister's daughter who knows the sixty-four arts will control her husband even if there are a thousand other women in the *antaḥpura* (*Kāmasūtra* 1.3.22).[18]

16 The description of lovers bears a resemblance to the well-known definition of an enemy in the texts on polity. The enemy, according to Kāmandakī, was one who pursued the same goal as the self (*ekārthābhiniveśa*) (*Nītisāra* 8.14).

17 Sinhala *visī* = Sanskrit *vaśa* (Paranavitana 1956 : 273, 166, see also 211, 494, 547).

18 See also *Nāṭyaśāstra* (24.224) for the woman whose husband is under her control (*svādhīnabhartṛkā*).

Exercising control over one's husband also entailed mastering the other women of the household, and Vātsyāyana advises the young wife to conquer her anger and cultivate herself in accordance with the *kāmaśāstra* in order to stand above and control her co-wives and husband (*Kāmasūtra* 4.2.90). Conversely, the *nāyaka* was also encouraged to bring a woman under his control. In his disquisition before the *goṣṭhī*, the *viṭa* Devilaka is asked the question of how one can bring under one's control a woman who does not disclose any sign of desire, who says 'enough', who does not draw near, and avoids one at the proper time. The *viṭa* approves of this question, and responds that one must first know the nature of the woman and then adopt a suitable means accordingly (*Dhūrtaviṭasaṃvāda* 46ff.).[19] When a man could not achieve this through the normal recommended method in the *kāmaśāstra*, methods he could have recourse to 'covert methods', which included the use of various special substances and rites from the *Atharva-veda*. The goal of many of these recipes was to enable a man to 'exert influence' over a woman (*Kāmasūtra* 7.12–3ff., 25–28, 31–35).[20] The significant aspect of these formulae is not their 'secrecy', but quite the opposite, their open revelation as to the ambitions of the normative strategies of courtship as a whole.

The Courtesan as Icon

The figure of the courtesan in the discourses of the court is worth pausing over, as among the non-conjugal sexual relations permitted by the Śāstras for men of rank, those with the courtesan are the most reflected upon in the didactic literature. It would seem that the courtesan was the *nāyikā* par excellence for those at court.[21] Inferior in rank to the wives and maidens of upper-caste men, nevertheless the courtesan could operate as an autonomous agent at court, unattached to the juridical identity of any male. She was capable of gaining the attachments of men and these attachments could in some cases have notorious and weighty consequences. Courtesans sought to make their own way in court circles by using their capacities. At one level, the courtesan differed little in the kinds of capacities she possessed from the various men who surrounded her (though the breadth of her capacities were considerably restricted). The discourse on courtesans is important because while they are often decried as being inferior to women of good standing, numerous aphorisms make the point that they were merely a sub-species of women as a whole, particularly women of the court. Courtesans are said to be better than women of good birth (*kulastrī*). Here the defamation of the courtesan links up with a wider denigration of women as 'fickle' and 'dangerous'.[22] And

[19] Devilaka recommends forcible seizure in the case of a proud woman.

[20] The whole of the fourteenth book of the *Ratirahasya* is devoted to *vaśīkaraṇa*, as well as specific mantras for various types of women in the sections on *nāyikābheda*. Also *s.v.* in Rai (1983), who draws heavily on Kalyāṇamalla's late-fifteenth century *Anaṅgaraṅga*.

[21] It is only in his book on courtesans that Vātsyāyana lays out the general characteristics of the *nāyikā* and *nāyaka*.

[22] The bad qualities of the courtesan are often indistinct from those of women in general. See *Gaṇikāvṛttasaṃgraha* (243–44, 359–416, 514–47, 525).

given what we know from Vātsyāyana's account of women enjoyed for pleasure outside of marriage, and the potential motives and dangers of such liaisons, we can easily see the basis for such perceptions.

In the *Kāmasūtra* (6.1.12) the male lover or *nāyaka* should be of 'independent means' (*svatantravṛtti*) and not subjected to women; he should be unattached (*anavasaṅkī*). The courtesan is advised by Vātsyāyana to put an end to all three of these conditions. Vātsyāyana repeatedly says that she was to attract, cause attachment and even excessive attachment in her lover and thus bring him under her will (*vaśa*) (*Kāmasūtra* 6.4.43). She was then, through various means, to extract as much wealth as possible from him. By draining her paramour of his wealth and destroying his financial independence the courtesan could bring him under the control of others through debt and penury – she turned him from a *nāyaka* to, in the worst cases, a *viṭa*. Bereft of his independence, the paramour was then summarily discarded.

The chief means of gaining the attraction of a client, according to Vātsyāyana, was dissemblance. Vātsyāyana suggests that courtesans go to men partly for pleasure, but more importantly for livelihood, which requires them to make their affections *seem* natural (*Kāmasūtra* 6.1.1–3).[23] She was to give her customer the impression that she was attached to him in order to gain his attachment to her (ibid.: 6.2.2). One of the most notable features of the aphoristic literature on courtesans is its obsession with deception. Her affections could sometimes be genuine. In the *Dhūrtaviṭasaṃvāda* (31, 32, 43), the *viṭa* named Devilaka resolves a controversy at a salon regarding the methods of detecting the sincerity of a courtesan's attraction to her would be paramour. Devilaka is adamant that the sentiments of courtesans were genuine. Physical states such as horripilation, crying and sweating were deemed involuntary bodily effects in the texts on dramaturgy. But courtesans, others maintained, were like actors and could induce these states in their bodies (*Kuṭṭanīmata* 312).[24] Indeed, the courtesan was an expert, according to Dāmodaragupta, at theatrics such as praiseworthy speech, gesturing with her limbs, decoration and indignation (*Kuṭṭanīmata* 657).[25]

The courtesan was skilled in displaying desire in different ways. Her agent, the *viṭa*, explains to the members of the salon that feminine desire could be classified as either 'open' or 'concealed' (*Dhūrtaviṭasaṃvāda* 53ff.). Wives concealed their desires, while courtesans could openly display or else hide their affections. Anticipating the question of why the courtesan's expression of passion which after all was permissible, would be concealed, the *viṭa* continues that various types of men – favourites of the king, those who had done some good for them or

[23] Much of Vātsyāyana's subsequent advice to the courtesan is aimed at creating confidence in her lover.

[24] See also *Kuṭṭanīmata* (98) and *Dhūrtaviṭasaṃvāda* (31–32). For other references to courtesans as actresses, see *Gaṇikāvṛttasaṃgraha* (222–29).

[25] These attributes correspond to the four modes of theatrical conveyance (*vācika, āṅgika, āhārya* and *sāttvika*) as set out in *Nāṭyaśāstra* (6.23). See the commentary on *Kuṭṭanīmata* (657) which cites the *Sāhityadarpaṇa*.

were gentle and devoted to them, or who showed respect – had to be served for her own interests even if she did not seek them out. In such cases the display of affection was 'feigned'. But when a courtesan sought the favours of a man secretly he had obtained the rarest reward of his life, for this was a true reflection of her desires: 'concealed love, growing out of attachment alone, and having little fault, is pleasing indeed in the case of courtesans'. Of course, Devilaka's optimism here is undermined by the elaboration in the erotic manuals of ever greater forms of dissemblance on the part of the courtesan.

The perennial debate about the authenticity of the courtesan is significant in light of the foregoing discussion. It is curious that the moralists of the court would decry her as the typical woman, faithless and deceptive. The aphorisms constantly bemoan how they attract, ensnare, and capture the minds of men, exert control over them, take their money and subject them to others. But such behaviour was more than familiar to the men of the court, as these were the very strategies open to them throughout their careers in their society. In her labours of dissemblance and calculations of disposition the courtesan differed little from other agents at court. This is recognized in the occasional verses which compare courtesans to men at court. The secret attentions that a courtesan might show a man were thus comparable to the secret devotions that the followers of an old king showed to princes to gain their favour when the king was dying (*Rājataraṅgiṇī* 7.619; cf. *Gaṇikāvṛttasaṃgraha* 462, 482, 484). Dependants and courtesans sell their bodies and words to anyone who will grant them favours. When it is said that 'like bitches, courtesans will display hundreds of sweet words, eat dirt, perform bad actions and live by deceit all for gifts' (*Gaṇikāvṛttasaṃgraha* 619), the author could be speaking of the necessities of dependence. Indeed, according to the *Mudrārākṣasa* (5.4) the courtier 'dependent on another' 'sold his body to the wealthy' and lost all ability to discriminate. Numerous maxims also compare the courtesan to the king, whose policies were unpredictable, concealed, and ultimately dangerous (*Gaṇikāvṛttasaṃgraha* 436–38, 529–36, 541).

One obvious conclusion that may be drawn from this invective against the courtesan, and women in general, is that relations between lovers were often fraught with the same complex tensions as those between lords and dependants. Indeed, this is because at one level marriage, concubinage and prostitution – the institutions that governed such relations – were in fact hierarchical relationships intimately associated with authority and property to begin with, which overlapped and were largely continuous with those which obtained between men. The contexts of courtship, in other words, were the contexts of the court, and were governed by the same principles and strategies.

This essay, however, has tried to suggest something more. Courtship had a special place in the society of the court, both as an institution and as an object of speculation and delectation. Courtship during youth allowed the men of the court to learn the strategies of conduct and forms of self-discipline necessary for their relations with men at court. The discernment and deployment of deception and indirection required in courtship prepared men for courtly existence as a whole.

In a world where discerning the strategies of others and concealing one's own was a necessity, the process of courtship could provide no better training. And judging from the sources, continued success at courtship was an indication of the self-perfection of a powerful man at court. The king as the most powerful man at court had to constantly present himself as the most perfectly skilled player in the contest of love. This was achieved by the various liaisons in which he engaged, but extended to his relations with the feminine qualities of sovereignty, which were sexualized in precisely this manner. As one inscription describes a king, he was 'freely chosen by the goddess of fortune, her mind being overpowered by passion for all his attractive royal qualities and other excellences' (*CII* IV: 24).

The conflictual elements in the discourses of courtship reveal the greater anxieties of courtly society around autonomy and dependence. It is not complete detachment from the world – typical of the ascetic – that underlies the courtly discourses, rather the idea of a hierarchical form of social engagement in which one subjected others by gaining their 'attachment' but remained relatively detached oneself. This was the dynamic between lord and retainer, which structured the affectations of court ethics. The problem, of course, was that each agent was typically caught in a web of such 'attachments'. Erotic love in part formed the palette upon which the underlying agonism entailed in relations of dependence and autonomy, wealth and poverty, service and mastery, was continually projected and thought about. Conversely, the particularities of this agonism, so essential to the representation of love in Sanskrit literature, may explain the prominence of this discourse as a whole at the courts of medieval India more than any civilizational conflict between the immanent and the transcendent.

References

Arthaśāstra by Kauṭilya (1988), edited and translated by R.P. Kangle (Delhi: Motilal Banarsidass).

Civajñāṉapōtam (1945), translated by Nallaswami Pillai (Dharmapuram: Gnanasambandam Press).

Corpus Inscriptionum Indicarum (*CII*), relevant volumes (New Delhi: Archaeological Survey of India).

Deśopadeśa by Kṣemendra (1961), in *Kṣemendralaghukāvyasaṃgraha*, edited by V.V. Raghavacarya and D.G. Padhye (Hyderabad: Sanskrit Academy).

Dhūrtaviṭasaṃvāda by Īśvaradatta (1975), edited and translated by Manomohan Ghosh as *Glimpses of Sexual Life in Nanda-Maurya India: Translation of the Caturbhāṇī Together with a Critical Edition of the Text* (Calcutta: Manisha Granthalaya).

Dasgupta, Surendranath (1922), *A History of Indian Philosophy* (Cambridge: Cambridge University Press).

Epigraphia Indica (*EI*), relevant volumes (New Delhi: Archaeological Survey of India).

Gaṇikāvṛttasaṃgraha (1953), compiled and edited by Ludwik Sternbach (Hoshiarpur: Vishveshvaranand Institute Publications).

Gathāsaptaśatī (1971), edited and translated by Radhagovinda Basak (Calcutta: Asiatic Society).

Grimes, John (1996), *A Concise Dictionary of Indian Philosophy* (Albany: SUNY Press).

Harṣacarita by Bāṇa *with the Commentary (Saṃketa) of Śaṅkara* (1925), edited by K.P. Parab, revised by W.L. Shastri (Bombay: Nirnaya Sagara Press).

Indika by Megasthenes (1877), translated by J.W. McCrindle (London: Trṃbner).

Kakar, Sudhir and John Munder Ross (1986), *Tales of Love, Sex and Danger* (Oxford: Basil Blackwell).

Kāmasūtra by Vātsyāyana (1929), edited by Goswami Damodar Shastri (Benares: Jaikrishnadas and Haridas Gupta).

Kuṭṭanīmatam by Dāmodaragupta (1991), edited by Tanusukharam Manusukharam Tripathi (Varanasi: Krishnadas Academy).

Mahābhārata (1961), edited by V.S. Sukthankar and S.K. Belvalkar (Poona: Bhandarkar Oriental Research Institute).

Meyer, Johann (1995) *Sexual Life in Ancient India* (New York: Dorset Press).

Mṛcchakaṭika (1937), edited and translated by R.D. Karmarkar (Poona: Aryabhushan Press).

Mudrārākṣasa by Viśākhadatta (1912), edited by A. Hillebrandt (Breslau: H. and M. Marcus).

Naiṣadhīyacaritam by Śrīharṣa (1952), edited by Narayana Rama Acharya (Bombay: Nirnaya Sagara Press).

Narayana Rao, Velcheru, David Shulman and Sanjay Subrahmanyam (1992), *Symbols of Substance: Court and State in Nāyaka Period Tamilnadu* (Delhi: Oxford University Press).

Nītisāra (1869), edited and translated by Rajendralal Mitra (Calcutta: Asiatic Society).

O'Flaherty, Wendy Doniger (1973), *Śiva: the Erotic Ascetic* (New York: Oxford University Press).

Pañcasāyaka by Jyotiśvara (1939), edited by Dhundhiraja Sastri (Benares: Jaikrishnadas and Haridas Gupta).

Pañcatantra (1924), edited and translated by Francis Edgerton (New Haven: American Oriental Society).

Paranavitana, S. (1956), *Sigiri Graffiti: Being Sinhalese Verses from the Eighth, Ninth and Tenth Centuries*, 2 Vols (London: Oxford University Press).

Puruṣaparīkṣā by Vidyāpati (1911), edited by Ganganatha Jha (Allahabad: Belvedere Steam Press).

Raghuvaṃśa by Kālidāsa (1982), edited and translated by G.R. Nandargikar (Delhi: Motilal Banarsidass).

Rai, Ram Kumar (1983), *Encyclopedia of Indian Erotics* (Varanasi: Prachya Prakashan).

Rājataraṅgiṇī by Kalhaṇa (1989), edited by Sir Aurel Stein, 3 Vols (Delhi: Motilal Banarsidass).

Ratirahasya by Kokkoka (1994), edited by Ramananda Sharma (Varanasi: Krishnadas Academy).

Shulman, David (1985), *The King and the Clown in South Indian Mythology* (Princeton: Princeton University Press).

Siegel, Lee (1983), *Fires of Love, Waters of Peace: Passion and Renunciation in Indian Culture* (Honolulu: University of Hawaii Press).

Sternbach, Ludwig, ed. (1963), *Cāṇakyarājanīti: Maxims on Rājanīti compiled from various Collections of Maxims attributed to Cāṇakya* (Madras: Adyar Library).

Subhāṣitaratnakoṣa by Vidyākara (1957), edited by D.D. Kosambi and V.V. Gokhale (Cambridge, Mass.: Harvard University Press).

Subhāṣitatriśatī by Bhartṛhari (1987), revised and edited by N.R. Acarya and D.D. Kosambi (Varanasi: Chaukhamba Sanskrit Sansthan).

Trautmann, Thomas (1981), *Dravidian Kinship* (Cambridge: Cambridge University Press).

Yadava, B.N.S. (1973), *Society and Culture in Northern India in the Twelfth Century* (Allahabad: Central Book Depot).

Zimmerman, Francis (1987), *The Jungle and the Aroma of Meats: An Ecological Theme in Hindu Medicine* (Berkeley: University of California).

Ideas and Communication

Medieval Sanskrit Drama as a Literate Medium for Non-Literate Communication*

Vishwa Mohan Jha

I

For most Sanskrit scholars and theatre experts, the decline of the Sanskrit drama in medieval times has been a self-evident truth. After Bhavabhūti (eighth century), it is held, there was a progressive decadence of the Sanskrit drama. The process of decline may be seen in the plays of Rājaśekhara and Murāri. After them, that is after the tenth century, the decline was complete. Sanskrit dramas continued to be written down the centuries in great numbers, but were not worth the name, being totally incapable of stage production.

The purpose of my paper is to provide (a) a brief outline of the writings through which the decline thesis has become a near truism; (b) a description of the main constituents of the thesis; (c) a critique of its conceptual base; and (d) evidence for the continuous performance of Sanskrit dramas through medieval India.

The elements of the theory of the decline appear as early as the nineteenth century in H.H. Wilson's work ([1871] 1984). Sylvain Levi ([1890] 1978, Vol. II: 95–96) provided a systematic exposition of the historical decline of the Sanskrit drama in his magnum opus. In a brief introduction to his bibliography of the Sanskrit drama, Montgomery Schuyler ([1906] 1977: 13) did not fail either to mention the decline. But it was in Keith's *Sanskrit Drama In its Origin, Development, Theory and Practice* (1924) that we see in English an emphatic and full-blown account of the decline that was, in fact, substantially indebted to Levi's work. It set the tone for the later treatment of the subject by scholars, as seen in the expansive descriptions in the very popular work of S.K. De (Dasgupta and De 1962).[1]

The account of Sanskrit drama given by M. Winternitz did not influence the scholars to the same extent as did Keith's work. Its English translation came

* The first version of this essay was presented in 1994 at a seminar on literacy and communication in Indian tradition organized by Prof. Kunal Chakrabarti of Jawaharlal Nehru University. The second, submitted in 1998, awaits publication (I understand) by the Indian Institute of Advanced Study, Simla, in a volume edited by him.

[1] De's contribution to this volume was written in 1946.

too late in the day to have done so. Winternitz was not as emphatic about the decline as Keith, but he did share most of Keith's judgments. He found the works of Bhavabhūti to be 'little dramatic' and called them 'book-dramas', 'more suitable for reading than staging purposes', and found Rājaśekhara's work 'lacking in taste'. In general, the dramas were 'meant only for persons with highly refined taste' (Winternitz 1963: 184, 259, 266–67). In 1960, Indu Shekhar published his *Sanskrit Drama: Its Origin and Decline.* It had the additional weight of J. Gonda's authority and guidance behind it. Thus firmly entrenched, the decline thesis has held the field ever since, being mentioned as a matter of course in surveys of Indian history, Sanskrit literature and allied pieces of research (Basham 1954: 442; Thapar 1966: 256; Bhattacharji 1993: 220–21, 273–96, 323–28; Mishra 1976: 143, n. 1; Neog 1980: 246–47; Bhat 1988: 1107; cf. Lienhard 1984: 160).

This theory was borrowed wholesale by the experts on theatre (Berthold 1972: 53, 56). In recent decades the numerous contributions of F.P. Richmond in standard works of reference and surveys have made it a part of received wisdom (Banham 1988; Richmond, Swann and Zarrilli 1993; Brandon 1993). Discerning critics like Girish Karnad have criticized Richmond's description of the Indian theatre in the modern period on many points, but find him 'good on the pre-modern theatre'.[2]

II

The prevalent ideas on medieval Sanskrit drama and its (lack of) relation to medieval theatre may be grouped into six main themes: (i) verses, which are basically undramatic, came to dominate the later Sanskrit drama; (ii) the fundamentals, that is the plot, dialogues, action and characterization are reduced to virtual insignificance; (iii) Sanskrit is understood by fewer and fewer persons; (iv) the Muslim conquest undermined the courtly patronage of drama; (v) medieval Sanskrit dramas are literary pieces, not meant for or capable of stage production; and (vi) there is a great revival of theatre from the sixteenth century onwards in the vernaculars.

The first symptom of the decline is stated to be the tendency to excessive versification, 'which in lesser [that is, later] dramatists overshadowed all that was dramatic in it' (Dasgupta and De 1962: 57). This demerit of having the rather undramatic element of verses had always been present, but had been kept under reasonable control: 'The older poets lived in the atmosphere of the poetry of the court and their dramatic instincts had always to fight against the tendency to introduce epic and lyric verses into their own works, heedless of the ruin thus wrought on the drama' (Keith [1924] 1970: 242). The induction of poetry had its rationale in the elite audience of classical Sanskrit drama: 'the audience for whose approval a poet looked was essentially one of men of learning, who were intent on discerning poetic beauties or defects. . .' (ibid.). So 'had the stage been a more popular one, this defect might have been counteracted' (ibid.). However, so far as

[2] *The Hindu*, Delhi edition, Sunday, 20 February 1994.

effective expression in verse is concerned, the later drama did achieve that with distinction: 'It would, however, be quite unjust to deny Rājaśekhara the power of effective expression: *like all the later dramatists* he is capable of producing elegant and attractive verses' (ibid.: 236–37, emphasis added).[3]

Second, as verse tended to dominate Sanskrit drama, there was a corresponding diminution of the importance of dialogue, action, plot and characterization. In place of these, the theorists of Sanskrit drama concentrated on *rasa* (sentiment) as the central theme of a drama, and poetry as a must for *rasa* (Keith [1924] 1970: 276–84; Dasgupta and De 1962: xlvi, 57–59). As such, they had 'little idea of what a drama really means' (Keith [1924] 1970: 242). The 'atmosphere of sentiment and poetry' prevailed 'at the expense of action and characterization' (Dasgupta and De 1962: 57). There was a dependence on the epics for source material, which discouraged creative thinking and led to threadbare plots and hackneyed characters. As Keith states, 'The drama suffered . . . from its close dependence on the epic and the failure of the poets to recognize that the epic subjects were often as a whole undramatic. Hence, frequently, as in the vast majority of the Rāma dramas and those based on the *Mahābhārata*, we have nothing but the recasting of the epic narrative into a semi-dramatic form, without real dramatic structure' (Keith [1924] 1970: 281). Thus in the *Anargharāghava*, 'there is no attempt to improve on the traditional narrative, though Vālin is honourably killed'; 'the characters are as stereotyped as ever'; 'for dialogue in general Murāri has no taste at all'; in sum, the play 'has no dramatic merit, being deficient in character, action, situations and interest' (ibid.: 229–30; Wilson [1871] 1984, Vol. II: 383). Likewise, the demerits of the plays of Rājaśekhara include lack of 'the power to create a character' and a 'poorly managed intrigue' (Keith [1924] 1970: 235–56).[4]

In the same critical vein, we are also often told about the 'lack of taste' or 'vitiation of taste' or 'deplorable taste' of the playwrights. In this respect scholarly judgement might seem downright ethnocentric at times, as in Wilson's statement, 'The Hindus of these days are little able to estimate purity of conception, delicacy of feeling, a brilliancy of fancy' (Wilson [1871] 1984, Vol. II: 383). There are hints, however, that the complaint was also about the lack of realism – rather non-adherence to unity of place – and a particular form of dialogue ('The taste which invents the visit to the world of the moon and Sumeru is as deplorable as that which substitutes the dull dialogue between Jāmbavant and Jaṭāyu for the

[3] See also Keith ([1924] 1970: 5–6, 229–30, etc).

[4] Drawing on this line of reasoning, later commentators would occasionally strengthen it by pointing to some other related elements of drama that they found missing in the later works. Thus the *Mahānāṭaka* was seen as a 'literary drama, a play never intended to be acted, as seems to be shown by the several peculiar features such as the prevalence of verse over prose, absence of Prakrit, the large number of characters, the omission of the Vidūṣaka, and its plagiarisms from earlier Rāma dramas' (Devasthali 1955: 182). Ingalls took 'action and the conflict (*agonia*) of character and principle as the essential factors' of a dramatic composition (Ingalls 1965: 38). The presence of conflict of principle in Sanskrit plays, according to Robert Goodwin, 'may indeed constitute their only authentically dramatic character' (Goodwin 1998: x).

vigorous conversation of Jaṭāyu and Sampāti in the *Mahāvīracarita.* For dialogue in general Murāri has no taste at all. . .' [Keith 1970: 229–30]).

The third important reason for the decline of Sanskrit drama was the Sanskrit language itself, increasingly distanced from the popular languages. 'In Bhāsa's day and even those of Kālidāsa, we may imagine that there was not too great a difficulty in following the main features of drama both in Sanskrit and in Prākrit, but the gulf between the popular languages and those of learning went on widening every year' (ibid.: 242–43) and 'it was clearly a very different thing to compose in Sanskrit and Prakrit in AD 1000, when the vernaculars were beginning to assume literary form' (ibid.: 243). As Sanskrit was 'banished' by the new languages, it 'found a refuge in centres of learning and became the monopoly of pedantic masters' (Levi [1890] 1978, Vol. II: 96). There thus inevitably occurred the 'realization that it was idle to seek fame . . . by the composition of the dramas, for which there was no popular audience and only a limited market' (Keith [1924] 1970: 243).

Even as the audience for the Sanskrit drama became progressively narrower, there was a gradual loss of court patronage, on which it had been dependent for survival (ibid.: 242, 371). This came as a result of Muslim conquests, which gradually substituted Muslim rulers for Hindu princes. 'Sanskrit culture had died when India ceased to be free' (Levi [1890] 1978, Vol. II: 96).

The fact, however, is that Sanskrit dramas continued to be composed on a considerable scale. This requires explanation, which is that these were only literary dramas, exercises in literary skill, and were not fit for dramatic representation (Keith [1924] 1970: 243–44, 253, 273). About *bhāṇas* (monologues) and *prahasanas* (farces), Keith agrees that they had a popular origin and character, but does not state whether they were meant for performance. Winternitz, however, makes the understanding explicit: 'The popular farcical comedies on the whole were never written down'; 'the monologues (*bhāṇas*) and the farcical comedies, that we possess, are probably just court-imitations in the *kāvya*-style and in Sanskrit, of popular models in popular dialects' (Winternitz 1963: 292, n. 2).

The point that the later dramas were literary pieces only, unfit for performance, is frequently illustrated, after Keith again, through the supposedly typical example of Kṛṣṇamiśra's *Prabodhacandrodaya.* It is 'perhaps the most interesting of the later dramas' as it is really a philosophical discourse, not a drama: 'It would be idle to pretend that the play has any dramatic force. Its chief merits are its effective and stately stanzas of moral and philosophical content' (Keith [1924] 1970: 253).

The exceptional cases when Sanskrit plays were performed only help to prove the rule:

> Although the birth, coronation or marriage of a Hindu prince would still inspire dramatic poets, their works composed with blind fidelity to the precepts of Bharata lacked interest. If, by chance, they reached the stage, they bore evidence to the decadence and death of a great art. Erudite men trans-

> formed for the circumstance into actors would painfully recite parts which they were unable to act. The public attended the performance without understanding. (Levi [1890] 1978: 96)

Finally, there is some speculation about the theatre between the tenth century and the fifteenth century. A great variety of theatrical forms after the fifteenth century have been studied in detail, in particular the ones connected with Vaiṣṇavism. This is seen as the 're-emergence' of the theatre, entirely unconnected with the Sanskrit drama:

> Thus with the tenth century a relatively dark period began in Indian theatre history. Little is known of the theatre of this period. For example, it is not known if the actors, once successfully patronized by the court of Hindu kings, took to the countryside, abandoned Sanskrit and performed plays in vernacular languages of the rural areas, catering to the less sophisticated taste of village spectators. To have done so would have been inconsistent and uncharacteristic, but entirely possible, given the will to survive.[5]
>
> It was only after the fifteenth century that 'theatre' re-emerged again in India with a dazzling array of village theatre forms, each with its unique manner of presentation, and, more importantly, in the vernacular language of a particular region.
>
> A major catalyst for the re-emergence of the theatre was Vaiṣṇavism. . . (Ibid.: 477; cf. Shekhar 1977: ix–x).

Even the commentators who have underlined the numerous structural similarities between Sanskrit drama and folk theatre have not found it difficult to reconcile that with the decline thesis. Thus Faubion Bowers, who laid great stress on those similarities, saw them as the product of the permeation of folk theatre with the spirit of Sanskrit drama after the latter had been 'forced to disappear from the stages of India' (Bowers 1956: 6, 17–19).[6]

On a related set of grounds, the reality of the performance of classical Sanskrit drama too has often been doubted. We must look into the issue, which may bear helpfully on our concern. Despite strong rebuttals from time to time, the view has persisted that any Sanskrit drama – whether classical or post-classical – was not fit to be performed. Levi ([1870] 1978, Vol. II: 74) summed up the case thus:

> Theatrical representation is by no means an indispensable condition for the development of the drama. Dramatic literature, like epic and lyrical poetry, can, in theory, live its own live [sic] independently of the stage. Hence the question: Was the Sanskrit drama ever anything but a sophisticated literary exercise? Many learned critics are inclined to believe so. Sanskrit, the language of the cultured elite, was reserved to a limited audience. Its sophisticated

[5] See Farley Richmond, in Banham (1988: 476).
[6] See also *Encyclopaedia Britannica* (1993, Vol. 27: 667).

> style, its subtle diction, its long compounds made of it a recondite medium more easily read than heard. The variety of the Prakrits, too, demanded specialized knowledge. Besides, the frequent changes of scenes, the richness of the *decor*, the abundance of accessories seemed to show that the drama was more a work of poetical imagination than a play meant for the stage.

Having posed the problem, Levi proceeded to demonstrate how 'the facts establish beyond doubt that the [pre-Muslim] Sanskrit drama was staged' by putting together (i) the hall/stage/preliminaries (ii) the troupe/actors, (iii) the direction and, (iv) stage management (ibid.: 74–95). Many decades later, it was still necessary for V. Raghavan to open his introduction on the *Āścaryacūḍāmaṇi* with the statement, 'The Sanskrit drama was written to be enacted upon the stage, as shown by both internal and external evidence' (Raghavan 1984: 1).

The sceptics' objections, however, remained. Levi and Raghavan said nothing about the issue of language communication. Nor did they relate how the 'frequent changes of scenes, the richness of the decor [and] the abundance of accessories' were or could be dealt with in stage performance. The Sanskrit playwrights were not particularly bothered about the three unities of classicist poetics, which the scholars generally held dear as an important condition for performance. The supposedly anti-dramatic elements were no less relevant for the later dramas than they were for the early. When one adds to this the acknowledged fact that the classical drama too was not known for novelty of plot[7] or characterization or action (Winternitz 1962: 189ff.; cf. Keith 1970: 276–81; Dasgupta and De 1962: 56–59), one cannot help noting a major anomaly in the general scholarly attitude towards classical and medieval drama respectively. When they dealt with the former, scholars passed over the issues regarding the anti-dramatic elements to emphasize the evidence for performance. For the latter, however, those very issues – along with a few others – became the centre of critical attention and the evidence for performance receded to the background. Quite simply, the truth, as Daniel Ingalls put it, is that 'the Sanskrit play is not a drama' (Ingalls 1965: 38). On the rare occasion when an exponent of the decline thesis evaluated the entire run of Sanskrit works in the light of his conception of the drama, he found it 'not surprising . . . that a modern critic should accept only *Mudrārākṣasa*, in the whole range of Sanskrit literature, as a drama proper' (Dasgupta and De 1962: 58).[8] Herein may be a reason for the persistence of the belief about the non-performance of Sanskrit plays.

[7] It is not true, *pace* Bhattacharji (1993: 221), that the 'plot had *become* derivative' during the period of the decline when 'most [plots] were borrowed from the epics and the Purāṇas and some from the biographies of the local kings and chieftains'; it had always been so.

[8] Ingalls' judgement is a shade different: 'The prose of the fifth Act of the *Śākuntala* is dramatic, I admit, and there are dramatic prose passages in the *Mudrārākṣasa*. Such passages are quite untypical of the Sanskrit theatre' (Ingalls 1965: 39, n. 36; see also ibid.: 216.)

III

How valid is the concept of drama that underlies the decline thesis, and, if pushed to its logical limits, indeed denies almost all the Sanskrit works a place in its ambit? An answer to this consists of three interrelated parts:[9]

1. The Indologists formed their notion of the drama by drawing, unwittingly it would seem, on a vast and extremely rich repertoire of theatrical theories in the West that had dialectically evolved over centuries, going back to the *Poetics* of Aristotle.
2. This theoretical tradition was normative, rather than scientific, in nature.
3. The Indological concept of drama does not measure up to the actual history of the theatre in the West, leave alone the East, which calls for a different definition of the term.

1

Each of the various strands in the Indological idea of drama, such as that plots should be original or that verses should be kept to the bare minimum in order to preserve the dramatic character, was taken from a theory of the theatre in the West. The point, however, is that in the Western critical tradition itself there was never any general agreement over any of these as the indispensable property of drama. The various constituents of the drama in our historiography were moreover drawn from mutually contrasted positions in this tradition. The Sanskritists' conception was accordingly formed out of a selection from theatrical theories that was as arbitrary as it was eclectic.

The element of plot was of highest importance for Aristotle, but the Renaissance commentators in Italy only rarely thought so. Novelty of plot could be frowned upon as antithetical to dramatic performance, to the principle of verisimilitude. Thus a major argument against having new plots was that 'tragedy must be based upon known stories, since these – *accepted as true* – would produce a deeper effect'.

Verisimilitude in turn did not bother Aristotle much, but became a major artistic concern during the Renaissance and the French neoclassical movement before being attacked by the romanticists (such as Victor Hugo). Samuel Taylor Coleridge famously countered it by ushering in the concept of the 'willing suspension of disbelief'. Even earlier, those who wanted to defend their right to write new plots had to question the principle of verisimilitude, at times severely:

> If we wish to concern ourselves with persuading the spectators that the thing represented is really true, it will no longer suffice to make the stage-settings of boards or in any other simulated way, but entire cities will have to be founded; nor will it be sufficient to dress in regal mantle the actors, but we shall

[9] While the argument remains mine, the details in the first two parts of the answer have been taken almost entirely from Marvin Carlson's study (1984: 49–51, 72–74, 119, 197–98, 215, 219–21, 223–24, 228, 237, 246–47, 288).

> have to go about resuscitating from their sepulchres the ashes of those Clytemnestras, of those Oedipuses . . . and place them once again, I do not say upon the stage, but in their royal palaces.

Frequent changes of scene, considered unsuitable for performance by Levi in the context of Sanskrit theatre, is by no means so, or is so at most with only some forms of theatre, rather than with theatrical performance as such. This was realized early in the Western critical tradition. For instance, in early nineteenth-century in Italy, it was pointed out that 'as theatrical conditions change . . . dramatic form must change as well. What was proper for a Greek outdoor, seating an entire population before a permanent scenic structure, with a great distance between spectator and performer, will not be suitable for modern audiences: a few hundred persons seated in a smaller, more intimate space where scenery can be rapidly and easily changed'. Despite this, a common point of criticism of romantic drama remained the multiplicity of scenes.

The romantic drama did not have much use also for – another regular point of its criticism by others – the three unities: of time, place and action. First enunciated in Renaissance Italy amidst some dissent, the three unities came to be established as essential features of drama in the classicist tradition, in France in particular. Romantics found these thoroughly dispensable. For reasons of patriotism, French neoclassical unites were supported in revolutionary France. For the same reasons, romanticism gathered force in Italy; it was pointed out that *Othello* 'with its multitude of characters and no unity whatever of time or place still excites compassion and terror, and is every whit as true a tragedy as the one which produces these same effects with three characters and all the most revered unities'.

Aristotle had insisted that a tragedy must be unified in action, action rather than narration on the stage being the feature of tragedy. The famous Renaissance commentator on Aristotle, Lodovico Castelvetro, did not quite agree. While he granted that unlike in an epic the scope for multiple action remained restricted in a drama, he argued that multiple actions is what pleased the audience. 'There is no doubt that it is more pleasurable to listen to a plot containing many and diverse actions than one which contains but a single one'. Accordingly, his creativity is all the greater 'if the dramatist can achieve this delight within his narrow compass'. In the same vein, another scholar argued: 'Certain things are by their nature such that they arouse greater marvel and compassion when we imagine them through somebody's narrative than when we see them, especially certain acts which last a very short time, such as wounding and killing'.

All this is enough to show that the theatrical theoretical tradition in the West does not entitle anyone *not* to call a piece a drama or to speak of decline of drama in the terms in which it has been done in South Asian studies. Most curious of all, however, is the insistence that poetry is by its very character undramatic. For drama as a form of poetry, a poetic genre, was as strongly rooted in Western critical tradition, where the dramatist was routinely called the poet, as in India. This was not questioned till the naturalist movement, and the birth of modern prose drama, in fact, dates to Henrik Ibsen. For this questioning the naturalists were criticized by the idealists who accused them of not realizing the supreme dramatic quality of poetry; one of them argued that neither scenic setting nor costume nor even the skill of the actor could be substitutes for the real power of the theatre, which is poetry, 'the great evoker, the great magician, the great maker of prodigies and miracles'. In the importance given to prose by Shakespeare, Oscar Wilde saw the decline of the drama in his plays.

2

It is also patent that the theories of the theatre in the West set out not so much to describe the performance of plays as to lay down norms for their composition and enactment; subjectivity was their hallmark. When a Hegel or a Coleridge wrote on theatrical theory, it was usually a statement on what drama should be, not a dispassionate analysis of what drama, actually performed, is as a medium of communication. Such theory, in other words, was a form of reasoning aimed at either justification or denunciation of a type of play that existed, or an advocacy of certain innovations that ought to be the concern of the future playwright.

The normative character of these theoretical works is strikingly brought home by the pronouncements of four literary giants – Johann Goethe, Charles Lamb, Oscar Wilde, and Leo Tolstoy – on Shakespeare. Goethe thought in his later years that Shakespeare's greatness lay precisely in the fact that he never cared for the demands of the stage, and dismissed the view of Ludwig Tieck, who maintained that his plays were tailor-made for enactment 'without revision or modification from beginning to end'. Lamb, who was fully acquainted with the fact of their performance, nevertheless thought as much as strongly: 'The plays of Shakespeare are less calculated for performance on a stage than those of almost any other dramatist whatever'. Wilde had his own set of reasons for detecting the unmistakable decline of the drama in the Bard: 'It shows itself by the gradual breaking-up of the blank verse in the later plays, by the predominance given to prose, and by the overimportance assigned to characterization'.

The most instructive of all, however, is the excoriation by Leo Tolstoy, which brings out the highly subjective (and therefore analytically worthless) character of all such pronouncements, of categories such as 'artificiality'. Tolstoy found little to appreciate in Shakespeare, and mounted a scathing attack on his many failures. Shakespeare failed to fulfil the technical requirements of his genre: his characters remain unmotivated, he was not careful enough to differentiate individual speech, and he indulged in anachronisms besides. Even more serious than these technical lapses were his lack of content and sincerity: apart from artificiality as seen in his obsession with word play, his plays betray a disdain for the masses and absolute lack of concern for improving the social order. All great dramatists must have a proper vision of life 'corresponding to the highest religious understanding of a given period', which Shakespeare did not and all significant drama must relate man to the cosmos, which his plays did not do. Yet if there is a flourishing Shakespeare industry today, it is an accidental by-product of the reaction of the German romantic movement against French classicism. Even more lamentable is his continuing baneful influence on the young dramatists, which has reduced this 'most important sphere of art' to 'merely an empty and immoral amusement for the empty and immoral crowd'.

3

Besides a vague and general familiarity with the theoretical tradition of the West, the other major source of the Sanskritists' view of drama was apparently their experience of the contemporary European stage; nothing else would explain their insistence on the importance of prose as the main feature of even ancient drama. As such their concept limits the genre of drama to one particular variety, one that has dominated the European stage in modern times. It dates back to the Renaissance period, when individualization of characters, novelty of themes and realism emerged as important concerns among playwrights. In England, for instance, it was with Shakespeare that individual characters came to the fore 'in place of the types and personified passions that had hitherto held the stage' (Trevelyan 1946: 203) such as the Miracle Plays and the Moralities. And even as he was perfecting the art of prose dialogue, 'it is no accident that Shakespeare's plays were more poetry than prose, for the audience he addressed, as indeed the common English in town and country alike, were accustomed to poetry as the vehicle of story-telling, entertainment, history and news of contemporary incidents and sensations' (ibid.: 202). For early Greek history too, 'the oral quality of literature' has been seen as 'probably an important part of the explanation' of the dominance of poetry in comparison to prose – 'the (to us) curious employment of poetry [even] in political and philosophical writing' (Finley 1984: 94–96).

The importance of poetry to the theorists of Sanskrit poetics was such that they saw the drama itself as a kind of poetry, one meant for watching (*dṛśya-kāvya*), and distinct from poetry meant for listening (*śravya-kāvya*). The theory was to all appearances a corollary of the actual traditions of performance: 'in Sanskrit expressions like *bharata* and *kuśīlava*, probably "bard-singers", can also be interpreted to mean "actor"' (Winternitz 1963: 180–81, n. 1),[10] and among the Cākyārs of Malabar who still perform Sanskrit drama, 'no sharp distinction is made between dramatic performances and epical recitations, between actors and bards (*naṭas* and *sūtas*)' (ibid.: 1963: 180–81).

The situation is closely paralleled in vernacular theatre. In the *jātrās* in eastern India, for example, 'until the beginning of the twentieth century, the dialogue was primarily sung' (*Encyclopaedia Britannica* 1993: 668). When Winternitz, in correspondence with Grierson, wondered about dramatic elements in early Indian poetry, especially the Buddhist *ākhyānas*, Grierson wrote to him (December 1912) that they

[10] Monier-Williams did not share the uncertainties of Winternitz. He gives 'bard, herald, actor, mime' and 'an actor, dancer, tumbler' as regular meanings of *kuśīlava* and *bharata* respectively (Monier-Williams [1899] 1990: 297, 747).

> reminded him of the *khyāls* of Rajasthan, written in the Marwar dialect. They contain a sort of popular sayings either in metrical dialogues or in prose narratives mixed with versified dialogues. They are either recited aloud by a single person or played on the stage in which the stage-manager speaks out the narrative part, whilst individual actors recite their own parts. There is neither a scenery nor an introductory act. Hence they are also literary documents that may be designated as 'ballads' or 'dramas' likewise. (Winternitz 1963: 180–81, n. 1)[11]

Besides repudiating the poetry-as-antithetical-to-drama thesis, this above passage brings out the importance of narrative as a specific mode of dramatic communication, an alternative to communication through action and scenery. Narration through dialogue rendered the condition of the three unities dispensable for stage performance. It made it possible to include 'frequent changes of scenes, the richness of the decor and the abundance of accessories' in a performance which the unfolding of a plot through action alone could never do. This may be seen almost ideally in the following from Keith's own summary of the *Anargha-rāghava*:

> [In Act I] the herald announces mid-day. In Act II a long-drawn-up conversation between Śunaḥṣepa and Paśumedhra . . . enlightens us on the history of Vālin, Rāvaṇa, the Rākṣasas, Jāmbavant, Hanumant and Tāḍakā. The entr'acte is followed by the appearance of Rāma and Lakṣmaṇa who describe the hermitage and the doings of its occupants, and then the heat of mid-day. Time, however, does not trouble the dramatist; though there is no further action and no interruption in the dialogue, we find ourselves transported to the evening; Viśvāmitra arrives and describes in converse with the boys the sunset. A cry behind the scenes announced the approach of the demoness Tāḍakā; Rāma hesitates to slay a female, but finally departs for the necessary duty; on his return he has to describe the rising of the moon. Viśvamitra then suggests a visit to Janaka of Mithilā, affording an opportunity for a description of the city and its ruler. (Keith [1924] 1970: 226–27)

In fact, the differences between the Indian performing traditions and those in the West were realized quite early by the persons who tried unsuccessfully to stage the *Abhijñāna-Śākuntalam*. Goethe, Schiller and many others felt 'as if the drama was just opposed to the European stage' (Winternitz 1963: 241–42). The performances failed to evoke much response from the audience (ibid.). The same was experienced with the Chinese theatre, where 'song and pantomime predominate, while the interest in traditional stock types leaves little room for creative dialogue; and as a result the occasional attempts to introduce Chinese plays onto the Western stage have proved uniformly unsuccessful' (Bab [1934] 1948: 599).

[11] Winternitz gathered all these pieces of information to show the origin of the drama in poetry; the evidence actually shows poetry as an integral feature of dramatic performance.

The incompatibility with the contemporary European stage of Indian and Chinese plays, as well as of the Moralities and Miracle Plays, naturally raised the question whether all of them could be said to belong to the category of drama. There were people who did not think so, and who tried to distinguish the 'real' plays from the rest (Hale 1977: 254).[12] Ultimately, however, it was the concept of the drama that was revised. Thus J.R. Hale called the pageant in Renaissance Europe 'a dramatic entertainment' on the ground that 'those taking part were representing someone other than themselves' (Hale 1977: 258.)

To reach this understanding of the drama – 'representing someone other than oneself' – was to have come full circle: Aristotle had defined 'tragedy' as 'an imitation . . . of action and life' and for Bharata the drama was 'an imitation/ representation of conditions/situations' (*avasth-ānukṛti*); Aristotle's *mimesis* and Bharata's *anukṛti* were subjected over the centuries to interminable critical discussion among the theorists, but the fact of representation does not seem usually to have been under doubt. Abhinavagupta's critique of Bharata was, for instance, meant to underline the fact of the representation, where the use of the term *anukṛti* in its sense of mimicry was seen as misleading (Dasgupta and De 1962: lxxvi–lxxvii).

The circle that had been completed was apparently irreversible. It seems to be writ large in the meanings of 'play'/'drama' that English dictionaries provide, aiming to capture its various forms in history: 'the stage representation of an action or story'/'a composition in verse or prose intended to portray life or character or to tell a story through action and dialogue and designed for theatrical performance' (Webster's 1969: s.v. play and drama).

4

There is a plethora of evidence, largely from the texts themselves but also from other sources, that the medieval Sanskrit drama was performed on stage. We sample the following in a chronological order:

1. In the ninth century, the *Anargharāghava* was staged on the occasion of the *yātrā* (religious procession) of Puruṣottama (Wilson [1871] 1984, Vol. II: 375).

2. Early in the tenth century, the *Bālabhārata* of Rājaśekhara was staged in the court of Gurjara-Pratihāra, Mahīpāla (Winternitz 1963: 279, n. 3).

3. Between the tenth and the eleventh centuries, the *Caṇḍa-kauśika* of Kṣemīśvara was staged for the patron king Mahīpāla (ibid.).

4. Between AD 1042 and 1098 (Nambiar 1971: 1), *Prabodhacandrodaya* was performed before Śrīkīrtivarman and his courtiers (ibid.: 4–5).

5. The *Tapatīsaṃvaraṇa* composed by the King Kulaśekharavarman (between AD 1050 and 1159) (Unni 1971: 40) was performed by the Cākyārs in Kerala (Sastri 1976: 346).

[12] Remarkably, however, Schuyler could see dramatic worth in the *Prabodhacandrodaya* despite its resemblance to 'the old English Moralities' (Schuyler [1906] 1977: 12).

6. The *Subhadrādhanañjaya*, also by Kulaśekharavarman, was performed by the Cākyārs (ibid.).

7. During the eleventh century, the *Rājarājanāṭaka* was performed annually in a Śiva temple by the order of the Coḷa king, Rājarāja (Keith [1924] 1970: 251, n. 3).

8. In the late eleventh century, the *Karṇasundarī* of Bilhaṇa was performed in the temple of Śāntinātha on the festival of Jina Ṛṣabha in Anhilvada (Winternitz 1963: 280).

9. The *Bhagavadajjuka* by Bodhyāna Kavi, written some time between the seventh and the twelfth centuries AD, was performed by the Cākyārs (Sastri 1976: 347; Dasgupta and De 1962: 494–95).

10. In the twelfth century, the *Dhanañjayavijaya* by Kāñcana was performed 'in the autumnal season at the close of the rains' (Wilson [1871] 1984, Vol. II: 374; Winternitz 1963: 277, n. 4).

11. The *Laṭakamelaka* was written by Śaṅkhadhara in the twelfth century 'for the entertainment of his patron king Govindacandra of Kanauj on the occasion of the spring festival' (Malathi Devi 1995: 95).

12. In the twelfth century, the *Prabuddharauhiṇeya* by Rāmabhadra Muni was 'written for performance in a temple of Yugādideva, that is, the *Tīrthaṅkara* Rishabhadeva, on the occasion of a procession festival' (Keith [1924] 1970: 259–60).

13. In the second half of the twelfth century, the *Rukmiṇīharaṇa* of Vatsarāja was performed at Kālañjara during the *yātrā* of Cakrasvāmin on order by the 'learned spectators' (*vidagdha-sāmājikaiḥ*) (ibid.: 266; Dalal 1972: 37).

14. Sometime during the second half of the twelfth and the first quarter of the thirteenth century, king Trailokyavarman ordered the performance (*abhinetum=ādiśati*) of the *vyāyoga* called *Kirātārjunīya* (Dalal 1972: 1).

15. The *bhāṇa Karpūracarita* of Vatsarāja was performed at the festival of Nīlakaṇṭha *yātrā* at the behest of the 'learned spectators' (ibid.: 23).

16. The *prahasana* called *Hāsyacūḍāmaṇi* of Vatsarāja was ordered by the king Parmarddideva, surrounded by learned spectators, to be performed at the festivity of Nīlakaṇṭha *yātrā* (ibid.: 118).

17. During the twelfth–thirteenth centuries, the *Pārthaparākrama* of Prahlādana was staged on the occasion of the festival of the sacred-thread ceremony of Acaleśvara, the tutelary deity of Mt. Abu (Keith [1924] 1970: 265).

18. In the early thirteenth century, the allegorical play *Moharājaparājaya* by Yaśaḥpāla was 'performed on the occasion of the festival of the idol of Mahāvīra at the Kumāravihāra, a temple erected by Kumārapāla, at Thārāpadra, where the author seems to have been a governor or resident' (ibid.: 254).

19. In the early thirteenth century, Jayasiṃha Sūri wrote the play *Hammīramadamardana* 'for performance at the festival of the procession of the god Bhīmeśvara at Cambay' (ibid.: 248).

20. The *Dūtāṅgada* by Subhaṭa 'was staged under an order of the Cālukya king Tribhuvanapāla of Gujarat on March 7 of the year 1243 during the spring-

festival on the day of the swing-feast in honour of a picture of Śiva obtained by Kumārapāla' (Winternitz 1963: 274).

21. In the fourteenth century probably, the *Unmattarāghava* of Bhāskarabhaṭṭa was staged 'before an assembly of learned men who had gathered for honouring Vidyāraṇya' (ibid.: 271, n. 3).

22. The *Āścaryacūḍāmaṇi* by was performed by the Cākyārs. It was composed before the fifteenth century (Raghavan 1984: 4–5).[13]

23. In the fifteenth century, the *Gaṅgādāsapratāpavilāsa* was staged in the court of Sultan Muhammad (AD 1443–51) of Ahmedabad (Winternitz 1963: 281–82; cf. Keith 1970: 251).

24. The *Kalyāṇasaugandhikā* of Nīlakaṇṭha was performed by the Cākyārs (Sastri 1976: 347). 'Nīlakaṇṭha may have lived as early as the tenth or as late as the fifteenth century' (Raghavan 1984: 5).

25. In the sixteenth century, the *Caitanyacandrodaya* by Paramānandadāsa Kavikarṇapūra was 'composed . . . and staged at the command of Gajapati Pratāparudra of Orissa at the Car festival (*guṇḍicā-yātrāyāṃ*) of Jagannātha at Purī' (De 1961: 570).

26. The *Lalita-Mādhava* of Rūpa Gosvāmin was 'enacted to entertain an assembly of Vaiṣṇava devotees, gathered at the temple of Mādhavī-Mādhava on the Rādhā-kuṇḍa at Vṛndāvana, on the occasion of the worship of the Govardhana hill during the Dīpāvalī festival' (ibid.: 585).

27. The *Jagannātha-vallabha* of Rāmānanda 'was composed and staged at the direction of Gajapati Pratāparudra' (ibid.: 577).

28. The different portions of *Vidagdha-Mādhava* by Rūpa Gosvāmin, in the sixteenth century, were meant to be staged at the festivals in honour of Kṛṣṇa in different seasons: the festival of spring in Caitra or Vaiśākha, the festival of the birth of Kṛṣṇa in Śrāvaṇa, and the Rāsayātrā in the autumn (Wilson 1984, Vol. II: 393–94).

29. In the late sixteenth century, the *Abhirāmamaṇi* by Sandaramiśra was performed at the festival of Puruṣottama (ibid.: 394).

30. Early in the seventeenth century, the *Madhurāniruddha* by Candraśekhara was 'represented at a festival in honour of Śiva', probably at Bundelkhand (ibid.: 398).

31. Early in the seventeenth century, the *Kaṃsa-vadha* by Kṛṣṇakavi was 'performed at a festival held in Benares in honour of Viśveśvara' (ibid: 401–02), that is, Lord Viśvanātha.

32. In the second half of the seventeenth century (De 1961: 489), the *Śṛṅgāratilaka* or *Ayyābhāṇa* by Rāmabhadra Dīkṣita was 'written for performance at the festival of the marriage of Mīnākṣī, the deity of Madura' and to rival the Vaiṣṇava play *Vasantatilaka* or *Ammābhāṇa* (Keith [1924] 1970: 263).

[13] On the grounds that Śaktibhadra is reputed to have been a pupil of Śaṅkarācārya and his *Āścaryacūḍāmaṇi* the first proper *nāṭaka* of the south, Nilakanta Sastri placed him in the late ninth–early tenth century (Sastri 1955: 687).

33. In the seventeenth century (ibid.: 262) the farce *Dhūrtanartaka* was written by Sāmarāja Dīkṣita 'for performance at a festival in honour of Viṣṇu. The chief object of this play is to ridicule the Śaiva saints, one of whom, Mureśvara, is represented in love with a dancing girl' (Wilson [1871] 1984, Vol. II: 407).

34. In the seventeenth century, Sāmarāja Dīkṣita wrote another play, *Śrīdāmacarita* 'for the amusement of Ānanda-Rāya, a petty Raja in Bundelkhand' (ibid: 404–06).

35. About the mid-eighteenth century, the *Pradyumna-Vijaya* by Śaṅkara Dīkṣita was 'written for performance at the coronation of Sabhā-siṃha, the Raja of Pannah . . . grandson of Chhatrasal' (ibid.: 403).

36. In the 1750s, Rāmapāṇivāda composed the *Sītārāghava* for enactment before an all-Kerala assembly of learned Brāhmaṇas (Malathi Devi 1995: 121).

37. The *Kṛṣṇābhyudaya* of Lokanātha was 'written for the rain time procession of the Lord of Hastagiri, Viṣṇu, in Kāñcī' (Keith [1924] 1970: 268).

38. The *Gopālakelicandrikā* by Rāmacandra, of unknown date, was meant to be staged 'in some festive congregation of the *bhaktas*, the faithful devotees of Kṛṣṇa' (Winternitz 1963: 275).

39. The *Yayāticaritra* by Rudradeva, of unknown date, was 'first performed at the Spring Festival' (ibid.: 388).

40. The *Hāsyārṇava* by Jagadīśa was 'represented at the vernal festival; but, where and when, it is not known' (ibid.: 409).

41. The *prahasana Kautukasarvasva* by Gopīnātha was written for performance at the festival of Durgāpūjā (ibid.: 410–12).

42. About the beginning of the nineteenth century probably, a *nāṭikā Mṛgāṅkalekha* by Viśvanātha was performed at the *yātrā* of Viśveśvara at Benares (ibid.: 391–92).

43. About 1820 (Keith [1924] 1970: 371, n. 2) the *Citrayajña* by Vaidyanātha Vācaspati Bhaṭṭācārya was 'composed for the festival of Govinda, by desire of Īśvaracandra, the Rājā of Nadiya' (Wilson [1871] 1984, Vol II: 414) in Bengal.

The reader will have realized that the majority of the instances are taken from the works of the votaries of the decline thesis. Imprisoned in its frame, an individual scholar, whenever he/she happened to recognize the bearing of his/her evidence on the decline thesis, would think that the evidence at his disposal was too exceptional to affect the thesis to an important extent, or, more frequently, that the elements of the decline were too conspicuously present in the instances of the works that were staged to provide any scope for regarding them as real dramas, much less for a critique of the decline thesis.[14] In any event, if it is possible to collect forty-three instances with so small an effort, it is only fair to expect much greater figures from a more sustained search at a deeper level.[15]

[14] See for example De (1961: 570, 575, 585, 590).

[15] While numbers are no doubt important, by themselves they cannot clinch the issue. For instance, the largest numbers of known *prahasanas*, more than 120, were composed exactly during that period (Malathi Devi 1995: 132–48) when the performance of Sanskrit plays was least important socially – the nineteenth and twentieth centuries.

If the above data are any indication, the performances were more intimately associated with temples and popular religiosity than with palaces and courts, although, given the close association of the central courtly figure (the king) with popular festivities in many instances, the contrast must not be overstated (cf. Pollock 2003: 116). There is evidence outside the texts too for the temples as the venue. The *Prabandhacintāmaṇi* of Merutuṅga (early fourteenth century) refers to the performance of plays at night in the temples in Malwa and Gujarat (*Prabandhacintāmaṇi* 1933: 8, 31, 70–71). On 26 October AD 980, the Paramāra king Vākpatirāja II gave away a village to the temple of goddess Bhaṭṭeśvarī at Ujjain for the expenses on the repairs of the temple, rituals and *prekṣaṇakas.*[16] In *c.* AD 1291–92, the leading citizens of the town of Palanpur issued a charter in which they referred to the revenues granted earlier by the state and by a private individual to the local temple of Śrīkṛṣṇa for the expenses on the worship, food offering and *prekṣaṇakas* and agreed to collect fresh taxes on themselves for the same ends (Bhandarkar 1912: 21, text lines 3–24).

Prekṣaṇaka can mean either a 'public show' or a 'drama'; the former meaning of course subsumes the latter. The *Kāmasūtra* refers to *prekṣaṇakas* during various festivities when the actors (*kuśīlavas*) 'came from different temples and gave performances at the temple of Sarasvatī'.[17] 'The two inscriptions thus bear witness not only to the continuation in medieval times of the early Indian practice but also to its strengthening in the medieval period: the need for fresh taxes in Palanpur town is more likely to have been due to an increase in the expenses on *prekṣaṇakas* than on worship and food offering (Majumdar 1956: 363).

Evidence for temple theatre is not wanting either. During the tenth to twelfth centuries, 'the greatest among the most glorious periods of temple building' in Tamil Nadu, several inscriptions record endowments to temple theatres (*nāṭaka-śālai*) (Panchal 1984: 20–23). The play *Rukmiṇīharaṇa* (above, no. 12) was performed before (the image/temple of) god Cakrasvāmin in the *candrodaya* (Dalal 1972: 37). *Candrodaya* has been taken as 'moonrise', but it perhaps makes better sense to see it as a particular type of open hall having only a roof (and no side walls).[18]

The Jalor Stone Inscription of Cāhamāna Samarasiṃhadeva (Jalor town, Rajasthan) refers to the installation of a golden cupola on the newly-made central hall, meant for dramatic performances, in *c.* AD 1211–12 (Bhandarkar 1911–12: 55, text lines 5–6). The famous Sun temple at Modhera in Gujarat had 'a detached open hall, variously called the *sabhā-maṇḍapa* (assembly hall), *raṅga-maṇḍapa* (theatre hall) or *nṛtya-śālā* (dancing-hall)' (Majumdar 1956: 368). The Jain minister of the Vāghelas, Vastupāla, is said to have had constructed a *raṅga-maṇḍapa* in the thirteenth century before the temple of Bakulasvāmīdeva (ibid.: 326).

Levi specifically referred to the eleventh-century *Kavikaṇṭhābharaṇa* as

[16] *Corpus Inscriptionum Indicarum* (VII.2: 17, text lines 8–19).

[17] *Kāmasūtra* (I.3.16, I.4.42), cited in Dasgupta and De (1962: 645).

[18] See (Monier-Williams [1899] 1990: q.v. *candrātapa* and *candrodaya*.)

the terminal allusion to the staging of Sanskrit plays, whereafter there were no professional actors of Sanskrit dramas. This is no longer admissible. In the *Karpūracarita,* the *sūtradhāra* states that the play, being a *bhāṇa*, needed only one actor, who was to be his younger brother, well-trained in acting (*abhinaye suśikṣito*) (Dalal 1972: 23). For twelfth-century Gujarat, Hemacandra refers to a *raṅgācārya* training women to play female roles,[19] which reminds one of the actresses in the *Kuṭṭanīmata.* And although there are gaps in the documentation of their existence, the performing traditions must have continued unbroken through the centuries; 'the art of traditional performances resides in the body of the living performer-teacher; if even one generation fails to learn, a theatre genre will be lost irrevocably' (Brandon 1993: 6).

A major fallacy of the decline thesis has been its conflation of the literary history of Sanskrit drama with the history of its performance. The need to distinguish the two histories is strikingly brought out by the plays of Bhāsa. The plays were lost to Sanskrit literary tradition, to be rediscovered in the early twentieth century, while the Cākyārs went on performing, right through these centuries, Act II of Bhāsa's *Pratijñāyaugandharāyaṇa,* calling it Mantrāṅkanāṭaka and 'with-out knowing its connection with the drama of Bhāsa' (Winternitz 1963: 221, n.1).

For the history of theatrical performance, the writing of new plays was undoubtedly important, but the result was an accumulation of the stock, and not the replacement of earlier plays. We may refer to the enactment of the seventh-century *Nāgānanda* later in the century, as reported by I-tsing, and to that of the seventh-century *Ratnāvalī* in the late eighth–early ninth century as reported by Dāmodaragupta in the *Kuṭṭanīmata* (ibid.: 251, n. 2). Śaṅkaradeva had the *Mahāvīracarita* performed in a temple in Assam in order to entertain a Brāhmaṇa visitor. The most interesting evidence, however, comes from the living tradition of the Cākyārs of Malabar, known from the time of the *Śilappadikāram.* They perform Sanskrit plays written all over the subcontinent and spanning tens of centuries: Act III of the *Pratijñāyaugandharāyaṇa* by Bhāsa[20] (third–fourth century AD), *Mattavilāsaprahasana* (AD 620) by Mahendravarman (Sastri 1976: 162, 347), *Nāgānanda* by Harṣa (seventh century AD) (Keith [1924] 1970: 371, n. 2), the *Tapatīsaṃvaraṇa* and the *Subhadrādhanañjaya* by Kulaśekharavarman (eleventh–twelfth century AD), the *Bhagavadajjuka* by Bodhāyana Kavi (dated between seventh and twelfth century AD), the *Kalyāṇasaugandhikā* by Nīlakaṇṭha (between tenth and fifteenth century AD) and the *Āścaryacūḍāmaṇi* by Śaktibhadra (before the fifteenth century, probably late ninth – early tenth century).

The belief that the coming of Islam caused the supposed decline of Sanskrit drama is a dogma that does not bear a moment's scrutiny; even the *History and Culture of the Indian People* series found it impossible to maintain this element of the mythology of the tyranny of Muslim rule (Mehendale and Pusalker 1957:

[19] *Dvyāśraya Mahākāvya,* Vol. I, vs.180, cited in Majumdar (1956: 363).

[20] A study by Herman Tieken concludes that the Trivandrum plays were not composed by Bhāsa but really belong to the time of the Pallava ruler Narasiṃhavarman II (AD 690–720) (cited in Ali 2004: 78, n. 33).

297–98). Shekhar brought attention to the Mughal patronage of Sanskrit learning (Shekhar 1977: 153–54). As stated, Act V of *Gaṅgādāsapratāpavilāsa* was staged in the court of Sultan Muhammad (AD 1443–51) of Ahmedabad (Winternitz 1963: 281–82; cf. Keith 1970: 251). Rūpa Gosvāmin, who wrote several Sanskrit dramas in the sixteenth century, was a minister of Husain Shah (Keith [1924] 1970: 247). A social history of Islam in India remains a desideratum, but the inherent weakness of the argument that Islam did not sanction the theatre may be seen in the fact that two theatre forms, the *Bhagat* of Agra and the *Bhand Jashna* of Kashmir, were specifically created for Muslim audiences (Richmond 1988: 477 and s.v. *Bhagat, Bhand Jashna*).

To be sure, it is probable that the output and social reach of the Sanskrit dramatic tradition did not remain the same everywhere and through the entire medieval period. However, the story of the shifting fortunes and the postulated eventual 'end' of Sanskrit literary culture, of which the composition of Sanskrit plays would be a part, is 'no straightforward matter'; it is far too complex for the 'commonest explanation, which traces the decline of Sanskrit culture to the coming of Muslim power' (Pollock 2003: 100–101).[21]

Finally, we come to the question of the social reach of the Sanskrit drama: the nature of the audience and the ways in which it understood the performances. The plays themselves often state or assume that the spectators are learned and cultivated, and the same critical admiration is expected of the ideal spectator by Bharata. At the same time, however, 'it is admitted [by Bharata] that there are the usual degrees among the spectators, good, medium and indifferent.'[22] According to the traditional story of the origin of the Sanskrit drama in the *Nāṭyaśāstra*, it was designed as something that would please both the eyes and the ears, and would be a fifth Veda that would be shared by the Śūdras too, and not be confined to the first three *varṇas* (Keith [1924] 1970: 12).

Despite the belief that the audience consisted of only those who could understand Sanskrit and Prākrit, scholars do allow for a wider gathering. Thus Keith could agree that at the performances organized by the temples during the great festivals, there must have been a great rush of common people.[23] The *Prabandhacintāmaṇi* evidence cited above refers to the king watching a drama in a temple, incognito, in the company of a petty trader, a seller of gram. Likewise, the citizens of the town of Palanpur who agreed to pay more for the *prekṣaṇakas* at the Śrīkṛṣṇa temple, a number of them being mentioned by name, may be supposed to have been foremost among the audiences.

21 Pollock has not addressed the theme of Sanskrit dramas in his accounts of the end of Sanskrit literary culture. The rise of the vernaculars and the coming of Arabic and Persian necessarily imply a shift in the importance of Sanskrit; that the shift meant the demise of Sanskrit literary culture must be contingent on empirical enquiry, one line of which leads Bronner and Shulman to 'disagree' and believe 'in short' that the 'rumours of the death of Sanskrit after AD 1000 are greatly exaggerated' (Bronner and Shulman 2006: 28, 1).

22 Cited in Keith ([1924] 1970: 369). See also the useful discussion in Ali (2004: 189–90).

23 Keith, of course, does not realize that this undermines the decline thesis.

According to a widely held, but unsubstantiated, belief, the text itself was of little importance to the majority of the people, who tried to make sense of the performances not so much by listening as by watching the conventional gestures. Thus, according to Keith:

> The fact that the dramas must have been largely unintelligible to all save a select few of the audience would not matter much; a drama was essentially a spectacle; in many cases its subject was perfect familiar to the Sanskrit audience, and the elaborate use of conventional signs must have been enough to aid many of the audience in following the nature of the proceedings. (Keith [1924] 1970: 370–71)

When the issue surfaced again in 1980 at an international seminar on the performance of Sanskrit drama, scholarly opinion reaffirmed the idea of the kinesic communication of the plays (representing the text through gestures). In a wider context, this opinion is part of a belief in the insularity of the Sanskrit texts in general. I examined these issues elsewhere in some detail (Jha 1996), to conclude as follows. There was a great concern with the textual – as distinct from kinesic – communication of the plays in the performances. At one level, there was adaptation of the text for the sake of performance. There is evidence for the staging of dramas by changing the text to make it more accessible, by preparing stage copies of texts through the insertion of songs in vernacular, and by abridgement or expansion of the texts (see Freeman 2003: 485–86). The performance of a Sanskrit drama was also aided by vernacularization of Sanskrit, which seems to be recognized in the major texts on dramaturgy in the medieval period. There were several other forms of code-switching for the purpose of communication. One may see in all this how the elite and the popular, the cosmopolitan and the regional, Sanskrit and vernaculars, could be closely interactive and mutually potentiating, rather than insular and mutually exclusive, entities.

References

Ali, Daud (2004), *Courtly Culture and Political Life in Early Medieval India* (Cambridge: Cambridge University Press).

Bab, Julius ([1934] 1948), 'Theatre', *Encyclopaedia of the Social Sciences*, Vol. 13 (New York: Macmillan).

Banham, Martin, ed. (1988), *The Cambridge Guide to World Theatre* (Cambridge: Cambridge University Press).

Basham, A.L. (1954), *The Wonder that was India* (London: Sidgwick and Jackson).

Berthold, Margot (1972), *A History of World Theatre*, translated by Edith Simmons (New York: Ungar Publishing Co.).

Bhandarkar, D.R., ed. (1911–12), 'Jalor Stone Inscription of Samarasiṃhadeva; [Vikrama-] Saṃvat 1242', *Epigraphia Indica*, Vol. 11, pp. 54–55.

——— (ed.) (1912), 'Anāvāḍā Stone Inscription of Sāraṅgadeva, [Vikrama] Saṃvat 1348', *Indian Antiquary*, Vol. 61, pp. 20–21.

Bhat, G.K. (1988), 'Drama – Sanskrit', *Encyclopaedia of Indian Literature*, Vol. II (New Delhi: Sahitya Akademi).

Bhattacharji, Sukumari (1993), *History of Classical Sanskrit Literature* (Delhi: Orient Longman).

Bowers, Faubion (1956), *Theatre in the East: A Survey of Asian Dance and Drama* (New York: Thomas Nelson & Sons).

Brandon, James R., ed. (1993), *The Cambridge Guide to Asian Theatre* (Cambridge: Cambridge University Press).

Bronner, Yigal and David Shulman (2006), 'A Cloud Turned Goose': Sanskrit in the Vernacular Medium', *The Indian Economic and Social History Review*, Vol. 63, No. 1, January–March 2006, pp. 1–30.

Carlson, Marvin (1984), *Theories of the Theatre: A Historical and Critical Survey, from the Greeks to the Present* (Ithaca and London: Cornell University Press).

Corpus Inscriptionum Indicarum (*CII*) (1978), Vol. VII, part II, edited by H.V. Trivedi (New Delhi: Archaeological Survey of India).

Dalal, C.D., ed. (1972), *A Collection of Six Dramas of Vatsarārja* (Baroda: Oriental Institute).

Devasthali, G.V. (1955), 'Language and Literature: Sanskrit', in Vol. III: *The History and Culture of the Indian People, The Age of Imperial Kanauj* (Bombay: Bhartiya Vidya Bhavan).

Dasgupta, S.N. and S.K. De (1962), *A History of Sanskrit Literature*, Vol. I (Calcutta: University of Calcutta).

De, Sushil Kumar (1961), *Early History of the Vaisnava Faith and Movement in Bengal, from Sanskrit and Bengali Sources* (Calcutta: Firma KLM).

Encyclopaedia Britannica (1993), Vol. 27 (Fifteenth edn.).

Finley, M.I. (1977) 1984, *The Ancient Greeks* (London: Pelican Books).

Freeman, Rich (2003), 'Genre and Society: The Literary Culture of Premodern Kerala', in S. Pollock, (ed.) *Literacy Cultures in History* (Delhi: Oxford University Press).

Goodwin, Robert (1998), *The Playworld of Sanskrit Drama* (Delhi: Motilal Banarsidass).

Hale, J.R. (1977), *Renaissance Europe: Individual and Society, 1480–1520* (Barkeley: University of California Press).

Ingalls, Daniel H.H. (1965), 'General Introduction', in *An Anthology of Sanskrit Court Poetry: Vidyākara's Subhāṣitaratnakoṣa*, Harvard Oriental Series, No. 44 (Cambridge: Harvard University Press).

Jha, Vishwa Mohan (1996), 'The Sociolinguistics of Medieval Sanskrit Dramas', paper presented at the National Seminar organized by the Department of History, University of Hyderabad.

Keith, A.B. ([1924] 1970), *Sanskrit Drama in its Origin, Development, Theory and Practice* (Delhi: Oxford University Press).

Levi, Sylvain ([1890] 1978), *Theatre of India*, Vol. II, translated by Narayan Mukherji (Calcutta: Writers Workshop Greybird Publication).

Lienhard, S. (1984), *A History of Classical Poetry: Sanskrit-Pali-Prakrit* (Wiesbaden: Otto Harrassowitz).

Majumdar, A.K. (1956), *Caulukyas of Gujarat* (Bombay: Bharatiya Vidya Bhavan).

Malathi Devi, K.K. (1995), *Prahasanas in Sanskrit Literature and Kerala Stage* (Delhi: Nag Publishers).

Mehendale, M.A. and A.D. Pusalker (1957), 'Language and Literature (Sanskrit)', in *The History and Culture of the Indian People*, Vol. V: *The Struggle for Empire* (Bombay: Bhartiya Vidya Bhavan).

Mishra, Jayakanta (1976), *History of Maithili Literature* (Delhi: Sahitya Akademi).

Monier-Williams, M. ([1899] 1990), *Sanskrit-English Dictionary* (Delhi: Motilal Banarsidass).

Neog, Maheshwar (1965), *Śaṅkaradeva and His Times; Early History of the Vaiṣṇava Faith and Movement in Assam* (Gauhaṭi: Gauhati University).

Panchal, Goverdhan (1984), *Kūttampalam and Kuṭiyāṭṭam* (Delhi: Sangeet Natak Akademi).

Pollock, Sheldon (2003), 'Sanskrit Literary Culture from the Inside Out', in S. Pollock (ed.), *Literary Cultures in History: Reconstructions from South Asia* (Delhi: Oxford University Press).

———, ed. (2003), *Literary Cultures in History: Reconstructions from South Asia* (Delhi: Oxford University Press).

Prabandhacintāmaṇi by Merutuṅga (1933), edited by Muni Jinavijaya.

Prabodhacandrodaya by Kṛṣṇa Miśra (1971), edited by Sita Krishna Nambiar (Delhi: Motilal Banarsidass).

Raghavan, V. (1984), 'Introduction to the Translation of the Play', in C. Reis Jones (ed.), *The Wondrous Crest-Jewel in Performance* (Delhi: Oxford University Press).

Richmond, F.P., D.L. Swann and Philip Zarrilli, eds (1993), *Indian Theatre: Traditions of Performance* (Delhi: Motilal Banarsidass).

Sastri, K.A. Nilakanta (1976), *A History of South India from Prehistoric Times to the fall of Vijayanagar* (Madras: Oxford University Press).

——— (1955), *The Cōḷas* (Madras: University of Madras).

Schuyler, Montgomery ([1906] 1977), *Bibliography of the Sanskrit Drama with an Introductory Sketch of the Dramatic Literature of India* (New Delhi: Asian Educational Services).

Shekhar, Indu (1977), *Sanskrit Drama: Its Origin and Decline* (Delhi: Munshiram Manoharlal).

Thapar, R. (1966), *A History of India*, Vol. I (London: Penguin Books).

Trevelyan, G.M. (1946), *English Social History* (London: Longmans, Green & Co.).

Unni, N.P. (1971), *Sanskrit Dramas of Kulaśekhara: A Study* (Trivandrum: Kerala Historical Society).

Webster (1969), *Webster's Seventh New Collegiate Dictionary.*

Wilson, H.H. ([1871], 1984), *Select Specimens of the Theatre of the Hindus* (Delhi: Munshiram Manoharlal).

Winternitz, M. (1963), *History of Sanskrit Literature*, Vol. III, translated by S. Jha (Delhi: Motilal Banarsidass).

New Intellectuals in Seventeenth-Century India

Sheldon Pollock

The intellectual history of Sanskrit in South Asia in the last centuries before European expansion poses serious obstacles to scholarly understanding. Indeed, if there is a dilemma about the last Sanskrit intellectuals beyond the crucial fact, and the causes of the fact, that they were to be the last, it is that they are so difficult for contemporary scholarship to approach.

The first problem is the complexity of the discourses that they produced. In idiom and subject matter, these surely represent some of the most sophisticated and refined texts known in human history. And this complexity is redoubled by the fact that the seventeenth-century intellectuals were the legatees of two millennia of brilliant thought, whose most important representatives, from the earliest among them onward, always remained partners in argument. Understanding anything later, therefore, always presupposes understanding everything earlier. A second obstacle pertains to the greater social world within which these discourses were produced, and, more particularly, to the relationship between them and other forms of intellectual production, whether Persianate or vernacular. For most of the key thinkers in question, we are confronted with what is virtually a total absence of context. In many cases not a shred of documentary evidence is available to help us give life to their writings, which we can only vaguely situate in time and place. An additional, and in some ways the most obstructive, problem is a higher-order question, namely, whether we can even reasonably speak of history for South Asia at all, intellectual or otherwise. Indeed, whether culture or polity or society in South Asia can be said to have a history before European colonialism and modernity blasted life in the subcontinent out of its putative continuum has been a central if sometimes tacit concern of both orientalist and post-orientalist humanistic scholarship. The conceptual terrain that scholarship on the question has covered in the twentieth century has been enormous, and deserves a brief recapitulation.

The dominant view at the beginning of the century was expressed by the Oxford Sanskritist whose argument, that the reason India has no written history is because it never made any, provided comfort to a colonial administration that conveniently discovered stagnation everywhere. This gave way, in the post-Independence period, to an obsessive search for historical dynamism, with the two or three centuries before colonialism coming under increasing scrutiny. At the present moment, by a *commodius vicus* of recirculation that is almost Joycean, we are told once again, only this time by the subjects of South Asian history, that the very mode of historically experiencing and knowing the world is alien to authentic India (Ashis Nandy, an unrefined argument) or inadequate for understanding the nonsecularity purportedly characteristic of it (Dipesh Chakrabarty, a subtle one).[1]

Among the many complexities that beset the problematic of an Indian history, intellectual, political or other, one of the most intractable is what we mean by the term history itself. Less self-evident but equally intractable are the different ideological commitments that press upon our analyses. For instance, the revelation of change as such in India's past, originating in the impulse to provide a counterpoint to the imperialist and vulgar Marxist belief that colonialism offered emancipation from archaic quiescence, has come to be regarded in post-orientalist historiography as something of an absolute good – and stasis as something akin to mortal sin. A third complication has to do with what we might call multiple temporalities, the possibility that in some worlds, culture (or polity or society) might be unevenly historical. As one example of these various complexities, consider Sanskrit literature. Can this be said to have a history (a beginning for example, or an end) whether from an external perspective or from the internal one of the producers of the literature? If, viewed from both the inside and the outside, Sanskrit literature has a history in one sense (as I believe it indisputably does), it seems to have none in another. Certain norms were considered as transhistorically valid; the expressive and aesthetic universe that seventeenth- and eighteenth-century writers aspired to inhabit was that of the fourth-century masters, an aspiration they sometimes, if rarely, achieved. And in this there may lie an analogy to be drawn with certain larger dimensions of pre-colonial polity. Whatever other innovations may be going on in the domain of early modern polity and economy broadly construed (in terms, for example, of the expansion of Mughal rule or of India's

[1] The Oxford Sanskritist was A.A. Macdonell (see Macdonell 1900: 10–11). The ideologeme has a much longer history (recall Marx: 'Indian society has no history at all' except of invasions into an 'unresisting and unchanging society'; see Avineri [1969: 132]), and it remains very much alive today. Consider Michel de Certeau, who compounds this error with another: 'in India, – la marche du temps n'a pas besoin de se certifier par la mise . . . distance de "passés", pas plus qu'il n'est nécessaire . . . un lieu de se définir en se distinguant d'"hérésies"' (Certeau 1975: 4). The quest for historical dynamism at all costs, but often with diminishing returns, may be perceived in a variety of texts on the late medieval/early modern period, for example, on Vijayanagara (Karashima 1992); the Telugu Nayakas (Narayana Rao, Shulman and Subrahmanyam 1992); even among Cambridge School historians (Bayly 1988: 7–14). The return of the repressed may be seen in Nandy (1995: 44–66) (I thank Sanjay Subrahmanyam for this reference), to which we must juxtapose the remarkable essay of Dipesh Chakrabarty (1997: 35–60). I omit discussion of lumpen 'history' as practised by, for example, RSS founder Savarkar, for whom seventeenth-century India was 'a veritable Pakistan', a view exploded by an ounce of historical knowledge.

incorporation into the nascent capitalist world-system), in the self-understanding of Sanskrit polity one could argue that a steady state of perfected governmentality, of very old stamp, was everywhere sought, and that in this domain, accordingly, 'stasis' represents not failure but achieved goal.

All these conceptual difficulties constrain our understanding of the remarkable transformations in the discursive and social world of South Asian intellectuals in the last centuries before colonialism, and no doubt help explain the fact that the intellectual history of this period – one that witnessed an explosion of scholarly production unprecedented for its quantity and quality – remains as good as unwritten. I should note at once that I am using the term 'intellectual' here in a wide and not very specific sense (as in the well-known essay of Edward Shils), and although I will break down the catch-all category 'South Asian intellectuals' at the end of this paper, suffice it here to say that I am concerned with that class of literati or 'prestige intellectuals' who expressed themselves through the medium of Sanskrit, still the premier code of discourse for systematic thought outside the Persianate order.[2] What is of interest to me here is the crucial (if little appreciated) fact that increasingly through the seventeenth century, these intellectuals in all the core disciplines, foremost among them the traditional trivium of knowledges of 'words, sentences, and reasons' (grammar, hermeneutics – that is, Mīmāṃsā and, by this date, *Dharmaśāstra* – and epistemology) as well as literary theory and rhetoric, began to identify themselves or their opponents as *navya* or 'new' scholars. The term appears to signify not just a different relationship with the past but a different way of thinking.

Sometimes *navya* will refer specifically to the remarkable innovations associated with the school of 'new philosophical analysis' (*navyanyāya*) that originated in late thirteenth- to early fourteenth-century Mithilā, spreading from there across India with extraordinary rapidity and appeal; typically, these innovations are associated with Gaṅgeśa, author of the founding text of the movement (*Tattvacintāmaṇi* [Wishing Stone of Philosophical Principles]), sometimes with later thinkers such as Raghunātha Śiromaṇi (about 1550). But very often, the use of the term by seventeenth-century scholars will have no reference whatever to the new philosophical analysis in this narrow sense. When, as we shall see, the great polymath Kamalākara sometime in the 1620s or 1630s identified the position of Kauṇḍa Bhaṭṭa (and others) on vernacular communicability as *navya*, what he is characterizing as new is an idea that is new as such, one that in fact stands in opposition to the *navyanyāya*. Moreover, many seventeenth-century thinkers, regardless of the label they may have adopted, began to produce what, historically viewed, are objectively innovative kinds of scholarship, and in such a way as to suggest that a new conception of the development of knowledge had come into being. In fact, I believe we are able to perceive a sharp line being drawn, for the first time in

[2] See Shils (1968: 1–23). The narrow sense of the term, as in, say, Bourdieu (1989: 99–110), is post-Dreyfus. The term 'prestige intellectuals' is borrowed from Masseau (1994: 38ff.).

Indian history, to systematically separate present knowledge from its past forms. At the same time, new social facts in the lifeworld of the Sanskrit intellectual begin to manifest themselves. Not least of these was the opportunity for increased circulation in unfamiliar conceptual universes, especially in Mughal north India but elsewhere as well, where interactions with Persianate intellectuals or Europeans became more common and more cordial.

I characterize and assess – very schematically, given the limits of this article, but also very provisionally given the complexities mentioned above – four thematics of a history of South Asian intellectuals and their discursive practices in the epoch that I will call (in a sense whose specificity will emerge from what follows) early modernity. These are: (a) the structure of the new historicality by which intellectuals began to organize their discourses; (b) the substance that was structured by this historicality, in other words, what is novel in the new intellectual movement; (c) the important transformations in the lifeworld of the early modern Sanskrit intellectuals, difficult though these are to capture with any specificity, and the possible effects of new ideas on Sanskrit cultural production; and (d) the history of intellectuals in seventeenth-century Europe, which, having run parallel to that of India for centuries, now diverged dramatically and produced a very different, uncompromising modernity that, through colonial dissemination, would eventually contest and undo the Sanskrit intellectual formation.

I

To appreciate the innovations in conceptions and discursive protocols, as these pertain to historicality, that we find among the writings of seventeenth-century intellectuals, we need some basic sense of the mentality they inherited. The first thing to remember is that for much of its existence and across most of its communities of practitioners, systematic thought in South Asia completely and utterly erased all evidence of its temporal being: it presented itself as something that took place entirely outside of time. In this, Sanskrit thought differed little from the theory and practice of European philosophy (modern no less than scholastic), which projects itself as discourse that transcends historicity as a relevant condition of its possibility.[3] In India this kind of transcendence was achieved most notably by the elimination of all historical referentiality. The names and times and places of participants in intellectual discourse across fields are largely excluded even where such exclusion makes it appreciably more difficult to follow the dialogue between disputants that forms the basic structure of most Sanskrit philosophical exposition. We never hear the name Dignāga, for example, when the hermeneutist Kumārila (seventh century) critiques the fifth-century Buddhist logician, or the name Kumārila when he is critiqued by the eighth-century Śantarakṣita. The names of the great Vedāntic philosophers, Śaṅkara, Rāmānuja, Madhva, Śripati, and so on from the ninth to the fifteenth centuries, are unspoken through

[3] See for example Chartier (1988: 53–73).

this entire half-millennium during which their mighty controversies with each other were conducted. This may seem like a simple case of the common 'forms of censorship specific to the field of philosophical production' that we can find elsewhere (Bourdieu 1991: 3–4, 70ff.). In India, however, this mode of discourse also implied that all intellectual generations, disembedded from any spatio-temporal framework, were coexistent: the past was a very present conversation partner. It was also viewed as a superior partner, the master who made the primary statements in a discussion upon which later participants could only comment. In the face of the grandeur of the past, intellectuals typically assumed an attitude of inferiority: the universe was systematically entropic, and intellectual effort could be nothing but a quest to recover what had once been known more perfectly, but now was lost.[4]

It is these elementary tendencies of South Asian thought – perhaps they have become by now among specialists even an intellectual-historical cliché – that appear to have been dramatically and fundamentally reversed in the late medieval or early modern period, beginning in the fourteenth century but gaining greater currency in the seventeenth. Now it is the very history of the development of thought-systems, the periodization of viewpoints, that becomes the principal method of organizing the presentation of intellectual discourse and at times also seems to constitute its very purpose. Concomitantly, 'new' has ceased to connote 'worse', and instead signifies the furthest point of advancement in a discourse.

This can be briefly illustrated by reference to a work exemplary of the procedure, and deserving of much wider appreciation than it appears yet to have received, the *Nyāyakaustubha.* This is a vast treatise on logic written by Mahādeva Punatambekara (fl. 1675), a Maharashtrian 'from Puṇyastambha' on the Godavari, as he tells us, but, like many of his intellectual compatriots, resident in Varanasi.[5] Mahādeva deals with matters that had long been standard in textbooks on epistemology and metaphysics, and follows the organization of the discipline canonized by the *Tattvacintāmaṇi,* for which the *Nyāyakaustubha* functions as both commentary and fuller exposition. Much of what in Mahādeva's text is symptomatic of the new intellectual method is already coded in the title. For the *kaustubha* (the gem made manifest at the primeval churning of the milk ocean by the gods and worn on the breast of Viṣṇu, figuratively pointing to the precious knowledge that is now believed to be uncovered as much as recovered) becomes something of a new scholarly genre in our period. In it the attempt is made to organize the totality of knowledge in a given discipline by determining the most significant positions that

[4] See my essay, Pollock (1985: 499–519).

[5] *Nyāyakaustubha Śabdakhaṇḍa* (1930, 1982). Mahādeva's genealogy is given in Vol. 1, p. 6; see also that of his grandfather, Ananta Pandita, at the conclusion of his commentary on the *Āryāsaptaśatī* (he was already resident in Varanasi when this work was completed in 1646, though he notes in his introduction to the *Rasamañjarī* that his father was still living in Maharashtra). On the Maharashtrian population of Varanasi during this period, see n. 30 below.

had been taken in the past, and by sorting these chronologically and indicating where advancements had been made, to produce a new synthesis.[6]

The mode of exposition in Mahādeva's treatise is thus dominantly historicist. He sets forth problems by differentiating the views of scholars, making very fine distinctions between schools, whom he often names and always positions in time. They are categorized – and such categories appear consistently throughout his work – as 'ancients' (*prācīna*), 'followers of the ancients' (*prācīnānuyāyin*), 'moderns' (*navīna*), 'most up-to-date scholars' (*atinavīna*), and 'contemporaries' (*ādhunika*). He links these categories to particular disciplines, such as 'followers of the Mīmāṃsā', and to specific individuals: for example, 'Raghunātha', 'the followers of Raghunātha', 'the recent followers of Raghunātha', and so on.[7]

Such designations are applied to hermeneutists, grammarians, literary theorists as well as logicians and cosmologists (Vaiśeṣika), demonstrating how vast, indeed culture-wide, was the temporal revaluation of forms of knowledge that was underway in the eyes of Mahādeva.

Other scholars of the period reproduce many of these, and add still more categories, including further grades of contemporaneity such as 'very new' and 'brand new' (*navyatara, abhinava*), as in the grammarian Kauṇḍa Bhaṭṭa (*c.* 1650, Maharashtra/Varanasi) and the hermeneutist Gāgā Bhaṭṭa (*c.* 1600–85, Varanasi) respectively, or further grades of antiquity such as 'the oldest' (*cirantana*), and *jīrṇa*, a term sometimes positively valorized ('the elders'), for example, Kamalākara Bhaṭṭa, sometimes negatively ('antiquated'), for example, Kamalakāra's nephew, Gāgā. A significant binary without obvious antecedent also comes into use now, which counterposes to 'traditionalists' (*sāṃpradāyika*) or the 'ancients' (*prāñcaḥ*) either 'independents' (*svatantra*), as in Kauṇḍa Bhaṭṭa, or 'moderns' (*navīna*), as in the logician, *mīmāṃsaka* and grammarian Annam Bhaṭṭa (fl. 1560, Andhra/Varanasi).[8] It is clear, too, that while for some scholars (as shown by Kamalākara's

[6] Thus we have well-known *kaustubha* works on Mīmāṃsā by Khaṇḍadeva (*c.* 1575–1665, Varanasi), on grammar by Bhaṭṭoji Dīkṣita (d. 1645, Varanasi/Keladi), and on moral order by Anantadeva (fl. 1675, Varanasi; see below), less well-known works on literary theory, one by Kavikarṇapūra (d. *c.* 1600, Navadvīp) and by Viśveśvara (d. *c.* 1750, Almora), and a little known text on Vedānta, the *Tattvakaustubha* of Bhaṭṭoji Dīkṣita (a Kumbhakonam edition of 1964 is inaccessible to me). Not all these works follow the same discursive procedures. (I profited from discussion on the genre of the *kaustubha* with Lawrence McCrea, University of Chicago, to whom I am also grateful for help in gathering various materials for this article.)

[7] The many complications in these identifications remain to be fully disentangled. The *mīmāṃsakānuyāyin,* for example, appears to refer elsewhere, as in the *Śaktivādavicāra* of Gadādhara (*c.* 1600), to certain 'deviant' schools of *navyanyāya.* See Gerschheimer (1996: 626).

[8] *Navyatara* (*Padārthadīpikā* 1900: 21); *abhinava* (*Bhaṭṭacintāmaṇi* 1933: 100); *jīrṇa,* 'the elders' (*Mīmāṃsākutūhala* 1987: 33); *jīrṇa*, 'antiquated' (*Bhaṭṭacintāmaṇi* 1933: 9) (their views often being set aside with a *vastutaḥ*, 'But in fact. . .'); *sāṃpradāyika/svatantra* in *Bṛhadvaiyākaraṇabhūṣaṇa* (1985: 47); *prāñcaḥ/svatantra* in *Pakṣatāprakaraṇa* of Jagadīśa (*c.* 1650) (*Pakṣatāprakaraṇa* 1930: 68, 75); *saṃpradāya/navīna* in *Tarkasaṃgraha* (1985: 10). One of Mahādeva's *ādhunika* authors, incidentally, is Jagannātha himself, whose views regarding the nature of idiomatic and etymological semantemes in reference to the

remarks cited below) the title 'new' intellectual could be a term of reproach, for others it was a proud self-description, as in the case of the literary theorist Siddhicandra (1587–1666, Delhi), who uses this description for his own position in his *Kāvyaprakāśakhaṇḍana*, a systematic attack on Mammaṭa's eleventh-century classic.

One should not infer from this evidence and my arguments based on it that prior to this period chronological thinking as such was never attested, that earlier knowledge was never described as earlier in scholarly discourse. Such is certainly not the case. A good example of how innovation was recognized as such and in contradistinction to past thought may be found in the literary theory that arose, during an epoch of profound intellectual ferment, in ninth- to twelfth-century Kashmir. Abhinavagupta, for example, who around AD 1000 introduced a radically new understanding of the very object of aesthetic analysis, contrasts his view on the subject of *rasa* with those of the 'most ancient' (*cirantana*) authorities (he has in mind the late seventh-century writer Daṇḍin). Both the category and the reference (but now with the addition of Bhāmaha, another seventh-century writer) are shared by Kuntaka, a second important literary theorist from around the same period. He too introduced what he believed to be a totally new departure in the analysis of literariness, and contrasted this with the view of the ancients, though this was largely to differentiate his views of certain tropes (*svabhāvokti*, *dīpaka*) – in short, only to provide new arguments in the contest over old questions.[9] It is also worth noting that in the *Tattvacintāmaṇi*, certain temporal divisions of knowledge were already articulated, with Gaṅgeśa's own logic designated as new and contrasted with old forms of knowledge, as for instance that of the 'antiquated *mīmāṃsakas*'.[10]

I am also not suggesting that the categories discussed above are always and everywhere to be understood as exact conceptual equivalents of the English translations I provide (no more than *moderni* in Carolingian Europe has the same meaning it has eight centuries later). The 'independent', for example, who breaks with the 'traditionalists' in Kauṇḍa Bhaṭṭa's work on language philosophy, corroborates his position by citing 'the blessed Patañjali', an authority from fifteen centuries earlier (Kauṇḍa Bhaṭṭa 1985: 47). Clearly in this case independence can connote not so much overthrowing tradition as renewing it by returning to foundational texts.

What I do wish to suggest is that in the seventeenth century, historical periodization for the first time becomes the very modality of understanding how knowledge is to be organized, and, more important, how new knowledge can

---

existence of suggestion he attempts to refute in *Nyāyakaustubha Śabdakhaṇḍa* (1982: 753); cf. *Rasagaṅgādhara* (1981, Vol. I: 252ff.).

[9] See *Nāṭyaśāstra* (1992: 266); *Vakroktijīvita* (1977: 153 et passim). Similarly, in the discourse on *dharma* from around the ninth century, we find the past signalled as the past by the use of the adjective 'old [authorities]' (*vṛddha*) in titles of works, cf. Derrett (1973: 40); there is a mere reference; the questions of periodicity here merit investigation.

[10] Gaṅgeśa refers to the *navyas* in *Tattvacintāmaṇi* (1990, Vol. IV, part 1) on p. 241, for example, and to the *jaranmīmāṃsaka* on p. 83.

actually be produced. The former finds expression in what I perceive to be an increase during this period in the production of independent treatises (*prakaraṇa-grantha*) and of works that directly comment on *sūtra* texts while summarizing the entire earlier history of interpretation, and in the concomitant decrease in ever more deeply nested commentaries on canonical works that had been a hallmark of the earlier schoolmen.[11] The complexity of the field of scholarly production is exemplified nowhere better than in the grammatical treatise of Bhaṭṭoji Dikṣita (*c.* 1575–1645), the *Prauḍhamanoramā* ([Exposition] Pleasing the Learned). This is a commentary on Bhaṭṭoji's own *Siddhāntakaumudī*, a grammar that helped revolutionize the teaching of Sanskrit by rearranging the venerable *sūtras* of Pāṇiṇi according to the logic of the language phenomena (phonology, morphology, nominalization and so on).[12] The commentary proceeds by systematically juxtaposing Bhaṭṭoji's explanations to the *prācāṃ mata,* the 'views of the ancients'. This juxtaposition of new and old knowledge constitutes the scientific logic of the work, to the same degree that the new architectonics constitutes its form. Note that it was Bhaṭṭoji's readiness here as elsewhere to criticize the work of his predecessors, specially the *Prakriyāprakāśa* of his own guru, Śeṣa [Śrī] Kṛṣṇa, that earned him the enmity of the great poet-scholar Jagannātha, who wrote a counterblast entitled, with intentional vulgarity, *Manoramā-kucamardana* (Fondling the Tits of the 'Pleasing [Lady]').

Evidently, knowledge is now thought to be better not just because it may be better (of greater coherence, economy, explanatory power), but also in part because it is new. Bhaṭṭoji, after all, could simply have called the positions he opposed the 'views of others', as had been the practice of centuries of earlier scholars. Why it is exactly now that this new periodicity enters Sanskrit discourse remains unclear. One might be inclined to look for inspiration in the first forms of cultural production newly made available in the immediate surroundings of the Sanskrit intellectuals, such as Islamic and Persianized historiography with their unfamiliar temporal sensibilities. But there is no evidence that this is so, and, in the case of this historiography in particular, nothing quite comparable is offered. What we may be observing instead are innovations in Sanskrit discourse generated from within the intellectual tradition but under conditions of intensified social change that rendered change itself the object of consciousness.

11 This is particularly well illustrated in the case of Mīmāṃsā with such works from seventeenth-century Varanasi (in chronological order, *c.* 1620ff.) as Kamalākara's *Mīmāṃsākutūhala*, Śaṅkara Bhaṭṭa's *Mīmāṃsābālaprakāśa*, Āpadeva's *Mīmāṃsā-nyāyaprakāśa*, which are all *prakaraṇagranthas*, and four *sūtravṛttis*: Gāgā's *Bhaṭṭacintāmaṇi*, Khaṇḍadeva's *Mīmāṃsākaustubha* and *Bhaṭṭadīpikā*, and (from mid-eighteenth-century Tanjavur) Vāsudeva Dīkṣita's *Adhvaramīmāṃsākutūhalavṛtti*.

12 The grammar that seems actually to have sparked the revolution was the *Prakriyākaumudī* of Rāmacandra Dīkṣita, composed probably in the mid-sixteenth century (often erroneously placed earlier). He was almost certainly the uncle of Śeṣa Kṛṣṇa, whose *Prakāśa* appears to be the earliest commentary on the text. The *prācāṃ mata* that Bhaṭṭoji criticizes in his commentary are those of Rāmacandra, whose work he appropriated without acknowledgement.

II

To determine what is objectively new in the substance of the work of the new intellectuals is a challenge. For, as mentioned at the start, it requires understanding some of the most exacting scholarly writing the world has ever seen and its development over centuries. Even judging what the intellectuals themselves thought to be new is far from simple. Accordingly, I must be sketchy in this preliminary review and diffident even about that.

What most immediately and forcefully strikes contemporary readers of this scholarship is the extraordinary innovation in style. This consists above all in a new philosophical metalanguage developed for specifying types of relationships that normal language and thought occlude. There is a prehistory to this style in Gaṅgeśa, but it reaches an extreme form in the writings of Raghunātha Śiromaṇi a century and a half later. In the eyes of many seventeenth-century writers, Raghunātha represents the new scholar par excellence, and his innovations in the search for ever greater precision and sophistication of definition and analysis were enormously influential. These innovations sometimes produced – as readers of, say, Heidegger would appreciate – the opposite of the intended result: Raghunātha's style makes his work undoubtedly the most challenging to read in the whole of Indian philosophy.[13] In addition to this transformation in discursive style, new or reinvigorated criteria of argument are employed. One example is the appeal to parsimony, in particular ontological as opposed to epistemological parsimony. Although by no means unknown earlier, a Sanskrit version of Occam's razor is now so frequently invoked as to signal an unmistakable change in standards of philosophical judgement.

A passage from Kauṇḍa Bhaṭṭa's little work, the *Padārthadīpikā* (Treatise on Categories), illustrates this criterion as well as the periodized exposition I have just mentioned. In his discussion of the exact mechanism of inference, a subject that profoundly concerned the new logicians, Kauṇḍa tells us that for the ancients (*prāñcaḥ*), the means of inference was to be identified with the inferential sign (*liṅga*). Gaṅgeśa then argued that it was the knowledge of invariable concomitance that was determinative, whereas the new intellectuals – whom Kauṇḍa thus distinguishes from Gaṅgeśa – believed this knowledge to require 'reflection mediated by latent traces'. This is a position, we are then told, that the most recent thinkers (*navyatara*) reject on the grounds of parsimony, differentiating reflection as a functioning of the organ of intellection, which in itself constitutes the means of inference.[14]

[13] A point made recently also by Karl Potter (1992: 521).

[14] Here is a literal translation of the passage: 'The ancients (*prāñcaḥ*) are those who hold inference to be that which provides the means of inferential knowledge, and this means the inferential sign (*liṅga*) one is cognizing. The author of the *Tattvacintāmaṇi*, however, holds the means of inference to be the knowledge of the invariable concomitance to which the sign pertains, because we can still have inferential knowledge when the sign itself is past or yet to come. The new intellectuals (*navya*) hold that the knowledge of the invariable concomitance with respect to inferential knowledge, the cause of which is not present – as in the case of inferential reflection that occurs only in recollection – cannot

Radically at odds, however, with the genuine innovations signalled by historicist exposition, discursive style and mode of argument is the traditional nature of the problematics. The universe of thought, it seems, did not expand in a way at all commensurate with the expansion of the instruments and styles of thought. It may be that the sometimes mind-numbing complexity of the discourses before us simply renders the newness of its content elusive. But the general tenor is certainly one of epistemic continuity. Consider, for example, Mahādeva's discussion of the *manas* (the seat of will and affect). He employs his new historicist framework to explicate a philosophical dispute on its physical dimensions. For the ancients, the *manas* had an atomic size (*paramāṇu*), whereas for the moderns (the reference here is to Raghunātha again) it is the minimally perceptible entity (*trasareṇu*). Mahādeva, apparently seeing himself as an *atinavīna*, finds the argument dubious and rejects it for lack of parsimony.[15] The exposition itself, the sophisticated conception of logical relationships, and to some degree the autonomy of judgement, especially temporalized as it is – implying that it is only now, at the end of the development, that one can see and adjudicate the whole matter – are strikingly new; the philosophical question itself, the method of analysis of the problem, and the actual judgement rendered, are archaic.

A second example, from the other end of the thought spectrum, is provided by Gāgā Bhaṭṭa's discussion of ultimate emancipation. The 'antiquated' scholars of the past (*jīrṇa*), he tells us, believed that emancipation was possible through either knowledge or action. The *navya* scholars, by contrast, hold that knowledge alone is able to produce genuine liberation. But the grounds Gāgā offers for this assertion are scriptural: two passages from the ancient Upaniṣads where the efficacy of means other than knowledge is flatly denied.[16] One might be inclined to see in

be the means since it is mediated by dispositions (*saṃskāras*) generated by an earlier reflection. Thus, the real means of inferential knowledge must be knowledge of an invariable concomitance (*vyāpti*) but only insofar as this generates a reflection (*parāmarśa*) commensurate with [or: common to] these dispositions. However, the most recent thinkers (*navyatara*) consider this explanation fundamentally to violate the law of parsimony (*atigauravagrastam*) . . . and hold the organ of intellection (*manas*) itself to be the means of inferential knowledge [and] reflection to be [its] functioning' (*Padārthadīpikā* 1900: 20–21).

[15] *Rasagaṅgādhara* (1981, Vol. I: 122). Raghunātha's position on the matter is found in his *Padārthatattvanirūpaṇa*, cf. Potter (1990: 529). Raghunātha's rejection of the hypothesized existence of imperceptible atoms in fact hearkens back to Kumārila, as he himself makes clear (cf. ibid.: 33).

[16] *Bhaṭṭacintāmaṇi* (1933: 44), and unless I am much mistaken, 'new' in this passage does not refer to the *navyanyāya* school. Gāgā does, however, take pains to add what earlier *mīmāṃsakas* would hardly have bothered to add, though it was a common position: 'Just because the knowledge of the truth to be derived from study of the Upaniṣads is accessible only to the three higher *varṇas* it by no means follows that Sūdras and so on are excluded from ultimate liberation. They can achieve liberation because they have access to the meaning of the Upaniṣads by learning those texts that reproduce it in another form, such as the *Purāṇas* and the like', though the actual texts of the Upaniṣads themselves are restricted. Perhaps one should not expect any less from the ritual adviser who transformed the Sūdra Shivaji into a Kṣatriya; see below.

Gāgā's argument a certain historically contingent resistance to the ever-expanding devotionalism of seventeenth-century north India. This was, after all, precisely the time and place of some of the most accomplished and articulate productions of theistic devotionalism, as exemplified in the works of, say, Tulsidās. In fact, Gāgā's own uncle, Kamalākara, had himself earlier mounted a very sustained and highly unusual defence of Mīmāṃsā theism, going so far as to assert that the way of devotion is perfectly in keeping with the strictest tenets and representatives of the philosophical system. He concludes, 'The atheism with which Udayanācārya has charged me and my fellows, or the [author of the] *Naiṣadha*, derives from their failure to examine our works or to understand our tenets, and can safely be ignored'.[17] But just as Kamalākara's principal argument here is with a tenth-century logician and a twelfth-century poet, so Gāgā's remains, in intellectual-historical terms, only the recapitulation of a very old position.

The mode of analysis of every topic on the philosophical menu between these two problems (on the one side, elementary categories such as the *manas*, and on the other, ultimate purposes such as emancipation) and the very topics selected for analysis – and this holds not just in epistemology and theology but across intellectual disciplines – are largely of a piece with what we find in Mahādeva and Gāgā. The new historicity and the awareness it seems to imply of the possibility of new truths are clearly in evidence, but remain securely anchored in a very old practice of thought, on an invariant set of questions.

These are, to be sure, assertions in need of sustained substantiation, and although that cannot be offered here in the requisite measure, a brief review can serve to indicate the general contours such a substantive account would take. This will allow us at the same time to flag some general trends in seventeenth-century intellectual discourse, to illustrate certain different styles of argument, and, where appropriate, to adduce the actual language of the texts. All this seems to me methodologically crucial, for we will hardly be taking the dilemma of the intellectuals seriously if we do not take seriously the nature of their intellectuality.

It is important to recognize, in the very first place, that the newness of historicity or periodicity by no means meant convergence with a newness of method (such as empiricism, for example), or a newness of ontology (such as a realist philosophy of nature), as trends in contemporaneous developments in European thought might lead us to expect. An illustration of the dominant tendency is provided by Mahādeva's discussion of the problem of yogic perception. He represents, as the tradition of thought on this matter, the view that the practice of

[17] *Mīmāṃsākutūhala* (1987: 44); the '*Naiṣadha*' verse (beginning *mīmāṃsayeva bhagavaty amṛtāṃśumaulau*) is not found in published editions of the *Naiṣadhīyacarita*, if that is in fact the text meant. (Other, earlier scholars had of course already addressed the problem of Mīmāṃsā atheism, notably the fourteenth-century scholar Vedāntadeśika in his *Seśvaramīmāṃsā*.) Similarly, the 'new' in Gadādhara's *Navamuktivāda* (New Discourse on Liberation, or, Liberation Discourse of the New [Logicians], of *c.* 1600 (Gadādhara n.d.) derives from Gaṅgeśa's *Īśvarānumāna*, and in this the work stands in contrast, as the editor points out, to Gadādhara's innovative intelligence in other domains of logic.

yoga produces a specific kind of non-phenomenal cognition that enables a *yogin* to cognize all objects. The *yogin* remains constrained by the fitness of objects to the sensory perception; mental cognition, however, is not constrained by the fitness of things to the mind. Kumārila's great *Ślokavārttika* (*c.* 650), which argues powerfully against the possibility and very intelligibility of omniscience, is adduced in corroboration of such phenomenal limitations: 'Even extraordinary sensory acuity operates on distant or subtle things without exceeding its appropriate object. The sense of hearing, for example, cannot operate on the visual' (*Codanāsūtra* 114). The *navya*s, however, respond that the perceptual capacity produced by yoga is a causal factor of cognition as such, irrespective of the distinction between its visual and mental varieties, and accordingly it is difficult to rule out the possibility that atoms and the like could be visual objects for *yogins*.[18]

Despite the historicized labelling of positions and the argumentation on the basis of such positions, it seems reasonably clear that these did not represent camps or schools; on the contrary, the new and old often show themselves to coexist in any given author. We might, in fact, even identify such intellectual independence as a second tendency among the new intellectuals. Most writers do not systematically reject the old or assert the new, but pick and choose among positions on grounds of consistency, rigour, economy and associated values of argumentation. No one instantiates this better than the mid-seventeenth-century poet and literary theorist Jagannātha, in his celebrated treatise *Rasagaṅgādhara* (The [Five-Faced] 'Śiva' of Aesthetic Emotion). In discussing whether a given trope (in this case, *sahokti)* should be recognized as a separate category of figure, he argues that the ancients constitute the final authority for the classification (they are said to have sensed some aesthetic difference in *sahokti* that set it apart from all others), and he criticizes the imaginary disputant who refuses to accept the ancients 'when they shut their eyes', by calling his arguments a mere exercise of arrogant authority and ungrounded in any actual aesthetic response. Elsewhere, by virtually the same argument, Jagannātha himself rejects the ancients' view completely: 'a claim of the ancients [in reference to a particular trope], when no adequate definition for it is provided, amounts to nothing more than a royal command'. When discussing the trope *utprekṣā* or poetic fantasy, he says that 'the statements neither of the ancients nor of present-day scholars can withstand criticism'. By contrast, he will just as frequently strive to preserve a position of the ancients (among whom he includes not only Bhāmaha and Udbhaṭa of the seventh-eighth centuries but also Mammaṭa and Ruyyaka of the eleventh–twelfth centuries) out of what seems to

[18] *yogābhyāsajanyādṛṣṭaviśeṣaḥ tenaiva sannikarṣeṇa yoginaḥ sarvaviṣayakasākṣātkārāḥ . . . yogajadharmasya . . . svaviśiṣṭasākṣātkāramātre hetutvaṁ na tu cākṣuṣamānasādibhedeneti paramāṇvādeś cākṣuṣādiviṣayatā durvārā* (*Nyāyakaustubha Pratyakṣakhaṇḍa* 1930: 192–93). 'Others' (perhaps *mīmāṃsaka*s) are shown to challenge this view on the grounds that both the 'natural way of understanding' (*svārasya*) the scriptural passages that are cited to prove yogic perception, and the fact that the knowledge of *yogins* at issue is knowledge of the transcendent principle (*brahma*), entail that the only cognition pertinent to the discussion is mental cognition.

be the anxiety that 'their taxonomy' would be 'destroyed' or even 'weakened'. Thus, on the question of whether *bhakti* should be considered the tenth *rasa* – note that devotion constitutes one of the few truly new sentiments in sixteenth-century poetry and theory – Jagannātha argues in line with the old school: 'The enumeration of *rasas* as nine is constrained by the declaration of the Sage [Bharata], and therefore the view of the *śāstra* is preferable'. What is decisive above all for Jagannātha, however, is the adequacy of categories and the consistency of definitions. A typical passage is his critique of the introduction of a new subspecies of the trope 'denial' (for example, 'that is not her face, it is rather the moon') by the late sixteenth-century scholar Appayya Dīkṣita in his treatise on tropology, the *Kuvalayānanda*. According to him the proposed subtype cannot be a form of denial to begin with, since it is not covered by the general definition of the category.

> First of all, it is clearly outside the definition given by the [eleventh-century] *Kāvyaprakāśa* . . . nor does the definition given by the [mid-twelfth-century] *Alaṅkārasarvasva* pertain to it. And the same holds true even of the definition contained in the *Citramīmāṃsā* that [Appayya Dikshita] himself wrote.

The subspecies, accordingly, turns out to be nothing more than a type of metaphor:

> If [Appayya] is prepared like [Śobhākaramitra, author of] the *Alaṅkāra-ratnākara* [thirteenth-fourteenth century] to ignore the view of the ancients and to include this subspecies in 'denial', why does he not simply subsume the whole species under metaphor, given that its specific features (including the non-reality of the perception, along with identification of source and target entities and certitude of the identification) are identical to what we find in metaphor? He could finally then give up his disingenuous deference to the ancients. Yet even in that case, the fact would remain that the definition of 'denial' that he provided in his own rhetoric, would not apply to the sub-species offered in *Kuvalayānanda* . . . whereas the definition of metaphor provided in the *Citramīmāṃsā* would. But perhaps he would say that in the *Citramīmāṃsā* his definition of metaphor follows the ancients, whereas in the *Kuvalayānanda* his account of 'denial' follows the *Ratnākara*. Somehow or other in this fashion he might put it all to rights.[19]

A third general observation is that whereas we can perceive a remarkable enthusiasm for rethinking a very wide range of important philosophical questions, these are all questions inherited from tradition. Consider, for example, Gāgā Bhaṭṭa's analysis of the cognitive status of semantic coherence. He notes that according to the old-fashioned scholars, among the three factors required for intelligible verbal

[19] See *Rasagaṅgādhara* (1981, Vol. II: 430): the ancients 'shut their eyes' presumably in pleasure, as testifying to the aesthetic experience, rather than in blindness to the truth. His remarks on Appayya are found on pp. 271–73 ('give up his disingenuous deference toward the ancients').

communication – the satisfying of syntactic expectation (*ākāṅkṣā*), semantic coherence or compatibility (*yogyatā*), and the contiguity of syntactically related items (*āsatti*) – the first two enable verbal cognition only when we actively understand them, whereas the third functions simply by its presence (we do not need to be actually aware of it). The new scholars disagreed about the function of the second factor, semantic coherence:

> According to the new logicians and hermeneutists, it is not the knowledge of semantic coherence that is a causal factor in verbal cognition. From a sentence like 'One should sprinkle [the sacrificial offering] with fire' we derive no verbal cognition, and from this we conclude (only) that the determination of semantic incoherence [since fire cannot act as an instrument in the act of sprinkling] obstructs verbal cognition . . . [not that] a [positive] knowledge of semantic coherence [is required for verbal cognition].

What is most significant about this discussion – it is in fact a standard question addressed in the new logic – is what follows. Gāgā goes on to discuss the view of the literary theorists, who hold that both positions are wrong:

> Neither does a knowledge of semantic coherence cause verbal cognition, nor does a determination of the lack of semantic coherence prohibit it. This is so because (a) even in the absence of the former and the presence of the latter we find such cognition to be produced, as for example in [what prima facie can be considered the semantically incoherent] metaphor 'Her face is the moon'; and (b) because we derive an unmistakable aesthetic pleasure through cognizing the meaning in such a [semantically incoherent line of verse as] 'The son of the barren woman passes by/crowned with a chaplet of flowers from the sky'. One cannot argue that in these two cases we are only recalling the meaning of the individual words, not experiencing 'verbal cognition'. The very notion of verbal cognition would thereby dissolve, since one could make the same claim about a sentence like 'fetch the pot'. It is only cognition other than verbal that is negated when [the statement is] known to be falsified. And it is no use raising the argument [against the cognizability of a false sentence] that action must follow [since action is held to be entailed by all real verbal knowledge]. The only knowledge that motivates action is knowledge free of doubt as to its own invalidity, that is to say, one that does not produce, at the moment the knowledge is coming into existence, a doubt about its invalidity through an earlier instance of falsification. And such knowledge is absent in the case of [a metaphor and the like; no one thinks they are true-as-stated in the first place]. As the *Khaṇḍana* puts it: 'Language can produce cognition even with respect to a thing/meaning that is totally non-existent'. In actual fact, however, a sentence like 'Her face is the moon' does not produce verbal cognition in a country bumpkin, but only in those familiar with Sanskrit rhetoric, and it brings aesthetic pleasure only to such people. For these reasons we must conclude that trace memories

from an earlier life are a stimulating factor here. And accordingly, we cannot regard as reasonable the view that the absence of a determination of semantic incoherence, when it is not qualified by such stimulating factors, is the cause of verbal cognition.[20]

This is highly sophisticated argumentation, and for those outside the discourse no doubt in some areas dark if not impenetrable. In extending a hitherto exclūsively philosophical problem to poetry, it is, so far as I can judge, altogether new. Moreover, the question Gāgā is addressing – the significance for a general philosophy of language of the possibility of grammatically acceptable but semantically incoherent sentences – is one that did not enter Western thought explicitly until Croce in 1910 (who, much less interestingly, denies aesthetic value to meaningless or irrational statements) and Chomsky in 1965 (one of whose concerns is to demonstrate that 'the notion of "grammaticalness" cannot be related to "interpretability" . . . in any simple way', or in Sanskrit terms, that *ākāṅkṣā* is relatively independent of *yogyatā*).[21] All that said, this remains a discourse that intimately cleaves to very old Sanskrit epistemic principles, rules of evidence and modes of argumentation.

It is in the realm of political thought, crucially, that we find the most compelling illustration of the persistence of the old among the new. In this connection the massive treatise on the moral order (*dharma*) called the *Smṛtikaustubha* (*c.* 1675) claims our attention. This is a work of Anantadeva, the son of the *mīmāṃsaka* Āpadeva, and perhaps a kinsman of Khaṇḍadeva, one of the leading new hermeneutists.[22] His patron was Baj Bahadur Chandra, lord of Almora, though the writer himself clearly lived in Varanasi (*Smṛtikaustubha* verse 25). Although a *kaustubha* by title, Ananta's work is really a standard law digest (*nibandha*) and

[20] *Rākāgama on Candrāloka* (1938: 8) ('It is only cognition other than verbal that is negated when [the statement is] known to be falsified,' 'one that does not produce . . . a doubt,' read *jananāt* for *jananāt). (*It is unclear what text Gāgā is referring to by the word *khaṇḍana*. The verse does not appear in Śrīharṣa's *Khaṇḍanakhaṇḍakhādya*.) For the standard *navyanyāya* analysis, as propounded in the generation before Gāgā, see *Siddhāntamuktāvalī* (1982: 309–11 = *Kārikāvalī* vss. 82–83). A brilliant if complex reprise of the whole question is found in *Rasagaṅgādhara* (1981, Vol. I: 313ff.), which I hope to treat on another occasion.

[21] Croce's essay 'This Round Table is Square' appears in his *Problem di estetica* (the essay was written in 1905); I know it from Gramsci's brief discussion (1991: 179–80). In his *Aspects of the Theory of Syntax*, Chomsky (1965: 148ff.) allows for, but is uninterested in, the possibility of aesthetically ordered semantic coherence (what he calls 'metaphorical' or 'allusive' interpretation) in such a sentence as 'Colorless green ideas sleep furiously', which is precisely the concern of Gāgā and many of Chomsky's later commentators.

[22] Āpadeva is the author of the *Mīmāṃsānyāyaprakāśa,* which quickly became a standard introduction to Mīmāṃsā across much of India. Of Khaṇḍadeva's family or birthplace, we know almost nothing, cf. Upadhyaya (1983: 32); Upadhyaya is oddly silent on both Āpadeva and Anantadeva. He is thought to have been a pupil of Gāgā Bhaṭṭa (1933, Bhumika: 2), but this seems dubious. if he was, as he certainly was, the teacher of Perubhaṭṭa, Jagannātha's father *(Rasagaṅgādhara,* vs. 2). We know he was alive at least as late as 1658 (see below).

incorporates little of the *navya* expository mode.[23] The reason I cite it here is the vision of the state it offers in its prodigious central section on 'The Moral Order of Kings'. Although this was written for a court that since 1587 had been incorporated into the new political order of the Mughals, and by a man living in the very midst of the new intellectuals, it is hard to identify anything in this text that could not have been written a millennium earlier, the time in which most of the sources it cites were composed.[24] In fact, nowhere in the writings of the seventeenth-century Varanasi intellectuals do we hear the faintest resonance of the incorporation of the region into the Mughal Empire at the beginning of the century (nor even of the depredations of Aurangzeb in Varanasi itself in 1669). Ananta's work is evidence of the astonishing resilience of ancient political theory – the steady state of governmentality I mentioned earlier – and of the fact that political reality often seems to have adapted to this theory, and not vice versa. Nothing shows this quite so vividly as the royal consecration famously invented for Shivaji in 1674 by one of the leading intellectuals of the period, Gāgā Bhaṭṭa himself.[25]

The remarkable new subtleties of argument and exposition directed toward the analysis of ancient categories and the establishment of archaic principles all suggest to me a serious tension in a newness that could not achieve innovation: a newness of the intellect constrained by an oldness of the will.

III

I have no space here to argue out the importance of a socially grounded contextual history of the Sanskrit intellectuals of the seventeenth century. Despite the strong emphasis in recent years on rational and language-centred reconstruction as a dominant mode of intellectual history – represented most prominently in the West by the work of scholars of political philosophy such as Quentin Skinner and John Pocock – others have felt the need, and argued powerfully, for an examination of the individual agencies out of which intellectual discourses emerge, the macro-societal institutions in which they are embedded, and the political consequences they entail.[26] Although our documentation from seventeenth-century India is

[23] Ananta does frequently use the argument based on parsimony (for example, *Smṛtikaustubha* 1985: 23). The fact that the distinction between old and new knowledge in *dharmaśāstra* was wholly clear to writers of the period is demonstrated by the introduction to the *Āsaucadīdhiti* of his younger brother Jīvadeva, who notes that he compared the *jīrṇagranthas* and the *navīnagranthas* in writing the chapter.

[24] The text (*Smṛtikaustubha* 1985) has been edited by Kamala Kṛṣṇa Smṛtitīrtha. Note that manuscripts of portions of Anantadeva's *Rājadharmakaustubha* are available in Bengal, Baroda, Tanjavur, Bikaner and Kashmir. One suspects that at least in some of these cases the presence of this text may have been the result of pre-colonial circulation, and that accordingly there was a demand for such works on the part of distant Hindu kingdoms.

[25] The rise of a new discourse on Śūdras, to which Śeṣa Kṛṣṇa, Kamalākara and Gāgā Bhaṭṭa contributed decisively, and the relation of this discourse to changes in polity and society in western India during the latter part of the sixteenth and through the seventeenth centuries, are the subject of a University of Chicago dissertation now in progress by Ananya Vajpeyi.

[26] See for example Wittrock (1999: 187–232).

wholly inadequate to a serious contextualization of this sort, I sought in an earlier paper to assemble materials that provide some sense of the remarkable transformations that were occurring in the social worlds of these intellectuals (Pollock 2001: 392–426). I summarize the relevant findings below.

Cross-cultural interactions that began to take place from the beginning of the Mughal period are without parallel for the distances bridged. Siddhicandra, for example, whose discussion of literature was noted earlier, was one of a number of influential Jain *sādhus* at the early Mughal court. His teacher, Bhānucandra, was Abū'l Faẓl's informant on Hindavī culture for the third book of the *Āīn-i Akbarī,* while Siddhicandra himself eventually became tutor to the sons of Akbar – before whom he recited works in Persian – and a favourite of Jahangir and Nūr Mahal. In the 1650s, Kavīndrācārya Sarasvatī, a Maharashtrian renunciant and leading Varanasi intellectual, became an intimate of Dānishmand Khān, the Mughal courtier, and companion of Francois Bernier, physician and translator of Descartes into Persian, who accompanied him to Varanasi, the 'Athens of India' in Bernier's idiom. Jagannātha, the best known of these intellectuals and a celebrated poet at the court of Shah Jahan, was the son of an orthodox Telangana Brāhmaṇa family and, according to some, a descendent of Vallabhācārya. Whether he actually married a Muslim woman and drowned in the Ganga at Varanasi in a kind of romantic agony (material available in an unpublished, late-seventeenth-century history of the Vallabhasampradāya makes some of this very likely), it is what the age of the new intellectuals somehow demanded that he do.

Inseparable from the new social circumstances of these scholars is the presence of a striking new subjectivity in their writing. Never before in Sanskrit literature had a writer constructed a self quite so vividly present as Siddhicandra does in his autobiography. The work itself, embedded in the biography of his teacher (*Bhānucandragaṇicarita*), almost objectifies the tension between a very old conception of heteronomy and a very new self-fashioning that the text thematizes throughout. Jagannātha composed verses on the death of his wife that were unprecedented and his lyrics on a Yavana woman he named Lavaṅgī (who almost certainly had become his wife) are probably an appropriation of the Persian motif of the *mahbūb,* the ever-unattainable beloved whose un-attainability is typically exaggerated by the code of otherness. At the level of literary expression, as well, the seventeenth century was a time of border-crossings we are just beginning to learn to perceive.

What seem to be new or intensified forms of social interaction among the intellectuals may also be glimpsed, if just barely. A minor but telling example is offered by the biography of Kavīndra. When this scholar was able to persuade Shah Jahan to rescind the *jizya* tax imposed on pilgrims travelling to Varanasi and Prayaga some time in the 1630s, what we may call with justice a *festschrift* was created in his honour, the *Kavīndracandrodaya* (Moonrise of Kavīndra), comprising poems of praise elicited from leading Sanskrit intellectuals across eastern India. Later undertakings, like the petitions to Warren Hastings by the pandits of Varanasi or those of the Maharashtrian pandits (in pursuit of the Peshwa's *dakṣiṇā* fund) in the early Bombay Presidency, suggest that wider structures for collective action may have come into being at an earlier date.

Certainly the dense concentration of intellectuals in urban centres would have encouraged such structures, and played a significant role in the new conversations taking place. Undoubtedly, Sanskrit scholars had long been peripatetic, and other cities, from Takshasila in the third century BC to Vijayanagara in the sixteenth, had acted as powerful magnets. But Varanasi in the seventeenth century witnessed a confluence of more or less free intellectuals – stipendiaries like Kavīndrācārya, clients of distant courts like Gāgā Bhaṭṭa, and no doubt rentiers – of a sort it had almost certainly never seen before, certainly not in such numbers; something similar, though on a smaller scale, may have held true elsewhere, as in Maratha Tanjavur.[27] Here, two important documents can be adduced in evidence of the remarkable transregional representation and vital interaction of intellectuals in Varanasi. Both are *vyavasthāpatra* or proclamations of legal judgments. The first dates from 1583 and lists as signatories scholars resident in Varanasi from Maharashtra (including Śeṣa Kṛṣṇa), Gurjara, Gauḍa and Tailamukta (Andhra?). The second, of 1658, shows an extraordinary array of scholars 'from Maharashtra, Karnataka, Konkana, Tailanga, Dravida, and so on'. These include, besides Gāgā, Anantadeva and Khaṇḍadeva, the great *dharmaśāstrin* Bhaṭṭa Nīlakaṇṭha (the youngest son of the brilliant *mīmāṃsaka* Śaṅkara Bhaṭṭa and cousin of Kamalākara), Jayarāma Nyāyapancānana, a leading *naiyāyika* from Bengal, Nṛsiṁhāśrama, an important *vedāntin,* and Appayya Dīkṣita III, grandnephew of the 'Bull of Draviḍa'.[28] We have no usable social history of Varanasi intellectuals before the period under consideration here. But it is hard not to believe that the city's incorporation into the Mughal Empire at the end of the sixteenth century, and the growth of pilgrimage, especially on the part of Maharashtrians, that may have been facilitated by the establishment of the empire, did not have something to do with the efflorescence of the intellectual class and its cosmopolitan mixture as represented in these documents.[29]

[27] On contemporaneous Tanjavur, see the introduction to Raghavan (1952).

[28] These documents are cited in *Bhaṭṭacintāmaṇi* (1933, Bhumika: 1–2). It is not clear what problem the first document adjudicates; the second, however, is a judgement on the 'true brahmanicalness' of the Devarṣi Brāhmaṇas. (I thank Lawrence McCrea for his suggestion as to the likely identity of Appayya Dīkṣita mentioned in the list.) These Brahmanical councils continued to activate subcontinental networks into the mid-eighteenth century. A *vyavasthāpatra* of 1750 mentions 133 pandits 'from various countries, Maharashtra and so on, who have been invited by Śrīmān Mahārājādhirāja Rājavallabha'. See Sastri (1968: 516–22).

[29] Maharashtrian clerics and intellectuals, as we have seen, were massively present in Varanasi in the seventeenth century. Estimates for the early nineteenth century exceed 11,000. See Sen and Mishra (1951: 4). Pilgrimage traffic had clearly increased under the Peshwas (Gordon 1993: 146), but one wonders if this is not a continuation of earlier trends.

IV

I conclude by considering the fate of Sanskrit intellectuals, and doing so by returning to the problem of historicity with which I began. I have three points to make and will do so very briefly, concerning (a) culture-internal representations and developments; (b) culture-external standards and the possibility and limits of synchronous comparativism; and (c) the irruption of those external standards into internal history, and the end of the creative Sanskrit intellectual tradition.

It should be clear that pre-colonial South Asia knew multiple temporalities (as it knew multiple spatialities, both pragmatic and cosmic) as well as multiple modes of representing and using the past, and of denying and arresting the past. Any theory of South Asian historicity (or dehistoricity) that fails to acknowledge this multiplicity will be fatally flawed. In the seventeenth century, systems of thought that for centuries had been seen as synchronic conversations were historically periodized in such a manner that altogether unprecedented ways of both organizing and evaluating knowledge came into being. If we accept the construction of modernity that judges it to be, among other things, a different mode of structuring temporality, whereby the 'continuous present' of tradition gives way to a world in which the past and the future are understood as discrete phenomena, a modernity of a certain sort must be said to confront us here.[30] In other domains of both thought and life, however, such as visions of polity, it is precisely rupture that is denied, with a very ancient continuum being stubbornly maintained. We are encountering, accordingly, a coexistence of radically different modes of being in time, resistant to theoretical purification. There is nothing mystical about such existence, I would insist; it is simply the ability to live simultaneously in several conceptual realities, however incompatible they would eventually come to be seen.

At exactly the same period of Indian history I have been describing, western Europe witnessed a series of strikingly comparable developments that impinge upon our evaluation of the Indian case. We notice, for example, a similar sense of intellectual renewal, one celebrated in the titles of some of the more famous books of the period: Kepler's *Astronomia Nova* (New Astronomy, 1609), Bacon's *Novum Organon* (1620), Galileo's *Discorsi e dimostrazioni matematiche, intorno à due nuoue scienze* (Discourses and Demonstrations concerning Two New Sciences, 1638) Pascal's *Expériences nouvelles touchant le vide* (New Experiments concerning the Void, 1647), and Boyle's *New Experiments* (1660).[31] This novelty was often at the same time to be a purification of older knowledge ('one was to get ahead by going back'), and it is almost banal to comment on the coexistence of very archaic with very new forms of knowledge, astrology with astronomy, for example, or alchemy with chemistry. The *Querelle des anciens et*

[30] See Giddens (1990: 104–05).

[31] On the vernacular shift visible in these titles, see further below. Steven Shapin, in *The Scientific Revolution*, remarks on the titles and also provides the source of the next sentence (Shapin 1996: 65–75; 4–5).

des modernes, which began in France in the last quarter of the seventeenth century and quickly spread to England, presents a range of additional parallels. Here the problem first posed in terms of transcending ancient science (as Descartes was believed to have done) soon became one of literary evaluation. Could contemporary writers transcend Cicero, whether in excellence of style or thought? Many thoughtful minds answered 'No', and demanded continued imitation of the classics. 'Style', or ways of being in the world, may be less important than ways of knowing the world, though I take it to be a serious historical fact that among Sanskrit writers, too, literary sensibilities, even Jagannātha's, remained largely continuous with the past. But the *Querelle* was also symptomatic of powerful changes in the ways of knowing, and if we compare these with India we shall find evidence of a major bifurcation in trajectories that had up to that point been remarkably parallel for centuries, from the origins of both in an axial moment some two millennia before, and classicized and shaped thereafter in a long and brilliant tradition of scholasticism. Among Sanskrit intellectuals we see nothing comparable to the moment in seventeenth-century England when scholars of natural philosophy decided to look at nature rather than read Aristotle and Galen – whose work from that moment on became chapters in a history of science and no longer science; and when they aspired, in addition, to turn this knowledge towards the transformation of social or political arrangements. In India, old limits on what could be known, or at least on what was worth discussing, and the ends to which this knowledge could be directed, remained securely in place. Characteristically, the ancients remained authoritative and living disputants (with independent scholars of the seventeenth century citing, as we saw, foundational texts from the beginning of the common era). While modes of analysis and the historicization of whole disciplines were new, the actual methods of producing knowledge remained unchanged. Nor did anyone seek, as Descartes did, to 'begin anew, from first principles'. This explains, or at least helps us register, the crucial fact that neither the new intellectuals nor their opponents ever thematized their new historicity or sought to make second-order sense of what made them new. And unlike some of the poets, they evinced no awareness of, let alone interest in, the new conceptual possibilities around them, whether Persianate or European. These and other differences can lead easily to normative judgments of the sort early colonial officials made ('revolving in perpetual circles of metaphysical abstractions never ending still beginning', as the education surveyor William Adam described Sanskrit intellectuals in 1835). It is only a self-authenticating ideology of progress, however, that prevents us from seeing how bizarre such normativity actually is.

Yet when these norms entered Indian history – when colonialism made the norms of Europe the norms of India – the Sanskrit intellectual formation melted like so much snow in the light of a brilliant, pitiless sun. Consider only the scholarship on *dharmaśāstra,* one of the most prolific and discursively central forms of knowledge in the seventeenth century. During this period, a dozen extraordinary works were produced, including the *Vīramitrodaya* under the direction of Mitramiśra at the Orchha court in the 1630s (the work is in twenty-two volumes, and twice the size of the *Mahābhārata).* Yet, following Nāgojī Bhaṭṭa, who wrote during the first half of the eighteenth century, the production of new work totally ceases throughout India (with the sole exception of Kāśīnātha Upādhye's *Dharmasindhu* of 1790). It is almost as if the intellectuals knew their world was being altered fundamentally and forever. This was not of course preordained, but clearly neither the newness in intellectual practices that was powerful enough to reorganize core knowledges of great antiquity and to mark an age as *navya,* nor the new kinds of fertilizing interactions, forms of subjectivity and social networks, proved sufficient to prevent it. In the face of European modernity, Indian systems of thought, or rather Sanskrit systems, simply vanished as a significant force in Indian history. I here introduce a distinction between Sanskrit and other South Asian systems of thought because the fate of the Sanskrit intellectuals cannot be understood without being seen in relationship to other forms of culture in India in the centuries preceding colonialism. Something in this relationship, I believe, may help us grasp why the kind of modernity self-generated in India proved resourceless against the European variant.

Over the course of what I have called the vernacular millennium – a profound but still poorly understood transformation of culture and polity in South Asia between 1000 and 1500 – a new or at least more powerful fissure in the intellectual class emerges as a fact of ever greater consequence. For the first time since the archaic split in religious consciousness that led Buddhists and Jains to develop alternative forms of communication, a split that had been wholly transcended in the course of the first millennium among both Jain and Buddhist literati, we find a growing divergence between what I would call *mārga* intellectuals, thinkers of the 'Great Way', and *deśi* intellectuals, thinkers of 'Place'.

An increasingly noticeable gap arose between those intellectuals who continued to cleave to a kind of cosmopolitan culture of Sanskrit (though the same argument would apply to Persianate intellectuals), and those who chose to think and write vernacularly. This is especially apparent in the domain of literary culture, which represented a mode of textualizing the world even more influential in South Asia than elsewhere, but it has powerful resonances across the wider field of intellectual production, and is closely linked – or so I have argued – with transformations in the political order.

Political-cultural transformations of an astonishingly comparable order are to be found in western Europe during the same period, running parallel to developments in India – again, until about the seventeenth century. At that moment, the vernacular both intellectualized itself and institutionalized its power, processes indissociably linked to new national and statist projects. Perhaps the most dramatic instance is provided again by Descartes: two years after the founding of the Académie française in 1635 (the first of eight national academies founded in western Europe before 1671) and undoubtedly connected to this event, Descartes decided to publish his *Discours de la methode* in French, an act of considerable risk (so much so that he felt compelled to publish a Latin version within a couple of years). His decision to write in French was also conditioned by the very philosophy he was promulgating – the universalism of natural reason, despite the fact that this stands in some tension with the particularity of the so-called natural language in which the philosophy was written – as well as by his sense of the market represented by an emergent cultivated public.[32] Similar developments, if not always quite so obvious in their causal sequence, are to be found throughout seventeenth-century Europe. In Italy, for example, the scientific Lincei Academy was founded in 1603 (the literary Accademia della Crusca had been established in 1582), and in 1638, as we noted earlier, Galileo published his *Discoursi* in Italian, probably the first significant scientific treatise in that language.[33] In England, the first important philosophical text in English, Francis Bacon's *Advancement of Learning*, appeared in 1605; here the fact that the Royal Society was founded only two generations later, in 1662, indicates just how overdetermined the shift in cultural consciousness was.[34]

Neither sort of transformation occurred in India. The political institutionalization of vernacularity in seventeenth-century Europe was the consequence of a kind of instrumentalization wholly unfamiliar to Indian patterns of culture and power both over the very long term of pre-modernity and late into the vernacular epoch. Not only did this not take place in India, but on the contrary, seventeenth-century intellectuals actively reasserted the Sanskrit monopoly on intellectual (and not just literary) production in the teeth of the growing challenge of vernacularity. Although many domains of systematic thought – logic-epistemology-ontology (*nyāya*), text-hermeneutics (*mīmāṃsā*), moral philosophy (*dharmaśāstra*) – had been wholly impervious to vernacular penetration, this was not true in other disciplines. Grammatical studies in the vernacular on the vernacular, for example, had been undertaken from at least the ninth century (if only in Tamil, Kannada and Telugu). Well known are the hagiographies and systematic theology in Kannada prose developed among Vīraśaivas from the fifteenth century (and even earlier among Jains), the religious treatises in the Tamil-Sanskrit idiolect (*Maṇipravāla*) among the Śrīvaiṣṇavas. But even in Marathi we find evidence of early philosophical prose (the thirteenth-century *Vivekasindhu*), while in Braj, beginning in the seventeenth century, we encounter the occasional work on metaphysics in expository prose, in addition to an important body of writing on rhetoric

32 On the first point see the reflections of Jacques Derrida (1984: 91–154). When, as earlier noted, Descartes announced the need to start anew from first principles, he announced it in Latin (a *primis fundamentis denuo inchoandum, Meditationes I* [1641]), the text having been addressed to the Jesuits of the University of Paris. A French translation appeared in 1647.

33 As Johan Heilborn (1995: 28) points out, Galileo's work 'bears the traces of the old duality', the mathematical deductions being discussed in Latin but the experiments in Italian. We should recall, however, that vernacular, political thought in Italy begins with Macchiavelli in 1513, a text whose exact contemporaneity with Kṛṣṇadevarāya's *Āmuktamālyada*, the Telugu work from late Vijayanagara that is based on texts composed more than a thousand years earlier, serves to point out both the extent and the limits of the vernacular parallel.

34 Recent work on the vernacularization of natural science discourse in early modern Europe is found in Chartier and Corsi (1996).

and metrics.[35] And all this is to say nothing of the vast and dynamic production across the subcontinent of vernacular *kāvya* of every imaginable sort, vernacular textualizations of the practical arts (medicine and the like), and the presence of Persian and Arabic intellectual production in the greatest profusion.

In the face of all this literary-cultural change – perhaps precisely on account of it – and despite the fact that many of their number had contributed centrally to the vernacular revolution or had affiliated with the new Persianate cultural order, Sanskrit intellectuals continued to reproduce a very archaic postulate about the inefficacy of non-Sanskrit languages, now with a new tone of contentiousness. For the controversy over the communicative power of the vernacular was obviously not simply about language as such but about the status of competing knowledges and the identities of, and relationships among, communities. And it is one of the more significant disputes in which the new intellectuals played a role that may be thought to have been objectively new and audacious. Strikingly, it was some philosophers of Sanskrit grammar who most powerfully articulated this *navya* position, or rather – since it was against the new logicians, among others, that they argued – the newest of the *navya* positions.

The history of language-philosophical analysis of the signifying capacity (*śakti*) of vernacular words is a very long one, stretching back to the last centuries before the common era, when grammarians and hermeneutists had begun to raise questions about the practical and ideological status of linguistic correctness, about how words transmit meaning, and related matters.[36] Yet it was only in the seventeenth century, so far as I can see, that some Sanskrit intellectuals were finally prepared to abandon the age-old notions about the vernacular capacity to signify, only if somehow mediated by grammatically correct (that is, Sanskrit) language, even if while doing so they sometimes resorted to much earlier arguments (such as those made in the sixth century by Bhartṛhari), and continued to maintain an ancient allegiance to the moral value of grammatical discipline.[37] The position against which these thinkers chiefly argue is that of the *navya naiyāyikas* starting with Gaṅgeśa himself. Here is how the seventeenth-century grammarian Kauṇḍa Bhaṭṭa sets out the problem:

> How can verbal knowledge be obtained from vernacular language (*bhāṣā-śabda*), since by definition there can exist in the vernacular neither primary nor secondary [tropological] signification (*śaktilakṣaṇayor abhavat*) [the two mechanisms by which grammatically correct language produces mean-

---

[35] Jasvant Simh, king of Jodhpur (fl. 1650), for example, and author of the well-known Braj (verse) treatise on rhetoric (the *Bhāṣābhūṣaṇ*), composed a *Siddhāntabodha* in Braj prose. See *Granthāvali* (1972: 152ff.).

[36] This topic has been reconsidered recently by George Cardona (1999), especially pp. 99–120.

[37] Bhartṛhari does not go precisely into the terms of the debate as they appear in later thinkers; see Cardona (1999: 114, n. 151). Cardona's article seems to be largely an attempt to show that Bhartṛhari did not in fact hold the view of direct signification of dialectal language.

ing]? Some people respond on the basis of the general consensus [that is, the entire earlier tradition] that such verbal knowledge is enabled by remembering the Sanskrit word [from which the vernacular word is thought to be corrupted]. The *navyas* respond by saying that, given the fact that those who have no knowledge of Sanskrit whatever nonetheless derive verbal knowledge [from vernacular communication], the knowledge must come from an 'illusion' of the presence of primary signification.[38]

The response that Kauṇḍa gives to the *navyanyāya* position that he here summarizes is, so far as I can see, dramatically new: 'Vernacular language signifies in precisely the same way as Sanskrit. Such is the view of the grammarians, which we have set out fully in our *Bhūṣaṇa*'. This larger treatise is the *Bṛhadvaiyāka-raṇabhūṣaṇa* (which exists in an abridged version as well, the *Sāra*), a commentary-cum-exposition of a work of his uncle Bhaṭṭoji Dīkṣita, the *Vaiyākaraṇa-matonmajjana* (Rescuing the Drowned Doctrines of the Grammarians).[39] There are a number of important new (or newly clarified) arguments that Kauṇḍa offers here; we should note in particular his understanding that it is precisely Sanskrit's cosmopolitan presence that in the eyes of previous writers endowed it the capacity of direct signification:

> [According to the *navya naiyāyika*] signifying power is found only in Sanskrit. It cannot exist in vernacular words even though the putative communicative exchange in the vernacular may be identical to what is found in Sanskrit. This is so because the vernaculars vary across regions [whereas Sanskrit words are thought to be everywhere the same]. . . . However, given the absence of any decisive argument one way or the other, we must conclude that vernacular language too possesses the power of signifying directly. Nor would this lead to any lack of parsimony [that is, the need to postulate multiple words – which is to say, multiple spellings of a single word – that all directly express the same meaning] since it is impossible to avoid attributing signifying power to Marathi *(mahārāṣṭrabhāṣā)* no less than Sanskrit. This is so because Marathi, too, remains self-identical in every single region. [*Sāra*: Like Sanskrit the vernacular of Maharashtra and all others are everywhere one and the same. (The *Prabhā* commentary adds: That is, all vernaculars produce meaning in one form only. None of them varies across regions, for when it does become truly transformed, it turns into another language.)] Thus, because there is no conclusive evidence for exclusion in the case of

38 Kauṇḍa Bhaṭṭa (1900: 32). The position reproduced is that of the *Tattvacintāmaṇi* (1990, Vol. IV, part 2: 639–40). Cf. also Gerschheimer (1996: 64). Kauṇḍa Bhaṭṭa, for his part, repeatedly calls this the *navya* position (*Vaiyākaraṇabhḥūṣaṇasāra* 1969: 249).

39 Also known as the *Vaiyākaraṇasiddhāntakārikā* (1901). Did Bhaṭṭoji's position evolve over time? In his *Śabdakaustubha* (1991: 25) he reports as the position of 'others' the belief in the communicative efficacy of dialectal words; in *Vaiyākaraṇasiddhāntakārikā* he tersely states: 'there is no distinction in communicative capacity' (*Vācakatvāviśeṣa*, vs. 37).

other languages, the rejection of signifying power with respect to any single one of the vernaculars is itself refuted. Indeed, even in the case of Sanskrit conclusive evidence for exclusion is absent. [*Sāra*: If by 'conclusive evidence' were meant acceptance by the learned everywhere that a given form is correct, then even in the case of Sanskrit there might be incorrect words, since the word *śava* is used as a verb of motion among the Kambojas, and as a noun meaning corpse in Āryāvarta, according to the *Mahābhāṣya*.]

One might argue further that it is not the fact of a language being Sanskrit or a vernacular that determines whether or not it has signifying power, but rather its orthographic stability, which [in the case of the vernaculars] is everywhere variable. But this would hardly differ from the case of Sanskrit synonyms: *ghaṭa* and *kalaśa* [are spelled differently but mean the exact same thing, 'pot']. Given this, the one [Sanskrit] cannot render the other [the vernacular] to be erroneously established [as having signifying power]. [*Sāra*: Moreover, (even if one were to agree that the vernaculars are marked by variation and argue that) it is orthography that defines a word as such (one could reply as follows): The variable orthography in the vernacular is like (the variability in Sanskrit) with respect to synonyms (that is, various spellings of a single vernacular word all mean the same thing, just as various spellings in Sanskrit in the case of synonyms all mean the same thing); what is the difference between the two (that is, that allows us to count the latter as correct and the former as incorrect)?] It is precisely for this reason [that is, that non-Sanskrit language can have signifying power] that the *Kāvyaprakāśa* quotes a Prakrit verse to illustrate a case of aesthetic implication of the expressed meaning [which demonstrates that other important authorities hold *śakti* to exist in *bhāṣā*].[40]

It is the position represented by Kauṇḍa Bhaṭṭa, which would now in its own right be characterized as *navya*, that came under attack from the widely influential Varanasi intellectual, Kamalākara Bhaṭṭa. Writing in perhaps the very decade in which the French Academy was founded, Kamalākara reiterates the old position in Mīmāṃsā language philosophy (though tinged in fact with *navyanyāya)*

[40] *Bṛhadvaiyākarṇabhūṣaṇa* (1985: 218, 220); *Vaiyākaraṇabhūṣaṇasāra* (1969: 341–42) ('thus, because there is no conclusive evidence for exclusion in the case of [lit., with] other languages' – that is, because just as in the case of Sanskrit, so in the case of the vernaculars the learned use one and the same form everywhere – 'the rejection of signifying power with respect to any single one [of the vernaculars] is itself refuted' (*bhāṣāntarair vinigamanāvirahād naikātra śaktir iti parāstam*); 'the one [Sanskrit] cannot render the other [the vernacular] to be erroneously established [as having signifying power]' (*naikenāparānyathāsiddhiḥḥ*). The Prakrit citation is from *Kāvyaprakāśa*, Chapter 2, vs. 6 (*māe gharovāraṇam*). This notwithstanding, it is more likely that Kauṇḍa Bhaṭṭa held Mahārāṣṭrī and Marathi as related, than that by *mahārāṣṭrabhāṣā* he meant the Prakrit (which for a thousand years had been called Mahārāṣṭrī). The presence of signifying power in non-Sanskrit is asserted by another *navya* grammarian of the preceding generation, Annam Bhaṭṭa (according to his sub-commentary on the *Mahābhāṣya* cited in Coward and Kunjuni Raja (1990: 237).

when arguing that the very capacity of vernacular language to produce meaning is a pure illusion, since authentic meaning presupposes language that does not change – that is, Sanskrit:

> The new intellectuals (*navya*) hold that [inherently expressive] words and sentences must exist in dialect, that is, in vernacular-language texts, as well as in [newly coined] technical terms and proper names, because these actually do communicate verbal knowledge. These men, however, fail to grasp the logic in the argument that 'a multiplicity of [equally expressive] speech forms cannot be logically posited' [*Pūrvamīmāṃsāsūtra* 1.3.26]. Nor do they understand that, by thereby rendering grammar itself irrelevant and accepting as valid words and meanings in use among the Mlecchas, they are destroying the Veda. There cannot exist in dialectal words such as *gavya* [instead of Skt *gau*, 'cow'] the expressive power conferred by divine will, because these dialectal words have no stable form [whereas the words stamped by God's will, that is, Sanskrit words, are invariable]. . . . In short, if direct signification is attributed to [a recently created] proper name one would have to attribute the power of signification to the sounds of seashells and bells. And by the same token, the vernacular can be said to possess real words only either by the illusion of their being expressive in themselves, or through the presence of the grammatically correct [Sanskrit] words that they suggest. Words are actually changeless-and-eternal, because the phonemes of which they are composed are such.[41]

We must not lose sight of what is ultimately at stake in this seemingly narrow discussion – which is nothing less, I think, than the possibility of creating a national–popular intellectual class, of the sort toward which the *philosophes*, for example, gestured in the century following Descartes's choice. But it is also worth stressing that while, as Kamalākara himself declares, it is against the *navyas* he mounts the argument, there is nothing to be found anywhere in this intellectual history to suggest that, even for new scholars like Kauṇḍa, the rebirth of the *mārga* as a *deśi* intellectual was not something excluded a priori from the realm of possibility by the kind of fundamental ideological precommitments expressed by

[41] *Mīmāṃsākutūhala* (1987: 77) ('dialect', *apabhraṃśa*; 'vernacular-language texts', *bhāṣāprabandha*; 'proper names and technical terms', *saṅketaśabda*). By and large, this is the dominant position across disciplines, from logic, see *Nyāyakaustubha Śabdakhaṇḍa* (1982: 549ff.) to literary criticism (*Alaṅkārakaustubha* of Kavikarṇapūra [*c.* 1600, Navadvip], pp. 30–31). Supporters of the new grammarians seem few and far between, though consider the following comments of Gāgā Bhaṭṭa in his commentary on the *Candrāloka* (p. 4). With regard to Mammaṭa's by then ubiquitous definition of poetry as *nirdoṣa . . . vāk* or 'faultless language,' Gāgā remarks: 'Some people hold that, even though faultless usage is absent from vernacular verse and the like (*bhāṣāślokādau*) given the presence there of phonological and morphological solecisms and so on (*cyutasaṃskṛtitva-*), people still apply the word "literature" to it, and accordingly "faultlessness" should be taken not as a defining property (*viśeṣaṇa*) of literature but as a secondary property (*upalakṣaṇa*).'

Kamalākara. As far as we know, Kauṇḍa himself wrote not a single word of scholarly Marathi. And we even encounter the occasional defection from the vernacular. Anantadeva, for example, the Sanskrit writer on moral law mentioned earlier, was the great-great-grandson of Eknāth, the vernacular sage of Maharashtra (d. 1609).[42] In the eyes of Sanskrit intellectuals of whatever stripe, for thought to be systematic, let alone true – thought on everything from polity to the expressive capacity of the vernacular (which in fact was never argued out in the vernacular) – was for thought to be *saṃskṛta.* All the rest was just poetry, if for some scarcely that.

I noted earlier that a crucial development in the intellectual modernity in western Europe was the rise of the royal academies and later secularized universities. What is additionally important about these institutions is the fact that, for the first time in centuries, knowledge could be produced outside the organizational framework of Christian theology (if still under the watchful eye of absolutist power). And here, not unparadoxically, European modernity seems to have been generated by moving closer to Indian pre-modernity (to adopt the prevailing idiom). A fact insufficiently emphasized in the scholarly literature is that intellectual freedom in pre-European India was virtually total. Institutional constraints or sanctions were as little known as compulsory dogma or censorship; the only censorship in India was failure of imagination, and the only dogma, uncritiqued tradition. The modernizing of Europe through greater approximation to pre-modern India is true, too, in the more particular case of philosophy, if we accept the account of the rise of Western philosophy as an academic discipline whereby its practitioners became 'institutionally-protected specialist[s] in esoteric disciplinary abstractions', both 'technically rigorous, and remote from the clear political and religious appeals of the lay-based philosophers whom they now displace' (Collins 1996: 141–62).[43] This is, I think, largely how the logicians, grammarians and other intellectuals of seventeenth-century India should be viewed.

Yet it is also beyond dispute that the social character of the modernity that would ultimately win in Europe, and perforce in colonial India, was of a very different sort. However else we may wish to characterize, it was undoubtedly a national and a vernacular modernity. In the realm of knowledge production, it brought the intellectual into a new public sphere with its far broader market and with demands eventually posed against the absolutist state, but also into a new pedagogical sphere, where vernacular cultivation was a central concern.[44] And against this, the Sanskrit scholars of seventeenth-century India, and their successors

[42] See *Smṛtikaustubha* (Anantadeva 1935, vs. 15), where Eknāth is called *srīkṛṣṇabhaktimān.* In this context it is worth recalling the legend that Eknāth was compelled by the Brāhmaṇas of Varanasi to destroy his Marathi *Bhāgavata* by throwing it in the Ganga (*Bhaktilīlāmṛta,* Chapter 21: 30–202; Chapter 22: 1–44).

[43] The quoted passages are found on pp. 152, 158.

[44] An account of the social transformation of the modern intellectual is offered in Heilbron (1995: esp. 26–77). On the vernacular 'pedagogical revolution' in seventeenth-century France, see also Blair (1996: 40ff.).

up to the end of the eighteenth century (Tanjavur was taken by Wellesley in 1799; Varanasi was ceded to the British by the Nawab of Awadh in 1803), had few resources to deploy.

As for the pedagogy, so far as we can tell from the thin data we possess, vernacular education in South Asia continued in the first instance to address practical needs (accountancy, clerical skills and the like); the formation of an intelligentsia remained the task of the Sanskrit *tol* and the Persian–Arabic *madrasa.* As for the public sphere, the new intellectuals did not and maybe could not, confront Europe as a political problem. In part this may have been because they believed they had long ago solved the enigma of power, in part because no theory of the vernacular polity had ever been produced and thus no national intellectual formation had ever autonomously generated itself. Whether or not I am right about this, it is a fact that Sanskrit intellectuals never directly confronted colonialism, whether as a political or an epistemological order; virtually without exception they simply ignored it. All they appeared able or willing to do, with the most remarkable resources of thought and expression they had ever developed – of a sort that in some cases would hardly be matched before the symbolic metalanguages of late (or post) modernity – was to reinvigorate and sustain an old ecumenical cultural order in a much-changed world where no other option was available.

References

Avineri, Shlomo, ed. (1969), *Karl Marx on Colonialism and Modernization* (Garden City, New York: Anchor Books).

Bayly, C.A. (1988), *Indian Society and the Making of the British Empire* (Cambridge: Cambridge University Press).

Bhaṭṭacintāmaṇi by Gāgā Bhaṭṭa (1933), edited by Surya Narayana Sukla (Varanasi: Chowkhamba Sanskrit Series Office).

Blair, Ann (1996), 'La persistance du latin comme langue de science . . . la fin de la Renaissance,' in Roger Chartier and Pietro Corsi (eds), *Sciences et langues en Europe* (Paris: Ecole des hautes ètudes en sciences sociales).

Bourdieu, Pierre (1989), 'The Corporatism of the Universal: The Role of Intellectuals in the Modern Word', *Telos*, Vol. 81, pp. 99–110.

——— (1991), *The Political Ontology of Martin Heidegger* (Stanford: Stanford University Press).

Bṛhadvaiyākaraṇabhūṣaṇa by Kauṇḍa Bhaṭṭa (1985), edited by Manudeva Bhattacharya (Varanasi: Chowkhamba Amarabharati Prakasana).

Cardona, George (1999), 'Approaching the Vākyapadīya', *Journal of the American Oriental Society,* Vol. 119, No. 1, pp. 88–125.

Chakrabarty, Dipesh (1997), 'The Time of History and the Times of Gods', in Lisa Lowe and David Lloyd (eds), *The Politics of Culture in the Shadow of Capital* (Durham: Duke University Press).

Chartier, Roger (1988), 'On the Relation of Philosophy and History', in *Cultural History: Between Practices and Representations* (Ithaca: Cornell University Press).

Chartier, Roger and Pietro Corsi, eds (1996), *Sciences et langues en Europe* (Paris: École des hautes études en sciences sociales).

Chomsky, Noam (1965), *Aspects of the Theory of Syntax* (Cambridge: M.I.T. Press).

Coward, Harold G. and K. Kunjuni Raja (1990), *The Philosophy of the Grammarians* (Princeton: Princeton University Press).

De Certeau, Michel (1975), *L'Ecriture de l'histoire* (Paris: Gallimard).

Derrett, J. Duncan M. (1973), *Dharmaśāstra and Juridical Literature* (Wiesbaden: Harrassowitz).

Derrida, Jacques (1984), 'Languages and Institutions of Philosophy', *Recherches Semiotiques/ Semiotic Inquiry,* Vol. 4, No. 2, pp. 91–154.

Gerschheimer, Gerdi (1996), *La théorie de la signification chez Gadādhara* (Paris: Institut de civilisation indienne).

Giddens, Anthony (1990), *The Consequences of Modernity* (Stanford: Stanford University Press).

Gordon, Stewart (1993), *The Marathas 1600–1818* (Cambridge: Cambridge University Press).

Gramsci, Antonio (1991), *Cultural Writings* (Cambridge: Harvard University Press).

Granthāvalī by Jasvant Simh (1972), edited by Vishvanathaprasad Mishra (Varanasi: Nagaripracarini Sabha).

Heilbron, Johan (1995), *The Rise of Social Theory* (Minneapolis: University of Minnesota Press).

Karashima, Noboru (1992), *Towards a New Formation: South Indian Society under Vijayanagar Rule* (Delhi: Oxford University Press).

Macdonell, A. (1900), *History of Sanskrit Literature* (London: W. Heinemann).

Masseau, Didier (1994), *L'invention de l'intellectuel dans l'Europe du XVIIIe siècle* (Paris: Presses Universitaires de France).

Mīmāṃsākutūhala by Kamalākara Bhaṭṭa (1987), edited by P.N. Pattabhirama Sastri (Varanasi: Sampurnanandasamskrtavisvavidyalaya).

Nandy, Ashis (1995), 'History's Forgotten Doubles', *History and Theory*, Vol. 34, No. 2, pp. 44–660.

Narayana Rao, Velcheru, David Shulman and Sanjay Subrahmanyam (1992), *Symbols of Substance: Court and State in Nāyaka-Period Tamil Nadu* (Delhi: Oxford University Press).

Nāṭyaśāstra with the commentary of Abhinavagupta by Kuntaka (1992), revised and edited by K. Krishnamoorthy (Baroda: Oriental Institute).

Navamuktivāda by Gadādhara (1959), edited by Kalipada Tarkacharya (Calcutta: Sanskrit College).

Nyāyakaustubha Pratyakṣakhaṇḍa by Mahādeva Punatāmbekara (1930), edited by Umesh Mishra (Varanasi: Varanaseya Sanskrit Vishvavidyalaya).

Nyāyakaustubha Śabdakhaṇḍa by Mahadeva Punatāmbekara (1982), edited by V. Subrahmanya Sastri (Tanjavur: Tanjavur Maharaja Sarabhoji Sarasvati Mahal Granthalaya).

Padārthadīpikā by Kauṇḍa Bhaṭṭa (1900), edited by Rama Krishna Sastri (Varanasi: Braj B. Das & co.).

Pakṣatāprakaraṇa by Jagadīśa (1930), edited by Shivadatta Mishra (Varanasi: Chowkhamba Sanskrit Series Office).

Pollock, Sheldon (1985), 'The Theory of Practice and the Practice of Theory in Indian Intellectual History', *Journal of the American Oriental Society*, Vol. 105, No. 3, pp. 499–519.

——— (1998), 'India in the Vernacular Millennium: Literary Culture and Polity, 1000–1500', in Samuel Eisenstadt and Wolfgang Schluchter (eds), *Early Modernities*, special issue of *Daedalus*, Vol. 127, No. 3, pp. 41–74.

——— (2001), 'The Death of Sanskrit', *Comparative Studies in Society and History*, Vol. 43, No. 2, pp. 292–426.

Potter, Karl (1992), *Indian Philosophical Analysis: Nyāya-Vaiśeṣika from Gaṅgeśa to Raghunātha Śiromaṇi* (Princeton: Princeton University Press).

Raghavan, V. (1952), *Śāhendravilāsa of Śrīdharaveṅkaṭeśvara* (Tiruchi: Kalyan Press).

Randall, Collins (1996), 'The Transformation of Philosophy', in J. Heilbron, L. Magnusson and B. Wittrock (eds), *The Rise of the Social Sciences and the Formation of Modernity: Conceptual Change in Contexts, 1750–1850* (Boston: Kluwer Academic Publishers).

Rākāgama on Candrāloka by Gāgā Bhaṭṭa (1938), edited by Ananta Ram Sastri Vetal (Varanasi: Chowkhambha Sanskrit Series Office).

Rasagaṅgādhara by Jagannātha Paṇḍitarāja (1981), edited by Kedarnath Ojha (Varanasi: Sampurnanandasamskrtavisvavidyalaya).

Śabdakaustubha by Bhaṭṭojī Dīkṣita (1991), edited by Gopal Sastri Nene and Mukund Sastri Puntamkar (Varanasi: Chowkhamba Sanskrit Series Office).

Sastri, Gaurinath (1968), 'Post-Gadādhara Naiyāyikas of Bengal (1600–1800 AD)', in J.C. Heesterman, G.H. Schokkerand V.I. Subramoniam (eds), *Pratidānam* (The Hague: Mouton).

Sen, Surendra Nath and Umesha Mishra, eds (1951), *Sanskrit Documents* (Allahabad: Ganganath Jha Research Institute).

Shapin, Steven (1996), *The Scientific Revolution* (Chicago: University of Chicago Press).

Shils, Edward (1968), 'The Intellectuals and the Powers: Some Perspectives for Comparative Analysis', *Comparative Studies in Society and History*, Vol. I, No. 1, pp. 15–22.

Siddhāntamuktāvalī by Viśwanātha Pañcānana (1982), edited by Atmaram Narayan Jere (Varanasi: Krsnadasa Akadami).

Smṛtikaustubha by Anantadeva (1935), edited by Kamala Kṛṣṇa Smṛtitīrtha (Baroda: Oriental Institute).

Tarkasaṃgraha by Annam Bhaṭṭa (1985), edited by Ramacandra Jha (Varanasi: Chowkhamba Sanskrit Series Office).

Tattvacintāmaṇi by Gangesa (1990), edited by Kamakhyanath Tarkavagisha (Delhi: Chowkhamba Sanskrit Series Office).

Upadhyaya, Baldev (1983), *Kāśī kī Pāṇḍitya Paraṃparā: 1200 CE–1950 CE* (Varanasi: Vishvavidyalaya Prakashana).

Vaiyākaraṇabhūṣaṇasāra by Kauṇḍa Bhaṭṭa (1969), edited along with the *Prabhā* and *Darpaṇa* Commentaries, by Balakrishna Pancholi (Varanasi: Caukhamba Samskrta Sirija Aphisa).

Vaiyākaraṇasiddhāntakārikā by Bhaṭṭojī Dīkṣita (1901) (Poona: Anandashrama).

Vakroktijīvita by Kuntaka (1977), edited by K. Krishnamoorthy (Dharwad: Karnataka University).

Wittrock, Bjorn (1999), 'Social Theory and Intellectual History: Rethinking the Formation of Modernity', in F. Engelstad and R. Kalleberg (eds), *Social Time and Social Change* (Oslo: Scandinavian University Press).

Conflicts and Adjustments

The Emergence of New Imprecations in Twelfth- and Thirteenth-Century Tamil Inscriptions and *Jāti* Formation

Noboru Karashima

Imprecations in the Gupta/Vākāṭaka Tradition

Although we do not know when the practice of granting lands to Brāhmaṇas began in India, it was common during the Gupta/Vākāṭaka period in the Gangetic valley and the northern Deccan plateau, and many kings and commoners left records of their charities inscribed on copper plates or stones. In these inscriptions (mostly copper plates) recording land grants, and sometimes other grants too, the imprecation to those who might give harm to the charity occurs near the end of the inscription following the details of the grant. Three examples of imprecations[1] in the Gupta copper-plate inscriptions are as follows:

1. Damodarpur inscription of Kumāragupta I (*Corpus Inscriptions Indicarum* [*CII*] III: 22), recording land purchase by a Brāhmaṇa for conducting Vedic rites: 'He who takes away land given by himself or by others, having become a worm in excreta, rots with his forefathers'.
2. Indore inscription of Skandagupta (*CII* III: 30), recording a lamp grant 'Whoever transgresses this grant that has been drawn up, that man [becoming as guilty as] the slayer of a cow, [or] the slayer of a spiritual preceptor, or the slayer of a Brāhmaṇa, shall go to the infernal region, being overpowered with those [well-known] five sins together with the minor ones'.[2]
3. Another Damodarpur inscription of Budhagupta (*Epigraphia Indica* [*EI*] XV: 7–3), recording a villager's land purchase for settling Brāhmaṇas: 'Whoever confiscates land given by himself or by another becomes a worm in ordure and rots with his forefathers, and the confiscator and he who approves resides for sixty thousand years in hell'.

Two examples of imprecations given in the Vākāṭaka copper-plate inscriptions recording royal grants are as follows:

[1] Imprecatory phrases (and also benedictory phrases often appearing together with them) in copper-plate inscriptions are usually given as the sayings of some sage(s), like Vyāsa as will be seen below, or as occurring in some religious texts (Sircar 1965: 141).

[2] Killing a Brāhmaṇa, drinking the liquor *surā*, stealing the gold of a Brāhmaṇa, adultery with a *guru*'s wife, and associating with such offenders are the five mortal sins (*mahāpātaka*) in the *Manusmṛti* (XI.55), and killing a cow is counted as one of the minor offences in the same text (XI. 60).

1. Poona inscription of Queen Prabhāvatigupta[3] (*CII* V: 1), recording a village grant by the queen to a Brāhmaṇa, quotes the following imprecatory couplets composed by Vyāsa: 'He who takes away the land given by himself or by others shall incur the sin of killing ten thousand cows'.
2. Siwani inscription of Pravarasena II (*CII* V: 7), recording a village grant by the king to a Brāhmaṇa, gives the following verse sung by Vyāsa: 'Those who give harm to the grant shall live in hell for sixty thousand years, and those who take away the land given by themselves or by others shall incur the sin of killing ten thousand cows'.

In the case of south India, the Pallava dynasty, which established its powerful rule in the Tamil country in the sixth century by following the ruling strategy of the Guptas and Vākāṭakas, employed the Gupta/Vākāṭaka practice of land grants. The Reyuru plates of Narasimhavarman II (*Thirty Pallava Copper Plates* [*TPCP*]: pp. 83–86) give the imprecation as follows: 'The property of a Brāhmaṇa is a dangerous poison; other poison is not poison (at all); (ordinary) poison kills one person only. (But) a Brāhmaṇa's property kills the whole lineage. Whoever takes away property given by himself or by others, he shall become a worm in the dung for sixty thousand years.'

The Kasakkudi plates of Nandivarman II (*TPCP*: pp. 155–69) also have a quite similar imprecation: 'Whoever takes back a property gifted by himself or by others, he shall become a worm in the dung for sixty thousand years'.

Strangely, however, none of the royal land-grant inscriptions of the Coḷas, who succeeded the Pallavas in the Tamil country in the ninth century, mention such imprecations, though there remain many copper-plate charters recording Coḷa kings' land grants to Brāhmaṇas. However, we do find imprecations in some of the Coḷa inscriptions that record charities made by common people, not kings, including land grants to Brāhmaṇas. The phrase most frequently seen in these imprecations is 'the person who would give harm to the charity shall incur all the sins committed in the land between the Ganges and Kanyakumari', reflecting the geographical circumstances of peninsular India, though we find some other expressions too. Examples are:

1. Tirumalpuram inscription of Rājarāja I (*South Indian Inscriptions* [*SII*] XIII: 29, NA) which records that the villagers (*ūrār*), having received money, agreed to supply oil for a lamp in a temple and to feed the collector of oil, gives the imprecation that if they violated this agreement, they would incur the sins committed between the Ganges and Kannyakumari.[4]
2. Ten-Mahadevamangalam inscription of Sundara Coḷa (*SII* XIII: Addendum 173A, NA), recording a tax grant for the maintenance of a tank, curses

[3] Prabhāvatigupta was a daughter of Candragupta II, a Gupta king, and married to Rudrasena II, a Vākāṭaka king. This indicates the close relationship between these two dynasties.

[4] There are many more inscriptions that record this type of imprecation. A variation of this type specifies the distance between the Ganges and Kannyakumari as 700 *kādam*. This variation is seen, for example, in *SII* XIII: 297 and 302, and *SII* XIX: 446.

the person who gives harm to this agreement by stating that he will go to a hell (*naraka*) lower than the seventh.

3. Tiruverumbur inscription of Sundara Coḷa (*SII* XIII: 114, Tp), recording the tax remission of temple land by the *sabhā*, gives a curse to the violator that he will be treated as an enemy (thorn) of the village.

Proliferation of Sins and New Imprecations

This situation seen in early Coḷa inscriptions continued for a few centuries under Coḷa rule, though some inscriptions of the middle period refer to actual punishment such as a fine for the person who goes against the decision.[5] In the latter half of the twelfth century, however, there occurred changes in the imprecatory expressions in inscriptions, and they become more conspicuous in the thirteenth century. A particular change is noticed in the employment of the term *drohī* (traitor). The word *drohī* appears in an inscription of Rājarāja I (*EI* XXI: 168) in the eleventh century, but this usage is not for the purpose of imprecation. The word *drohī* appears in twelfth- and thirteenth-century inscriptions in the imprecatory section of an inscription in combination with such terms as *rāja* (king), *nāḍu* (locality), *ina* (community), Śiva, and *guru* (religious preceptor). Here are five examples:

1. An Arpakkam inscription (*SII* VI: 456, AD 1168, Cg), recording the grant of a village by a chief to Arpakkam temple praying that the Sri Lankan army which had invaded the Pāṇḍyan country would not come into the Coḷa country, gives the imprecation that the person who harms this grant will fall into the sin of killing parents and Brāhmaṇas and will be a traitor to Śiva (*Śiva-drohī*). The Sri Lankan army that damaged the Ramesvaram temple is also condemned as *Śiva-drohī*.
2. A Kudumiyamalai inscription (*Inscriptions of the Puddukkotai State* [*IPS*]: 285, AD 1229, Pd), which records the decision made by various communities in their assembly to share the money for the repair of a temple, contains the curse that those who violate their decision are traitors to *Śiva*, *nāḍu* (*nāṭṭu-drohī*), and *ina* (*ina-drohī*).
3. A Mannargudi inscription (*SII* VI: 58, AD 1239, Tj), recording the agreement between Brāhmaṇa landowners and Veḷḷāḷa cultivators on the payment of *kuḍimai* by the latter, warns the violator of this agreement that he will be a traitor to *nāḍu* and *guru* (*guru-drohī*).
4. A Chengama inscription (*SII* VII: 118, AD 1258, NA), recording a feud between a local chief and the three sons of his brother that involved whole communities in the locality, states that the three brothers who joined the enemy of the chief are traitors to *rāja* (*rāja-drohī*) and *nāḍu*.
5. A Tiruvorriyur inscription (*Annual Report on [South] Indian Epigraphy*

[5] For example, *SII* VIII: 805 (AD 996) records a fine of 25 *kaḻañju* of gold to be collected by the village assembly (*sabhā*) from a person who will not pay for tank maintenance.

[*AR*] 1912: 203; Thangavelu and Thyagarajan, *History of Sambuvarayar* [*HS*]: pp. 468–71, AD 1342, Cg) records the assignment of tasks among temple servants (*padiyilār* and *devaraṭiyār*) by the religious authority headed by a *maṭhādipati*, ending with the warning that a violator of this decision will be treated as a traitor to *Śiva*, *nāḍu*, and *ina*.

It is clear from these examples that arrangements for the protection of which any future violator is threatened with an imprecation, are not confined to land grants to Brāhmaṇas or lamp burning in temples, but also include agreements made between hostile parties and resolutions made in an assembly of various groups of a locality. We can gather from these inscriptions, including those above, some eight terms used as a prefix or an attribute of a *drohī*, indicating to whom or to what the cursed person will be a traitor, namely, what sort of sin the person who harms the endowment or violates the agreement, will commit. The eight terms are: *Śiva*, *rāja*, *guru*, *nāḍu* (locality), *grāma* or *ūr* (village), *ina* (community) and *mātru* (mother). Some of these prefixes may indicate the vast horizons of newly appearing values stretched beyond their apparent and conventional meanings in Brāhmaṇical ideology, but their study must await research in the future.

Up to the twelfth century, the sin referred to in inscriptions meant giving harm to the charity, which was practically confined to grants to Brāhmaṇas and to deities. In Brāhmaṇical ideology charity has great meritorious value[6] and its hindrance was thought to be equal to the five mortal sins prescribed in the *Manusmṛti*. In the twelfth and thirteenth centuries, however, the idea of sin becomes more elaborate, and, therefore, it became necessary to specify against whom or what the sin was committed. This change towards a proliferation or specification of sin seems to have moved apace with, or to have been caused by, an increase in the number of inscriptions that record various arrangements other than grants, including agreements or decisions made by various groups of people (Karashima 1996).

Accordingly, this proliferation and specification of sins brought about the emergence of various new imprecatory expressions in inscriptions, along with the employment of the term *drohī* during the twelfth and thirteenth centuries. There continued to be a standard or stereotyped expression of imprecation in inscriptions, but the expression itself changed from the earlier 'receiving of the sin committed between the Ganga and Kanyakumari' to the new 'falling into the sin of killing a tawny cow on the bank of the Ganga'. This new stereotype is found in many inscriptions, including in *SII* VII:150 (AD 1147, SA) recording a tax grant to a temple by a chief; *SII* V: 492 (AD 1187, Nl) recording a tax (*āyam*) grant to a temple by a military chief and merchants (*nagaram*); *SII* IV: 849 (AD 1204, Cg) recording a tax grant to a temple by a chief; and *SII* V: 504 (AD 1208, Nl) recording a land grant to a temple as *tiruviḍaiyṭṭam* by a chief's agent.

[6] As stated earlier, there are often benedictory verses also in the inscriptions recording grants, especially land grants to Brāhmaṇas. For example, the Damodarpur inscription of Budhagupta quoted above gives the benediction, 'the grantor of land enjoys pleasure in heaven for sixty thousand years' (*EI* XV: 136).

The most remarkable change, however, occurred in the emergence of various free and more vivid – often vulgar – expressions of imprecation. In contrast to the stereotyped phrase quoted above, which still lies within the frame of Brāhmaṇism,[7] many of these new coarse expressions are deviations from Brāhmaṇical ideology, or at least something new within the orbit of Brāhmaṇism. Eight examples are as follows:

1. A Tirumaiyam inscription (*IPS*: 340, AD 1223, Pd), recording reconciliation reached by two long-hostile temples in a large assembly of the locality, states that people who violate the agreement will die young without issue, being traitors to the ruler (*rāja*), mother (*mātru*), and locality (*nāḍu*).
2. A Valikandapuram inscription (*AR* 1943/44: 276, AD 1227, Tp), recording a solidarity pact of the *iḍaṅgai 98* groups[8] comprising the Nattamakkal, Malaiyamāṅgal and others, stipulates that everybody will share the good and bad fortune of the members and that if anyone goes against this pact, he/she will be degraded lower than other low *jāti*s.
3. Another Valikandapuram inscription (*AR* 1943/44: 268, AD 1233, Tp), recording an agreement concerning contributions by local people to a temple festival, states that the person who goes against this agreement will be dismissed from the village as a *Śiva-drohī* and *nāṭṭu-drohī*.
4. A Tiruvannamalai inscription (*SII* VIII: 80, AD 1233, NA) recording a village grant by a chief, warns the person who gives harm to this charity by stating that his beard and breasts will grow,[9] and he will not be born as a legitimate child, will eat beef, and incur the sin of killing a tawny cow on the bank of the Ganga and on the shore of Kanniyakumari.
5. A Valikandapuram inscription (*AR* 1943/44: 279, AD 1240[?], Tp), recording the remission of tax for four villages by military leaders, states that the wife of the person who gives harm to this charity will be given to a Pulaiyar[10] who cuts grass for our horses.
6. Another Valikandapuram inscription (*AR* 1943/44: 281, AD 1243[?], Tp), recording a village grant to a temple by a chief, states that the person who changes this endowment will fall into a hell below the seventh and his wife will be given to the Panmaiyān[11] who cuts grass for my horse.
7. A Chengama inscription (*SII* VII: 118, AD 1258, NA) already referred to, recording a feud between a local chief and the three sons of his brother involving whole communities in the locality, states that the three brothers

7 As stated earlier, killing a cow is counted as one of the minor offences in the *Manusmṛti* (XI: 60).

8 *Iḍaṅgai* means 'left hand'. *Valaṅgai* meaning 'right hand' also appears in inscriptions. These two groups, often combined with the numbers 98, 79, etc., are the large assemblies of various lower *jāti*s, mostly of artisans, merchants and hill-tribe soldiers. For these, see Chapter 8 of Karashima (1992) and Karashima and Subbarayalu (2002).

9 The expression 'his beard and breasts will grow' means that he will be a hermaphrodite.

10 Pulaiyars were one of the outcaste groups of Tamil Nadu during the British period.

11 Panmaiyār(n) seem to have been a low *jāti*.

are traitors to the ruler (*rāja*) and locality (*nāḍu*), and that people who help them will be killed and thrown away, being treated as lower than the pig and dog, and the noses and breasts of their wives will be cut off.

8. A Ratnagiri inscription (*AR* 1914: 153, date lost, probably thirteenth century, Tp), recording an agreement made between the *nāḍu* (local assembly), *grāmam* (village assembly), and *nagaram* (town assembly), states that if a future violator of this agreement is a Brāhmaṇa, his eyes will be taken out and his nose will be cut . . . he will be regarded as a pig . . . and he will be killed by soldiers. . . . If those who violate the agreement die, 'their bodies will be treated as those of pigs and dogs'. The inscription is so badly damaged that we cannot determine the full content of the agreement or the true meaning of the imprecation.

Some of these vivid expressions may even be considered to refer to the actual punishment to be given or revenge to be taken, exceeding the psychological inhibition intended by imprecation, but here we shall pay attention to the changes that occurred in the imprecatory expressions without going into the psychology. What caused this change in twelfth- and thirteenth-century inscriptions? As stated above, the proliferation of sins mentioned in inscriptions seems to have kept pace with the multiplication of matters recorded in inscriptions, resulting from an increase in decisions made in various group assemblies including proclamations of solidarity by some community and decisions about sharing festival expenditure by merchant groups.

Emergence of New Social Groups Organized in Assemblies

These changes in their turn appear to have been related to the weakening of state control towards the end of Coḷa rule. It is noticeable that among the various *drohīs* the *nāṭṭu-drohī* is mentioned most frequently in inscriptions, implying that people became more conscious about matters concerning the locality (*nāḍu*), particularly its safety. Owing to the decline of state power, it became necessary for the local people to defend the locality themselves.[12] The formation of so-called supra-local organizations, such as *chittiramēḻi-periyanāḍu* (peasant organization), *iḍaṅgai* and *valaṅgai* groups (supra-community organization, often headed by ex-hill-tribes), and *ainnūṟṟuvar* (merchant organization with soldiers under them as guards),[13] conspicuous from the twelfth century onwards, appear to be closely related to this instability of the political power of the state.

[12] This situation may be well illustrated by a Tirukkachchur inscription of Jaṭāvarman Sundarapāṇḍya (*SII* XXVI: 333, 1263 AD, Cg), which records the local people's decision taken on the atrocities of five Brāhmaṇa brothers. According to this inscription some chiefs caught the brothers at the request of the local people, but soon trouble started again and another chief sent soldiers to catch them. Though they caught two of them, the remaining three brothers continued to fight in the forest and killed even the soldiers sent by the Pāṇḍyan king.

[13] On these organizations, see Karashima and Subbarayalu (2004); Chapter 8 of Karashima (1992); and Karashima and Subbarayalu (2002).

Once people became conscious about the locality, particularly its safety, they began to concern themselves more with the social order in the locality. Previously, till the middle of the Coḷa period, society was stable under the hegemony of the Brāhmaṇas and Veḷḷāḷas who constituted the ruling class in agrarian society as landowners, even though there seems to have been hostility also between the Brāhmaṇa landlords and Veḷḷāḷa cultivators in the case of Brāhmaṇa villages (*brahmadeyas*).[14] A Tirukkachchur inscription, mentioned in note 13 and recording the atrocities of five Brāhmaṇa brothers, deplores the fact that these brothers ceased to observe the normally good behaviour of Brāhmaṇas and Veḷḷāḷas and instead began to behave in the manner of lower *jātis*. This statement indicates social cooperation and coordination between the two upper communities.

This situation recorded in the Tirukkachchur inscription is certainly a reflection of the increase of the power of social groups other than Brāhmaṇas and Veḷḷāḷas during the latter half of Coḷa rule, particularly from the twelfth century onwards. They were either men of the ex-hill-tribes who had been recruited into the Coḷa army, subsequently becoming landholders in the plains by acquiring land by purchase or coercion (Karashima 1984: 30), or merchants and artisans, who increased their strength with the development of foreign trade under the Coḷas from the eleventh century onwards (Karashima 1992: 171–80; Karashima, Subbarayulu and Shanmugam 2008). They formed such supra-local organizations as mentioned above and recorded in inscriptions the various agreements or resolutions they made in the large assembly (*peruniravi*).

The Valikandapuram inscription of AD 1227 quoted above mentions caste-like groups,[15] such as the Yādavar, Nattamakkaḷ, Malaiyamāṅgal, Andanar, and Pannāṭṭār, as constituents of *chittiramēḻi-periyanāḍu*, and Vāniya-nagaram and Kaikkoḷar, as part of merchant guild (*padineṉ-viṣayam*[16]), as well as Pirāmaṇar and Ariyar probably as members of the highest social group, though not grouped under any name. The Kudumiyamalai inscription of AD 1229, quoted above, mentions caste-like groups such as Brāhmaṇa, Ceṭṭi, Veḷḷāḷa, Ilamaiyar, Paḍaiparrugal, Tanḍi, Paṛaiyar, and Paṭṭar,[17] besides some administrative groups such as *nāḍu* (local assembly), *nagaram* (town assembly), *grāmam* (village assembly), *vanniyar* (soldiers), and *paḍaipaṟṟugaḷ* (soldiers). The Chengama inscription of AD 1258,

[14] The hostility is indicated to some extent by the agreement recorded in the Mannargudi inscription quoted above. On this point, see Subbarayulu (2001b), and Karashima and Subbarayalu (2004).

[15] It is extremely difficult to identify these groups, and so I use this vague expression deliberately. A technical term for them may be *jāti*, as it is often used in inscriptions to indicate these groups, but we have to avoid confusion with its present-day usage by sociologists.

[16] *Padineṉ-viṣayam* is synonymous with *ainnūṟṟuvar* (Karashima and Subbarayalu 2002).

[17] There is a gap between Brāhmaṇa and Ceṭṭi in the inscription owing to damage to the stone. The first three groups are described as *kāṇiyāḷar* (hereditary-right holders/landholders) and the next three groups as *kuḍimakkaḷ* (farmers/cultivators). Paṛaiyar and Paḷḷar are not grouped together under any name, but they must have composed the lowest social stratum.

quoted above, enumerates, besides various administrative bodies of the locality, the following groups under the head 'all the *jātis*':[18] '*Aḍivārattu-malaiyāḷar, Malaiyāḷa-mudaligaḷ, Mudunīr-malaiyāḷar, Malaiyāṉ-mudaligaḷ, Ceṭṭigaḷ, Vāṇigar, Kaṇakkar, Karumappēr, Pannāṭṭavar, Pannāṭṭu-mudaligaḷ, Poṟkoṟṟa-kaikkōḷar, Āṇḍārgaḷ, Śivabrāhmaṇar, Manṟāḍigaḷ, Uvachchar, Vadatalai-nāṭṭavar and Tenmalai-nāṭṭavar of Tenkarai-nāḍu, Tella . . . Pulavar, Paṇṇuvār, Niyāyattār, Pannirandu-paṇimakkaḷ, Perumvēḍar, Pāṇar, Paṟaiyar, Paṟai-mudaligaḷ, Chekkiliyar,* and *Iruḷar*'. The rough and vulgar impre-catory expressions appearing in twelfth- and thirteenth-century inscriptions are a reflection of the strength of some of these caste-like groups, who increased their power greatly and formed supra-local organizations in and after the twelfth century.

Increased Reference to *Jātis* in Inscriptions

Although a study of these groups and the process of caste formation is not the aim of this paper, I would like to make three points for future discussion in caste studies. Cynthia Talbot has recently discussed the caste-like terms appearing in Andhra inscriptions (Talbot 2001), about which she stresses two points. First, in Andhra inscriptions there are no references to specific sub-castes (*jātis*) by name, and the word *jāti* is rarely found in thirteenth-century inscriptions (ibid.: 52). Second, some caste-like terms appearing in Kakatiya inscriptions are terms showing status based primarily on occupation and cannot be taken as representing castes or sub-castes (ibid.: 55ff.). Generally, there is much difference between Tamil inscriptions and Andhra inscriptions, and also between Tamil inscriptions and Karnataka inscriptions, in the matters recorded as well as in the way of recording them. Probably the difference comes from the different socio-cultural setting in these regions. It is no surprise, therefore, to find practically no reference to the term *jāti* or to actual *jātis* in Andhra inscriptions, though as we have seen, we have plenty of references to *jāti* (and *ina*), as well as specific *jāti* groups in thirteenth-century Tamil inscriptions.

However, the second point discussed by Talbot should be considered carefully here, as it is very difficult in the case of Tamil inscriptions also to understand what sort of social categories those groups represented. Although they are mentioned as *jātis* in inscriptions, *jāti* does not necessarily denote what present-day sociologists understand by this term. Here, taking into consideration the analysis made by Talbot, we may discern three codes possessed by the caste-like groups appearing in Tamil inscriptions: 1) social status shown by titles, 2) profession, and 3) lineage or kinship relation. Among the groups mentioned in the Chengama inscription, *Nāṭṭu-mudaligaḷ* seems to indicate the social status code, *nāṭṭu-mudali* being a title. *Kaṇakkar* (accountant) indicates the professional code and *Paṟaiyar,* who may not marry with any other group, the lineage code. However, as will be

[18] The expression 'all the *jātis*' (*uḷḷṭṭa anaittu jātigaḷ*) appearing at the end of this enumeration may include the various administrative groups of the locality enumerated in the preceding part of the inscription, summed up at the end as *palajanattom* (we various people).

inferred from the appearance of all these different codes in one enumeration, it is extremely difficult to identify a particular group with a particular code. In the Chengama inscription there are enumerated many groups whose identification with these codes is either not easy or impossible. Moreover, a particular group can be identified as possessing more than one code in many cases. This difficulty or ambiguity probably comes from the fact that *jātis* were still in their formative stage in the thirteenth-century Tamil country.

In the fifteenth-century inscriptions, however, the differences between the above three codes seem to have been blurred or merged, and the *jāti* groups enumerated in the revolt inscriptions of *iḍaṅgai* and *valaṅgai* groups[19] are less in number and less complicated than those given in the Chengama inscription. They are closer to those appearing in British documents. However, if we see the caste-like or *jāti* groups appearing in twelfth- and thirteenth-century inscriptions in the context of their activities, the ex-hill-tribe groups, such as Paḷḷi and Nattamakkaḷ, seem to reveal one of the salient characteristics that later *jātis* came to show, namely, group solidarity, by proclaiming their unity (*orumai*) in inscriptions. Anyway, thirteenth-century Tamil inscriptions do illustrate that *jāti* formation was progressing in the Tamil country.

The second point I wish to add here for future discussion concerns the caste system based on hierarchy. These last thirty or forty years scholars have been discussing the issues of caste hierarchy, concentrating their arguments on the question of which of the two, Brāhmaṇas or Kṣatriyas, occupied the pinnacle of the hierarchy, or which of the two, religion or politics, played a crucial role in maintaining social order in traditional India. Scholars follow Hocart and/or Dumont. It seems to be more important, however, to realize the interdependence of the two, Brāhmaṇas *and* the king, or the religious *and* the political, if we consider empirically the function of the so-called caste hierarchy. In the long course of Indian history the opposition between the allies of Brāhmaṇas and the Kṣatriyas (or dominant castes), as the rulers on the one hand, and the other groups (classified theoretically as Vaiśya or Śūdra), as the ruled on the other, has had much significance in society. Though no communities properly called Kṣatriyas have existed in south India, we are able to regard the Veḷḷāḷas, the dominant caste, as having played the role of the Kṣatriyas in ancient and medieval Tamil country.[20] A good

[19] Though the term *jāti* does not appear in these inscriptions, we can gather from the Korukkai and Tiruvaigavur inscriptions the following community names as belonging to *valaṅgai 98* or *iḍaṅgai 98 groups*: *Seṭṭigaḷ, Kaikkoḷar, Sēnaikkaḍaiyār, Sāligar, Niyāyattār, Seṇiya, Manṟāḍi, Iḍaituṟai, Koyilaṅgāḍigaḷ, Sivanpaḍavar, Vāṇiyar, Sekkuvāṇiyar, Kammāḷar, Kollan, Tachchan, Taṭṭān, Vaṇṇattār, Kusavan, Nāvitan, Vaṇṇān, Kāvalkāṟan, Kaivvinai-paṟaiyar, Sārvakkāṟar, and Iḷampuñjai.* We can ascribe a profession to most of these groups (Karashima 1992: 145).

[20] Although the Coḷa royal family do not seem to have been Veḷḷāḷa, the Veḷḷāḷas composed the ruling class in the Coḷa state and society as the most important dominant caste. Mūvendaveḷan, which means a Veḷḷāḷa who served the three Tamil royal families, is the title conferred by the king on important and distinguished officers of the state.

example of Brāhmaṇa/Veḷḷāḷa coordination can be seen in the Tirukkachchur inscription, quoted above, contrasting the (good) behaviour of Brāhmaṇas *and* Veḷḷāḷas with the (lowly) behaviour of the lower *jāti*s and missing the former. The best example of the confrontation between the Brāhmaṇa/Veḷḷāḷa allies and other communities organized as *iḍaṅgai* and *valaṅgai* may be found in the revolt inscriptions of the fifteenth century referred to above.

Political Instability and *Jāti* Formation

The actual regulation of the caste hierarchy seems to have been carried out by the kings, state officers, or local chiefs,[21] so that it was political power that regulated the caste hierarchy to maintain the social order. In the course of history, however, there were sometimes periods when the king's power waned and social disorder prevailed. Did the regulation of caste relations then disappear? Was it relaxed during these periods? In this connection, we may recall Inden's observations on the relationship between caste formation and political instability:

> There (Inden 1976) I showed that it was the collapse of Hindu kingship which led to the formation of 'castes' in something resembling their modern form (albeit not as usually described). That is, the distinctive institution of Indian civilization does not appear until the thirteenth or fourteenth century, at the earliest; and castes are not the *cause* of the weakness and collapse of Hindu kingship, but the *effect* of it. (Inden 1990: 92)

However, the situation in medieval Bengal studied by Inden, where mixed marriage among various caste-like groups produced many *jāti*s, seems to have been quite different from that in contemporary Tamil Nadu. In the Tamil country the formation of *jāti*s and the consequent rearrangement of the hierarchy had been accelerated during the period of political instability and social disorder around the thirteenth century as stated above.[22] But the process of *jāti* formation was not by mixed marriage. It was through the incorporation of some new communities who had gained power in the local social order. The struggle for hegemony between the new and old groups, or amongst new groups, caused the reshuffling of the

[21] The best example is seen in the regulation made by the Bengal king Vallāla Sena (Inden 1976: 60ff.). We can find examples in Maratha administrative documents of the seventeenth and eighteenth centuries, though Kotani differentiates the king from the state (Kotani 2002: 192ff.). In Tamil Nadu some Vijayanagar inscriptions record that *nāyaka*s (state officials in charge of a certain territory) regulated the privileges given to some communities (Karashima 1992: 165). There are also inscriptions recording a *nāyaka*'s decision on privileges disputed by two communities (Karashima 1992: 24).

[22] The formation of the so-called 'little kingdom' in Pudukkottai may be considered to have also started in this process of political disturbance around the thirteenth century (Dirks 1987: 139–55). However, Pudukkottai was an exceptional area where no regular administration was introduced by the powerful states like the Coḷas, Pāṇḍyas and Vijayanagar (Subbarayalu 2001a), which seems to have left the field open for Pudukkottai to form its little kingdom in succeeding centuries.

caste hierarchy. And this establishment of a new hierarchy was not regulated by the king, but by the local people organized as assemblies.

Whatever was the agency, king or local assembly, we notice here the working of Brāhmaṇical ideology in regulating the caste (*jāti*) hierarchy. If we look back over the course of history, the *Manusmṛti* had been the authority for protecting grants made by kings as well as ordinary people. New imprecations in inscriptions during the political crisis of the thirteenth century also make mention of the *jāti* hierarchy by inserting a phrase such as 'all *jātis*, *Andaṇan* (Brāhmaṇa) at the top to *Arippan* (Paraiya?) at the end' (Chengama, AD 1258), or by saying that if anyone goes against the pact, he will be degraded lower than other and low *jātis* (Valikandapuram, AD 1227), and that the wife of the person who does harm to the endowment will be given to a Pulaiyar (untouchable) who cuts grass for his horse (Valikandapuram, AD 1240). In the process of the absorption of new groups into local society, the boundaries of each group must have been demarcated and their relative positions decided, to a certain extent, on the basis of the pure/impure opposition of Brāhmaṇical ideology.

At the same time we can also recognize the people's antagonistic feelings against Brāhmaṇas, and probably against Brāhmaṇical ideology too. This is evident, for example, in the hatred shown in the Ratnagiri inscription examined above, which suggests taking out the eyes and cutting off the noses of Brāhmaṇas. Behind the formation of *iḍaṅgai/valaṅgai* groups in the twelfth and thirteenth centuries we may perceive the challenging idea that the people conceived of changing the Brāhmaṇical hierarchy by bifurcating the *jāti* groups horizontally into *iḍaṅgai* (left hand) and *valaṅgai* (right hand), though their own hierarchical arrangement of *jātis* in each group may betray this interpretation or show limitations in the efforts to realize the idea. Their challenge, if any, must have been made possible by their growing in political and economical power, but we should also recognize the effect of an orthodox ideology in this process of rearrangement of caste-hierarchy.

The third point I wish to touch on here is the Hocartian aspect of the caste system, namely, its political aspect, particularly the role played by local powers in *jāti* formation. While Dirks (1987, 1989) assigns the central role in caste formation to the king, Kotani and Tanabe pay more attention to local political power in this connection (Kotani 2002; Tanabe 2003; Tanabe 2005). As regards caste formation and the rearrangement of its hierarchy, seen in south India around the thirteenth century when the powerful kingdom disappeared, I also partially follow the line of argument put forward by Kotani and Tanabe, rather than that by Dirks.

The material relevant to the discussion on this point is once again inscriptions recording decisions made on some matters in a large assembly of various local groups. A Tittagudi inscription (*SII* VIII: 291, AD 1167, SA), recording the decision made in a large assembly of *chittiramēḻi-periyanāḍu* and *ainnūṟṟuvar*, states that for the worship and renovation expenses of a Viṣṇu temple in their locality the members should contribute a quantity of paddy and money annually in the following way: a *padakku* of paddy for each plough, a *kuṟuni* of paddy for each person, five *kāśu* of money for each of the garland sellers, two *kāśu* for each of low class servants (*kīḻ-paṇimakkaḷ*), and four *nāḻi* of oil for each family (*kuḍi*) of cowherds.

In this inscription, no member groups of either *chittiramēḻi-periyanāḍu* or *ainnūṟṟuvar* are enumerated, but the former was the organization of peasant groups, including Veḷḷāḷas and sometimes Brāhmaṇas too, and the latter was an organization of various merchant and artisan groups. The groups comprised by these organizations are often clubbed into some graded divisions[23] or seem to have been arranged hierarchically for enumeration, as seen in the above Kudumiyamalai inscription, which begins the list with Brāhmaṇa and ends with Paḷḷar. Considering this hierarchical arrangement of the groups and their allotment of contributory shares to their members, in some cases according to the profession and grade of the member groups, we may conclude that these supra-local and/or supra-community organizations did indeed exercise power in regulating *jāti* relations.

From the fact that contributory shares were basically decided on the basis of plough and person, we could also argue that there was an aspiration among the people who founded these organizations for an egalitarian society; yet the reverse may also be argued, from the mention of lower class servants, in this inscription: Further discussion on these three points, however, is beyond the scope of this study. We have to satisfy ourselves by saying that caste formation in the Tamil country around the thirteenth century opened an arena where the ruling and the ruled and traditional ideology and a renovating ideology vied with each other for hegemony. The emergence of new kinds of imprecations in inscriptions reveals this confrontation.[24]

Acknowledgements

I am grateful to Professors G. Yamazaki, Y. Subbarayalu, and A. Tanabe, who kindly went through the draft of this paper and gave useful suggestions for improvement, and also to Directors of Epigraphy, Archaeological Survey of India, who kindly permitted me to read unpublished inscriptions preserved in their office in Mysore.

Abbreviations

Cb= Coimbatore, Cg= Chingleput, NA= North Arcot, Nl= Nellore, Pd= Pudukkottai, SA= South Arcot, Tj= Thanjavur, Tp= Tiruchirapalli.

[23] In the Sarkar Periyapalaiyam inscription (*Avanam* 6/12: AD 1289, Cb), for example, two soldier groups are categorised as 'our sons' (*nammakkaḷ*), indicating their subordinate position. On this division, see also Karashima and Subbarayalu (2002: 82).

[24] No change has been made in the text completed in 2004, but a few articles published afterwards have been added to Footnotes and References.

References

Annual Report on (South) Indian Epigraphy (*AR*), relevant volumes (New Delhi: Archaeological Survey of India).

Corpus Inscriptionum Indicarum (*CII*), relevant volumes (New Delhi: Archaeological Survey of India).

Dirks, Nicholas B. (1987), *The Hollow Crown: Ethnohistory of an Indian Kingdom* (Cambridge: Cambridge University Press).

——— (1989), 'The Original Caste: Power, History and Hierarchy in South Asia', *Contributions to Indian Sociology*, Vol. 23, No. 1, pp. 55–77.

Inden, Ronald B. (1976), *Marriage and Rank in Bengali Culture: A History of Caste and Clan in Middle Period Bengal* (Berkeley: University of California Press).

——— (1990), *Imagining India* (Oxford: Basil Blackwell).

Inscriptions (Text) of the Pudukkottai State Arranged According to Dynasties (*IPS*), (first edn 1929, published by Pudukkottai State).

Karashima, Noboru (1984), *South Indian History and Society: Studies from Inscriptions* AD *850–800* (New Delhi: Oxford University Press).

——— (1992), *Towards a New Formation: South Indian Society under Vijayanagar Rule* (New Delhi: Oxford University Press).

——— (1996), 'South Indian Temple Inscriptions: A New Approach to Their Study', *South Asia: Journal of South Asian Studies*, New Series, Vol. 19, No. 1, pp. 1–12.

———, ed. (2002), *Ancient and Medieval Commercial Activities in the Indian Ocean: Testimony of Inscriptions and Ceramic-sherds* (Tokyo: Taisho University).

——— (forthcoming), 'Commercialisation of Pāḍikāval seen in the 13th and 14th-century Pudukottai inscriptions.'

Karashima, N. and Y. Subbarayalu (2002), 'Ainnurruvar: A Supra-local Organization of South Indian and Sri Lankan Merchants' in N. Karashima (ed.), *Ancient and Medieval Commercial Activities in the Indian Ocean* (Tokyo: Taisho University).

——— (2004), 'The Emergence of the Periyanadu Assembly in South India during the Chola and Pandyan Periods', *International Journal of Asian Studies*, Vol. 1, No. 1, pp. 87–103.

Karashima, N., Y. Subbarayulu and P. Shanmugam (2008), 'Nagaram during the Chola and Pandyan Period: Commerce and Towns in the Tamil Country', AD 850–1350', *The Indian Historical Review*, Vol. 35, No. 1, pp. 1–33.

Kotani, Hiroyuki (2002), *Western India in Historical Transition: Seventeenth to Early Twentieth Centuries* (New Delhi: Manohar).

Sircar, D.C. (1965), *Indian Epigraphy* (Delhi, Motilal Banarsidass).

South Indian Inscriptions (*SII*), relevant volumes (New Delhi: Archaeological Survey of India).

Subbarayalu, Y. (2001a), 'Arasus of the Pudukkottai Region and the Nayaka System' in Kenneth R. Hall (ed.), *Structure and Society in Early South India: Essays in Honour of Noboru Karashima* (New Delhi: Oxford University Press).

——— (2001b), 'Inscriptions as Sources for History', in Francois Grimal (ed.), *Les Sources et le Temps (Sources and Time):* A Colloqium, Pondicherry, January 1997 (Pondicherry: Institut Fracais de Pondicherry and Ecole Francaise d'Extreme-Orient), pp. 229–241.

Subrahmaniam, T.N., ed. (1966), *Thirty Pallava Copper Plates* (*TPCP*) (Chennai: Tamil Varalatru Kazhagam).

Talbot, Cynthia (2001), *Precolonial India in Practice: Society, Region, and Identity in Medieval Andhra* (New York: Oxford University Press).

Tanabe, Akio (2003), 'The Sacrificer State and Sacrificial Community: Kingship in Early Modern Khurda, Orissa, Seen Through a Local Ritual' in G. Berkemer and Margret Frenz (eds), *Sharing Sovereignty. The Little Kingdom in South Asia* (Berlin: Klaus Schwarz Verlag Berlin).

——— (2005), 'The System of Entitlements in Eighteenth-century Khurda, Orissa: Reconsideration of 'Caste' and 'Jajmani System' in Pre-colonial India', *Journal of South Asian Studies*, Vol. 28, No. 3, pp. 345–85.

Thangavelu, G. and I. Thiyagarajan (1990), *History of Sambuvarayar* (*HS*) (in Tamil) (Madras: Gopalanarayanan Memorial Educational Trust).

Conflict and Conversion

Religious Trends in Early Medieval India

D.N. Jha

It is proclaimed often and loudly that, unlike Christianity and Islam, Hinduism is a tolerant and non-proselytizing religion; and this idea receives an easy popular acceptance. The present paper argues just the opposite of this proposition, focusing on some trends in early medieval Indian religious history. It examines the evidence, especially early medieval literary and epigraphic material, to show just how wrong this perception is. Looking at instances of theological antagonism as well as violent clashes between the different Brāhmaṇical sects as well as between them and the heterodox religions Buddhism and Jainism, it seeks to suggest that sectarian rivalries may have led to a process of religious conversion and transformation.

I

The idea that Hinduism is a tolerant religion is rooted to a certain extent in European writings on India. Thus Francois Bernier, the French doctor who travelled widely in India during the 1660s, stated that Hindus 'did not claim that their law is universal' (Halbfass 1990: 407). Similarly, Herder (1744–1803), the forerunner of the Romantic glorification of India, referred to the Hindus as 'mild' and 'tolerant' and as 'the gentlest branch of humanity'; and Immanuel Kant (1724–1804) said that they 'do not hate the other religions but they believe they are also right' (ibid.). Such views find a more prominent place in the writings of Orientalists like William Jones, according to whom 'the Hindus . . . would readily admit the truth of the Gospel but they contend that it is perfectly consistent with their Sastras' (Marshall 1970: 245). In the nineteenth century, religious reformers emphasized the idea of tolerance in Hinduism. For example, Vivekananda (1863–1904) picked up the famous Ṛgvedic statement '*ekamsad viprā vahudhā vadantī*' to support his vision that 'India alone [was] to be . . . the land of toleration' – a vision which, in reality, did not conform to his view that 'all creeds may be equal but Hinduism [was] more equal' and to his projection of Hinduism as a 'standard by which to measure both the theological and philosophical content as well as the histories of the other religions' (Brekke 2002: 41–42). The Ṛgvedic quote, which has been 'milked for all its worth' since the time of Vivekananda, has become a cliché, and his prophecy itself, if seriously meant, has repeatedly been shown to be ill-founded.

Even so, the supposedly tolerant nature of Hinduism has been the subject of considerable debate in academic circles in the twentieth century. Paul Hacker, for example, used the word 'inclusivism' in his discussion of tolerance/intolerance in Indian religions and considered it exclusively an Indian phenomenon (Hacker 1957: 167–79; 1983: 11–28). Others like J.W Hauer (1961: 90ff.) and Karl-Heinz Golzio (1990: 89–102) have, however, questioned his views – Golzio, in fact, refers to the statement of the Dvaita philosopher Madhva (AD 1199–1278) according to whom the king should punish those who are against the Vaiṣṇavas (ibid.: 92). During the period of the Indian freedom struggle the supposed inclusive and tolerant nature of Hinduism was emphasized by many leaders, important among them being Jawaharlal Nehru and Mahatma Gandhi. While according to the former 'its essential spirit seems to be to live and let live' (Nehru 1947: 75), according to the latter Hinduism is a ceaseless search for truth and is the most tolerant of all religions. This understanding of Hinduism has elicited conflicting responses from the scholarly community. Scholars such as the late Nirad C. Chaudhuri (1965: 39) virtually ruled out the idea of religious tolerance and asserted that 'if the familiar words about the tolerance and capacity for synthesis were true, one would be hard put to it to explain why there are such deep suspicions and enmities among the human groups in India'. On the other hand, there are many historians and social scientists who have emphasized the inclusive character of Hinduism. The influential literature generated by them in recent years, most notably by Amartya Sen (2005: 3–33), has glorified religious tolerance and inclusiveness in early India.

It is true that religious sects in early India, especially in the early medieval period, showed a certain degree of mutual accommodation, and one may offer several examples to illustrate this process. Thus, judging from the Purāṇic evidence, much of which belongs to the early medieval period or even later, the Buddha, founder of a heretic religion, emerged as an *avatāra* of Viṣṇu around the middle of the sixth century AD (Hazra 1975: 41–42; O'Flaherty 1988: 187–88, 204–11) and figured as such even in several later sources including the *Daśāvatāracarita* of Kṣemendra and *Gītagovinda* of Jayadeva (Hazra 1975: 41; Chakrabarti 2001: 153). Similarly, Ādinātha (Ṛṣabha), the first *Tīrthaṅkara* of another heretic religion, Jainism, was accepted as an incarnation of Viṣṇu in the *Bhāgavatapurāṇa* (Jaini 2000: 325–49). Although sacrifice to the Buddha was recommended for worshippers desirous of beauty (*rūpakāmo yajed buddhaṃ*) (*Varāhapurāṇa* 48.22) and a way was thus opened for Brāhmaṇa priests to officiate at Buddhist temples (Jaini 2001: 90), it is forgotten that Śiva is believed to have appeared on earth in the form of Śaṅkara to combat the Buddha *avatāra* (O'Flaherty 1988: 208–09). Likewise, the acceptance of Ṛṣabhanātha as an *avatāra* of Viṣṇu was an effort at Vaiṣṇavising a Jain deity and an ingenious, albeit unsuccessful, 'drive towards the syncretism of the two rival faiths' (Jaini 2000: 343–44). Further, the Vedāntist philosopher Mādhava Ācārya (fourteenth century) is often said to have displayed an exemplary tolerance of opposing points of view in his *Śarvadarśanasaṃgraha* (Collection of All Systems), which begins by presenting the school of Cārvākas, criticizes it and ends with Śaṅkara's Advaita 'as the conclusion and crown of all philosophical systems' (Grimes 2005: 539). But scholars have missed out on the fact that this was in keeping with the traditional practice of presenting the opponent's view before refuting it. Similar examples are available from subsequent periods as well. The Muslim sect of Imam Shahis believed that the Imam was himself the tenth *avatāra* of Viṣṇu and that the Quran was a part of the *Atharvaveda* (Ivanow 1936: 19–70). Christ was sometimes included in the incarnations of Viṣṇu (Danielou 1964: 12), just as Queen Victoria was accepted as a Hindu goddess when a plague broke out in Mumbai following an insult to her statue by some miscreants (Hopkins 1913: 314). It is missed, in all this, that neither the Imam, nor Christ, nor Victoria occupied an important place in the Brāhmaṇical scheme of things.

II

Even if we accept these instances as evidence of Brāhmaṇism giving space to heterodoxies, there are valid reasons and much historical data, especially from the early medieval period onwards, to question the view that India has been a land of religious tolerance and that the large number of sects covered by the umbrella term 'Hinduism' have stood for non-violence. Apart from the fact that a religion with a caste system and untouchability as characteristic features was and is inherently incapable of promoting tolerance, sources indicate antagonism between the various Brāhmaṇical sects as well as between Brāhmaṇism, which accepted the Vedic authority, and the heterodox non-Brāhmaṇical sects, which rejected it. Thus the legend of Dakṣa, which evolved from the *Ṛgveda* through Brāhmaṇa literature to the *Mahābhārata* and further to the early medieval Purāṇas, has been interpreted by scholars as a saga of conflict between Vaiṣṇavism and Śaivism (O'Flaherty 1975: 118; Bhattacharji 2000: 124). It has also been construed as evidence of the struggle between the two cults over a holy place called Kanakhala (near Haridwar), which is highly spoken of in the *Mahābhārata*, and access through which to the river Ganga during the Kumbhamela was given much importance by their adherents.

The Purāṇic and other early Indian texts are, in fact, unambiguous about the Śaiva–Vaiṣṇava antagonism. The *Viṣṇupurāṇa* (I.9.56) claims the superiority of Viṣṇu over Brahmā and Śiva, and the *Kūrmapurāṇa* considers the various Śaiva sects – Bhairavas, Kāpālikas, Vāmas – as deserving censure for deluding the world (Gonda 1976: 92–93). Similarly, the *Varāhapurāṇa* devotes two chapters to a negative portrayal of the Śaiva sect of the Pāśupatas (Gonda 1976: 92–93; 196 note 55), and the *Padmapurāṇa* (6.234.27) makes the general statement that even a Brāhmaṇa is a *pāṣaṇḍa* if he is not a Vaiṣṇava (*avaishnas tu yo viprah sa pāṣaṇḍaḥ prakīrtitah*) – an exclusivist position supported by the *Vṛddhahārita*, a medieval legal text, according to which a Vaiṣṇava reciting a *mantra* received from a non-Vaiṣṇava guru will be cooked in the fire of hell for millions of years

(Gonda 1976: 93). The *Śaṅkaradigvijaya* recalls a meeting between Mādhava and Śaṅkara, accompanied respectively by the king Sudhanvan and the Kāpālikas. The Kāpālika preceptor reproached the philosopher Mādhava for not worshipping Bhairava, leading to a fight between king Sudhanvan and the Kāpālikas, who were all killed (Gonda 1976: 196–97). Some early medieval legal authorities even prescribed purificatory rites for those touching a Śaiva or entering a Śaiva or Buddhist temple (Gonda 1976: 92–93; Kane 1974: 168–69). The Vaiṣṇava aversion to the Śaivas is evident from the practice that a 'good' Vaiṣṇava would not use even the common word 'to sew' (*siv*) because it resembled the name of Śiva – a practice that has prevailed among Vaiṣṇavite families until recently (Gonda 1976: 196, n. 58).

The Śaivas seem to have reciprocated in full measure. They sometimes regarded Viṣṇu as a sorcerer (Meinhard 1928: 38, cited in Gonda 1976: 196 n. 8); and the *Saurapurāṇa* (3.6) seeks to prove the superiority of Śiva, who gave the *sudarśanacakra* to Viṣṇu. The *Padmapurāṇa* extols the worship of Vāsudeva in one place but discourages it strongly at another, and states, let not the name of Viṣṇu ever be pronounced (Rocher 1986: 22). The followers of Śaṅkara 'opposed and persecuted' the Vaiṣṇava philosopher Madhu/Madhva (O'Flaherty 1988: 209), and in two chapters the *Saurapurāṇa* bitterly attacks him and describes him 'as a Charvaka, a most malignant, disguised promulgator of the defamation of Śiva' and his followers as 'wicked creatures . . . *mlecchas*, śūdras' (Rocher 1986: 20–21).

Important evidence of Śaiva intolerance and fanaticism is found in the attitude of the Coḷa ruler Kulottunga II, who removed the statue of Viṣṇu from the courtyard of the Chidambaram temple (Sastri 1975: 644–45) and also in the story of the twenty Śaiva priests committing suicide to protest the introduction of Vaiṣṇavite symbols in it (Gonda 1976: 196, n. 57). This fits in with the story of the persecution of Rāmānuja (1017–1137), who, according to the conventional account, was forced to withdraw from Srirangam (Tamilnadu) in 1098 and take his activities to Mysore (Karnataka) for nearly twenty-five years (Sastri 1975: 644; Sastri 1987: 432); and there is the story of the bigoted Coḷa king who ordered the eyes of one of his disciples to be put out (Gonda 1976: 196, n. 49).

Śaiva malice towards the Vaiṣṇavas is evident from an epigraph of 1160 which records the decision of the *mahāsabhā* of Tirukkaḍaiyur that the property of a Śaiva who engaged in social interaction with the other group would be forfeited and made over to the local temple (257 of AR 1925, cited in Sastri 1975: 645). So great was the enmity that a Vaiṣṇava Nāgā, according to one tradition, took a vow not to eat without killing at least one Śaiva monk, and a Śaiva in turn swore never to eat unless he had slain one Vaiṣṇava (Klostermaier 1990: 335; Ghurye 1964: 177). According to another tradition, two Gosain leaders had taken a vow to slay two Vairāgīs daily before tasting food (Orr 1940: 86). The most unambiguous example of religious intolerance is, however, provided by a Vīraśaiva hagiographical text which tells how a Vedāntist was humiliated by Bāsava at the court of Bijjala and how a Vedic scholar was ridiculed by the Liṅgāyats, who had the Vedas recited by dogs (Nandi 2000: 485, n. 47).

The Śaiva–Vaishnava hostility was evident among the lower social ranks as well. An eighteenth-century Tamil work, for example, describes how in a quarrel the Śaiva and Vaiṣṇava wives of a low-caste man dragged their gods in a most unseemly manner (Jesudasan and Jesudasan 1961: 246; Gonda 1976: 94). Similarly, in the nineteenth century J.A. Dubois refers to 'numerous troops of religious mendicants and vagabonds always ready to provoke each other and to hurl gross and obscene abuse at each other's heads' (Gonda 1976: 94). It may not be far from the truth to suggest that these 'mendicants and vagabonds' included members of higher as well as lower castes and that different social segments were involved in the Śaiva–Vaiṣṇava conflicts.

III

While instances of the Śaiva–Vaiṣṇava hostility in the early medieval and subsequent centuries can be multiplied to almost any degree, early Indian sources provide plentiful evidence of conflict between Brāhmaṇism and the heterodox sects. Early testimony comes from the Jain canonical text, *Āyārāṅga-suttam* (XXII, II.3.1.10), according to which Jain monks hid themselves during the day and travelled by night lest they be suspected of being spies. Similarly, the *Arthaśāstra* of Kauṭilya contemptuously describes the followers of non-Vedic sects such as *Vṛṣala* or *pāṣaṇḍa* (?) (for example, Śākyas, Ājīvikas), assigns them residence at the end of, or near the cremation ground (*pāṣaṇḍacaṇḍālānām śmasānānte vāsaḥ*) and prescribes a heavy fine for inviting them to dinners in honour of the gods and the manes (II.4.23; III.20.16).

The word *pāṣaṇḍa* in the edict of Asoka 'is not necessarily pejorative', because he appointed *dharmamahāmātras* to look after the affairs of not only the Buddhist Sangha, the Brāhmaṇas and Ājīvikas, but also 'some other religious sects' (*pāṣaṇḍesu*). Tolerance of dissenting faiths, which was the hallmark of Aśoka's policy, is not seen, however, in subsequent times. The celebrated grammarian Patañjali (second century BC) observed that 'the Śramaṇas and Brāhmaṇas are "eternal enemies" like the snake and the mongoose (*virodhaḥ śāśvatikaḥ*)' (*Mahābhāṣya* 2.4.9; Jaini 2001: 337). The Buddhist work *Divyāvadāna* (of the third–fourth centuries) describes Puṣyamitra Śuṅga as a great persecutor of Buddhists who not only destroyed their stupas but also announced a prize of one hundred *dīnār* for every head of a Śramaṇa (*Divyāvadāna* 1886: 433–44).

Brāhmaṇical animosity towards Buddhism and Jainism seems to have intensified in the early medieval period, as is evident from the textual evidence of theological antagonism and the persecution of their adherents. Uddyotakara (seventh century) refuted the Buddhist logicians Nāgārjuna and Dignāg, and his arguments were further reinforced by Vācaspati Miśra (ninth century). Udayana, another anti-Buddhist logician and the founder of the Navya Nyāya school, launched a sharp attack on the atheistic thesis of Buddhism in his *Ātmatattvaviveka*, a text also known as the *Bauddhadhikāragrantham* on account of its outright rejection of the ideas of Buddhists. He also demolished the ideas of the Saugatas, Digambaras, Cārvākas, Mīmāṃsakas and Sāṃkhyas in his *Kusumānjaliprakaraṇa*, which he wrote as a commentary on his own work *Nyāyakusumānjali* (Thakur 1964: 72).

Outside the school of Nyāya, several Brāhmaṇical thinkers attacked Buddhism and Jainism. For example, Kumārila Bhaṭṭa (eighth century), the south Indian dialectician, rejected the views of all unorthodox religious movements, especially Buddhism and Jainism, because, according to him, whatever is contradicted by a Vedic statement has to be rejected. He goes to the extent of saying that the heterodox sects 'are like ungrateful and alienated children who refuse to acknowledge what they owe to their parents' because they 'use the [Vedic] idea of *ahimsā* as an instrument of their anti-Vedic propaganda'. Śaṅkara, Kumārila's younger contemporary, is even more rigid and uncompromising. He categorically rejects all traditions outside the Vedas, including those of the Bhāgavatas or Pañcarātrins, and accuses the Buddha of 'incoherent prattling (*asambaddhapralāpitvāpitvā*) or even deliberately and hatefully leading mankind into confusion. . . .' (Halbfass 1991: 57, 59, 61, 95–96). Similarly, while an inscription dated 1035 (*EI* V: 227) describes a Śaiva temple priest (Lakulīṣapaṇḍita [?] by name) as 'a submarine fire in the ocean of Buddhists' (*bauddhābdhi_baḍavāmukham*), Madhusūdana Sarasvatī, the sixteenth-century Bengali commentator of the *Bhagvadgītā*, tells us that the teachings of the materialists and the Buddhists *et al.* are like those of the Mlecchas and excludes them from his consideration (Halbfass 1990: 361).

The attitude of the orthodox philosophers found an echo in the Purāṇic texts as well. According to the *Devīpurāṇa*, Buddhists were a symbol of evil, the right of whom could result in disaster; and their appearance even in dreams was inauspicious (Chakrabarti 2001: 149). The denigration of dissenting faiths was extended to Jains, Kāpālikas, and Cārvākas, as is evident from a passage of the *Devībhāgavatapurāṇa* (ibid.: 149, 163 n. 152). The *Saurapurāṇa* (64.44; 38.54) says that the Buddhists, Jains and Cārvākas should not be allowed to settle in a kingdom (Chakrabarti 2001: chapter IV; Sircar 1971: 183–205).

Similarly, early medieval literary texts provide highly negative portrayals of these groups. The *Mattavilāsa Prahasana*, a farce written by the Pallava ruler Mahendravarman (seventh century), depicts Buddhists as morally depraved, dishonest and the scum of the earth. A corrupt Buddhist monk is made to ask, 'Why did [the Buddha] not think of sanctioning the possession of women and the drinking of *surā* (*kinnukhalu strīparigrahaḥ surāpānavidhānam ca na dṛṣṭam*)?' (*Mattavilāsa Prahasana* 1973: 48). The *Prabodhacandrodaya*, a drama written by Kṛṣṇa Miśra (eleventh century), describes both Buddhism and Jainism as *tāmasika* (arising out of darkness), depicts a Buddhist monk as indulging in worldly pleasures (Act III, vs. 9) and a Jain monk as naked, devoid of manliness (*nivīrya*), the hair of his head plucked out and carrying a peacock feather in his hand (Nambiar 1998: 44–45); and it speaks of a battle between good and evil in which Buddhists, Jains, *pāṣaṇḍas* (heretics) and materialists (*Lokāyatas*) were defeated and all the anti-Vedic schools were 'uprooted by the sea of the Vedic thoughts' (ibid.: 126).

The heterodox sects did not lag behind in their own denunciation of Brāhmaṇical literature and thought. The Jain logician Akalaṅka (seventh–eighth centuries) was full of scorn for the Vedic animal sacrifice, and the famous scholar Hemacandra (twelfth century) dubbed Manu's verses supporting ritual violence as a part of *himsāśāstra.* In the seventh century the Jain commentator Jinadāsa described Maheśvara (Śiva) as 'the son of a nun who had been magically impregnated by a wizard seeking a suitable repository for his powers' (Dundas 1992: 201); and in the sixteenth century the *Pāṇḍavapurāṇas,* which are the Jainized version of the *Mahābhārata,* show Viṣṇu in a negative light and portray Kṛṣṇa as 'scheming and selfish' (Jaini 2000: 353; cf. Dundas 1992: 200–206). While the Jain sources are replete with hostile statements about the Brāhmaṇical sects, they frequently refer to great Jain teachers defeating Buddhists in debate (Dundas 1992: 206–08), and the famous Jain philosopher Haribhadra (eighth century) critiques Buddhism and Vedanta. The hostility of the Jains towards the Buddhists is also borne out by their appropriation of the caves of the latter (Bhattacharya 1998: 204).

Similarly, the Buddhist contempt for Brāhmaṇism was never a secret. As is well known, the Buddha himself described the three Vedas as 'foolish talk' and 'a waterless desert', and their wisdom as 'a pathless jungle' and 'a perdition' (*Dīghanikāya* 1967, Vol. I: 240). In early medieval times, the Buddhist hostility towards Brāhmaṇism and other religions like Jainism became sharp. At a theoretical level this is evident from works like the *Tattvasaṃgraha* of Śāntarakṣita (eighth century) who critically reviewed Nyāya, Mīmāṃsā, Sāṃkhya and Jain philosophies from the Buddhist point of view (Jha 2006: 34, n. 174). Buddhists disdained the Brāhmaṇical deities and treated them, especially the Śaiva ones, as subordinate to and even servants of the Buddhist gods and goddesses. They are thus often portrayed in some early medieval sculptures as being trampled upon (Sharma 1970: 655–66). Evidence of Buddhist and Jain antipathy towards Śaivism, however, appears to be less voluminous in comparison to the copious references to Śaiva hostility towards the heterodox sects. So fierce was the opposition of the Śaivites to the heterodox sects that they possibly went to extent of destroying Buddhist and Jain literary works. There is much substance in the view that religious fanaticism explains the disappearance of important Buddhist works like the *Kuṇṭalakeci* and the *Vimpicārakatai* and of Jain works like the *Vaḷaiyāpati* and the Jain *Rāmāyaṇa,* and even the wilful destruction of the Tamil Siddha corpus by the orthodox Śaivas (Zvelebil 1992: 46–7).

The Brāhmaṇical *odium theologicum* and the invective against Buddhists and Jains were not empty words; their persecution from around the middle of the first millennium is amply borne out by the early medieval sources. Hsüan Tsang states that the Gauḍa king Śaśānka, a contemporary of Harṣavardhana, cut down the Bodhi tree at Gaya and removed the statue of the Buddha from the local temple. He also tells us that the Huṇa ruler Mihirakula, a devotee of Śiva, destroyed 1,600 Buddhist stupas and monasteries and killed thousands of Buddhist monks and laity (Beal 1969: 171–72). This is corroborated by Kalhaṇa (eleventh century), who makes a reference to the persecution of Buddhists by a Kashmir king in the earlier period. Although the references to the plunder and destruction of temples found in the *Rājataraṅgiṇī* (I.140–44) of Kalhaṇa relate generally to the royal greed for wealth, some of them are certainly indicative of hostility towards the Buddhists. An early example of this is the destruction of a Buddhist *vihāra* by Aśoka's son Jalauka, who was a Śaivite.

Important evidence of the persecution of Buddhists in Kashmir belongs to the reign of the king Kṣemagupta (AD 950–58), who destroyed the Buddhist monastery Jayendravihāra at Śrīnagara and used its ruins in constructing a temple called Kṣemagaurīśvara (VI.171–73). In Uttar Pradesh, forty-seven deserted sites of fortified towns in Sultanpur district, we are told, are ruins of Buddhist cities destroyed by fire when Brāhmaṇism won its final victory over Buddhism (Yadava 1973: 346). Some Purāṇic passages and inscriptions from northern India also provide evidence of persecution. A Tibetan tradition has it that the Kalacuri king Karṇa (eleventh century) destroyed many Buddhist temples and monasteries in Magadha, and the Tibetan text *Pag-sam-jon-zang* refers to the burning of the library of Nalanda by some 'Hindu fanatics' (Yadava 1973: 346), not by Bakhtiyār Khalji as is commonly believed. An interesting example of antagonism to Buddhists comes from south India. The Vaiṣṇava poet-saint Tirumankai, according to a thirteenth century Ālvār text, stole a large gold image of the Buddha from a *stūpa* at Nagapattinam and had it melted down for reuse in the temple which he was commissioned by the god Viṣṇu himself to build (Davis 1999: 83).

IV

While all this points to hostility towards Buddhists, there is much more evidence of antipathy towards and persecution of Jains, especially from south India, where proponents of devotional Śaivism (Nāyanārs) and Vaiṣṇavism (Alvars) consistently portrayed them as hated 'others' from the sixth–seventh centuries onwards. Evidence of this is available from the *Tevāram* (tenth century), a collection of hymns attributed to the three early and prominent Nāyanār saint-poets. Two of them, Appar (seventh century) and Sambandar (seventh century), denigrated the Jains in abusive language. Appar speaks of them as the 'shameless Jain monks', 'naked Jains who fast by night', 'wicked monks who eat in barbaric ways', 'the weak and filthy Jains with their yellowing teeth'. Sambandar's denunciation of the Jains is in no better language. He refers to them as 'mad Jain monks who wear mats, and pluck their hair and eat their food standing' (Peterson 1998: 171). A vivid description of the encounter of these two Nāyanār saints with Jains is available from the twelfth century hagiography, the *Periyapurāṇam,* of Cekkilār. The most important and well known event mentioned in his narrative relates to how Sambandar defeated the Jains in all contests and succeeded in converting the Pāṇḍyan king of Madurai from Jainism to Śaivism, eventually leading to the impalement of eight thousand Jain monks.

Although there is no record of a massacre having taken place (Dundas 1992: 109–19; Davis 1998: 213–24), Śaiva intolerance towards the Jains is corroborated by several legends narrated in the *sthalapurāṇa* of Madura (Desai 1957: 82). Similarly, the conversion of the earliest known Jain cave temple in Tirunelveli district (Tamilnadu) into a Śaiva shrine in the seventh century (Thapar 1987: 17;

cf. Champakalakshmi 1978: 69–81), the portrayal of the scenes on the walls of the Kailashnath temple of Kanchipuram (Nandi 1986: 97) and those of the *maṇḍapam* of the Golden Lily tank of the Meenakshi temple at Madurai all bear testimony to the persecution suffered by the Jains in Tamilnadu.

In Karnataka, the Jains were a perpetual *bete noir* to the militant Śaivite Liṅgāyat sect which emerged in the twelfth century. The hagiographies of Bāsava furnish evidence of the slaughter of Jains (Narayana Rao 1990: 200–213), and the conversion of Jain temples at several places in Karnataka into Śaiva shrines and the vandalizing of Jain images are well documented (Thapar 1987: 18). A notable episode of the desecration of a Jain religious establishment, recorded in a Karnataka inscription as well as the *Cennabāsava Purāṇa*, took place in 1160 at Ablur when the Vīraśaiva Ekāntada Rāmayya defeated the Jains in debate, demolished their temple and built a shrine in honour of Vīra Somanātha which contains sculptured panels depicting scenes of his encounter with the Jains (*EI* V: No. 25, lines 69–80; Desai 1957: 182; Lorenzen 1978: 64–65). Their victimization became so severe that the Jains had to seek the intervention of the Vijayanagara ruling family in the fourteenth century. Yet the Vīraśaivas continued to persecute them in subsequent times. This is borne out by several sixteenth-century inscriptions from the Srisailam area of Andhra Pradesh, one of which tells us that a chief named Liṅga took pride in cutting off the heads of Śvetāmbara Jains (Desai 1957: 23). The Jains remained a hated lot until very late, and Dev Raj Chanana (1965: 65) cites a passage according to which one should not enter a Jain temple even under threat of being trampled upon by an elephant (*hastinā taḍyamāno pi na gacched jaina-mandiram*).

V

There is thus considerable evidence to show that the Brāhmaṇical sects did not routinely practise religious tolerance. On the contrary, the increasingly frequent portrayal of Brāhmaṇas as engaged in soldierly activities and as receiving military training implies their emergence as a militant group. References to arms-bearing Brāhmaṇas are found in several early Indian texts. Pāṇini (*c.* 500 BC) uses the word 'Brāhmaṇaka' for the country in which Brāhmaṇas adopted the military profession (*Aṣṭādhyāyī* IV.2.104), Kauṭilya refers to the recruitment of Brāhmaṇa soldiers (*Arthaśāstra* IX.2), and Patañjali (200 BC) speaks of a Śiva Bhāgavata as carrying an iron lance (*Mahābhāṣya* V.2.76).

Such references as these are plentiful in the early medieval period. Bāṇabhaṭṭa (seventh century), for example, describes the meeting of Puṣpabhūti with the ascetic Bhairavācārya and his three disciples who were valiant fighters and says how two of them became personal bodyguards of the king (Agrawal 1964: 56–60). Inscriptions testify to the fact that the early medieval ruling houses like the Candellas, Kalacuris, Cālukyas and Rāṣṭrakūṭas quite often employed Brāhmaṇa military officers (*EI* IV: 158; *IA* XXV: 205; *IHQ* 1928: 35). According to a record of AD 888, a Brāhmaṇa called Gaṇaramma laid down his life while defending his village during the reign of Kṛṣṇa III of the Rāṣṭrakūṭa dynasty (*EI* XIII: No. 15 [I], line 4), which had enlisted the service of several Brāhmaṇa generals (*EI*

XIII: No. 29, lines 9–13). The Coḷa rulers conferred the title *brahmādhirāja* on those Brāhmaṇas who distinguished themselves in battle (Mahalingam 1954: 263; Sastri 1975: 456, 465).

Brāhmaṇas continued to occupy important military positions in the subsequent period; Kopaṇṇa, a Brāhmaṇa general, is said to have been instrumental in extending Vijayanagara power into the Tamil countryside (Shulman 1985: 111). Rummaging through the sources, one gets the impression that the number of arms-bearing Brāhmaṇas increased in the early medieval period and that they came to enjoy much respect in society – which is in keeping with the disdain for temple priests often seen in the early medieval normative and narrative texts (Chattopadhyaya 1966: 58). Not surprisingly, it was during this period that the concept of *kṣatra-brāhmaṇa* received much attention from jurists.

The frequent mention of arms-bearing Brāhmaṇas is indicative of martial skills acquired through military education – a fact amply supported by the early medieval epigraphic evidence. According to an analysis of the inscriptional data the term *caṭṭa*, which occurs in inscriptions along with the word *bhaṭṭa*, stands for the Brāhmaṇas who received training in martial arts. The word *caṭṭa* found in a record from Parthivapuram (AD 866) has been interpreted to mean Brāhmaṇa students who were required not only to study the Vedic lore but also to receive military training in the centres called *śālai* attached to local Viṣṇu temples (Veluthat 1978: 102–15). Several similar temple-supported establishments existed in Kerala during the early medieval period, an important one being the Kāntalūrśālai, which became famous for its military role in the Coḷa-Cera conflict (Narayanan 1970: 125–36).

In the Cālukya and Pallava territories, the counterparts of *śālais* were called *ghaṭikā*, the most famous being the one at Kanchi. That the *śālais* and *ghaṭikā* imparted military education to Brāhmaṇas is borne out by literary texts from both north and south India. The Jain work *Kuvalayamālā* of Udyotanasūri (eighth century) describes a *maṭha* at Vijaya where students from different parts of India (Lāṭa, Karnāṭaka, Mālava, Kanauj, Mahārāṣṭra, Saurāṣṭra, Śrīkaṇṭha and Sindha) received instruction in such diverse subjects as archery (*dhanurveda*), manoeuvring with a shield (*phalakakrīḍā*), use of the sword and the bow (*asi dhanu praveśa*), fighting with a spear (*kuntayuddha*), fighting with clubs (*lakuṭi-yuddha*), fighting with arms (*bāhuyuddha*), etc. (Sharma 1996: 231). Similarly, several *maṇipravāla* texts, especially the *Candrotsavam* (fifteenth century) and the *Keralolpatti* (seventeenth century), indicate the association of Brāhmaṇas with martial arts. Somadeva (tenth century) in his *Kathāsaritasāgara* (LXXIV: 155; LXXIII: 69; LVI: 9) makes several references to Brāhmaṇas receiving military training. Thus Śrīdarśana, Mahīpāla and Akṣakṣapaṇaka are said to have acquired training in the use of weapons (Chattopadhyaya 1966: 52–9); and some celebrated heroes who figure in this work (for example, Guṇaśarmaṇa, Aśokadatta, Śaktidatta and Śrīdatta) as experts in the art of warfare also find mention in Kṣemendra's *Bṛhatkathāmañjarī* (Chattopadhyaya 1966: 52).

Similar evidence is available from the *Rājataraṅgiṇī* of Kalhaṇa (twelfth century) who refers to several brave Brāhmaṇa soldiers who died in battle (VII.675; VIII.1071, 1345, 3018). The practice of imparting military training to Brāhmaṇas led to the emergence of groups of them taking to arms for their livelihood, and to the growth of temple militias necessary for the protection of the wealth which the early medieval religious institutions acquired through land grants and other kinds of donations.

Martial training also paved the way for the emergence of the military ascetic orders of the Śaṅkara school, known as Dasanāmī Nāgās (Ghurye 1964: chapter VI) and organized around what are known as *akhāḍās*. Col. James Tod confirms the existence of numerous naked militant ascetics called *nāgās* throughout Rajputana before the thirteenth century, and J.N. Farquhar, who was one of the first to study militant asceticism, speaks of their presence throughout north India from at least the seventh century (Farquhar 1925a: 479–86; Farquhar 1925b: 431–52; Orr 1940: 81–100; Gross 1992: Chapter 2). Similarly Jadunath Sarkar, on the basis of a nineteenth-century Hindi manuscript, dates the establishment of the six armed bands or *akhāḍās* of the Dasanāmī Nāgās between AD 547 and AD 1146 (Sarkar 1958: 82–90; Lorenzen 1978: 69). While these dates are uncertain and call for a separate study, there is little doubt that they emerged as an important socio-religious factor in the early medieval period. Their counterparts, the militant Vaiṣṇava Nāgās, may have organized themselves around *akhāḍās* somewhat later.

In any case, contrary to the view of some scholars (Lorenzen 1978: 61–75; Pinch 1996: *passim*), the growth of these militant ascetic orders indicates the existence of warrior ascetics and soldier sadhus in India before the coming of Islam. They spawned antagonism and armed hostilities between the numerous Brāhmaṇical and non-Brāhmaṇical religions and between the various Brāhmaṇical sects in the early medieval and subsequent periods, when several instances of armed conflict between the Śaivas and Vaiṣṇavas are recorded. Jadunath Sarkar, on the basis of a traditional account, tells us that the Nāgā Sanyāsīs – Bhavānanda, Surasurānanda and Kamalānanda – inflicted a crushing defeat on the Vaiṣṇava Vairāgīs at Haridwar in 1266 and gained precedence in taking a bath at the Kumbhamela (Ghurye 1964: 103). The Śaiva and Vaiṣṇava Nāgās again fought at the same place in 1760, and this finally settled the issue of precedence in favour of the former (Klostermaier 1991: 112).

A large number of Vairāgīs were massacred at the Simhasta fair at Nasik in 1690 (Ghurye 1964: 178) and another open confrontation between the Śaiva Sanyāsīs and Vaiṣṇava Vairāgīs took place at Ayodhya, after the death of Aurangzeb, over control of religious places and pilgrims' fees and gifts (Sharma 2000: 14–15; Bakker 1986: 149). In fact there is evidence of regular battles between the Dasanāmīs and Vaiṣṇava Vairāgīs till as late as the nineteenth century. All this suggests that, like medieval Christianity and Islam, Brāhmaṇism and its various forms were intolerant and that this intolerance, often violent, may have received much sustenance from the martialization of the religious sects in the early medieval period. It is thus difficult to agree with the view that 'Hinduism' has 'a propensity to assimilate rather than to exclude' or that tolerance is the very essence of 'Hinduism *qua* Hinduism' (Sharma 1978: 145). Equally, to say that Islam brought violence to a land which until then had not known it, is to blind oneself to a mélange of available evidence.

VI

Several Brāhmaṇical and heterodox religious sects existed in India in the early medieval period before the coming of Islam. In this atmosphere of religious pluralism marked by competing soteriological perspectives, the Brāhmaṇical religious preceptors often tried to convert people to their own sects. Since the Brāhmaṇical sects – covered by the modern term 'Hinduism' – did not have a founder, a basic text or an organized monastic establishment, they may not have proselytized in the same manner as Christianity or Islam. But sources indicate that conversion was indeed practised in early times before as well as after the advent of Islam. As early as the later Vedic period, the *Tāṇḍya Brāhmaṇa,* also known as the *Pañcaviṃśa Brāhmaṇa,* describes the *vrātyastoma* sacrifice which the *vrātyas* (the people living outside the pale of the Brāhmaṇical religion) were required to perform for becoming eligible to have social interaction with the orthodox *Āryas* (Kane 1974: 385–89; Gonda 1977: 539, 641; Heesterman 1962–63: 2). First mentioned in the *Atharvaveda*, the *vrātyas* continued to figure in many post-Vedic texts. Some medieval works like the *Vrātyatāprāyaścitanirṇaya* and the *Vrātyatāśuddhisaṃgraha* provide for the purification of *vrātyas* even after twelve generations, though the latter states categorically that they can be admitted into Brāhmaṇical society only in accordance with prescribed purificatory methods (Choudhary 1964: 77).

Mention may also be made of the *dīkṣā* ceremony, generally understood in the sense of initiation or consecration, which 'implies death to profane existence, enables man to gain sacred knowledge and wisdom, a higher stage of existence and access to heavenly life' (Gonda 1965: 316). Without expatiating on the meaning and significance of this ceremony in the various ritual contexts, it may be pointed out that its importance in different Indian religions can hardly be exaggerated. In Vaiṣṇavism, for example, its main object is purification, without which an individual cannot be admitted to the religious order or community and cannot be allowed to read such texts as the *Rāmāyaṇa* or the *Śrībhāṣya* of Rāmānuja (Gonda 1965: 398, 402). The *Bhāgavatapurāṇa*, a fundamental Vaiṣṇava text, states that 'those desirous of *mokṣa* must put themselves under the care and guidance of a preceptor', just as the *Haribhaktivilāsa*, the basic text of the Caitanya movement, asserts that 'a man without *dīkṣā* is not entitled to worship, for the act of initiation destroys all sins and bestows divine knowledge' (Gonda 1965: 422, 427). Similarly, in Śaivism in Kashmir, *dīkṣā* is 'the most important method of attaining integral Śivahood'; and in Vīraśaivism it is mandatory for each member of the Vīraśaiva community because it opens the door of Vīraśaivism not only for members of the community but, more importantly, for non-Vīraśaivas seeking admission to the fold (Gonda 1965: 433; Sadasivaiah 1967: 104–106).

Thus, in some cases at least, *dīkṣā* may be treated as a precondition of conversion to a faith. Even if there are some differences of opinion about the nature and significance of this ritual (Heesterman 1962–63: 2), the practice of conversion in Śaivite sects seems to have been common, as can be inferred from a variety of sources: myths, religious texts, secular literature. Among the early myths the legend of Dakṣa Prajāpati implies religious conversion within the fold of Brāhmaṇism. It has many versions, but its core element is 'the conflict between the Vedic sacrificial religion and the Rudra-Śiva religion which . . . was reconceived into a conflict between Vaiṣṇavism and Śaivism' in the epics and in the Purāṇas, the latter belonging mostly to the early medieval and subsequent centuries. The climax of the story is represented by Śiva destroying the sacrifice performed by Dakṣa followed by the latter's realization of the superiority of the former and conversion to him (Klostermaier 1991: 110, 125, 128; Bhattacharji 2000: 124).

Besides, the actual conversion procedure is laid down in some texts. For example, the *Somaśambhūpaddhati*, a manual compiled by Somasambhū in the second half of the eleventh century (von Stietencron 1995: 51–81), prescribes a procedure called the *liṅgoddhāra* (conversion ritual), for conversion from other creeds to Śaivism by the ritual removal of earlier religious affiliation, the purpose of the conversion being the realization that without becoming a Śaiva salvation is unattainable (Michaels 2005: 20–21). Similarly, a Tāntric text called the *Kubjikā-nityāhnikatilaka* (AD 1197) mentions the conversion of nine Buddhists to the Kaula religion. When Śrīnātha alias Tūṣṇīśa alias Unmanīśanātha, the first of the ancient *gurus* of the Kubjikā school of Tantra, went to *gandharvaloka*, he was questioned by some Buddhists living there. He told them that he was a *siddha* (perfect) and possessed the supreme divine instruction (*divyajñānavaralabdhaka*), upon which the Buddhists laughed at him and challenged him to prove his statement. Śrīnātha, as the story goes, uttered the syllable 'HUM' and all the Buddhist monasteries collapsed. The monks then acknowledged his authority, and later he converted them (*Ṣaṭasāhasra Saṃhitā* 1982: 38; Goudrian and Gupta 1981: 149). Among the secular works, the *Prabodhacandrodaya* of Kṛṣṇa Miśra (eleventh century) depicts how, after an interesting conversation with a Buddhist and a Jain, and after offering them wine and women, a Kāpālika succeeds in converting them to Śaivism (Act III).

Several legends indicate that religious conversion may have been of central importance to the many *bhakti* saints and *gurus* who appeared on the religious scene with the development of the various devotional sects, especially in early medieval south India, and who were inspired by a strong zeal to convert the people to a life of spiritual surrender to the highest god. This is corroborated by the instances of conversion recorded in the early medieval Śaiva hagiographies. The twelfth-century *Periyapurāṇam* of Sekkilār tells us that the Nāyanār saint Appar was born in an orthodox Śaiva family of the Veḷḷāḷa community but became a Jain monk at an early age. Agitated, his elder sister sought Śiva's help. Appar was then afflicted with a serious abdominal disorder, which was cured not by the Jain physicians and their mantras but only by the grace and miracle of Śiva. The repentant Appar returned to the fold of his family faith. Enraged at this, the Jains brought charges against him before the Pallava king Mahendravarman, a Jain. Appar, however, succeeded in convincing the king of the truth of Śaivism, whereupon Mahendravarman himself became a Śaiva. Although the various assumptions underlying this narrative, related in the *Periyapurāṇam* five centuries after the events, have been rightly questioned (Davis 1998: 213–24), it is true that Appar and Mahendravarman changed their religions.

Sekkilār also gives an account of the encounter between another Śaiva saint, Sambandar, and the Jains. As the story goes, the queen and the minister of the Pāṇḍyan king invited Sambandar to Madurai to drive out the Jain monks who exercised a hold over the king. The saint went to Madurai, proved the superiority of his miracles over those of the Jains, and converted the king to Śaivism. The king later impaled 8,000 Jains. Like the story of the conversion of Mahendravarman, this may be a tall tale told by Sekkilār; but in neither of the two cases can the fact of conversion be questioned.

In addition to miracles, theological disputations also seem to have played a role in the spread of Brāhmaṇical religious and philosophical ideas. Of the many early medieval Indian philosophers to whom attention has been drawn, Śaṅkara (eighth century) was by far the most important. A peripatetic mendicant (*parivrājakācārya*), he travelled from place to place and engaged in debate with various sects like the Jains and the Buddhists and refuted their philosophies. He is also said to have converted some individuals to his Advaita philosophy. For instance, he won arguments with Viśvarūpa in Magadh and Maṇḍana in Prayag, the two disciples of the Mīmāṃsā philosopher Kumārila (Pandey 1994: 278–81, 342). Śaṅkara is also credited with the setting up of four, five or even six monastic establishments in different parts of the country for the mendicants following his doctrines. Despite the conflicting chronological sequence of their establishment, the Śaṅkarite monasteries, in all probability, played an important role in converting people, especially several centuries later under the Vijayanagara rulers whose generous patronage added wealth and feudal authority to their traditional religious prestige and influence (ibid.: 361). Śaṅkara's early disciples founded the Dasanāmī orders, to which they converted mendicants and ascetics. This receives corroboration from the *Nāradaparivrājakopaniṣad*, a medieval text which sets out in detail the way in which renouncers were to be converted or admitted to these groups (Ghurye 1964: 93; Chakraborti 1973: 58, 61, 119, 144).

Despite the fact that people could be converted by theological debate and disputation, the use of force in drawing people into Śaivite cults was not unknown. In a story related in the *Māghamāhātmya*, which claims to be part of the *Padmapurāṇa*, the Śaivas instigated the Kṣatriya king Citrasena of '*Draviḍa viṣaya*' to prohibit the worship of Viṣṇu in his kingdom, to persecute his devotees, and to have his images thrown into the ocean. As a result, many Vaiṣṇavas fled the country and those staying back became Śaivas (Hazra 1963: 362). One is also reminded of the legend about the battle between Khaṇḍobā, the principal non-Brāhmaṇa god of the Western Deccan, and the two demon brothers Malla and Maṇi preserved in the *Mallārimāhātmya*, which is part of the *Brahmāṇḍapurāṇa*. In this narrative, all of Malla's generals were defeated until only Maṇi was left. Maṇi too was defeated, and just as the sole of Khaṇḍobā's feet touched the head of this demon, he experienced a total change of heart (Stanley 1990: 271–98; cf. Sontheimer 1997: 208–35).

The most unambiguous evidence of forced conversion, however, comes from Karnataka and relates to the persecution of Jains by Vīraśaivas. According to a tradition supported by epigraphic evidence, large-scale conversions from Jainism to Vīraśaivism took place in Karnataka in the wake of Ekāntada Rāmayya's victory over the Jains (Desai 1957: 182–83), and these could not have been different from forced ones. The Vīraśaivas, in fact, engaged in conversion in a systematic manner; for the chief function of the monastery founded by Bāsava at Kalyana in 1156, as well as that of the five traditional Vīraśaiva monasteries established in the different parts of India after the twelfth century, was to convert people to Vīraśaivism (Sadasivaiah 1967: 88–89). Such testimony as cited above certainly indicates that the Brāhmaṇical sects forced people to convert, and one feels that Islam and Christianity have undeservedly earned the sole credit for such conversions.

While the evidence cited indicates that sometimes people were coerced to convert, there is also much to show that this was not always the case. The Purāṇas. most of which were composed in the early medieval and subsequent centuries, played a crucial role in changing the religion of the people in large parts of the country. As noted earlier, they launched bitter attacks on heterodox sects like Buddhism and Jainism, which engaged in proselytizing activities, as can be inferred from a passage of the *Viṣṇupurāṇa* (III.8) which tells us that the Buddha came to the earth in order to brainwash the *daityas* against the Vedas (Nath 2001: 195). The Purāṇas thus provided an ideological resistance to the conversion of people to non-Brāhmaṇical sects and were 'anxious to ensure that at least Brāhmaṇas did not become Buddhists which, they feared, would happen in the degenerate Kali age' (Chakrabarti 2001: 149) . But in resisting the heterodoxies they acted also as an instrument for the diffusion of Brāhmaṇical religious ideas among a variety of ethnic groups living in the peripheral areas (Nath 2001: chapter 8; Chakrabarti 2001: chapter 4). Thus, while the Purāṇas played a dual role, it does not seem to have been accompanied by the use of force.

The importance of the Purāṇas in the religious and cultural transformation of non-Brāhmaṇical people should be viewed in conjunction with the evidence from the large number of inscriptions which record gifts of land and other objects to temples and to priests. These give the unmistakable impression that the practice of making donations to priests and temples in peripheral areas became widespread in the early medieval period. As a result, Brāhmaṇa settlements mushroomed in different parts of the country and acquired a special significance in the economically backward regions inhabited by culturally marginalized tribal people. In these areas, the Brāhmaṇas, living as they did at a higher level of material existence, were able to disseminate their own world view, especially religious beliefs and practices rooted in the Purāṇas. The popularization of the Purāṇas and the practice of making land grants in the peripheral areas thus went hand in hand and acted as agents of religious transformation as well as of the integration of a large number of ethnic groups into Brāhmaṇical society. This is clear from the fact that the land charters often specified the donees' obligations, which included not only the teaching of Vedic lore but, more importantly, the performance of Brāhmaṇical rites and rituals which enabled them to make inroads into tribal society and religion. An interesting eighth-century inscription from the Raipur district in Chhattisgarh mentions two Śaiva ascetics, Sadyaḥśivācārya and Sadāśivācārya, and records the dedication of a temple to the latter and his spiritual successors along with several plots of black-soil land (*kṛṣṇatalā*) in different villages. It states that in return for the endowment, the ascetics were to arrange a free feeding house (*annasya sattram*), a sacrificial rite (*yāga*), the exposition of the Śaiva doctrine (*vyākhyāyaḥsamayasya*) and the ceremony of initiation (*dīkṣā*) into the Śaiva faith which was capable of securing salvation (*nirvāṇadakśa*) (Senkapat Stone Slab Inscription of the time of Sivagupta Balarjuna, vs. 15–22; Sastri 1995: 154–59). This inscription clearly indicates that land gifts were made to priests in the peripheral areas often with the specific purpose of transmitting religious beliefs and practices to tribal groups and converting them to Brāhmaṇical sects.

The growing hegemony of the Brāhmaṇas, who received donations of land and other objects in the economically backward areas, led not only to the drawing of various non-Brāhmaṇical groups into the Brāhmaṇical social and religious order through the dissemination of Purāṇic lore and other Brāhmaṇical ideas, but also to the appropriation and Brāhmaṇization of more and more of the tribal cults in different parts of the country. In Bengal, for example, Manasā was integrated into the Brāhmaṇical pantheon in the early phase of the Pāla rule; and in Orissa, Maṇināgeśvarī was elevated to a place of importance in the fifth–sixth centuries through royal donations just as Stambheśvarī, a goddess associated with the Śaulika tribe, was absorbed through the patronage of the Śulki rulers. In Tamilnadu the goddess Mīnākṣī was brought into the fold because of the patronage of the Pāṇḍya rulers and in Andhra Pradesh, Padmāvatī, a goddess with Tāntric affiliations, became important in the eighth century when a temple was built for her at Tirupati. Almost all the temples of the sixty-four *yoginīs* (the mother goddess in sixty-four forms) were built in the tribal belt of eastern Madhya Pradesh and Orissa during early medieval times, not to mention several other tribal deities who were drafted into the Tāntric Brāhmaṇical tradition (Jha 2004: 205). The conversion of tribal peoples and the Brāhmaṇization or Sanskritization of their cult deities has been going on till our own times. Scholars often prefer to describe this as acculturation, but in reality it is no different from conversion. The difference is that the former is a protracted process while the latter involves, at least ideally, an abrupt and total switching of religious loyalties.

Religious conversion, through choice and conviction or through coercion and cajolery, was practised by Brāhmaṇical sects in early India and may have received ideological support from normative texts, some of which give sanction to the conversion of those who voluntarily or under compulsion had given up the religions into which they were born. For example, the *Devalasmṛti* states that if Brāhmaṇas and members of other castes are carried off by Mlecchas and indulge in forbidden acts, they can be purified by the performance of appropriate penance (*prāyascitta*) (Kane 1974: 389–91). Its reconstructed text (Wadekar 1996) devotes one full chapter to *mlecchitaśuddhi* and lays down detailed procedure for the purification of those who were taken away by Mlecchas or stayed with them for five to twenty years. According to Devala and other early medieval lawgivers, anyone who had left his religion could be reconverted (Kane 1974: 391). Reconversion (*parāvartana*), equated with the ancient ritual of *Vrātyastoma* (Kane 1974: 118), was no different from conversion. There is nothing to show that the Mlecchas, as distinct from those who joined their ranks by pollution, were not allowed to convert to the Brāhmaṇical religions, because the word Mleccha remained a generic term for exclusion and stood for specific tribes or groups of tribes till as late as the fifteenth century, when it came to be used extensively for Muslims (Thapar 2000: 259). This idea of reconversion certainly anticipated the *śuddhi* movement led by the Arya Samaj. It is the same as the religious conversion supported by the Ramakrishna Mission, founded in 1897 by Vivekananda, who 'wished to flood the country of the Yankees with idolatrous missionaries' and had 'grandiose ideas of how the US and Europe could be converted . . . in a matter of decades' (Brekke 2002: 48; cf. Hacker 1978: 565–79). Nor, finally, does it differ from what is being aggressively pushed by the Vishwa Hindu Parishad and its affiliates in India and abroad.

In conclusion, it may be pointed out that one notices several important trends in the religious life of the people during the early medieval period. In the first place, there existed numerous religious sects in different parts of the country. Second, religious pluralism led to antagonism not only between the different Brāhmaṇical sects but also between them and the heterodox religions like Buddhism and Jainism. This resulted in theological and philosophical disputations and also in violent clashes between them. Third, the competing and antagonistic soteriologies inspired religious preceptors to convert people to their faiths. Brāhmaṇical sects were thus inherently intolerant, and they engaged in converting people during the early medieval period. All this does not deny the fact that religious sects borrowed a great deal from one another, leading to the growth of a composite culture over the centuries. But that is a different story.

References

Acārāṅgasūtra (1884), translated by H. Jacobi (Oxford: Sacred Books of the East Series).

Agrawal, Vasudev Sharan (1964), *Harśacarita: Ek Sāmskritik Adhyayan* (Patna: Bihar Rashtra Bhasha Parishad).

Ātmatattvaviveka by Udayanācārya (1995), translated by N.S. Dravid (Shimla: Indian Institute of Advanced Study).

Ayengar, N.S.R. (2000), *Gītagovindam, Sacred Profanities: A Study of Jayadeva's Gītagovinda* (original Sanskrit text with English translation) (Delhi: Penman Publishers).

Bakker, Hans (1986), *Ayodhyā* (Groningen: John Benjamins Pub. Co).

Beal, Samuel (1981), *Si-yu-ki: Buddhist Records of the Western World: translated from the Chinese of Hiuen Tsiang* (Delhi: Motilal Banarsidass).

Bhattacharji, Sukumari (2000), *The Indian Theogony* (New Delhi: Penguin Books).
Bhattacharya, Ranjana (1998), 'Religion in Early Medieval Gujarat (AD 600–1300)', PhD Thesis, Department of History, University of Delhi.
Brekke, Torkel (2002), *Makers of Modern Indian Religion in the Nineteenth Century* (New York: Oxford University Press).
Candrotsavam (1955), edited by E.P.N. Kunjan Pillai (Kottayam: National Book Stall).
Chakrabarti, Kunal (2001), *Religious Process: The Purāṇas and the Making of a Regional Tradition* (Delhi: Oxford University Press).
Chakraborty, Haripada (1973), *Asceticism in Ancient India* (Calcutta: Punthi-Pustak).
Champakalakshmi, R. (1978), 'Religious Conflict in the Tamil Country,' *Journal of the Epigraphical Society of India*, Vol. 4, pp. 69–81.
Chanana, Dev Raj (1965), 'The Sanskritist and Indian Society', *Enquiry*, New Series, Monsoon, Vol. 2, No. 2, pp. 49–67.
Chapple, Christopher Key and John Casey (2004), *Reconciling Yoga: Haribhadra's Collection of Views on Yoga with a new translation of Haribhadra's Yogadṛṣṭisamucca* (Albany: SUNY Press).
Chattopadhyay, Aparna (1966), 'Martial Life of Brāhmaṇas in Early Medieval India', *Journal of the Oriental Institute*, Vol. 16, pp. 52–59.
Chaudhuri, Nirad C. (1965), *The Continent of Circe* (London: Chatto and Windus).
Danielou, A. (1964), *Hindu Polytheism* (New York: Parthenon).
Daśāvatāracarita by Kṣemendra ([1891] 1983), edited by Pandit Durgaprasada and Kashinath Panduran Parab (Bombay: Kavyamala No. 26; [reprint] Delhi: Munshiram Manoharlal).
Davis, Richard. H. (1998), 'The Story of the Disappearing Jains: Retelling the Śaiva–Jaina Encounter in Medieval South India' in John Cort (ed.), *Open Boundaries: Jain Communities and Cultures in Indian History* (Albany: SUNY Press).
——— (1999), *Lives of Indian Images* (Delhi: Motilal Banarsidass).
Devīpurāṇa (BS 1384), edited and translated (into Bengali) by Tarkaratna Panchanan and Srijib Nyayatirtha (Calcutta: Navabharat Publishers).
Desai, P.B. (1957), *Jainism in South India and Some Jaina Epigraphs* (Sholapur: Jaina Samskriti Samrakshaka).
Dīgha Nikāya (1958), 3 Vols, edited by Bhikhhu Jagdish Kassap (Nalanda: Pali Publication Board, Bihar Goernment).
Divyāvadāna (1886), edited by E.B. Cowell and R.A. Neil (Cambridge: University Press).
Doniger O'Flaherty, Wendy (1970), 'The Origin of Heresy in Hindu Mythology', *History of Religions*, Vol. 10, No. 4, pp. 271–333.
——— (1975), *Hindu Myths* (Baltimore: Penguin).
——— (1983), 'The Image of the Heretic in the Gupta Purāṇas', in Bardwell L. Smith (ed.), *Essays on Gupta Culture* (Delhi: Motilal Banarsidass).
——— (1988), *The Origin of Evil in Hindu Mythology* (Delhi: Motilal Banarsidass).
Dundas, Paul (1992), *The Jains* (London & New York: Routledge).
Dvyāśrayakāvya by Hemacandra (1915–21), edited by Abhaya-Tilaka Gani and Abaji Vishnu Kathavate (Bombay: Government Central Press).
Epigraphia Indica (EI), relevant volumes (Delhi: Archaeological Society of India).
Farquhar, J.N. (1925a), 'The Organization of the Sannyasis of the Vedanta', *Journal of the Royal Asiatic Society*, July, pp. 479–86.
——— (1925b), 'The Fighting Ascetics of India', *Bulletin of the John Rylands Library*, Vol. 9, pp. 431–452.
Ghosh, A., ed. (1975), *Jaina Art and Architecture*, 2 Vols (Delhi: Bharatiya Jnanapith).
Ghurye, G.S. (1964), *Indian Sadhus* (Bombay: Popular Prakashan).
Golzio, Karl-Heinz (1990), 'Das Problem von Toleranz und Intoleranz in indischen Religionen anhand epigraphischer Quellen' in Helmut Eimer (ed.), *Frank-Richard Hamm Memorial Volume* (Bonn: Indica et Tibetica Verlag).
Gonda, J. (1965), *Change and Continuity in Indian Religion* (The Hague: Mouton & Co.).
——— (1976), *Viṣṇuism and Śivaism: A Comparison* (Delhi: Munshiram Manoharlal).
——— (1977), *The Ritual Sūtras* (Wiesbaden: Otto Harrassowitz).
Goudriaan, Teun and Sanjukta Gupta (1981), *Hindu Tāntric and Śākta Literature* (Wiesbaden: Otto Harrassowitz).

Grimes, John A. (2005), 'Darśana', in Sushil Mittal and Gene Thursby (eds), *The Hindu World* (New York & London: Routledge).

Gross, Robert Lewis (1992), *The Sadhus of India* (Jaipur: Rawat Publications).

Gundert, Herman, ed. (1961), *Keralolpatti* (Trivandrum: Balan Publications).

Hacker, Paul (1957), 'Religiose Toleranz und Intoleranz in Hinduism', *Saeculum*, Vol. 8, pp. 167–79.

——— (1978), 'Der religiose Nationalismus Vivekanandas', in L. Schmithausen (ed.), *Kleine Schriften* (Wiesbaden: Steiner).

Halbfass, Wilhelm (1990), *India and Europe: An Essay in Philosophical Understanding* (Delhi: Motilal Banarsidass).

——— (1991), *Tradition and Reflection: Exploration in Indian Thought* (Albany: SUNY Press).

Harśacarita by Bāṇa (1961), translated by E.B. Cowell and F.W. Thomas (Delhi: Motilal Banarsidass).

Hauer, J.W. (1961), *Toleranz und Intoleranz in den nichtchristlichen Religionen* (Stuttgart: W. Kohlhammer).

Hazra, R.C. (1958), *Studies in the Upapurāṇas*, Vol. 1 (Calcutta: Sanskrit College).

——— (1963), *Studies in the Upapurāṇas*, Vol. 2 (Calcutta: Sanskrit College).

——— (1975), *Studies in the Purāṇic Records on Hindu Rites and Customs* (Delhi: Motilal Banarsidass).

Heesterman, J.C. (1962–63), 'Vrātya and Sacrifice', *Indo-Iranian Journal*, Vol. 6, pp. 1–37.

Hopkins, E.W. (1913), 'The Divinity of Kings', *Journal of the American Oriental Society*, Vol. 51, No. 4, pp. 309–16.

Ivanow, W. (1936), 'The Sect of Imam Shah in Gujrat,' *Journal of the Bombay Branch of the Royal Asiatic Society*, Vol. 12, pp. 19–70.

Indian Antiquary (*IA*), relevant issues.

Indian Historical Quarterly (*IHQ*), relevant issues.

Jaini, P.S. (2000), *Collected Papers on Jaina Studies* (Delhi: Motilal Banarsidass).

——— (2001), *Collected Papers on Buddhist Studies* (Delhi: Motilal Banarsidass).

Jesudasan, C. and H. Jesudasan (1961), *A History of Tamil Literature* (Calcutta: YMCA Publishing House).

Jha, D.N. (2004), *The Early India: A Concise History* (Delhi: Manohar).

——— (2006), *Looking for a Hindu Identity* (General President's Address) (Visva Bharati: Indian History Congress).

Kane, P.V. (1974), *History of Dharmaśāstra*, Vol. II, Part 1 (Poona: Bhandarkar Oriental Research Institute).

Kangle, R.P. (1963), *The Kautīlīya Arthaśāstra*, Part 1 (Bombay: University of Bombay).

Kathāsaritasāgara by Somadeva (1960), edited and translated by Kedarnath Sharma (Patna: Bihar Rashtra Bhasha Parisad).

Klostermaier, Klaus K. (1990), *A Survey of Hinduism* (Delhi: Munshiram Manoharlal).

——— (1991), 'The Original Dakṣa Saga', in Arvind Sharma (ed.), *Essays on the Mahābhārata* (Leiden: Brill).

Kuvalayamālā by Udyottanasūri, Part I (1959), edited by A.N. Upadhye, (Bombay: Bharatiya Vidya Bhavan).

Lorenzen, David N. (1978), 'Warrior Ascetics in Indian History', *Journal of the American Oriental Society*, Vol. 98, No. 1, pp. 617–65.

Mahalingam, T.V. (1954), *South Indian Polity* (Madras: University of Madras).

Marshall, P.J. (1970), *The British Discovery of Hinduism in the Eighteenth Century* (Cambridge: Cambridge University Press).

Mattavilāsaprahasana by Mahendravikramavarman (1973), edited and translated by N.P. Unni (Trivandrum: College Book House).

Meinhard, H. (1928), *Beiträge zur Kenntnis des Sivaismus nach den Purana's*, PhD Thesis, University of Bonn.

Michaels, Axel (2005), *Hinduism: Past and Present* (Delhi: Orient Longman).

Nandi, R.N. (1986), *Social Roots of Religion in Ancient India* (Calcutta: K.P. Bagchi).

Narain, A.K. (1983), 'Religious Policy and Toleration in Ancient India with particular reference to the Gupta Period', in Bardwell L. Smith (ed.), *Essays on Gupta Culture* (Delhi: Motilal Banarsidass).

Narang, S.P. (1972), *Hemacandra's Dvyāśrayakāvya: A Literary and Cultural Study* (Delhi: Munshiram Manoharlal).

Narayanan, M.G.S. (1970), 'Kantallur Salai – New Light on the Nature of Aryan Expansion to South India,' *Proceedings of the Indian History Congress*, 32nd Session, Jabalpur.

Nath, Vijay (2001), *Purāṇas and Acculturation: A Historico-Anthropological Perspective* (Delhi: Munshiram Manoharlal).

Nilakanta Sastri, K.A. (1975), *The Coḷas* (Madras: University of Madras).

——— (1987), *A History of South India* (Delhi: Oxford University Press).

Nyāyakusumānjali by Udayanācārya (1996), translated by N.S. Dravid, Vol. 1 (New Delhi: Indian Council of Philosophical Research).

Oberhammer, G. (1983), *Inclusivismus. Eine indische Denkform* (Vienna: De Nobili Research Library).

Orr, W.G. (1940), 'Armed Religious Ascetics in Northern India', *Bulletin of the John Rylands Library*, Vol. 24, No. 1, pp. 81–100.

Padmapurāṇa (1893–94), edited by Hari Narayan Apte (Poona: Anandasrama Sanskrit Series).

Peterson, Indira Viswanathan (1989), *Tevāram* (*Poems to Śiva*) (Princeton: Princeton University Press).

——— (1998), 'Śramaṇas Against the Tamil Way', in John Cort (ed.), *Open Boundaries: Jain Communities and Cultures in Indian History* (Albany: SUNY Press).

Pinch, William R. (1996), *Peasants and Monks in British India* (Delhi: Oxford University Press).

Prabodhacandrodaya by Kṛṣṇa Miśra (1998), edited and translated by Sita Nambiar (Delhi: Motilal Banarsidass).

Periyapurāṇam (1990), translated into English by T.N. Ramachandran (Thanjavur: Tamil University).

Rao, Velcheru Narayana (1990), *Śiva's Warriors: The Bāsava Purāṇa of Pālkurriki Somanātha* (Princeton: Princeton University Press).

Rocher, Ludo (1986), *The Purāṇas* (Wiesbaden: Otto Harassowitz).

Sadasivaiah, H.M. (1967), *A Comparative Study of Two Vīraśaiva Monasteries* (Mysore: University of Mysore).

Sarkar, Jadudunath (1946), *A History of Dasnāmī Nāgā Sanyāsīs* (Allhabad: Mahanirvani).

Sastri, Ajay Mitra, ed. (1995), *Inscriptions of the Sarabhapurias, Pāṇḍuvaṃśins and Somavaṃśins* (Delhi: Indian Council of Historical Research & Motilal Banarsidass).

Sharma, Arvind (1978), 'Some Misunderstandings of the Hindu Approach to Religious Plurality', *Religion*, Vol. 8, No. 2, pp. 133–54.

Sharma, B.N. (1970), 'Religious Tolerance and Intolerance as reflected in Indian Sculptures', *Journal of the Ganganath Jha Research Institute*, Umesh Mishra Commemoration Volume.

Sharma, R.S. (2000), *Communal History and Rama's Ayodhya* (Delhi: People's Publishing House).

Sharma, Shanta Rani (1996), *Society and Culture in Rajasthan c.* AD *700–900* (Delhi: Pragati Prakashan).

Ṣaṭsāhasra Saṃhitā (1982), translated and edited by J.A. Schoterman (Leiden: Brill).

Sen, Amartya (2005), *The Argumentative Indian* (London: Allen Lane).

Shulman, David Dean (1985), *The King and the Clown in South Indian Myth and Poetry* (Princeton: Princeton University Press).

Śarvadarśanasaṃgraḥ (1997), translated into Hindi by Udya Narain Singh (Bombay: Khemraj Shrikrishandass Publication).

Saurapurāṇa (1924), edited by V.G. Apte (Poona: Anandasrama Sanskrit Series).

Sircar, D.C. (1971), *Studies in the Religious Life in Ancient and Medieval India* (Delhi: Motilal Banarsidass).

Śrīmad Śaṅkaradigvijayam by Vidyāraṇya (1985–86), 2 Vols, translated by K. Padmanaban (Madras: Padmanaban).

Stanley, John M. (1990), 'The Capitulation of Maṇi: A Conversion Myth in the Cult of Khaṇḍobā', in Alf Hiltebeitel (ed.), *Criminal Gods and Demon Devotees* (Delhi: Manohar).

Stein, M.A. (1979), *Kalhaṇa's Rājataraṅgiṇī* (Delhi: Motilal Banarsidass).

Tattvasaṃgraha by Śāntarakṣita (1937–39), 2 Vols, translated by Ganganath Jha (Baroda: Gaekwad Oriental Series).

Thakur, Upendra (1964), *Studies in Jainism and Buddhism in Mithila* (Varanasi: Chowkhamba).

Thapar, Romila (1987), *Cultural Transaction and Early India* (Delhi: Oxford University Press).

Varāhapurāṇa (BS 1313), edited by Panchanan Tarkaratna (Calcutta: Vangavasi Press).

Viṣṇupurāṇa (BS 1331), edited by Panchanan Tarkaratna (Calcutta: Vangavasi Press).

Veluthat, Kesavan (1978), *Brāhmaṇa Settlements in Kerala* (Calicut University: Sandhya Publications).

von Stietencron, H. (1995), 'Religious configurations in Pre-Muslim India and the Modern Concept of Hinduism', in Vasudha Dalmia and Stietencron von H. (eds), *Representing Hinduism* (Delhi: Sage Publications).

Vyākaraṇa Mahābhāṣya by Patanjali (1962–72), 3 Vols, edited by F. Kielhorn (Poona: Bhandarkar Oriental Research Institute).

Wadekar, M.L. (1996), *Devalasmṛti Reconstruction*, 2 Vols. (Delhi: Chowkhamba).

Yadava, B.N.S. (1973), *Society and Culture in Northern India in the Twelfth Century* (Allahabad: Central Book Depot.).

Yogaśāstra by Hemacandra (1977–86), 3 Vols, edited by Muni Jambuvijaya (Mumbai: Jain Sahitya Vikas Mandal).

Zvelebil, Kamil (1992), *Companion to Studies in Tamil Literature* (Leiden: Brill).

Temple Desecration and Indo-Muslim States

Richard M. Eaton

Framing the Issue

In recent years, especially in the wake of the destruction of the Baburi Mosque in 1992, much public discussion has arisen over the political status of South Asian temples and mosques, and in particular the issue of temples desecrated or replaced by mosques in the past. While Hindu nationalists like Sita Ram Goel have endeavoured to document a pattern of wholesale temple destruction by Muslims before the colonial period (Goel 1990, 1991), few professional historians have engaged with the issue, even though it is a properly historical one. This essay aims to examine the available evidence of temple desecration with a view to asking: what temples were in fact desecrated in India's pre-modern history? When, and by whom? How, and for what purpose? And above all, what might any of this say about the relationship between religion and politics in pre-modern India?

Much of the contemporary evidence on temple desecration cited by Hindu nationalists is found in Persian materials translated and published during the rise of British hegemony in India. Especially influential has been the eight-volume *History of India as Told by its Own Historians,* first published in 1849 and edited by Sir Henry M. Elliot, who oversaw the bulk of the translations, with the help of John Dowson. Elliot, keen to contrast what he understood as the justice and efficiency of British rule with the cruelty and despotism of the Muslim rulers who had preceded that rule, was anything but sympathetic to the 'Muhammadan' period of Indian history. As he wrote in the preface,

> The common people must have been plunged into the lowest depths of wretchedness and despondency. The few glimpses we have, even among the short Extracts in this single volume, of Hindus slain for disputing with Muhammadans, of general prohibitions against processions, worship, and ablutions, and of other intolerant measures, of idols mutilated, of temples razed, of forcible conversions and marriages, of proscriptions and confiscations, of murders and massacres, and of the sensuality and drunkenness of the tyrants who enjoined them, show us that this picture is not overcharged. . . . (Elliot and Dowson n.d.: xxi)

With the advent of British power, on the other hand, 'a more stirring and eventful era of India's History commences . . . when the full light of European truth and discernment begins to shed its beams upon the obscurity of the past, (ibid.: xvi). Noting the far greater benefits that Englishmen had brought to Indians in a mere half century than Muslims had brought in five centuries, Elliot expressed the hope that his published translations 'would make our native subjects more sensible of the immense advantages accruing to them under the mildness and the equity of our rule' (ibid.: xxii, xxvii).

Elliot's motives for delegitimizing the Indo-Muslim rulers who had preceded English rule are thus quite clear. Writing on the pernicious influence that this understanding of pre-modern Indian history was to have on subsequent generations, Mohammad Habib once remarked, 'The peaceful Indian Mussalman, descended beyond doubt from Hindu ancestors, was dressed up in the garb of a foreign barbarian, as a breaker of temples, and an eater of beef, and declared to be a military colonist in the land where he had lived for about thirty or forty centuries. . . . The result of it is seen in the communalistic atmosphere of India today' (Habib 1974: 12). Although penned many years ago, these words are relevant in the context of current controversies over the history of temple desecration in India. For it has been through selective translations of pre-modern Persian chronicles, together with a selective use of epigraphic data, that Hindu nationalists have sought to find the sort of irrefutable evidence – one of Goel's chapters is titled 'From the Horse's Mouth' – that would demonstrate a persistent pattern of villainy and fanaticism on the part of pre-modern Indo-Muslim conquerors and rulers.

Each scrap of evidence in the matter requires scrutiny. Consider an inscription dated 1455, found over the doorway of a tomb-shrine in Dhar, Madhya Pradesh, formerly the capital of Malwa. The inscription, a 42-verse Persian *ghazal,* mentions the destruction of a Hindu temple by one 'Abdullāh Shāh Changal during the reign of Rājā Bhoja, a renowned Paramāra king who had ruled over the region from 1010 to 1053. Goel takes the inscription's words more or less at face value, as though it were a contemporary newspaper account reporting a temple destruction as an objective fact (Goel 1991: 115–16).[1] However, the text is concerned not with documenting an instance of temple destruction, but with narrating and celebrating the fabulous career of 'Abdullāh Shāh Changal, the saint who lies buried at the site of the tomb. A reading of a larger body of the text reveals, in fact, a complex historiographical process at work:

> This centre became Muhammadan first by him [that is, 'Abdullah Shah Changal], (and) all the banners of religion were spread. (I have heard) that a few persons had arrived before him at this desolate and ruined place. When the muazzin raised the morning cry like the trumpet-call for the intoxicated *sufis,* the infidels (made an attack from) every wall (?) and each of them

[1] Goel does, however, consider it more likely that the event took place during the reign of Rājā Bhoja II in the late thirteenth century than during that of Rājā Bhoja I in the eleventh century.

> rushed with the sword and knife. At last they (the infidels) wounded those men of religion, and after killing them concealed (them) in a well. Now this (burial place and) grave of martyrs remained a trace of those holy and pious people.
>
> When the time came that the sun of Reality should shine in this dark and gloomy night, this lion-man ['Abdullah Shah Changal] came from the centre of religion to this old temple with a large force. He broke the images of the false deities, and turned the idol-temple into a mosque. When Rāi Bhoj saw this, through wisdom he embraced Islam with the family of all brave warriors. This quarter became illuminated by the light of the Muhammadan law, and the customs of the infidels became obsolete and abolished.
>
> Now this tomb since those old days has been a famous pilgrimage-place of the world. Graves from their oldness became leveled (to the ground), (and) there remained no mount on any grave. There was also (no place) for retirement, wherein the distressed *darvish* could take rest. Thereupon the king of the world gave the order that this top of Tur [Mount Sinai] be built anew. The king of happy countenance, the Sultan of horizons (that is, the world), the visitors of whose courts are Khaqan (the emperor of Turkistan) and Faghfur (the emperor of China), 'Alau-d-din Wad-dunya Abu'l-Muzaffar, who is triumphant over his enemies by the grace of God, the Khilji king Mahmud Shah, who is such that by his justice the world has become adorned like paradise, he built afresh this old structure, and this house with its enclosure again became new. (Yazdani 1909: 1–5)

The narrative divides a remembered past into three distinct moments. The first is the period before the arrival of the hero, 'Abdullāh Shāh Changal. At this time a small community of Muslims in Malwa, with but a tenuous foothold in the region, were martyred by local non-Muslims, their bodies thrown into a well. The second moment is the period of the hero, who comes from the 'centre of religion' (Mecca?), smashes images, transforms the temple into a mosque, and converts to Islam the most famous king of the Paramāra dynasty – deeds that collectively avenged the martyred ṣūfīs and, most importantly, served to (re)establish Islam in the region. The third moment is the period after the hero's lifetime when his grave-site, although a renowned place of pilgrimage, had suffered from neglect. Now enters the other hero of the narrative, Sultan Maḥmūd Khaljī – the 'king of the world' and 'of happy countenance,' to whose court the emperors of China and Central Asia pay respect, and by whose justice the world has become adorned like paradise. His great act was to patronize the cult of 'Abdullāh Shāh by (re)building his shrine. This, we are told at the end of the text, included a strong vault, a mosque, and a *caravansarai*. The inscription closes by offering a prayer that the soul of the benevolent Sultan may last until Judgment Day and that his empire may last in perpetuity.

Although Indo-Muslim epigraphs are typically recorded near in time to the events they describe, the present one is hardly contemporary, as it was composed some 400 years after the events to which it refers. Far from being a factual account of a contemporary incident, then, the text presents a richly-textured legend elaborated over many generations of oral transmission until the story of 'Abdullāh Shāh Changal and his deeds in Malwa became frozen in the written word that we have before us. The narrative reveals how a particular community at a particular time and place – Muslims in mid-fifteenth century Malwa – constructed their origins. Central to the story are themes of conversion, martyrdom, redemption, and the patronage of sacred sites by Indo-Muslim royalty, as well as, of course, the destruction of a temple. Whether or not any temple was actually destroyed four hundred years before this narrative was committed to writing, we cannot know with certainty. However, it would seem no more likely that such a desecration had actually occurred than that the renowned Rājā Bhoja had been converted to Islam, which the text also claims.

In any event, it is clear that by the mid-fifteenth century the memory of the destruction of a temple, projected into a distant past, had become one among several elements integral to how Muslims in Malwa – or at least those who patronized the composition of this *ghazal* – had come to understand their origins. The case thus suggests that caution is necessary in interpreting claims made in literary sources to temple desecration. It also illustrates the central role that temple desecration played in the remembered past of an Indo-Muslim state or community.

Early Instances of Temple Desecration

During the two centuries before 1192, which was when an indigenous Indo-Muslim state and community first appeared in north India, Persianized Turks systematically raided and looted major urban centres of South Asia, sacking temples and hauling immense loads of movable property to power bases in eastern Afghanistan.[2] The pattern commenced in AD 986, when the Ghaznavid Sultan Sabuktigin (reigned 977–97) attacked and defeated the Hindu Shāhī rājā who controlled the region between Kabul and northwest Punjab. According to Abu Nasr 'Utbi, personal secretary to the Sultan's son, Sabuktigin 'marched out towards Lamghan [located to the immediate east of Kabul], which is a city celebrated for its great strength and abounding in wealth. He conquered it and set fire to the places in its vicinity which were inhabited by infidels, and demolishing the idol-temples, he established Islam in them' (*Tārīkh-i Yāminī*: 22).[3]

Linking religious conversion with conquest – with conquest serving to facilitate conversion, and conversion serving to legitimize conquest – 'Utbi's brief notice established a rhetorical trope that many subsequent Indo-Muslim chroniclers would repeat, as for example in the case of the 1455 inscription at Dhar, just discussed. Notwithstanding 'Utbi's religious rhetoric, however, subse-

[2] A good summary of the political history of this period is found in Wink (1997: 111–49).

[3] For a thirteenth-century Persian translation of 'Utbi's original Arabic, made in 1206, see Abu Sharaf Nasih al-Jurfadqani (1345 AH: 31).

quent invasions by Sabuktigin and his more famous son Maḥmūd of Ghaznī (reigned 998–1030) appear to have been undertaken for material reasons. Based in Afghanistan and never seeking permanent dominion in India, the earlier Ghaznavid rulers raided and looted Indian cities, including their richly endowed temples loaded with movable wealth, with a view to financing their larger political objectives far to the west, in Khurāsān (Bosworth 1992: 32, 68). The predatory nature of these raids was also integral to the Ghaznavid political economy: their army was a permanent, professional one built around an elite corps of mounted archers who, as slaves, were purchased, equipped, and paid with cash derived from regular infusions of war booty taken alike from Indian and Iranian cities.[4] From the mid-eleventh century, however, Maḥmūd's successors, cut off from their sources of military manpower in Central Asia first by the Seljuqs and then by the Ghurids, became progressively more provincial, their kingdom focused around their capital at Ghazni in eastern Afghanistan with extensions into the Punjab. While the later Ghaznavids continued the predatory policies of raiding the Indian interior for booty, these appear to have been less destructive and more sporadic than those of Sabuktigin and Maḥmūd.[5]

The dynamics of north Indian politics changed dramatically, however, when the Ghūrids, a dynasty of Tajik (eastern Iranian) origin, arrived from central Afghanistan toward the end of the twelfth century. Sweeping aside the Ghaznavids, Ghūrid conquerors and their Turkish slave generals ushered in a new sort of state quite unlike that of the Ghaznavids. Aspiring to imperial dominion over the whole of north India from a base in the middle of the Indo-Gangetic plain, the new Delhi Sultanate (1206–1526) signalled the first attempt to build an indigenous Muslim state and society in north India. With respect to religious policy, we can identify two principal components of this project: (a) state patronage of an India-based Ṣūfī order, and (b) a policy of selective temple desecration that aimed not, as earlier, to finance distant military operations on the Iranian plateau, but to de-legitimize and extirpate defeated Indian ruling houses. Let us consider these in turn.

[4] Maḥmūd did not hesitate to sack Muslim cities. His plunder of the Iranian city of Ray, in 1029, brought him 500,000 dinars' worth of jewels, 260,000 dinars in coined money, and over 30,000 dinars' worth of gold and silver vessels. India, however, possessed far more wealth than the more sparsely populated Iranian plateau. Somnath alone brought in twenty million dinars' worth of spoil (Bosworth 1963: 78).

[5] The contemporary historian Baihāqī recorded the first attack on Benares conducted by a Turkish army, carried out in 1033 by the Ghaznavid governor of Lahore. 'He marched out with his warriors and the army of Lahore,' wrote Baihāqī, 'and exacted ample tribute from the Thakurs. He crossed the river Ganges and went down the left bank. Unexpectedly (*na-gah*) he arrived at a city which is Banaras, and which belonged to the territory of Gang. Never had a Muslim army reached this place. . . The markets of the drapers, perfumers, and jewellers were plundered, but it was impossible to do more. The people of the army became rich, for they all carried off gold, silver, perfumes, and jewels, and got back in safety' (*Tārīkh-i Baihāqī*, n.d.: 123–24; 1971: 517).

Ṣūfism and State Building

'The world is bound up closely with that of the men of faith,' wrote the Bahmani court-poet 'Abd al-Malik 'Isāmī in 1350. 'In every country, there is a man of piety who keeps it going and well. Although there might be a monarch in every country, yet it is actually under the protection of a fakīr [Ṣūfī shaikh].'[6]

Here we find a concise statement of one of the leading medieval Perso-Islamic conceptions of how religion and politics interrelate. In 'Iṣāmī's view, what had saved the Delhi Sultanate from Mongol conquest was the respect showed by Sultan Muḥammad bin Tughluq (reigned 1325–51) for the memory of the founder of the Chishti order of Ṣūfīs in India, Shaikh Mu'in al-Din Chishti (d. 1236), to whose tomb in Ajmer the Sultan had made a pilgrimage just after engaging with a Mongol army.[7] 'Isāmī also felt, however, that the decline of Delhi, and of the Tughluq empire generally, had resulted in a large part from the demise in 1325 of Shaikh Nizām al-Din Auliyā, Delhi's most renowned Ṣūfī shaikh. Conversely, he considered that the arrival in the Deccan of one of Nizām al-Din Auliyā's leading spiritual successors, Burhan al-Din Gharīb (d. 1337), was the cause of that region's flourishing state at mid-century.[8]

Among all the South Asian Ṣūfī orders, the Chishtis were the most closely identified with the political fortunes of Indo-Muslim states, and especially with the planting of such states in parts of South Asia never previously touched by Islamic rule. The pattern began in the first several decades of the fourteenth century, when the rise of the Chishti order to prominence among Delhi's urban populace coincided with that of the imperial Tughluqs. The two principal Persian poets in India of that time, Amīr Hasan and Amīr Khusrau, and the leading historian, Zia al-Dīn Baranī, were all disciples of Delhi's principal Chishti shaikh, Nizām al-Din Auliyā. As writers whose works were widely read, these men were in effect publicists for Nizām al-Din and his order. And since the three were also patronized by the Tughluq court, the public and the ruling classes alike gradually came tc associate dynastic fortune with that of the Chishti order.[9] Moreover, as the spiritual power of a charismatic Ṣūfī was believed to adhere after his lifetime to his tomb-site, shrines at such tombs were patronized by Indo-Muslim rulers just as they were frequented by Muslim devotees. And since the tomb-shrines of the greatest shaikhs of this order were located within South Asia, and not in distant Central Asia or West Asia as was the case with those of other orders, a ruling dynasty's patronage of Chishti shrines could bolster its claims to being both legitimately Islamic and authentically Indian.

[6] *Futūhu's-salātīn*, 1948: 455; *Futuhu's-salātīn*, 1967, Vol. III: 687).

[7] *Futūhu's-salātīn* (1948: 466; 1967, Vol. III: 702).

[8] *Futūhu's-salātīn* (1948: 456, 458; 1967, Vol. III: 689, 690–92). 'As soon as that holy man of virtue [Nizām al-Din Auliyā] departed from Dehli to the other world', he wrote, 'the country, in general, and the city, in particular, fell into a turmoil and were subjected to ruin and destruction.'

[9] See Digby (1986: 69–70).

Thus Chishti shaikhs repeatedly participated in the launching of new Indo-Muslim states. At the core of ‘Iṣāmī’s narrative of the Bahmani revolution, which in 1347 threw off Tughluq overlordship and launched an independent Indo-Muslim state in the Deccan, is a narrative of the passing of the Prophet Muḥammad’s own mantle *(khirqa)* from Abū Bakr, the first caliph, down to Burhān al-Dīn Gharīb’s leading disciple, Zain al-Dīn Shīrāzī (d. 1369). It was from that very mantle – ‘by whose scent one could master both worlds’ – that the founder of the Bahmani Sultanate, Sultan Hasan Bahman Shāh (reigned 1347–58), was said to have received his own power and inspiration (*Futūhu ‘s-salātīn*, 1948: 7–8; *Futūhu ‘s-salātīn*, 1967, Vol. I: 11–13). We see the same pattern in Bengal, another former Tughluq province that asserted its independence from Delhi in the mid-fourteenth century. The earliest-known monument built by the founder of Bengal’s Ilyās Shāhī dynasty (1342–1486) was a mosque dedicated in 1342 to Shaikh ‘Ala al-Haq (d. 1398), a Ṣūfī shaikh whose own spiritual master was – like Zain al-Dīn’s spiritual master – a disciple of the great shaikh of imperial Delhi, Nizām al-Dīn Auliyā (d. 1325). What is more, the political ascendancy of the Ilyās Shāhī dynasty coincided exactly with the spiritual ascendancy of shaikh ‘Ala al-Haq and his own family. Down to the year 1532, fully fourteen successive sultans of Bengal enlisted themselves as disciples of the descendants of this Shaikh, while the tomb-shrine of ‘Ala al-Haq’s own son and successor, Nur Qutb-i ‘Ālam, became in effect a state shrine to which subsequent sultans made annual pilgrimages (Eaton 1993: 86, 91).

In short, within the space of just five years, between 1342 and 1347, founders of independent Indo-Muslim dynasties in both Bengal and the Deccan patronized local Chishti shaikhs whose own spiritual masters had migrated from Delhi where they had studied with the imperial capital’s pre-eminent Nizām al-Dīn Auliyā. The pattern was repeated elsewhere, as the Tughluq empire continued to crumble, giving rise to more provincial successor-states. In 1396, the Tughluq governor of Gujarat, Muzaffar Khān, proclaimed his independence from Delhi immediately after marching to Ajmer, where he paid his respects to the tomb of Mu‘in al-Dīn Chishti, the ‘mother-shrine’ of the Chishti order in India (*Tārīkh-i Fīrīshta*, 1966, Vol. IV: 4). In 1404, soon after proclaiming his own independence from Delhi, the former Tughluq governor of Malwa, Dilāwar Khān, described himself as ‘the disciple of the head of the holy order of Nāsir Dīn Mahmūd’.[10] The reference here was to Nizām al-Dīn Auliyā’s most eminent disciple to have remained in Delhi – Shaikh Nāsir al-Dīn Mahmūd (d. 1356), over whose grave Sultan Fīrūz Shāh Tughluq (reigned 1351–88) had raised a magnificent tomb several decades earlier (Siddiqui 1989: 21).

Nor did the pattern cease with the launching of Tughluq successor states. On entering Delhi in 1526, Babur prayed at the shrine of India’s second great Chishti shaikh, Bakhtiyār Kāki (d. 1235), while his brother-in-law rebuilt the

[10] Zafar Hasan (1909: 12).

tomb of Nizām al-Dīn Auliyā. In 1571, Akbar built a tomb for his father Humāyūn near Nizām al-Dīn's shrine, and in the same year he began building his new capital of Fatehpur Sikri at the hospice-site of Salim Chishti, the shaikh who had predicted the birth of his son. Towards the end of his life this same shaikh tied his turban on the head of that son, the future Jahāngīr, and pronounced him his spiritual successor. As for Jahāngīr, as Emperor he built gates and other buildings at or near the shrine at Ajmer, as did Shāh Jahān as part of his victory celebrations after defeating the raja of Mewar. Shāh Jahān's daughter, Jahān Ārā, even wrote a biography of Mu'in al-Dīn Chishti. Shāh Jahān's son and successor Aurangzeb, who sought to build another pan-Indian empire on the Tughluq model, visited and made sizeable contributions to Chishti tomb-sites in former Tughluq provinces such as at Gulbarga or Khuldabad in the Deccan, in addition to sites in Ajmer and Delhi. Even the later Mughals patronized those Chishti shrines to which they had access in their dwindling domains, as when 'Ālamgīr II repaired and made additions to the tomb of Nizām al-Dīn Auliyā. Bringing the pattern to a full circle, the last Emperor, Bahādur Shāh II (deposed 1858), built his own mansion adjacent to the shrine of Bakhtiyār Kāki, the very site where Babur had prayed more than three centuries earlier (Asher 1992).

In sum, the entire Mughal dynasty, believing that the blessings of Chishti shaikhs underpinned their worldly success, vigorously patronized the order. Two of Akbar's fourteen pilgrimages to the shrine of Mu'in al-Dīn Chishti at Ajmer, those of 1568 and 1574, were made immediately after conquering Chitor and Bengal respectively (Curie 1992: 100). Discussing his military successes with the historian 'Abd al-Qādir Badāūnī, Akbar remarked, 'All this (success) has been brought through the Pīr [Mu'in al-Dīn]' (*Muntakhab al-tawārīkh*: 243). Vividly dramatized by Akbar's pilgrimages from Agra to Ajmer, several of them on foot, the Mughal–Chishti partnership even survived the collapse of the Mughal state. In a sense it persists to this day. The ceremonies, the terminology, and the protocol still found at Chishti shrines generally, and at the Ajmer shrine particularly, all reflect the extraordinary intrusion of Mughal court culture into that of the Chishti order.[11]

[11] It has been noted recently that the *qawwālī* protocols observed during the annual *'urs* ceremonies at Ajmer, which commemorate the death date of Mu'in al-Dīn Chishti, 'betray the impact of Mughal court etiquette. The diwan, dressed Mughal fashion, represents in fact the Mughal king rather than a religious dignitary, and comes escorted by the torch-bearers and mace-bearers wearing Mughal costumes. He takes his seat on the cushion *(gadela)* under a special tent *(dalbadal)* erected for the occasion. . . . On his arrival in the shrine the diwan kisses the tomb and offers flowers, and then one of the *khadims,* who happens to be his *wakil,* like the other pilgrims, ties a *dastar* (turban) over his head, spreads the cloth sheet over his bowed head, prays for him, and then gives him *tabarruk,* consisting of flowers, sandal and sweets. . . . Then he [the diwan] sits down and the *fatiha khwans,* who are permanently and hereditarily employed, recite the *fatiha*, as well as prayers for the sovereign *(badshah-i Islam),* the diwan, the mutawalli and other officials, and for the general public' (Moini 1989: 72, 74).

Temple Desecration and State Building

By effectively injecting a legitimizing substance into a new body politic at the moment of its birth, the royal patronage of Chishti shaikhs contributed positively to the process of state-building. Equally important to this process was the sweeping away of all prior political authority in newly-conquered and annexed territories. When such authority was vested in a ruler whose own legitimacy was associated with a temple – typically one that housed an image of a ruling dynasty's state-deity, or *rāshtra-devatā* (usually Viṣṇu or Śiva) – that temple was often looted, redefined, or destroyed, any of which would have had the effect of detaching a defeated rājā from the most prominent source of his legitimacy. Temples that were not so identified, or temples formerly so identified but abandoned by their royal patrons and thereby rendered politically irrelevant, were normally left unharmed. Such was the case, for example, with the famous temples at Khajuraho south of the Middle Gangetic plain, which appear to have been abandoned by their Candella royal patrons before Turkish armies reached the area in the early thirteenth century (Wink 1997: 324).

It would be wrong to explain this phenomenon by appealing to an essentialized 'theology of iconoclasm' felt to be intrinsic to the Islamic religion. For, while it is true that contemporary Persian sources routinely condemned idolatry (*but-parastī*) on religious grounds, it is also true that attacks on images revered by enemy kings had been, from about the sixth century AD on, thoroughly integrated into Indian political action. With their lushly sculpted imagery vividly displaying the mutual interdependence of kings and gods and the mingling of divine and human kingship, royal temple complexes of the early medieval period were thoroughly and pre-eminently political institutions. It was here that, after the sixth century, human kingship was established, contested, and revitalized.[12] Above all, the central icon housed in the sanctum and inhabited by the state-deity of the temple's royal patron, expressed the shared sovereignty of king and deity. Moreover, notwithstanding that temple priests endowed a royal temple's deity with attributes of transcendent and universal power, that same deity was also understood to have a very special relationship, indeed a sovereign relationship, with the particular geographical site in which its temple was located.[13] As revealed in temple narratives, even the physical removal of an image from its original site could not break the link between deity and geography (Davis 1997: 122, 137–38).[14] The bonding

[12] 'The need to link one's royal origins to religious and divine forces,' writes Chattopadhyaya (1993: 40) referring to the period 700–1200, 'led to the extraordinary temple building of this period'.

[13] Michael Willis suggests that one of the reasons the imperial Pratīhāras did *not* build great monumental temple complexes was precisely their determination to avoid the localization of sovereign power in this manner. According to this reasoning, the most active patrons of temple construction in this period were subordinate kings who did not have such vast imperial pretensions as did the Pratīhāras (Willis 1993: 58–59).

[14] Davis here cites David Shulman: 'A divine power is felt to be present *naturally* on the spot. The texts are therefore concerned with the manner in which this presence is revealed and with the definition of its specific attributes' (Shulman 1980: 48, emphasis mine).

between king, god, temple, and land in early medieval India is well illustrated in a passage from the *Bṛhatsaṃhitā,* a sixth-century text: 'If a Śiva linga, image, or temple breaks apart, moves, sweats, cries, speaks, or otherwise acts with no apparent cause, this warns of the destruction of the king and his territory'.[15] In short, after the sixth century, images and temples associated with dynastic authority were politically vulnerable.

Given these perceived connections between temples, images, and their royal patrons, it is hardly surprising that early medieval Indian history abounds in instances of temple desecration that occurred amidst inter-dynastic conflicts. In AD 642, according to local tradition, the Pallava king Narasimhavarman I looted the image of Ganeśa from the Cālukyan capital of Vātāpi. Fifty years later armies of those same Cālukyas invaded north India and brought back to the Deccan what appear to be images of Ganga and Yamuna, looted from defeated powers there. In the eighth century, Bengali troops sought revenge on king Lalitāditya by destroying what they thought was the image of Viṣṇu Vaikuṇṭha, the state deity of Lalitāditya's kingdom in Kashmir. In the early ninth century the Raṣṭrakūṭa king Govinda III invaded and occupied Kanchipuram, which so intimidated the king of Sri Lanka that he sent Govinda several (probably Buddhist) images that had represented the Sinhala state, and which the Raṣṭrakūṭa king then installed in a Śaiva temple in his capital. About the same time the Pāṇḍyan king Śrīmāra Śrīvallabha also invaded Sri Lanka and took back to his capital a golden Buddha image – 'a synecdoche for the integrity of the Sinhalese polity itself' – that had been installed in the kingdom's Jewel Palace. In the early tenth century the Pratīhāra king Herambapāla seized a solid gold image of Viṣṇu Vaikuṇṭha when he defeated the Sāhī king of Kangra. By the mid-tenth century the same image was seized from the Pratīhāras by the Candella king Yaśovarman and installed in the Lakshmana temple of Khajuraho. In the early eleventh century Rājendra I furnished his Coḷa capital with images he had seized from several prominent neighbouring kings: Durgā and Ganeśa images from the Cālukyas; Bhairava, Bhairavī, and Kālī images from the Kalingas of Orissa; a Nandī image from the Eastern Cālukyas; and a bronze Śiva image from the Pālas of Bengal. In the mid-eleventh century his successor, Rājādhirāja, defeated the Cālukyas and plundered Kalyāṇī, taking a large black stone door guardian to his capital in Thanjavur, where it was displayed to his subjects as a trophy of war.[16]

[15] Cited in Davis (1997: 53).

[16] Davis (1997: 51–83). The same pattern continued after the Turkish conquest of India. In the 1460s, Kapilendra, the founder of the Sūryavaṃśī Gajapati dynasty in Orissa, sacked Śaiva and Vaiṣṇava temples in the Kaveri delta in the course of wars of conquest in the Tamil country (see Wagoner 1993: 146). Somewhat later, in 1514, Kṛṣṇadevarāya looted an image of Bāla Kṛṣṇa from Udayagiri, which he had defeated and annexed to his growing Vijayanagara state. Six years later he acquired control over Pandharpur, where he seems to have looted the Viṭṭala image and carried it back to Vijayanagara, with the apparent purpose of ritually incorporating this area into his kingdom (Davis 1997: 65, 67).

While the dominant pattern here was one of looting royal temples and carrying off images of state deities,[17] we also hear of Hindu kings engaging in the destruction of the royal temples of their political adversaries. In the early tenth century, the Rāṣṭrakūṭa monarch Indra III not only destroyed the temple of Kala-priya (at Kalpa near the Jamuna River), patronized by the Rāṣṭrakūṭas' deadly enemies the Pratīhāras, but they took special delight in recording the fact (Willis 1993: 59).

Thus it is clear that Turkish invaders, when attempting to plant their own rule in early medieval India, were following established patterns. The table and the corresponding maps in this essay by no means give a complete picture of temple desecration after the establishment of Turkish power in upper India. Undoubtedly other temples too were desecrated but the facts in the matter were never recorded, or the facts were on records that no longer survive. Conversely, later Indo-Muslim chroniclers, seeking to glorify the religious zeal of earlier Muslim rulers, sometimes attributed temple desecration to rulers even when no contemporary evidence supports the claims.[18] As a result, we shall never know the precise number of temples desecrated in Indian history. Nonetheless, by relying strictly on evidence found in contemporary or near-contemporary epigraphic and literary sources spanning a period of more than five centuries (1192–1729), we can identify 80 instances of temple desecration whose historicity appears reasonably certain.

First, acts of temple desecration were carried out by military officers or ruling authorities; that is, such acts that we know about were undertaken by the state. Second, the chronology and geography of the data indicate that acts of temple desecration typically occurred on the cutting edge of a moving military frontier. From Ajmer in Rajasthan, the former capital of the defeated Cāhamāna Rajputs – also, significantly, the wellspring of Chishti piety – the post-1192 pattern of temple desecration moved swiftly down the Gangetic plain as Turkish military forces sought to extirpate local ruling houses in the late twelfth and early thirteenth century (Table and Map 1: Nos. 1–9). In Bihar, this included the targeting of Buddhist monastic establishments at Odantapurī, Vikramaśila, and Nalanda. Detached from a Buddhist laity, these establishments had by this time become dependent on the

[17] In the late eleventh century, the Kashmiri king Harṣa even raised the plundering of temples to an institutionalized activity; and in the late twelfth and early thirteenth century, while Turkish rulers were establishing themselves in north India, kings of the Paramāra dynasty attacked and plundered Jain temples in Gujarat (Thapar, Mukhia and Bipan Chandra 1969: 14, 31; Willis 1993: 59).

[18] In 1788, for example, the author of the *Riyāz al-sālātin* claimed that Muḥammad Bakhtiyār demolished local temples after he conquered Bengal in 1204, though no contemporary evidence suggests that he did so (Salim 1975: 64). Even contemporary sources could make false claims. An inscription on a mosque in Bidar, dated 1670, claims that the Mughal governor Mukhtar Khān had destroyed a temple and built the mosque on its site. 'But as a matter of fact,' noted the epigraphist who published the inscription, 'the mosque is a new construction, and the rock does not seem to have been disturbed, for it still survives' (*Epigraphia Indo-Moslemica* 1927–28 1931: 32).

patronage of local royal authorities, with whom they were identified. In the 1230s Iltutmish carried the power of the Delhi Sultanate into Malwa (Nos. 10–11), and by the onset of the fourteenth century the Khalji sultans had opened up a corridor through eastern Rajasthan into Gujarat (Nos. 12–14, 16–17).

Raids on peninsular India, on which the Khaljis embarked between 1295 and the early decades of the fourteenth century (Nos. 15, 18–19), appear to have been driven not by the goal of annexation but by the need for treasure with which to defend northern India from Mongol attacks.[19] For a short time, then, peninsular India stood in the same relation to the north – namely, as a source of plunder for financing distant military operations – as the north had stood in relation to Afghanistan three centuries earlier. After 1323, however, a new dynasty, the Tughluqs, sought permanent dominion in the Deccan, which the future Sultan Muḥammad bin Tughluq established by uprooting royally patronized temples in western Andhra (Nos. 20–22). Somewhat later, Sultan Fīrūz Tughluq did the same in Orissa (No. 23).

From the late fourteenth century, after the tide of Tughluq imperialism had receded from Gujarat and the Deccan, emergent successor states sought to expand their own political frontiers in those areas. This, too, is reflected in instances of temple desecration, as the ex-Tughluq governor of Gujarat and his successors consolidated their authority there (see Table and Map 1: Nos. 25–26, 31–32, 34–35, 38–39, 42), or as the Bahmani sultans challenged Vijayanagara's claims to dominate the Raichur doab and the Tamil coast (Nos. 33, 41). The pattern was repeated in Kashmir by Sultan Sikandar (Nos. 27–30), and in the mid-fifteenth century when the independent sultanate of Malwa contested renewed Rajput power in eastern Rajasthan, after Delhi's authority there had waned (Nos. 36–37). In the early sixteenth century, when the Lodī dynasty of Afghans sought to reassert Delhi's sovereignty over neighbouring Rajput houses, we again find instances of temple desecration (Nos. 43–45). We find the same pattern in the late sixteenth and early seventeenth centuries, when Bijapur and Golconda challenged the territorial sovereignty of Orissan kings (Nos. 55, 59; Maps 2 and 3), of Vijayanagara (No. 47), and of the latter's successor states – especially in the southern Andhra country (Nos. 50–51, 53–54, 60–61; Maps 2 and 3).

Unlike the Deccan, where Indo-Muslim states had been expanding at the expense of non-Muslim states, in northern India the Mughals under Bābur, Humāyūn, and Akbar – that is, between 1526 and 1605 – grew mainly at the expense of defeated Afghans. As non-Hindus, the latter had never shared sovereignty with deities patronized in royal temples, which probably explains the absence of firm evidence of temple desecration by any of the early Mughals, in Ayodhya or elsewhere.[20]

[19] In 1247 Balban, the future sultan of Delhi, had recommended raiding Indian states for precisely this purpose. See Juzjani (1970, Vol. II: 816).

[20] The notion that Bābur's officer Mīr Bāqī destroyed a temple dedicated to Rama's birthplace at Ayodhya and then got the emperor's sanction to build a mosque on the site – the

However, whenever Mughal armies pushed beyond the frontiers of territories formerly ruled by the Delhi sultans and sought to annex the domains of Hindu rulers, we again find instances of temple desecration. In 1661, the governor of Bengal, Mīr Jumla, sacked the temples of the neighbouring raja of Kuch Bihar, who had been harassing the northern frontiers of Mughal territory (No. 64; Map 3). The next year, with a view to annexing Assam to the imperial domain, the governor pushed far up the Brahmaputra valley and desecrated temples of the Ahom rajas, replacing the principal one at Garhgaon with a mosque (Nos. 65–66).

All these instances of temple desecration occurred in the context of military conflicts when Indo-Muslim states expanded into the domains of non-Muslim rulers. Contemporary chroniclers and inscriptions leave no doubt that field commanders, governors, and sultans viewed the desecration of royal temples as a normal means of decoupling a former Hindu king's legitimate authority from his former kingdom, and more specifically, of decoupling that former king from the image of the state-deity that was publicly understood as protecting the king and his kingdom. This was accomplished in one of several ways. Most typically, temples considered essential to the constitution of enemy authority were destroyed. Occasionally, temples were converted into mosques, which more visibly uprooted the earlier sovereignty in favour of a new one.[21]

The form of desecration that showed the greatest continuity with pre-Turkish practice was the seizure of the image of a defeated king's state-deity and its abduction to the victor's capital as a trophy of war. In February 1299, for example, Ulugh Khān sacked the famous temple of Somnath and sent its largest image to Sultan 'Alā al-Dīn Khaljī's court in Delhi (No. 16; Map 3). When Fīrūz Tughluq invaded Orissa in 1359 and learned that its most important temple was that of Jagannath, in the raja's fortress in Puri, he carried off the stone image of the god and installed it in Delhi 'in an ignominious position' (No. 23). In 1518, when the court in Delhi came to suspect the loyalty of a tributary Rajput chieftain in Gwalior, Ibrāhīm Lodī marched to the famous fortress, stormed it, and seized

notorious Baburi Masjid – was elaborated in 1936 by S.K. Banerji. However, the latter offered no evidence that there had ever been a temple at this site, much less that it had been destroyed by Mīr Bāqī. The mosque inscription records only that Bābur had ordered the construction of the mosque, which was built by Mīr Bāqī and was described as 'the place of descent of celestial beings' (*mahbiṭ-i qudsiyān*). This commonplace rhetorical flourish in Persian can hardly be construed as referring to Rāma, especially since it is the mosque itself that is so described, and not the site or any earlier structure on the site. See Banerji (1936: 76–83).

[21] For example, a 1406 inscription records that after Sultan Fīrūz Shāh Bahmani had defeated the forces of Vijayanagara in the much-contested Raichur doab region, 'a mosque has been converted out of a temple as a sign of religion'. It then records that the Sultan himself had 'conquered this fort by the firm determination of his mind in a single attack (lit. on horseback). After the victory of the emperor, the chief of chiefs, Safdār (lit. the valiant commander) of the age, received (the charge of) the fort' (*Epigraphia Indica* 1964: 57–58).

Map 1 Temple desecrations: Imperialism of the Delhi Sultanate, 1192–1394
(See table at the end of the chapter)

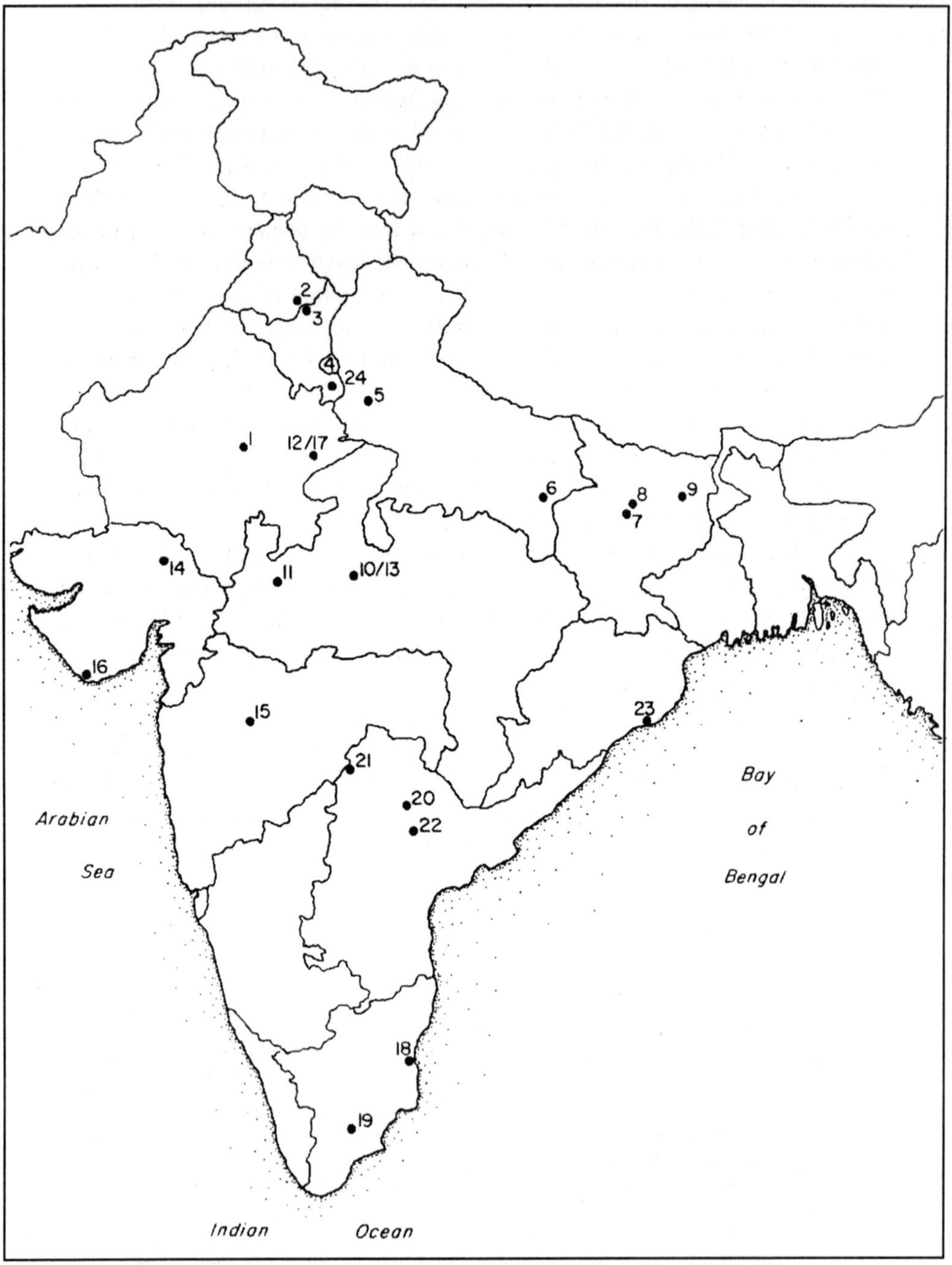

Map 2 Temple desecrations: The growth of regional sultanates, 1394–1600 (See table the end of the chapter)

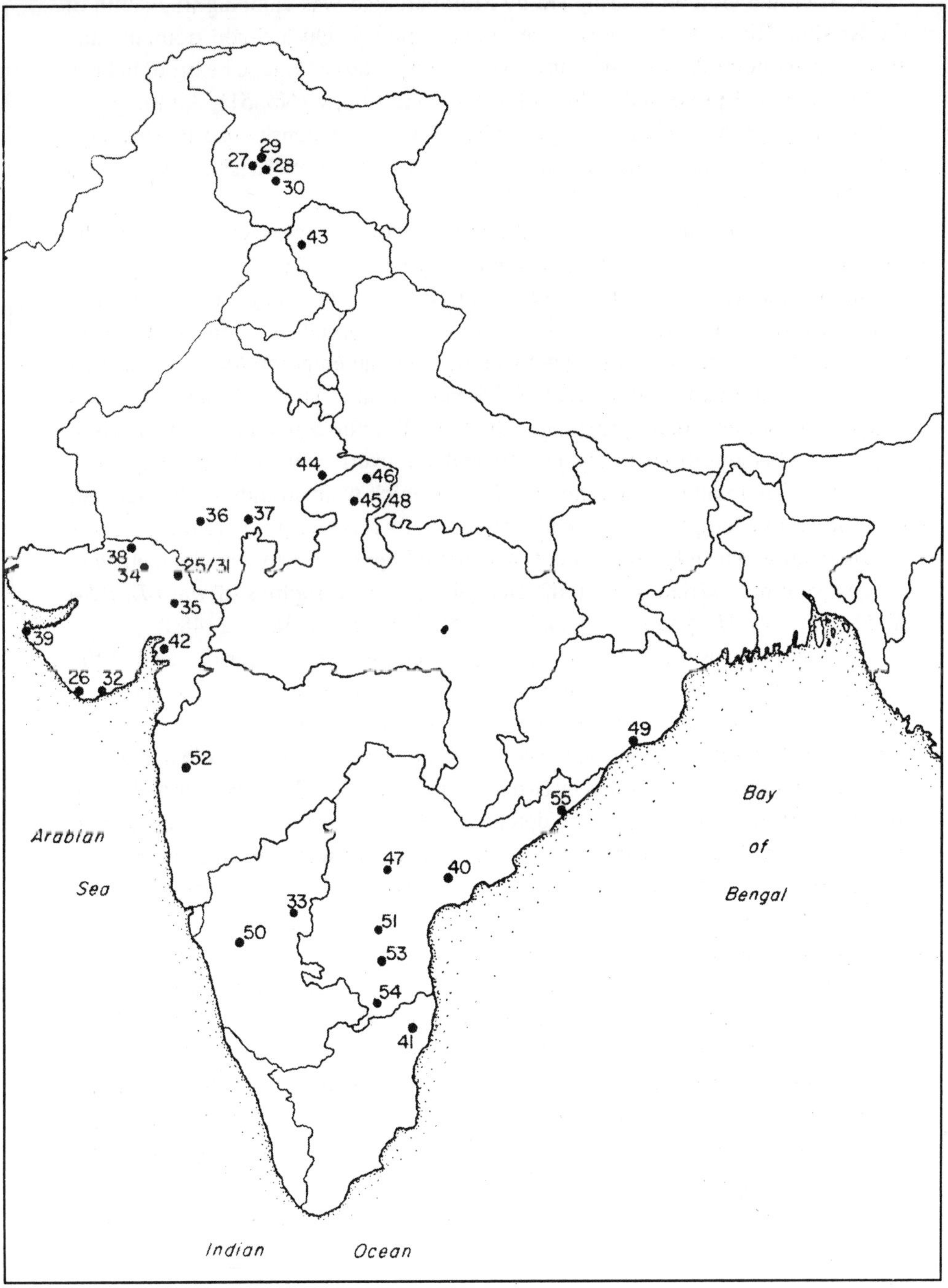

a brass image of Nandī at the local Śiva temple. The Sultan brought it back to Delhi and installed it in the city's Baghdad Gate (No. 46; Map 2). Similarly, in 1579, when the Golconda army led by Murahari Rao was campaigning south of the Krishna River, Rao annexed the entire region to Quṭb Shāhī domains and sacked the popular Ahobilam temple, whose ruby-studded image he brought back to Golconda and presented to his sultan as a war trophy (No. 51). Although the Ahobilam temple had only local appeal, it had close associations with prior sovereign authority since it had been patronized and even visited by Krishna Deva Rāya (*Tārīkh-i Fīrīshta*, Vol. III: 267).[22]

In each of these instances, the idol or icon, taken as war trophy to the capital of the victorious ruler, became radically detached from its former context and in the process was transformed from a living to a dead image. However, sacked images were not always abducted to the victor's capital. In 1556, the Gajapati rājā of Orissa had entered into a pact with the Mughal emperor Akbar, the distant adversary of the sultan of Bengal, Sulaimān Karrani. The rājā had also given refuge to Sulaimān's more proximate adversary, Ibrāhīm Sūr, and offered to assist the latter in his ambitions to conquer Bengal and overthrow the Karrani dynasty. As reprisal Sulaimān sent an army into Orissa which went straight to the Gajapati kingdom's state temple of Jagannath and looted its images. But here the goal was not annexation but only punishment, which might explain why the Gajapati state images were not carried back to the Bengali capital as trophies of war (*Tārīkh-i Khān Jahānī va Makhzān-i Afghānī*: 413–15; *Akbarnāma*: 381–82, 480).

Whatever form they took, attacks on temples were never directed at the people, but at the enemy king and the image that incarnated and displayed his state-deity. A contemporary description of a 1661 Mughal campaign in Kuch Bihar, which resulted in the annexation of the region, makes it clear that the Mughal authorities were guided by two principal concerns. The first was to destroy the image of the state-deity of the defeated rājā, Bhīm Nārāyan. And the second was to prevent Mughal troops from looting or in any way harming the general population of Kuch Bihar. To this end, we are informed, the chief judge of Mughal Bengal, Saiyid Muḥammad Sādiq, 'was directed to issue prohibitory orders that nobody was to touch the cash and property of the people, and he should go personally and establish order everywhere. He was asked to confiscate the treasure of Bhīm Nārāyan, break the idols and introduce the laws of Islam. Sayyid Sādiq issued strict prohibitory orders so that nobody had the courage to break the laws or to plunder the property of the inhabitants. The punishment for disobeying the order was that the hands, ears or noses of the plunderers were cut. Sayyid Sādiq busied himself in giving protection to the life and property of the subjects and the destitutes' (*Muntakhab al-lubāb*: 142–43).

In newly annexed areas formerly ruled by non-Muslims, as in the case of

[22] The temple's political significance, and hence the necessity of desecrating it, would have been well understood by Murahari Rao, himself a Marathi Brāhmaṇa.

Kuch Bihar, Mughal officers took appropriate measures to secure the support of the common people who had created the material wealth on which the imperial edifice rested.

Temple Protection and State Maintenance

If the idea of conquest became manifest in the desecration of temples associated with former enemies, what happened once the land and the subjects of those enemies were integrated into an Indo-Muslim state? On this point, the data are quite clear: pragmatism as well as time-honoured traditions of both Islamic and Indian statecraft dictated that temples lying within such states be left unmolested. We learn from a Sanskrit inscription, for example, that in 1326, thirteen years after he annexed the northern Deccan to the Tughluq empire, Muḥammad bin Tughluq appointed Muslim officials to repair a Śiva temple in Kalyāna (in Bidar District), thereby facilitating the resumption of normal worship that had been disrupted by local disturbances (Desai 1957–58: 165–68). According to the Sultan's interpretation of Islamic Law, anybody who paid the poll-tax *(jizya)* could build temples in territories ruled by Muslims (Ibn Battūta 1986: 214).

Such views continued to hold sway until modern times. Within several decades of Muḥammad bin Tughluq's death, Sultan Shihāb al-Dīn (1355–73) of Kashmir rebuked his Brāhmaṇa minister for having suggested melting down Hindu and Buddhist images in his kingdom as a means of obtaining quick cash. In elaborating his ideas on royal patronage of religion, the Sultan referred to the deeds of figures drawn from classical Hindu mythology. 'Some [kings]', he said,

> have obtained renown by setting up images of gods, others by worshiping them, some by duly maintaining them. And some, by demolishing them! How great is the enormity of such a deed! Sagara became famous by creating the sea and the rivers. . . . Bhagiratha obtained fame by bringing down the Ganges. Jealous of Indra's fame, Dushyanata acquired renown by conquering the world; and Rama by killing Ravana when the latter had purloined Sita. King Shahvadina [Shihab al-Din], it will be said, plundered the image of a god; and this fact, dreadful as Yama [death], will make the men in future tremble. (Sadhu 1993: 44–45)

About a century later, Muslim jurists advised the future Sikandar Lodī of Delhi (reigned 1489–1517) that 'it is not lawful to lay waste ancient idol temples, and it does not rest with you to prohibit ablution in a reservoir which has been customary from ancient times' (*Tabaqāt-i Akbarī*: 386).

The pattern of post-conquest temple protection, and even patronage, is especially clear when we come to the imperial Mughals, whose views on the subject are captured in official pronouncements on Maḥmūd of Ghaznī, one of the most controversial figures in Indian history. It is well known that in the early eleventh century, before the establishment of Indo-Muslim rule in north India, he had made numerous, and very destructive, attacks on the region. Starting with the writings of his own contemporary and court poet, Firdausī (d. 1020), Maḥmūd's career soon became legend, as generations of Persian poets lionized Maḥmūd as a paragon of Islamic kingly virtue, celebrating his infamous attacks on Indian temples as models for what other pious sultans should do.[23] But the Ghaznavid Sultan never undertook the responsibility of actually governing any land whose temples he had wantonly plundered. Herein lies the principal difference between the careers of Maḥmūd and Abū'l Faẓl, Akbar's chief minister and the principal architect of Mughal imperial ideology. Reflecting the sober values that normally accompany the practice of governing large, multi-ethnic states, Abū'l Faẓl attributed Maḥmūd's excesses to fanatical bigots who, having incorrectly represented India as 'a country of unbelievers at war with Islam', incited the Sultan's unsuspecting nature, which led to the 'wreck of honour and the shedding of blood and the plunder of the virtuous' (*Ā'īn-i Akbarī*: 377).

Indeed, from Akbar's time onward, Mughal rulers treated temples lying within their sovereign domain as state property. They undertook to protect both the physical structures and their Brāhmaṇa functionaries. At the same time, by appropriating Hindu religious institutions to serve imperial ends – a process involving complex overlappings of political and religious codes of power – the Mughals became deeply implicated in institutionalized Indian religions, in dramatic contrast to their British successors, who professed a hands-off policy in this respect. Thus we find Akbar allowing high-ranking Rajput officers in his service to build their own monumental temples in the provinces to which they were posted (Asher 1992: 183–201). His successors went further. Between 1590 and 1735, Mughal officials repeatedly oversaw, and on occasion even initiated, the renewal of the cult of Jagannath in Puri. By sitting on a canopied chariot in the annual chariot festival, Shāh Jahān's officials ritually demonstrated that it was the Mughal emperor, operating through his appointed officers *(manṣabdār),* who was the ultimate lord and protector of the temple and hence the god (Acharya 1961: 46). Such actions in effect projected a hierarchy of political and religious power that descended from the Emperor to his mansabdar, from the *manṣabdār* to Jagannath and his temple, from Jagannath to the local king who patronized the god, and from the king to his subjects. For the Mughals, politics within their sovereign domains never meant annihilating prior authority, but appropriating it within a hierarchy of power that flowed from the Peacock Throne to the mass of commoners below.

Such ideas continued in force into the reign of Aurangzeb (1658–1707), whose orders to local officials in Benares in 1659 clearly indicate that Brāhmaṇa temple functionaries there, together with the temples at which they officiated, merited state protection:

> In these days information has reached our court that several people have, out of spite and rancour, harassed the Hindu residents of Benares and nearby places, including a group of Brahmans who are in charge of ancient temples

[23] A useful discussion of Maḥmūd, his legend, and the question of iconoclasm prior to the establishment of Islamic states in India is found in Davis (1997: Chapters 3 and 6).

> there. These people want to remove those Brahmans from their charge of temple-keeping, which has caused them considerable distress. Therefore, upon receiving this order, you must see that nobody unlawfully disturbs the Brahmans or other Hindus of that region, so that they might remain in their traditional place and pray for the continuance of the Empire.[24]

By way of justifying this order, the Emperor noted that, 'According to the Holy Law (*shari'at*) and the exalted creed, it has been established that ancient temples should not be torn down'. On this point, Aurangzeb aligned himself with the theory and the practice of Indo-Muslim ruling precedent. But then he added, 'nor should new temples be built' – a view that broke decisively from Akbar's policy of permitting his Rajput officers to build their own temple complexes in Mughal territory.[25] Although this order appears to have applied only to Benares – many new temples were built elsewhere in India during Aurangzeb's reign[26] – one might wonder what prompted the Emperor's anxiety in this matter.

Temple Desecration and State Maintenance

It seems certain that Indo-Muslim rulers were well aware of the highly charged political and religious relationship between a royal Hindu patron and his client-temple. Hence, even when former rulers or their descendants had been comfortably assimilated into the ruling class, there always remained the possibility, and hence the occasional suspicion, that the latent political significance of a temple might be activated and serve as a base to further the patron's political aspirations. Such considerations might explain why it was that, when a subordinate non-Muslim officer in an Indo-Muslim state showed signs of disloyalty – and especially if he engaged in open rebellion – the state often desecrated the temple(s) most clearly identified with that officer. After all, if temples lying within its domain were understood as state property, and if a government officer who was also a temple's patron demonstrated disloyalty to the state, from a juridical standpoint ruling authorities felt justified in treating that temple as an extension of the officer, and hence liable for punishment.

Thus in 1478, when a Bahmani garrison on the Andhra coast mutinied, murdered its governor, and entrusted the fort to Bhīmrāj Oriyyā (who until that point had been a Bahmani client), the Sultan personally marched to the site and, after a six-month siege, stormed the fort, destroyed its temple, and built a mosque on the site (No. 40). A similar thing occurred in 1659, when Shivaji Bhonsle, the son of a loyal and distinguished officer serving the 'Ādil Shāhī sultans of Bijapur, seized a government port on the northern Konkan coast, thereby disrupting the

[24] Order to Abu'l-Hasan, Benares, dated 28 Feb, 1659 (Order 1911: 689–90). My translation. The 'continuance of the empire,' or course, was always forefront on the minds of the Mughals, regardless of what religious functionary was praying to which deity.

[25] *'Az rū-yi shar'-i sharif wa millat-i munif muqarrar chunīn ast, ki dair-hāyi dīrīn bar andākht nashavad, wa but-kada-hā tāza banā nayābad'* (ibid., my translation).

[26] See Eaton (1993: 184–85, 263).

MAP 3 Temple desecrations: Expansion and reassertions of Mughal authority, 1600–1760 (See table at the end of the chapter).

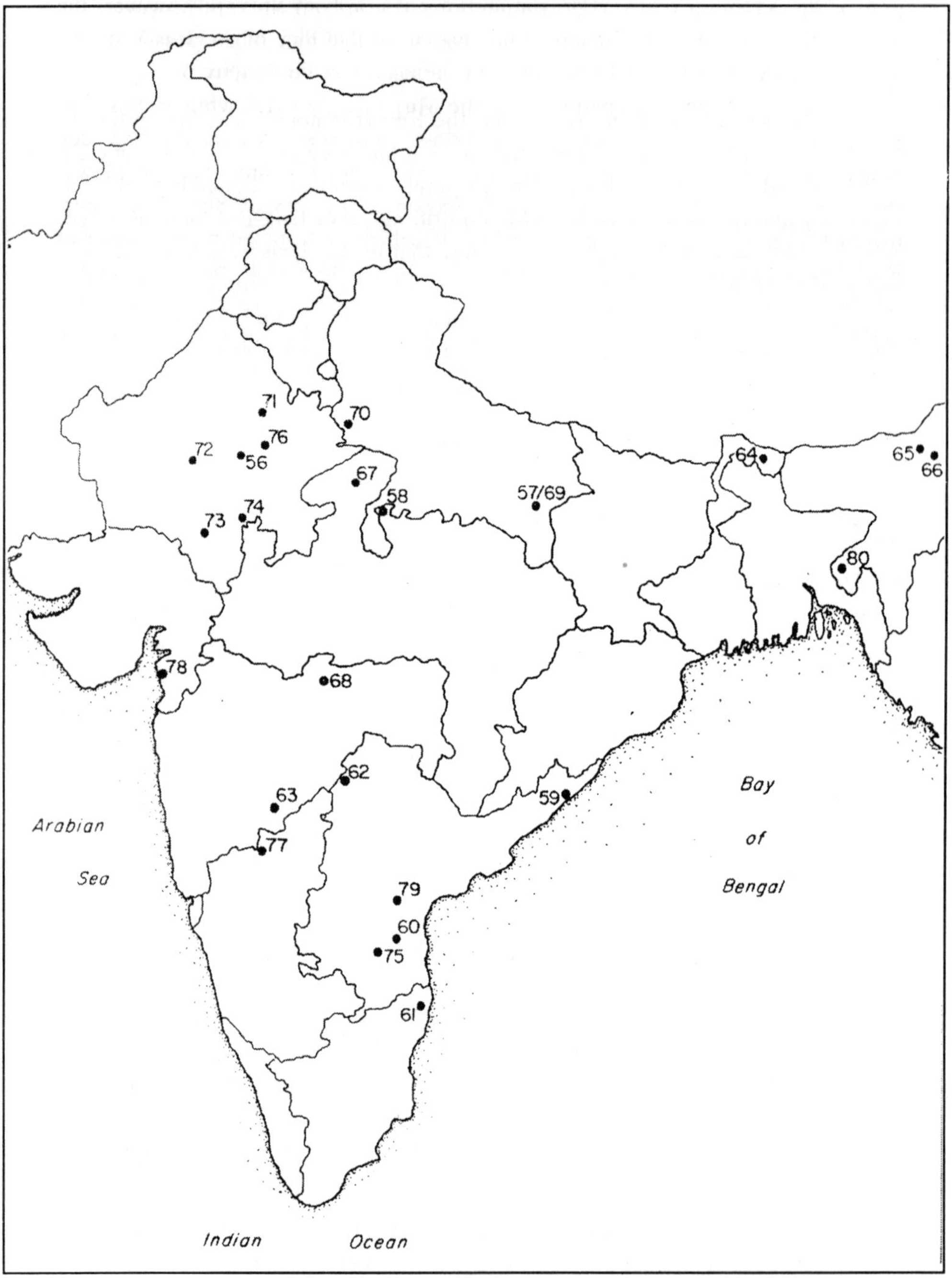

flow of external trade to and from the capital. Responding to what it considered an act of treason, the government deputed a high-ranking officer, Afẓal Khān, to punish the Maratha rebel. Before marching to confront Shivaji, however, the general first proceeded to Tuljapur and desecrated a temple of goddess Bhavānī, to which Shivaji and his family had been personally devoted (No. 63; Map 3).

We find the same pattern with the Mughals. In 1613, while at Pushkar, near Ajmer, Jahāngīr ordered the desecration of an image of Varāha that had been housed in a temple belonging to an uncle of his enemy, Rānā Amar of Mewar (See Table and Map 3: No. 56). In 1635, his son and successor, Shāh Jahān, destroyed the great temple at Orchha, which had been patronized by the father of Rājā Jajhar Singh, a high-ranking Mughal officer who was at that time in open rebellion against the emperor (No. 58). In 1669, there arose a rebellion in Benares among landholders, some of whom were suspected of having helped Shivaji escape from imperial detention. It was also believed that Shivaji's escape had been initially facilitated by Jai Singh, the great grandson of Rājā Mān Singh, who almost certainly built the great Vishvanath temple. It was against this background that the Emperor ordered the destruction of that temple in September, 1669 (No. 69) (Sinha 1974: 65–68; Asher 1992: 254, 278; Saqi Must'ad Khan 1871: 88). About the same time, serious Jat rebellions broke out in the area around Mathura, in which the patron of the local congregational mosque had been killed. So in early 1670, soon after the ring-leader of these rebellions had been captured near Mathura, Aurangzeb ordered the destruction of the Keshava Deva temple of Mathura and built an Idgah on the site (No. 70) (*Maasir-i 'Ālamgirī*, 1947: 57–61; Asher 1992: 254). Nine years later, the Emperor ordered the destruction of several prominent temples in Rajasthan that had become associated with imperial enemies. These included temples in Khandela patronized by refractory chieftains there; temples in Jodhpur patronized by a former supporter of Dara Shikoh, the Emperor's brother and arch-rival; and the royal temples in Udaipur and Chitor patronized by Rānā Rāj Singh after it was learned that that Rajput chieftain had withdrawn his loyalty to the Mughal state (Nos. 71–74).

Considerable misunderstanding has arisen from a passage in the *Maāthir-i 'Ālamgirī* concerning an order on the status of Hindu temples that Aurangzeb issued in April 1669, just months before his destruction of the Benares and Mathura temples. The passage has been construed to mean that he ordered the destruction not only of the Vishvanath temple at Benares and the Keshava Deva temple at Mathura, but of all temples in the empire.[27] The passage reads as follows: 'Orders respecting Islamic affairs were issued to the governors of all the provinces that the schools and places of worship of the irreligious be subject to demolition and that with the utmost urgency the manner of teaching and the public practices of the sects of these misbelievers be suppressed' (Saqi Must'ad Khan 1871: 81).[28]

The order did not state that schools or places of worship be demolished,

[27] See Goel (1991, Vol. II: 78–79, 83); Sharma (1962: 132–33); Athar Ali (1966: 98n).

[28] My translation. Cf. *Maasir-i 'Ālamgirī* (1981: 51–52).

but rather that they be *subject* to demolition, implying that local authorities were required to make investigations before taking action. More importantly, the sentence immediately preceding this passage provides the context in which we may find the order's overall intent. On 8 April 1669, Aurangzeb's court received reports that in Thatta, Multan, and especially in Benares, Brāhmaṇas in 'established schools' (*mudāris-i muqarrar)* had been teaching 'false books' *(kutub-i bāṭila)* and that Hindu and Muslim 'admirers and students' had been travelling great distances to study the 'ominous sciences' taught by this 'deviant group' (Saqi Must'ad K͟hān 1871: 81; *Maasir-i 'Ālamgirī,* 1981: 51). We do not know what sort of teaching or 'false books' were involved here, or why both Muslims and Hindus were attracted to them, though these are intriguing questions. What is clear is that the court was primarily concerned, indeed exclusively concerned, with curbing the influence of a certain 'mode' or 'manner' of teaching (*taur-i dars-o-tadrīs*) within the imperial domain. Far from being, a general order for the destruction of all temples in the empire, then, the order was a response to specific reports of an educational matter.

In sum, apart from his prohibition on building new temples in Benares, Aurangzeb's policies on temples within imperial domains generally followed those of his predecessors. Viewing temples within their domains as state property, Aurangzeb and Indo-Muslim rulers in general punished disloyal Hindu officers in their service by desecrating the temples with which they were associated. How, one might then ask, did they punish disloyal Muslim officers? Infractions short of rebellion normally resulted in demotions in rank, while serious crimes like treason were generally punished by execution, regardless of the perpetrator's religious affiliation.[29]

No evidence, however, suggests that ruling authorities attacked mosques or Ṣūfī shrines patronized by disloyal or rebellious officers. Nor were such monuments desecrated when one Indo-Muslim kingdom conquered another and annexed its territories. On the contrary, new rulers were quick to honour and support the shrines of those Chishti shaik͟hs that had been patronized by those they had defeated. As we have seen, Bābur, upon seizing Delhi from the last of the city's ruling sultans in 1526, lost no time in patronizing the Chishti tomb-shrines of the city. The pattern was repeated as the Mug͟hals expanded into provinces formerly ruled by Indo-Muslim dynasties. Upon conquering Bengal in 1574, the

[29] Consider the swift and brutal punishment of Bahā al-Dīn Gurshāsp, a high-ranking officer in Tug͟hluq imperial service and a governor in the Deccan. In 1327, Gurshāsp joined forces with the rājā of Kampila in an unsuccessful rebellion against Sultan Muḥammad bin Tug͟hluq. When captured, the Rājā, who had never sworn allegiance to Tug͟hluq authority, got the relatively light punishment of a beheading. But the rebel governor, who was not only a former Tug͟hluq officer but the emperor's first cousin, was spat upon by his female relatives and flayed alive; then his skin was stuffed with straw and paraded throughout the imperial provinces as a cautionary tale to the public, while his body was mixed with rice and fed to elephants (see *Futūhu's salātin,* 1967, Vol. III: 658–59; Ibn Battūta 1953: 96). As a final indignity to Gurshāsp, we are told by Ibn Battūta that the elephants refused to eat the meal that had been mixed with the rebel's body.

Mughals showered their most lavish patronage on the two Chishti shrines in Pandua – those of Shaikh 'Alā al-Haq (d. 1398) and Shaikh Nūr Qutb-i 'Ālam (d. 1459) – that had been the principal objects of lavish state patronage by the previous dynasty of Bengal sultans (Eaton 1993: 176–77). And when he extended Mughal dominion over defeated Muslim states of the Deccan, the dour Aurangzeb, not-withstanding his reputation for eschewing the culture of saint-cults, made sizeable contributions to those Chishti shrines in Khuldabad and Gulbarga that had helped legitimize earlier Muslim dynasties there.

Temples and Mosques Contrasted

Data presented in the foregoing discussion suggest that mosques and shrines carried political meanings very different from those of royal temples in independent Hindu states, or temples patronized by Hindu officers serving in Indo-Muslim states. For the Muslim rulers, building mosques was considered an act of royal piety, even a duty. But all actors, rulers and ruled alike, seem to have recognized that the deity worshipped in mosques or shrines had no personal connec-tion with a Muslim monarch. Nor were such monuments thought of as under-pinning, far less actually constituting, the authority of an Indo-Muslim king. This point is well illustrated in a reported dispute between the Emperor Aurangzeb and a Ṣūfī named Shaikh Muḥammadī (d. 1696). As a consequence of this dispute, in which the shaikh refused to renounce views that the Emperor considered theolo-gically deviant, Shaikh Muḥammadī was ordered to leave the imperial domain. When the Ṣūfī instead took refuge in a local mosque, Aurangzeb claimed that this would not do, since the mosque was also within imperial territory. But the shaikh only remarked on the Emperor's arrogance, noting that a mosque was the house of God and therefore only His property. The standoff ended with the imprisonment of the shaikh in Aurangabad fort – property that was unambiguously imperial (Alam 1996: 177).

This incident suggests that mosques in Mughal India, though religiously potent, were considered detached from both sovereign terrain and dynastic authori-ty, and hence politically inactive. As such, their desecration could have had no relevance to the business of de-establishing a regime that had patronized them. Not surprisingly, then, when Hindu rulers established their authority over territories of defeated Muslim rulers, they did not as a rule desecrate mosques or shrines, as, for example, when Shivaji established a Maratha kingdom on the ashes of Bijapur's former dominions in Maharashtra, or when Vijayanagara annexed the former terri-tories of the Bahmanis or their successors.[30] In fact, the rājās of Vijayanagara, as

[30] Examples of mosque desecrations are strikingly few in number. In 1697–98 in Sambhar, in Rajasthan's Jaipur District, Shāh Sabz 'Ali built a mosque on the site of a temple. In the reign of Shāh 'Ālam (1707–12), however, non-Muslims came to dominate the region and demolished the mosque, which was subsequently rebuilt in the reign of Farrukhsiyar, see Desai (1971: 157). Similarly, there is evidence that in 1680, during Aurangzeb's inva-sion of Rajasthan, the Rajput chief Bhīm Singh, seeking to avenge the emperor's recent destruction of temples in Udaipur and elsewhere, raided Gujarat and plundered Vadnagar,

is well known, built mosques, evidently to accommodate the sizeable number of Muslims employed in their armed forces. By contrast, monumental royal temple complexes of the early medieval period were considered politically active, inasmuch as the state-deities they housed were understood as expressing the shared sovereignty of king and deity over a *particular* dynastic realm.[31] Therefore, when Indo-Muslim commanders or rulers looted the consecrated images of defeated opponents and carried them off to their own capitals as war trophies, they were in a sense conforming to customary rules of Indian politics. Similarly, when they destroyed a royal temple or converted it into a mosque, ruling authorities were building on a logic that, they knew, placed supreme political significance on such temples. That same significance, in turn, rendered temples just as deserving of peace-time protection as it rendered them vulnerable in times of conflict.

Temple Desecration and the Rhetoric of State Building

Much misunderstanding over the place of temple desecration in Indian history results from a failure to distinguish rhetoric from practice. Whereas the former tends to be normative, conservative, and rigidly ideological, the latter tends to be pragmatic, eclectic, and non-ideological. Rhetorically, we know, temple desecration figured very prominently in Indo-Muslim chronicles as a necessary and even meritorious constituent of state-formation.[32] In 1350, for example, the poet-chronicler 'Iṣāmī gave the following advice to his royal patron, 'Alā al-Dīn Hasan Bahman Shāh, the founder of the Bahmani kingdom in the Deccan: 'If you and I, O man of intellect, have a holding in this country and are in a position to replace the idol-houses by mosques and sometimes forcibly to break the Brāhmaṇic thread and enslave woman and children – all this is due to the glory of Mahmud [of Ghazni]. . . . The achievements that you make today will also become a story to-morrow' (*Futūhu 's-salātīn*, 1967, Vol. I: 6–7).

But the new Sultan appears to have been more concerned with political stability than the glorious legacy his court-poet would wish him to pursue. There is no evidence that he converted any temples to mosques. After all, by carving

---

Vishalnagar, and Ahmedabad, in the latter place destroying thirty smaller mosques and one large one *(Rāja-sumudra-praśasti,* XXII, v. 29, an inscription composed *c.* 1683, which appears in Kavirāj Shyāmaldas, *Vīr Vinod* [Udaipur: Rajayantralaya, 1886]; cited in Majumdar [1974: 351].

[31] One can hardly imagine the central focus of a mosque's ritual activity, the prayer niche *(mihrāb),* being taken out of the structure and paraded around a Muslim capital by way of displaying Allāh's co-sovereignty over an Indo-Muslim ruler's kingdom, in the manner that the ritual focus of a royal temple, the image of the state-deity, was paraded around many pre-modern Hindu capitals in elaborate 'car' festivals.

[32] Aiming to cast earlier invaders or rulers in the role of zealous and puritanical heroes, later chroniclers occasionally attributed to such figures the desecration of staggering numbers of temples. Maḥmūd of Ghaznī, for example, is said to have destroyed 10,000 temples in Kanauj and 1,000 in Mathura, his grandson Ibrāhim 1,000 in the Delhi Doab and another 1,000 in Malwa, Aibek 1,000 in Delhi, and Muḥammad Ghūrī another 1,000 in Benares – figures that Hindu nationalists like Sita Ram Goel have accepted at face value (Goel 1990: 269).

out territory from lands formerly lying within the Delhi Sultanate, the founder of the Bahmani state had inherited a domain void of independent Hindu kings and hence void, too, of temples that could pose a political threat to his fledgling kingdom.

Unlike temple desecration or the patronage of Chishti shaikhs, both of which figured prominently in the contemporary rhetoric on Indo-Muslim state-building, a third activity, the use of explicitly Indian political rituals, found no place whatever in that rhetoric. Here we may consider the way Indo-Muslim rulers used the rich political symbolism of the river Ganga, whose mythic associations with imperial kingship had been well established since Mauryan times. Each in its own way, the mightiest imperial formations of the early medieval peninsula – the Cālukyas, the Rāṣṭrakūṭas, and the Coḷas – claimed to have 'brought' the Ganga down to their southern capitals, seeking thereby to legitimize their claims to imperial sovereignty. Although the Cālukyas and the Rāṣṭrakūṭas did this symbolically, probably through their insignia, the Coḷas literally transported pots of Ganges water to their southern capital (Davis 1997: 71–76). And, we are told, so did Muḥammad bin Tughluq in the years after 1327, when that Sultan established Daulatabad as his second capital (Ibn Battūta 1953: 4). In having Gangā water carried a distance of forty days' journey from north India 'for his own personal use', the Sultan was conforming to an authentically Indian imperial ritual. Several centuries later, the sultans of Bengal, on the occasion of their own coronation ceremonies, would wash themselves with holy water that had been brought to their capital from the ancient holy site of Gangā Sāgar, located where the Gangā empties into the Bay of Bengal (Manrique 1927: 77).

No Indo-Muslim chronicle or contemporary inscription associates the use of Gangā water with the establishment or maintenance of Indo-Muslim states. We hear this only from foreign visitors: an Arab traveller in the case of Muḥammad bin Tughluq, a Portuguese friar in the case of the sultans of Bengal. Similarly, the image of a Mughal official seated in a canopied chariot and presiding over the Jagannath car festival comes to us not from Mughal chronicles, but from an English traveller who happened to be in Puri in 1633 (Acharya 1961: 46). Such disjunctures between the rhetoric and the practice of royal sovereignty also appear, of course, with respect to the founding of non-Muslim states. We know, for example, that Brāhmaṇa ideologues, writing in chaste Sanskrit, spun elaborate tales of how warriors and sages founded the Vijayanagara state by combining forces for a common defence of *dharma* from assaults by barbaric (Mleccha) Turkic outsiders. This is the Vijayanagara of rhetoric, a familiar story. But the Vijayanagara of practical politics rested on very different foundations, which included the adoption of the titles, the dress, the military organization, the ruling ideology, the architecture, the urban design, and the political economy of the contemporary Islamic world (Wagoner 1996: 851–80).[33] As with Indo-Muslim states, we hear of such

[33] See also Wagoner (2000: 300–26).

practices mainly from outsiders – merchants, diplomats, travellers – and not from Brāhmaṇa chroniclers and ideologues.

Conclusion

One often hears that between the thirteenth and eighteenth centuries, Muslim rulers, driven by a Judeo-Islamic 'theology of iconoclasm,' by fanaticism, or by sheer lust for plunder, wantonly and indiscriminately indulged in the desecration of Hindu temples. Such a picture cannot, however, be sustained by evidence from original sources for the period after 1192. Had instances of temple desecration been driven by a 'theology of iconoclasm', as some have claimed,[34] such a theology would have committed Muslims in India to destroying all temples everywhere, including ordinary village temples, as opposed to the highly selective operation that seems actually to have taken place. Rather, the original data associate instances of temple desecration with the annexation of newly-conquered territories held by enemy kings whose domains lay on the path of moving military frontiers. Temple desecrations also occurred when Hindu patrons of prominent temples committed acts of treason or disloyalty to the states they served. Otherwise, temples lying within Indo-Muslim sovereign domains, viewed normally as protected state property, were left unmolested.

Finally, it is important to identify the different meanings that Indians invested in religious monuments, and the different ways these monuments were understood to relate to political authority. In the reign of Aurangzeb, Shai<u>kh</u> Muḥammadī took refuge in a mosque believing that that structure – being fundamentally apolitical, indeed above politics – lay beyond the Emperor's reach. Contemporary royal temples, on the other hand, were understood to be highly charged political monuments, a circumstance that rendered them fatally vulnerable to outside attack. Therefore, by targeting for desecration those temples that were associated with defeated kings, conquering Turks, when they made their own bid for sovereign domain in India, were subscribing to, even while they were exploiting, indigenous notions of royal legitimacy. It is significant that contemporary inscriptions never identified Indo-Muslim invaders in terms of their religion, as Muslims, but most generally in terms of their linguistic affiliation (most typically as Turk, *turuṣka*). That is, they were construed as but one ethnic community in India amidst many others.[35] In the same way, Chattopadhyaya (1998: 49–50, 53, 60, 84) locates within early medieval Brāhmaṇical discourse an 'essential urge to legitimize' any ruling authority so long as it was effective and responsible. This urge was manifested, for example, in the perception of the Tu<u>gh</u>luqs as legitimate successors to the Tomaras and Cāhamānas; of a Muslim ruler of Kashmir as having a lunar, Pāṇḍava lineage; or of the Mu<u>gh</u>als as supporters of *rāmarājya* [the 'kingship of Lord Rāma'] (Chattopadhyaya 1998: 49–50, 53, 60, 84). It is likely that Indo-Muslim

[34] See Wink (1997, Vol. II: 294–333).

[35] See Talbot (1995: 701).

policies of protecting temples within their sovereign domains contributed positively to such perceptions.

In sum, by placing known instances of temple desecration in the larger contexts of Indo-Muslim state-building and state-maintenance, one can find patterns suggesting a rational basis for something commonly dismissed as irrational vandalism. These patterns also suggest points of continuity with Indian practices that had become customary well before the thirteenth century. Such points of continuity in turn call into serious question the sort of civilizational divide between the 'Hindu' and 'Muslim' periods of Indian history first postulated in British colonial historiography and subsequently replicated in both Pakistani and Hindu nationalist schools. Finally, this essay has sought to identify the different meanings that contemporary actors invested in the public monuments they patronized or desecrated, and to reconstruct those meanings on the basis of the practice, and not just the rhetoric, of those actors. Hopefully, the approaches and hypotheses suggested here might facilitate the kind of responsible and constructive discussion that this controversial topic so badly needs.

References

Abu Sharaf Nasih al-Jurfadqani (AH 1345), *Tarjuma-yi tārīkh-i Yāminī* (Teheran: Bangah-i Tarjomeh va Nashr-i Kitab).

Acharya, P. (1961), 'Bruton's Account of Cuttack and Puri', *Orissa Historical Research Journal*, Vol. 10, No. 3, pp. 25–50.

Ā'in-i Akbarī by Abū'l Faẓl 'Allāmī (1977–78), translated by H.S. Jarrett, edited by Jadunath Sarkar, Vol. III (Calcutta: Asiatic Society of Bengal).

Akbarnāma by Abū'l Faẓl 'Allāmī (1979), translated Henry Beveridge (New Delhi: Ess Ess Publications).

Asher, Catherine B. (1992), 'The Architecture of Raja Man Singh: A Study of Sub-Imperial Patronage,' in Barbara Stoler Miller (ed.), *The Powers of Art: Patronage in Indian Culture.* (Delhi: Oxford University Press).

——— (1992), *Architecture of Mughal India*, Vol. 1, No. 4 in *The New Cambridge History of India Series* (Cambridge: Cambridge University Press).

Athar Ali (1966), *The Mughal Nobility under Aurangzeb* (Bombay: Asia Publishing House).

Banerji, S.K. (1936), 'Babur and the Hindus', *Journal of the United Provinces Historical Society*, Vol. 9, pp. 76–83.

Bosworth, C.E. (1963), *The Ghaznavids: Their Empire in Afghanistan and Eastern Iran, 994–1040.* (Edinburgh: Edinburgh University Press).

——— (1992), *The Later Ghaznavids, Splendour and Decay: The Dynasty in Afghanistan and Northern India, 1040–1186* (New Delhi: Munshiram Manoharlal).

Chattopadhyaya, Brajadulal (1998), *Representing the Other? Sanskrit Sources and the Muslims (8th–14th century)* (New Delhi: Manohar).

——— (1993), 'Historiography, History, and Religious Centers: Early Medieval North India, circa AD 700–1200,' in Vishakha N. Desai and Darielle Mason (eds), *Gods, Guardians, and Lovers: Temple Sculptures from North India, AD 700–1200* (New York: Asia Society Galleries).

Currie, M. (1992), *The Shrine and Cult of Mui'n al-Dīn Chishti of Ajmer* (Delhi: Oxford University Press).

Davis, Richard H. (1997), *Lives of Indian Images* (Princeton: Princeton University Press).

Desai, Z.A. (1971), *Published Muslim Inscriptions of Rajasthan* (Jaipur: Government of Rajasthan).

Desai, P.B. (1957–58), 'Kalyana Inscription of Sultan Muhammad, Saka 1248', *Epigraphia Indica*, Vol. 32.

Digby, Simon (1986), 'The Sufi Shaikh as a Source of Authority in Mediaeval India', in Marc

Gaborieau (ed.), *Islam and Society in South Asia*, in *Puruṣārtha*, No. 9 (Paris: Ecole des Hautes Etudes en Sciences Sociales).
Eaton, Richard M. (1993), *The Rise of Islam and the Bengal Frontier, 1204–1760* (Berkeley: University of California).
Elliot, H.M. and John Dowson (n.d.), *The History of India as Told by Its Own Historians*, Vol. I (Allahabad: Kitab Mahal).
Epigraphia Indica, Arabic and Persian Supplement (1962, 1964), (Delhi: Manager of Publications).
Epigraphia Indo-Moslemica (1927–28, 1931) (Calcutta: Government of India).
Futūhu 's-salātīn by 'Abd al-Malik 'Iṣāmī (1948), edited by A.S. Usha (Madras: University of Madras).
Futūhu 's-salātīn by 'Abd al-Malik 'Iṣāmī (1967), translated and edited by Agha Mahdi Husain as *Shāh Nāmah-i Hind of Iṣāmī* (London: Asia Publishing House).
Goel, Sita Ram (1990) *Hindu Temples: What Happened to Them*, Vol. I: *A Preliminary Survey* (New Delhi: Voice of India).
——— (1991), *Hindu Temples: What Happened to Them*, Vol. II: *The Islamic Evidence* (New Delhi: Voice of India).
Habib, Mohammad (1974), *Politics and Society during the Early Medieval Period: Collected Works of Professor Mohammad Habib*, Vol. I, edited by K.A. Nizami (New Delhi: People's Publishing House).
Ibn Battūta (1953), *The Rehla of Ibn Battūta (India, Maldive Islands and Ceylon)*, translated by Mahdi Husain (Baroda: Oriental Institute).
——— (1986), *Travels in Asia and Africa, 1324–1354*, translated by H.A.R. Gibb (New Delhi: Oriental Books Reprint Corporation).
Manrique, Sebastiao (1927), *Travels of Fray Sebastien Manrique, 1629–1643*, translated by E. Luard and H. Hosten, Vol. I (Oxford: Hakluyt Society).
Maāsir-i 'Ālamgirī by Saqi Must'ad Khān (1947), translated by Jadunath Sarkar (Calcutta: Royal Asiatic Society of Bengal).
Maāsir-i 'Ālamgirī by Saqi Must'ad Khān (1981), translated by Jadunath Sarkar as *Maasir- i 'Ālamgirī : A History of the Emperor Aurangzeb 'Ālamgīr* (Lahore: Suhail Academy).
Moini, Syed Liyaqat Hussain (1989), 'Rituals and Customary Practices at the Dargah of Ajmer', in Christian Troll (ed.), *Muslim Shrines in India: Their Character, History and Significance* (Delhi: Oxford University Press).
Muntakhab al-lubāb by Muhammad Hashim Khafi (1975), translated by S.M. Haq as *Khafi Khan's History of Ālamgīr* (Karachi: Pakistan Historical Society).
Muntakhab al-tawārīkh by 'Abd al-Qādir Badāūnī (1973), translated by W.H. Lowe, Vol. II (Delhi: Idarah-i Adabiyat-i Delli).
Muzaffar Alam (1996), 'Assimilation from a Distance: Confrontation and Sufi Accommodation in Awadh Society,' in R. Champakalakshmi and S. Gopal (eds), *Tradition, Dissent, and Ideology: Essays in Honour of Romila Thapar* (Delhi: Oxford University Press).
Order (1911), 'Aurangzeb's Order to Abu'l-Hasan. Benares, dated 28 February 1659,' *Journal of the Asiatic Society of Bengal*, pp. 689–900.
Majumdar, R.C., ed. (1974), *The Mughal Empire* (Bombay: Bharatiya Vidya Bhavan).
Sadhu, S.L., ed. (1993), *Medieval Kashmir, Being a Reprint of the Rajataraṅgiṇīs of Jonarāja, Shrivara and Shuka*, translated by J.C. Dutt (New Delhi: Atlantic).
Salim, Ghulam Hussain (1975), *Riyāz-us-Salātīn: A History of Bengal*, translated by Abdus Salam (Delhi: Idarah-i Adabiyat-i Delhi).
Saqi Must'ad Khan (1871), *Maathir-i 'Ālamgirī* (Calcutta: Bibliotheca Indica).
Sharma, Sri Ram (1962), *The Religious Policy of the Mughal Emperors* (second edn.) (London: Asia Publishing House).
Shulman, David D. (1980), *Tamil Temple Myths: Sacrifice and Divine Marriage in the South Indian Saiva Tradition* (Princeton: Princeton University Press).
Siddiqui, Iqtidar Husain (1989), 'The Early Chishti Dargahs,' in Christian W. Troll (ed.), *Muslim Shrines in India: Their Character, History and Significance* (Delhi: Oxford University Press).
Sinha, Surendra Nath (1974), *Subah of Allahabad under the Great Mughals* (New Delhi: Jamia Millia Islamia).

Tabaqāt-i-Akbarī by Nizamuddin Ahmad (1937–39), Vol. I, translated by B. De (Calcutta: Bibliotheca Indica).

Tabakāt-i-Nāsirī by Minhāj Sirāj Jūzjānī (1970), translated by H.G. Raverty (New Delhi: Oriental Books Reprint Corporation).

Talbot, Cynthia (1995), 'Inscribing the Other, Inscribing the Self: Hindu-Muslim Identities in Pre-Colonial India,' *Comparative Studies in Society and History,* Vol. 37, No. 4, pp. 692–722.

Tārīkh-i Khān Jahānīva Makhzan-i Afghani by Khwajah Ni'mat Allāh (1960), Vol. I, translated by S.M. Imam al-Din (Dacca: Asiatic Society of Pakistan).

Tārīkh-i Yāmini by 'Utbi (n.d.), in Elliot and Dowson, *The History of India as Told by its Own Historians,* Vol. II (Allahabad: Kitab Mahal).

Tārīkh-i Baihāqi by Baihāqi (1971), edited by Ali Akbar Fayyaz (Mashhad: University of Mashhad).

Tārīkh-i Baihāqi by Baihāqi (n.d.), in Elliot and Dowson, *The History of India as Told by its Own Historians,* Vol. II (Allahabad: Kitab Mahal).

Tārīkh-i Fīrīshta by Muḥammad Qāsim Firishta (1966), translated by John Briggs as *History of the Rise of the Mahomedan Power in India* (Calcutta: Editions Indian).

Thapar, Romila, Harbans Mukhia and Bipan Chandra (1969), *Communalism and the Writing of Indian History* (Delhi: People's Publishing House).

Wagoner, Phillip B. (1993), *Tidings of the King: A Translation and Ethnohistorical Analysis of the Rayavucakamu* (Honolulu: University of Hawaii Press).

——— (1996), '"Sultan among Hindu Kings": Dress, Titles, and the Islamicization of Hindu Culture at Vijayanagara', *Journal of Asian Studies,* Vol. 55, Vol. 4, November, pp. 851–880.

——— (2000), 'Harihara, Bukka, and the Sultan: the Delhi Sultanate in the Political Imagination of Vijayanagara,' in David Gilmartin and Burce B. Lawrence (eds), *Beyond Turk and Hindu: Rethinking Religious Identities in Islamicate South Asia* (Gainesville: University Press of Florida).

Willis, Michael (1993), 'Religion and Royal Patronage in north India,' in Desai and Mason (eds), *Gods, Guardians, and Lovers.*

Wink, Andre (1997), *al-Hind: The Making of the Indo-Islamic World,* Vol. II: *The Slave Kings and the Islamic Conquest, 11th–13th Centuries* (Leiden: Brill).

Yazdani G., ed. and tr. (1909), 'The Inscription of the Tomb of 'Abdullah Shah Changal at Dhar', *Epigraphia Indo-Moslemica.*

Zafar Hasan (1909), 'The Inscriptions of Dhar and Mandu', *Epigraphia Indo-Moslemica.*

Instances of Temple Desecration, 1192–1760

No.	Date	Site	District	State	Agent	Source
For nos. 1–24 see Map 1: Imperialism of the Delhi Sultanate, 1192–1394						
1	1193	Ajmer	Ajmer	Rajasthan	Md. G͟hūri (s)	23: 215
2	1193	Samana	Patiala	Punjab	Aibek	23: 216-17
3	1193	Kuhram	Karnal	Haryana	Aibek (g)	23: 216–17
4	1193	Delhi		U.P.	Md. Ghūrī (s)	1(1911): 13; 23: 217,222
5	1194	Kol	Aligarh	U.P.	G͟hurid army	23: 224
6	1194	Benares	Benares	U.P.	G͟hurid army	23: 223
7	*c.* 1202	Nalanda	Patna	Bihar	Bakhtiyār K͟haljī (c)	20: 90
8	*c.* 1 202	Odantapuri	Patna	Bihar	Bakhtiyār K͟haljī	22: 319; 21:551–2
9	*c.* 1202	Vikramasila	Saharsa	Bihar	Bakhtiyār K͟haljī	22: 319
10	1234	Bhilsa	Vidisha	M.P.	Iltutmish (s)	21: 621–2
11	1234	Ujjain	Ujjain	M.P.	Iltutmish	21: 622–3
12	1290	Jhain	Sawai Madh.	Rajasthan	Jalal al-Dīn K͟haljī (s)	27: 146
13	1292	Bhilsa	Vidisha	M.P.	'Alā al-Dīn K͟haljī (g)	27: 148
14	1298–1310	Vijapur	Mehsana	Gujarat	K͟haljī invaders	2(1974): 10–12
15	1295	Devagiri	Aurangabad	Maharash.	'Alā al-Dīn K͟haljī (g)	24: 543
16	1299	Somnath	Junagadh	Gujarat	Ulugh Khān(c)	25: 75
17	1301	Jhain	Sawai Madh.	Rajasthan	'Alā al-Dīn K͟haljī (s)	25: 75–6
18	1311	Chidambaram	S. Arcot	Tamilnad	Malik Kāfūr (c)	25: 90–1
19	1311	Madurai	Madurai	Tamilnad	Malik Kāfūr	25: 91
20	*c.* 1323	Warangal	Warangal	A.P.	Ulugh Khān (p)	33: 1–2
21	*c.* 1323	Bodhan	Nizamabad	A.P.	Ulugh Khān	1(1919–20): 16
22	*c.* 1323	Pillalamarri	Nalgonda	A.P.	Ulugh Khān	17: 114
23	1359	Puri	Puri	Orissa	Firuz Tug͟hluq (s)	26: 314
24	1392–93	Sainthali	Gurgaon	Haryana	Bahādur Khān Nahar (c)	3(1963–64): 146
For nos. 25–55, see Map 2: Growth of Regional Sultanates, 1394–1600						
25	1394	Idar	Sabar-K.	Gujarat	Muzaffar Khān (g)	14–3: 177
26	1395	Somnath	Junagadh	Gujarat	Muzaffar Khān	6–4: 3
27	*c.* 1400	Paraspur	Srinagar	Kashmir	Sikandar (s)	14–3: 648
28	*c.*1400	Bijbehara	Srinagar	Kashmir	Sikandar	34: 54
29	*c.* 1400	Tripuresvara	Srinagar	Kashmir	Sikandar	34: 54
30	*c.* 1400	Martand	Anantnag	Kashmir	Sikandar	34: 54
31	1400-1	Idar	Sabar-K	Gujarat	Muzaffar Shāh (s)	14–3: 181
32	1400-1	Diu	Amreli	Gujarat	Muzaffar Shāh	6–4: 5
33	1406	Manvi	Raichur	Karnatak	Firuz Bahmani (s)	2(1962): 57–58
34	1415	Sidhpur	Mehsana	Gujarat	Ahmad Shāh (s)	29: 98–99
35	1433	Delwara	Sabar-K.	Gujarat	Ahmad Shāh	14–3: 220–1
36	1442	Kumbhalmir	Udaipur	Rajasthan	Maḥmūd K͟haljī (s)	14–3: 513
37	1457	Mandalgarh	Bhilwara	Rajasthan	Maḥmūd K͟haljī	6–4: 135
38	1462	Malan	Banaskantha	Gujarat	'Alā al-Dīn Suhrab (c)	2(1963): 28–29 39
39	1473	Dwarka	Jamnagar	Gujarat	Maḥmūd Begdha (s)	14–3: 259–61
40	1478	Kondapalle	Krishna	A.P.	Md. II Bahmani (s)	6–2: 306
41	*c.* 1478	Kanchi	Chinglepur	Tamil Nadu	Md. II Bahmani	6–2: 308

No.	*Date*	*Site*	*District*	*State*	*Agent*	*Source*
42	1505	Amod	Broach	Gujarat	Khalil Shāh	3(1933): 36
43	1489–1517	Nagarkot	Kangra	Himachal Pradesh	Khawwās Khān (g)	35:81
44	1507	Utgir	Sawai Madh.	Rajasthan	Sikandar Lodī (s)	14–1: 375
45	1507	Narwar	Shivpuri	M.P.	Sikandar Lodī	14–1: 378
46	1518	Gwalior	Gwalior	M.P.	Ibrāhīm Lodī (s)	14–1: 402
47	1530–31	Devarkonda	Nalgonda	A.P.	Quli Quṭb Shāh (s)	6–3:2 12
48	1552	Narwar	Shivpuri	M.P.	Dilāwar Khān (g)	4 (Jun 1927): 101–4
49	1556	Puri	Puri	Orissa	Sulaimān Karrani (s)	28: 413–15
50	1575–76	Bankapur	Dharwar	Karnataka	'Alī 'Ādil Shāh (s)	6–3: 82–4
51	1579	Ahobilam	Kurnool	A.P.	Murahari Rao (c)	6–3: 267
52	1586	Ghoda	Poona	Maharashtra	Mīr Md. Zaman (?)	1: (1933–34) 24
53	1593	Cudappah	Cudappah	A. P.	Murtazā Khān (c)	6–3: 274
54	1593	Kalihasti	Chittoor	A. P.	I'tibār Khān (c)	6–3: 277
55	1599	Srikurman	Visakhapatnam	A. P.	Quṭb Shāhī general	32–5: 1312

For nos. 56–80 see Map 3: Expansion and Reassertions of Mughal Authority, 1600–1760

No.	*Date*	*Site*	*District*	*State*	*Agent*	*Source*
56	1613	Pushkar	Ajmer	Rajasthan	Jahāngīr (e)	5: 254
57	1632	Benares	Benares	U.P.	Shāh Jahān (e)	31: 36
58	1635	Orchha	Tikamgarh	M.P.	Shāh Jahān	7: 102–3
59	1641	Srikakulam	Srikakulam	A.P.	Sher Md. Kh. (c)	3(1953–54) 68–9
60	1642	Udayagiri	Nellore	A.P.	Ghazi 'Alī (c)	8: 1385-86
61	1653	Poonamalle	Chingleput	Tamilnad	Rustam b. Zulfīqar (c)	1(1937–38): 53–2
62	1655	Bodhan	Nizamabad	A.P.	Aurangzeb (p, g)	1(1919–20): 16
63	1659	Tuljapur	Osmanabad	Maharash.	Afzal Khān (g)	16: 9–10
64	1661	Kuch Bihar	Kuch Bihar	W. Bengal	Mīr Jumla (g)	9: 142–3
65	1662	Devalgaon	Sibsagar	Assam	Mīr Jumla	9: 154, 156–57
66	1662	Garhgaon	Sibsagar	Assam	Mīr Jumla	36: 249
67	1664	Gwalior	Gwalior	M.P.	Mu'tamad Khān (g)	10. 335
68	1667	Akot	Akola	Maharashtra	Md. Ashraf (c)	2(1963): 53–54
69	1669	Benares	Benares	U.P.	Aurangzeb (e)	11: 65-8; 13:88
70	1670	Mathura	Mathura	U.P.	Aurangzeb	12: 57–61
71	1679	Khandela	Sikar	Rajasthan	Darab Khān (g)	12:107; 18:449
72	1679	Jodhpur	Jodhpur	Rajasthan	Khān Jahān (c)	18:786; 12: 108
73	1680	Udaipur	Udaipur	Rajasthan	Ruhullāh Khān (c)	15: 129–30; 12: 114–15
74	1680	Chitor	Chitorgarh	Rajasthan	Aurangzeb	12: 117
75	1692	Cuddapah	Cuddapah	A.P.	Aurangzeb	1(1937–38): 55
76	1697–98	Sambhar	Jaipur	Rajasthan	Shāh Sabz 'Alī (?)	19: 157
77	1698	Bijapur	Bijapur	Karnatak	Hamid al-Dīn Khān (c)	12: 241
78	1718	Surat	Surat	Gujarat	Haidar Qulī Khān (g)	1(1933): 42
79	1729	Cumbum	Kurnool	A.P.	Muḥammad Salih (g)	2(1959–60): 65
80	1729	Udaipur	West	Tripura	Murshid Qulī Khān	30:7

Note: (e) = emperor, (s) = sultan, (g) = governor, (c) = commander, (p) = crown prince

Key to Sources

1: *Epigraphia Indo-Moslemica.*
2: *Epigraphia Indica, Arabic & Persian Supplement.*
3: *Annual Report of Indian Epigraphy.*
4: *Indian Antiquary.*
5: Jahangir, *Tūzuk-i-Jahāngirī,* tr. A. Rogers, (Delhi, 1968), Vol. 1.
6: Firishta, *Tārīkh-i Fīrīshta* tr. J. Briggs, *History of the Rise of the Mahomedan Power in India* (Calcutta, 1971), 4 vols.
7: Kanbo, *'Amal-i Sālih* (text: Lahore, 1967), Vol. 2.
8: A. Butterworth and V.V. Chetty. *A Collection of the Inscriptions on Copper-Plates & Stones in the Nellore District* (Madras, 1905), Vol. 3.
9: Khāfī Khān, *Khāfī Khān's History of' Ālamgīr,* tr. S.M. Haq (Karachi, 1975).
10: A. Cunningham, *Four Reports Made during 1862-65* (Varanasi, 1972).
11: S.N. Sinha, *Subah of Allahabad under the Great Mughals* (New Delhi, 1974).
12: Sāqī Must'ad Khān, *Maāsir-i 'Ālamgirī,* tr. J. Sarkar (Calcutta, 1947).
13: Sāqi Must'ad Khān, *Maāsir-i 'Ālamgirī* (text: Calcutta, 1871).
14: Nizamuddīn Ahmad, *Tabaqāt-i Akbarī,* tr. B. De (Calcutta, 1973).
15: Ishwardas Nagar, *Futuhat-i 'Ālamgirī,* tr. T. Ahmad (Delhi, 1978).
16: Surendranath Sen, ed. & tr., *Śiva Chhatrapati* (Calcutta, 1920), vol. 1.
17: P. Sreenivasachar, ed., *Corpus of Inscriptions in the Telingana Districts of H.E.M. the Nizam's Dominions,* pt. 2 (Hyderabad, 1940).
18: Shāh Nawāz Khān, *Maāthir-ul-Umarā,* tr. H. Beveridge (Patna, 1979), vol. 1.
19: Z.A. Desai, *Published Muslim Inscriptions of Rajasthan* (Jaipur, 1971).
20: G. Roerich, tr., *Biography of Dharmaswāmin* (Patna, 1959).
21: Minhāj-i Sirāj, *Tabakāt-i Nāsirī,* tr. H. Raverty (New Delhi, 1970), vol. 1.
22: Chattopadhyaya, D., ed., *Tāranātha's History of Buddhism in India* (Calcutta, 1980).
23: Ḥasan Nizāmī, *Tāj al-ma'āthir,* in Elliot & Dowson, *History,* vol. 2.
24: Amīr Khusrau, *Miftāḥ al-futūḥ,* in Elliot & Dowson, *History,* vol. 3.
25: Amīr Khusrau, *Khazā'in al-futūḥ,* in Elliot & Dowson, *History,* vol. 3 .
26: Shams-i Sirāj, *Tārikh-i Firūz Shāhī,* in Elliot & Dowson, *History,* vol. 3.
27: Zia al-Dīn Baranī, *Tārikh-i Firūz Shāhī,* in Elliot & Dowson, *History,* vol, 3.
28: Khwajah Ni'mat Allah, *Tārikh-i Khān-Jahani wa makhzan-i-Afghani* (text: Dacca, 1960), vol. 1.
29: Sikandar bin Muḥammad, *Mirāti-i Sikandarī,* in E.C. Bayley, *Local Muhammadan Dynasties: Gujarat,* ed. N Singh (repr. New Delhi, 1970).
30: Āzād al-Husaini, *Nau-Bahār-i Murshid Quli Khāni,* tr., Jadu Nath Sarkar, *Bengal Nawabs* (1952, repr. Calcutta, 1985).
31: 'Abd al-Hamīd Lāhorī, *Bādshāh-nāma,* in Elliot & Dowson, *History,* vol. 7.
32: *South Indian Inscriptions* (New Delhi: Archaeological Survey of India).
33: George Michell, 'City as Cosmogram,' *South Asian Studies* vol. 8 (1992).
34: Jonarāja, *Rājataraṅgiṇī,* ed. S.L, Sadhu, trans. J.C. Dutt (repr. New Delhi, 1993).
35: Iqtidar Husain Siddiqui, tr., *Waqi'at-e-Mushtaqui of Shaikh Rizq Ullah Mushtaqui* (New Delhi, 1993).
36: Jagadish Narayan Sarkar, *Life of Mīr Jumla* (Calcutta, 1952).

Obsessed by *Doṣa*

People's Inner World in Later Medieval Deccan

Hiroyuki Kotani

The mind or inner world of an individual is revealed by various acts the person undertakes in daily life. Of all such daily acts, rituals give the most information about how a person thinks. Such rites include those marking passage through life–birth rites and funeral rites, for example, as well as community-related rites like village rituals.

Prāyaścitta was one of the most important rituals in later medieval India[1] (the sixteenth to eighteenth centuries). Performed on a sinner, it was meant to remove the sin from the body. A sinner who did not undergo expiation through *prāyaścitta* was believed doomed to face the dreadful results of the sin in a future life. Thus, *prāyaścitta* was an indispensable ritual for people.

By studying the ritual of *prāyaścitta* as performed in later medieval Deccan, this essay will examine the inner worlds of the people. Sin in later medieval Deccan, most commonly termed *doṣa* (not *pāpa* or *pātaka*) in Marathi documents, included a much wider range of offensive acts than in the modern period. It was assumed to be transmittable through *saṃsarga* (social association) to other persons who had associated with the original sinner, making *prāyaścitta* obligatory for a wider circle of people. As a result, the ritual was frequently performed.

Thus, Marathi documents of the period, official state papers as well as private papers, contain many references to *prāyaścitta*.[2]

Prāyaścitta and *Saṃsarga*: Provisions in Śāstras

Importance of Prāyaścitta

In describing the dreadful results of a sin, the *Manusmṛti* (XI.48) prescribes: 'Some wicked men suffer a change of their (natural) appearance in

[1] The periodization of medieval period of Indian history in this essay is as follows: Early medieval: eighth to twelfth centuries; medieval: thirteenth to fifteenth centuries; later medieval: sixteenth to eighteenth centuries.

[2] In references to Marathi documents, Roman numerals indicate the volume number and Arabic numerals indicate the document number. All the insertions in parentheses added to the translated texts of Marathi documents are the author's. In the texts quoted from English works in this essay, the insertions in parentheses are original, while those in square brackets [ ] are added by the author for explanation.

Saṃsarga with Those Suffering Discrimination

The *Manusmṛti* does not contain a provision declaring that a sin is caused by *saṃsarga* with outcastes like the Caṇḍāla, except for a provision (XI.176) which prescribes: 'A Brāhmaṇa who unintentionally approaches a woman of the Kandala [Caṇḍāla] or of (any other) very low caste, who eats (the food of such persons) and accepts (presents from them) becomes an outcaste [*patita*]; but (if he does it) intentionally, he becomes their equal'. It seems, thus, that the concept of the sin caused by *saṃsarga* with those discriminated against is a rather new development in later Śāstras. Kane points out:

> *Āpastambasmṛti* (III.1–3) states: 'if a Caṇḍāla stays in the house of any one of the four castes [*varṇa*] without being known, the latter on coming to know of the fact should undergo expiation, which is *Cāndrāyaṇa* or *Parāka* for a member of the first three varṇas and *Prājāpatya* for a śūdra. Those who partook of cooked food in that man's house should undergo *Kṛcchra*; one should prescribe one half of *Kṛcchra* for those who took cooked food in the house of the second associator and for those who partook of cooked food in the house of these last one fourth of *Kṛcchra* is prescribed'. (Kane 1968–77, Vol. IV: 28)

As medieval society developed and untouchability became firmly established, the sin caused by *saṃsarga* with those discriminated against developed into a sin caused by *saṃsarga* with untouchables in general. In later medieval Deccan, cases of a *saṃsarga* with an untouchable were mainly caused by unknowingly employing an untouchable woman as a slave or servant, known as a *baṭīk* or *kuṇbiṇ* (see below).

Saṃsarga with Mlecchas

In the *Manusmṛti* there is no provision stating that a sin is caused by *saṃsarga* with a Mleccha. The concept of the sin caused by *saṃsarga* with a Mleccha seems to have begun to develop in the early eighth century when the Umayyad army under Muḥammad ibn Qāsim first invaded Sind and occupied the Indus valley area up to Multan. This invasion and occupation by Muslims, a new group of Mlecchas, gave rise to a difficult legal question concerning *saṃsarga* with Muslims. Kane remarks as follows:

> The *Devalasmṛti* opens with a question by the sages put to Devala who was sitting on the banks of the Sindhu [Indus] at ease as to how brāhmaṇas and members of the other varṇas when carried off by Mlecchas were to be purified and restored to caste. The following verses of the *Devalasmṛti* are very instructive on this point. Verses 7–10 declare that when a Brāhmaṇa is carried off by Mlecchas and he eats or drinks forbidden food or drink or has sexual intercourse with women he should not have approached, he becomes purified by doing the penance of *cāndrāyaṇa* and *parāka*, that a kṣatriya becomes pure by undergoing *parāka* and *pādakṛcchra*, a vaiśya by half of *parāka* and a Śūdra by the penance of *parāka* for five days. Then verses 17–22 are most

> important. 'When persons are forcibly made slaves by Mlecchas, Caṇḍālas and robbers, are compelled to do dirty acts, such as killing cows and other animals or sweeping the leavings of the food (of Mlecchas) or eating the leavings of the food of Mlecchas or partaking of the flesh of asses, camels and village pigs, or having intercourse with their women, or are forced to dine with them, then the penance for purifying a *dvijāti* that has stayed for a month in this way is *prājāpatya*. . . ; for one who stays a year (with Mlecchas in this condition of things) it is both *cāndrāyaṇa* and *parāka*; a Śūdra who stays (in this condition) for a month becomes pure by *kṛcchrapāda*; a Śūdra who stays a year should drink *yāvaka* for half a month. The appropriate *prāyaścitta* should be determined by learned brāhmaṇas when a person has stayed (in the above circumstances among Mlecchas) for over a year; in four years the person (who stays in the above circumstances among Mlecchas) is reduced to their condition (that is, becomes a Mleccha and there is no *prāyaścitta* for him)'. (Kane 1968–77, Vol. II: 389–91)

As the *Devalasmṛti* is deemed to have been written in the ninth or tenth century, Mlecchas in the *Devalaṣmṛti* meant, without doubt, Muslims. Thus, such legal questions that developed as a result of the Muslim invasion of Sindh involved the readmission to the *varṇa* or caste (*jāti*) of a person who had been forcibly made to commit the sin of *saṃsarga* with Muslims. The above-cited verses of the *Devalasmṛti* seem to impose a four-year time limit during which readmission is possible for all members of the four *varnas*. Other verses of the *Devalasmṛti*, however, state: 'One who was forcibly seized by Mlecchas for five, six, or seven years or from ten to twenty years, is purified by undergoing two *prājāpatyas*. Beyond this there is no purification; these penances are meant only for him who has simply stayed among Mlecchas' (Kane 1968–77, Vol. II: 391).

Kane understands this as an exception meant only for one who has 'not done any of the forbidden things such as eating *ucciṣṭa* or the flesh of asses' (ibid.).[5] The time span for readmission to a caste remained a difficult legal question even in later medieval Deccan as will be discussed below.

Doṣa and *Prāyaścitta* in Later Medieval Deccan

Horrors of Naraka

As we have seen, a sinner whose sin had not been removed from his or her body by *prāyaścitta* was assumed to go to hell in the next life. People in later medieval Deccan were actually obsessed by the horror of going to *naraka*. In one case, a Kunbī (peasant) named Vithūji Valekar of the village Kamthadi, Khedebare district, presented himself before the government office in Pune. He had been driven by the horrors of *naraka* to confess his *doṣa* of *gohatyā* (cow killing):

[5] Discussing the problem of readmission to his/her original caste of a person forcibly converted to Islam, A.R. Kulkarni indicates that the time limit for readmission was removed by the *Agni Purāṇa* which states that a person of any *varṇa* who associated with Mlecchas could be purified after the performance of certain rituals (Kulkarni 1996: 139).

> I was milking my cow, as she was a milch cow, when she did some mischief against me. So, in a lighthearted mood, I beat her, and as an unexpected result of this, she died. I am now under the curse (*abhiśrāp*, from *abhiśāpa* in Sanskrit) resulting from this act. If I conceal this act, I shall go to *naraka*. I am afraid of this and so I told government soldiers and village officers what happened. I have come to Pune to describe (my *doṣa*) to the government. So, Saheb (Peshwa) must inflict an appropriate punishment (*śāsana*) on me. (Oturkar 1950: No. 191)

As a response, the Peshwa government decided:

> The government fine (*sarkārdaṇḍa*) shall be waived, because he is too poor to pay it. He shall be sent to a sacred place on the Krishna River as a supplicant for the *devabrāhmaṇa*'s protection (*devabrāhmaṇās śaraṇ jāūn*) to be released (from his *doṣa*). Then, he shall be made to host a caste commensal meeting (*jāti jevaṇa*) in his village according to his ability and in conformity with the rules, and after doing so, he shall be readmitted to his caste. This decision of the government was duly communicated to the headman (*mokadam*) of the village who was ordered to execute it.

Thus this peasant asked the government for a punishment, fearing that without it he would go to *naraka* in the next life. The punishment had three aspects: the government fine was waived, but Brāhmaṇas of a sacred place along the Krishna river were to perform the *prāyaścitta* for him (though the term *prāyaścitta* was not used in this document) and a caste commensal meeting was to be held to acknowledge his readmission to the caste.

This document clearly shows that people who lived in later medieval Deccan greatly feared the horrors of *naraka*. It might also be said that the horrors of *naraka* were more real to people than the fear of transmigration into lower creatures or being again born as a human with handicaps.

Doṣa and Śuddhi

In the society of later medieval Deccan, Brāhmaṇas who lived in a sacred place thus played a crucial role in performing rituals for sinners to remove sins from their bodies. In such a sacred place as Nasik, there were certain Brāhmaṇa families who held the office of *Dharmādhikārī*, one of the hereditary offices (*vatan*) of the local society.[6] Sinners who wanted to undergo *prāyaścitta* to remove their *doṣa* submitted a *doṣapatra* (statement of sin) to the *Dharmādhikārī*. Upon receipt, the latter convened a meeting of the principal Brāhmaṇas in the sacred place to examine the *doṣapatra* and determine an appropriate method. After performing *prāyaścitta*, the *Dharmādhikārī* issued a *śuddhipatra* (certificate of purification)

[6] It has been so far ascertained that a *Dharmādhikārī* existed not only in Nasik but also in Kolhapur (*MIS*, Vol. XX: 185–90), Pune (Oturkar 1950: No. 159), and Karad (*MIS*, Vol. XXI: 84–336).

to certify that the sin had been expiated. Thus, two types of documents, *doṣapatra* and *śuddhipatra*, have been preserved by *Dharmādhikārī* families in sacred places.

One *doṣapatra* preserved by one of the two *Dharmādhikārī* families in Nasik, the Prabhū Dharmādhikārī family, reads as follows:

> *Doṣapatra.* I, Gaṅgājī at present living in the village Shivade, the son of Ranoji Jadhav, an inhabitant of Nasik, write about my *doṣa* to Prabhū Dharmādhikārī and Deva Dharmādhikārī (of Nasik).
>
> My father went mad and began eating with people of other castes as he was suffering from a famine, and as a result our caste excommunicated my father and myself. We went to the village Gavade and lived there for two years, at which time my father died while still in a mad state. I have repented for this and decided to get *prāyaścitta* performed on my father's bones as well as on myself, and then to perform my father's funeral rites on the Ganga (Godavari) river, so that I may be released from the *doṣa* and freed of my obligations to my father (*vaḍilāñce utarāī hoūn*). As a result, I hope, I would no longer be excluded from the commensal and marital relationships of the caste.
>
> With this in mind, I have presented myself before you to describe my *doṣa*. So please perform *prāyaścitta* on me and remove the *doṣa* from me. (*Aitihāsik Saṃkīrṇa Sāhitya* [*ASS*], Vol. I: 194, AD 1795)

In this case, the father of the person who wanted to undergo *prāyaścitta* violated the commensal rule of his caste (probably the Maratha, judging from their family name) by eating with persons of other castes. This *doṣa* of the father was assumed to have been transmitted to his son through *saṃsarga*. To avoid transmission of the *doṣa* to others of the caste, they were ex-communicated, and so the son was obliged to undergo *prāyaścitta*. The son decided to get *prāyaścitta* performed on his father's bones, probably to save the father from *naraka*. This was the duty of a son to his father.

This *doṣapatra*, though informative, does not describe the actual method of *prāyaścitta*. But another *śuddhipatra*, also preserved by the Prabhū Dharmādhikārī family, clarifies these points.

The *Dharmādhikārīs* and principal Ṛgvedī and Yajurvedī Brāhmaṇas, all Brāhmaṇas, assembled together. Hari Yādav and Rāmacandra Yādav Bhāgvat, two brothers of the town Pimpalgamv, Chandvad district, came to Janasthan (Nasik) and prostrated themselves before the Brāhmaṇas to state their *doṣa* as follows:

> As a result of a quarrel with a maidservant (*kuṇbīṇ*), our mother committed suicide by throwing herself in a well. (We were excommunicated by our caste, as our mother's *doṣa* of suicide was assumed to have been transmitted to us through *saṃsarga*.). . . . We passed one year in this state and have repented. . . . So we have prostrated ourselves before a meeting of Brāhmaṇas (*Brahmavṛnda*) and stated our *doṣa* before all of them.

In response to this, the Brāhmaṇas performed *prāyaścitta* on them at

Rāmakuṇḍa at the *saṅgam* of the Aruna (with the Godavari river) to release them from the *doṣa*. Then they were made to pay (for the caste commensal meeting), according to their resources, in order to become fit for caste commensality (*paṅkti-pāvana*). The following *śuddhipatra* was issued:

> *Prāyaścitta* having been performed, you are now fit for the commensality of the caste. No *doṣa* remains on you. Everybody should communicate with you as before in every location and in every country. You two brothers are now pure. Nobody should have doubt about this in any location or country. As proof of this, this *śuddhipatra* has been issued. (*ASS*, Vol. I: 203, AD 1806)

This *śuddhipatra*, together with the above-cited *doṣapatra*, shows that without any order of the government, the sons whose father or mother had committed *doṣa* presented themselves before the *Dharmādhikārīs* of Nasik to describe the *doṣa* transmitted to them through *saṃsarga* with their parents. This shows that they wanted to get rid of the hardships endured in this world as a result of the excommunication from their caste, but they were also frightened of the terrible punishments which would occur in a future life if the *doṣa* remained unpurified.

Schools and Castes of Brāhmaṇas in Nasik

In Nasik, there were Brāhmaṇas who followed two schools, the Ṛgvedīs and the Yajurvedīs. The *Dharmādhikārīs* were the representatives of all the Brāhmaṇas, regardless of the difference of school. Brāhmaṇas assembled to determine an appropriate method of *prāyaścitta* to be performed on a sinner, most probably with one *Dharmādhikārī* as the chair.

Prāyaścitta was actually performed at the Rāmakuṇḍa, the conference of the Aruna and Godavari rivers, but the actual method is not mentioned in the documents. The Rāmakuṇḍa was the most important pool (*kuṇḍa*) for ritual ablutions in Nasik. According to legend, it is the place where Rāma used to bathe. The Rāmakuṇḍa referred to in the above-mentioned *śuddhipatra*, however, was constructed by Chitrarao, a landholder of Khatav in the Satara district in 1696 and repaired by Gopikābāī, the mother of the fourth Peshwa, Madhavrao (in office, 1761–72), in 1782. It was eighty-three feet by forty feet (40 X 20m) (*Nasik Gazetteer* 1883: 526). *Prāyaścitta* used to be performed at the Rāmakuṇḍa (*Śiva Caritra Sāhitya* [*SCS*], Vol. II: 315, 316) which must have been maintained by all the Brāhmaṇas of Nasik as the common ritual place.

In the early years of the seventeenth century, when Nasik was under the rule of the Nizāmshāhī dynasty, a quarrel broke out among the Ṛgvedī and Yajurvedī Brāhmaṇas in Nasik about who would become the *tīrthaguru* for pilgrims. One Gomajibhat Kshemkalyani went to Malik 'Ambar, the well-known minister of the Nizāmshāhī, and stated: 'Many pilgrims come to Gautami (Godavari). The Ṛgvedī or Caturvedī Brāhmaṇa who first meets a pilgrim, attends to him as a *tīrthaguru* to officiate at the rites to be performed in the sacred place (*tīrthavidhi*) for him. . . . This is the longstanding custom. This custom is no longer observed since quarrels have started to break out among Brāhmaṇas.' Accordingly, Malik

'Ambar issued an order to the *kārkūn* and the Deśmukh of the Gulshanabad district that the Brāhmaṇas should be made to observe the longstanding custom' (*SCS*, Vol. IV: 706, AD 1617).

This custom continued up to the late nineteenth century. 'A pilgrim who is the first of his family to visit Nasik accepts as a rule the offer of the first man who accosts him' (*Nasik Gazetteer* 1883: 528). Each *tīrthaguru* family (*kṣetra upādhyā* or *tīrthopādhyā* in the *Gazetteer* [ibid.: 528, 650]), however, knew a certain number of families of different castes and from various parts of the country, for whom he or his forefathers had acted as *tīrthaguru*. These families were called the *yajmān* (*yajamāna*) of the *tīrthaguru* family. The *tīrthaguru* was paid well by the *yajmāns* and this caused keen competition among them. To prevent any of his *yajmāns* from leaving for a rival Brāhmaṇa, each *tīrthaguru* family kept a record of its *yajmāns* which often spanned 300 years and had entries relating to 10,000 to 500,000 families (ibid.: 528).

In the middle of the seventeenth century, trouble of this same kind broke out in Trimbak (Triambakeśvara), and in 1650 the Mughal government issued the following order to 'all the Brāhmaṇas of the great sacred place (*mahāsthala*) of Trimbak': because Ṛgvedī and Yajurvedī Brāhmaṇas were quarrelling with each other, the Huzūr decided as follows: 'When *yajmān*s of Ṛgvedī or Yajurvedī come on a pilgrimage, Brāhmaṇas of the respective schools shall officiate at the rites for them. . . . When any *yajmān* holds a *samārādhana* (Brāhmaṇa feast), any Brāhmaṇa who is favourably disposed toward this can attend' (*SCS*, Vol. IV: 707).

At the same time, the Brāhmaṇa population of a sacred place was composed of various castes. A decree issued by the Peshwa government about a quarrel among them in Nasik shows the composition in AD 1779–1780.

According to this document, a Brāhmaṇa of Nasik was accused of murdering another, but some Brāhmaṇas, continued to have *saṃsarga* with the accused even though he did not undergo *prāyaścitta*. Again, some other Brāhmaṇa was accused of having been the ringleader in a plot to kill a Brāhmaṇa. These acts caused a quarrel. The Peshwa government summoned the principal members of the contending sides to Pune for arbitration. An agreement about appropriate behaviour for Nasik Brāhmaṇas was drawn up. Three copies of this agreement were prepared and ordered to be preserved as follows:

> One copy shall be preserved by the *kamāvīsdār* (collector of a district) in *daftar*. Another copy shall be kept by the Pāṭil and Kulkarṇi of Nasik. The third copy shall be handed over to the *Dharmādhikārī*, who shall prepare five more copies of the same, put his signature and that of other *Dharmādhikārīs* if these exist on them, and write on the reverse side that he possesses the original copy of the agreement. He shall then give one copy to each of five castes (*dñāti, jñāti*) of Nasik Brāhmaṇas:
>
> If Deshastha, to Upasni Hingne,
> If Chitpavan, to Yajnanesvara Diksit Patvardhan,

If Karhada, to Chintaman Diksit Bhadkambhkar,
If Yajurvedi, to the family who used to keep the documents,
If Kanva (Kannav), to the family who used to keep the documents.
(*Selections from the Satara Rajas' and Peshwas' Diaries* [*SSRPD*], Vol. VIII: 1121).

This document shows that five castes of Brāhmaṇas existed in Nasik, namely Deśastha, Citpāvan, Karhāda, Kaṇva (Kannav) and Yajurvedī, and that each of them had a representative. Though Yajurvedī is not a caste, the Yajurvedī Brāhmaṇas of Nasik were treated as separate, probably because they formed a group distinct from other Brāhmaṇa castes. This might indicate that the other four castes of Brāhmaṇas in Nasik were followers of the Ṛgvedī school. According to the *Nasik Gazetteer* too, there were five Brāhmaṇa castes in Trimbak: Yajurvedī (about 150 families); Deśastha and Citpāvan (seventy-five families each); Kaṇva (Kannav) (five families); Karhāda (two families) (*Nasik Gazetteer* 1883: 650).

Dharmādhikārī Families of Nasik

The agreement discussed above also provides information about the *Dharmādhikārī*. The Peshwa government ordered the *Dharmādhikārī* of Nasik to prepare five more copies of the agreement and distribute them to each of the five Brāhmaṇa castes. This means that the *Dharmādhikārī* was the representative of all the five groups. He thus unified all the Brāhmaṇas, regardless of the differences in caste and school. When *prāyaścitta* was performed on people to purify their *mahādoṣa*, the fees paid by these people were allotted to the five Brāhmaṇa castes, again proving the unity of the Nasik Brāhmaṇas (also see *SSRPD*, Vol. VIII: 1121).

As indicated earlier, the office of *Dharmādhikārī* of Nasik was shared by two families, the Prabhū Dharmādhikarī and the Deva Dharmādhikarī. In the early decades of the seventeenth century, a dispute arose among the members of the Prabhū Dharmādhikarī family. To find an amicable solution to this problem, a meeting of the local community[7] was convened and a *mahzar* (written statement of the case) was drawn up in 1625. According to this *mahzar*, the *dharmādhikārī vatan* belonging to Govind Prabhū, the ancestor of the Prabhū Dharmādhikarī family, had been inherited by his two sons, Bāl and Koṇḍ, by dividing it in half (see the family tree below). Bāl Prabhū's share of the *dharmādhikārī vatan* was again divided in half by his two sons, Mahāḍ and Govind. Govind Prabhū died without a son, leaving his wife, Hirāī, and a daughter, Phulāī. Hirāī and Phulāī entrusted to Bāl Prabhū, the son of Mahād, the duties of their half share of the

[7] The local community called *gota* in Marathi was the social unit composed, in general, of 50–100 villages with Deśmukh as its head (representative) and Deśpāṇḍe as its scribe. If trouble occurred in the local community, the Deśmukh convened a meeting of the local community (*gota sabhā*) to find a solution to it. The *gota sabhā* was attended by the Deśmukh, Deśpāṇḍe, Pāṭils (village headmen), Kulkarṇis (village scribes) and headmen (*mehtars*) of each caste.

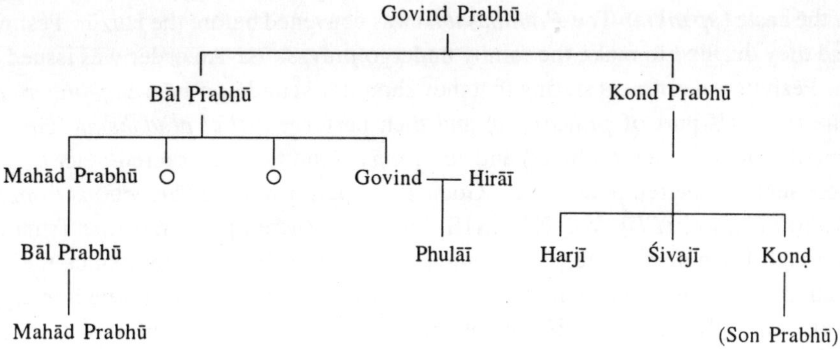

dharmādhikārī vatan. He also received the proceeds of their half share of the *dharmādhikārī vatan* from which they were given an annual payment of fourteen *ṭakā*.

Because the *gayāvarjana* (funeral rites performed in Gaya) for Govind and other expenses left them impoverished, Hirāī and Phulāī demanded that Bāl Prabhu increase their yearly payment, saying: 'You are eating our *mirāsī* (*vatan* of *dharmādhikārī*), and so you must pay our debts'. Bāl Prabhū refused. A meeting of the local community was convened to find a solution to this dispute. At the meeting, it was decided: 'Bāl Prabhū shall give Hirāī and Phulāī one *khaṇḍī* of grain and two *hon* of money to pay for food and clothing as well as a share (*takṣīm*) in a house to live in every year for the rest of their lives'. In return for this, the half share of the *dharmādhikārī vatan* that belonged to Hirāī and Phulāī was most probably transferred to Bāl Prabhū, though there remains some ambiguity on this point since the last portion of this document is damaged (*SCS*, Vol. II: 290).

In most cases, there were several *Dharmādhikārīs* from the same family line in a sacred place, since *vatans* were divided among family members into shares as families increased in size over the generations. In such a case, one male member of the main family, or the senior in the family line, acted as the representative. Female holders of a share of a *dharmādhikārī vatan* without a male heir entrusted a male member of the same family line to perform the duties of *Dharmādhikārī* and received a portion of the proceeds. As mentioned earlier, among the most lucrative sources of payment for the *Dharmādhikārī* were the fees paid by those upon whom *prāyaścitta* was performed.

Pūrvottaraṅgaprāyaścitta and *Pradakṣiṇā* at Brahmagiri

The most formal type of *prāyaścitta* was *pūrvottaraṅgaprāyaścitta* and *pradakṣiṇā* at a sacred place, especially meant for those who committed a grave sin (*mahādoṣa*). For Brāhmaṇas, eating meat and drinking liquor were such a *mahādoṣa*. In one case, a Brāhmaṇa named Bālājī Dhoṇḍdev began to live with a dancer (*kaḷavaṇṭīṇ*) and took to drinking liquor and eating meat. He was thus regarded as *patita*, and all of his kin were also excluded from the commensal row of the caste (*apaṅkta*). The *Brahmasabhā* was convened before the Huzūr (Peshwa) and they decided to make the family undergo *prāyaścitta*. An order was issued by the Peshwa government stating that they should first undergo *pūrvaṅgaprāyaścitta* (the first half part of *prāyaścitta*) and then perform *pṛthvī pradakṣiṇā* (circumambulation of a sacred object) and *tīrthasnāna* (ablution at a sacred place). They were sent to a sacred place on the Godavari to perform these (*Selections from the Peshwa Daftar* [*SPD*], Vol. XXXXIII: 29). (This sacred place must be Trimbak, although the name of the place cannot be found in the document since the last section is damaged.) They then returned home and must have undergone *uttaraṅga-prāyaścitta* (the second half part of *prāyaścitta*). This can be inferred from the following case.

When a Brāhmaṇa was murdered, the formal procedure of *prāyaścitta* was rigidly followed. The wife of a Brāhmaṇa, Mahādevbhaṭṭ Joshi, killed a relative, and as a result, Mahādevbhaṭṭ Joshi, his wife, and all his kin were excommunicated. He petitioned the Peshwa to be allowed to undergo *prāyaścitta*. In response, an order was issued that his wife be made to do *saṅkalpa* (solemn enunciation of the purpose of the ritual), to be followed by the performance of the *pūrvaṅga* rituals. She should then go to Trimbak to perform the *pradakṣiṇā* here; on returning home, she should be made to undergo the *uttaraṅga* rituals; *prāyaścitta* shall be performed on her husband and relatives thereafter (*SPD*, Vol. XXXXIII: 151).[8]

In this formal type of *prāyaścitta*, *pradakṣiṇā* at a sacred place was important. In the northern Deccan, Trimbak was the sacred place where *pradakṣiṇā* was most often performed. In the following letter, the Peshwa government asked all the Brāhmaṇas of Trimbak to make a Brāhmaṇa perform *pradakṣiṇā* at Trimbak:

> Naro Trimbak Umbaralkar, the *kārkūn* of Ganapatrav Raste, once went mad and ate the food of Śūdra (*śūdrānna*). After recovering he was made to undergo *prāyaścitta*. He again lost his senses and ate *śūdrānna* for a month's time. Later, he recovered and came (before the government) as a supplicant for protection (*śaraṇ*). Thus, it has been decided that he should be made to undergo *pūrvaṅga* and be sent to the sacred place (Trimbak) to perform twelve *pradakṣiṇās* of joy (*harṣacā bārā pradakṣiṇā*) at Brahmagiri. Accordingly, he has been sent to you. Please make him perform twelve *pradakṣiṇās* under your supervision, as has been decided, and send him back upon completion with your certificate. (*SPD*, Vol. XXXXIII: 113)

This document shows that *pradakṣiṇā* in Trimbak was a circling of Brahmagiri, the sacred hill and presumed source of the Godavari. According to

[8] The phrase *dvādaśabda pūrvottaraṅga* used in this document might refer to six *pūrvaṅga* rituals and six *uttaraṅga* rituals, though the actual procedures followed for these rituals were not mentioned. The criminal wife in this case was first ordered to go on a pilgrimage to Varanasi and Rameshvara, as was usual with a sinner who had committed a *mahādoṣa*. Later this was replaced by *pradakṣiṇā* at Triambakeśvara on the ground that the culprit was a female (*strījāti*).

legend, a small stream trickles from a fissure of Brahmagiri and then flows out from a stone cow's mouth. This water mysteriously disappears and reappears in the Kuśāvarta pond at the foot of the hill. This is the source of the Trimbak branch of the Godavari (*Nasik Gazetteer* 1883: 651).[9] Brahmagiri is said to be 'ten miles around the base and about four miles around the top' (ibid.: 655). Thus, the *pradakṣiṇā* course at Brahmagiri most probably meant circling ten miles around the base of the hill. In other words, one *pradakṣiṇā* in Trimbak was a walk of ten miles (about sixteen kilometres). That a *pradakṣiṇā* course of a sacred place was of such a distance as this can be corroborated by the fact that there were two *pradakṣiṇā* courses in Nasik, one of six miles and the other of ten miles (ibid.: 531). In this case, the sinner was ordered to circle the ten-mile course of *pradakṣiṇā* twelve times, making the total *pradakṣiṇā* a distance of 120 miles (about 192 km). These must have taken at least one or two weeks to complete. This *pradakṣiṇā* was, however, not as hard as other examples of *pradakṣiṇā* at Brahmagiri which could total several thousand miles, as will be shown below (*Marāthyāñcyā Itihāsācīṃ Sādhaneṃ* [*MIS*], Vol. VIII: 40; *SPD*, Vol. XXXXIII: 107).

Saṃsarga Doṣa in Later Medieval Deccan

Saṃsarga Doṣa with a Sinner

As indicated earlier, the concept of *saṃsarga* shows a clear development in later Śāstras. Family members and relatives of the sinners were made to undergo *prāyaścitta* in order to purify *doṣa* transmitted to them through *saṃsarga* with the culprits.

In medieval Marathi, the term *saṃsarga doṣa* or *sāṃsargik doṣa* referred to *doṣa* transmitted through interaction with a sinner, an untouchable, or a Muslim. *Saṃsarga doṣa* was assumed either to be 'acquired' (*prāpt hoṇeṃ*) by a person or to 'stick' (*lagṇeṃ*) to a person.

The following case of *bad-amal* (an evil deed, specifically rape or adultery), involving Gaṅgājī Jagthap, the Deśmukh of the Sasvad district, and six others (three Kunbīs, a Sali, a Māli and a Muslim), is a good example, even though the charge was later proven to be false. Shāhū, the fourth king of the Maratha kingdom (reigned 1708–49), issued the following order to the Deśmukh, Deśpāṇḍe and all the members of the local community of the Pune district:

> Gangaji Jagthap Deshmukh and a Sali (weaver), a Mali (gardener) and others, in all seven men of the *kasbe* (town) Sasvad, committed *badamal* (rape) upon a Mahar woman. These men were summoned before the king for an inquiry. As a result, they have been ordered to go on a pilgrimage to Varanasi and Rameshvara. Upon returning home, you must hold a *gotapata* (ritual for re-admission to caste) for expiation. Existing relatives should be tonsured and made to observe a three-night fast. Furthermore, those who have 'acquired'

[9] For the legendary topography of Brahmagiri see Feldhaus (2000: 18–19, 24–25, 39).

> *saṃsarga doṣa* must observe a one-day fast as *prāyaścitta* (Oturkar 1950: No. 152, AD 1732).

In this case, the six accused men, but not the Muslim, were ordered to go on a pilgrimage to Varanasi and Rameshvara, both of which are several thousand miles away. This very severe *prāyaścitta* was inflicted because the *doṣa* was grave: *bad-amal* on an untouchable woman. Due to the gravity of their *doṣa*, *saṃsarga doṣa* was 'acquired' by a very wide circle of people. This document shows that not only the relatives of the accused, but many inhabitants of the *kasbe* Sasvad were assumed to have 'acquired' the *saṃsarga doṣa*, though the degree of *doṣa* was less serious.

The following order of Sachiv, one of the Aṣṭapradhān (eight ministers) of the Maratha kingdom, was addressed to the Deśmukh of the Supe district regarding this case. It shows that *saṃsarga doṣa* was assumed to have 'stuck' to the town of Sasvad itself:

> Gangaji Jagthap and Sali, Mali, Kunbi and others, in total seven men of the *kasbe* Sasvad, committed *badamal* in the *kasbe* Sasvad. . . . Since the *sāṃsargik doṣa* resulting from this stuck to the town (*gāv*), it has been decided to perform *prāyaścitta* on the town to purify it and to convene the Deshmukhs and *gotas* of all the Mahals for this purpose. Thus, the king's letter regarding this was sent separately to (the districts of) the Maval province and to you. . . . Therefore, you should go to the above-mentioned town, and perform *prāyaścitta* on the town to purify it. (Oturkar 1950: No. 156)

A similar letter must have been sent to the Deśmukhs of neighbouring districts, ordering them and the *gotas* to assemble to perform *prāyaścitta* on the *kasbe* Sasvad. *Bad-amal* on an untouchable woman was so grave a *doṣa* that this wide circle of people was required to attend the ritual in the town, which the Brāhmaṇas must actually have performed. Thus, *saṃsarga doṣa* (*sāṃsargik doṣa*) in later medieval Deccan was assumed to stick not only to human beings, but to the town as well. In another case concerning a *saṃsarga doṣa* of a woman who had committed adultery with an untouchable man, the *saṃsarga doṣa* was likewise assumed to have stuck not only to people but also to the house in which the woman lived, the furniture and cooking utensils used by her, as well as the land on which the house stood (*SSRPD*, Vol. VIII: 1125).

As indicated earlier, this case of sin proved to be a false accusation; in spite of this, the accused men were obliged to undergo *prāyaścitta.* The king, in fact, ordered the *Dharmādhikārī* and the Brāhmaṇas of Pune to proceed to Sasvad to perform *prāyaścitta* on the men and make them fit to dine with other Brāhmaṇas, though the actual method of expiation was not mentioned (Oturkar 1950: No. 159). In addition, the following order was sent by the Sachiv to the Deśmukhs of neighbouring districts: 'You make the Deshmukh, Kunbi, Sali and Mali, in all six men, fit for commensality (*paṅktipāvana*) and readmit them to their castes.' (ibid.: No. 155). This seems to mean that the Deśmukhs and the members of the Kunbī,

Sali and Māli castes of the Sasvad district were ordered to hold separate meetings to readmit respective caste member(s) to their castes, after the *prāyaścitta.*

Doṣa and Untouchability

Doṣa caused by Sparśa with an Untouchable

Physical contact with an untouchable was called *sparśāsparśa.* In popular understanding today, people of those days were assumed to dread *sparśāsparśa* because of the impurity acquired by such contact. In later medieval Deccan, however, *sparśāsparśa* was dreaded more because it involved the *doṣa* of touching a person with whom *sparśa* was prohibited. While an impurity caused by *sparśāsparśa* could be purified by private ritual bathing at home, the *doṣa* of *sparśāsparśa* had to be purified by *prāyaścitta* performed by Brāhmaṇas in a sacred place. In one case, a Nhāvī (barber) unknowingly cut the hair of an untouchable, and as a result was obliged to submit the following *doṣapatra* to the *Dharmādhikārīs* of Nasik to ask that *prāyaścitta* be performed on him:

> *Doṣapatra.* To Prabhu Dharmadhikari, Deva Dharmadhikari and all (the Brāhmaṇas of Nasik).
>
> I, Vithu, the son of Mayaji Nhavi (barber), from the village Khandale near the village Karandi, at present living in Nasik, write about my *doṣa,* as I have been ordered.
>
> When I was sitting on the banks of the Ganga (Godavari) river waiting for a guest, a man of Budhalakar (an untouchable caste of animal-skin vessel [*budhalā*] makers) approached and asked me to cut his hair. I did not inquire about his caste, and he, as well, did not inform me that he was a Budhalakar. So I wet his hair and began to cut it, when one of the members of my caste happened to come along and said to me: 'He is a Budhalakar. Why do you cut his hair? You should not cut his hair!' Thus, I (stopped cutting and) returned home. Some days later, I went for a meal at the house of a member of my caste, where some members accused me of the *doṣa* of having had contact with a Budhalakar's head. So, I walked out while the meal was still in progress. I have, on these grounds, come to you. The *doṣa* of touching a Budhalakar's head is on my body, and I must be released from this.
>
> Thus, I have written about my *doṣa* to you all. (*ASS,* Vol. II: 193, AD 1795)

This document is notable because there is no mention of the contamination believed to have been acquired by physical contact with an untouchable. This barber was accused of committing the *doṣa* of touching a man with whom physical contact was unlawful. He was excommunicated by his caste, not because of contamination but because of the *doṣa* of *sparśāsparśa.* Had he not been ousted from the caste, his *doṣa* would have spread to all the members of the caste. This would not have happened with an impurity caused by physical contact with an untouchable, since an impurity was not believed to be transmittable to other persons in later medieval Deccan.

Also in the aforementioned false case of *bad-amal* assumed to be committed by Gaṅgājī Jagthap and others, there was no mention of the impurity assumed to be acquired by physical contact with an untouchable woman. Thus, in our period a *doṣa* was much more important and dreadful to society than impurity.

Saṃsarga Doṣa with an Untouchable

In later medieval Deccan, a person acquired *saṃsarga doṣa* or *sāṃsargik doṣa* as a result of *saṃsarga* (social association) with an untouchable. Though the most common forms of *saṃsarga* were *annavyavahāra* (pertaining to food) and *lagnavyavahāra* (marital relationship), people would not be likely to have such relationships with untouchables. Thus, *saṃsarga doṣa* with an untouchable was committed under particular circumstances. Typically, a woman, who was a *baṭīk* or *kuṇbīṇ* (both meaning a female slave or maidservant), was employed by a family and she later proved to be an untouchable. This was a woman who had been sold by her family or sold herself, as the result of such reasons as the poverty of her family or excommunication from her caste. She did the domestic chores in the home of the family who had bought her. Such a person was sold repeatedly, and in that process her caste origins could become obscure. As a result, a woman who had been bought and worked in a home could later be proven to be an untouchable. In such cases, the family members and other servants were believed to have committed *saṃsarga doṣa* with an untouchable, as a result of living together in the same house. As cited earlier, the *Āpastambasmṛti*, in referring to a case in which a member of the four *varṇas* has unwittingly had a Caṇḍāla in the house, describes the respective methods of *prāyaścitta* to be undergone by members of each *varṇa* once they realize what has happened. Similar cases could occur in later medieval Deccan too.

In one such case, Rāmacandra Govind Prabhune, the Kulkarṇi and Joshi of a village in the Vai area, submitted the following *doṣapatra* to Lakṣmaṇbhaṭṭ Prabhū Dharmādhikārī and Gaṅgārām Deva Dharmādhikārī of Nasik (*SCS*, Vol. II: 315, AD 1791–92):

> A wandering *kuṇbīṇ* (*phirastī kuṇbīṇ*) had been staying in my home, working for her daily bread. A commotion arose about her being an untouchable (*atiśūdra*) woman. Once I found out about this, I was very much disgusted. Thus, I have come with my family members and servants to Janasthan (Nasik) as a supplicant for protection before you and all the principal Brāhmaṇas of this sacred place. Full of remorse (*anutāp*), I plead with you to purify me, a *patita*. You must perform *prāyaścitta* on me in order to make me fit for commensality of the caste.

After this first portion of the document, there follows a lengthy and rather confusing explanation of how he committed *saṃsarga doṣa* with an untouchable woman. In short, a woman of unknown identity was handed over to Rāmacandra Govind Prabhune by an official of the Peshwa government. Three or four months after he had taken her to Rajapur, his residence, a *kuṇbīṇ* from the village Kuradgamv happened to see her in the bazaar and identified her as an untouchable (*anāmika*) from the same village. Rāmacandra Govind Prabhune asked her whether it was true, and she claimed that the charge was false. At night, however, she secretly fled from his house. This convinced him that she was an untouchable woman.

This must be a typical example of *saṃsarga doṣa* with an untouchable in later medieval Deccan. In these cases, all the members of the family, as well as their servants, had to undergo *prāyaścitta* to purify the *saṃsarga doṣa*.

Upon receiving a *doṣapatra* such as the one cited above, the *Dharmādhikārī* and Brāhmaṇas of a sacred place assembled to prescribe the method of *prāyaścitta* and actually performed it on the party concerned. To certify that this had been done, the *Dharmādhikārī* issued a *śuddhipatra*. The following is an example of one such *śuddhipatra*.

> *Śuddhipatra* from the *Dharmadhikari* and all of the principal Rgvedi and Yajurvedi Brahmans.
>
> Balajipant, Makundpant, and Shankarajipant, the Joshis and Kulkarnis of the village Pokhali, Parner district, Junnar province, have come to the sacred place (Nasik) with all the members of their family, as well as their male and female slaves. They made proper greetings to all the Brahmanas and stated that they had committed the *doṣa* of *saṃsarga* with a woman of the Chandala skinners (*carmakī Cāṇḍālī*). As a result, they submitted a *doṣapatra* to the Dharmadhikari, and they have come before all the Brahmanas as supplicants for protection, requesting that they purify them all. They petitioned in this manner.
>
> Thus, all the Brahmanas assembled at the *saṃgam* of the Aruna (and the Godavari river) and decided upon the ritual in accordance with the sastras, taking into consideration the supplicants' means of livelihood. The Brahmanas then ordered them to undergo *prāyaścitta* to purify themselves. *Prāyaścitta* was duly performed on them before all the Brahmans, and the commensal meeting of the Brahmanas was also held at their expense. Thus, they have become fit to sit in a row to eat with other Brahmanas. No *doṣa* remains on them. Everybody should communicate with them as before in every location and in every country. They and their family members have become pure. In every location and in every country, nobody should have any doubt about this. This is the *śuddhipatra*. Written by Bhaskarbhatt Prabhu Dharmadhikari. Witness, Gadi Ḍeva Dharmadhikari, *kasbe* Nasik, on the Ganga (Godavari) river. (*ASS*, Vol. I: 200, AD 1756)

There was discrimination against the Caṇḍālas, a well-documented group, since ancient times. In later medieval Deccan, however, there was no caste called Caṇḍāla, so that 'Caṇḍāla' in this document may be a Brāhmaṇical way of referring to the Chambhar (tanner). Though the document does not make clear how *saṃsarga*

all Brāhmaṇas of the *kasbe* Harsul, Aurangabad province, about the *prāyaścitta* to be performed on a Brāhmaṇa named Gangādhar Rangnāth, who had been forcibly converted to Islam by the Mughals. The first portion of this order reads as follows:

> Gangadhar Rangnath, the Kulkarni of Harsul, was in the service of the Mughals. After a while the Mughals forcibly polluted (*bātvilā*, that is, converted) him. They caused him to fall (*bhraṣṭa*, from the caste) and then put him in prison for three months. In the prison he had *annodakasaṃsarga* (relationships of food and water) with Yavanas (Muslims). After that, the Mughals gave him the mansab of 250 and took him into their service. He served the Mughals for five years. During this period, he was prohibited from performing *snāna* and *sandhyā*, but did not have *annodakasaṃsarga* with Muslims. Though he made a fortune, . . . he felt remorse in his heart and wished to be readmitted to his *dñāti*. Abandoning all his fortunes and possessions, he has come before the king (Sambhaji, the second king of the Maratha kingdom) at Raigad. For one year . . . he has been asking that *prāyaścitta* be performed for him.

At last, an assembly of Brāhmaṇas was convened, which ordered a *prāyaścitta*. The actual methods of *prāyaścitta* were: 360 *pradakṣiṇās* around Śrīgiri (Brahmagiri) in Trimbak; twenty-four rituals of the first half and the second half (*pūrvottaraṅga prāyaścitta*), though further details are not known. As discussed earlier, the *pradakṣiṇā* course of Brahmagiri extended for more than ten miles. Thus, 360 *pradakṣiṇās* around Brahmagiri totalled 3600 miles (about 5760 km). It would have taken at least a year for Gangādhar to complete this extremely severe *prāyaścitta*. The document continues:

> 'Gangadhar . . . underwent *prāyaścitta* in the manner prescribed in Śāstras. He performed *tīrthavidhi* at the sacred place (Trimbak) with the approval of the Dharmadhikari and other Brahmans. He then hosted a *brāhmaṇabhojana* and became fit for the *annaprasādapaṅkti* (row-wise sitting arrangement for commensal eating).
>
> He came to my (Panditrao's) place with the certificate from the Brahmans of the sacred place (Trimbak) stating that a *śuddhibhojana* had been held and *prāyaścitta* and *pradakṣiṇā* had been duly performed. He also had a letter from the *deśādhikārī* (Deshmukh and Deshpande). He handed over the certificate and letter to me.

On receiving the certificate from Gangādhar, Panditrāo gave him *bhojana* in his *paṅkti* and then gave him a *śuddhipatra* to certify that he was free of sin and fit for *vyavahāra*. Panditrao proclaimed that 'all the Brāhmans should have relationships of food, water and other things (*annodakādi vyavahāra*) with him as they have done in the past' (*MIS*, Vol. VIII: 40).

Maratha government was the one most closely related to *prāyaścitta*. After the death of Shāhū in 1749, the Peshwa government allowed the office of the Panditrāo to exist in name only under the puppet Maratha kings.

In this case, a Brāhmaṇa who had lived more than five years as a Muslim among Muslims was readmitted to his caste, but only after very severe expiatory rituals. In another case of forcible conversion to Islam (1721–22), however, the procedure for expiation was much simpler. A Putaji bin Mudhoji Vadghar was taken prisoner by the Mughals in Surat. Forcibly converted, he lived as a Muslim for six years. He then fled from the Mughals and joined the Peshwa's army when Bālājī Viśvanath Peshwa (in office, 1713–20) passed close to Surat on his way home from the Delhi expedition. Once home, this man pleaded with his caste to readmit him, and the caste agreed. For decisions of this sort, approval from the king or the Brāhmaṇas of a sacred place was required, and so the caste asked Shāhū for approval. Shāhū approved on the grounds that the Mughals had forcibly converted the man. The Maratha government's order was sent to the Patil and others of his town. It said that all the caste members (*samast gota*) should assemble and purify the man in accordance with Śāstra and then readmit him to the caste (*SSRPD*, Vol. I: 373). No arduous *prāyaścitta* like the *pradakṣiṇā* of more than three thousand miles was required, even though the man had spent six years as a Muslim. The difference, most probably, stemmed from the fact that in the latter case the individual was not a Brāhmaṇa and rigid ritual purity was not required of him.[12]

Under the rule of the Peshwas in the second half of the eighteenth century, conditions for readmission to a caste seem to have become stricter. Narhari Rānālekar's case serves as a good example of this. Narhari Rānālekar, a Brāhmaṇa from Paithan, was taken prisoner by the Afghans in the battle of Panipat in 1761 and forcibly converted to Islam. After being detained for ten to twelve years, he was released and allowed to return home. Upon his return, there arose questions about whether he could be readmitted to his caste after undergoing *prāyaścitta*. The following letter sent to the Peshwa (probably Mādhavrāo) by a district official of Ahmadnagar provides much information about this case.

> Yavana (Muslims) captured Narhari Ranalekar in Panipat, carried him away, and converted him (*bhraṣṭa kele*). He lived among Muslims for ten to twelve years, so that he had become a thorough *yavana* (*yavanamaya*). In spite of this (once he returned home), some Brāhmaṇas purified him in Paithan. This caused a dispute which was brought before the Peshwa. An assembly of *vaidiks* and *paṇdits* was convened to investigate the problem. The assembly decided that it was not proper to submit a man who had been *yavanamaya* for ten to twelve years to expiation. (*SPD*, Vol. XXXXIII: 25, probably AD 1772)

[12] Another case of forcible conversion to Islam was caused by the Siddis (Muslims who had migrated from Ethiopia to the Konkan area). In this case, Śāmājī, a Kāyastha Prabhū by caste, had been captured by the Siddis and forcibly converted. He later fled from the Siddis and, on returning home, asked his caste to readmit him. The caste assented to this. The decision of the caste, however, was not based on Śāstra, and so the caste sent a letter to the Brāhmaṇas of an anonymous sacred place asking for their approval (*Mahārāṣṭretihāsācī Sādhanem̐* [*MS*], Vol. II: 200).

This dispute was not settled, and continued for more than ten years. Finally the Peshwa government ordered Naro Yeshvant, the paternal cousin of Narhari Rānālekar, to perform the ritual of ex-communication on Narhari. Ramashastri, the well-known Nyāyādhish under the Peshwas, sent the following to all the Brāhmaṇas of Trimbak.

> Narhari Ranalekar, a Brāhmaṇa, was converted to Islam and became *yavanamaya.* Shamacharya and some other Brāhmaṇas of Paithan, however, performed *prāyaścitta* on him, though they had no authority to do so, and had a commensal relationship (*paṅktivyavahāra*) with him. This was not proper. Therefore, Naro Yeshvant, the paternal cousin of Narhari, has been ordered to perform *ghaṭasphoṭa* (literally the breaking of a pitcher, the ritual of ex-communication) on him. It has been decided that the *prāyaścitta* of Naro Yeshvant should be 121 *pradakṣiṇās* of ten *kos* at Sri Triambakesvara. Accordingly, he has been sent to the sacred place (Trimbak). Please make him continually (*nitya*) perform *snāna* in the Ganga (Godavari) river and *pradakṣiṇā* at Śrī(giri), and, when the *pradakṣiṇā* is completed, send him back with your certificate. (*SPD*, Vol. XXXXIII: 107, probably 1786)

Thus Narhari Rānālekar was actually ex-communicated from his caste following the formal procedure known as *ghaṭasphoṭa.* The *Manusmṛti* (XI.184) prescribes the ritual which makes a man *patita* as follows: 'A female slave shall turn over a pot [*ghaṭa*] filled with water with her foot, as if it were for a dead person.' The ritual performed in later medieval Deccan may have been similar to this.[13]

Furthermore, Naro Yeshvant, who performed *ghaṭasphoṭa* on Narhari, had to undergo *prāyaścitta* because of the *saṃsarga doṣa* with Narhari. The actual *prāyaścitta* involved *snāna* in the Godavari and 121 *pradakṣiṇās* of ten *kos* (twenty miles) around Śrīgiri (Brahmagiri). The total of 121 *pradakṣiṇās* of ten *kos* amounted to 2,420 miles (about 3870 km). Naro must have stayed a long time in Trimbak to do all this.

Saṃsarga Doṣa Transmitted from a Bāṭgī Musalmān

Saṃsarga doṣa with a Muslim was also believed to be transmittable to other persons. In one case, Rānojī Pāṭil of the village Sonke near Vai bought a *baṭīk*, Udi by name, but it was later discovered that she had had a commensal relationship (*annavyavahāra*) with 'a polluted Muslim woman' (*bātgī musalmān*), that is, a woman who had converted to Islam of her own accord. Because Rānojī lived in the same house as his *baṭīk*, it was believed that the *saṃsarga doṣa* with a Muslim committed by the *baṭīk* had been transmitted to him. Thus, Rānojī was

[13] As another example of *ghaṭasphoṭa*, Narasiṃha Bhāratī, the head monk of the Karvir Math of the Śaṅkara school, wrote a letter addressed to the *Dharmādhikārī* and all the Brāhmaṇas of Kolhapur. The letter gave notice that the widow of a Bhimbhaṭṭ Joshi had fallen from her caste by joining the group (*yātī*) of Jaṭil Gosāvī, and had been formally excommunicated from her caste by the performance of the *ghaṭasphoṭa* ritual (*MIS*, Vol. XX: 189).

ordered to undergo the rites of *prāyaścitta* (*SSRPD*, Vol. I: 399, AD 1752–53). This is another example of the chain transmission of *doṣa* in later medieval Deccan.

Conclusion

In the Maratha country of the later medieval period, people seem to have been obsessed with *doṣa.* Fearing the dreadful results in this life and in a future life of unpurified *doṣa,* they were driven to seek expiation through *prāyaścitta.* In addition, *doṣa* was not a personal or private matter involving only the sinner. It was transmittable to the rest of the family, relatives, co-inhabitants, caste members and even to the inhabitants of a village or town in which the sinner lived. People were constantly menaced by this chain of transmission originating with persons virtually unknown. *Doṣa* therefore was a public issue. As the concept of *saṃsarga* expanded, there was a rise in the importance of *prāyaścitta* to ward off the terrible results of unpurified *doṣa.*

In later medieval Deccan, when political conditions were always unstable and wars constant, the social order was maintained in the main by society itself. Thus, each constituent social unit, such as the local community (*gota*), village, caste and family, had its own self-regulating devices. These involved mutual vigilance of members' conduct and joint responsibility for members' misconduct. The concepts of *doṣa* and *saṃsarga* provided a religious component to the mutual vigilance and joint responsibility that kept the social fabric from falling into chaos. Hence the acute awareness of *doṣa* and *saṃsarga*, was rooted in a perilous political environment.

The expiation of sin has often been confused with purificaton of impurity or contagion. This can be seen in the following remarks of Dumont:

> [A] man made impure by serious contacts with impure substances or people, jeopardizes by what Hutton [J. Hutton, *Caste in India* (1961)] calls 'contagion' the status not only of his family but of his whole group [caste]: thus he must be separated [ex-communicated] from the rest. . . . One can also understand the fact which Abbe Dubois . . . found striking, that serious crimes against one's fellow men and public order, like murder or theft, not jeopardizing the caste's status, can appear much less serious than an infringement of the rules about food. (Dumont 1980: 179–180)

In later medieval Deccan, however, there is no evidence of people being ex-communicated because of physical contact with an untouchable. It was such sins (*doṣa*) as murder and violation of caste commensal rules that counted. *Doṣa* did not count as impurity or contagion; the latter was not thought transmittable to other persons, and could be purified or removed from one's body merely by ritual bathing in private. In other words, contamination (*sparśāsparśa*) was a personal or private matter, not jeopardizing the status of others. By contrast, *doṣa* or sin was a public matter which had a negative effect upon a much wider circle of people, especially members of the family and caste.

Thus, when studying the inner worlds of people who lived in later medieval

India, it is better to analyse their responses to *doṣa*, *pāpa*, and *pātaka* and the necessary expiatory rituals (*prāyaścitta*), rather than focus, as Dumont has done, on the concepts of purity and impurity.

References

Aitihāsik Patreṃ Yādī Vagaire (1930), edited by G.S. Sardesai, Y.M. Kale and V.S. Vakskar, (Pune: Chitrashala Press).

Aitihāsik Saṃkīrṇa Sāhitya (1934–67), 13 Vols, edited by Bharat Itihas Samshodhak Mandal (Pune: Bharat Itihas Samshodhak Mandal).

Dumont, L. (1980), *Homo Hierarchicus: The Caste System and Its Implications* (Chicago: The University of Chicago Press).

Feldhaus, A. (2000), 'Mountains, Rivers, and Shiva: Continuity among Religious Media in Maharashtra', in M. Kosambi (ed.), *Intersections: Socio-Cultural Trends in Maharashtra* (New Delhi: Orient Longman).

Hutton, J.H. (1961), *Caste in India: Its Nature, Function, and Origins* (London: Oxford University Press).

Kane, P.V. (1968–77), *History of Dharmaśāstra*, 5 Vols, second edn. (Poona: Bhandarkar Oriental Research Institute).

Kotani, H. (2002), *Western India in Historical Transition: Seventeenth to Early Twentieth Centuries* (New Delhi: Manohar).

Kulkarni, A.R. (1996), *Medieval Maharashtra* (New Delhi: Books & Books).

Mahārāṣṭretihāsācī Sādhaneṃ (1967), 3 Vols, edited by V.S. Bemdre (Mumbai: Mumbai Marathi Grantha Samgrahalaya).

Manusmṛti with Manubhāṣya of Medhātithi (1992), 2 Vols, edited by G. Jha (New Delhi: Parimal Publications).

Marāthyāṃmcyā Itihāsācīm Sādhaneṃ (1898–1919), 22 Vols, edited by V.K. Rajvade (Poona and Bombay: Maharashtra Sahitya Parishad).

Nasik Gazetteer (1883), *Gazetteer of Bombay Presidency*, Vol. 16: *Nasik* (Bombay: Government of Bombay).

Oturkar, R.V., ed. (1950), *Peśve Kālīn Sāmājik va Ārthik Patravyavahār* (Pune: Bharat Itihas Samshodhak Mandal).

Selections from the Peshwa Daftar (1930–34), 45 Vols, edited by G.S. Sardesai (Bombay: Government Central Press).

Selections from the Satara Rajas' and the Peshwas' Diaries (1905–11), 9 Vols, edited by G.C. Vad (Poona and Bombay: Deccan Vernacular Translation Society).

Sen, S. (1925), *Administrative History of the Marathas* (Calcutta: University of Calcutta).

Śiva Caritra Sāhitya (1926–65), 13 Vols, edited by Bharat Itihas Samshodhak Mandal (Pune: Bharat Itihas Samshodhak Mandal).

The Laws of Manu (English translation of the *Manusmṛti*) (1886), translated by G. Bühler, *The Sacred Books of East*, XXV (Oxford: Oxford University Press).

Contributors

DAUD ALI is Senior Lecturer in Early Indian History, Department of History, School of Oriental and African Studies, University of London, London.

RICHARD M. EATON is Professor of History, Department of History, University of Arizona, Tucson.

IRINA GLUSHKOVA is Leading Research Scholar, Centre for Indian Studies, Institute of Oriental Studies, Moscow.

STEWART GORDON is Research Scholar at the Centre for South Asian Studies, University of Michigan, Ann Arbor.

IRFAN HABIB is Emeritus Professor of History at Aligarh Muslim University, Aligarh.

NAJAF HAIDER is Associate Professor, Centre for Historical Studies, Jawaharlal Nehru University, New Delhi.

D.N. JHA is former Professor of History, University of Delhi, Delhi.

VISHWA MOHAN JHA is Reader in History, A.R.S.D. College, University of Delhi, Delhi.

HIROYUKI KOTANI is former Professor of History at the Tokyo Metropolitan University, Tokyo, and presently Member of the Science Council of Japan.

NOBORU KARASHIMA is Professor Emeritus, University of Tokyo, Tokyo.

VIJAY NATH is former Reader in History, Janki Devi Mahavidyalaya, University of Delhi, Delhi.